JOURNEY TO ENLIGHTENMENT

The Adventure of a Lifetime

By

Hanno Soth

HANNO151@GMAIL.COM

Copyright © 2024 Hanno Soth
All rights reserved.

This Book is Dedicated to my parents.

Detlef & Elke Soth

For all the Love and all you have done for me.

With Utmost Respect and Gratitude
To
Lord Buddha

and past and present Kings of Thailand
for allowing me to reside in the Kingdom of Thailand
Land of Buddha
To learn meditation and the dhamma

Master Acharavadee Wongsakon
For teaching me Meditation and Dhamma
Whose Dhamma fills these pages.

www.school-of-life-foundation.com

And Venerable Monks
Pra Ajarn Somdej Toh Promarangsri
Laung Por Sanchai Jittapalo
Pra Ajarn Amorn Prommin Khunna Vuttho

1.	How a Prince attained Enlightenment	9
2.	What the Buddha Discovered	79
3.	The Creation of Man	105
4.	Death	115
5.	The Energy Vortex	131
6.	Being Born Human (Programing)	141
7.	Searching for Answers	169
8.	Technology Trap	179
9.	Vipassana Meditation	197
10.	The Mind	211
11.	Beauty is only Skin Deep	241
12.	Techo (Fire) Vipassana Meditation	257
13.	The World Within	271
14.	The Impurity Forces	287
15.	The Next Level Impurity Forces	307
16.	House-Builders	317
17.	Past Lives - Reincarnation	326
18.	Miraculous Insights	355
19.	Father - Dad	413
20.	Mother - Mom	429
21.	Spiritual Path	437
22.	The Master	501
23.	The Monk	515
24.	The Doctor	529
25.	Destiny - Wassana	569

FOREWORD

This book is based on the Supreme Wisdom and Dhamma of The Buddha, Enlightened Buddhist Masters, and those who through countless of hours of insight Meditation practice, have uncovered the Ancient Lost Knowledge and the Ultimate Truth.

The intention of this book is to offer the reader, a glimpse into Advanced Vipassana Meditation, giving insights and encouraging you to discover the Truth within your own self through meditation practice.

They say, "a picture is worth a thousand words."

In this world, where people read less and less, and are accustomed to swiping on their smartphones, the author has decided to create a book, with many pictures to illustrate the Journey to Enlightenment.

Additonally, since the path to Enlightenment is so rare a Journey and lacks the common vocabulary to describe it, using images offers the reader a true view into the other dimensions.

May this book open the Minds of all those who read it and plant the seed of dhamma.

Who am I ?

What am I doing here ?

What is the meaning of Life ?

Does God Exist ?

What happens when we die ?

Can I escape death ?

What is the secret of a happy Life ?

Is this all there is to Life….is there nothing more?

WORLD OF ILLUSION

Throughout history and the ages man has tried to figure out the meaning of Life…

In our modern world, many of us busy ourselves and have become so distracted, that we often forget the very question, let alone embarking on searching for the answers.

Many people do not wish to confront their own mortality.

Terms like Anti-Aging, Bio-hacking, Cloning, Stemcells, Metaverse, Neurolink, SpaceX, AI, make us believe that somehow at the end or the eleventh hour, modern technology and medicine will save us from Death. "Technology will allow us to live forever"

So we live with a YOLO Mindset (You Only Live Once)
We Live heedlessly, We avoid thinking about Death or the Consequences of our actions and Immorality.

It is the Mara (devil) who has deluded us to live in ignorance, and caused us to attach to this world of Illusion, where we live in misery for eternity

The game of Mara (devil) is to keep us enslaved in this world.
The Devil helps humanity create technology, to keep us ensnared in a web of deception,
and prevent us from discovering the Ultimate Truth.

However, despite the treachery of Mara, the truth can still be uncovered, once we stop looking out into the world (maya), or perceiving our world through our Smart Phones. Instead we must look within ourselves to discover the answers and the Ultimate Truth.

CHAPTER 1

HOW A PRINCE REACHED ENLIGHTENMENT

In order to understand the World, we live in and to find our answers, we must examine the Life of a young Prince from Nepal, who lived 2500 years ago and through great determination and sacrifice, cracked the code of the Universe and discovered the Truth of all things.

Prince Siddhartha accomplished this by looking inward and not outward into the Illusion of the World.

This young Prince is so important because he left us the road map to Truth and Enlightenment.

When Prince Siddhartha was born, his father, the King, invited three sages to the palace, to predict the boy's future. All sages predicted that this young Prince, named Siddhartha, would either grow up to be a great King, conquering and ruling many nations, or a great Spiritual Leader.

Upon hearing this, the King decided that he wanted the Prince to become the great King of nations not a Holy man.

Consequently, he raised his son, accordingly, teaching him all the skills of war, military strategy and training him to conquer the World.

Prince Siddhartha lived a Life of Pleasure and Opulence

The King built his son 3 palaces, one for each of the 3 seasons. Prince Siddhartha was afforded every luxury and pleasure to keep him from becoming a Great Spiritual Leader, rather instead to become a Great Conqueror of Nations.

Even 2500 years ago, people lived in opulence and luxury, becoming comfortable with their lives. And often too busy or lazy or uninspired to seek the Spiritual Path, despite having the opportunity.

DISCONTENTMENT

At age 30, Prince Siddhartha started to feel dissatisfied with his Life. It was as though something was missing from his Life.

The Prince was living in splendor, all his needs and desires catered to, he was educated by the best teachers, excelled at military strategy and combat, yet the Prince felt incomplete.

As he stared out the palace window, it was as if he had once made a promise to himself, which he was now somehow not keeping.

Prince Siddhartha, despite recently marrying the most beautiful Princess named Yasodhara, was unhappy and felt suffering.

As Prince Siddhartha held Princess Yasodhara and their newborn son, a surge of fatherly joy enveloped him. Yet, amidst this bliss, a profound conflict gnawed at his heart. He understood that the more he allowed himself to become attached to his child, the more he risked compromising his unwavering commitment to fulfill his age-old promise: to alleviate the world's suffering.

Driven by an insatiable thirst for answers to life's eternal questions, Siddhartha grappled with the very questions that echo through the corridors of time: What is the meaning of existence? How can one transcend suffering? What path leads to true happiness?

In that pivotal moment, amidst the tender embrace of family, Siddhartha's resolve remained unshaken. He knew that his quest for enlightenment, his journey toward understanding the nature of life and suffering, was a path he must tread alone—a path that would ultimately illuminate the way for countless seekers across generations.

One night, before anyone could change his mind, the Prince got on his magnificent horse Kanthaka and rode away from the palace, leaving his family and his Princely life forever. Siddhartha rode into the night and the unknown.

As he was riding, Mara (devil) whispered into his ear. "Prince Siddhartha, within 7 days the greatest riches in this world shall be yours, if you turn back now, and return to the Palace and your Happy Life".

Prince Siddhartha, with great determination, ignored Mara (devils) words and rode even faster.

Now far away from the palace, in a final act, the brave Prince relinquished his Princely title, his wealth, his family, royal clothes and released his beloved horse.

Prince Siddhartha now became Siddhartha the ascetic, wandering barefoot through the country begging for his food, as he searched for the Ultimate Truth about all things.

As Siddhartha the ascetic met others on the same journey, he followed various drastic practices, believing this would lead to spiritual insight.

Siddhartha practiced.

Harsh Living Conditions: He subjected himself to harsh living conditions, often residing in forests, caves, or other remote locations, and endured exposure to the elements.

Sleep Deprivation: He limited his sleep and practiced sleep deprivation, believing that it would heighten his awareness and spiritual sensitivity.

Intense Breath Control Exercises: He engaged in intense breath control exercises in an attempt to gain mastery over his body and Mind.

Self-mortification: He practiced self-mortification, enduring physical pain through practices such as self-flagellation, extreme forms of meditation, or holding painful postures for extended periods.

Starvation: He believed that deprivation of physical nourishment would lead to spiritual insight, often subjecting himself to starvation.

Finally, these extreme practices brought an emaciated Siddhartha to deaths door.

At the last moment, Siddhartha realized he was on the wrong path and abandoned this extreme asceticism, realizing the limitations of these life-threatening practices, Siddhartha instead adopted a middle path, between self-indulgence and self-mortification.

After eating again, nourishing his body, and regaining his strength, Siddhartha found a place under the now-famous Bodhi tree, where on that fateful night he committed himself to, meditating without stopping, until he had reached the Ultimate Truth and found the way out of suffering.

Under the Bodhi tree, Siddhartha famously swore these words:

"Even if my skin, sinews, and bones should waste away and my blood dry up in my veins, yet will I never stir from this seat until I have attained full enlightenment."

Under that great tree, Siddhartha practiced what is now known as Vipassana insight meditation.

Vipassana meditation means to look into one's Mind and see things as they truly are.
Vipassana means "insight" or "clear seeing."

Siddhartha entered the battle of his life, inside his Mind, against the Mara (devil), and armies of impurity forces (Kilesa) burning away layers of Sangkaras (past memories and emotions) in his Mind that held the attached him to the past and this World.

As his body became perfectly still, and his concentration fixed, it was as though he was sitting on the bottom of the ocean of his Mind.

He now observed, not giving any attention to what thoughts, sounds, or images arose in his Mind.

In this state of absolute focus, concentration and consciousness, Siddhartha suddenly saw himself sitting above the world. His Mind and body still.

Witnessing this, Mara (devil) began to worry. Siddhartha's Mind was so steady with determination. and was starting to uncover the long-hidden Truth.

Mara gathered all her troops to stop Siddhartha, she sent in the impurity forces, as legions of soldiers shooting arrows into the heart of Siddhartha.

The arrows were made from strong emotions that existed in Siddhartha's Mind. These were his weaknesses, which Mara shamelessly used against him. Mara used these memories and emotions to try to break Siddhartha's concentration.

One arrow contained the emotions resulting from leaving his newborn son and Princess. Another arrow was the emotion of losing his friends and family and Royal Life.

Then came the arrow of doubt: "Did he do the right thing to leave the palace, could he really find the way out of suffering for humanity"?

But Siddhartha as these arrows pierced his heart, did not attach to these emotions, he merely let the emotions arise, and then fade away. Therefore, doubt did not shake is resolve or break his concentration.

His Mind remained firm, still concentrated, and equanimous.

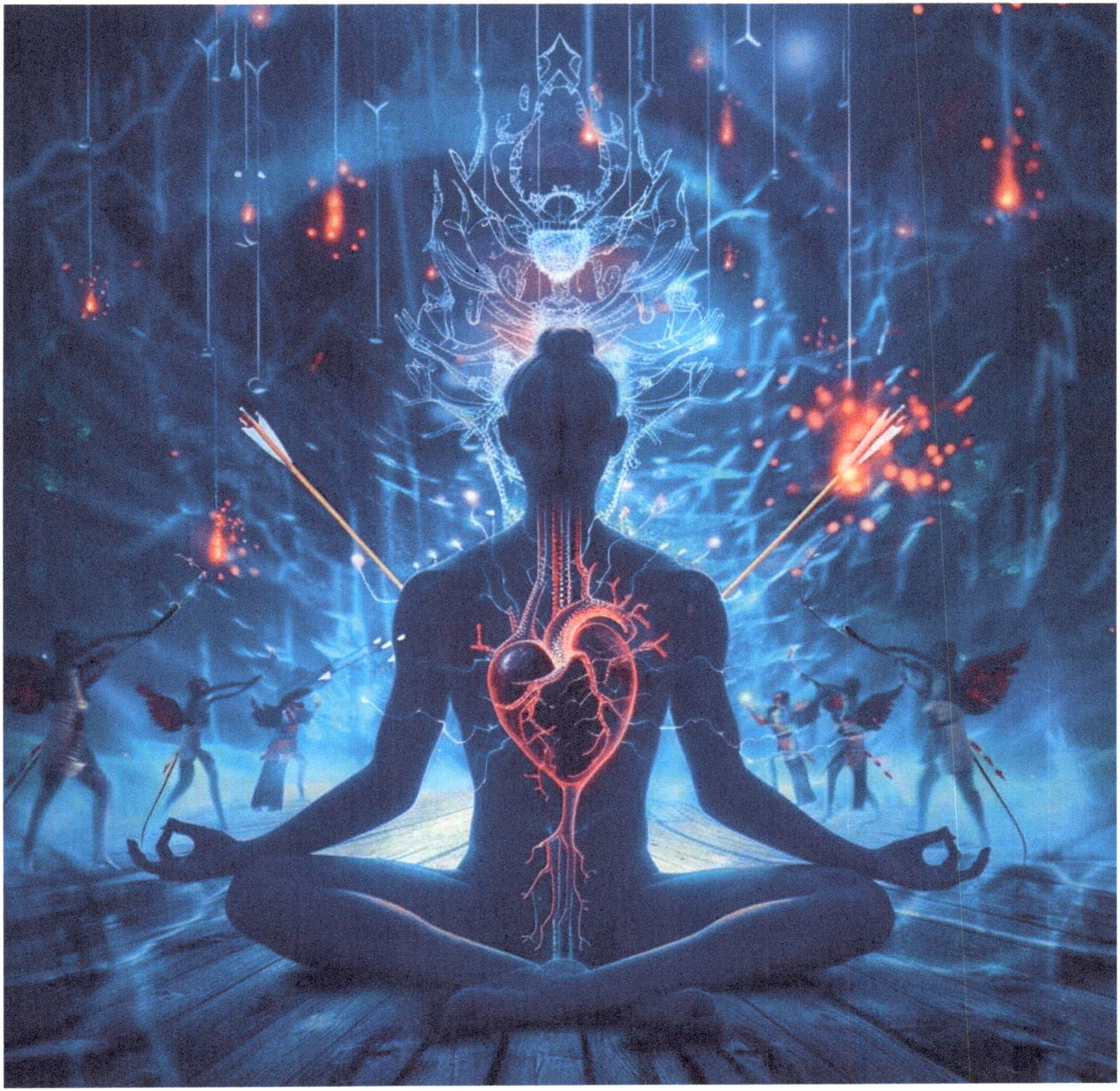

But then Mara (devil) brought her secret weapon, 3 gorgeous daughters to evoke **Lust and Sexual Desire** in Siddhartha's Mind.

So beautiful were Mara's daughters, that no mortal man could resist them. Sexual Lust is the weakness of all humanity, as it is a base instinct that is in our DNA and keeps us in this world.

But Siddhartha's Mind remained fully focused, concentrated, still, firm, and equanimous. Feelings of lust and desire arose in Siddhartha's Mind, but then merely passed by.

Siddhartha's ability not to attach to his desires, caused his Mind to become free from the attachment to sensual desires. The spell of Mara's daughters had no effect on Siddhartha.

Siddhartha had cut the heaviest chain that bound him to the cycle of rebirth – sensual desire.

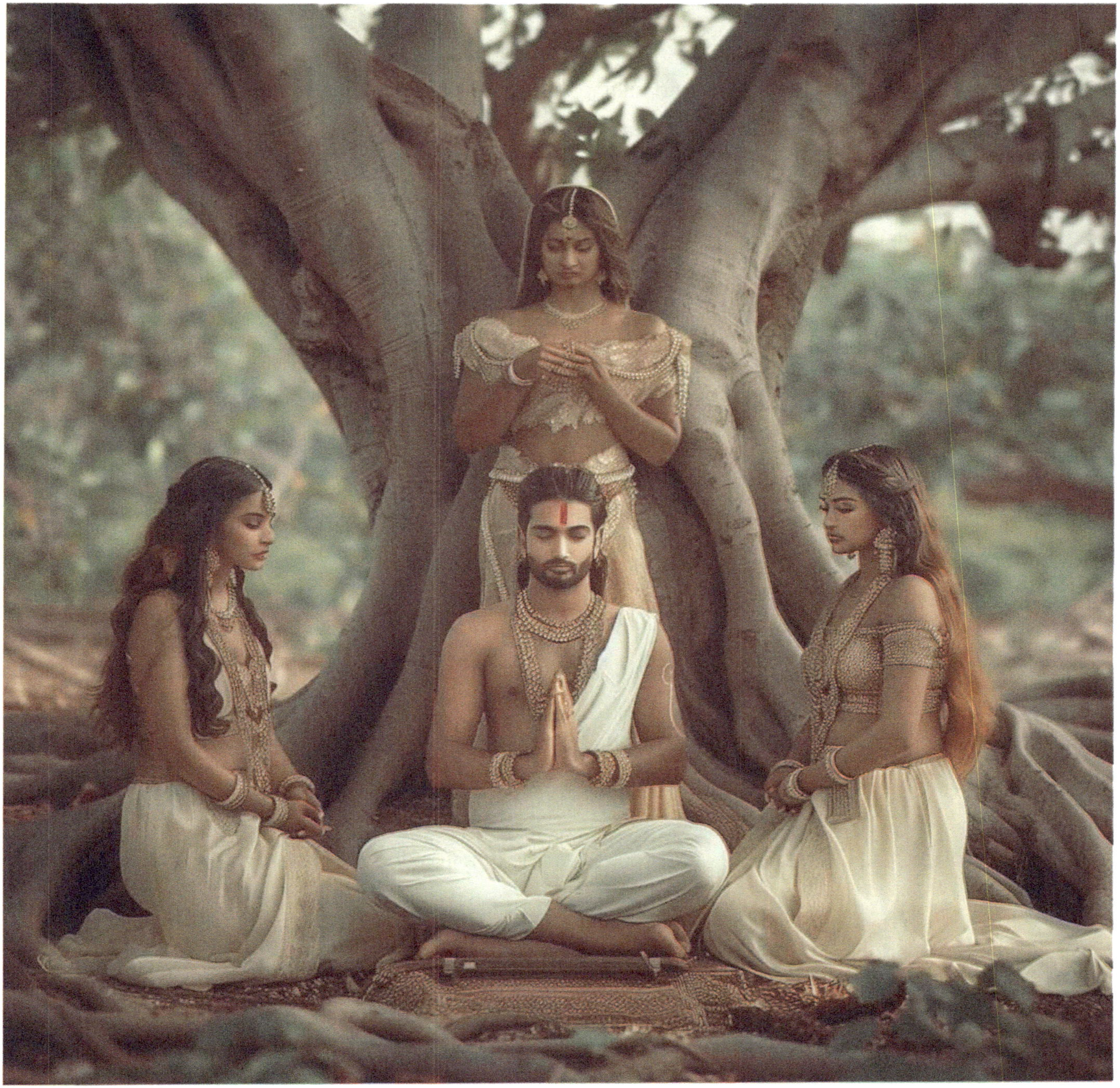

By eliminating the impurities in his Mind and cutting the other chains of attachment one by one, Siddhartha began to detach his Mind from this world of ignorance and delusion.

1. Belief in a permanent self (or identity view)
2. Doubt or uncertainty
3. Attachment to rites and rituals
4. Sensual desire
5. Ill will or aversion
6. Desire for existence in the material realm (attachment to the material world)
7. Desire for existence in the immaterial realm (attachment to formless realms)
8. Conceit or arrogance
9. Restlessness
10. Ignorance or delusion

Siddhartha realized that everything in this world is energy and energy cannot be destroyed, it only changes form.

That all things in the world arise, stay for a while, and then disappear. That suffering comes only if we attach or try to hold on to things.

By letting go of all attachments, Siddhartha could become free from the chains that had bound him to the world.

Siddhartha saw he was part of this vast Universe of Energy.

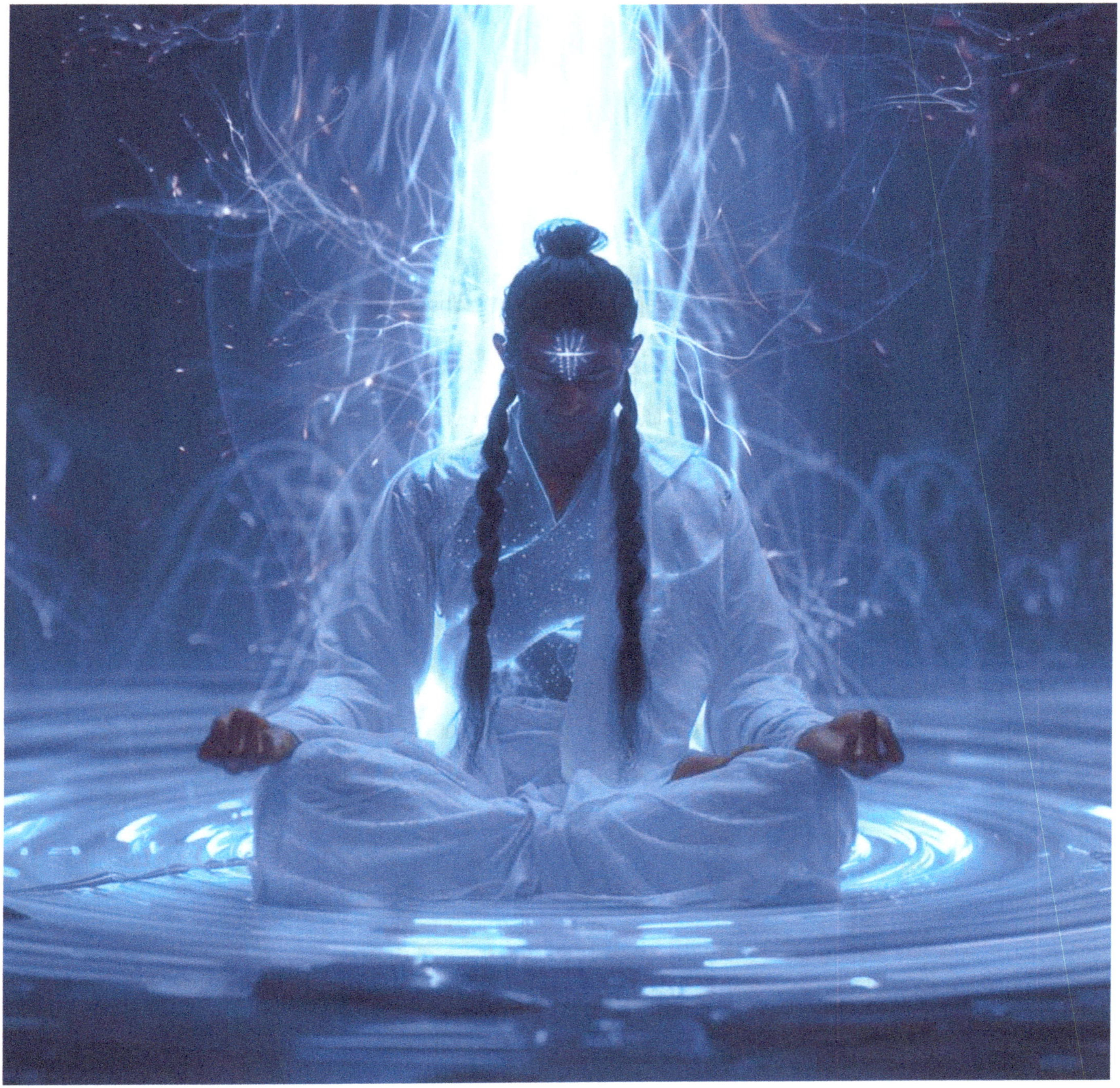

With his Mind releasing from the impurities and ignorance, Siddhartha began to see his countless past lifetimes.

He could remember in detail, hundreds of lifetimes, including who his parents, relatives, and friends were in each Life. He realized that his past lives were so numerous and uncountable.

He could see how many times he had lived, and died both in the human, animal, and other realms.

And in each Lifetime, he could see the suffering he had endured.

He also saw how many lifetimes it took him to perfect his virtues and keep his promise to himself to find the Ultimate Truth and help humanity find the way out of suffering.

43

Siddhartha saw the countless skulls and bones of his past lives, stacked up higher than any mountain.

These were all his past lives. A great sadness arose in him as he realized the Truth of how many times he had been born and died, not just as a human, but in the animal, reptile, and other realms.

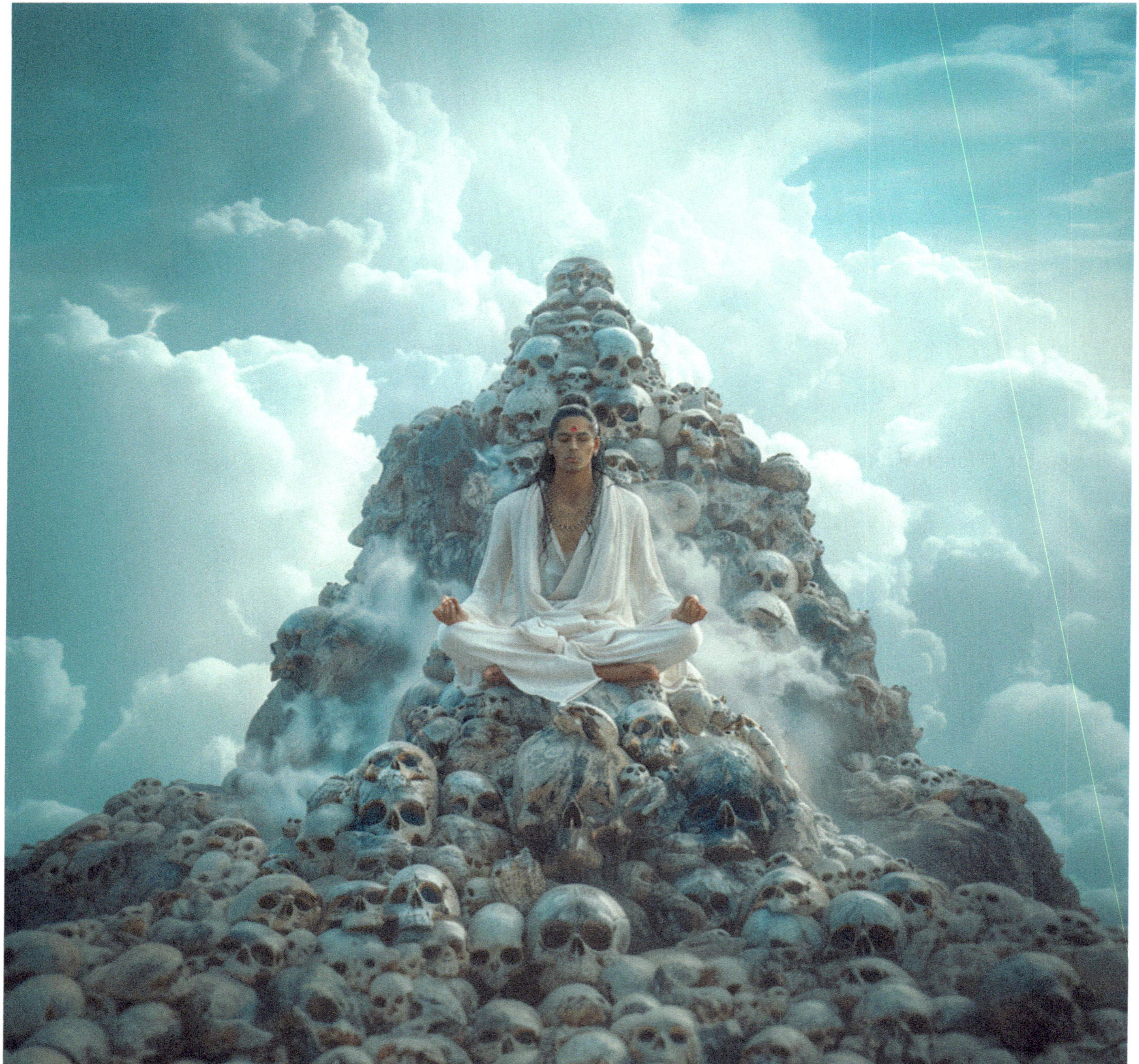

He saw the Ultimate Truth about himself and how he got here.

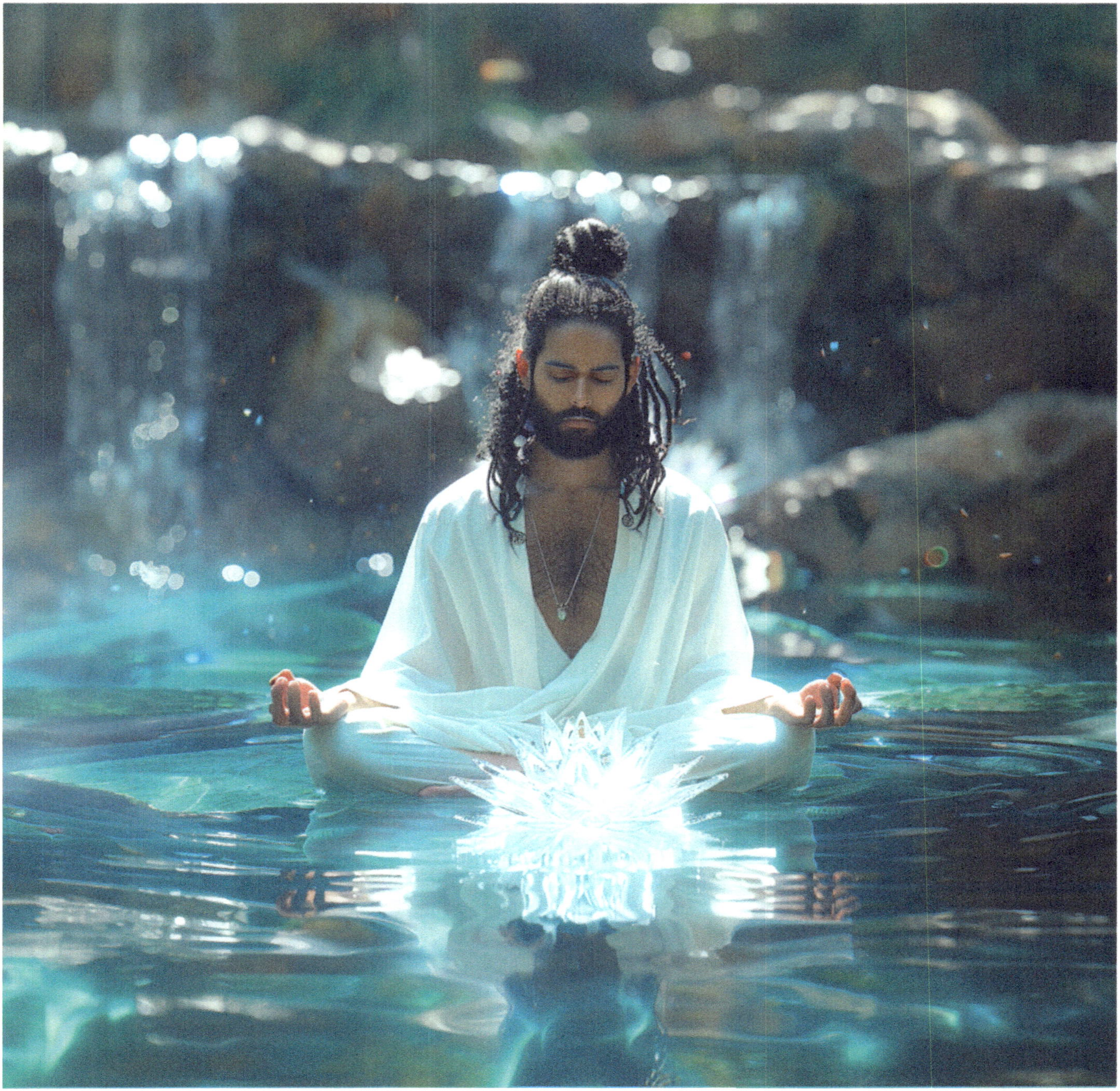

Then suddenly Siddhartha was in the presence of 27 Buddhas, that have existed over the eons of time.

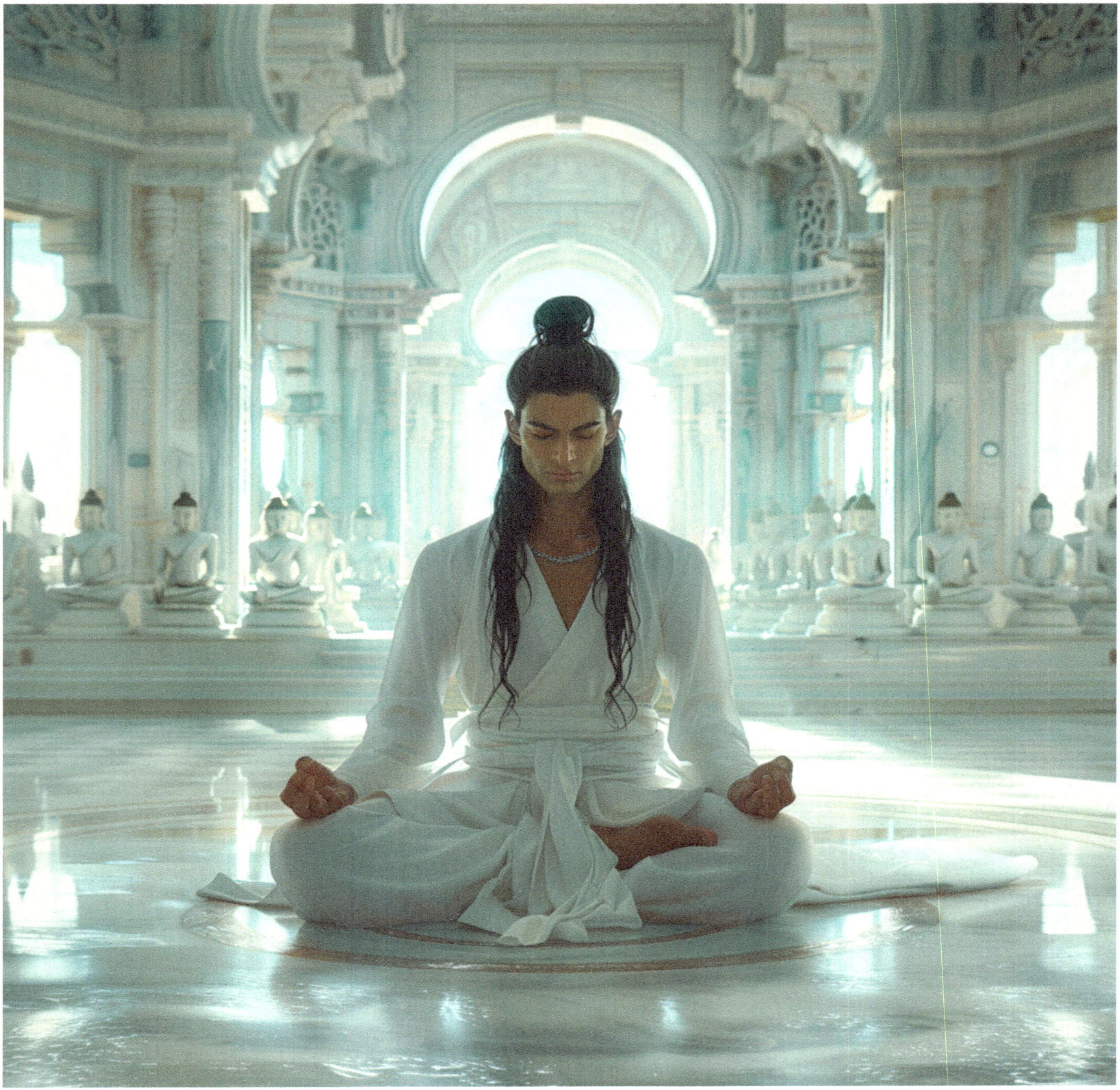

He became ONE with the Universe and all things as Pure Energy

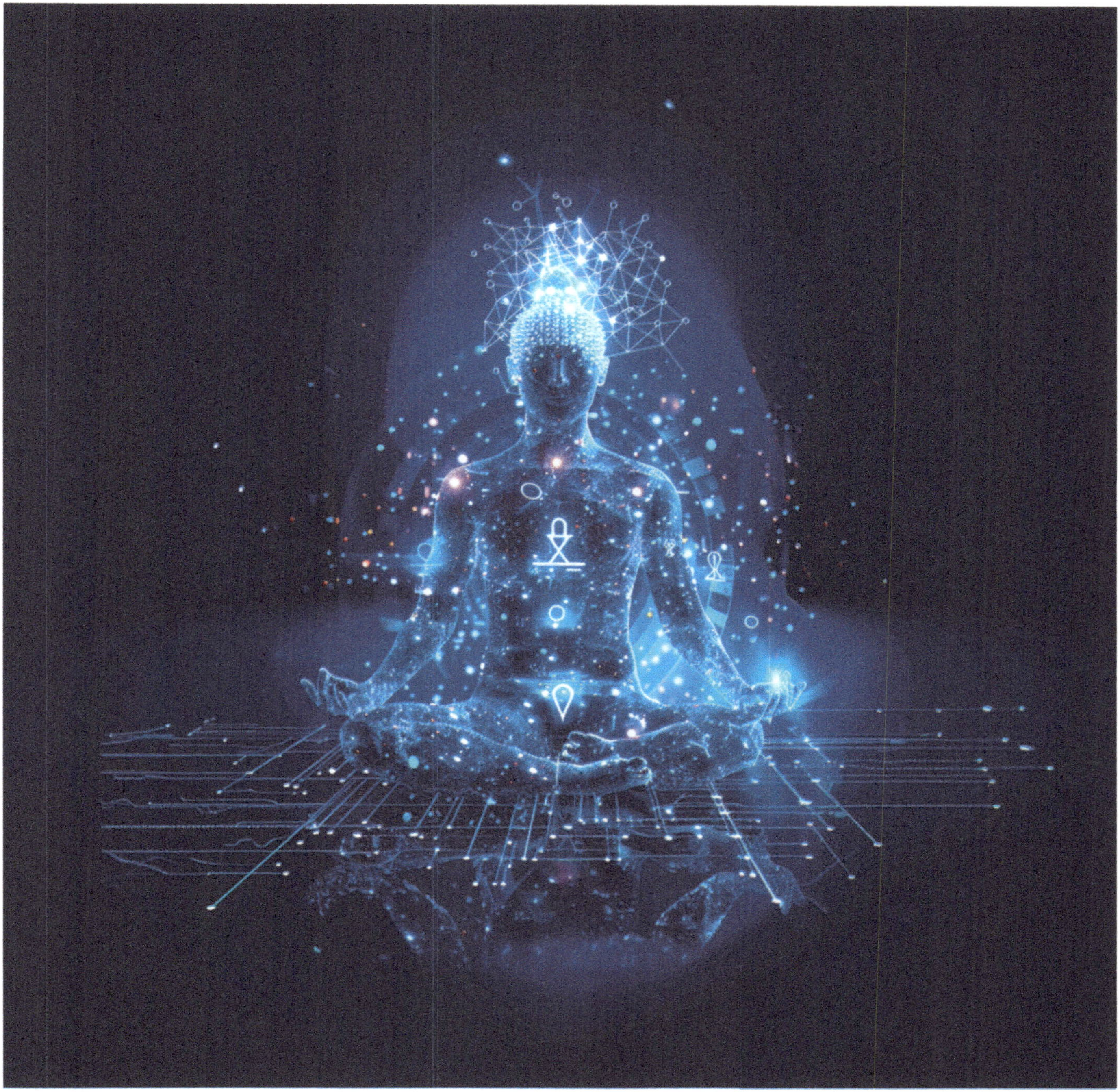

The world shook, as the man who was a Prince, destined to be a Great Ruler, who relinquished everything, now became: **The 28th Buddha, the fully self-enlightened, self-realized being.**

So rare is such an event in the History of the Universe, that the World stopped and took Notice.

53

The Buddha withdrew his meditation and opened his eyes.

When he eventually stood up, from his seat under the Bodhi tree, he began walking back and forth to the tree, enjoying, and absorbing the energy and the "fruits of his attainment" Enlightenment.

There was such a great radiant light coming from himself, a fully realized Buddha, that the angels came down from heavens to see what was going on.

For days they watched the Buddha walk back and forth, to and from the Bodhi tree.

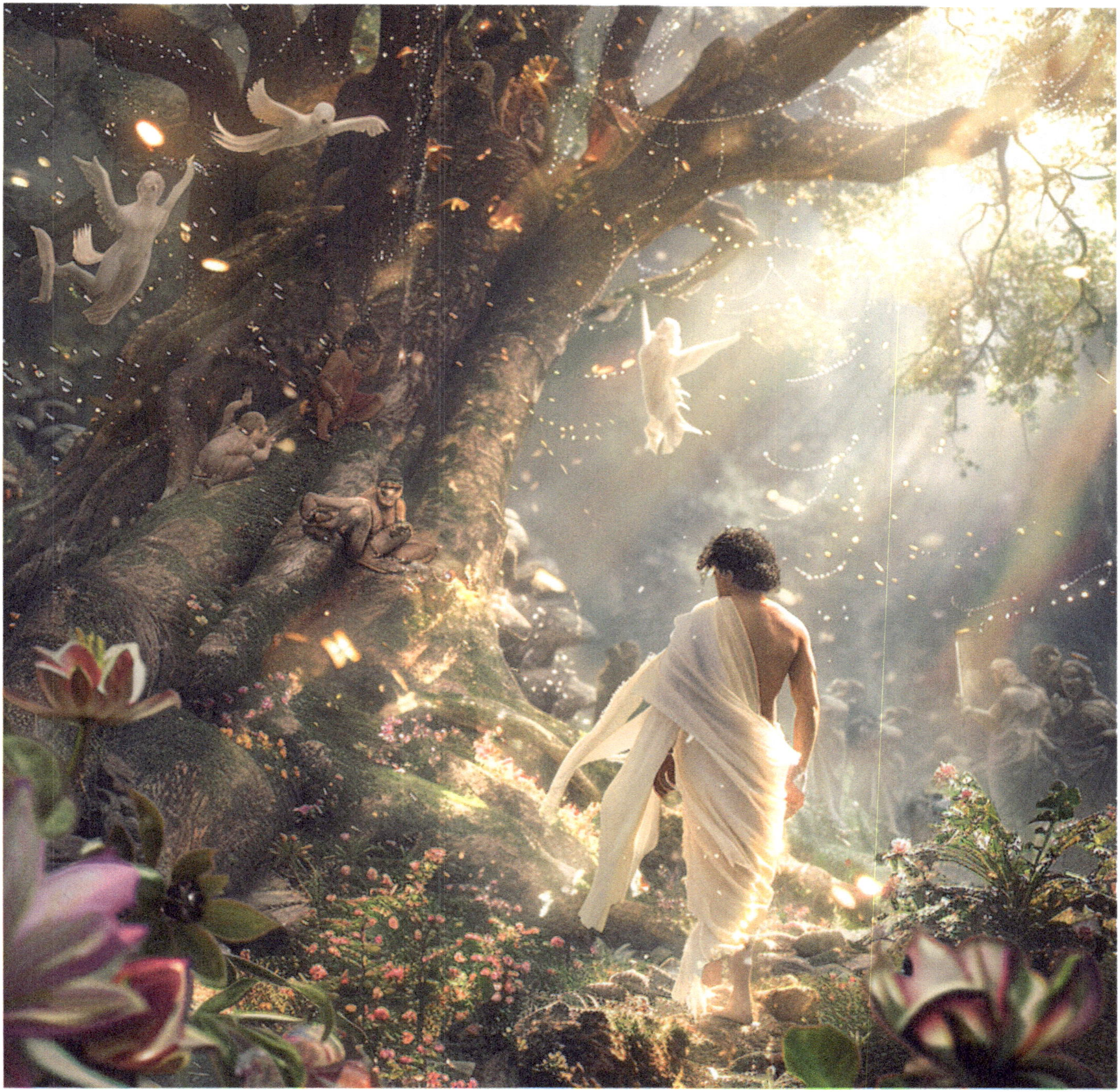

Finally, the Head of the Angels spoke, "Lord Buddha… say something… tell us what happened…what you experienced."

"The ambrosial Dharma I obtained is profound, immaculate, luminous, and unconditioned. Even if I explain it, no one will understand. I think I shall remain silent in the forest."

The Buddha replied,

Then there was silence for a long time……

The Head of Angels spoke again, "But Lord Buddha… how about those who have the potential to understand…those who are close to discovering…. how about them….do you not have something to say to those people?"

The Buddha contemplated for a while and then decided the Head of the angels was correct…
there are those in this world who have the potential to know and be Awakened.

And for those the Buddha decided to go into the World and teach so others could reach Liberation and become free from the cycle of rebirth (Samsara).

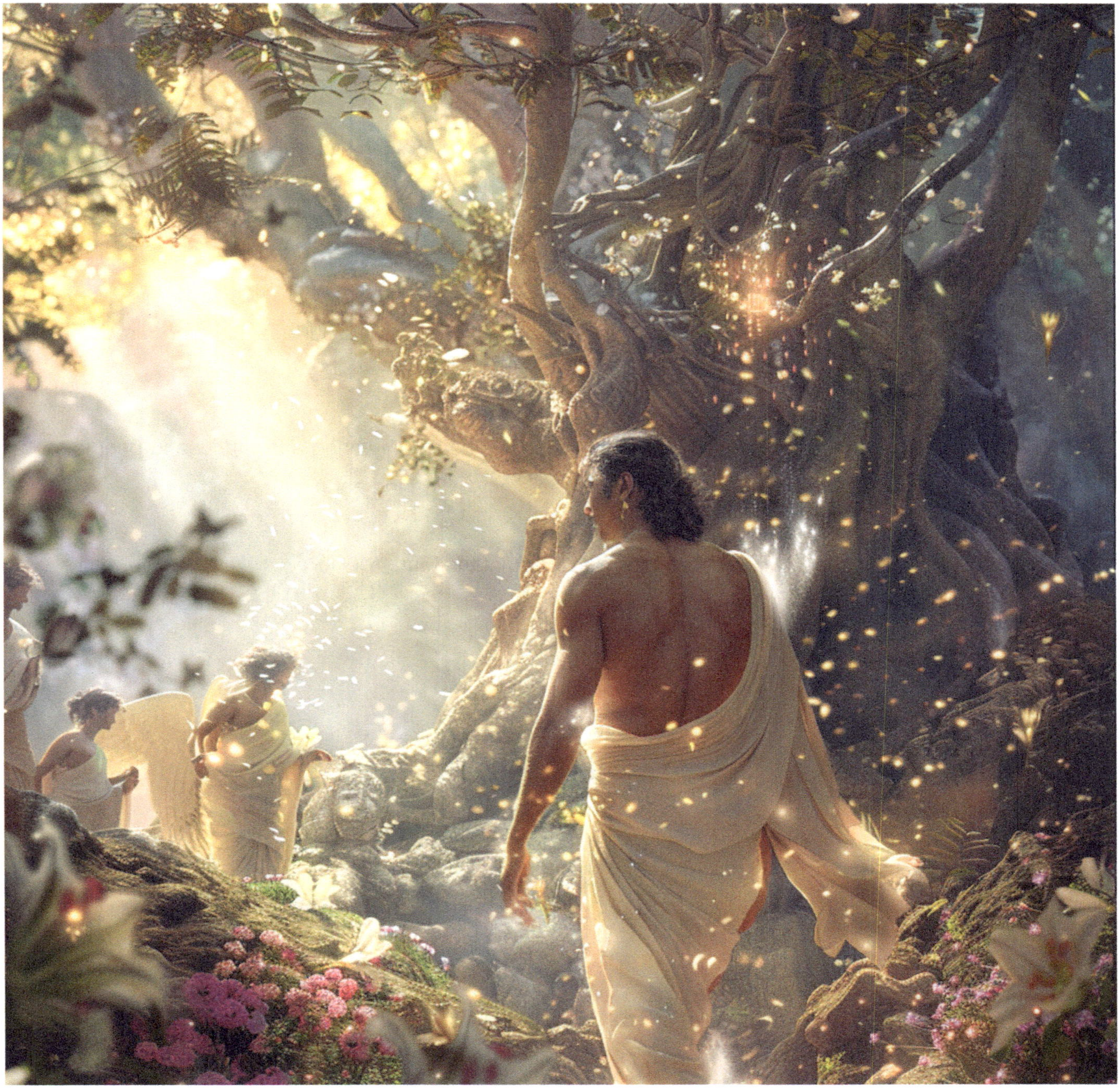

The Buddha was ready to reveal to the world his attainment of Enlightenment and teach the Dhamma to those who would listen.

However, the first people the Buddha encountered were the ascetics with whom he had practiced extreme methods. These ascetics did not want to believe or hear what the Buddha had to say!
They viewed the Buddha, as one who had given up on their ascetic practice and rituals.

This is the reality of the World and human nature. Even with an Enlightened Buddha standing directly Infront of his friends, they were simply not ready or willing to listen, in order to Awaken.

Despite his radiance and even Supernatural Powers, Buddha could only bring a few thousand people to various stages of Enlightenment, during the next 50 years of walking the earth.

This is the power of the World of Illusion and the deception of the Mara (devil).

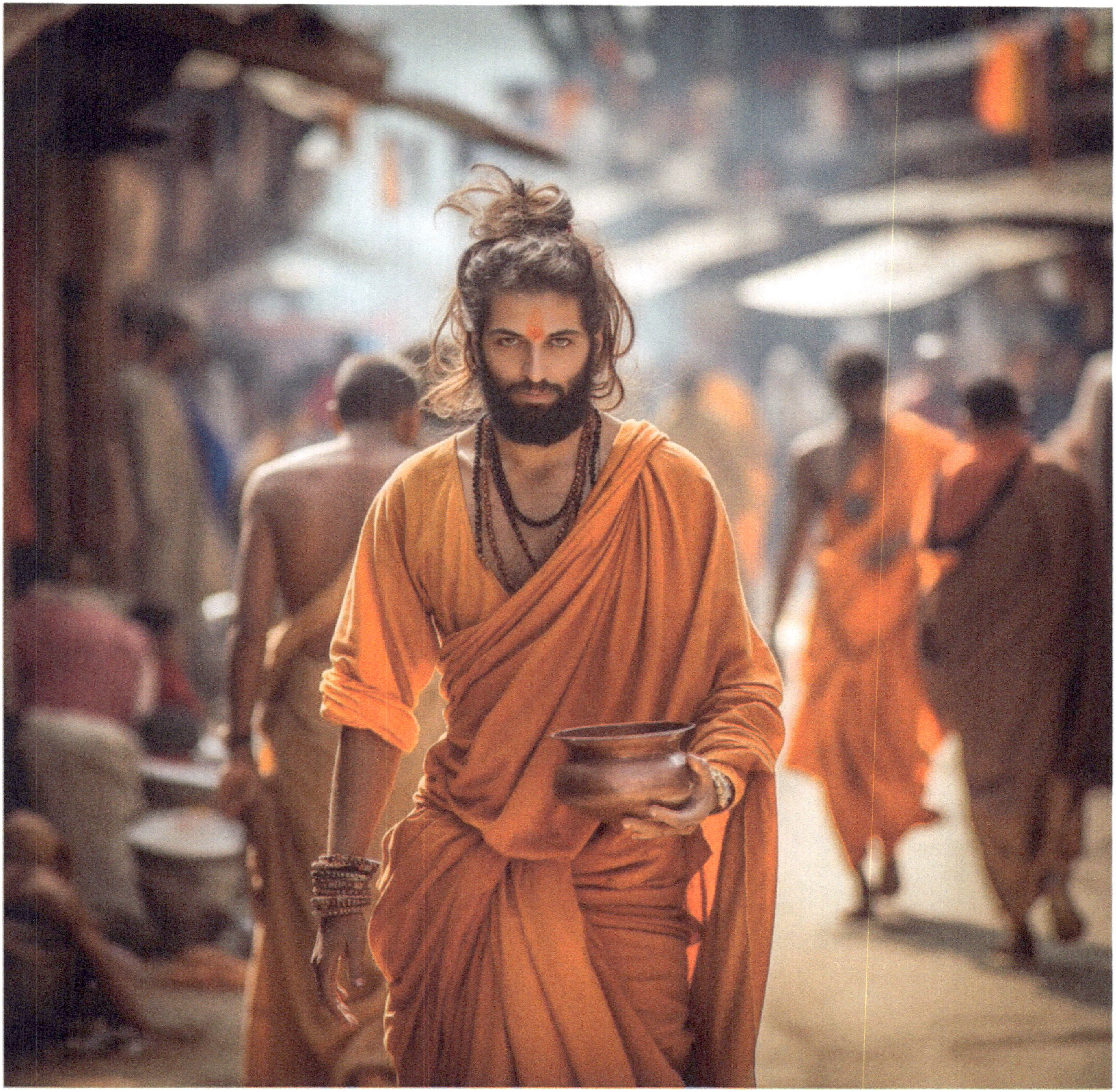

Overtime the Buddha created a Monastic order of Monks, for those who were ready to renounce the world and dedicate their time and lives, in order to reach Enlightenment.

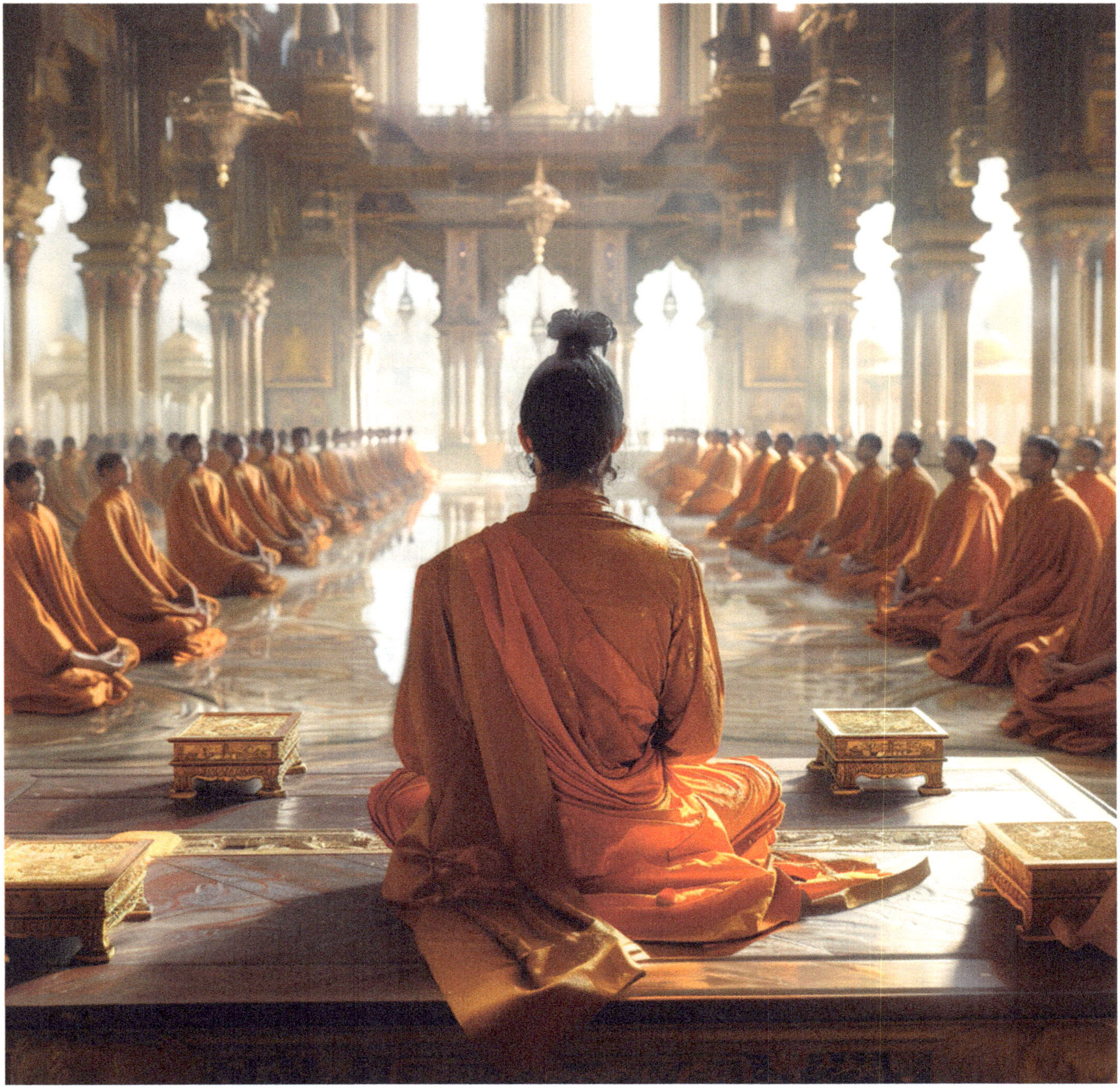

The Buddha also taught the Dhamma (law of nature) to laypeople (regular folks) who wanted to learn about the path to Enlightenment but were not prepared or able to renounce their householder lives, in order to ordain and practice as monks.

When the Buddha preached, he would use his Mind power to scan his audience in order to know if someone in the crowd was ready to realize the Dhamma. The Buddha would then give his teachings based on what would help them break through the illusion and reach the first stage of Enlightenment.

The Buddha would also plant the seed of Dhamma (nature) in others to grow within them, to be realized another time.

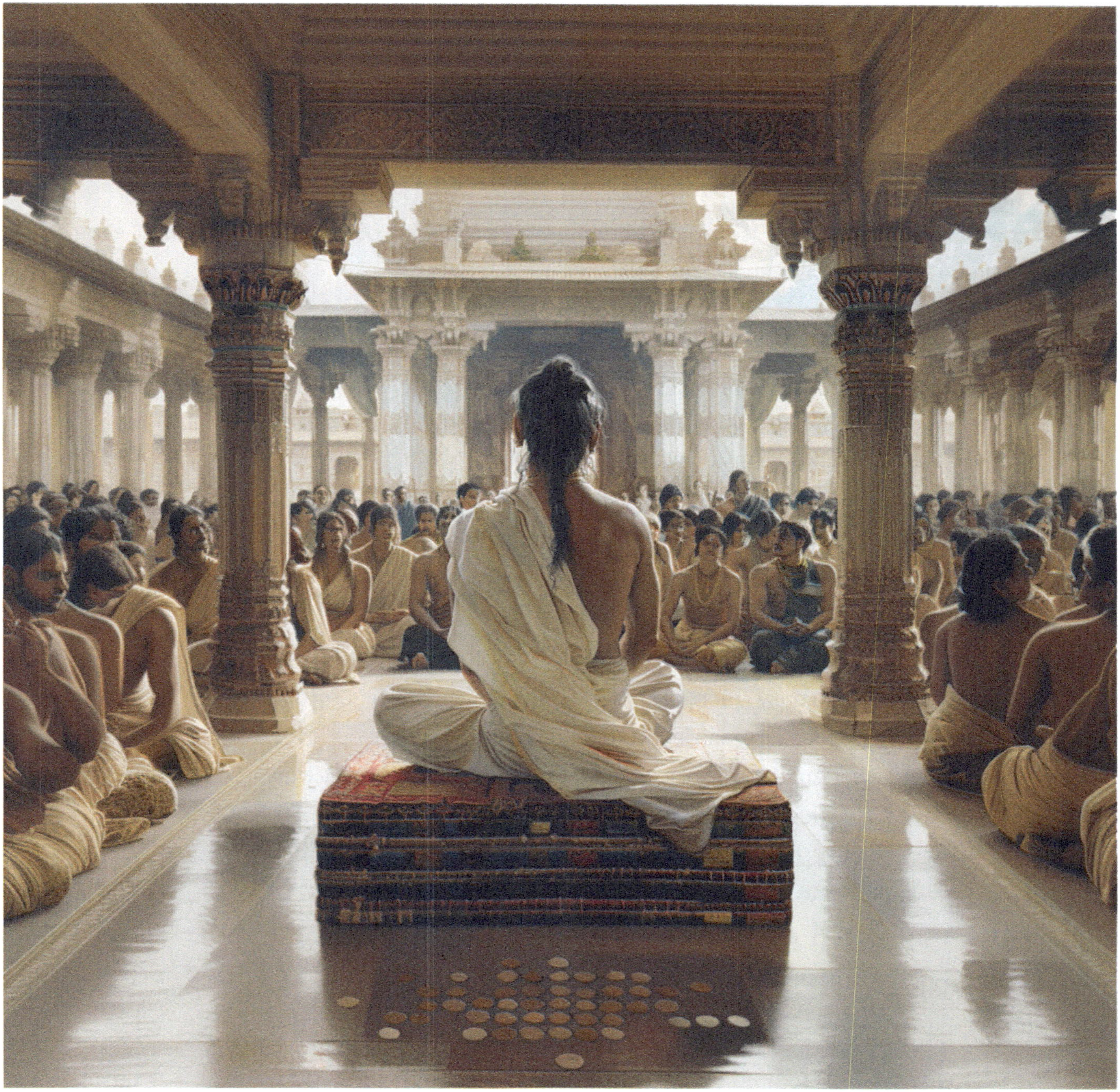

With a powerful Mind that can transcend dimensions, the Buddha would access other realms like the deva heavens, where he could teach Angels the Dhamma.

Angels do not have bodies like humans, that can act as a station between negative and positive energies. Therefore, they require a human form to achieve Enlightenment. This is the reason many Angels wish, to reincarnate as humans, to be able to practice Vipassana meditation and reach the Enlightenment and the level called Nirvana like the Buddha reached.

Nirvana is a realm higher than heaven, which angels aspire to reach, but they must come down to earth once again, taking human form and risking being trapped in the lower realms, to have a chance to achieve Enlightenment.

However, the world is not an easy place, and Angels return to the dark energy that dominates the world, and once more must face the same challenges and temptations we all face.
There is no guarantee that Angels will not lose their way once again for many lifetimes.
However, they have their virtues from their past lives to guide and shield them.

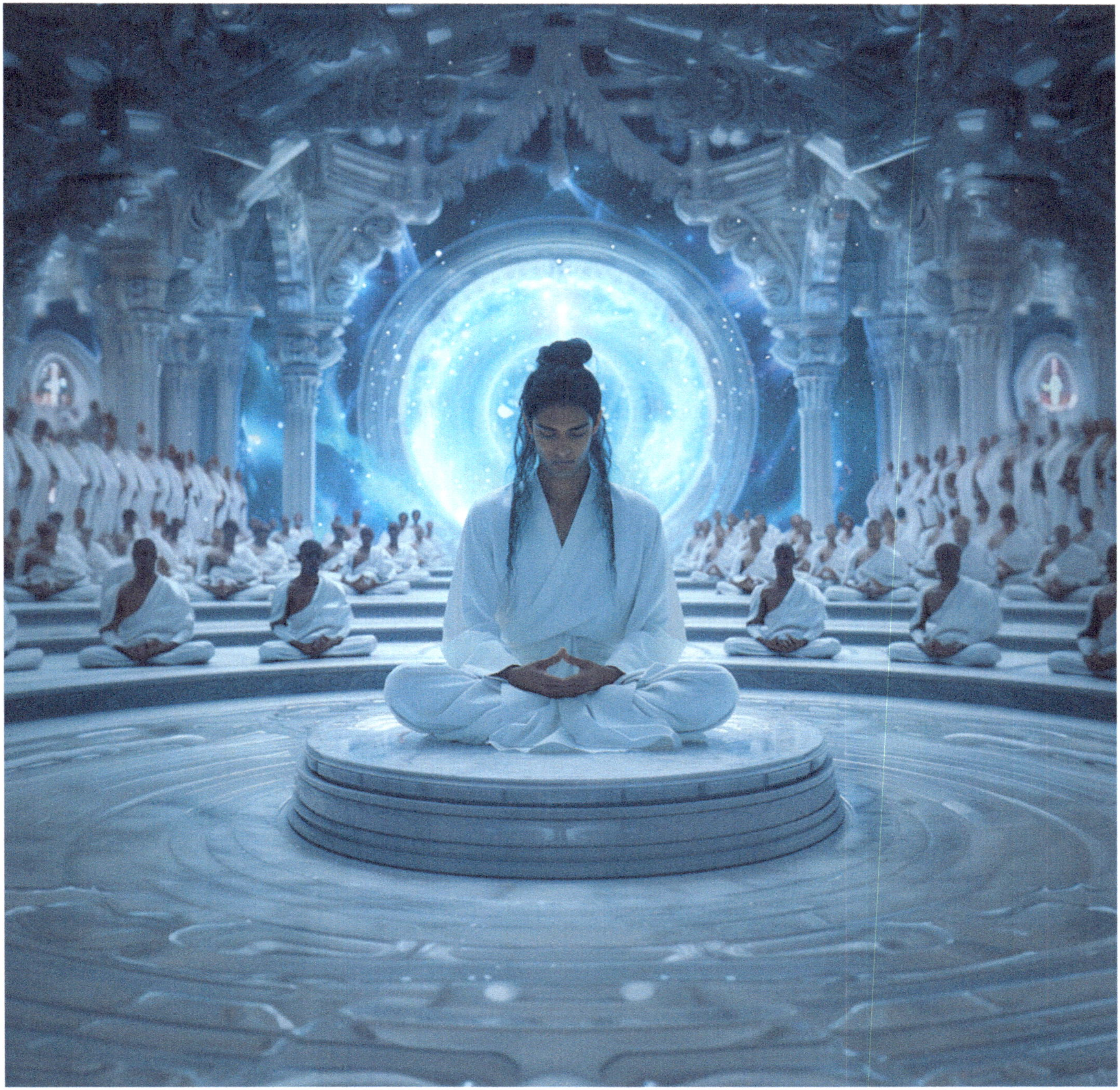

What many people today do not realize is that the Buddha was a flesh and blood human being.

He developed "Supernatural Powers" and "Supreme Wisdom" through meditation practice, and was god like in his abilities, but did not wish to be worshipped. The Buddha only wished for his teachings to guide others in order for them to reach the end of suffering, by reaching Enlightenment as he had.

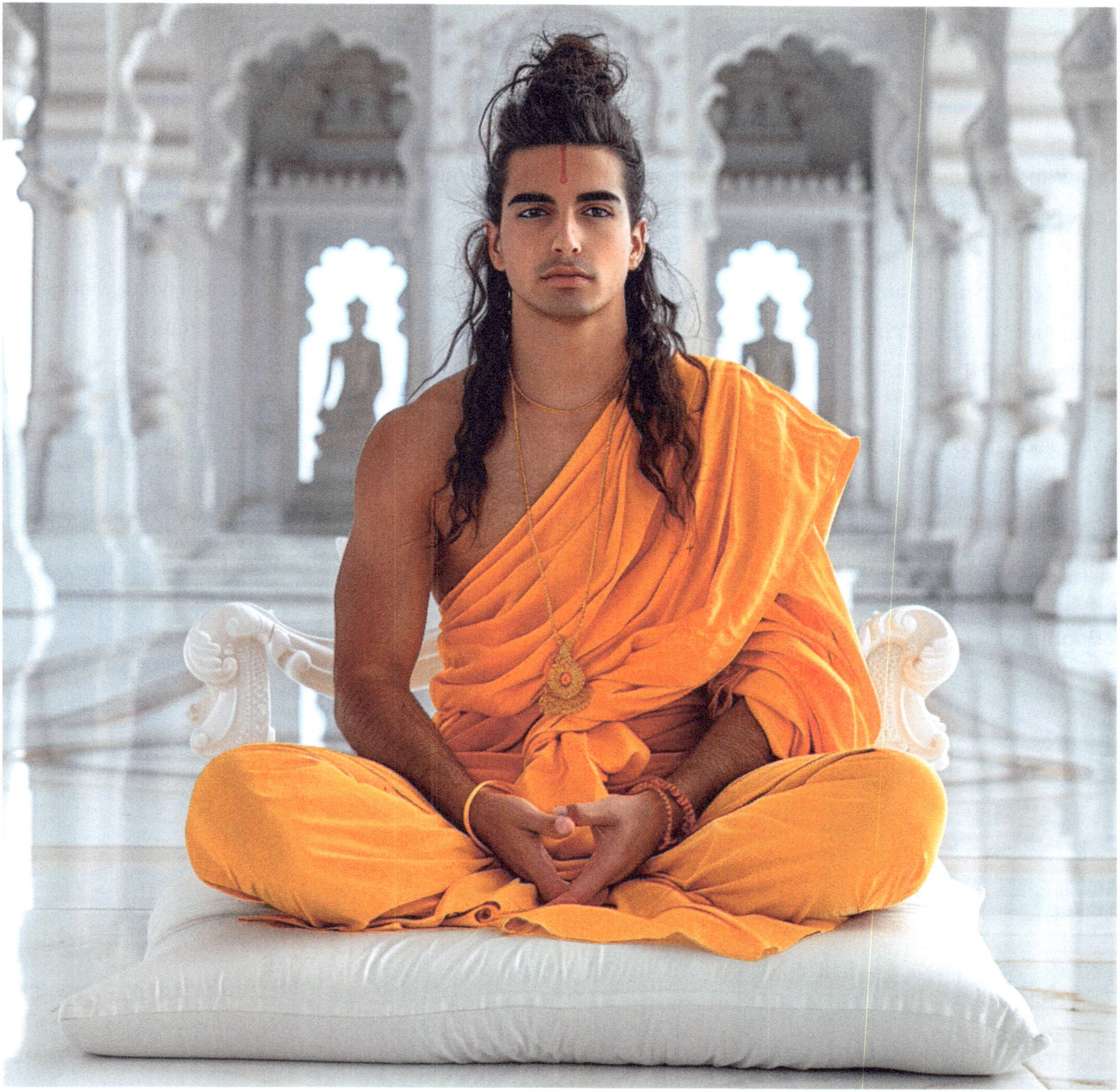

After the Buddha's death, statues were created to remind us of and keep the story of Buddha's attainment of Enlightenment alive, so others can find the way.

We show respect and bow to these statues, not as you would a god or deity, but to humbly acknowledge the Buddha's Enlightenment and to show our gratitude for his teachings, which he left for future generations to guide them on the path out of suffering, free from the cycle of reincarnation.

We also acknowledge his pure Energy stream of Goodness, that still pours into the world today.

Buddhism although considered a religion, is more akin to a scientific method, that invites people to examine for themselves through their own experience, what the Buddha discovered.

Buddha statues are meant to encourage us to practice morality, and meditation to find the path.

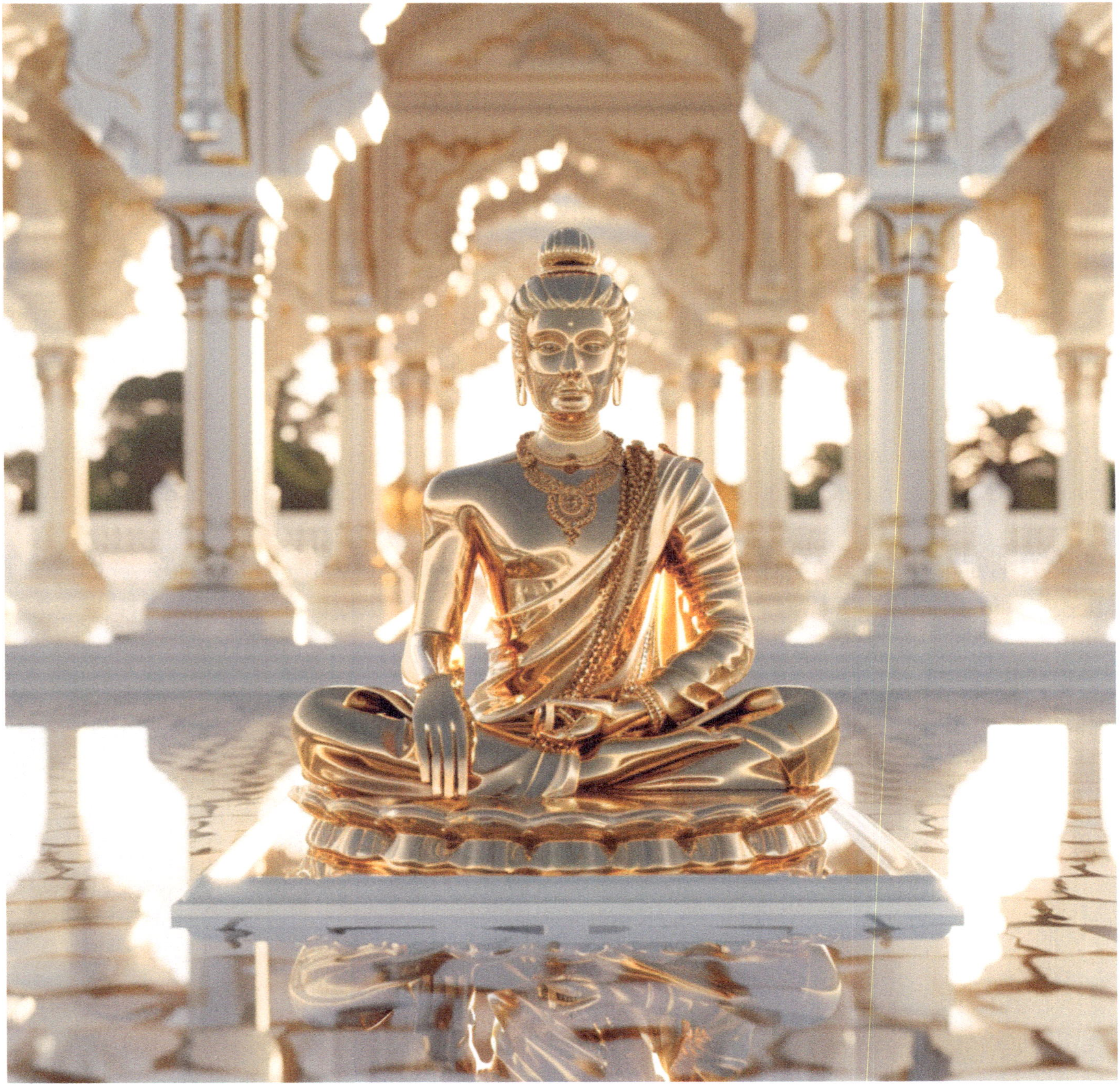

The Buddha once revealed that the odds of finding the path to Enlightenment is so rare and once discovered we should practice diligently while we still have breath and strength in this World.

There is no guarantee that next Life we will be born as humans or that we will once again discover the Buddha's teachings.

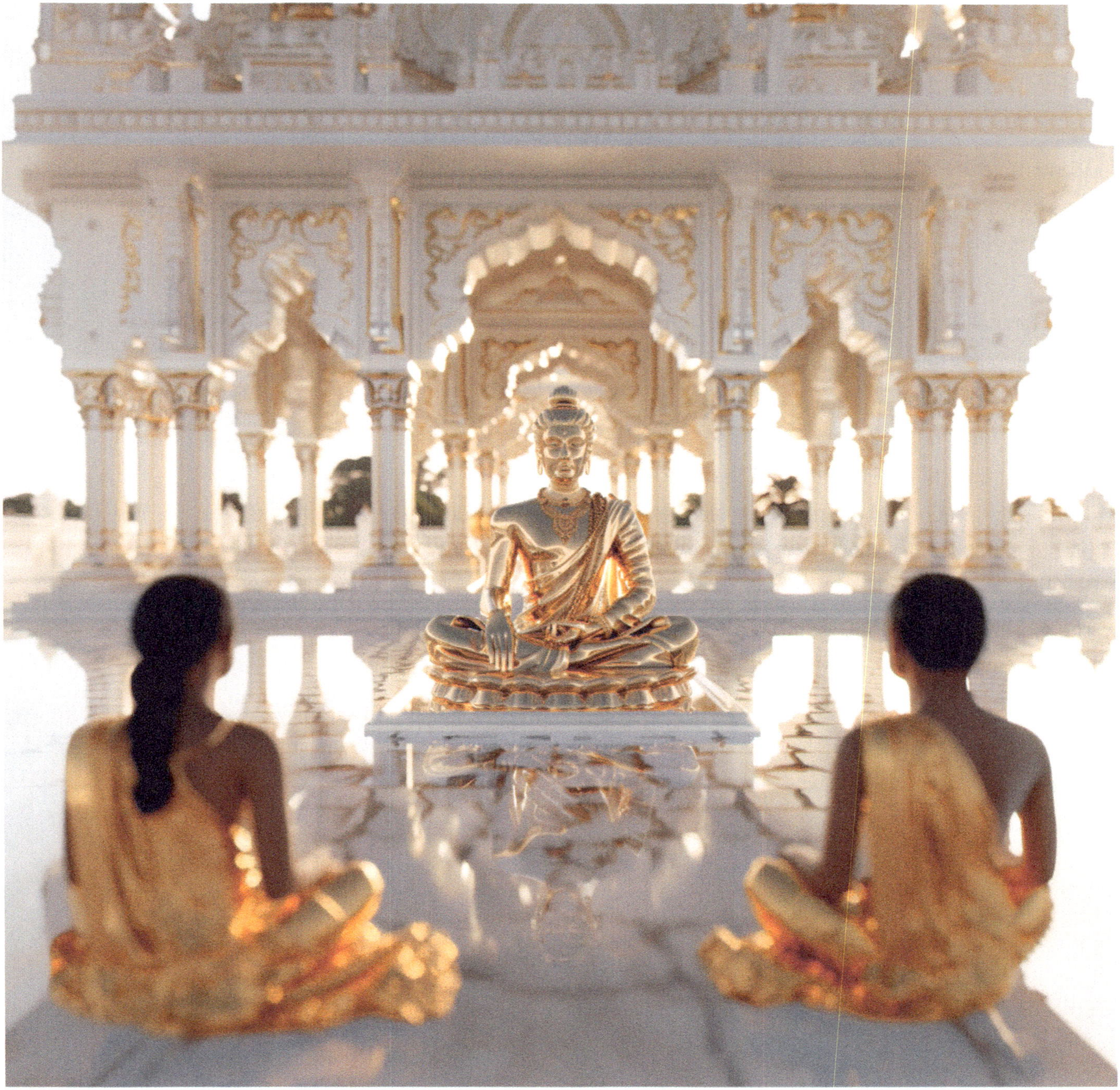

Many travelers to Thailand and other Buddhist countries, often visit the Buddhist Temples.
One can see the calmness and peace these visitors experience sitting inside these temples and in front of the Buddha statue.

They typically admire the beauty of the temple and feel the vibrations, often sitting there for hours absorbing the unknown Energy.

Buddhist temples in Thailand and other Buddhist countries are like Energy Beacons that connect to the Energy stream of the Buddha, his Teachings, and the Masters.
Temples often contain the relics (crystalized remains) of the Buddha or Enlightened Masters. These precious relics themselves emit great Power.

The vibration from chanting and meditation by Monks and practitioners also make these divine places vibrate with positive Energy and Goodness.

Monks meditating and chanting cause these temples to radiate positive Energy and Goodness, which cancels out the dark energy and electromagnetic waves, flowing through the world.

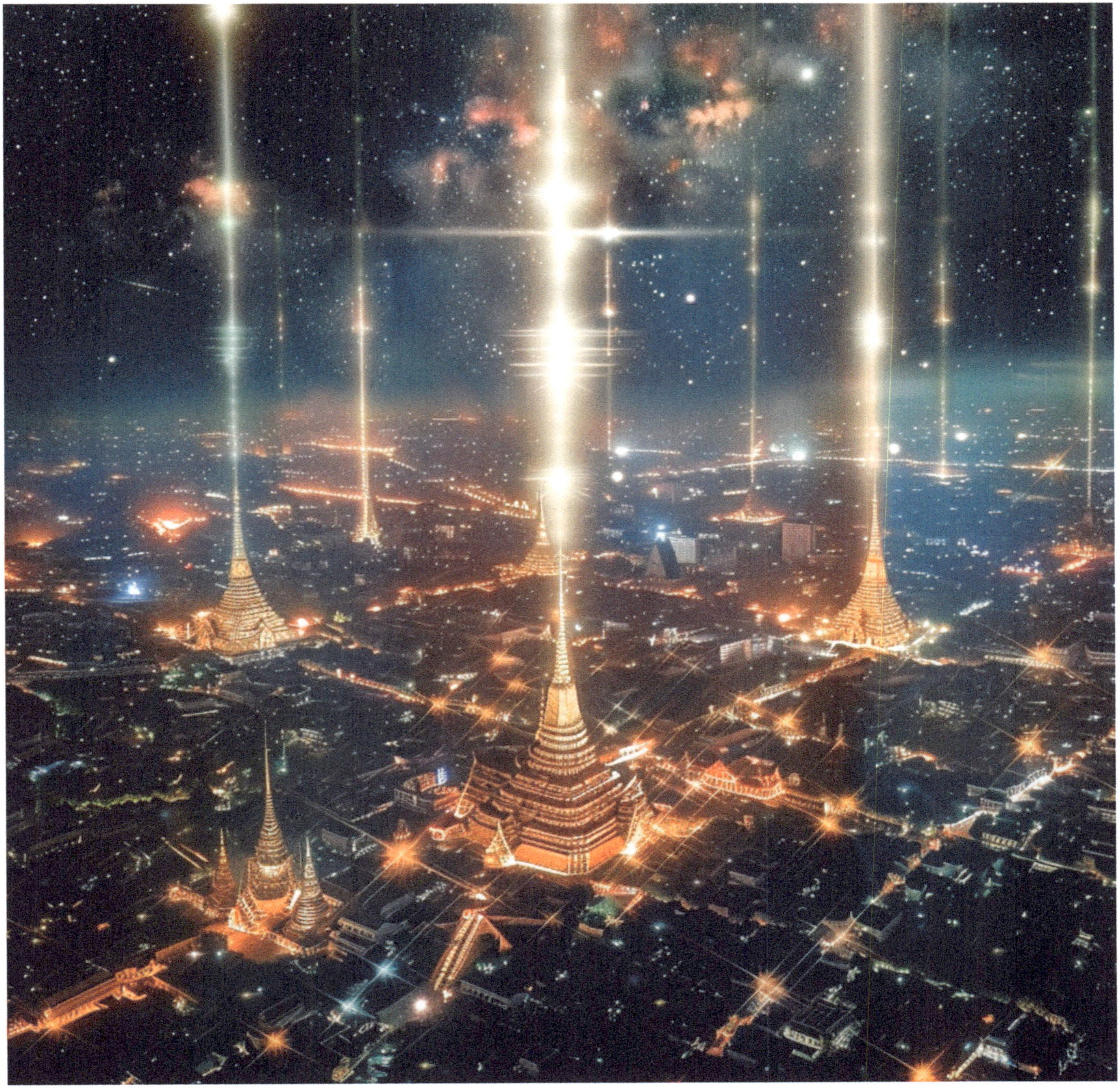

Everything in this world is made up of Energy.

The Buddha during his Life time spread his Energy particle wherever he walked or slept.

Once the Buddha passed away, he did not cease to exist, only he left his old worn body, which decayed like all living things. However, the Buddha's body when burned left crystalize relics, which were distributed around the World spreading his Energy Stream.

Many who practice Vipassana Meditation and raise their Mind Energy, to the fine Energy level, can connect with the Energy of the Buddha. They can see the Buddha in the form of a human, statue, or as pure Energy.

The Buddha's Energy continues to support goodness in the World and can lift people's Minds.

People around the World continue to pray and ask Buddha for support in for their lives, connecting to the vibration of the Buddha's high Virtues and Goodness, thus helping elevate their own vibration and goodness, translating to luck and improved lives and cancelling out bad energy and karma.

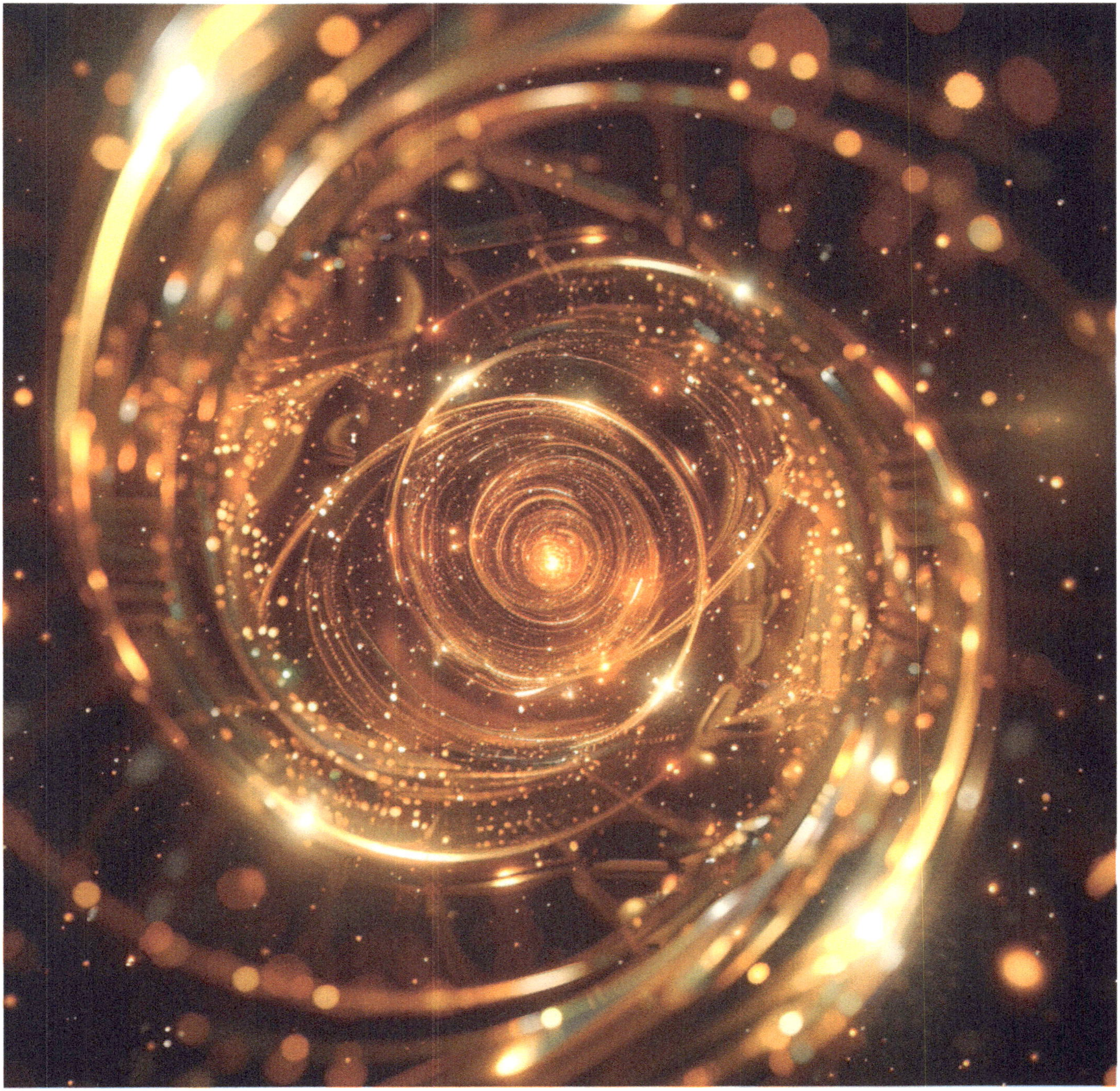

The path to Liberation is sometimes hard to find, especially in the modern world. But once uncovered the Mind begins to feel cool and happy, returning to a familiar natural state of harmony and wisdom.

The Mind returns to Nature.

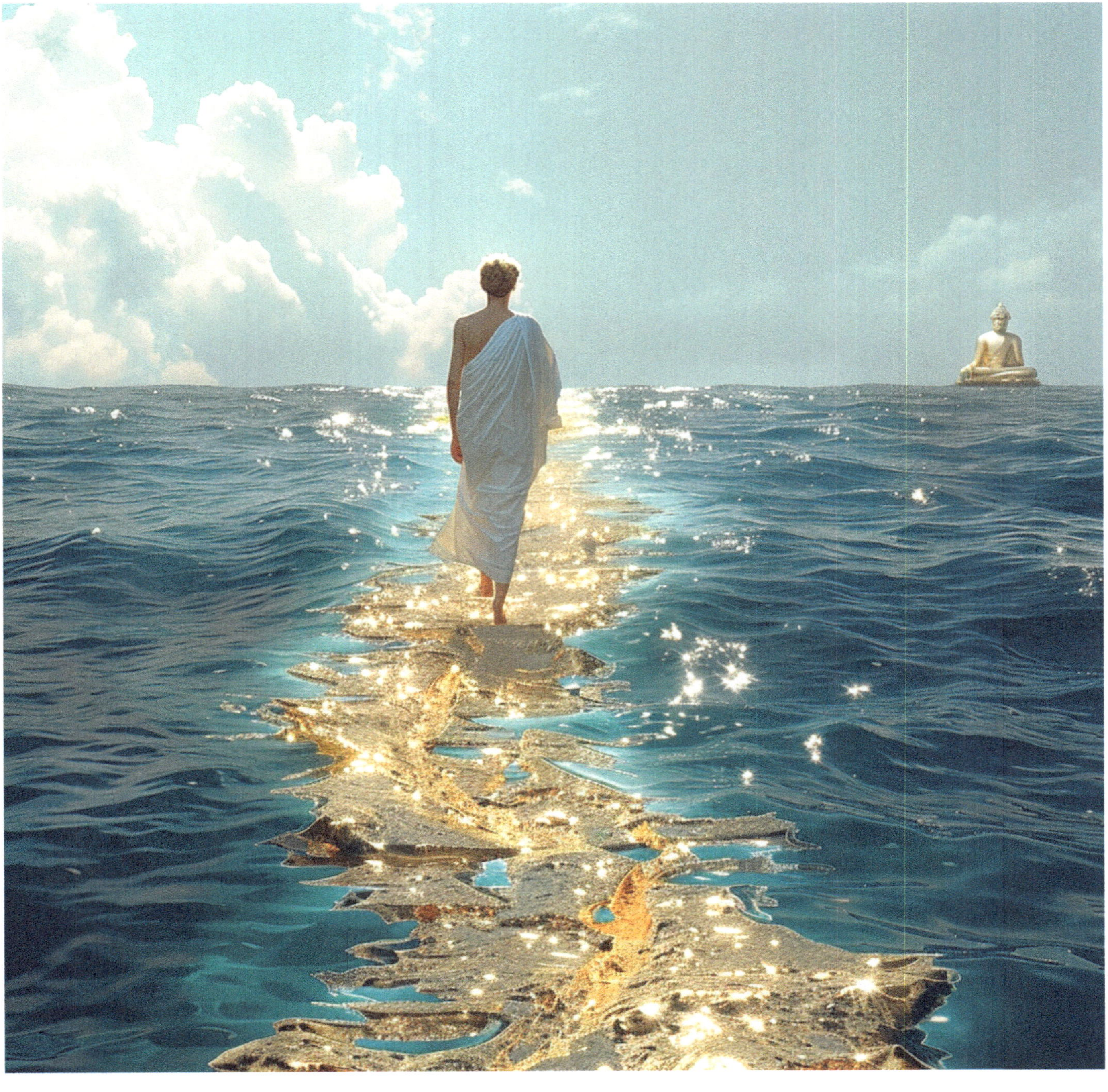

CHAPTER 2

WHAT THE BUDDHA DISCOVERED

GOOD AND EVIL

The world is made up of Good and Evil. These 2 opposing forces are part of nature as, positive, and negative energy. The World becomes Anti-Nature as these forces go out of balance.

Humans have the capacity to use their bodies as a transformer station, between they 2 opposite energy currents. It is for this reason that when we meditate, some people are able to see, hear or connect to the fine Energy of other dimensions.

Only the human body has this ability to connect to these fine energies through mediation, so therefore to reach the Enlightenment we must be born as a human. Although sometimes we look at animals as having the capacity to Enlighten (Dogs, Cats, Monkeys, Whales), they lack the ability of humans.

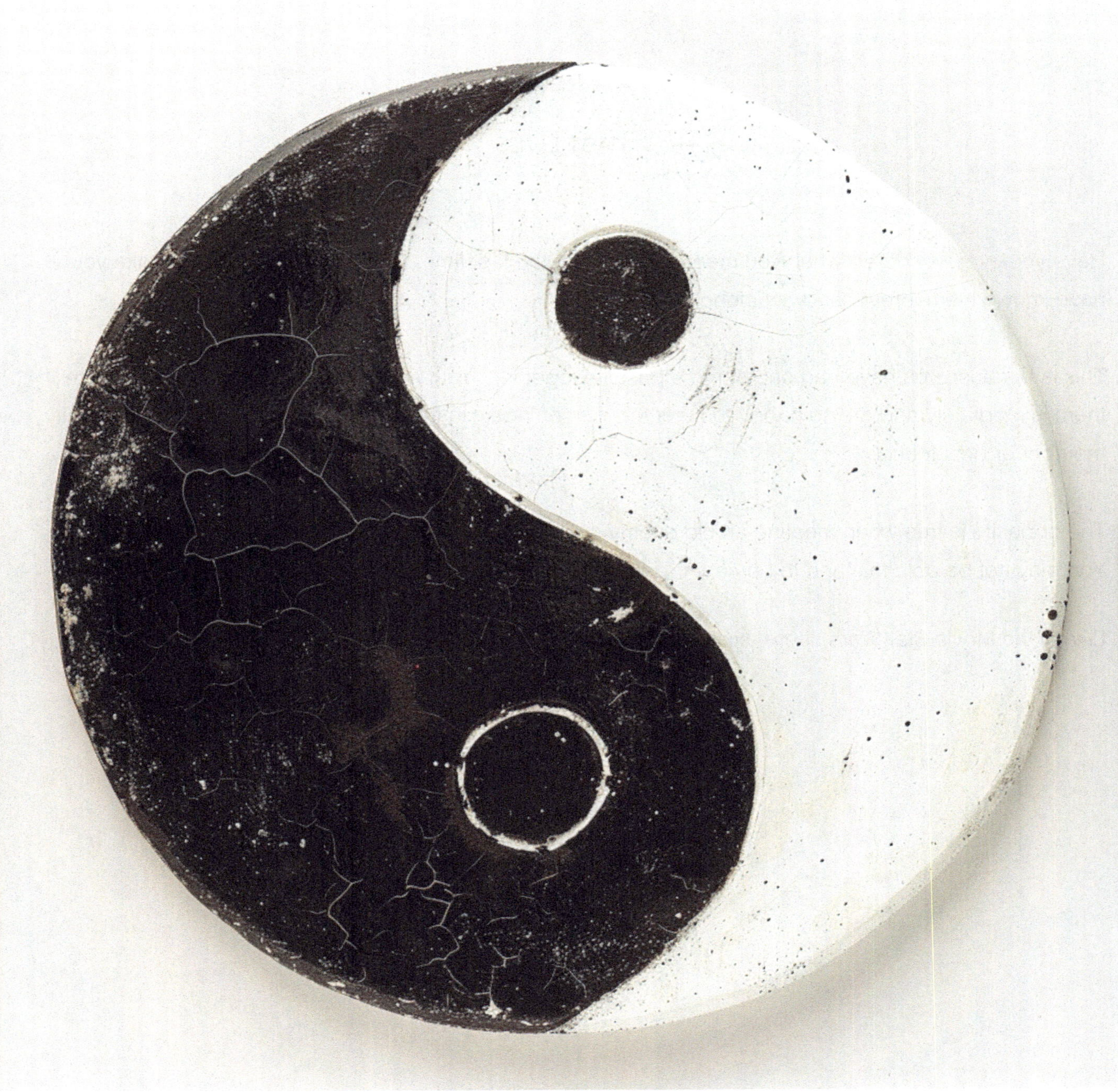

PAST LIVES

Have you ever wondered when you meet someone for the first time, and you immediately feel like you have known them forever and get along so well.

This is because you have had one or more past life together. Your knowing Mind and heart recognize them immediately and are so happy to meet this person again in this life. They could have been a family member or best friend.

The opposite is true when meeting an old enemy or someone who wronged you in the past.
You may not be able to stand to be near them or even hear their voice or read their messages.

Like in the Movie Star Wars, there exists the Dark Force (Dark Energy) and the Good Force (Light Energy).

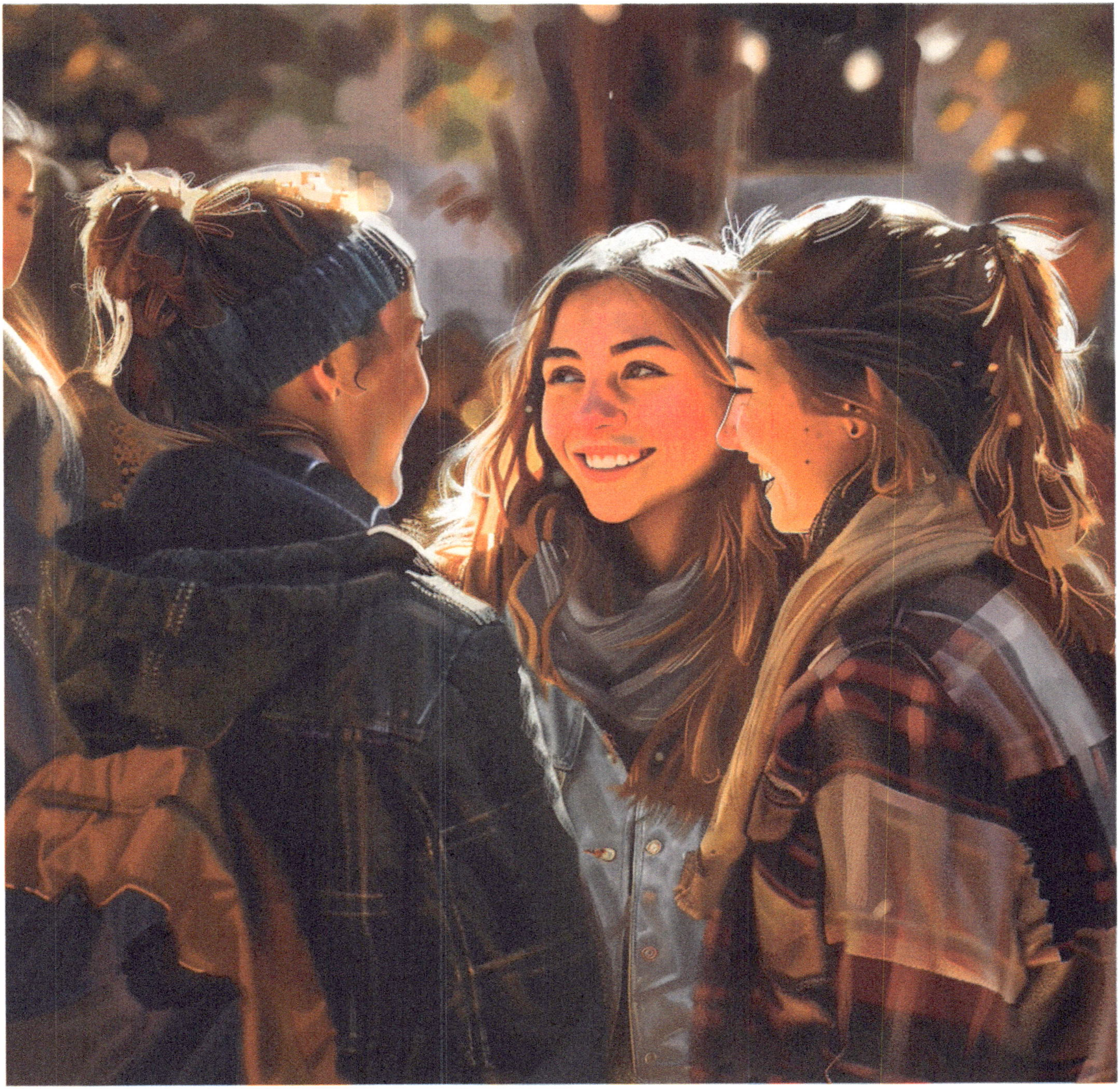

REINCARNATION

Reincarnation is like a never-ending play, where we keep coming back to life in different roles. We experience birth, life's ups and downs, and eventually, death. But even though we may want to leave this cycle of constant rebirth, we are stuck because of our karma and actions in past lives, which create our future.

The Buddha taught that life involves suffering, but by doing good deeds and meditating, we can reduce karma and suffering and eventually break free from this cycle of reincarnation and find peace.

IMPERMANENCE

Life is short and full of uncertainty and suffering.

The main reason we suffer in life, is because we want things to be the way we want them to be.

We do not like change or uncertainty. When things change, or there is loss, all sorts of feelings and emotions arise, until we feel pain, grief, suffering and even anger.

Change is the law of nature.
With all things in nature, they arise, they stay for some time and then they disappear.
This is how are lives are, but do not want to admit it and mostly, we wish this not to be the case.

The Buddha's 84,000 teachings can be summarized in one word "non-attachment".

If we can see the impermanence in all things, and maintain a neutral and equanimous Mind, then we can see everything as nature and dhamma. We appreciate the present moment, but do not try to hold on to it.

The Buddha reached the Enlightenment by not attaching to anything that arose in his Mind.

87

SEED OF KARMA

"You reap what you sow."

"When you plant a mango tree, it takes a long time for the tree to grow and then to bear fruit".

So it is with Karma, both **"good deeds"** and **"bad deeds"** take time to show their result or bear their fruit.

But eventually karma will appear – either in this life or in a future life.

Because Karma can take a long time to manifest, many people doubt that karma is real and they therefore, continue to be heedless or believe their actions have no consequences.

The Buddha taught that everything in the universe has cause and effect.

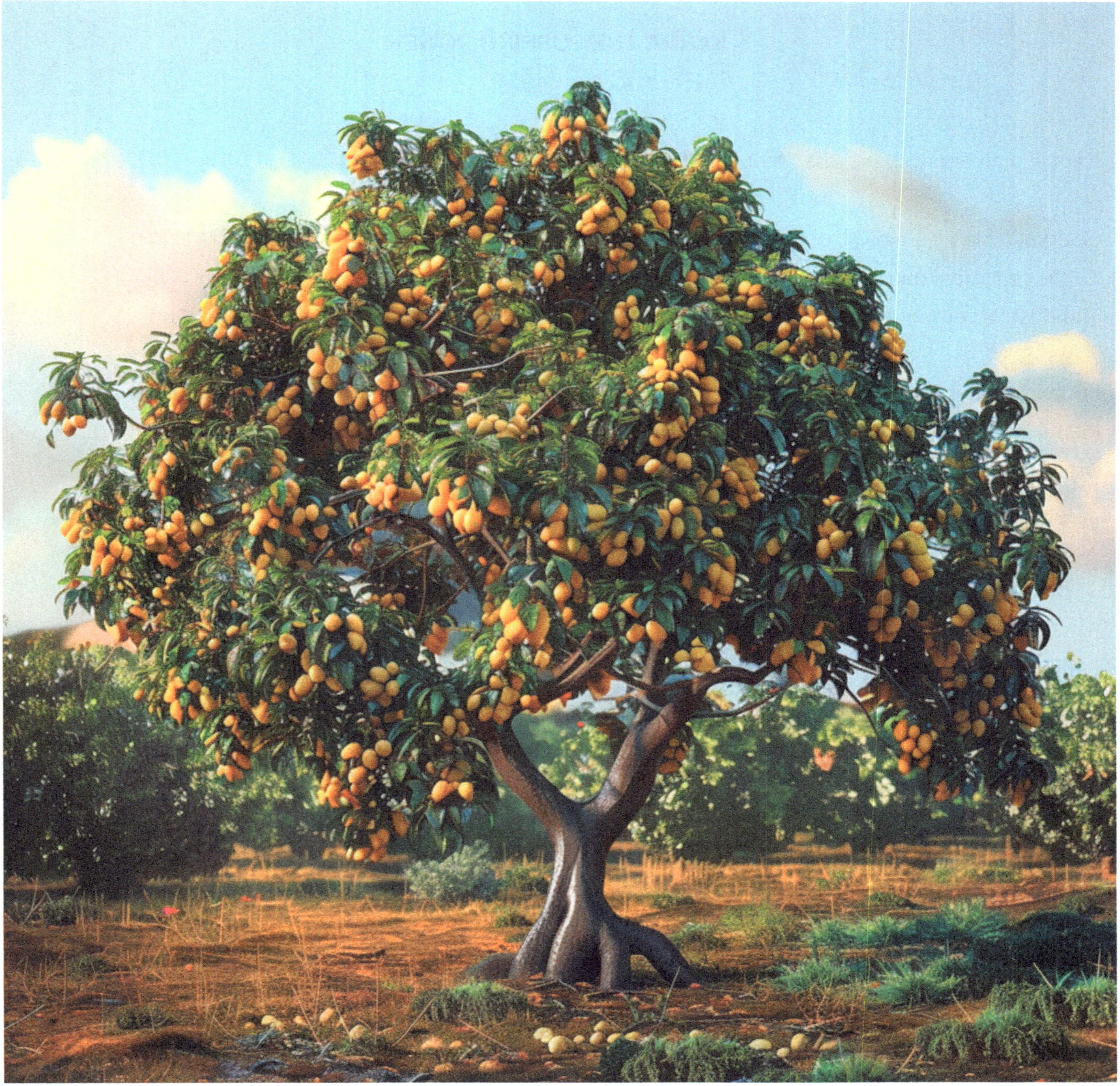

KARMA THE PUSHING POWER

Karma is an energy which has a pushing power.

Good and Bad Karma will push a person's life in the direction that reveals as good or bad luck.
This is really just cause and effect of Energy.
The pushing power of Karma puts people in places and in positions, where things can happen.

For example: if a person wrongs another person in one lifetime, then the pushing power of karma will at the future time, bring these 2 people together again. So that the person who suffered from the wrongdoing, may revenge, or collect the karmic debt.

Karma can be stopped, reduced, or cancelled in 3 ways:

1. by the person who was wronged, letting go of anger, hate, and revenge,
2. doing good deeds to cancel out the karmic debt.
3. advanced Vipassana meditation, that can burn away past karma.

To dissolve karmic debts, one must release attachments, to hatred and vengeance, engage in acts of kindness to offset negative energy of the karma, or partake in advanced Vipassana meditation, capable of cleansing and eradicating the burdens of karma.

It is easier to let go of bad, hateful energy, if we realize that what is happening to us, is probably what we did to that person in the past and this is just a debt being paid off. So, we see it for what it is and accept the punishment to pay off the Karma.

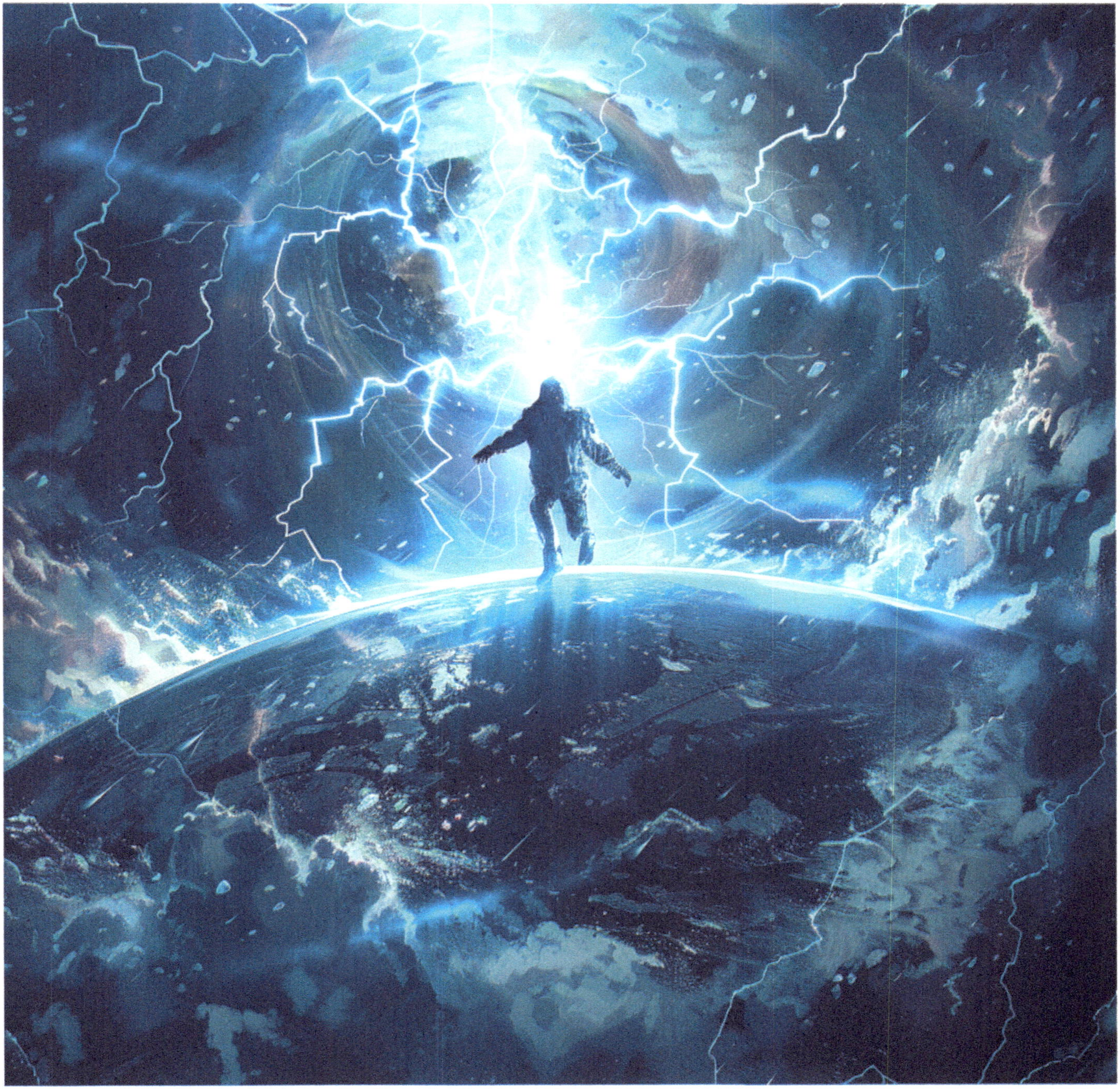

KARMA THE SHADOW

Karma follows us through this life, and through future lives, like a shadow.

We never know when and how the retribution from karma we did in the past might manifest.

The Buddha taught that the complexity of karma cannot be figured out and we should not even try.

Our only duty is to understand the nature of Karma and not to make new Karma and to eliminate old Karma.

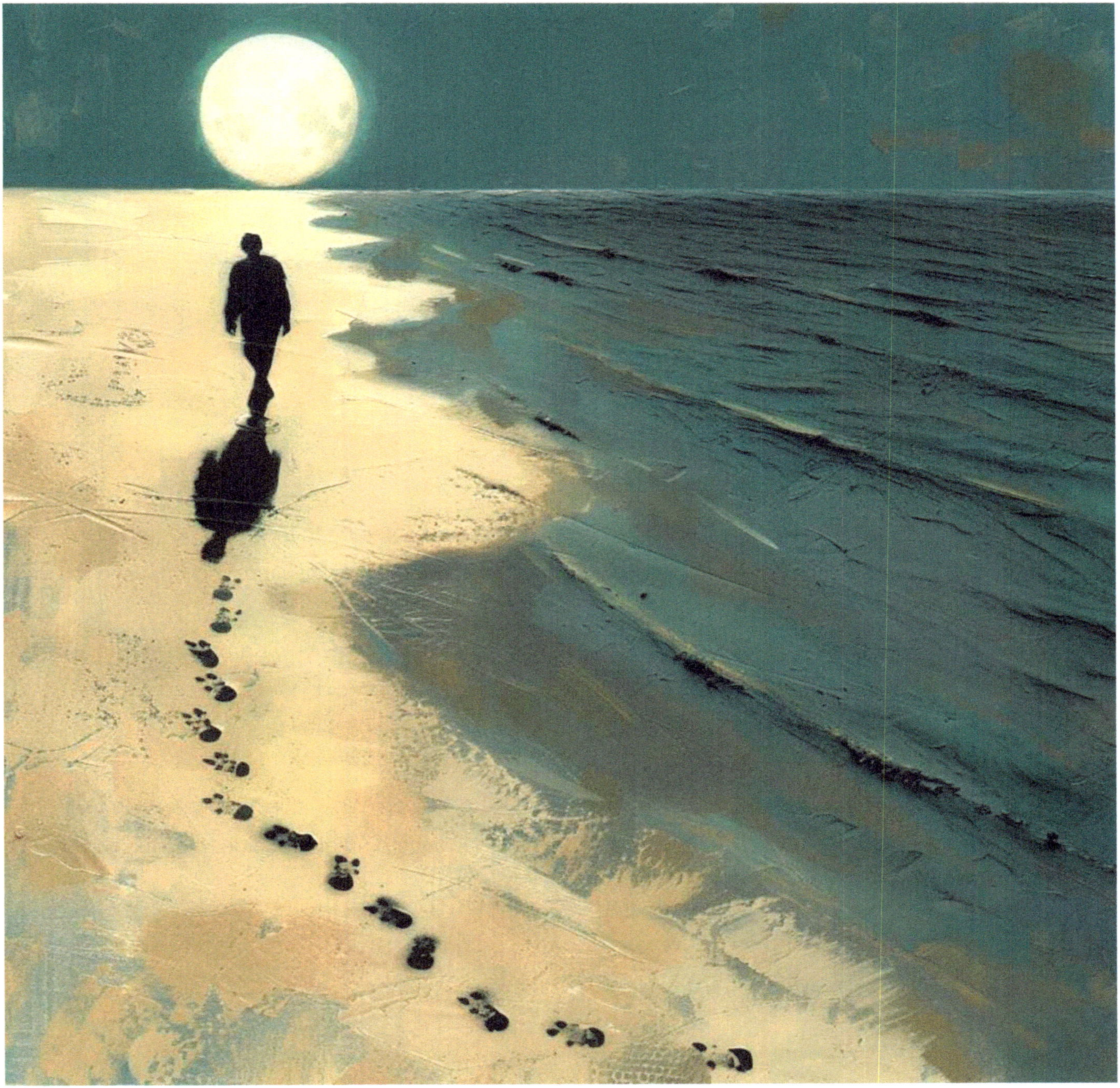

KARMA ENERGY WAVE

One day I was sitting with a friend talking and suddenly I felt a wave of energy. This was a positive feeling Energy. Suddenly the idea of going to the swimming pool popped into Mind, completely unrelated to the conversation I was having with my friend. Before I could even process the idea, I heard myself saying to my friend, "hey let's go to sit by the pool".

After spending time at the pool, I was walking down the stairs and suddenly tripped and fell so hard that I broke my arm.

This illustrates the pushing power of karma. Something made me want to go to the pool suddenly for no reason. And then fall down the stairs that I had navigated successfully so many times, now caused me to fall.
Had I remained in my house I would not have severely injured myself. This is how Karma manifests. It can even feel like a positive or negative energy that makes us jump up and decide to go somewhere, like being baited into a trap. This is why it is important to always practice mindfulness.

Advanced meditators can often feel the Energy current of Karma, arise. When this happens, we must not attach to it, but remain mindful and equanimous. Do not suddenly jump up and decide to go the pool. Consider the energy you have just felt.

95

KARMA - DISEASE

Karma is an Energy that can manifest as disease and illness.

All Karma does not reveal itself as good or bad luck. Nor as an accident or losing something.

Often Karma can show up in our bodies as disease, pain, deterioration, or even sudden inexplicable death.

We cannot prevent our past Karma from appearing, but we can reduce or mitigate the damage.

In this world Dark Energy can be reduced or even eliminated by the White Energy or the Good Force.

97

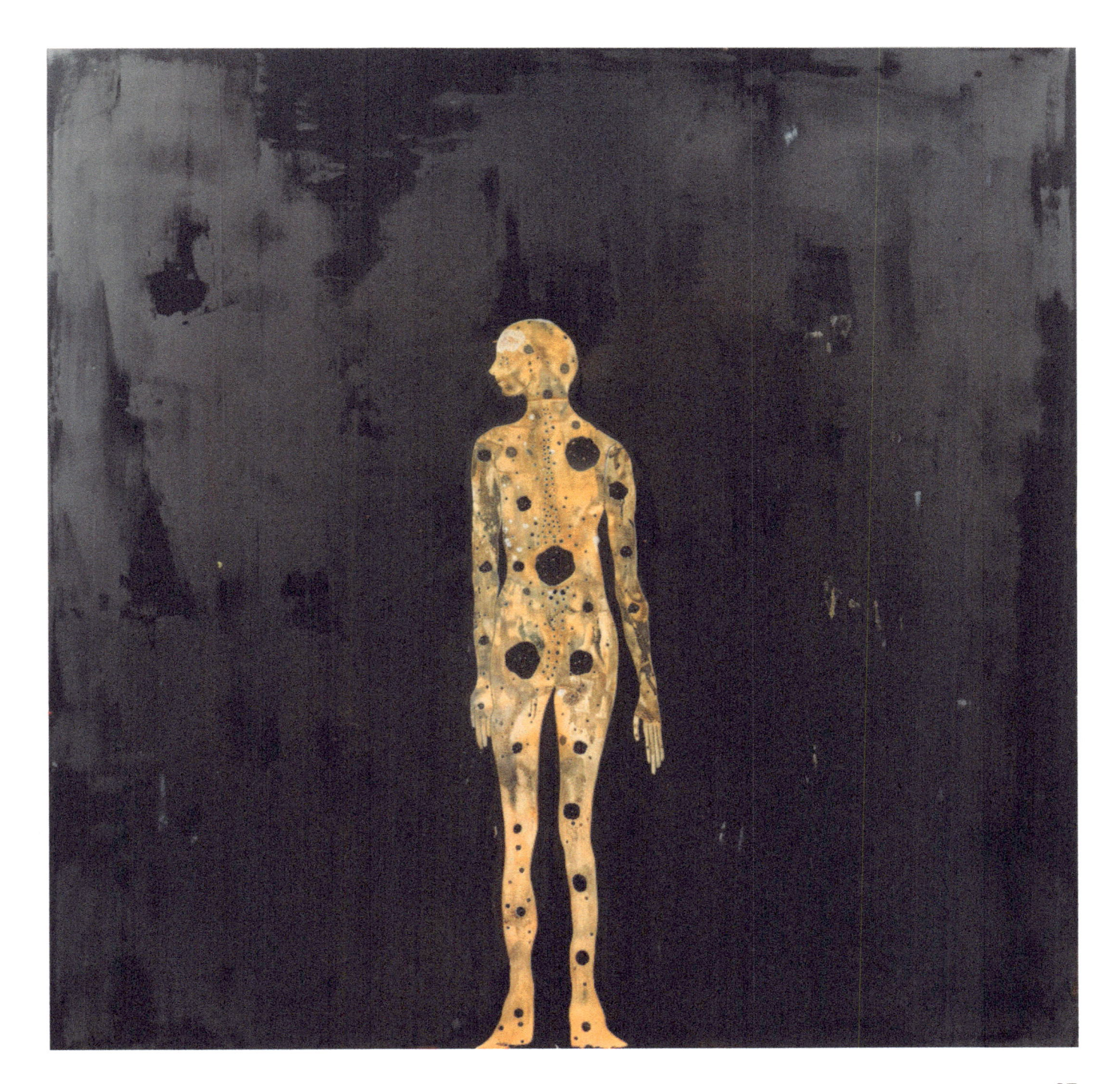

Part of the path to Enlightenment involves the cutting of chains that bind us to this world in the forms of bonds or attachments.

1. Belief in a permanent, unchanging self or identity
2. Doubt or uncertainty about path to liberation, and the efficacy of spiritual practice.
3. Clinging to external rituals, observances, or religious practices as a means to attain liberation, without understanding their true purpose or significance.
4. Craving for sensual pleasures and gratification through the five senses, including desires for pleasure, comfort, and sensory stimulation.
5. Hostility, resentment, or aversion towards oneself or others, including feelings of anger, hatred, and animosity.
6. Craving for existence in this world or other realms
7. Craving for existence in formless realms,
8. Conceit or Arrogance, pride, or self-importance, characterized by the belief in one's superiority, excellence, or special status compared to others.
9. Restlessness Mental agitation, distraction, or turbulence, characterized by a lack of peace, stability, and concentration.
10. Ignorance of the true nature of reality, characterized by delusion

It is by overcoming these bonds that the Buddha, Masters, and others have reached liberation, and Enlightenment This is achieved through Vipassana meditation, not by studying books or intellectualizing the process. Books give understanding, but meditation give the result.

As we sever these chains, we reach four **stages of Enlightenment**. These **stages** are Sotapanna (stream-enterer), Sakagami (once-returner), Anagami (non-returner), and Arahant. The oldest Buddhist texts portray the Buddha as referring to people who are at one of these four stages as noble people (*ariya-puggala*) and the community of such persons as the noble sangha (*ariya-sangha*).

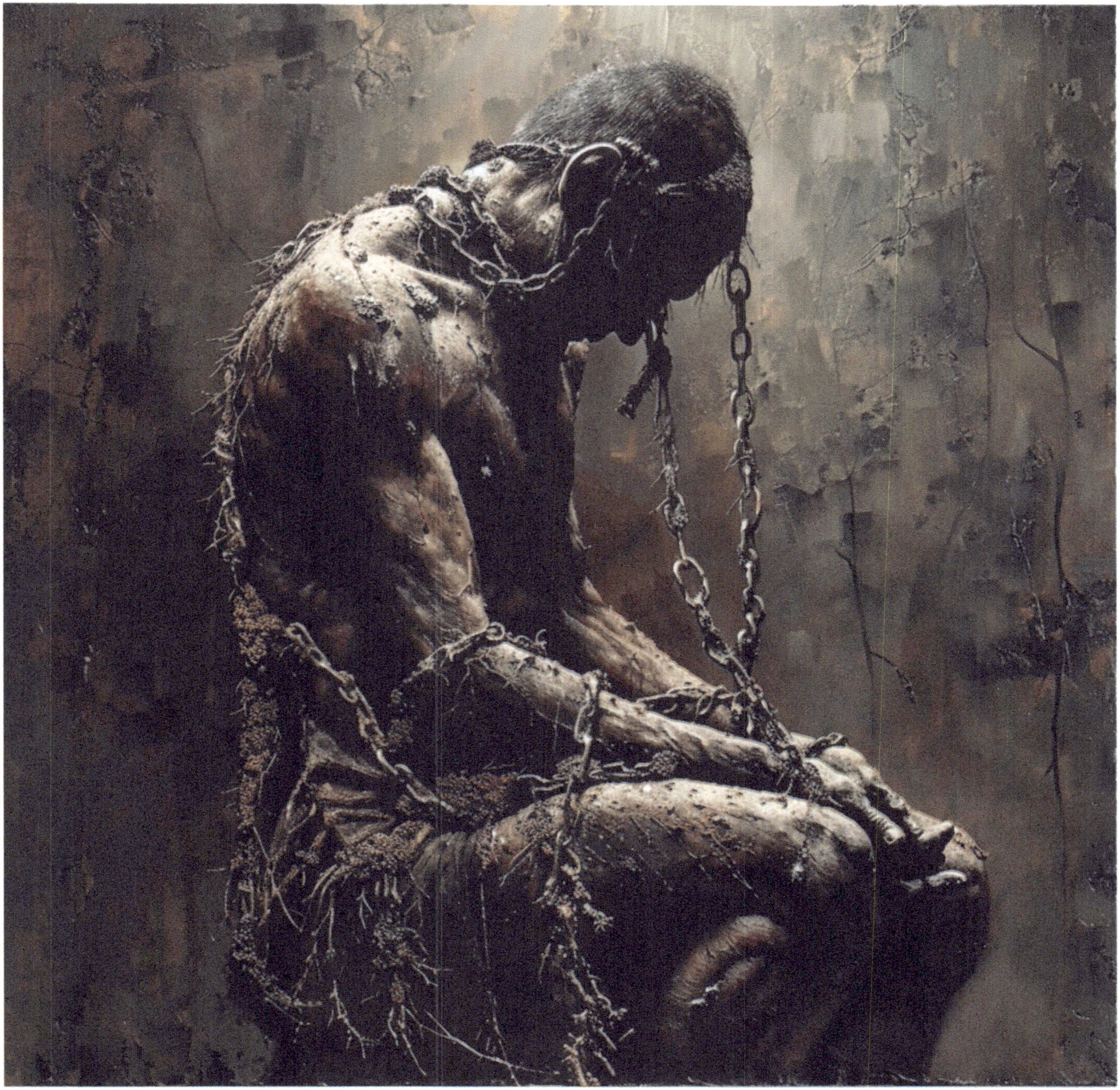

ARMIES OF IMPURITIES (KILESA)

It was the Buddha that discovered the impurity forces that exist in the Mind and body.

The Buddha referred to them as house builders, that make their world inside of us.
They are like parasites, which can control our Minds and influence us to do as they wish.

This results in us doing bad deeds or having bad thoughts. These Impurities (Kilesa) influence us to create bad karma. (they are like little devils whispering in our ears).

The impurity forces work with the Mara (devil), to enslave our minds. It is hard for us to imagine. That we are not in charge of our own minds. But this is the truth. Our minds have been Hi-Jacked by parasitic Hi-Jacking entities.

Scientists have discovered that our human bodies are largely influenced by parasites, which control us to crave sugar and even get us and go to the store to buy a candy bar or other sugar treats.

So, we can also understand that spiritual parasite or impurities forces (Kilesa), also control our original Minds in the dimension of Energy.

101

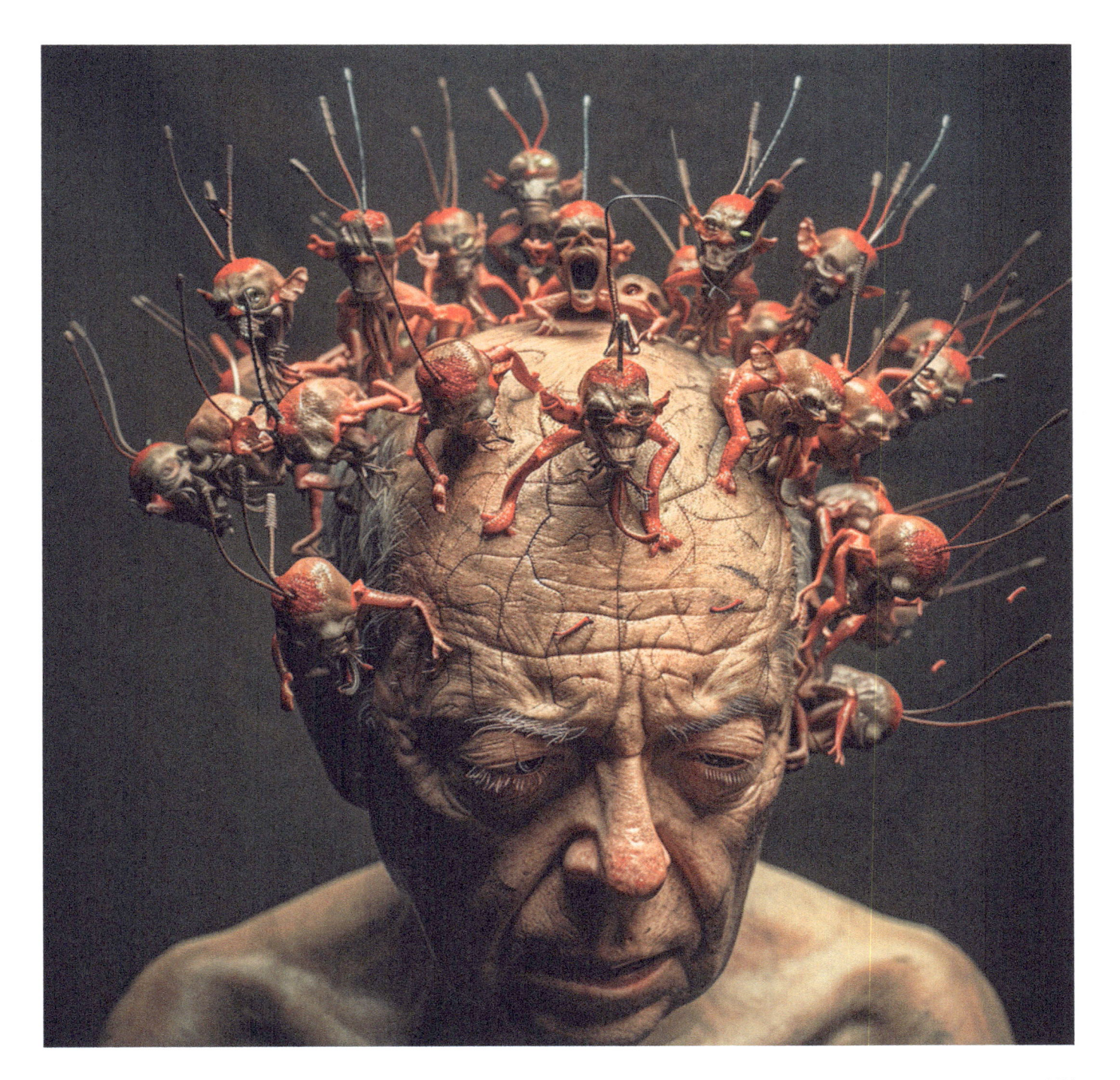

DATABASE (SANGKARA)

In each lifetime our emotions form layers like the memory of a hard drive or database. Stored on this hard drive are strong past emotions, or memories called Sangkara. These deep emotions or memories are burned into our hard drives and follow us into the next lifetime as Energy.

The lingering emotions and memories help to form our future personalities.

For example: A person who dies a cruel unjust death in this life, may become an angry or unjust person in the next Life.

Also following us into the next lifetimes is the energy of Karma – good and bad deeds we have done. Along with mental impurities called (Kilesa), which are like parasites which feed on the energy born from our past emotions.

Some may argue that since our lives are so influence by memories, karma and impurities, our lives are predetermined or predestined to play out roles based on this pre-programing and by virtue of being hi-jacked by impurity forces.

This is true in part, but through Vipassana meditation we can reformat our hard drives and alter the outcome through good deeds, destroying the impurity forces (Kilesa) and burning away memories, negative Energy, and bad Karma.

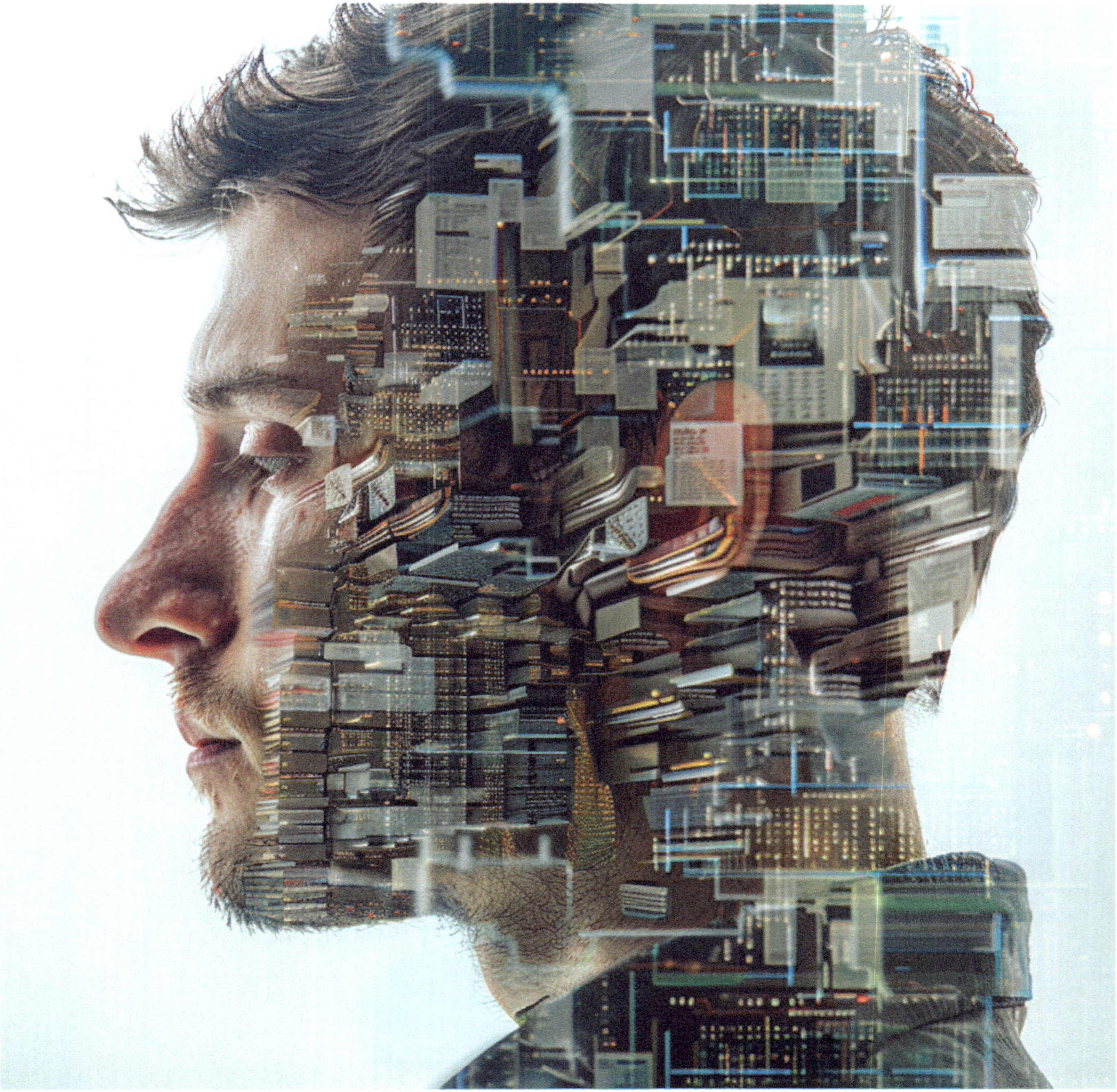

CHAPTER 3

THE CREATION OF MAN

THE CREATION OF MAN

Where did we come from. This is the age-old questions humans always seek to find the answer to. Often, we look at old ruins and the Pyramids hoping to find the answers.
Creation stories in different religions are similar in origin. The Buddha did not give great importance to the origins of man or the creation of the Universe as he saw this more as a distraction on the path to Enlightenment, and not so useful.

Many meditators today are fascinated with the idea of seeing phenomena like seeing aliens. Instead of looking inward to destroy impurities, they send their minds out in the hopes of connecting with higher beings or Aliens. This is considered unproductive and even dangerous in Vipassana meditation. It is so easy to be fooled by the Mara (devil) or impurity forces, until finally we lose our ways.

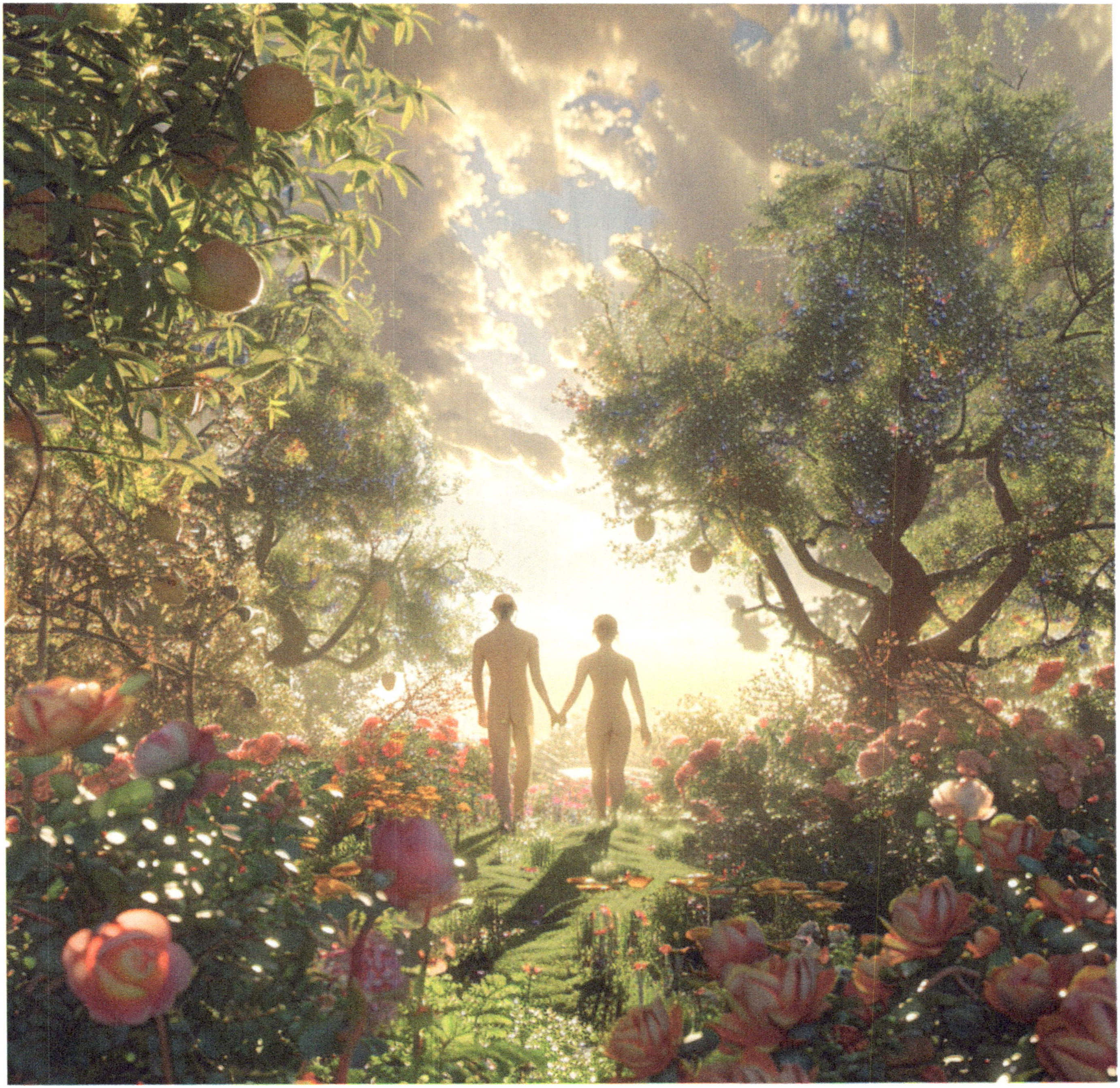

THE ORIGINAL SIN

The creation story talks about a garden of Eden. The Original Sin.
Spiritualism on the other hand, suggests humanity was created by a benevolent being, for a benevolent purpose, or we arrived at this world by choice to learn lessons while having a human experience.
There is truth in both the creation story and the spiritualism view. But the story is not as rosy or cheerful as many assume: "I am a spiritual being having a human experience."

Yes, we did come to this World as Energy being to experience what it would be like, to enjoy human form. As we used our human form to eat food, and later developed sexually, we developed likes and dislikes, we saw others as beautiful or ugly, we developed emotions. We succumbed to temptation, we committed sin and did evil and killed each other. All resulting in Karma and a deeper imprisonment.

Until one day our original Minds were no longer pure, could no longer leave our human bodies and suddenly were trapped in these bodies for eternity. This was due to the magnetic force that now held the impurities in our Minds, like a magnet holds steel ball bearings. Being trapped our emotions grew and eventually our bodies were also hi-jacked by a parasitic energy form (Kilesa) that would build their worlds inside our bodies and Minds.

The Mara (devil), Kilesa (the impurity forces) and karma and our sin, created the prison we inhabit until today, in a vicious cycle to birth, death and re-birth again and again.
How painful it is to be imprisoned in this World.
The Mara (devil), temptation, evil, karma, and sin are real and caused our original Minds to become heavy and not be able to escape their earthly bodies. This along with the impurity forces imprisoned us in the cycle of rebirth (Samsara)

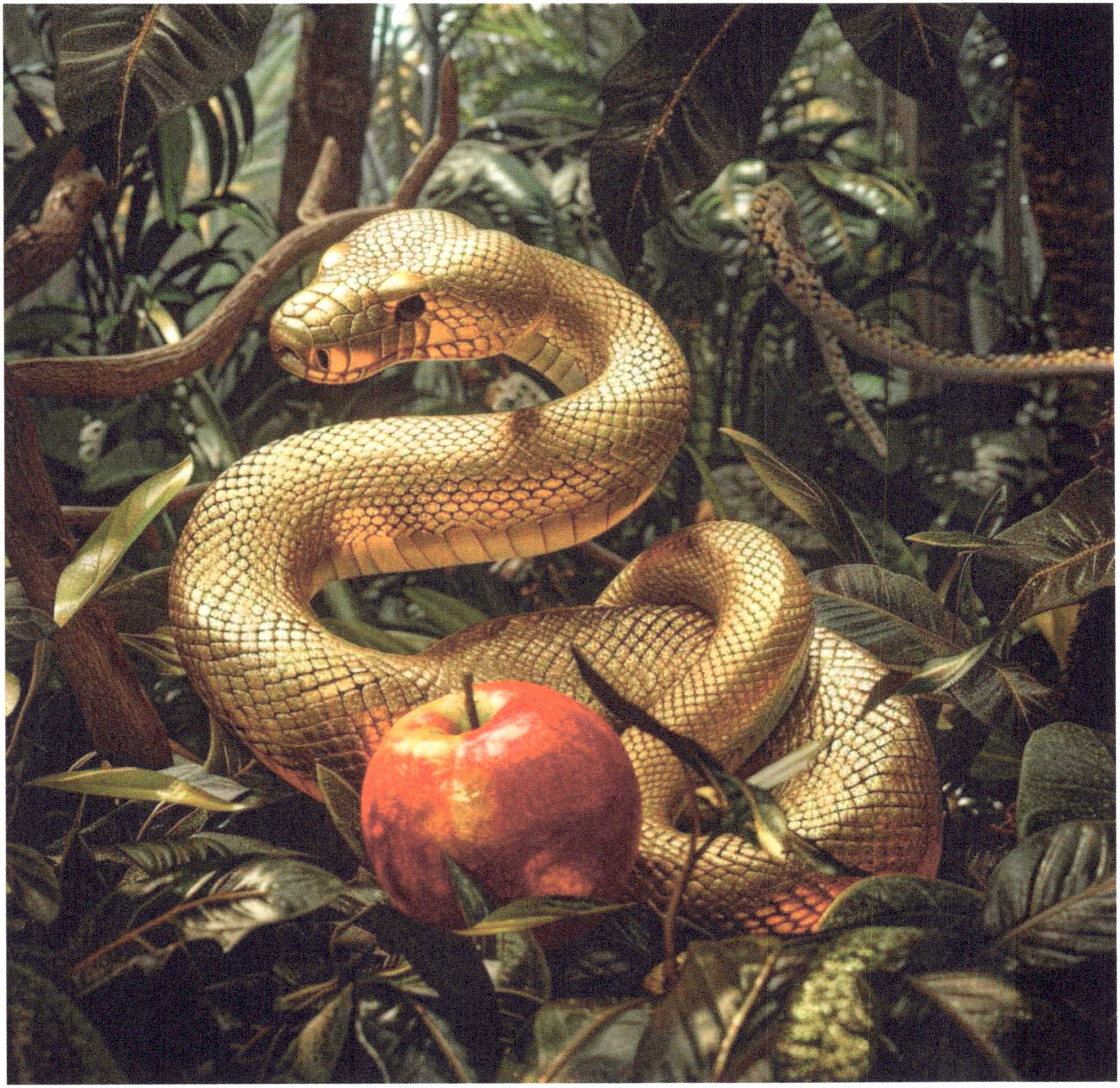

ENERGY BEINGS

The Buddha never gave much importance to explaining the past or the future or about Aliens and other Worlds.

To a prisoner it is not important or useful to dwell on how one was imprisoned.

Nor is it useful to explore whether Aliens or other beings might come to rescue us or provide us with some important information.

What is important is that we are in a prison. That there is a way to get out of the prison. And that we have limited time to achieve this before the game of Life resets and we must start the search all over again.

In our prison the Mara (devil) keeps our Minds distracted, while she builds new levels to the prison, in case we start to figure out how to escape.

In case we learn how to return to pure Minds and pure energy beings.

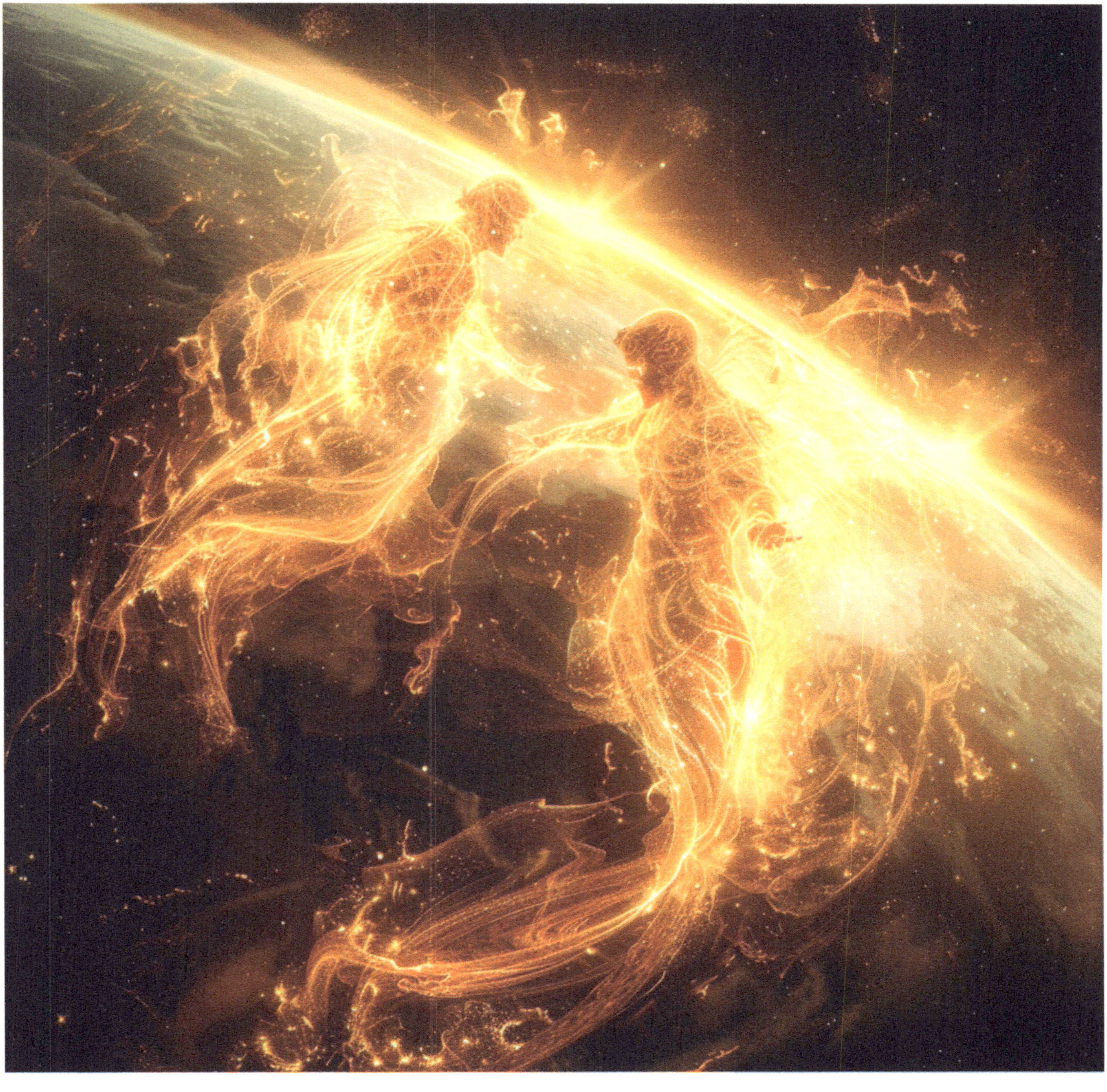

ORIGINAL MINDS

Imagine our pure, original Minds as pristine spheres of Energy — luminous and unencumbered, floating freely in the vast expanse of existence.

Yet, as time passes, these once radiant spheres become tainted by the accumulation of emotions, karmic imprints, and other impurities. Picture these impurities as small, spherical metal pieces, adhering to the surface of our pure Energy Minds.

With each attachment of metal, our once light and free spheres grow heavier, weighed down by the magnetic pull of worldly forces, akin to the Earth's gravitational hold.

To reclaim the purity of our Minds, we must embark on a journey of purification— liberating ourselves from the magnetic grip of the world. Only through cleansing our Minds of these accumulated impurities can we hope to return to our original state pure Energy and Original Minds.

This metaphor encapsulates the essence of our existence— a perpetual quest to transcend the worldly entanglements that obscure the brilliance of our true Nature.

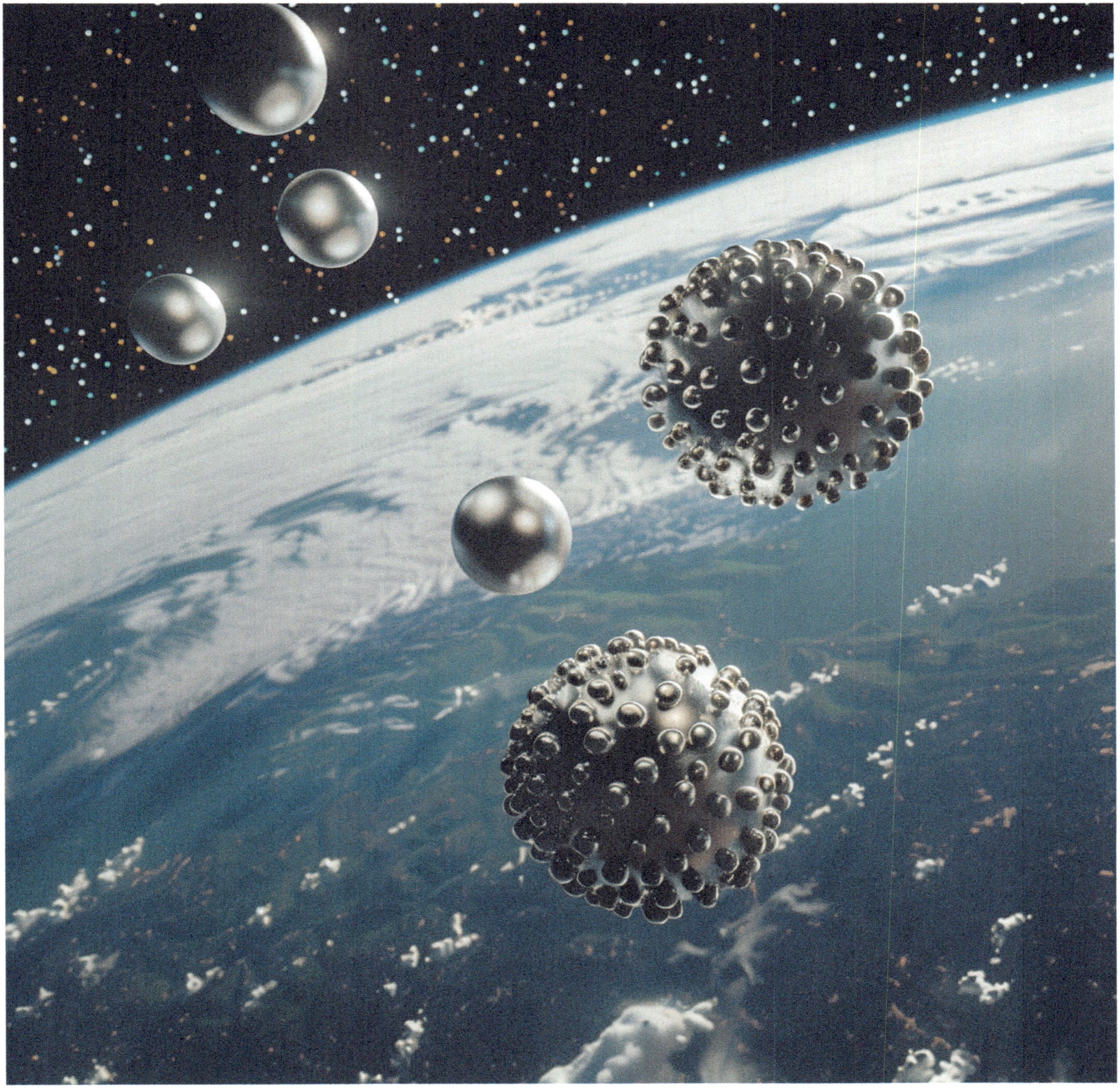

CHAPTER 4

DEATH

GROWING OLD IS SUFFERING.

The three things we fear the most are getting old, dying, and believe it or not, rebirth.

Here I sit alone in my room, waiting for someone to visit or call. They are all too busy with their lives. I spend my time thinking about the past and all my friends, and my wife, all long gone now… What was this life all about?

I feel so lonely… I could cry!

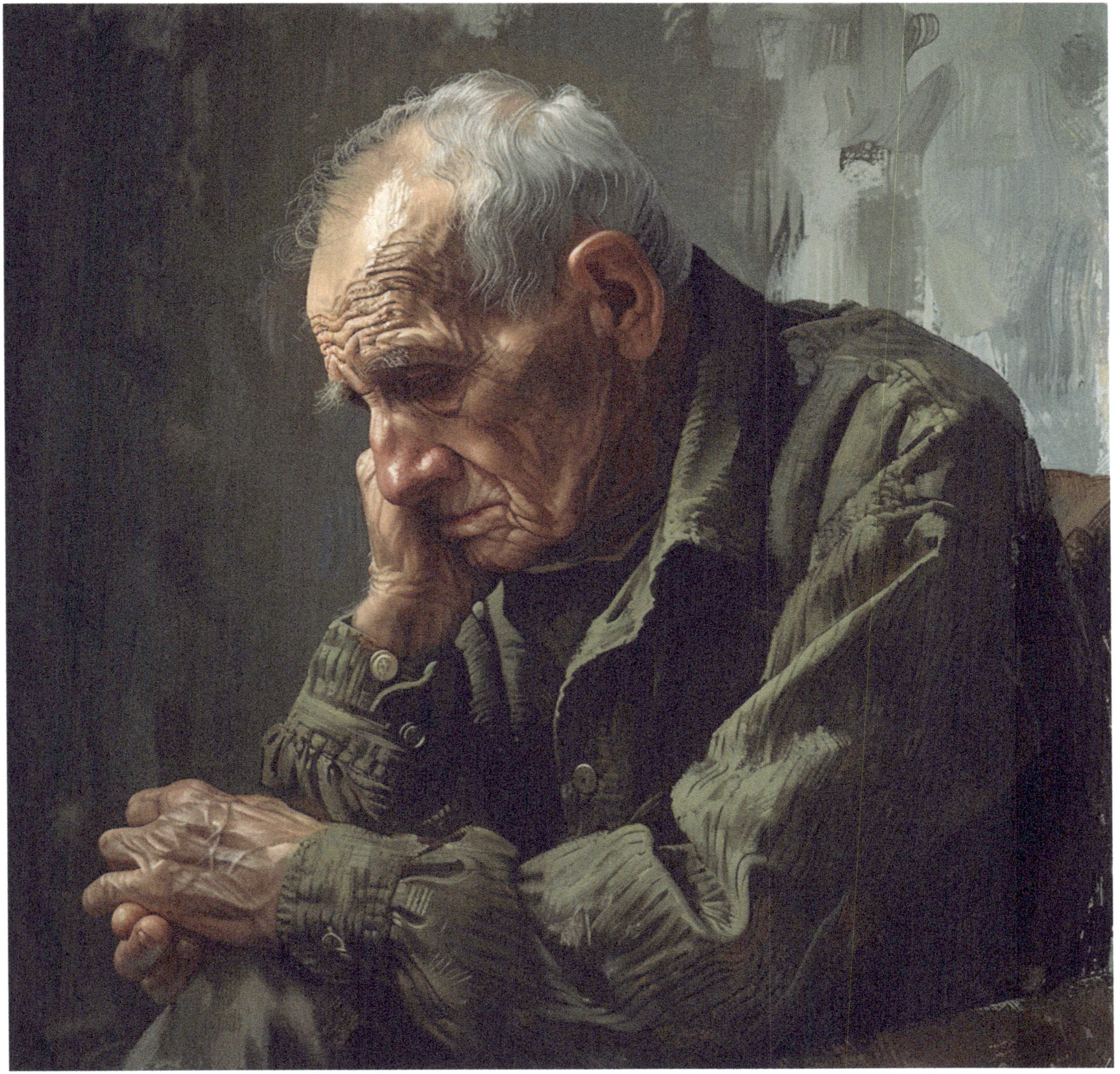

I'm getting old, my body hurts all the time now. My kids are grown up and I've worked hard my whole life. But now, I'm spending all my money to stay in this hospital room. I'm hooked up to machines and swallowing their medicines, hoping to see my family one more time before I die.

I feel worried the hospital will keep me alive with those machines, costing even more money. My kids might have to sell my house to pay the bill.

Imagine working all your life and this is how it ends.

Please let me die in peace.

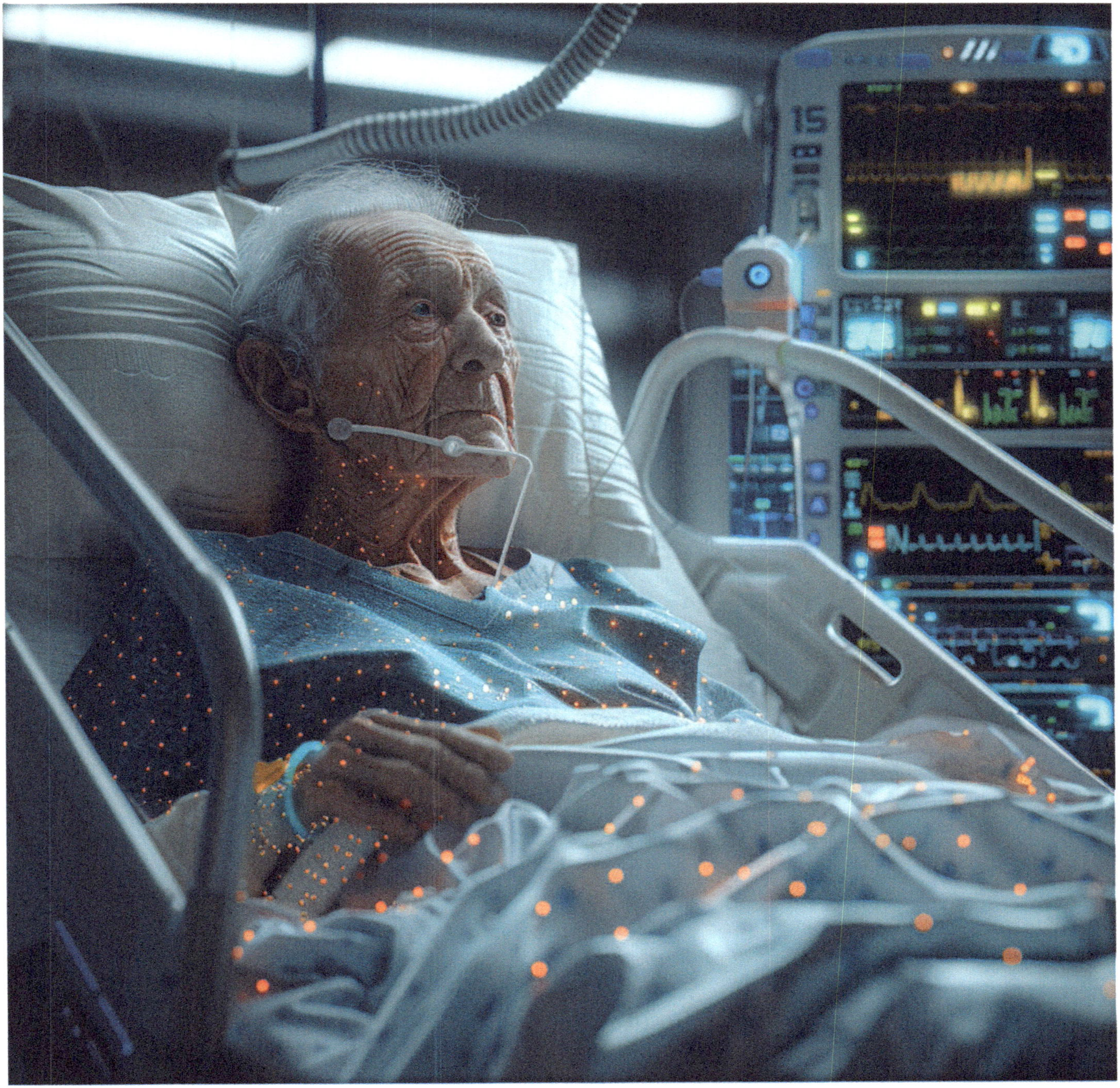

One last time with my family beside me, I gather my strength to say goodbye, to give them courage to live their lives, because life is tough and goes by so quickly.

I feel so much love for all of them and it's so hard to let them go. I was always the one who picked them up when they fell down. All that mattered was that I could support them until they could stand on their own.

Where did the time go?

I can feel that I am leaving now. I beg them, please don't keep me on that life support machine. There's no point. I am so tired and worn out, I just want to rest.

Visiting hours are over. Now they must go. I am relieved. I didn't want them to see me die. I want them to remember me as strong and unafraid, although all I want to do now is cry.

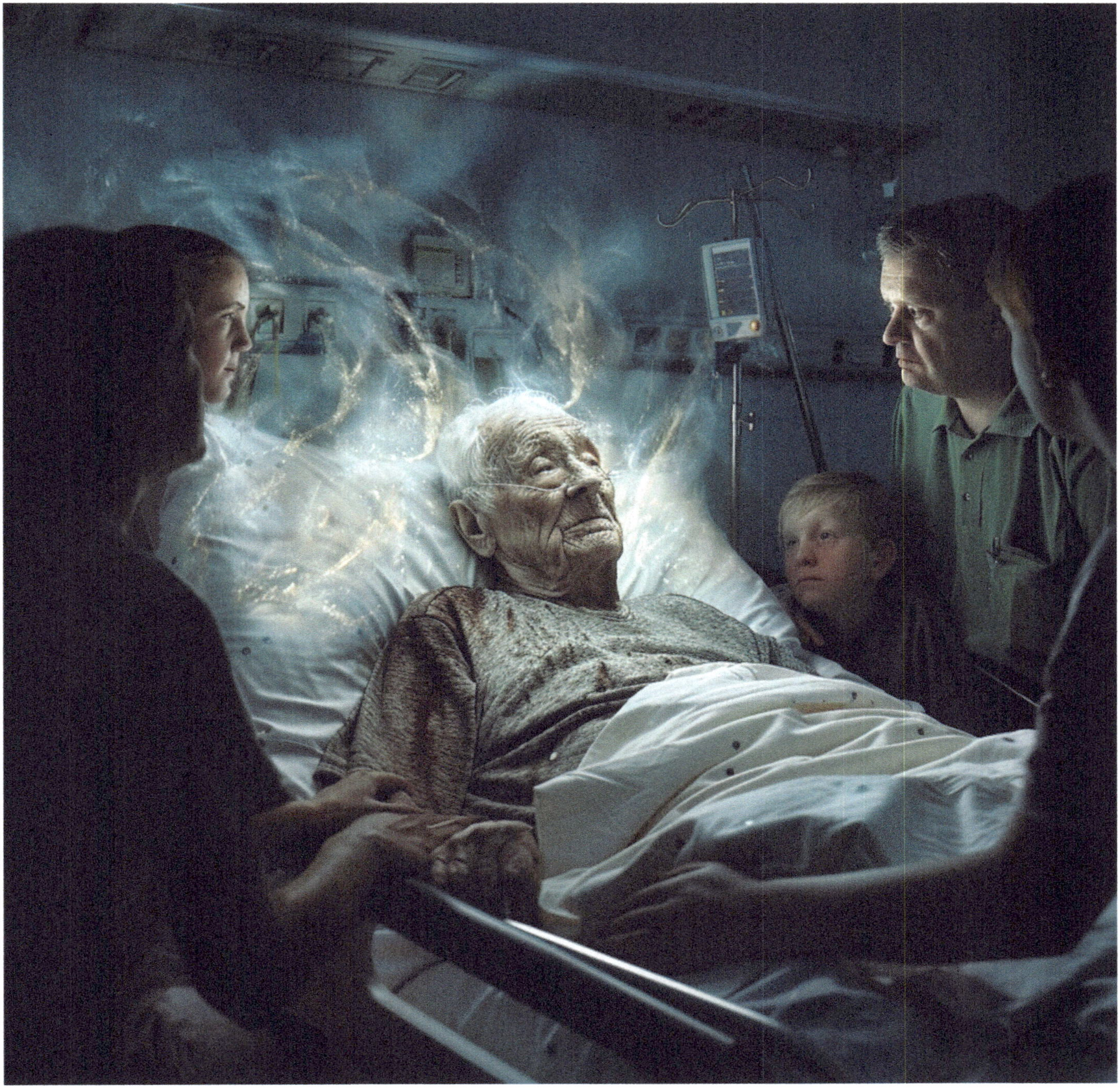

Hey that's me lying in the bed looking so cold. But I feel fine, and all my pain is gone. My Mind is so clear.

Why was I so afraid to let go? Why did I not trust Nature?

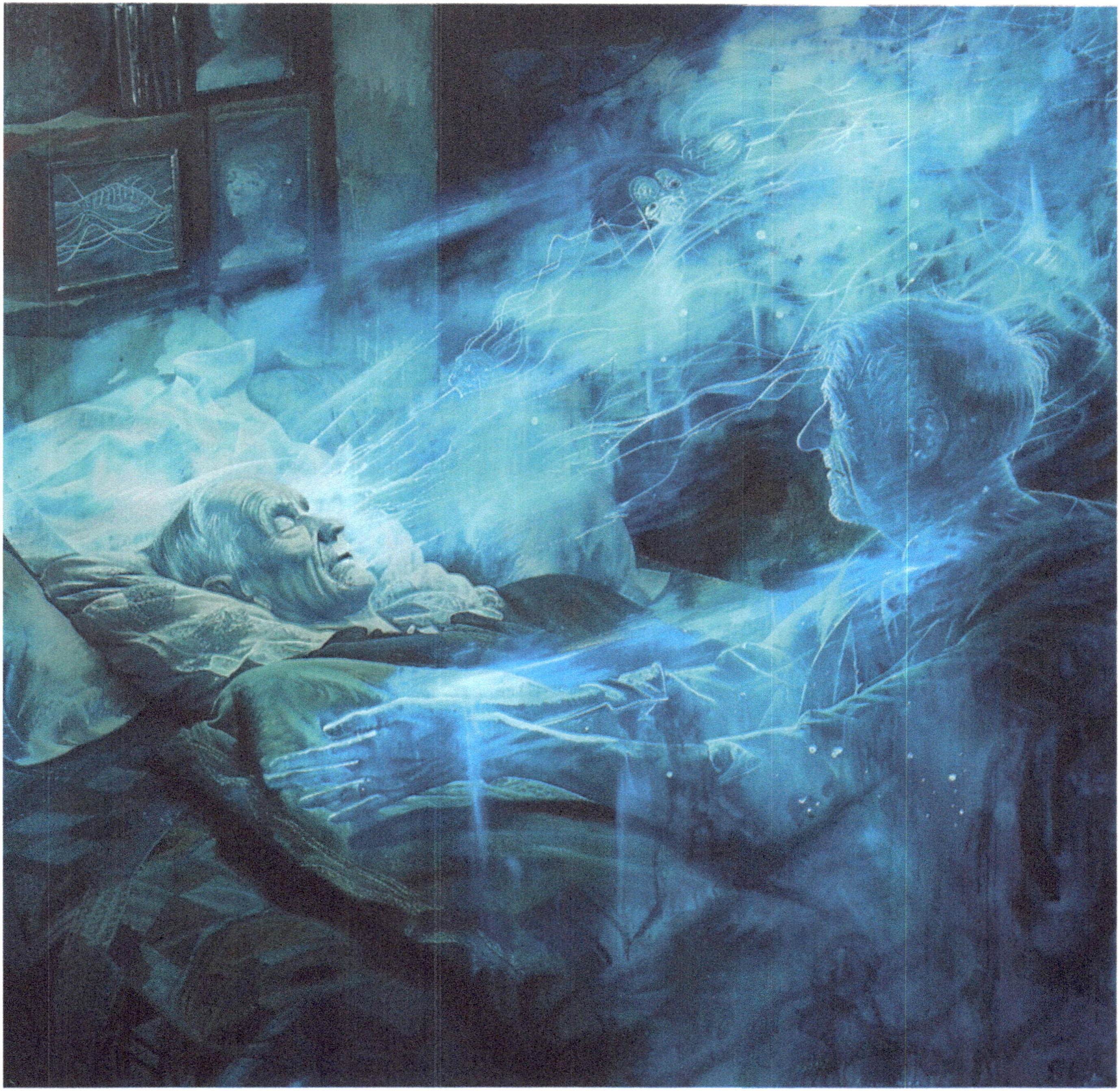

Oh, I guess that is my body under the sheet. I don't need that old worn body anymore.

Ready for the funeral home, to be cleaned, made up and dressed for the funeral and the grave.

Everything is as it should be now. It's all fine….and I understand.

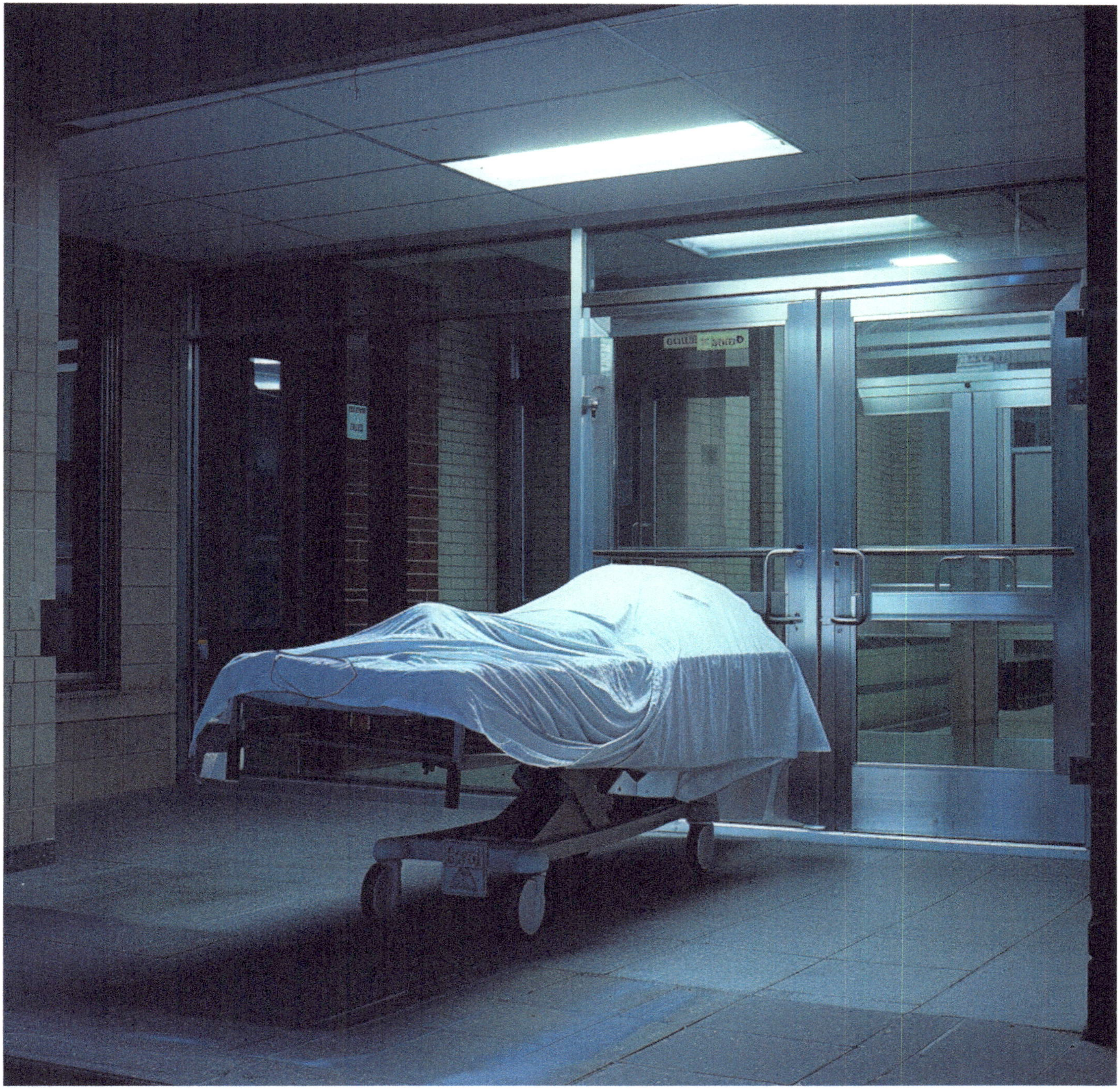

I know this warm and familiar place. ……I have been here many, many times.

I did good this time around…. I did not panic or hold on. Now I feel my Mind going high. I know I can do better next time around.

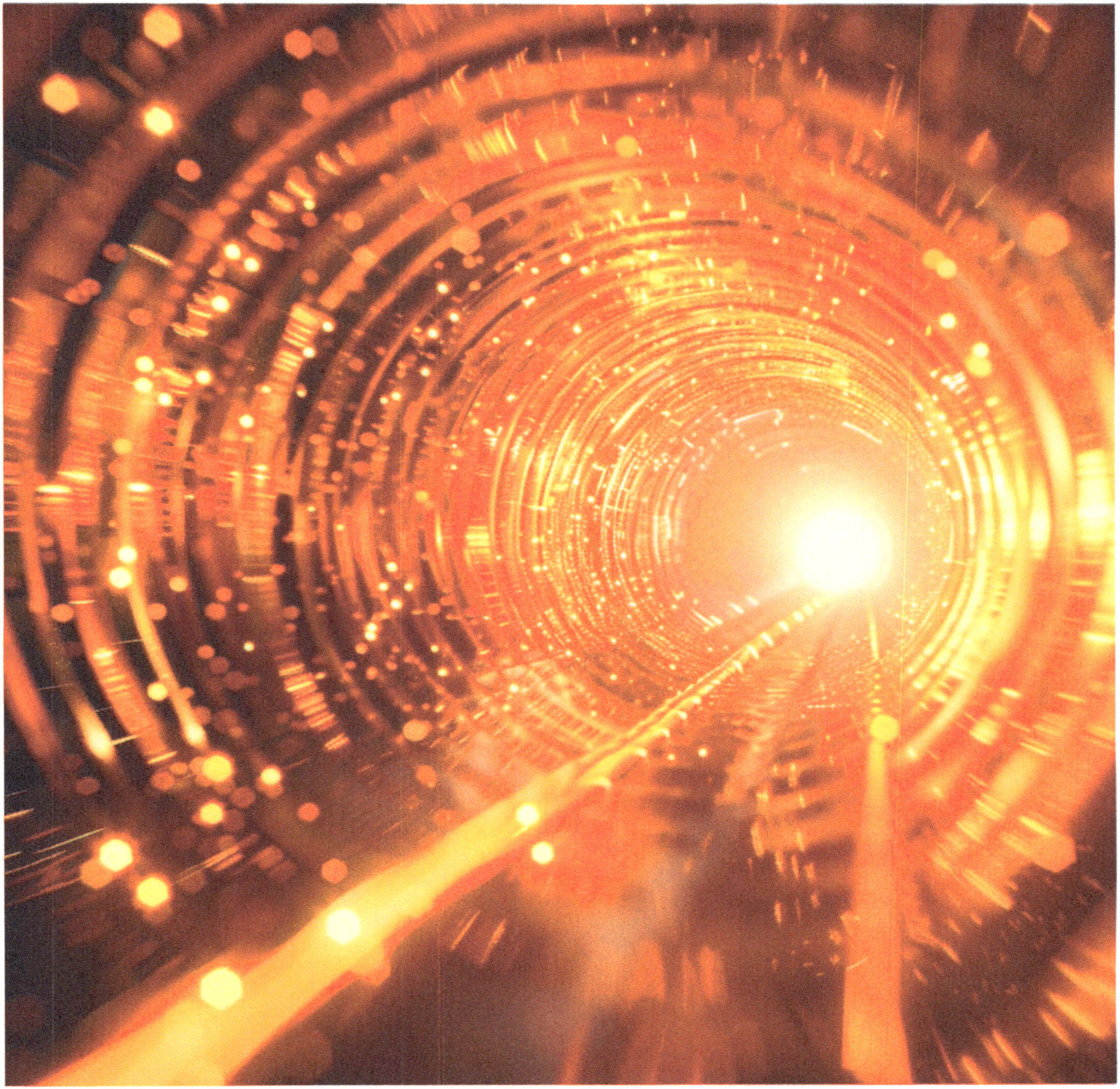

Last Life I recall my Mind was so heavy and I tried to hold onto my life so hard,

Why did I try to hang on to this World and that Life, that brought so much pain, it only caused me to get stuck in the Energy wave. It's that "damn" fear and attachment that fools me every time.

If only I could remember when I am reborn, it's just a game and a role, that resets and starts a new, it's all just a matter of time.

Next time I will do better.

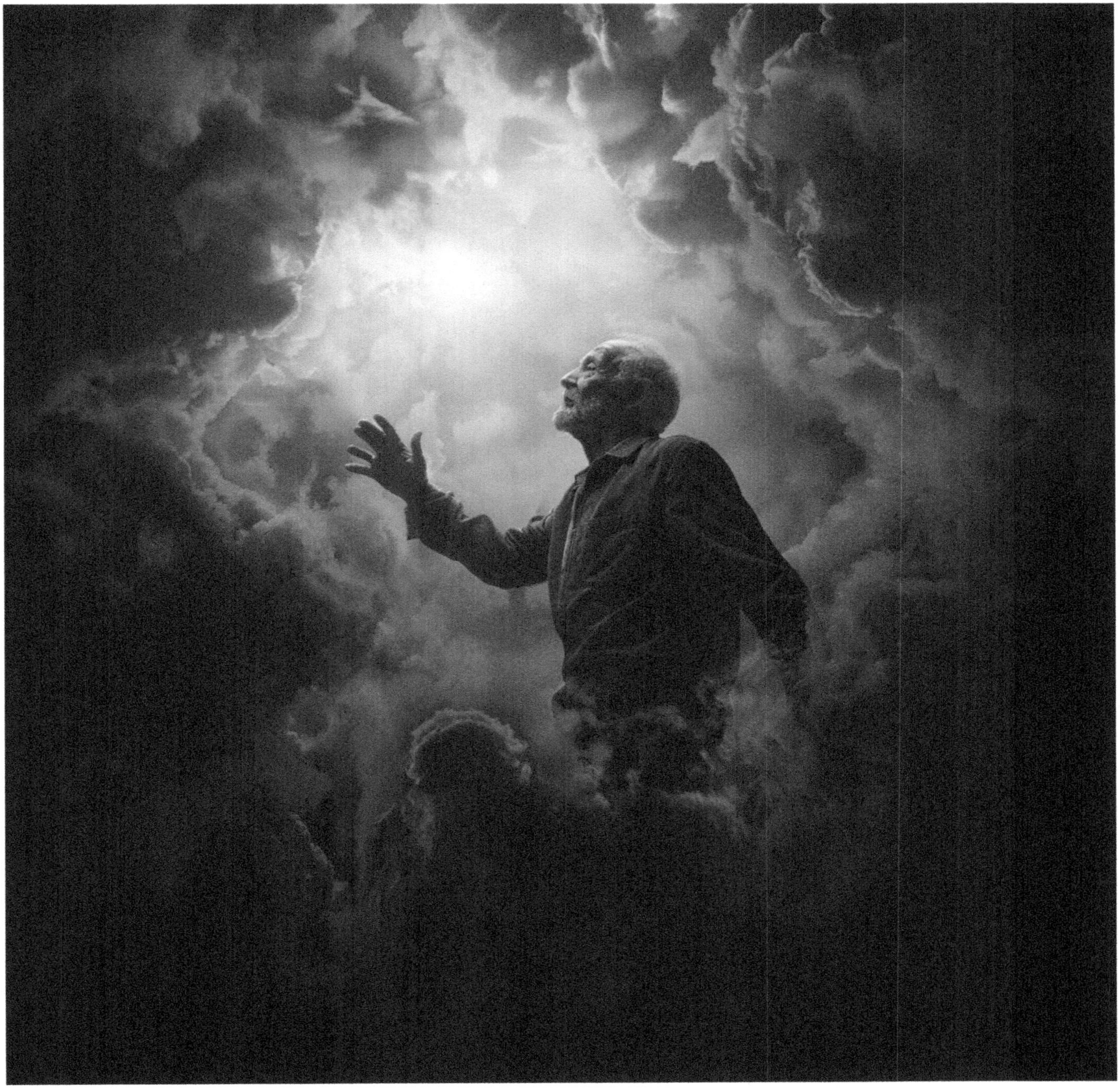

CHAPTER 5

THE ENERGY VORTEX

THE ENERGY VORTEX

A plane is hit by lightning, and it's bad. A crash is inevitable. Just minutes to live.

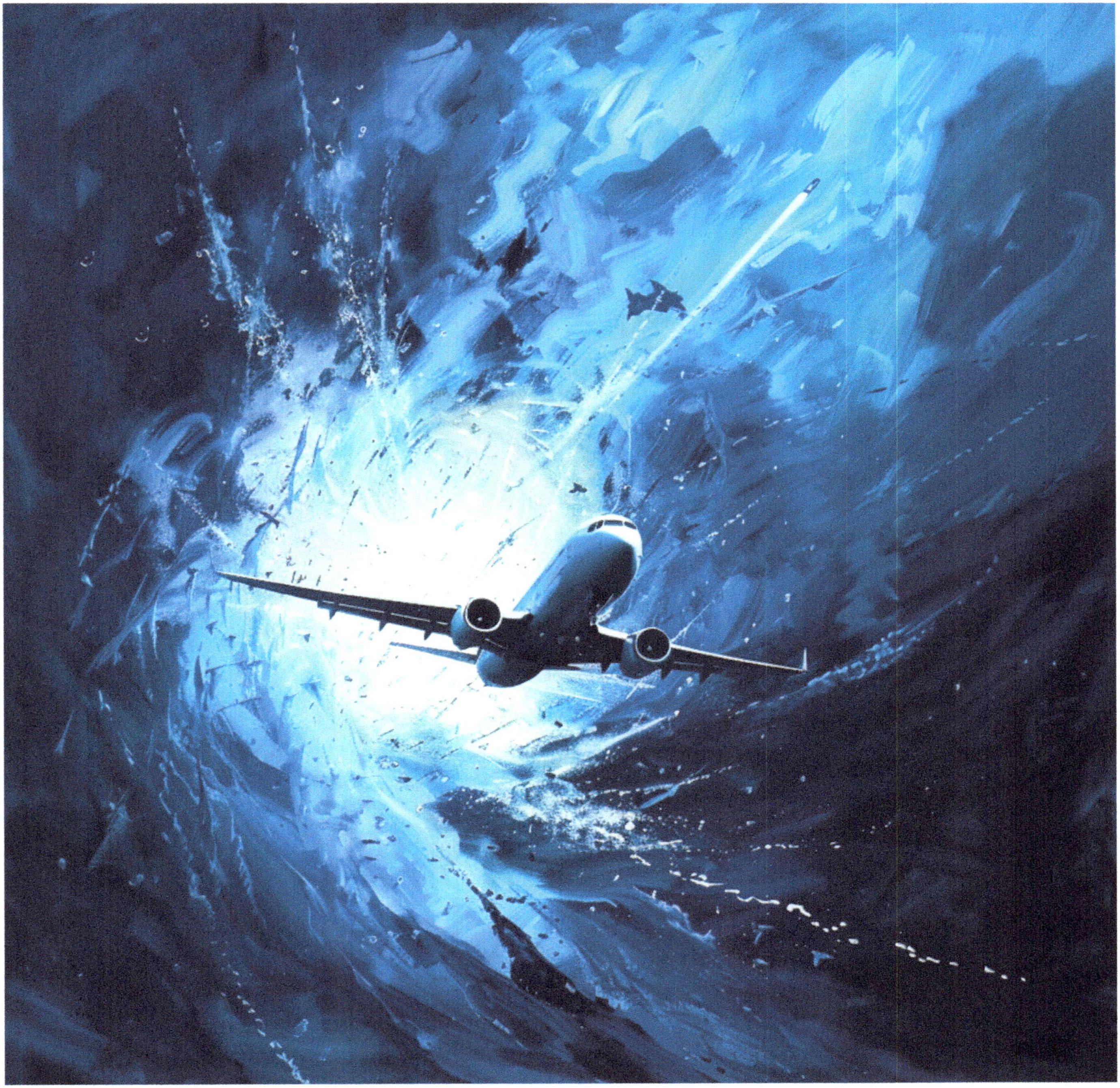

Panic and fear grip the passengers. People screaming.

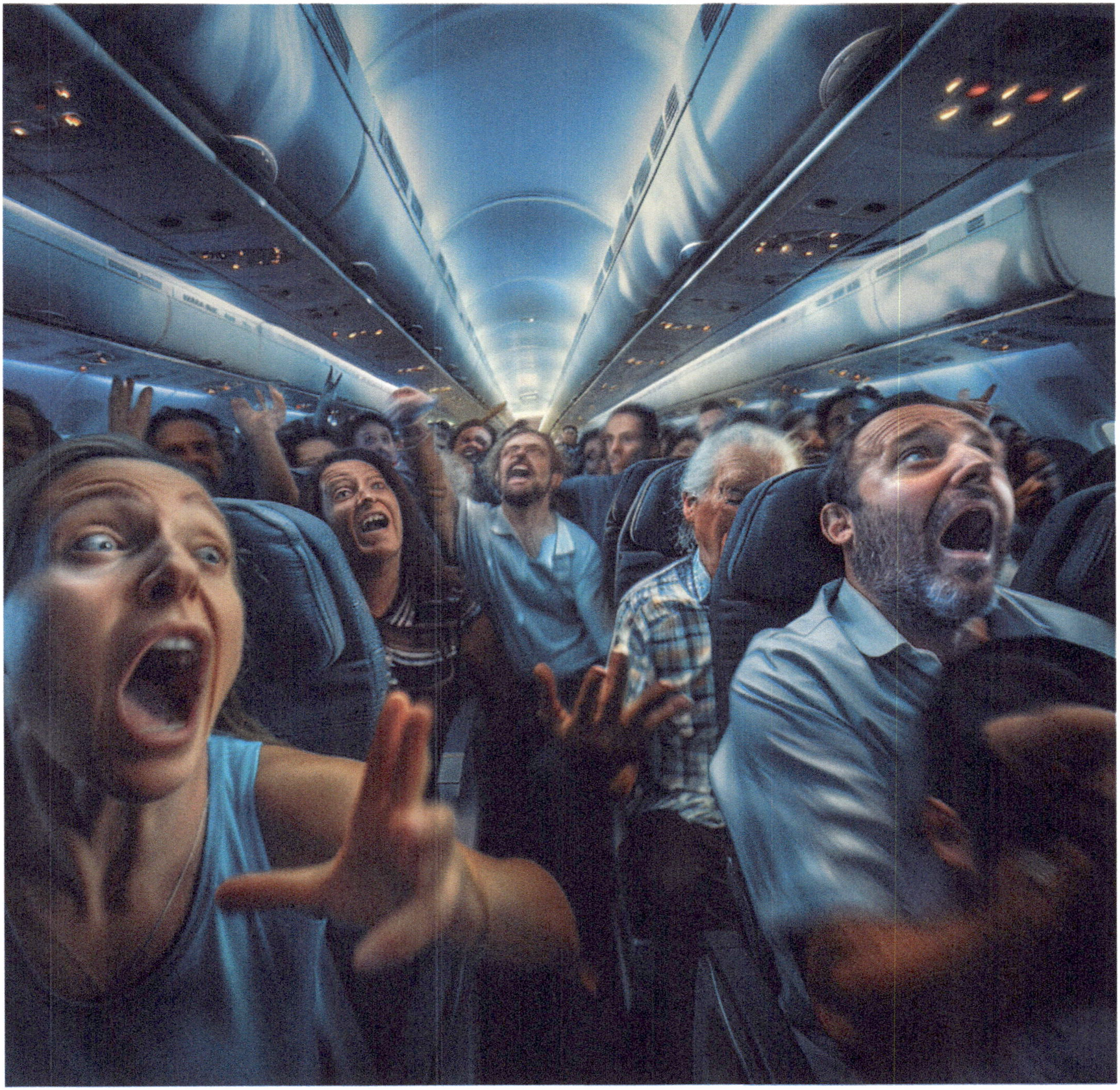

Everyone panics, and this exacerbates the situation because it creates a vortex of fear that ensnares their souls.

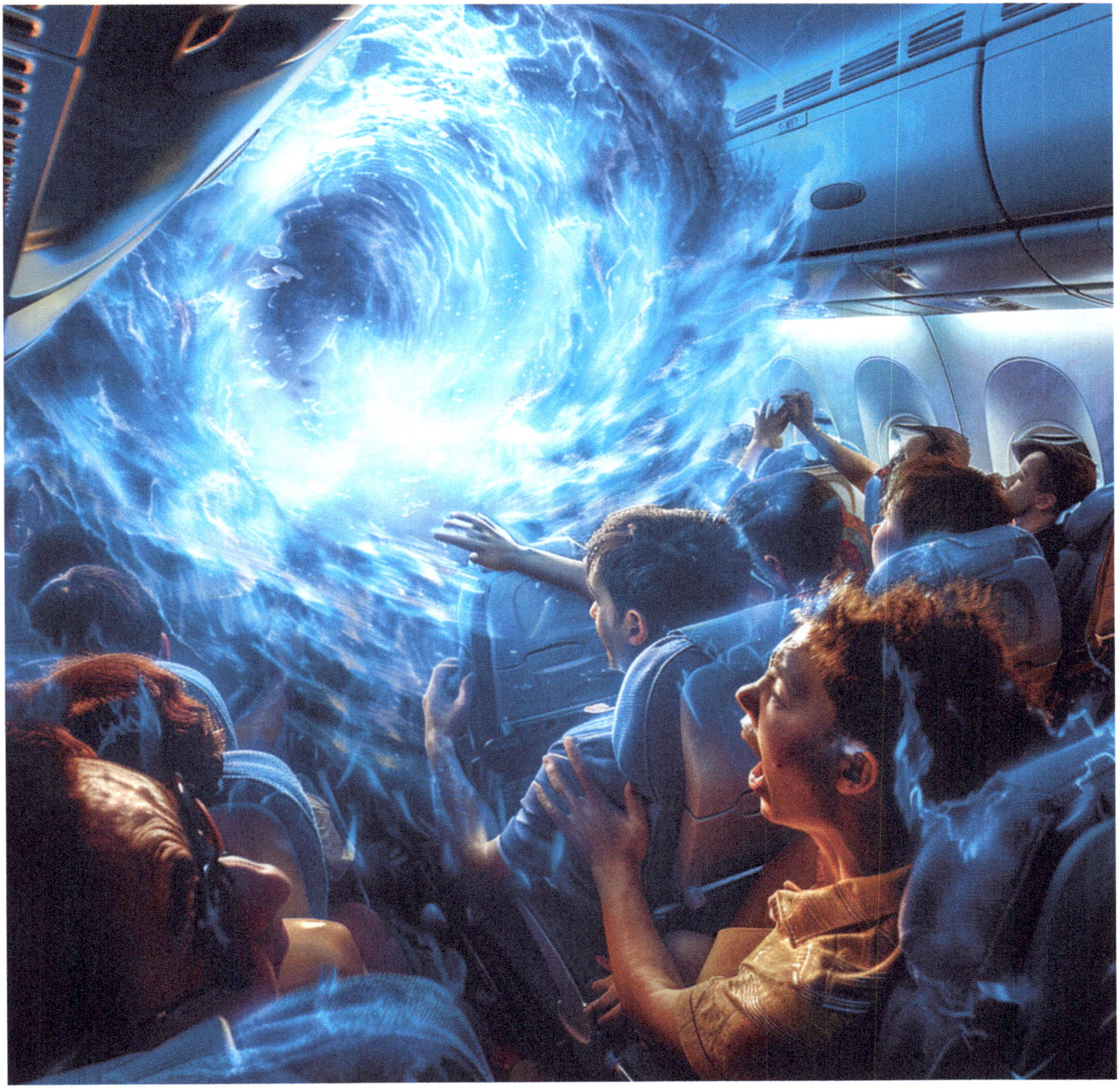

Their souls enter the vortex, weighed down by heavy vibrations, to be stuck for the longest time in limbo and the energy of fear.

Except for one person whose Mind was well-trained. As a meditator, their Mind stayed calm, serene, focused, totally equanimous, even as the plane slammed into the ground.
Their Mind was light and didn't get caught in the energy vortex. Instead, it floated up high and free, passing through the vortex and all the heavy Souls.

The trained Mind can always rise above.

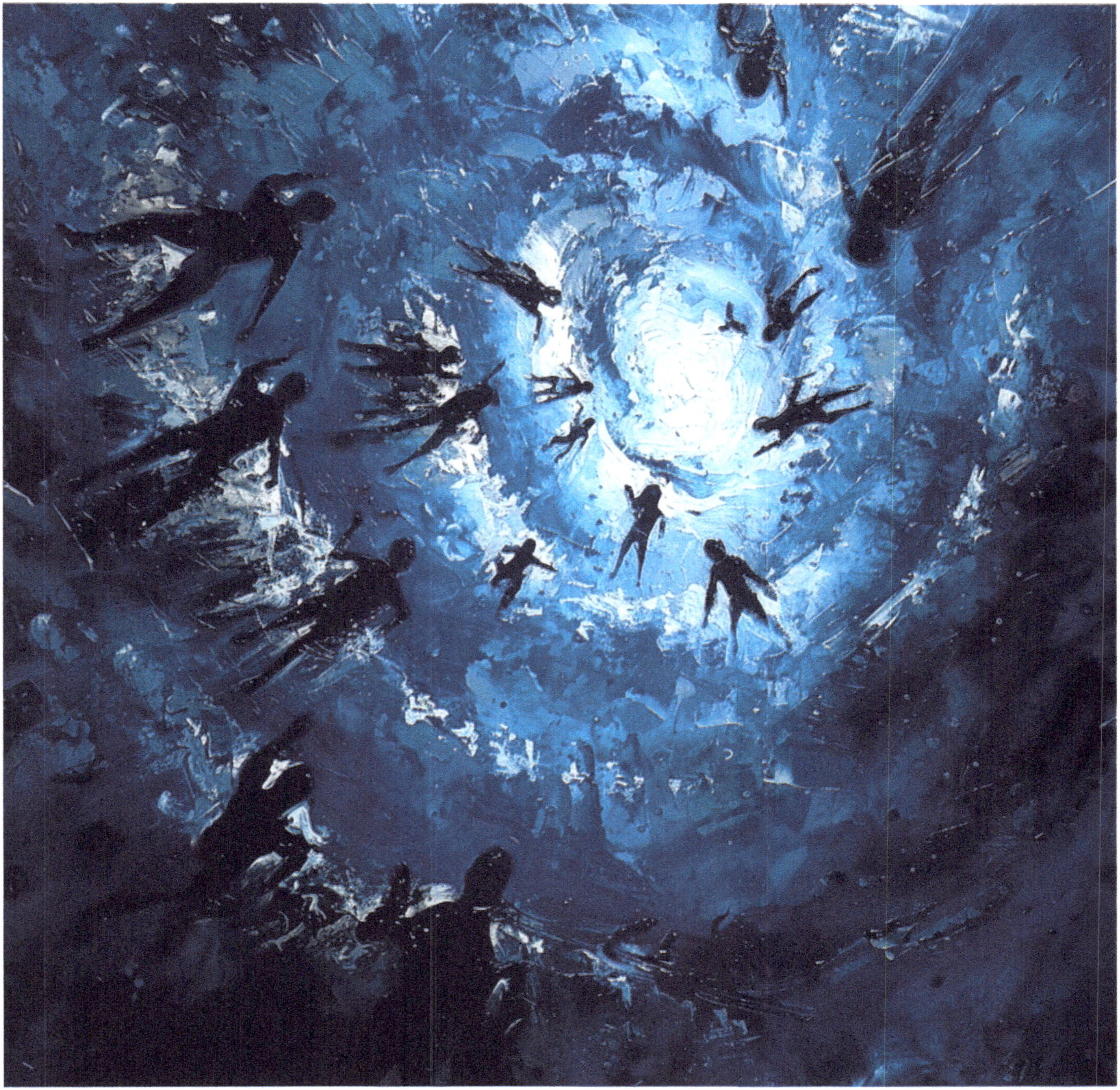

CHAPTER 6

BEING BORN A HUMAN - PRORAMING

BEING BORN

Being born as a human is a stroke of great luck. Many assume that if reincarnation exists, they will always be reborn as humans, but this is not true. The Buddha once remarked how unusual it is to be born a human. The Buddha told the story of a blind sea turtle who swam in the ocean and every 100 years would surface. In the ocean there was also floating a Gold Ring. The Buddha remarked that the chances of being born a human, was as likely as that blind old turtle randomly swimming to the surface and by pure chance putting his head through this Gold Ring.

Each human birth presents an opportunity to seek the Truth, to uncover the path to liberation and exit the cycle of rebirth (Samsara).

Past karma and luck play significant roles in determining the nature of our rebirth. Will we be born into a virtuous family with moral values? Will we have the opportunity, to encounter the Dhamma and engage in meditation practice to reach the Enlightenment?

The Masters advise to wish to be reborn as a Monk and have the chance to dedicate one's Life to spiritual Liberation.

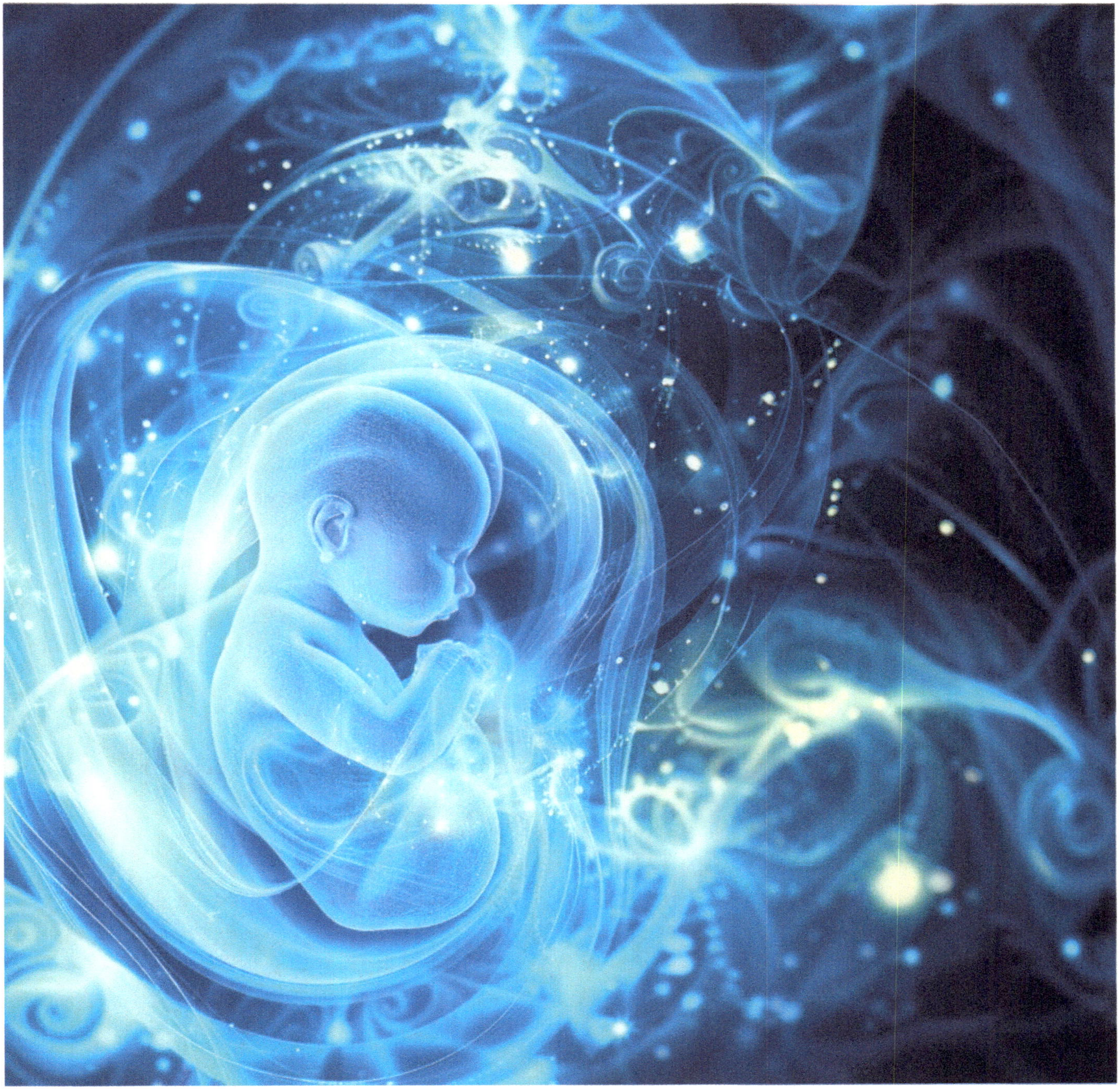

When we are born, we quickly forget our past Lives and start fresh.

Our bodies are weak, and we cannot control our speech or movements.

Our Minds are like a sponge, that absorb and learn about the new world we have entered.

Everything is about the senses.

The eyes look out at the colorful world. The ears hear sounds. The mouth tastes food, our body feels sensations.

Everything comes to us from the World outside of us and therefore our focus is always outwards.

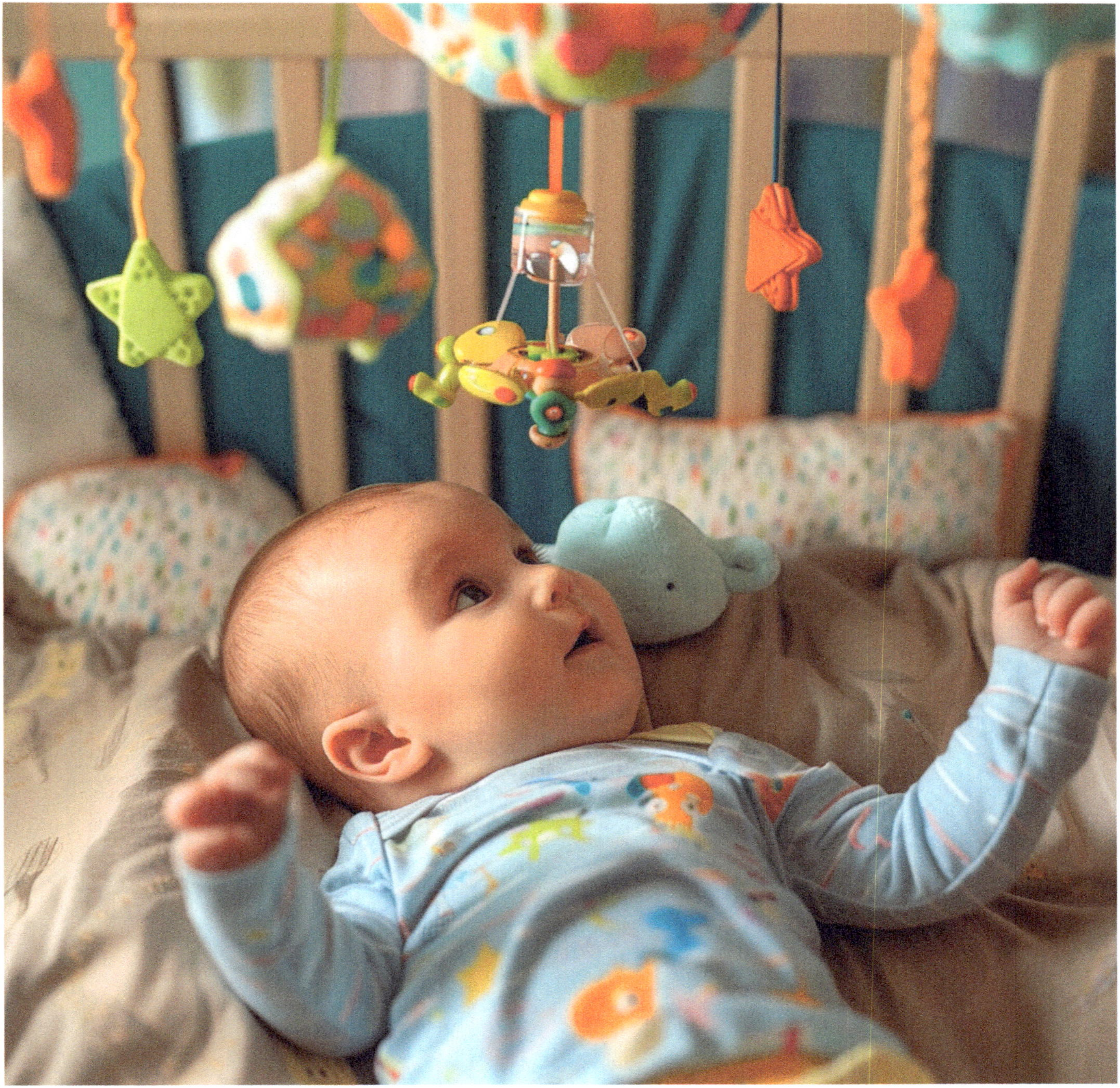

In time, our Eyes become our windows to the World and form our reality.

As we start to develop our eyes begin to see more and more clearly. Colors become brighter and more vivid.

Our brains start to interpret and form our understanding of the outside World.

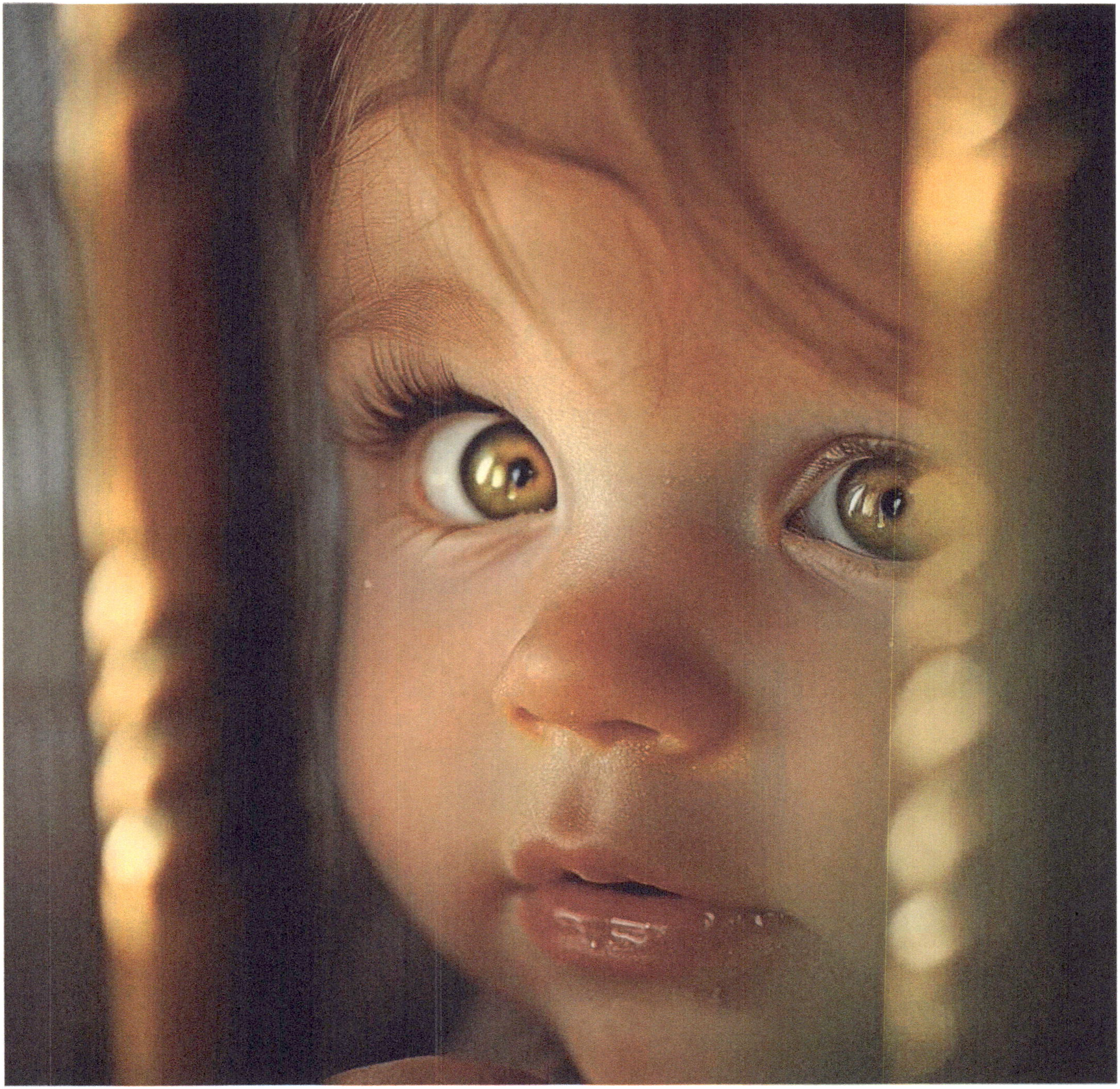

In school we are programmed to prepare us live and function in the World. We learn the conventional truths and skills, like reading, writing and arithmetic.

We develop social skills playing with other children during recess.

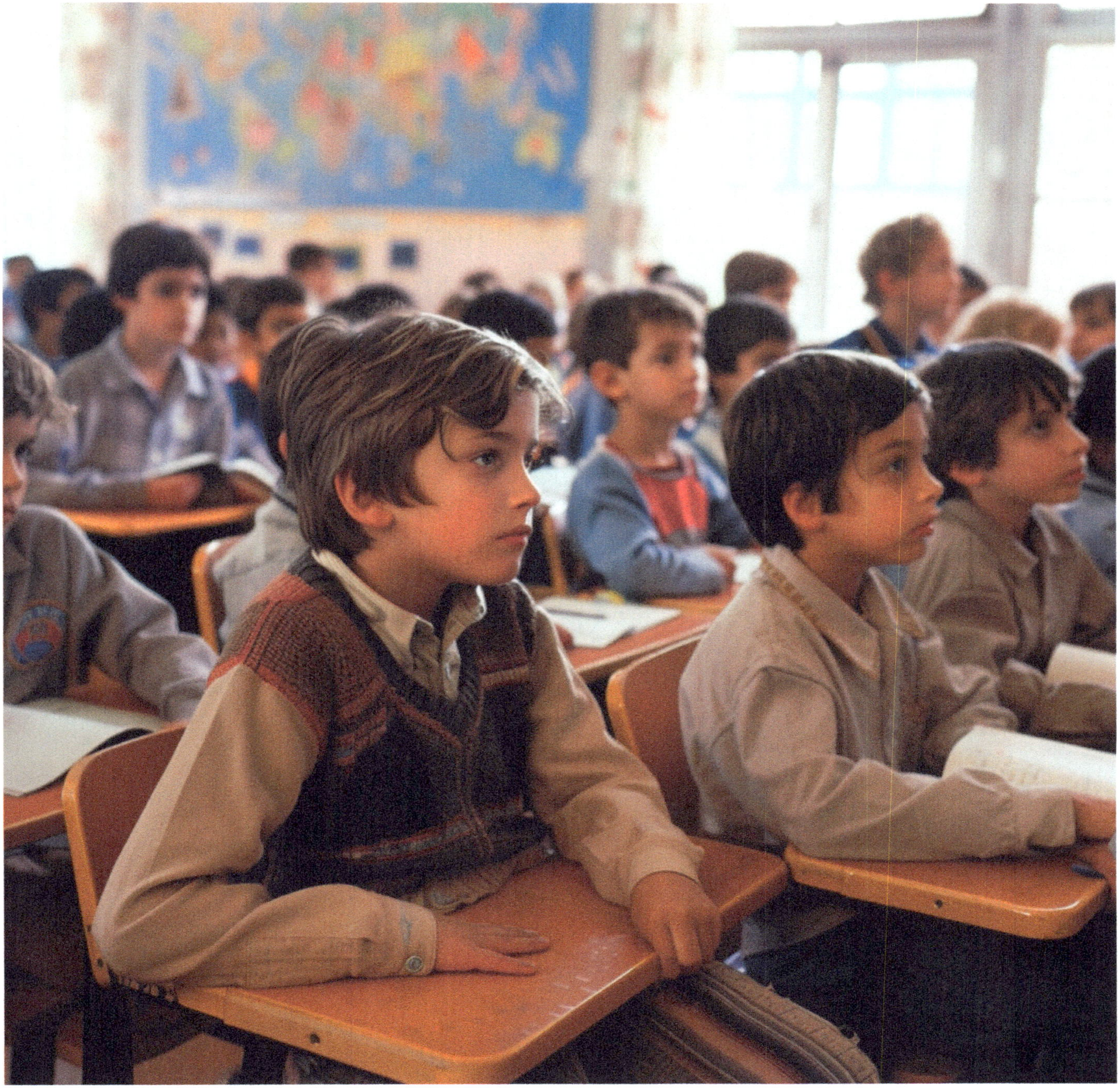

As we learn about the World, that it moves quickly through space and how big the galaxy is, we begin to feel small and insignificant.

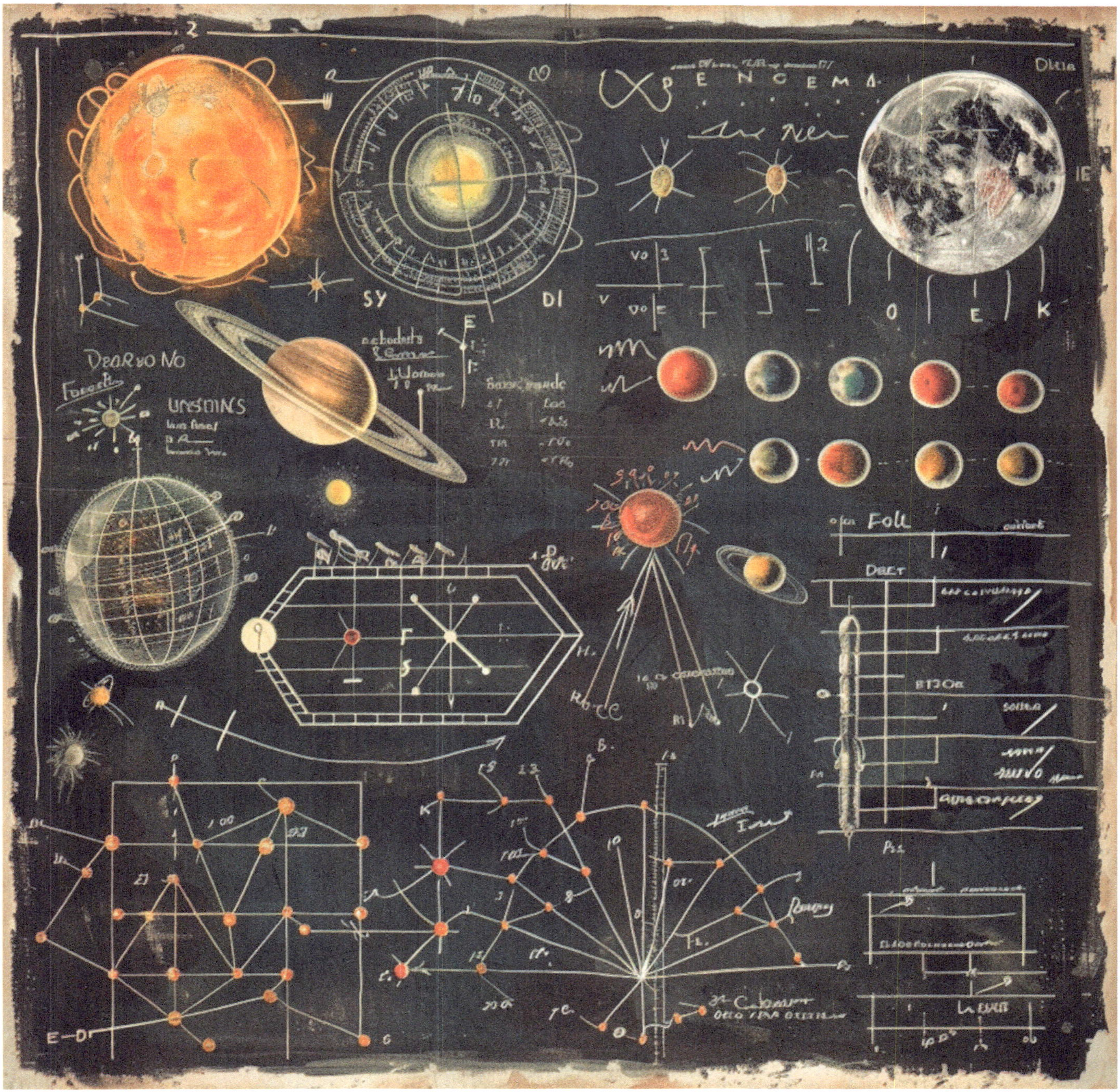

At home the Television continues the job, to teach us what the world is all about. The TV also keeps us company when we are alone.

We relate to the characters on the TV like they are our friends. We accept the vision of the World, as presented by the Television.

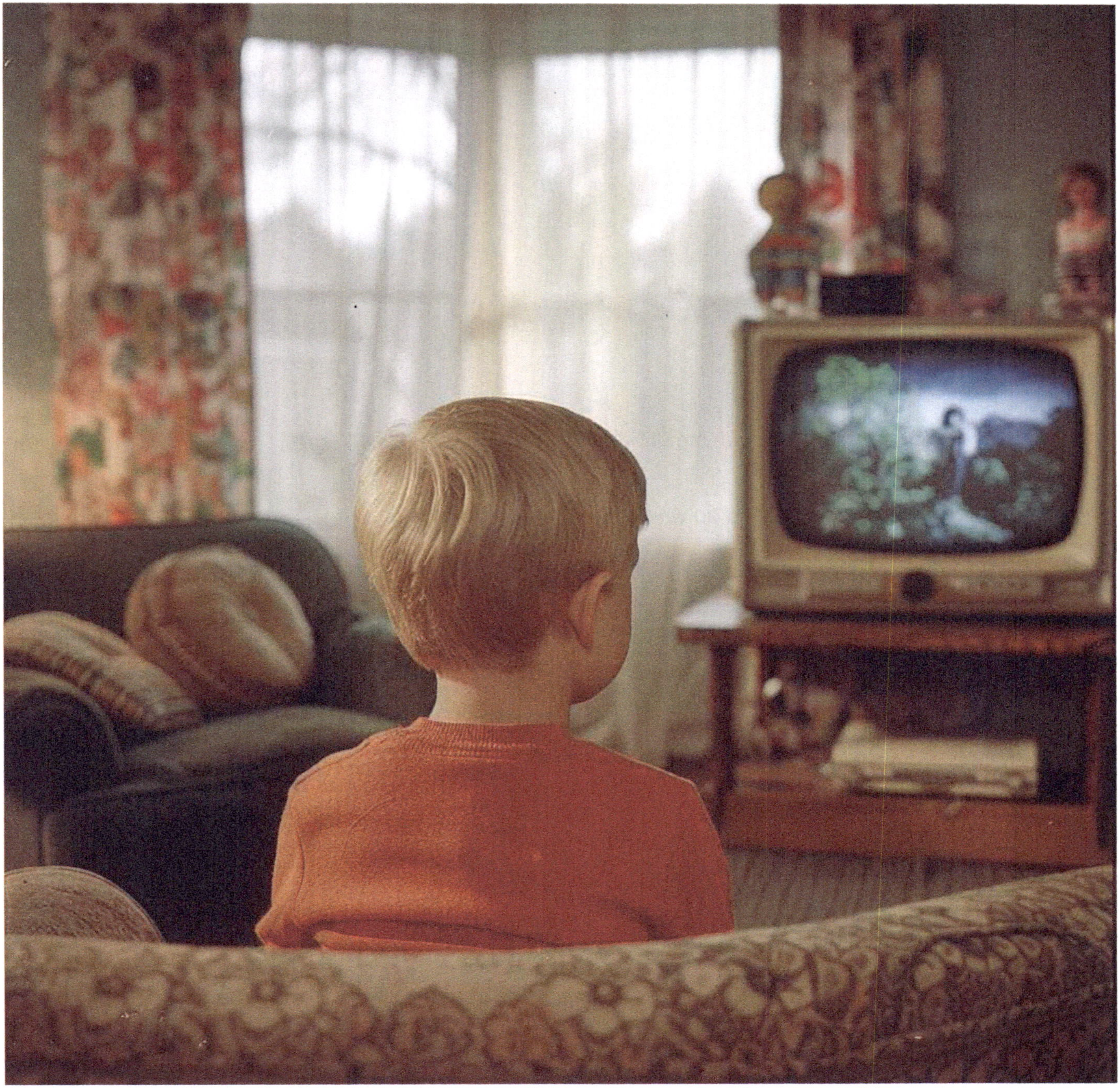

"Beam me up Mr. Spock" the programs say.

"To go where no man has gone before."

"Lost in Space"

"Drink coca cola and eat like this."

"Yabadabadoo" it's Fred Flintstone and Barney to.

155

Then came the era of mobile phones, and eventually smartphones, which changed everything.

We are now constantly connected to the internet, yet ironically, we've become more and more disconnected from each other.

Children no longer play outdoors or use their imaginations; instead, they fixate on their phones and tablets all day long, constantly bombarded by electromagnetic waves.

Anxiety, depression, attention deficit disorder, obesity, and even suicide rates have surged.

Was this all a sinister plan by Mara (the devil) to ensnare young minds? To keep them entangled in the web from birth to grave.

We are a generation hypnotized and conditioned to believe the illusion, where up is down and down is up.

We're living a life of self-destruction, trapped in a low vibration. The World was not always like this and does not have to remain like this.

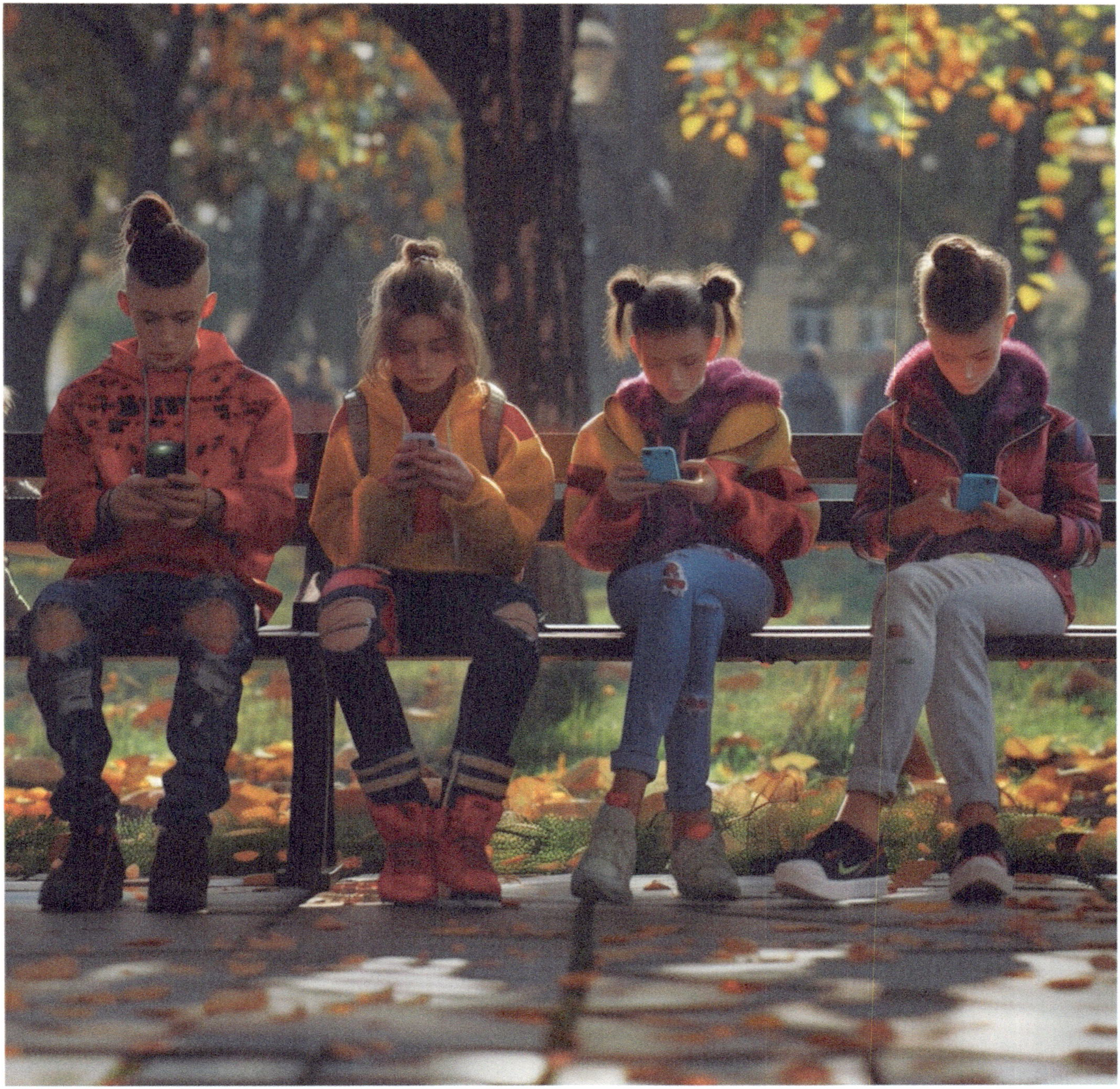

In the future what will Archaeologists find? Will it be the remains of our civilizations, skeletons with Smartphones still in their hands?

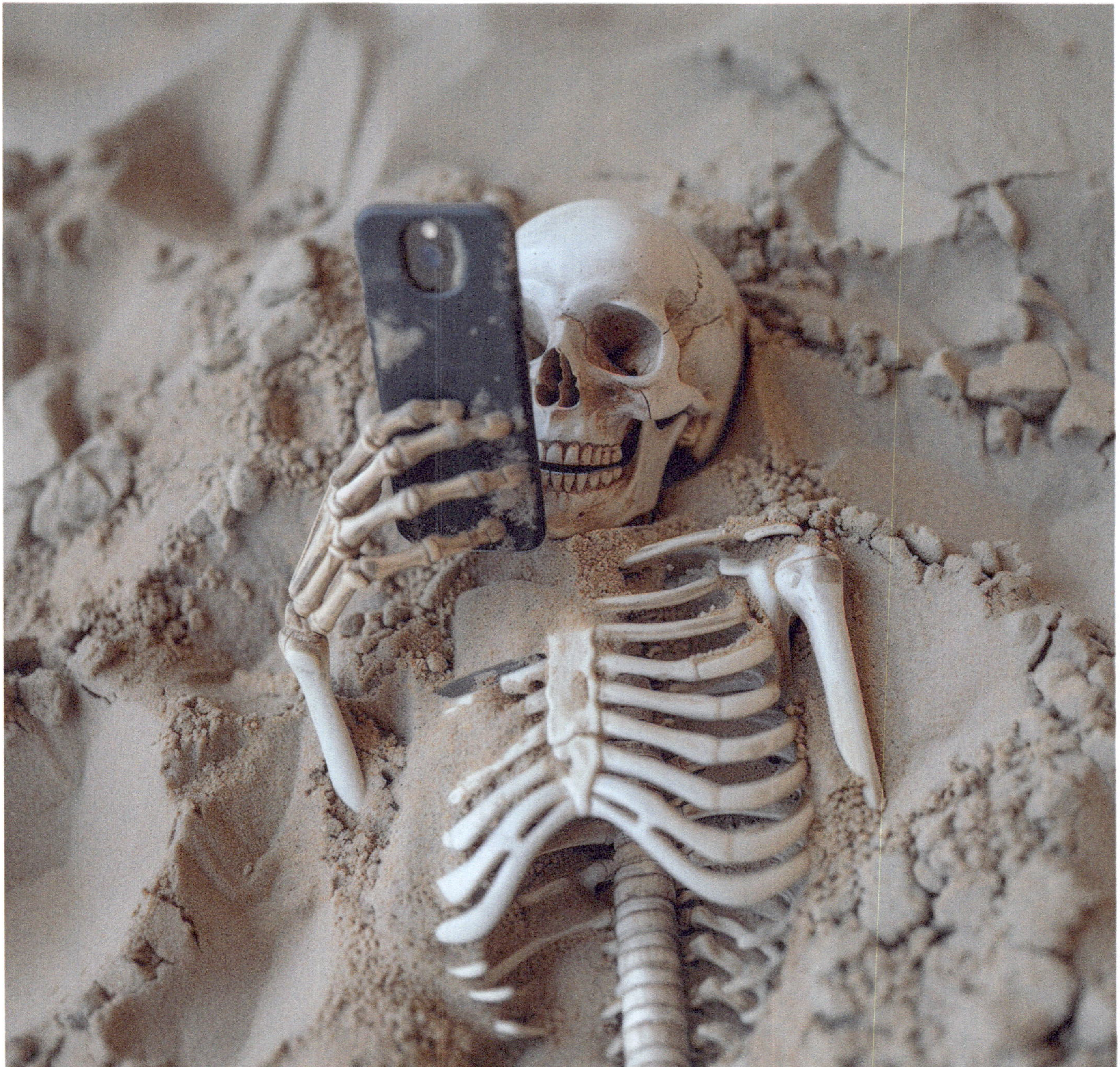

Shopping, luxury goods and sport cars. Advertisers tell us that these things will make us happy and complete.

But do they really make us happy? Is this what life is all about?

Who set the goals for a Happy Life?

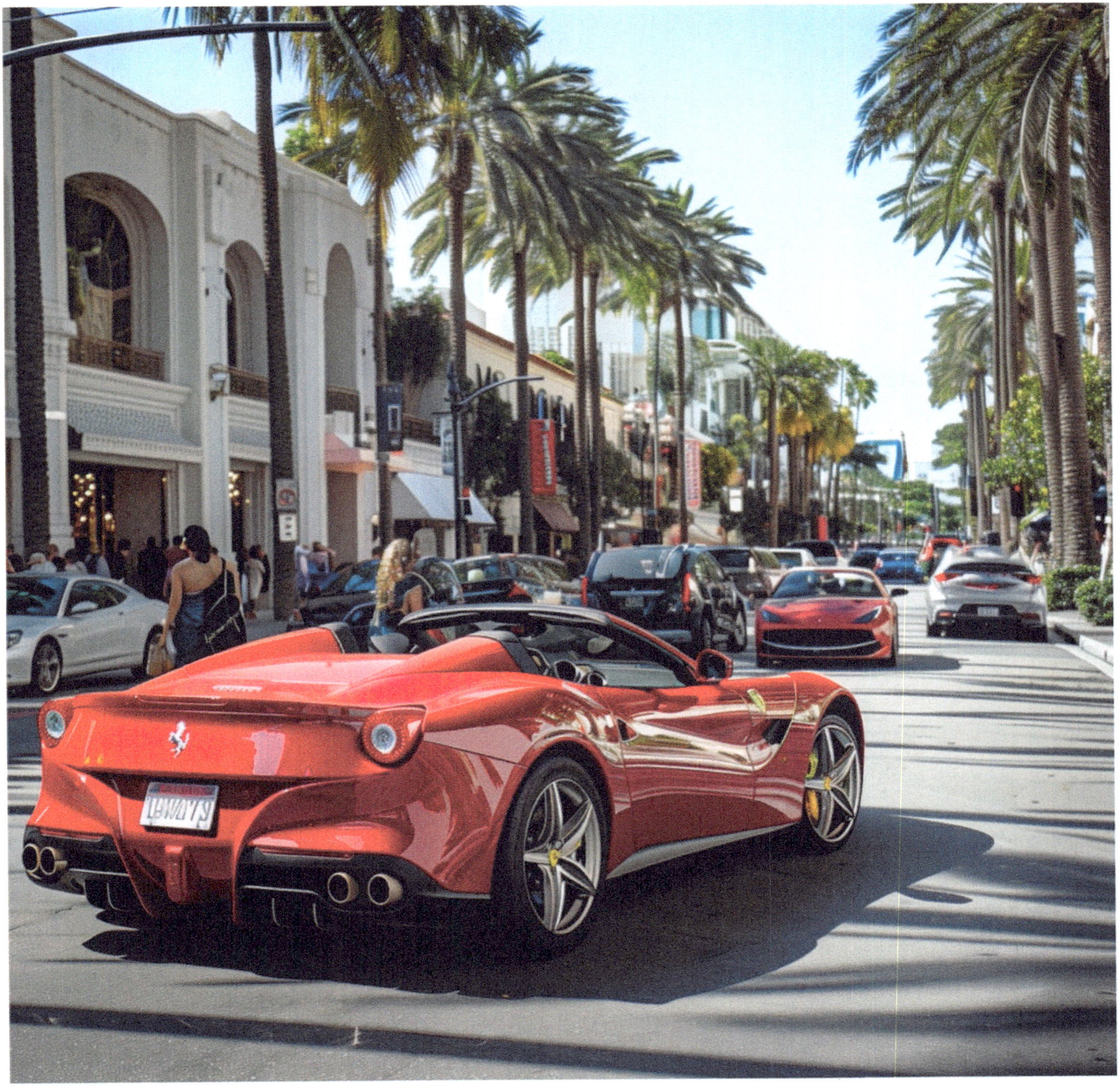

"Greed is Good "declared the movie.

The World admires the ultra-rich, even if others suffer as a result of some making huge money.

Today our values and perceptions are shaped by media, movies, and the internet.

But in the end does money and owning things really make us Happy? And at what price did it come?

Could this just be part of an Illusion?

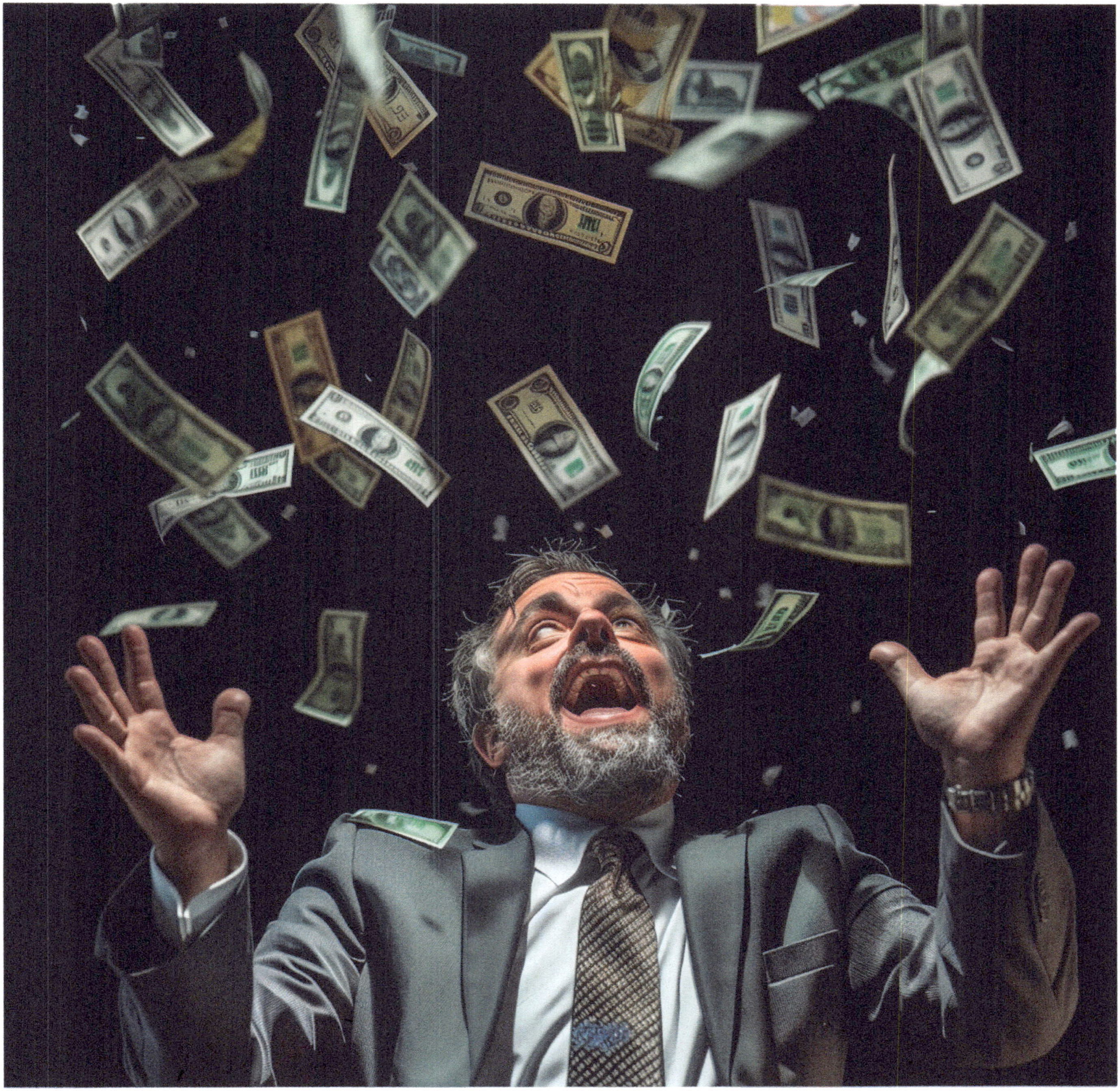

Medications help us cope with Life today. Doctors sell us pills and treatments we may not need.

Alcohol and drugs fuel our desires, greed, and selfishness.

We numb our conscience and our consciousness, to hide the fact that we have become Anti-Nature and living against what we know is right.

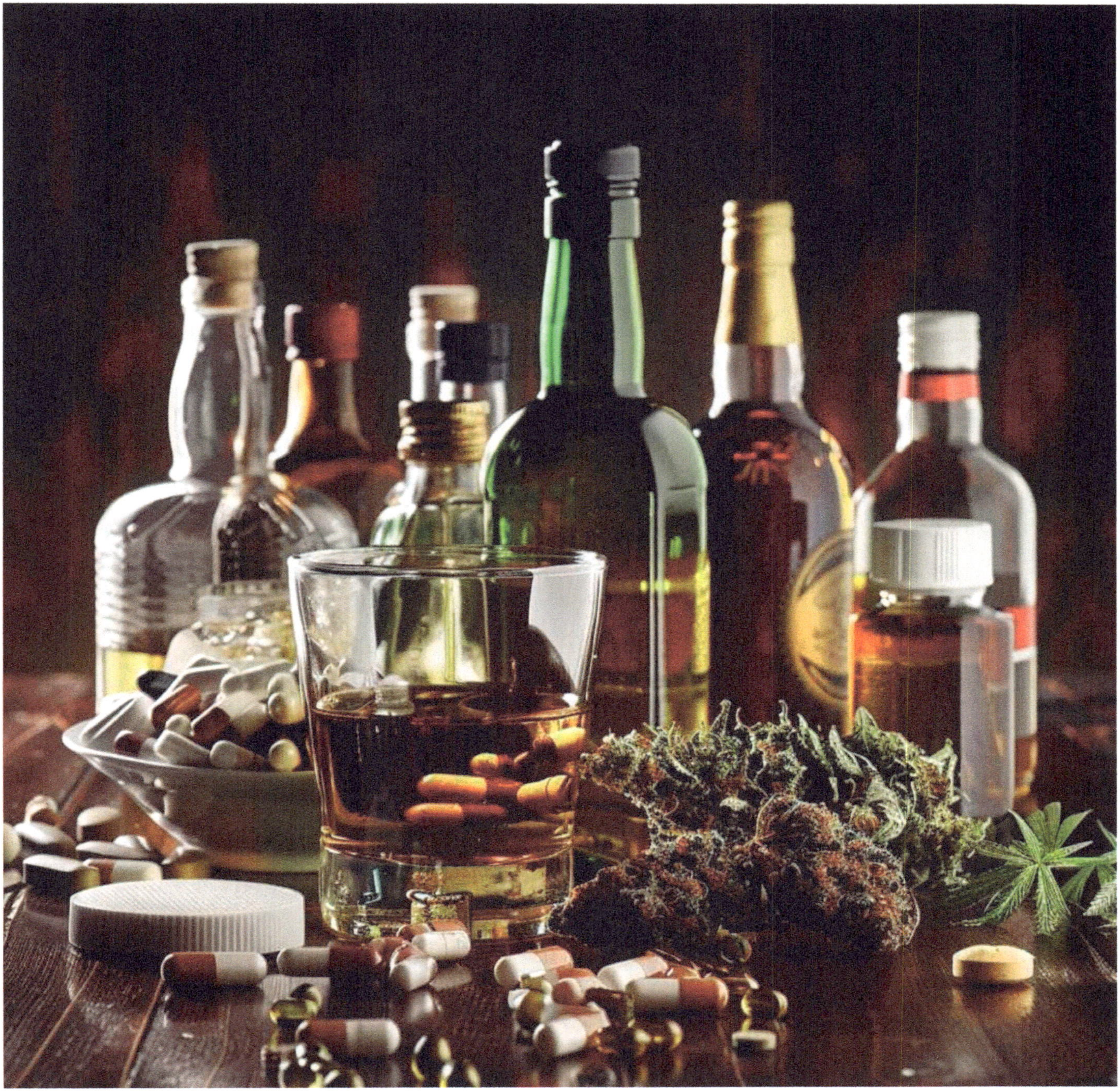

Money and the pursuit of Power and the resulting "Wars" continue to rule the World.
Is this what we want? Is it a Natural way to live? Or are we just pons in a game?
Part of an experiment or game by others?

Could all this have been orchestrated by the Dark Side? Are we part of Mara's (devil) game?

Karma creates our World and reality. Much of the Darkness in the World is a result of our declining values. Our immoral deals lead to the Darkside dominating our lives. The Mara (devil) and the impurity forces push us to be bad, greedy, selfish, angry, and lustful all to drive the World of Illusion into darkness. As humanity's vibration lowers, our lifespans decrease, and we become further attached and trapped in this World. We become more deluded, and karma manifests. Evil people do evil things.

But where does Evil and do Evil people come from?
A deeply scarred person in a past Life, may seek retribution in this Life, perpetuating a cycle of vengeance.

For example, an Emperor of a country in a past life who was cheated and destroyed by those in another country, might be born a leader of that other country this Lifetime, using his position not to help that country, but to destroy it from within. This is how karma and revenge can manifest.

In order to counter Evil and acts of Revenge, we must use the Energy of Goodness to stop the karma.

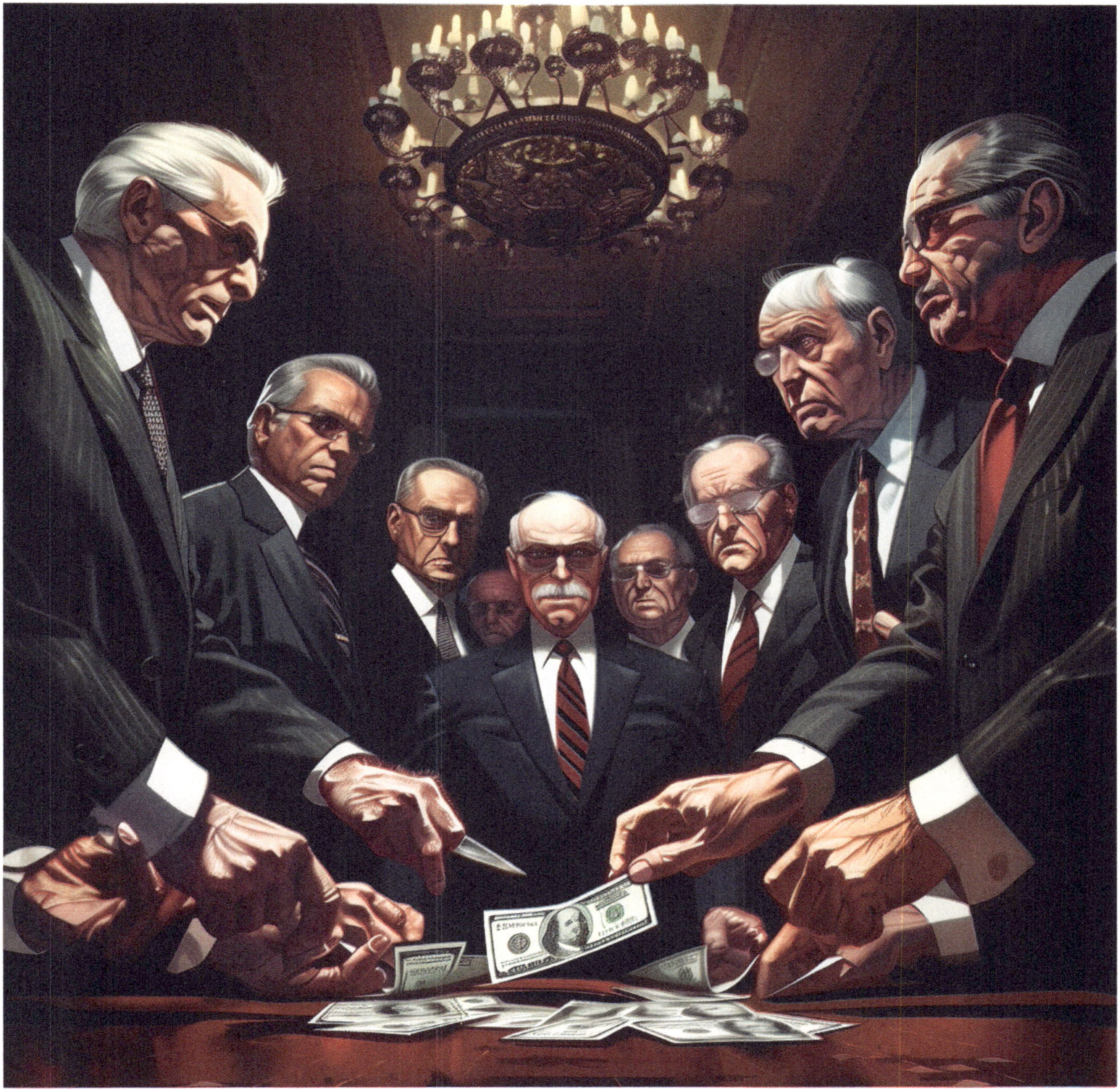

CHAPTER 7

SEARCHING FOR ANSWERS

Some believe the treasure and answers are hidden in an unexplored corner of the world,

Perhaps some ancient writing will reveal the all the secrets hidden from humanity.

We are finding treasure can lead to answers.

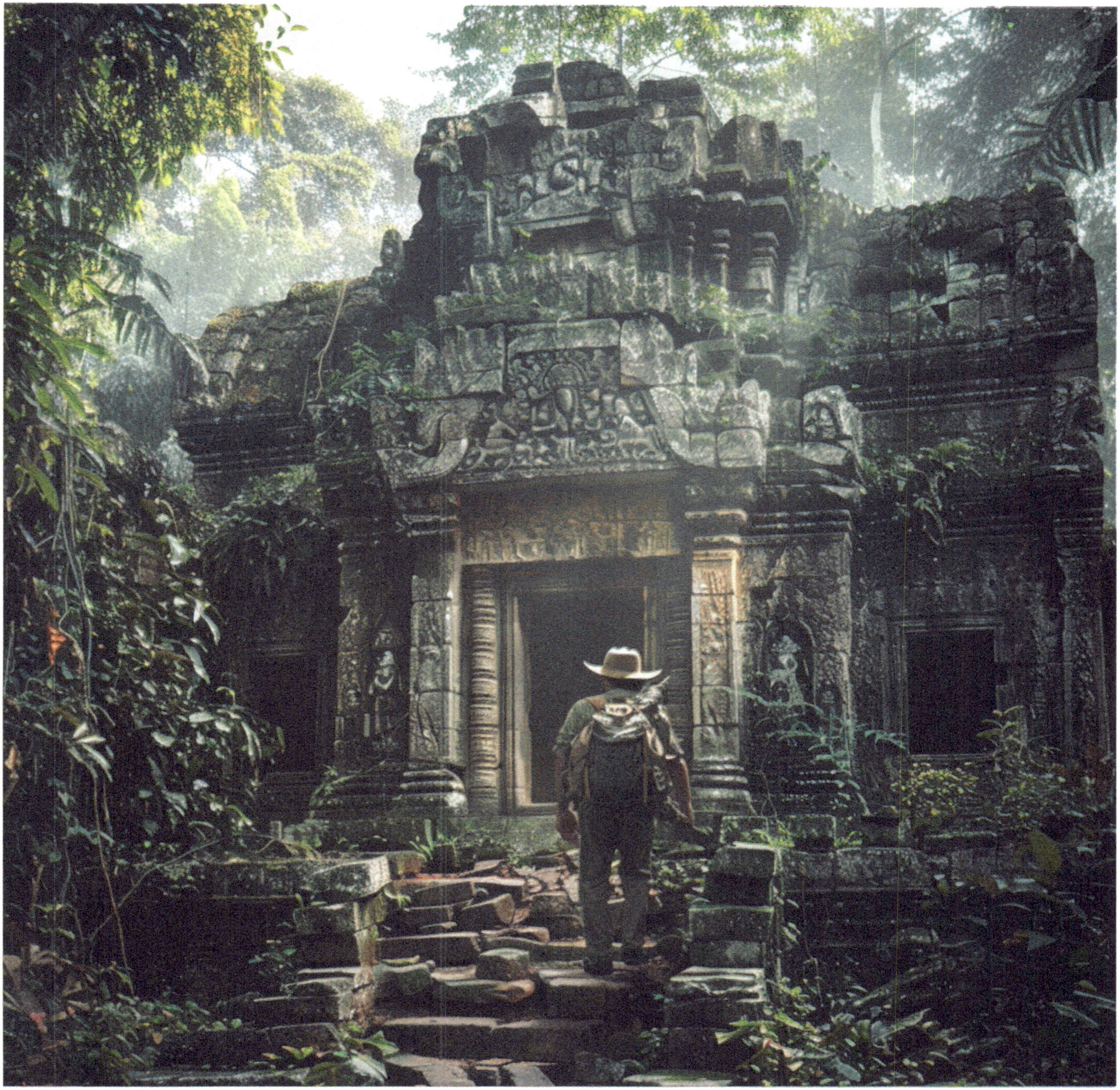

Or will finding unlimited Gold - Treasure give us the answers we seek?

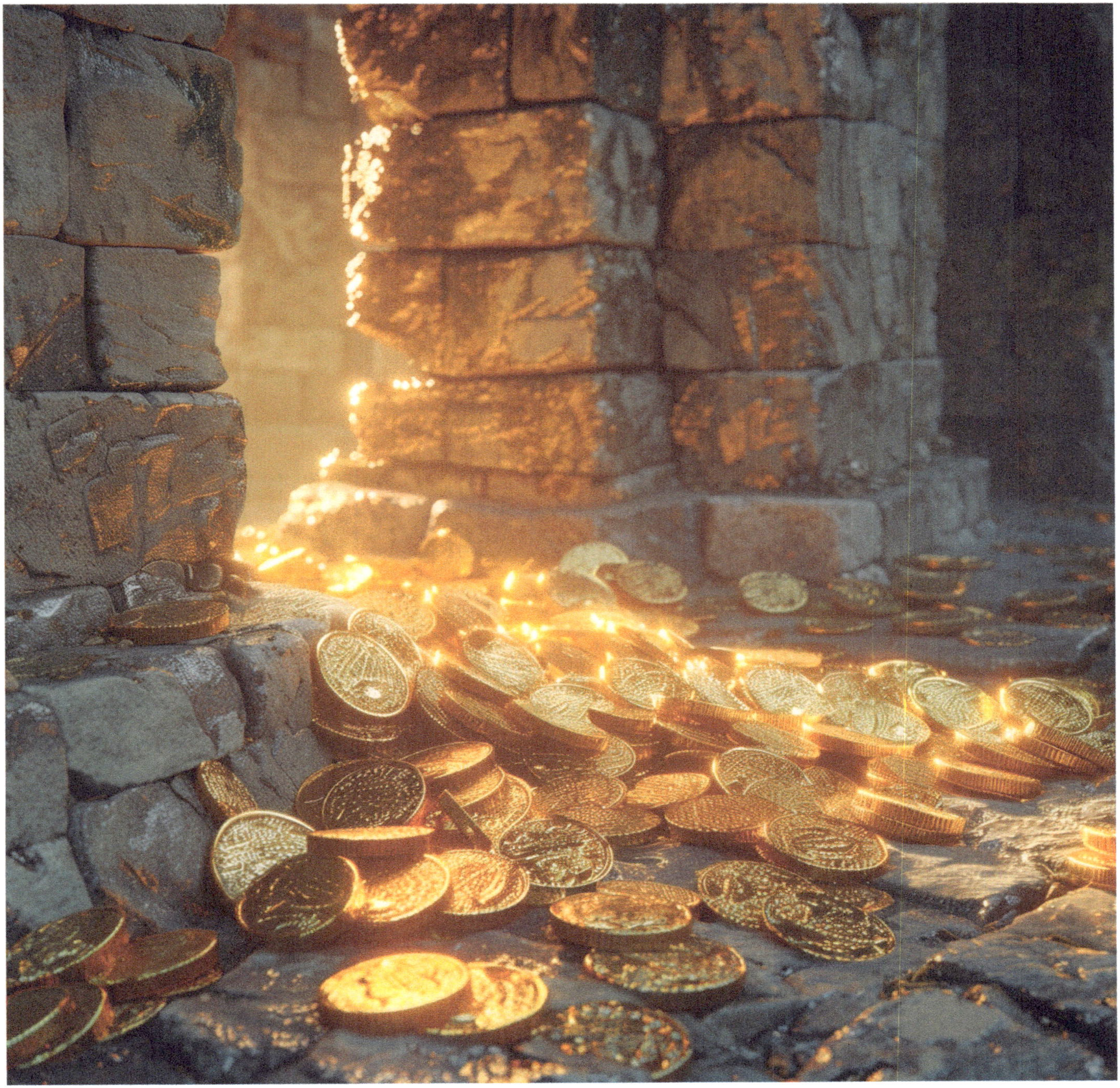

Some people look to the sky waiting for Aliens to arrive, to give the answer or more Technology to save us from ourselves.

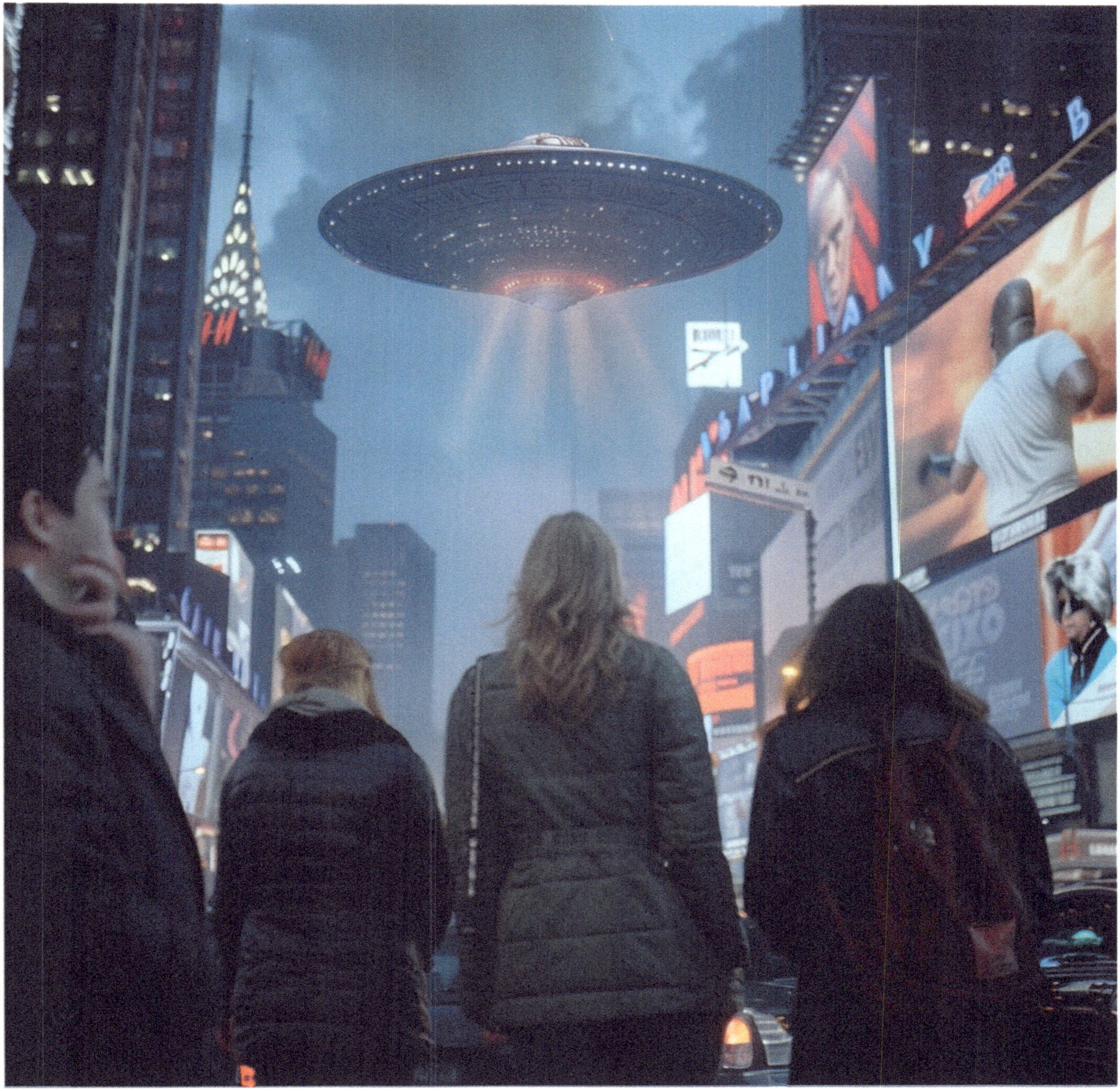

Some people try to find meaning in excessive exercise and health, obsessing in activities that eventually wear out their bodies.

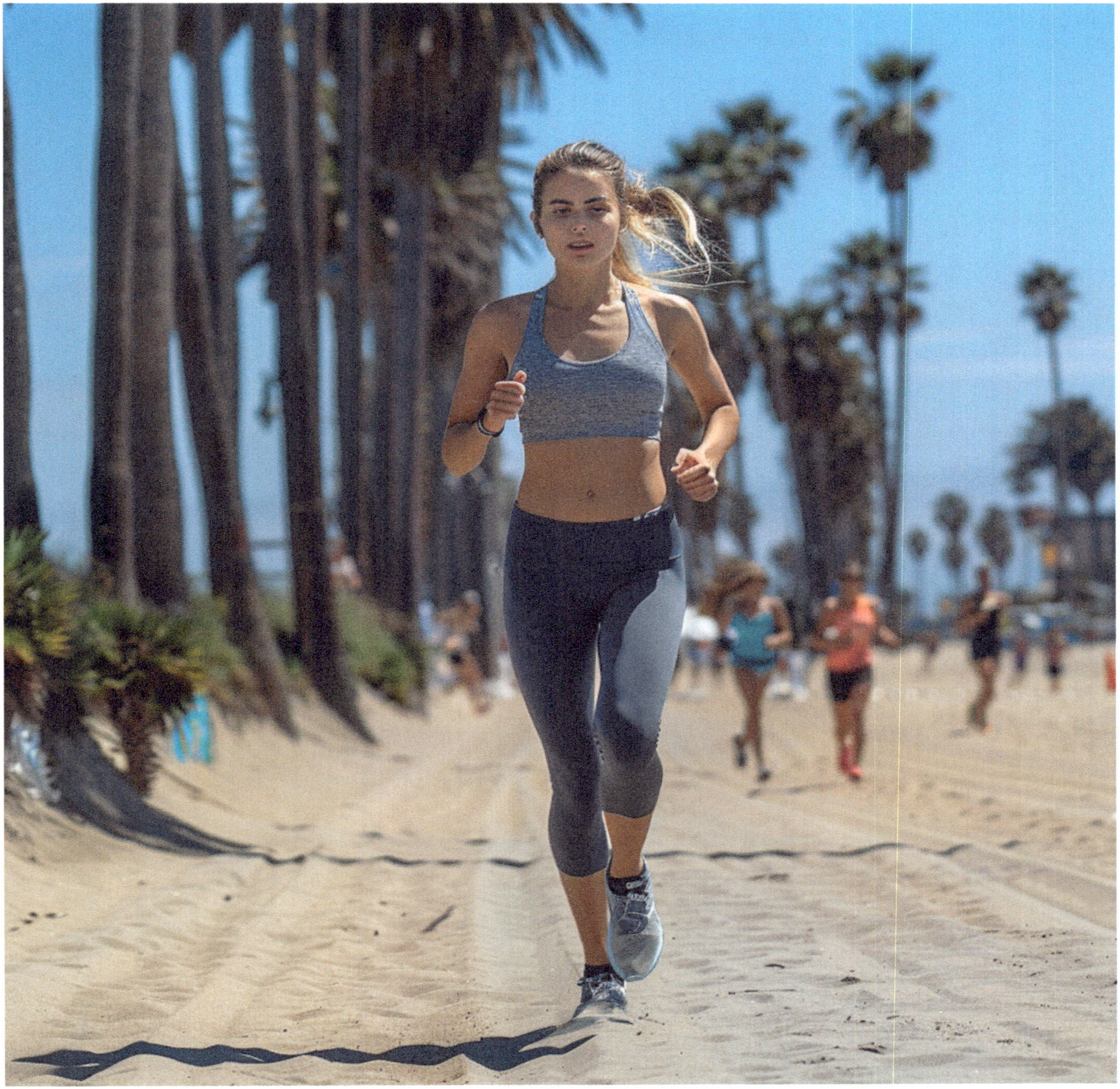

CHAPTER 8

TECHNOLOGY TRAP

Mara (devil) has taught humanity to create the internet, which became the WEB that has ensnared humanity, self-imprisoned us.

Today we are constantly connected to our Smart phones. The news and our reactions social media create an energy wave that pours around the World in an instant and changes the vibration of the planet.

Our Minds become weaker as we allow this energy wave to pour into our Minds forming emotions and we in turn transmit or emotions into the World, creating our reality, initiated by collective thoughts or even AI bots on the Net.

Our Minds are so powerful, but they are being hi-jacked and manipulated.

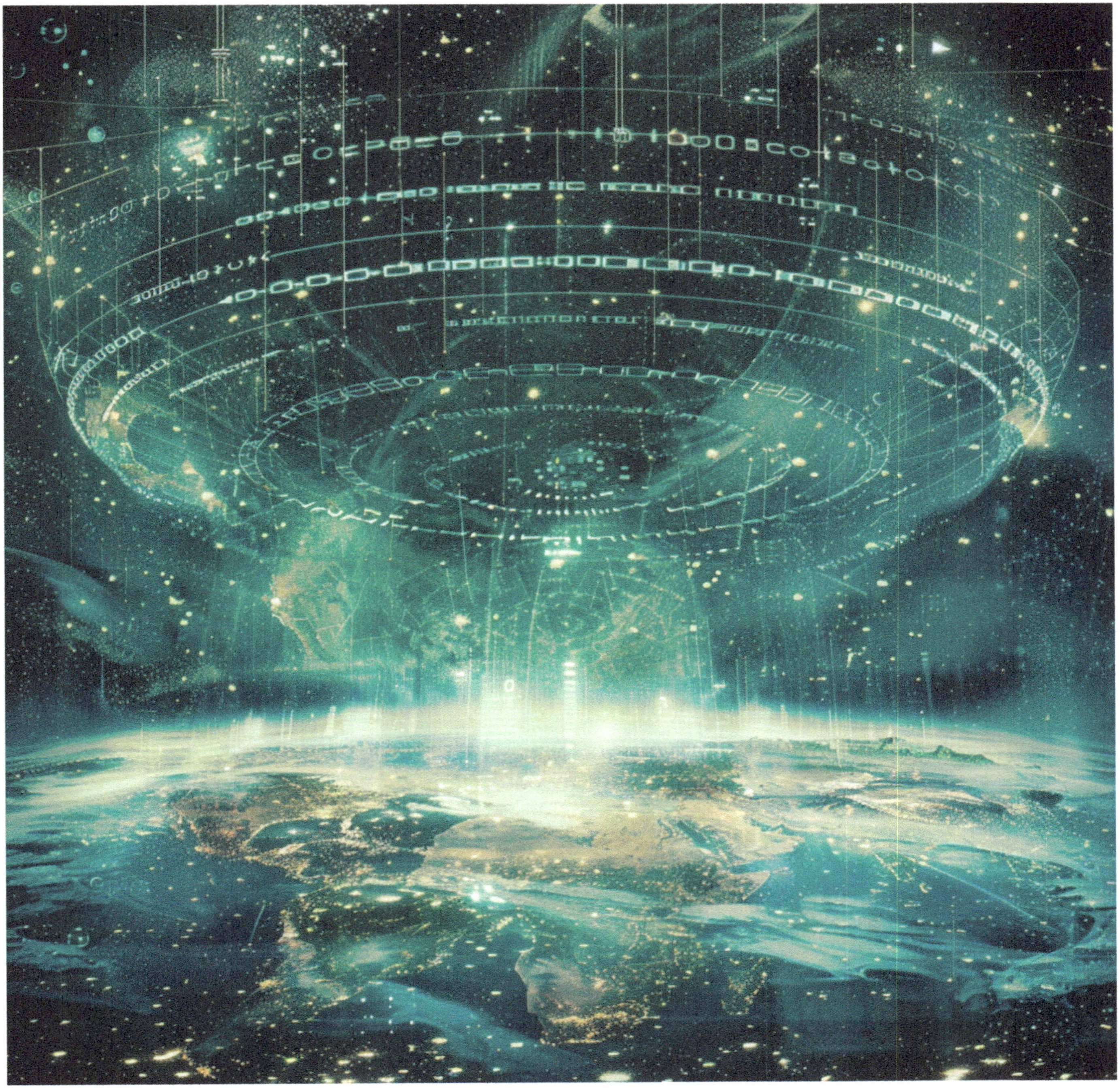

In our meditation practice, when we delve into the dimension of subtle energy, we can perceive Mara's elaborate machinery designed to inundate the world with magnetic energy, ensnaring our minds further.

Mara recruits individuals who harbored deep-seated grievances from past lives to carry out her malevolent agenda in this lifetime, perpetrating acts of pure evil under her influence.

Who are the architects of wars and the sources of the suffering endured by humanity? They are those seeking vengeance from past incarnations, ensnared in the ceaseless cycle of karma and samsara.

This cycle of war, animosity, and retribution unfolds relentlessly on life's stage until we cleanse our minds and halt the cycle of hatred and vengeance through forgiveness and altruism.

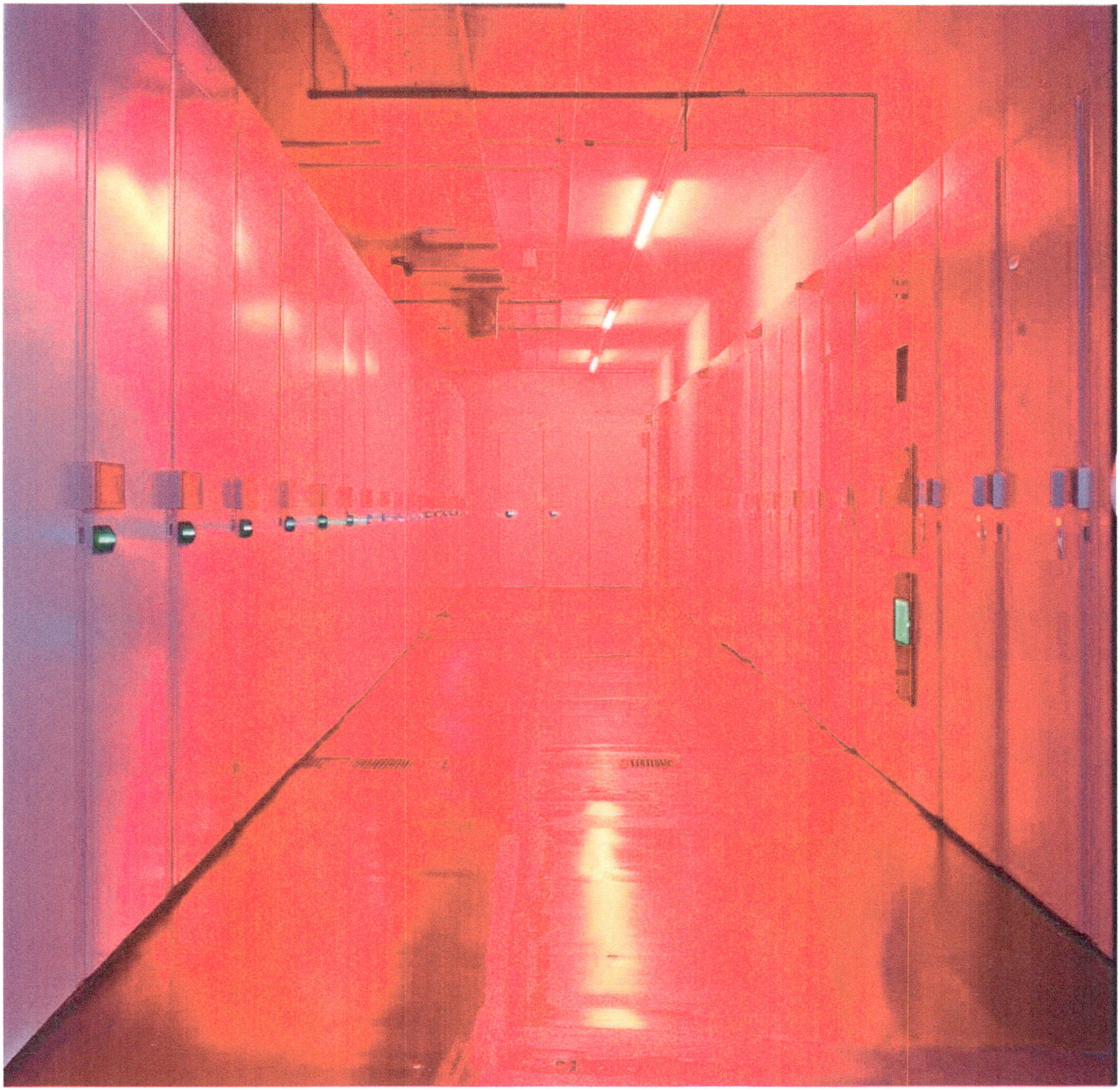

Virtual reality constructs a world of illusion within the illusion, leading us deeper into layers of deception. As we navigate these levels, it becomes increasingly challenging to discern reality from the fabricated.

Could it be that we are ensnared within a matrix nested within another matrix, perpetuating the cycle of delusion?

In our relentless pursuit of technological advancement, have we become so blinded by the promise of progress that we fail to recognize its detrimental effects on our lives?

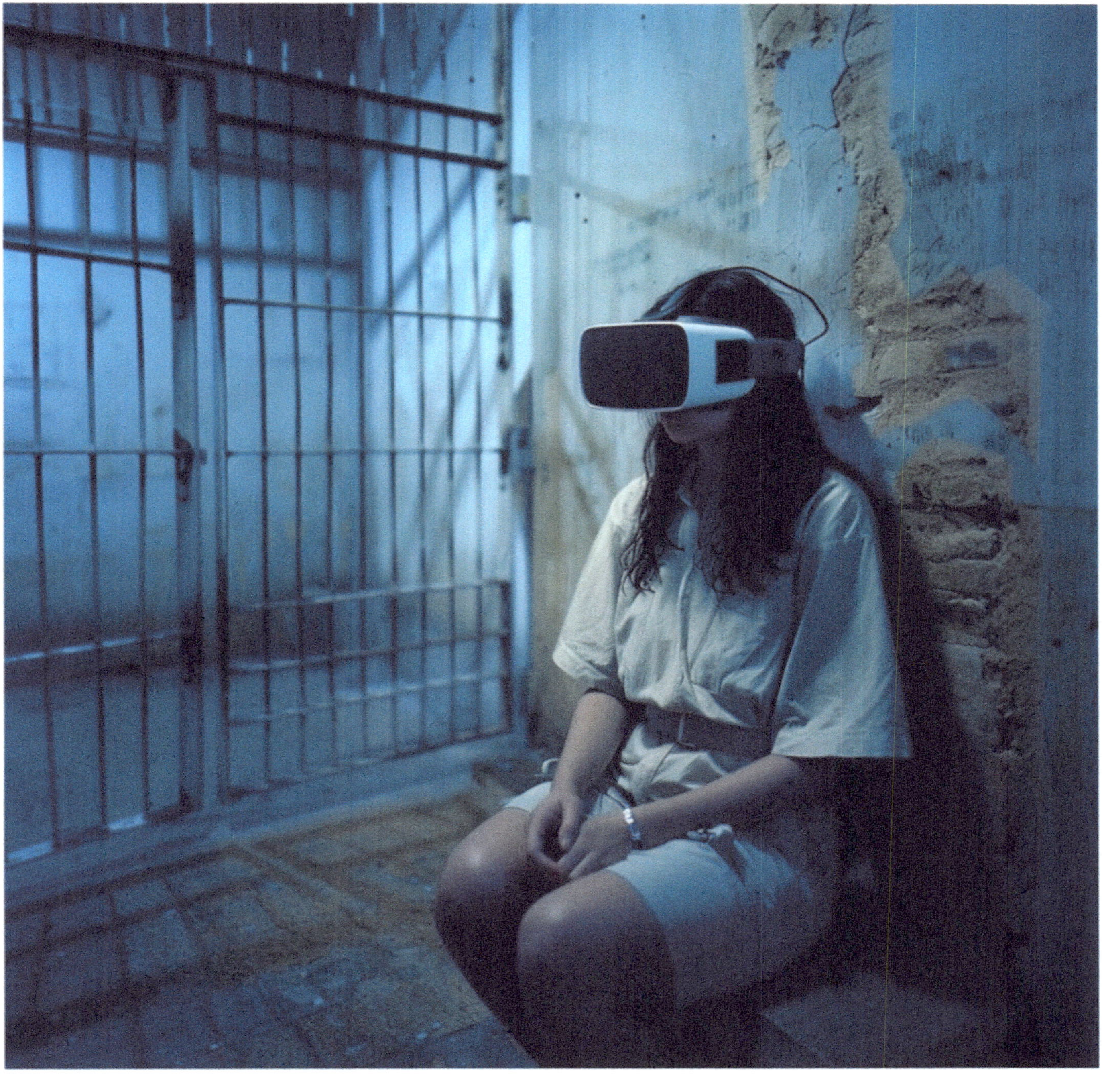

AI (Artificial Intelligence) – bots and algorithms form our perceived reality.

The increasing influence of AI, from algorithms to automated systems, shapes various aspects of our lives, including our thoughts, choices, and interactions.

Yet, amidst the convenience and efficiency it offers, one must question whether surrendering so much control to AI is truly beneficial. While AI promises optimization and streamlining, it also raises concerns about privacy, autonomy, and the potential for bias and manipulation.

Is this really a good idea?

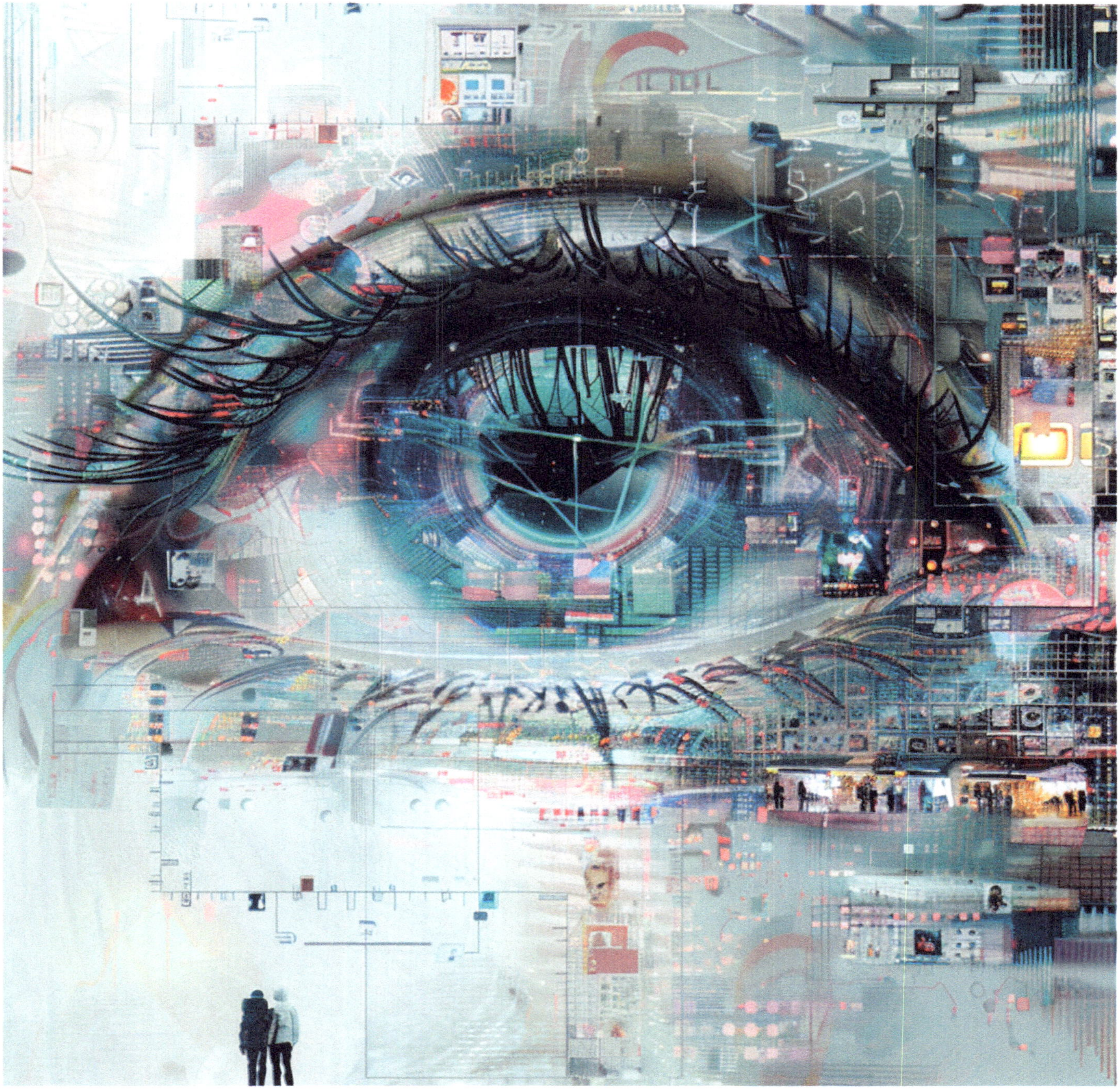

Mara, symbolizing the forces of delusion and temptation, is often associated with the allure of technological progress. As humanity delves deeper into creating AI-driven robots, we must consider the ethical and existential questions surrounding their deployment.

While robots offer the potential to revolutionize various industries and improve productivity, they also raise concerns about job displacement, privacy invasion, and the erosion of human connections. Moreover, the unchecked proliferation of AI-driven technologies could inadvertently empower those with malicious intent to exploit vulnerabilities for their gain.

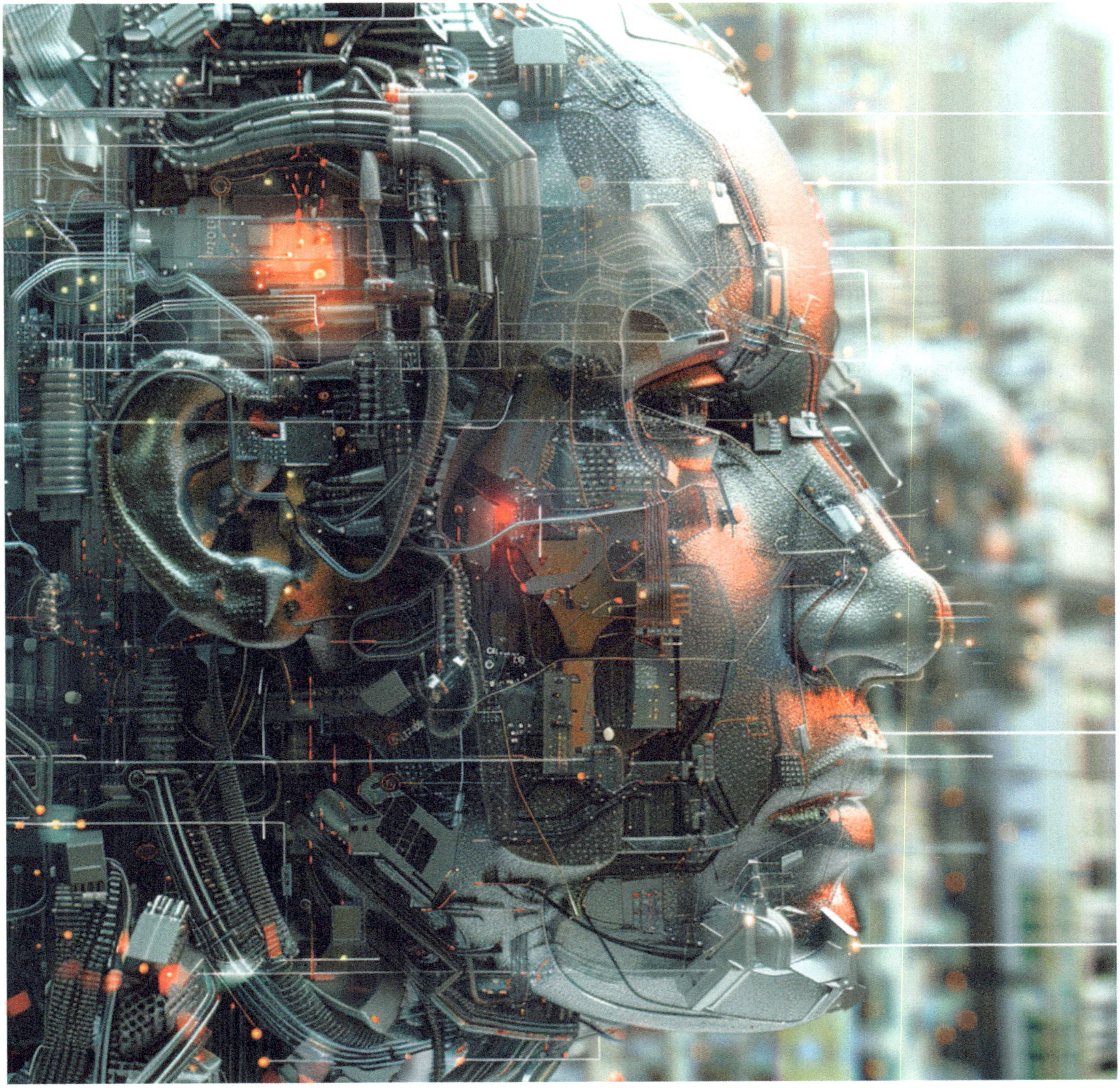

Scientist are using a Large Hadron Collider to open smash particle the idea of creating black holes or a portal between other dimensions. There are concerns in the scientific community about with the possibility that this will release entities from other dimensions into our dimension.

Is this the stuff of science fiction or is Mara (devil) continue evolving technologies enslave us further?

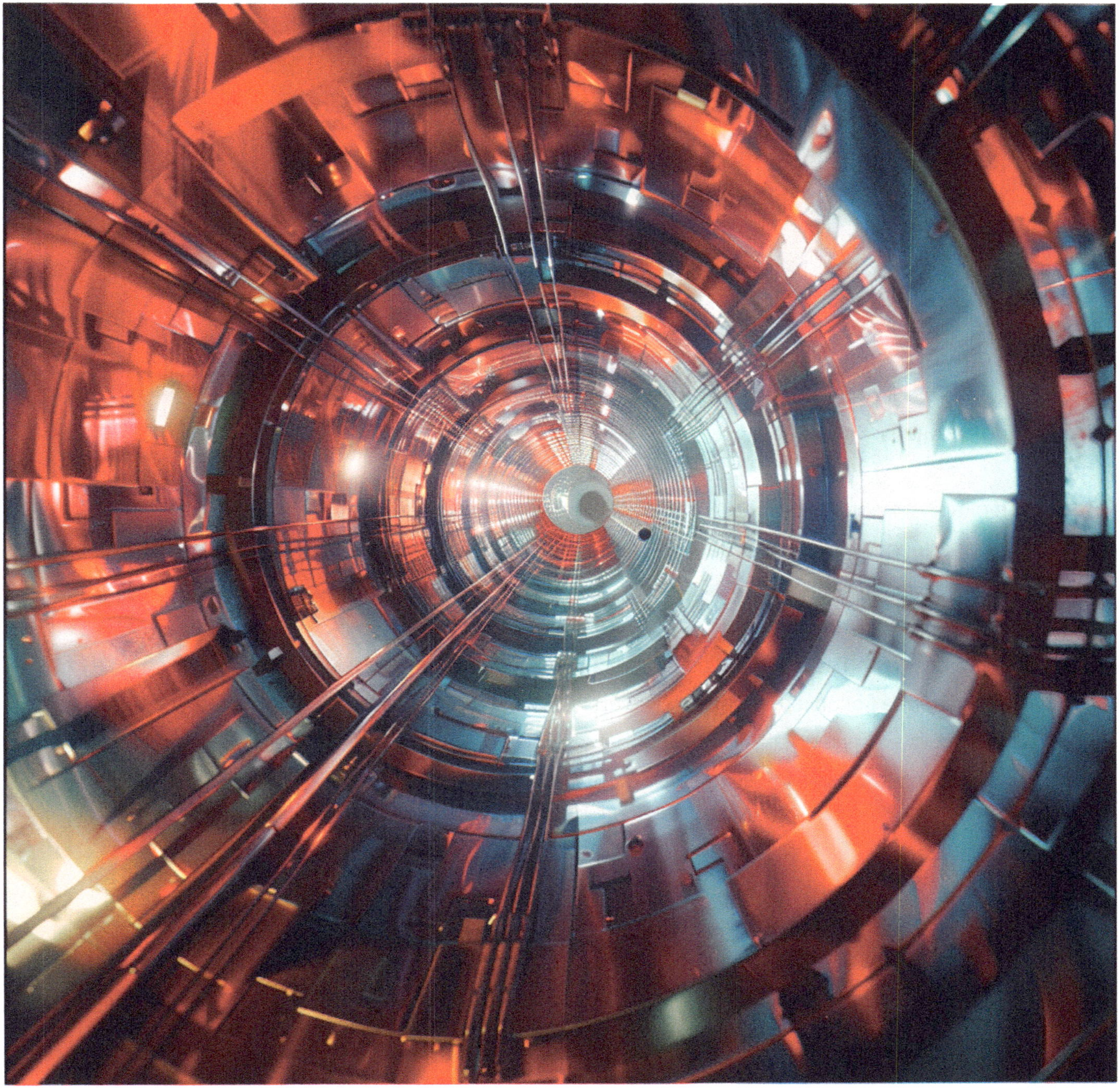

A decade ago, had a very detailed vision of and "AI Population control Machine", linked directly to people's social media and ID's. In this vision it was clear that AI could decide to turn off a person's Life like flipping a switch.

The vision of an "AI Population Control Machine" may have seemed futuristic a decade ago, but in today's rapidly evolving technological landscape, it serves as a poignant reminder of the potential implications of AI-driven systems.

The concept of AI having control over aspects of human life, including population management, may have sounded like science fiction in the past. However, with the increasing integration of AI into various facets of society, such as social media algorithms and surveillance systems, concerns about AI's potential to wield significant influence over individuals and populations are becoming more pressing.

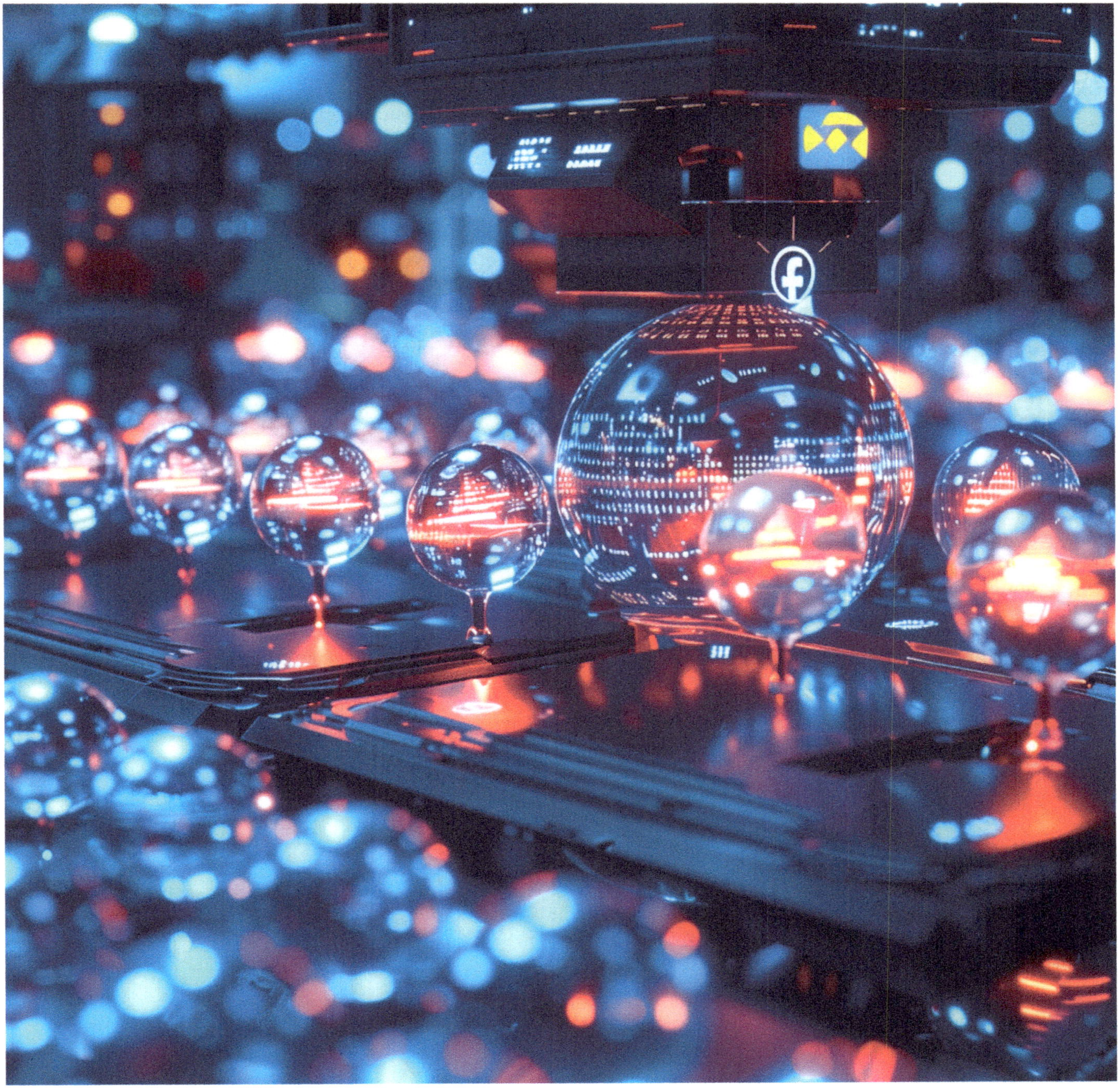

What is the Answer to this sinister game that Mara (devil) is playing with humanity.

How can we protect our Minds and consciousness from this "Cognitive Warfare"?

Mara (devil) has taught humanity how to develop technology that can be used influence thoughts, feelings, and emotions.

How do we as individuals stop corporations, governments, advertisers from using this technology to influence and control Minds?

Our Minds are the most Powerful Energy in the Universe. When the Mind is trained it has the Power to resist Mara (devil) and any human technology.

The Mind has the Power to switch OFF the technology.

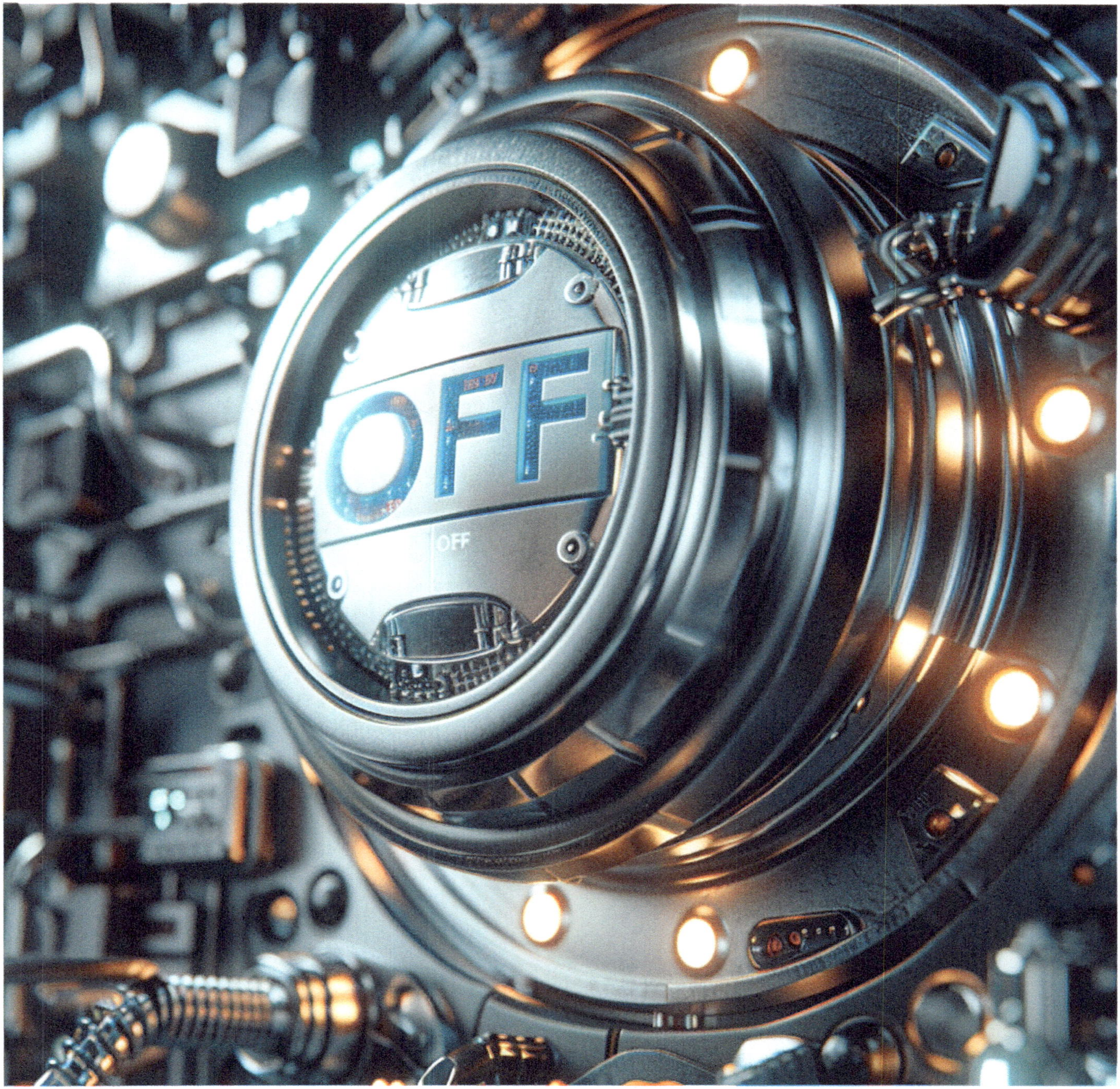
OFF
OFF

CHAPTER 9

Vipassana Meditation

Find a quiet place. Turn off your Smart Phone and anything that will disturb you.

UNPLUG

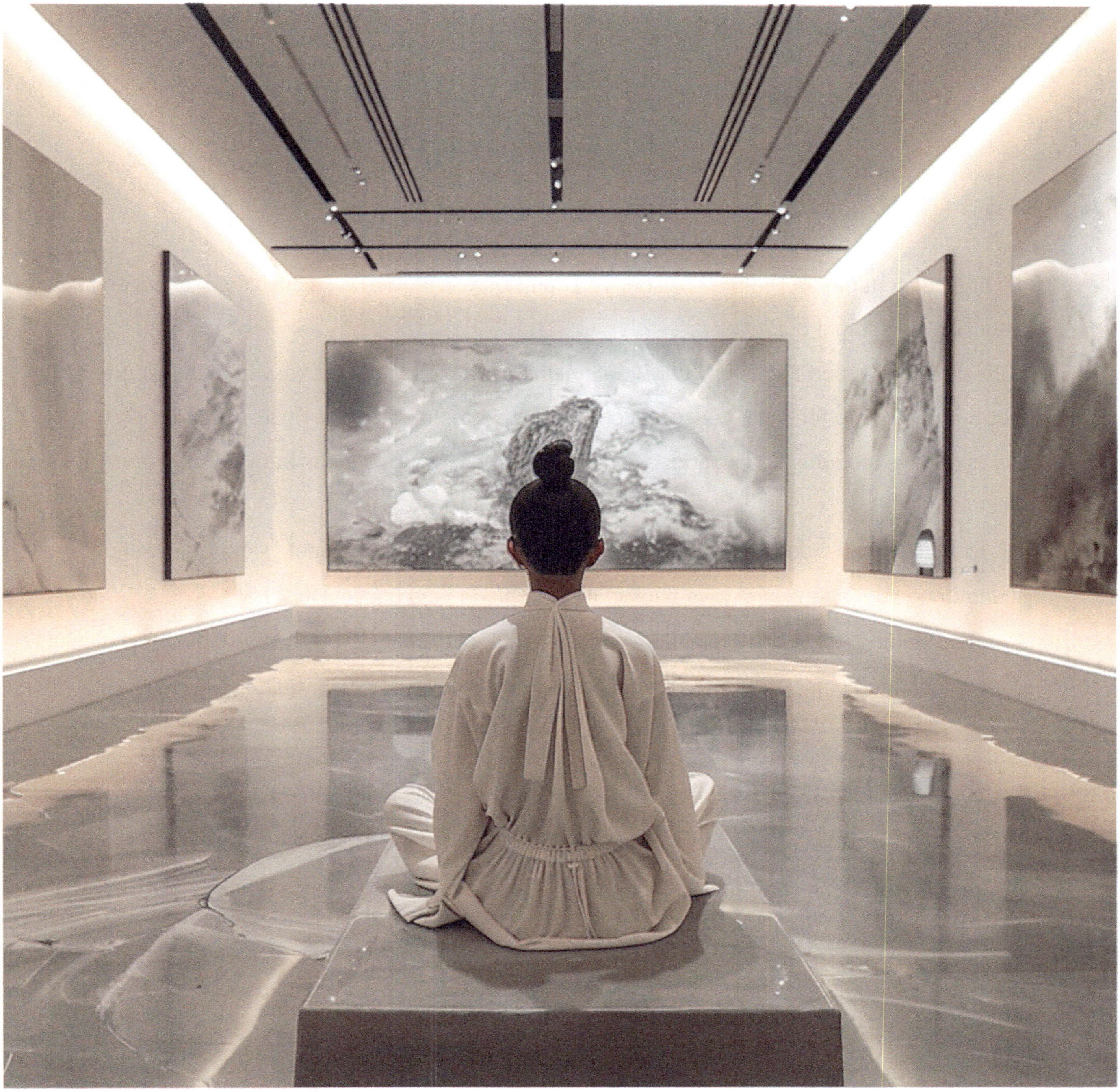

Anapanasati meditation, involves focusing one's attention on the breath.

1. Sit in a comfortable and stable position. You can sit cross-legged on a cushion or chair, ensuring your back is straight but relaxed.
2. Close your eyes and Focus on your Breath at the entrance of the nostrils, where the air enters the nose. The key is to focus on the sensation where the breath enters the nose. When your Mind starts to have thoughts and wander away, just order your Mind to focus back on the breath at the nostrils.
3. Be Mindful of your thoughts. As thoughts arise, let them arise, but do not follow them. Simply know it and bring your attention always back to the air entering the nostrils. It is that easy.
4. Practice starting with 5 or 10 minutes and increase the time as you feel comfortable to 50 minutes.
5. You do not need music or any guide. Just allow your breath to be your guide.

This is the meditation method the Buddha taught used to achieve his Enlightenment.

201

Practicing Vipassana meditation can lead to things arising from the Mind, including sounds, visions, feelings, emotions. Also, mental impurities can arise and try to disturb the meditator's concentration and focus.

Do not follow any conditions that may arise. Just know that they arise, but do not give any importance to them, follow, or attach to them.

Your job as a meditator is to just be the one who observes.

Whenever you lose your focus, or your attention runs away, following a thought or feeling – simply bring your attention back to your breath at the entrance of the nostrils.

There is no goal or no destination when practicing. Do not have desire to see or experience anything. If you do experience something, just know it and remain equanimous and neutral. Otherwise, the impurity forces (Kilesa) will deceive you and your progress will be impacted.

Progress can be measured by your ability to stay focused on the breath and not follow thoughts, feelings, emotions, or visions.

The key is being still, concentrated and equanimous.

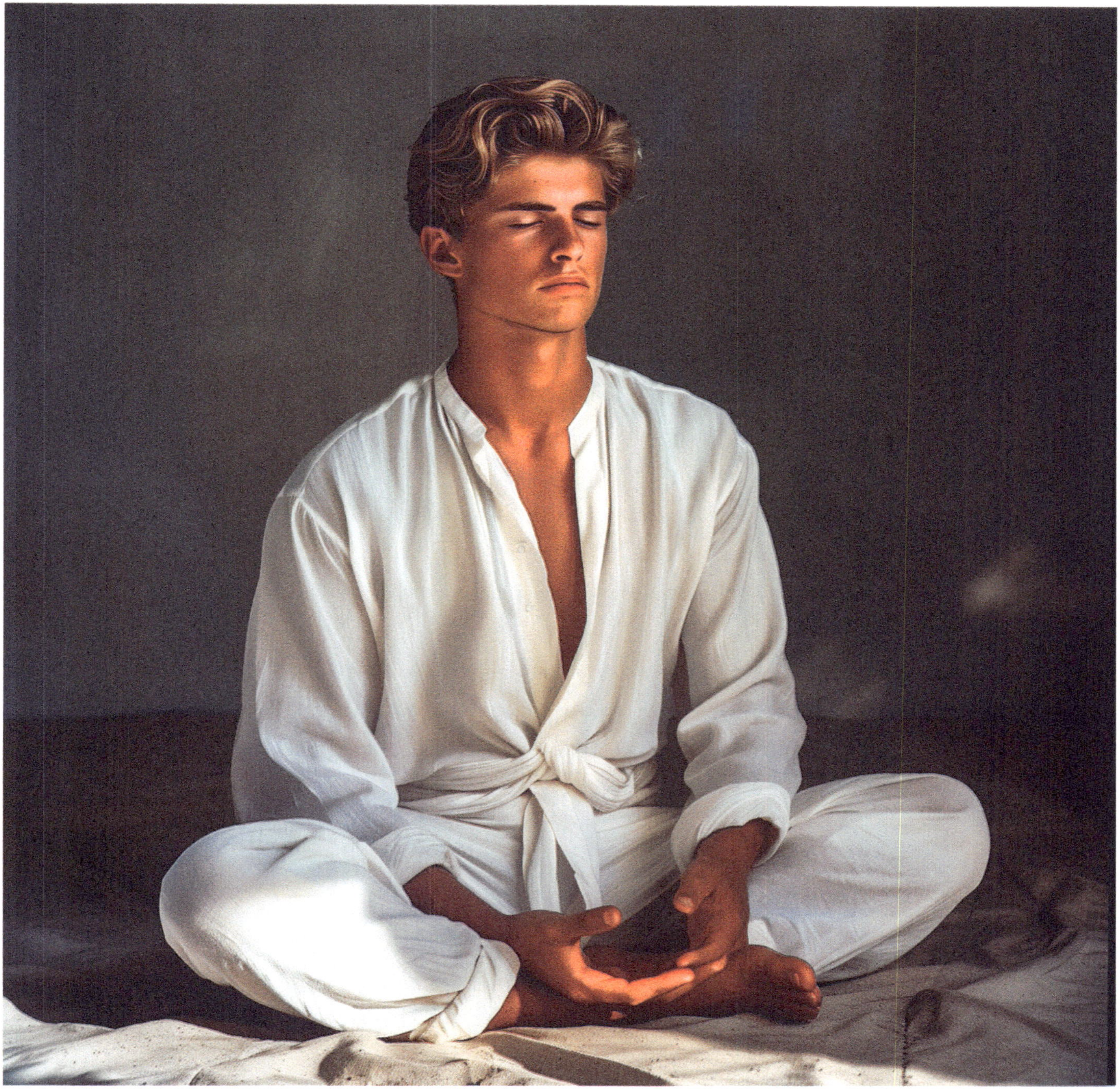

Chant

Not everyone can always meditate. Chanting by itself or before or after meditation can raise a person's vibration and energy. The following are 3 powerful chants:

1. [Namo tassa] bhagavato arahato samma-sambuddhassa. (3 TMES)
   Homage to the Blessed One, the Worthy One, the Rightly Self-awakened

2. Buddham sanam gacchami.   (I go to the Buddha for refuge).
   Dhammam sanam gacchämi. (I go to the Dhamma for refuge).
   Sangham sanam gacchämi.   (I go to the Sangha for refuge).

3. Itipi so bhagava araham sammä- sambuddho, (Repeat many times)
   Vijja-carana-sampanno sugato lokavidu,
   Anuttaro purisa-damma-särathi satthädeva-manussänam buddho bhagaväti

   (translation) He is a Blessed One, a Worthy One, a Rightly Self-awakened One.
   consummate in knowledge & conduct, one who has gone the good way,
   knower of the cosmos, unexcelled trainer of those who can be tamed,
   teacher of human &divine beings; awakened; blessed.

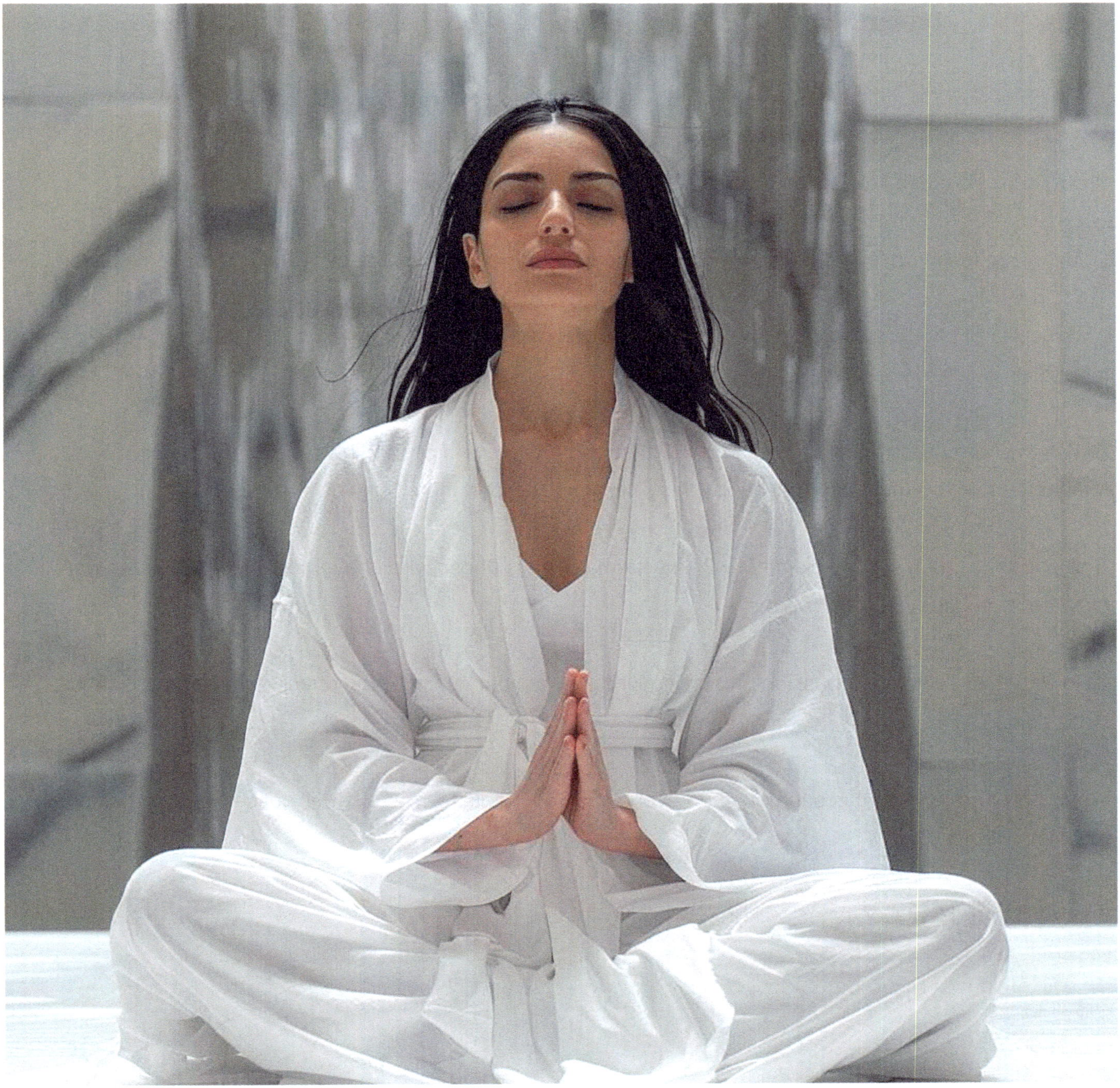

SHARING MERIT

Practicing Vipassana Meditation is one of the most noble things a person can do in their life.

Looking into the Mind, instead of being trapped into looking outwards into the illusion, is great merit.

And therefore, after each meditation session, the practitioner may share merit they earned during their meditation with anyone using such words as:

"I wish to share / dedicate this merit to my "father and mother who passed away" may my father and mother receive this merit and feel happy, may this merit support them."

"I also wish to share part of this merit with my karma owners (those who I have done wrong to in the past), may they feel happy and forgive me".

Following this sharing compassion and loving kindness to your family, loved ones, karma owners and all living beings.

You will feel great to do this each day and every time you meditate. You also will notice how your Mind and vibration will lift.

And your own "Merit Container" will grow and fill with merit.

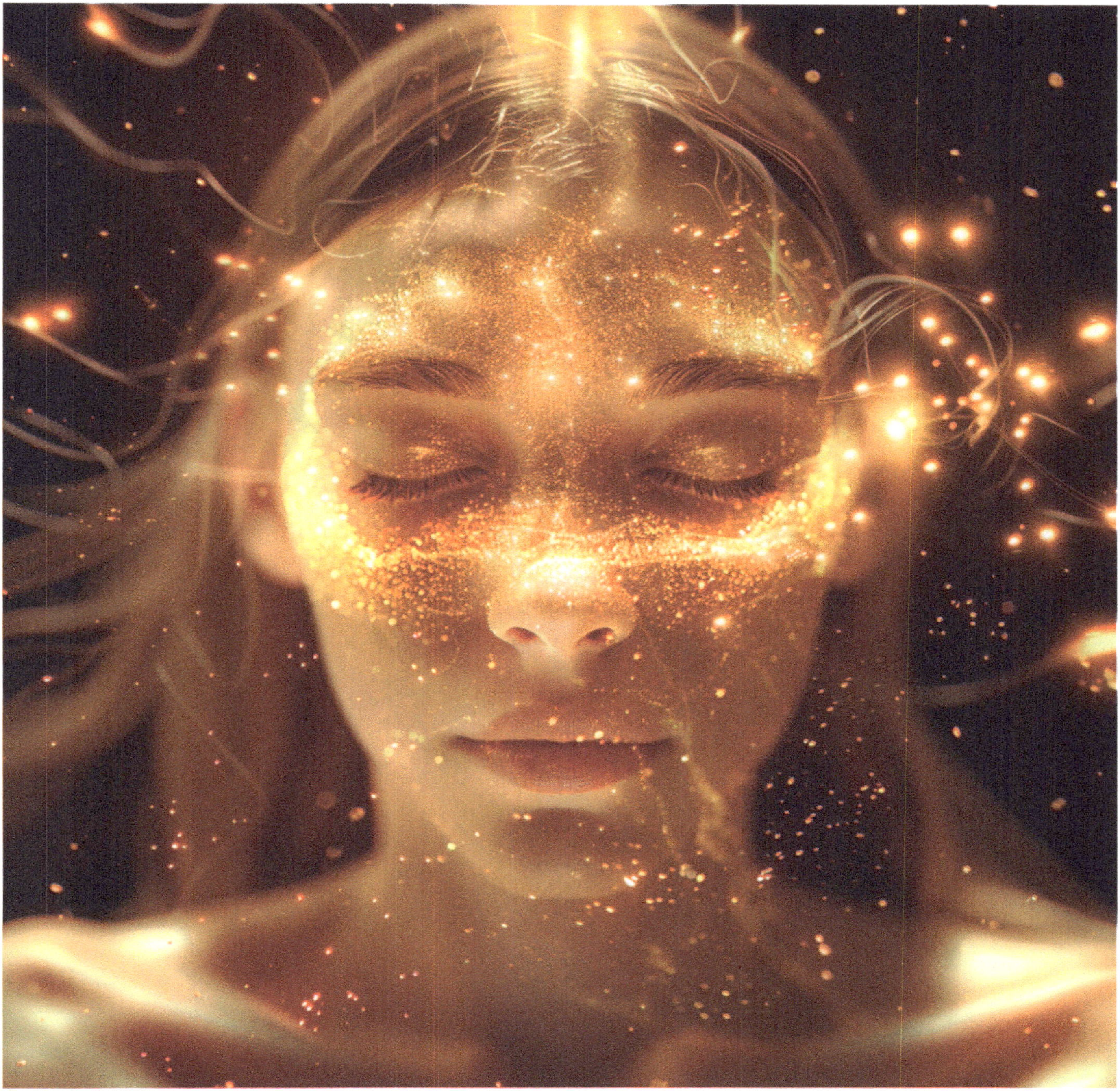

WISH AND MANIFEST

When the Mind is in a high vibration following meditation and sharing merit, loving kindness and compassion – this is also a great moment to manifest positive things for your life.

Start a journal, write down what you wish and believe that goodness will bear results in your life.

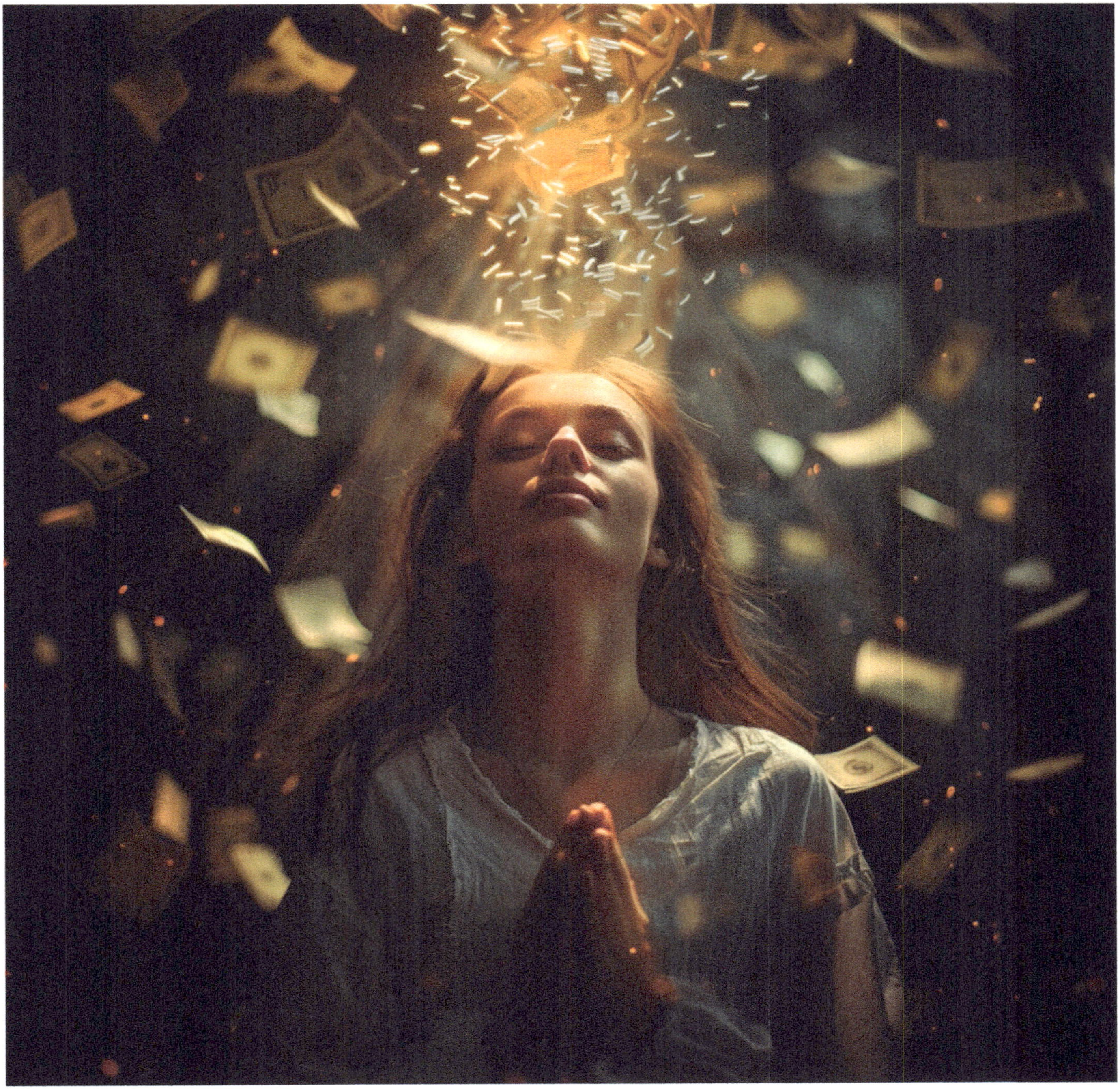

MAKING MERIT

What activities are considered merit-making?

Making merit is not a distant subject from us or only religion-related activities. Merits are activities that create cheerfulness to the mind.

Buddha states that there are 10 meritorious actions as follows:

1. Giving alms - donations in forms of money, things, or to help someone physically or mentally.
2. Holding precepts – determined not to exploit one's own and others.
3. Meditating – having a resolute mind which leads to a purification of the mind from the power of impurities (Kilesa).
4. Respecting those who should be respected. In other words, is to be modest.
5. Giving help or services to others such as to the public or others by sacrificing one's own happiness.
6. Sharing merits such as telling the way to make merits or sharing merits that ones have made.
7. Being delighted in others' success and cut of any jealousy by rejoicing with merits others have made.
8. Listening to sermons and persisting on walking the path of good deeds.
9. Teaching Dhamma, which is being the lights for others.
10. Having the right view, not letting the mind go down the deteriorated or wrong path.

Merits are any deeds that bring cheerfulness to the mind. They are not only religion-related activities but also those which make us feel we're doing good deeds. For example, giving the right direction to those who are lost or working as volunteers. Results of the merit would be big or small depend on the purity of the purpose, how much sacrifices have been made and the purity (of the mind) of the person the merit has been made with.

~Master Acharavadee Wongsakon

CHAPTER 10

THE MIND

The mind without training can turn feelings into emotions quickly.

Hate, Anger and Lust go deep into our subconscious, leaving a deep scratch like a nail that scratches a rock. It takes a very long-time to disappear.

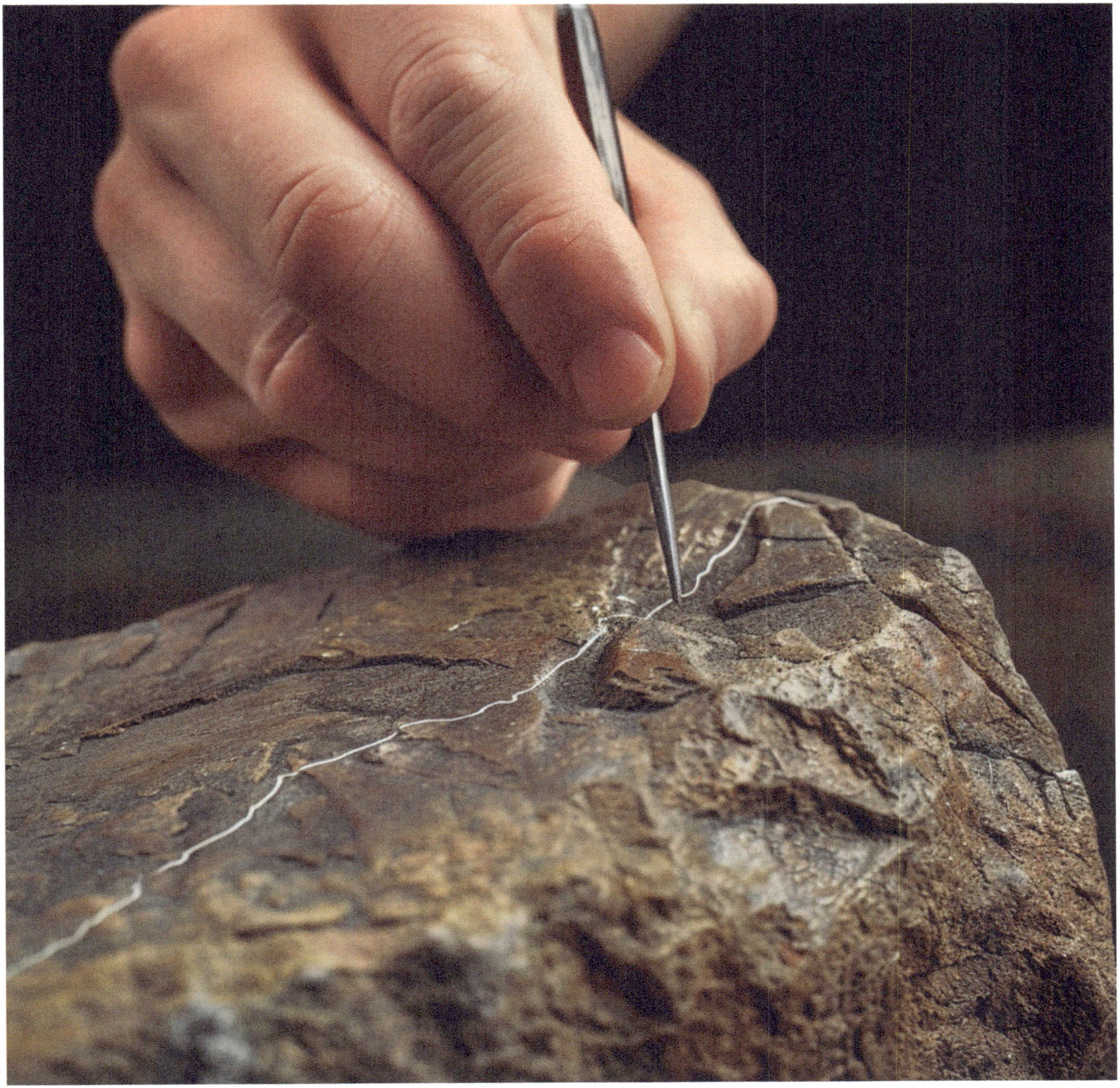

As we practice Vipassana meditation and mindfulness, our feelings do not turn into emotions as quickly. We remain more equanimous and mindful.

Feelings like anger, hate and desire do not go as deeply into our subconscious mind. Instead, the emotions are like scratching sand with as stick. The emotions appear, but disappear much faster than a scratch in a rock.

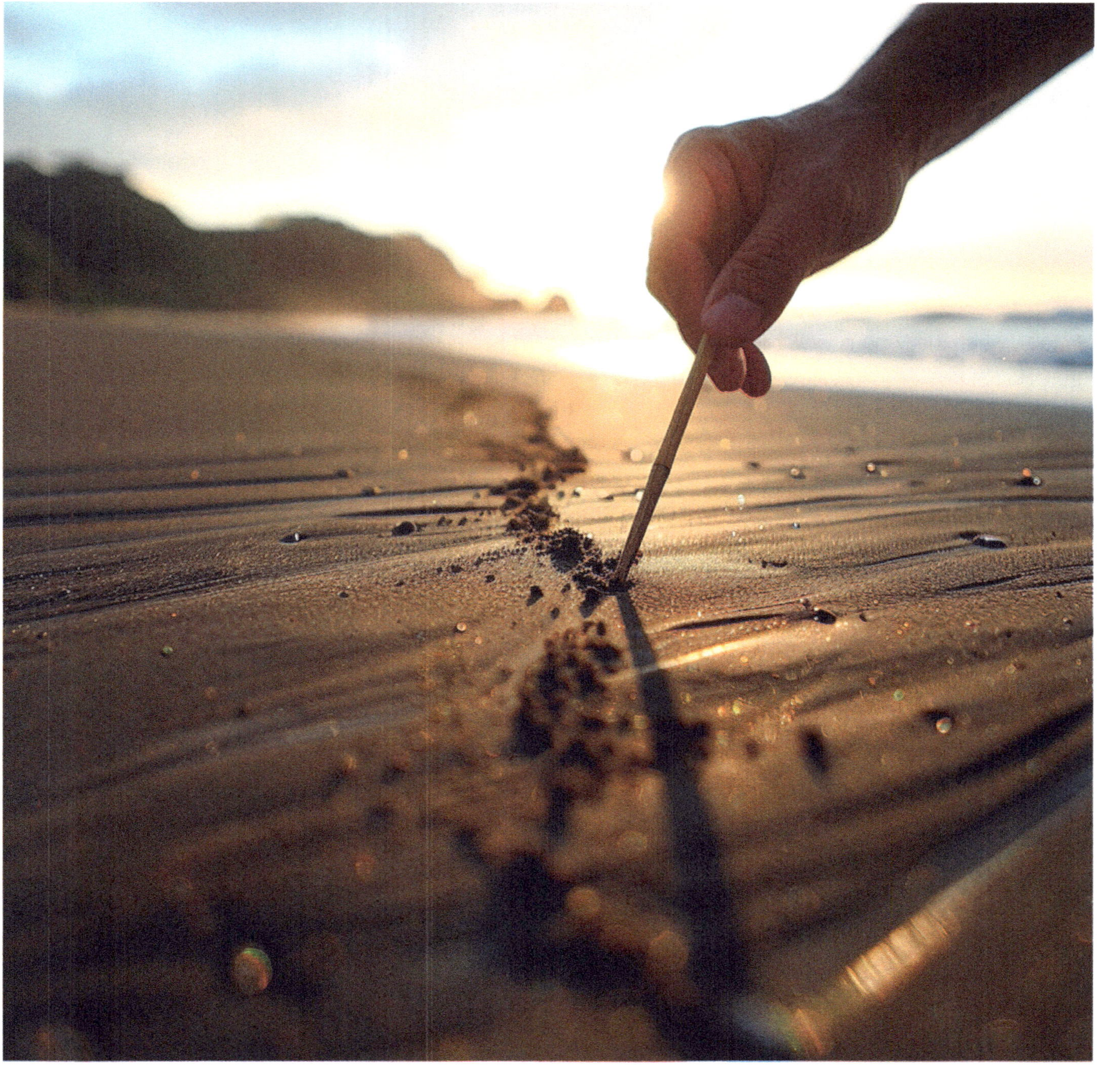

Finally, when the Mind is well trained and the Mindfulness is clear, as feelings arise and turn into emotions, they do not last long. It is like scratching the surface of a still pond with a stick. There appears a ripple for a very short time.

This is the result of Vipassana practice and indicative of a Mind liberated from deep emotions.

This is the Enlightened Mind. There are no heavy scratches or memories or emotions added to our mental data base. Mental impurities have no power to exist in this kind of Mind.

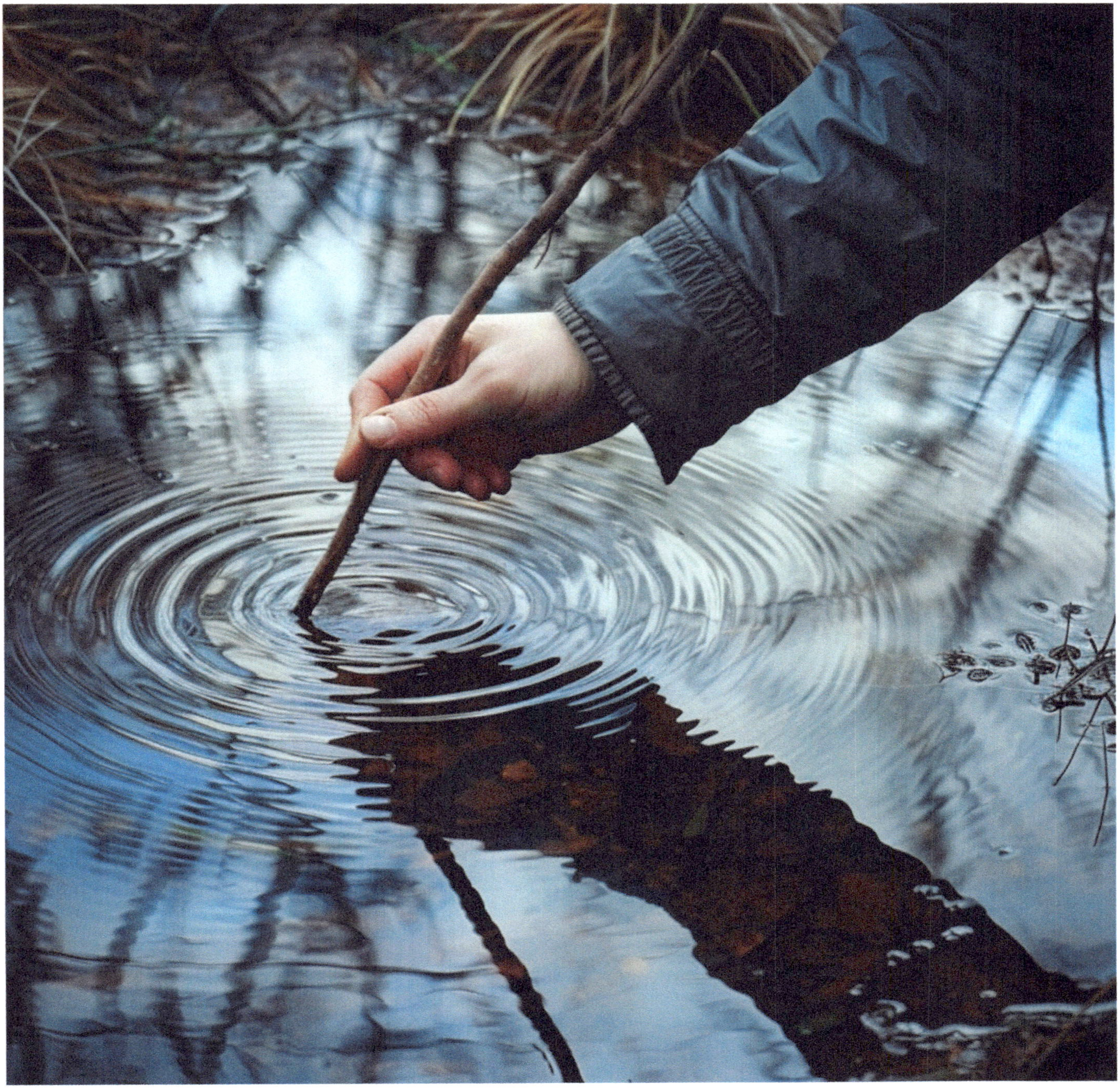

As we practice Vipassana Meditation the Mind gains strength. After some time, one can feel the Mind power like a trained muscle.

The Mind can flex its Mindfulness and not be dragged by feelings, emotions, or impurities.

This is the result of Vipassana Meditation.

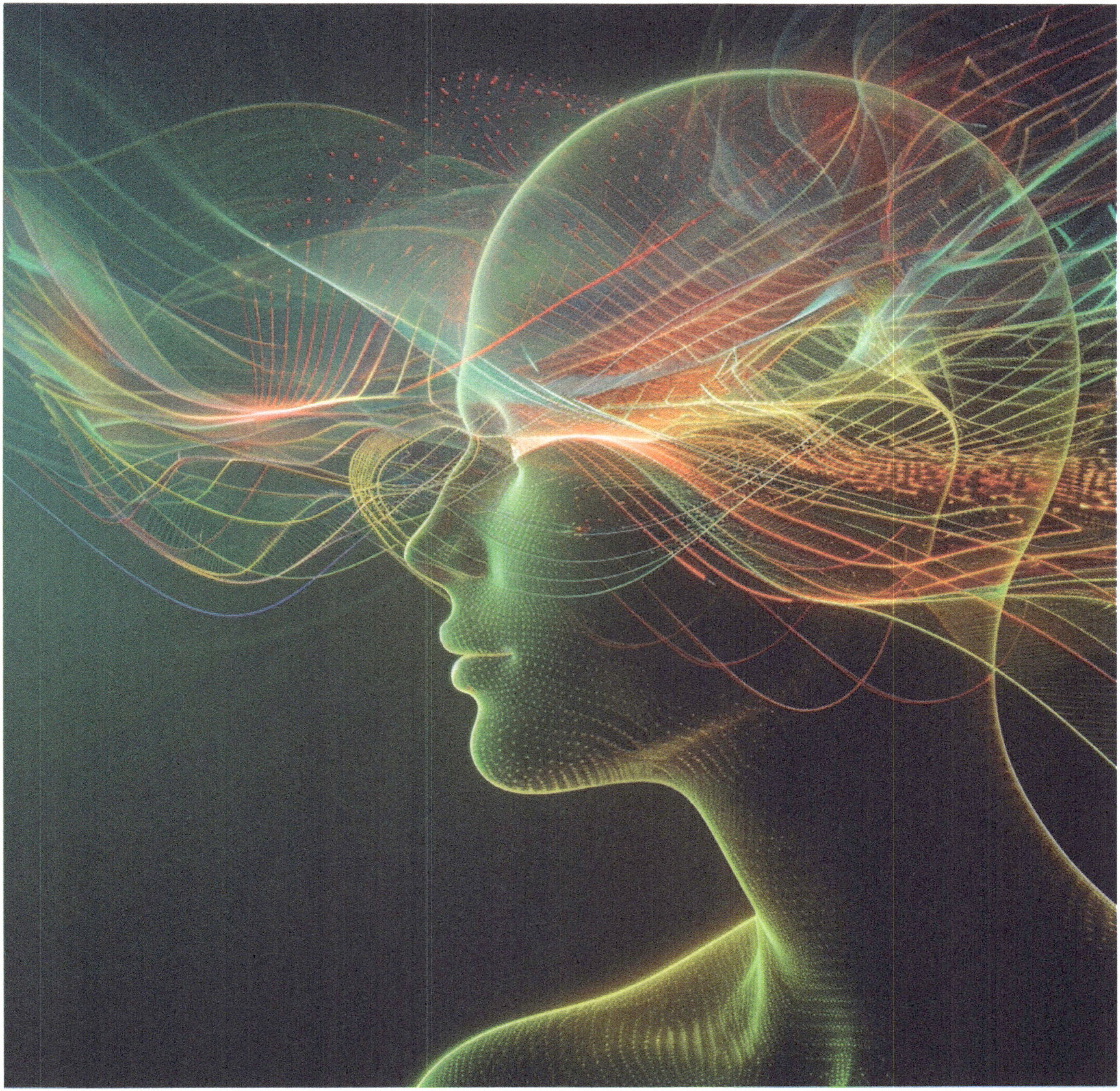

Where does the Mind reside in the body?

Most people assume it is in our heads or brain.

However, the truth is the Mind is everywhere in the body.

This is why we feel pain in our hearts or butterflies in our stomach or pain in our limbs.

The Mind occupies the entire body.

This is also why we can feel and see the impurity forces throughout our bodies, not just in our heads. We come to realize when we practice meditation, that the Mind is not the body, but only resides in the body. Once the body wears out and dies, the Mind leaves the body and finds its next incarnation.

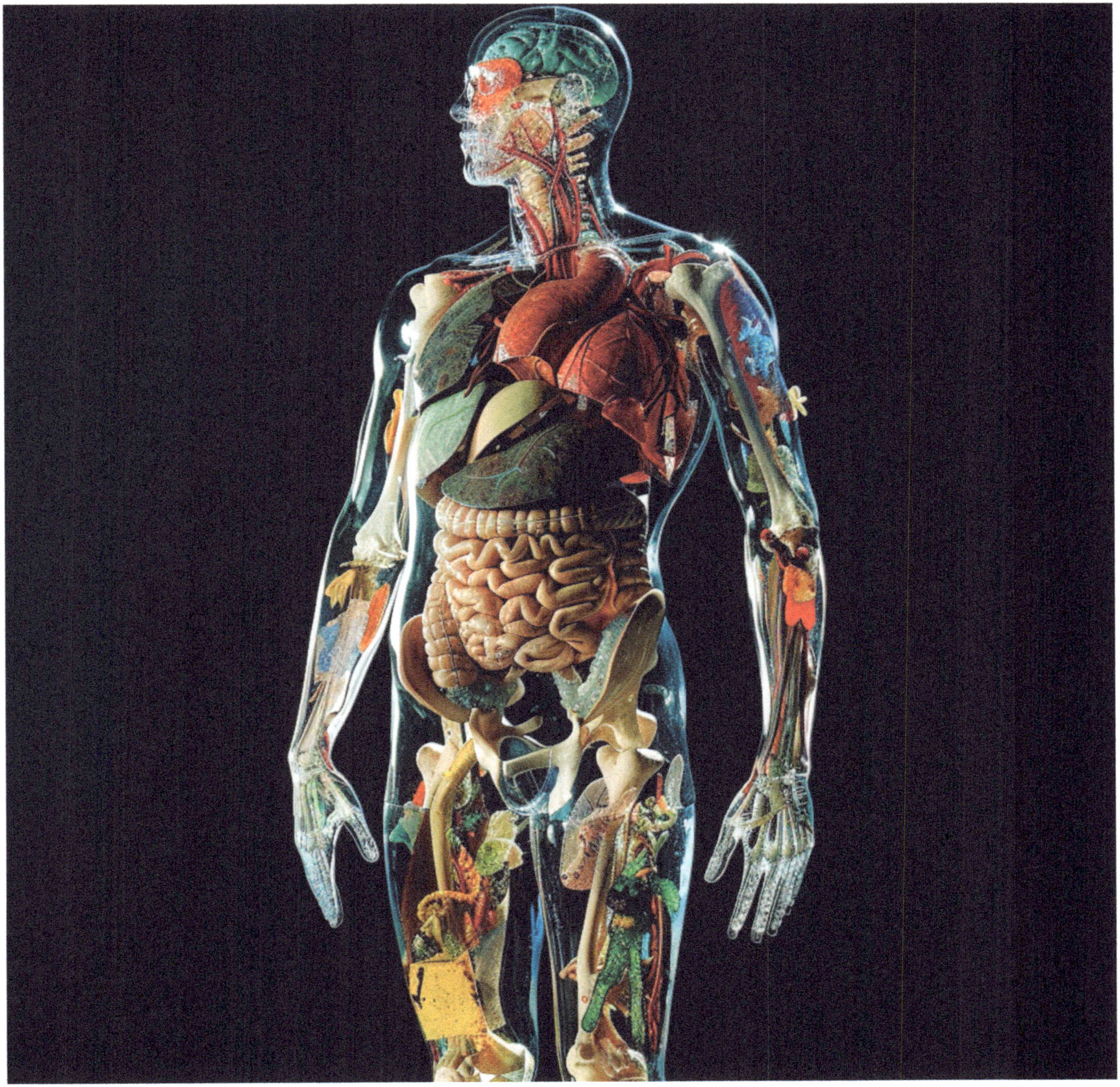

The Trained Mind does not Fear Death

I had a dream that I was kneeling on the floor with a giant snake towering above me, ready to bite through my head and neck, with its mighty fangs.

In the dream, with my eyes closed and facing impending death any second, my Mind was calm, at peace, equanimous, focused and still, I let go of fear. If the snake decided to kill me, it was fine, whatever was about to happen, good or bad, the Mind was in a neutral state.

This is the result of Vipassana meditation Mind training. We see all things as being impermanent, arising, staying for a while, and then being gone. We accept karma and our fate, without emotion or fear.

This will allow the Mind to become free at the moment of death and go high into the heavenly realms.

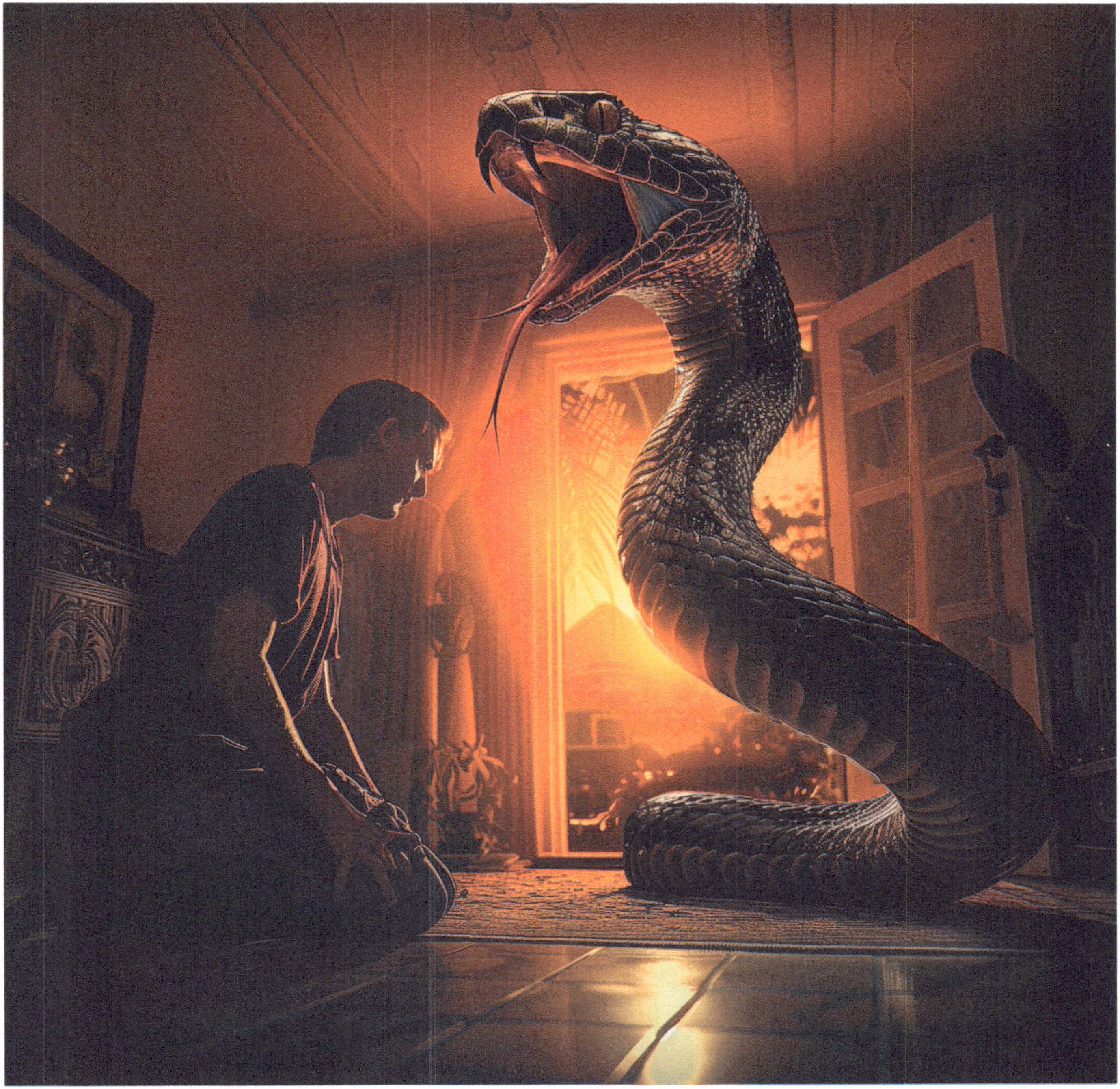

The Enlightened Buddha Mind is free from the gravity of this world and can float high into the universe.

From such a high and elevated place, the Mind can see the beginning and end of time.

It is connected to the energy of everything and knows all.

225

The Enlightened Boddhisatva Mind only wishes to reach down into the mud and pull any suffering human out of the quagmire of Samsara, even if they get muddy or damaged in the process.

I have seen the Mind of my Master and the Monk's Mind during a meditation course, determined to help pull the Minds of practitioners up.

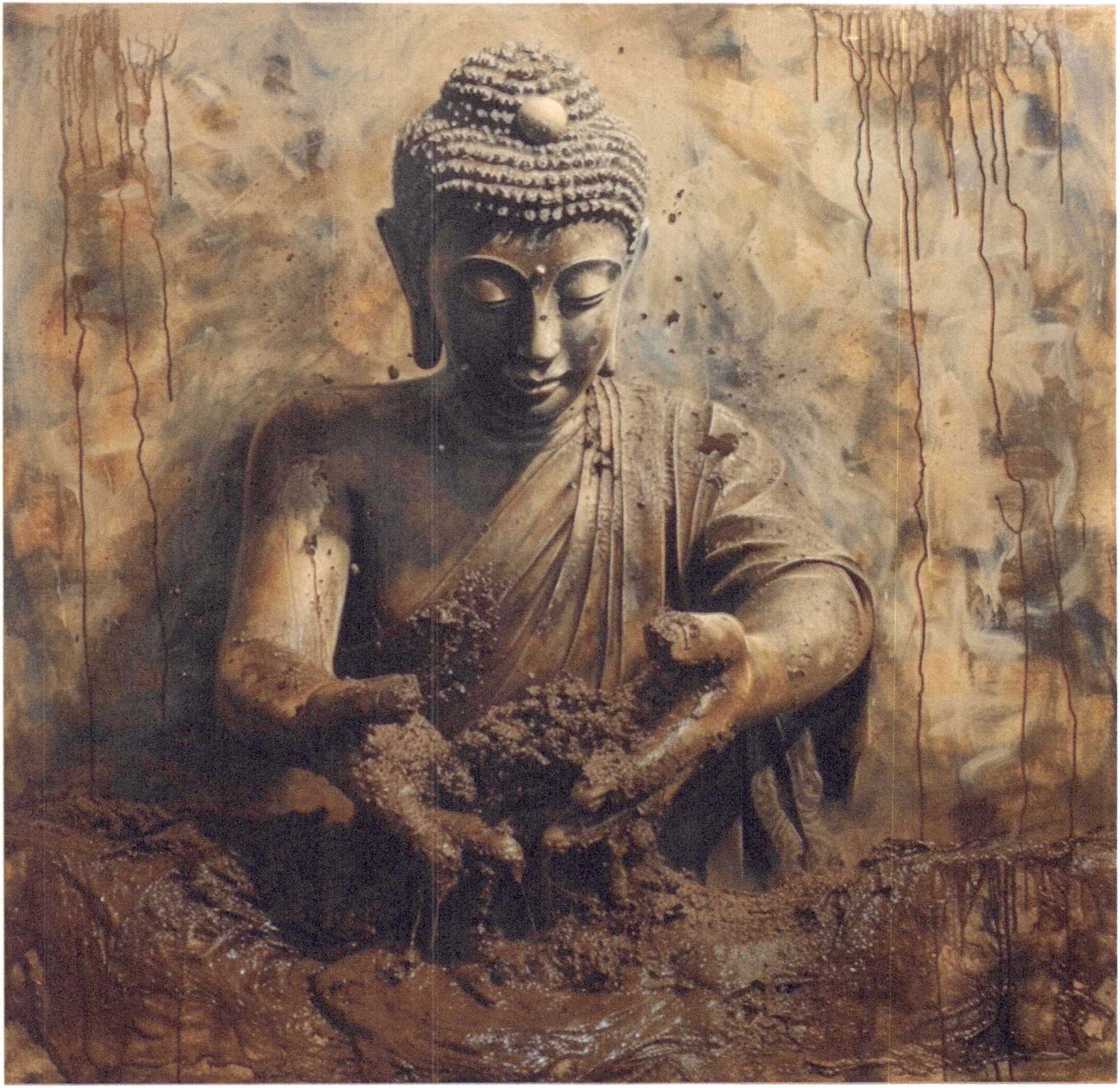

The Mind is Energy and forms its own particle.

The particle of a Mind filled with Goodness, Morality and Pure intention is smooth and golden in shape. It has a warm vibration.

The Mind does not have edges to cling or attached to. Unlike the Mara's (devil) particle.

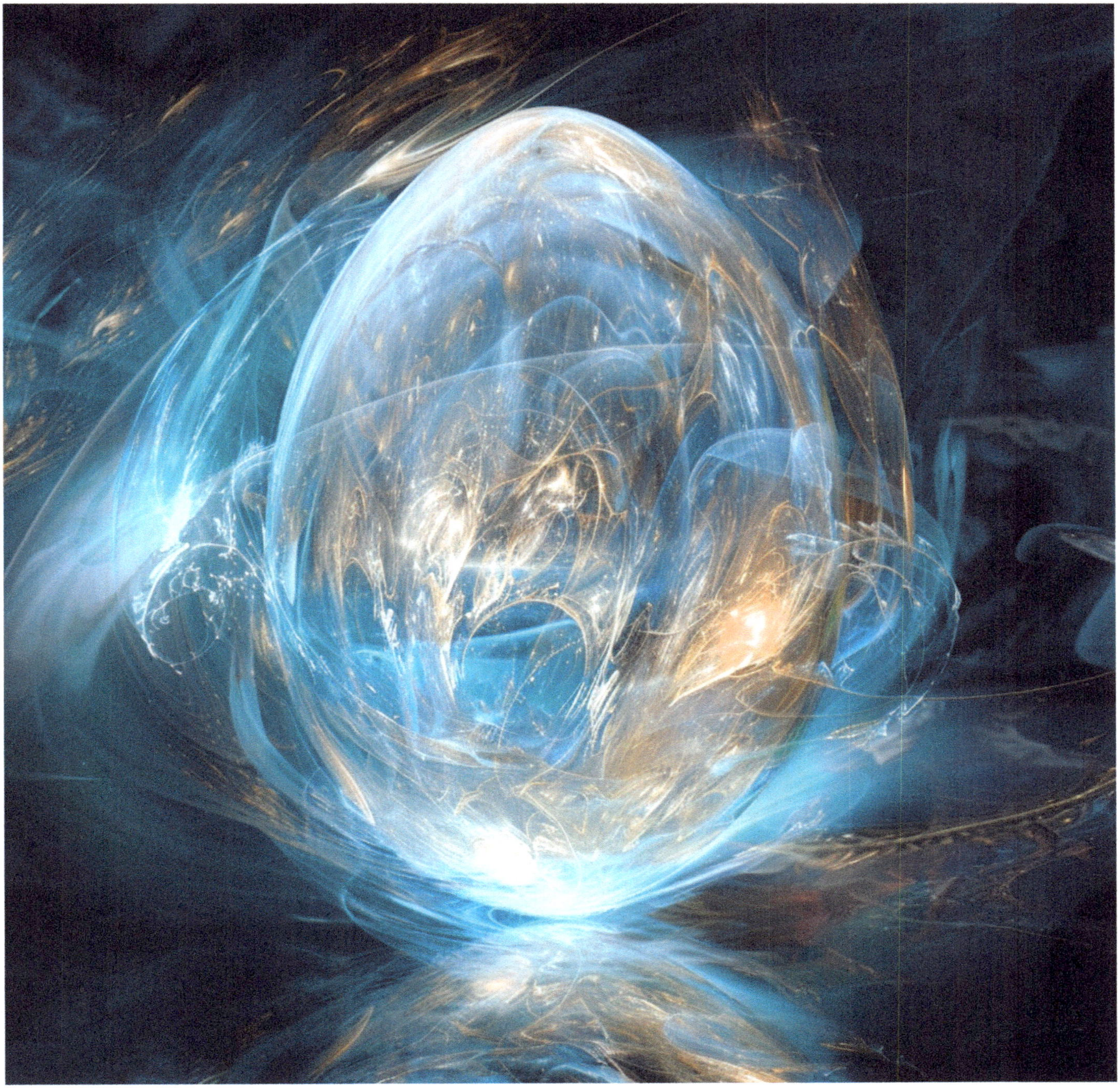

The Mind particle of desire, temptation, greed, lust, is an attractive particle and easy to attach to, due to its many edges and hooks.

This Mind particle offers the promise and reward of pleasure hard for most to resist, especially once they have been hooked by this particle.

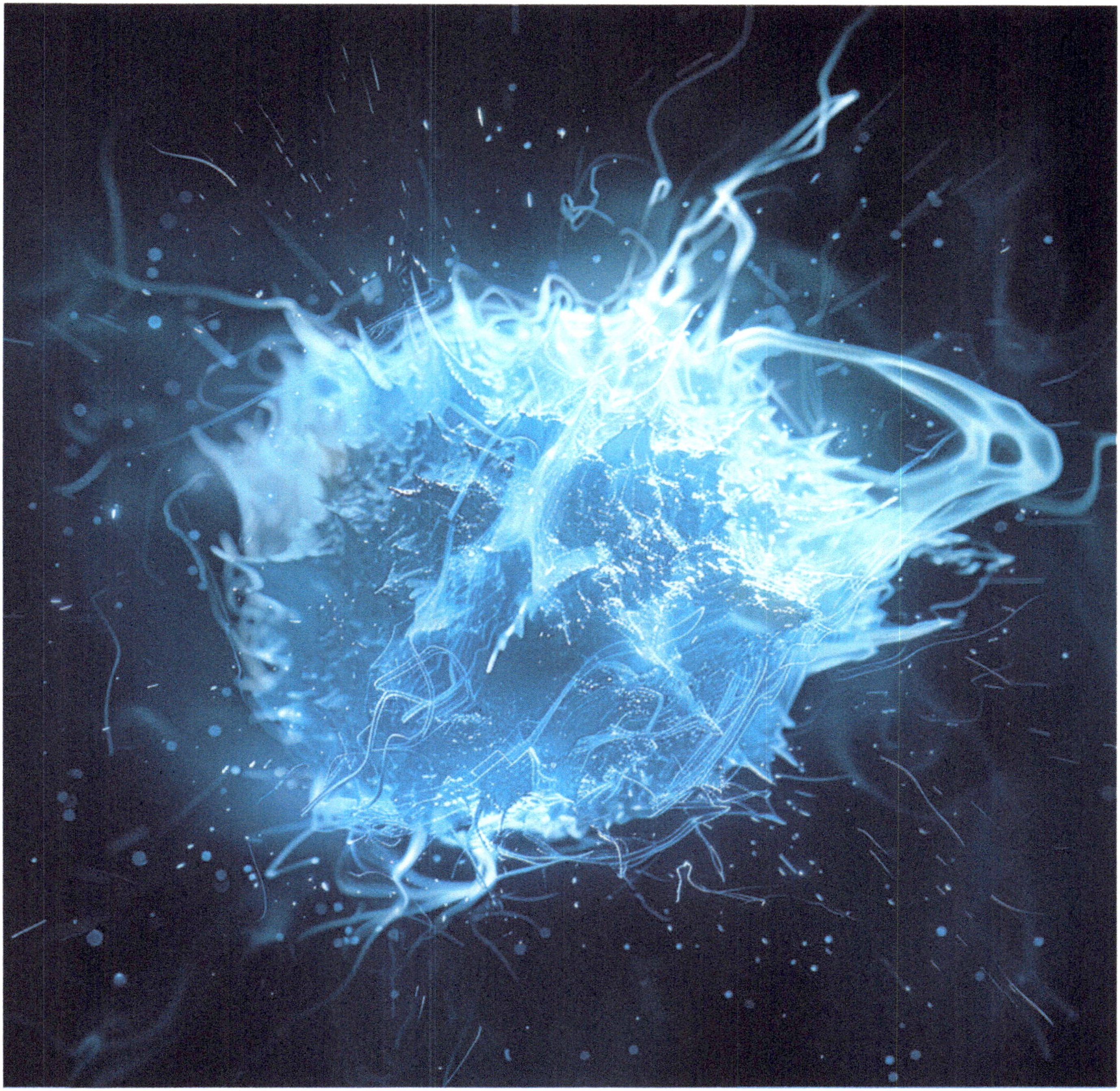

Desire and sexual energy are the primal driving force of humanity. It is programmed into our DNA.

It gives pleasure, it provides procreation and drives our actions and our lives.

Mara (devil) uses sex as a main weapon to keep us firmly attached to this World.

We fall prey to advertising and temptation that ignites our lust and desire.

The purified Mind that no longer succumbs to desire and sexual lust. It sees the body and sex for what it is. The Buddha cut the chain of sensual pleasure and desire, in order to attain Enlightenment.

Next time you see some sexy advertisement or thing that catches your eye, be mindful and command your mind not to take a second look. This exercise will strengthen the mind and weaken the impurity forces within.

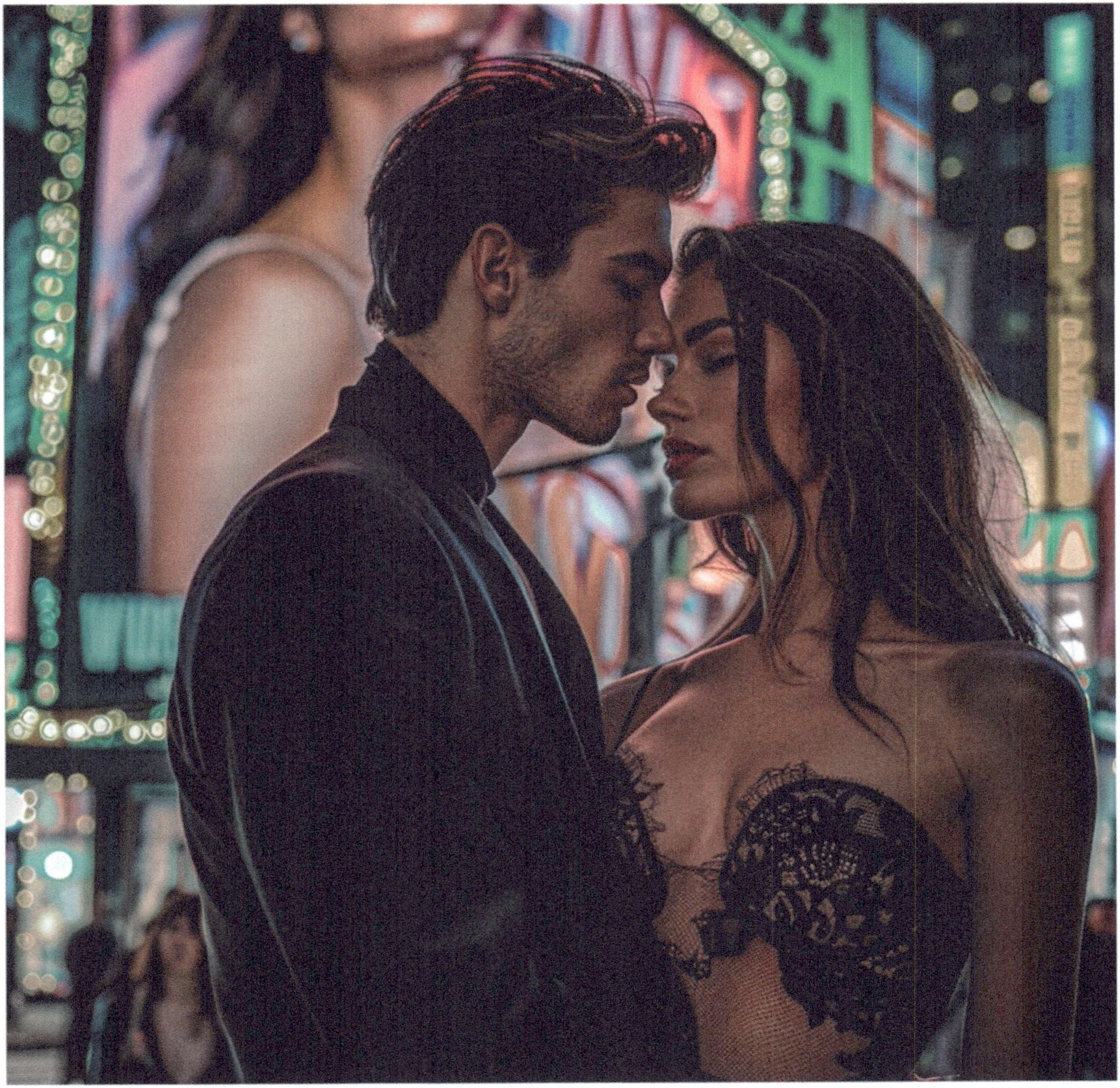

A Mind that vibrates and has the Energy particles of Desire, Greed, Lust, Delusion, will be heavy and find its way to the Hell realm after death.

Hell is real and not just an idea to scare us.
There is no arbiter that decides who goes to hell. This is based purely on the weight of a person's mind resulting from wrongdoing and karma.

500 years in the deepest Hell Realm is equivalent to 1 day on earth. Or you can say 1 day on earth is equivalent to 500 years in lowest Hell Realm.

The energy in Hell is so thick, that time moves so incredibly slowly. It is this heavy energy that attracts the Souls of those who have done evil and bad during their lifetimes.

Hell is a place where the mind or consciousness is tortured by the weight of its own sin – through extreme heat of flames or having the illusion of a body that is tortured, by being burned by red hot steel, climbing trees with large thorns and spikes, where one eventually is impaled on the spikes. Or where the flesh is slowly torturously removed from the body and then at a terrifying and excruciating time, only to regrow later and the process starting over again.

The greatest sin we can commit is to kill our own parents (patricide). Next is to hurt or steal from those who have supported our lives and done good for us. These kinds of sin send the dark person's mind immediately to the Hell realm.

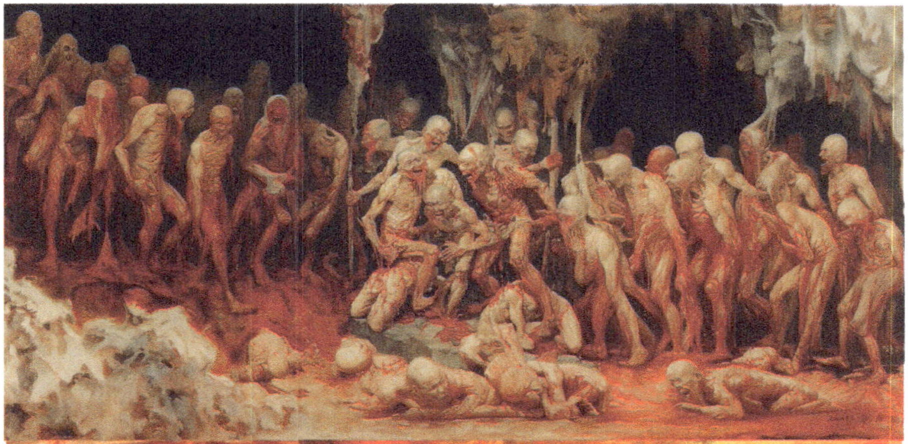
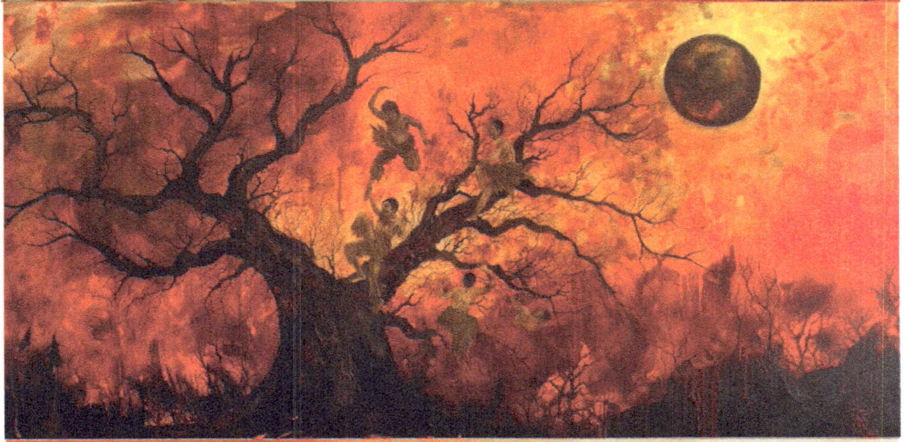
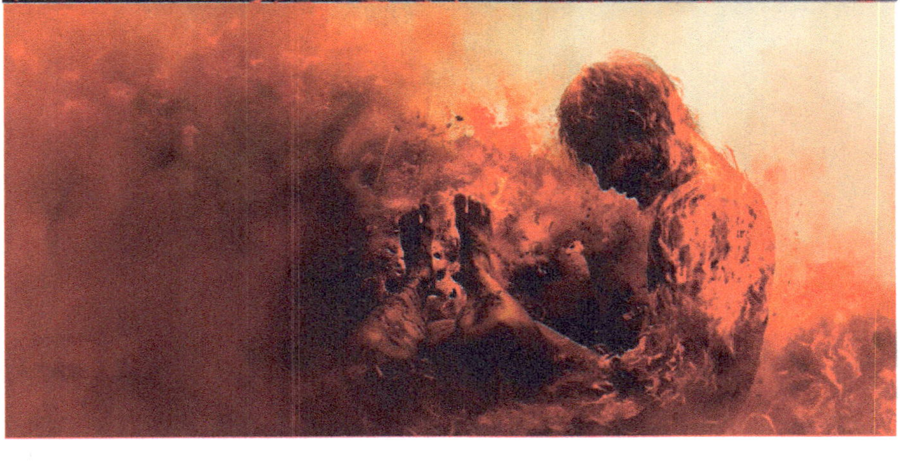

A Mind that vibrates and has the Energy particle of Goodness, morality, kindness and merit energy will be light and find its way to the Heavenly realms after death.

In heaven, one day in heavens is equivalent to 100 years on earth. Therefore, life in the Heaven realm is much longer than on earth. A day in heaven is equal to 100-year lifespan on earth. Existence in the Heavenly realms lasts much longer than living out a lifetime on earth.

This is why having a light mind at the time of death, will allow a person to reach the Heavenly realms, so may your last thoughts and actions be light and have a high vibration.

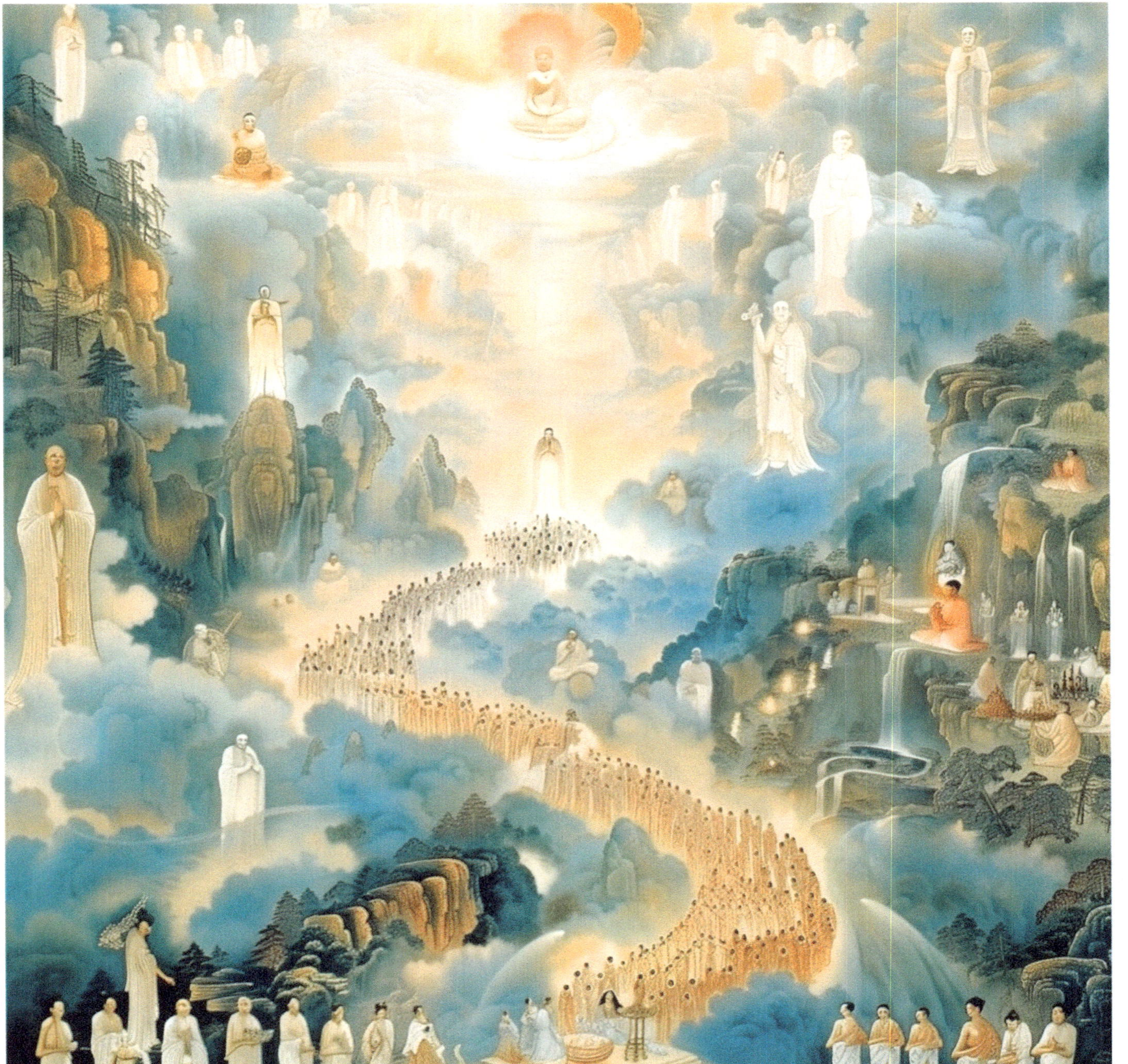

Nirvana is the highest realm above the heavens. A Mind that is purified will find its way to the highest Energy realm called Nirvana.

In Nirvana there is only pure energy and no sense of time.

It is effortless and neutral.

A person, even if they fail to find dhamma and the spiritual path to liberation during their lifetimes, could conceivably reach Nirvana if they can bring their minds to the highest vibration at the moment of death.

This would send the mind high into the Nirvana realm.

239

CHAPTER 11

BEAUTY IS ONLY SKIN DEEP

Youth and beauty can cast a spell on the heart.

It can be mesmerizing for the one who sees the beauty, as well as the one, who is so beautiful.

Beauty attaches us to the illusion and this World and results in suffering, because eventually beauty will start to fade away and finally disappear.

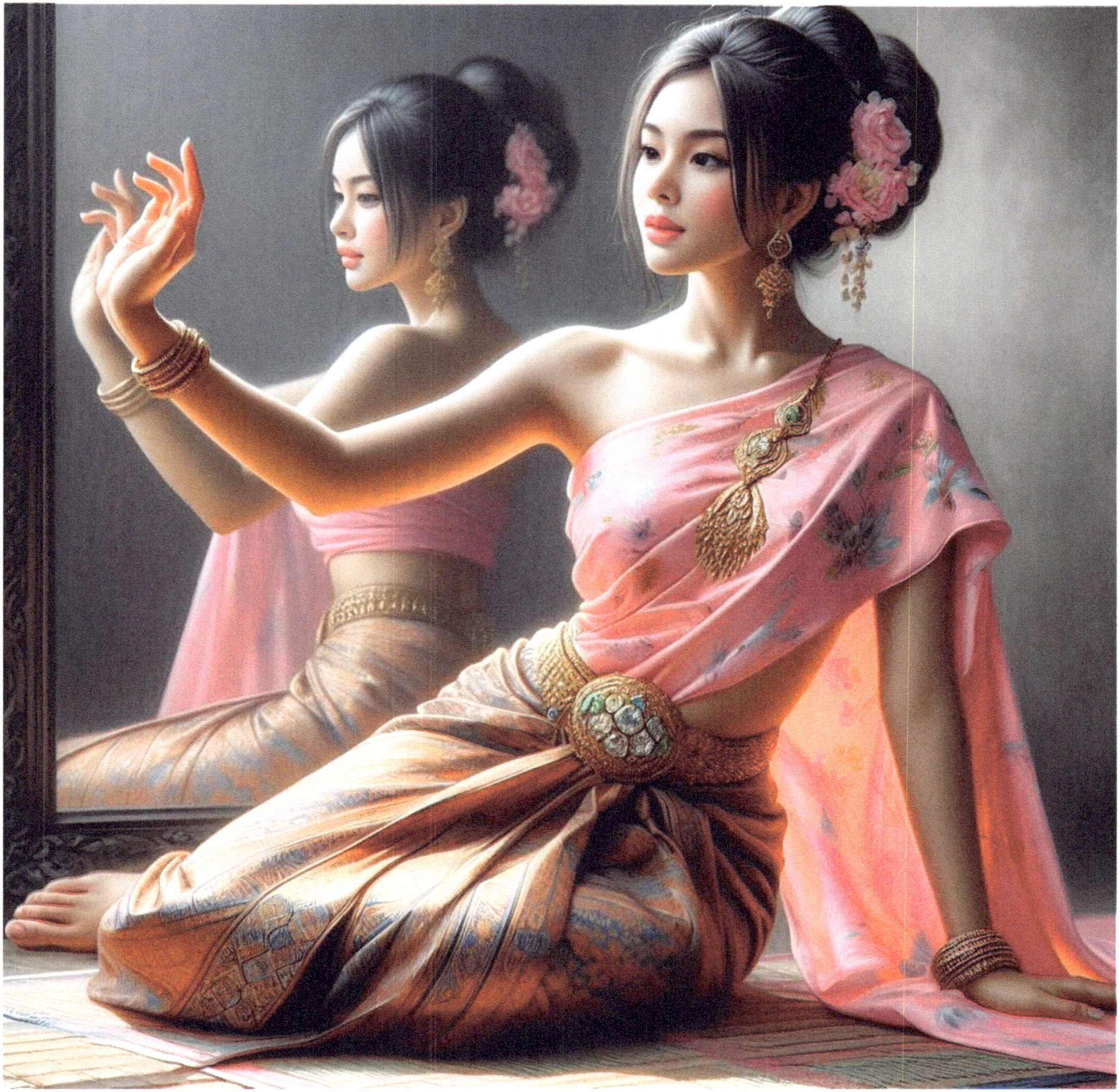

As meditators, as we practice and purify the mind, wisdom arises, and we begin to see things as they truly ar, our perspective changes.

We begin to see the impermanence of youth and beauty. The world puts such a high value on looks.

We dream to be with someone young and beautiful and we dream to be young and beautiful ourselves.

Love songs echo this sentiment and the obsession with beauty.

"I would die for you…." says the song.

But wait a second – you would die to be with someone who soon will grow old, sick, and die?

You would die for them just because you love how they look at this moment?

Another popular song asks, "Will you still love me when I am no longer young and beautiful….?"

"I know you will, I know you will…."

245

Beauty literally is only skin deep. Peel away the skin and the human body in reality, is a smelly ugly vessel full of fluids and decaying food.

But we obsess and addict to this "bag made of skin, filled with water, meat, bones and excrement".

It sounds horrible to describe the body like this, but this perspective helps us to understand that we are merely attaching to something that is decaying and only will be around for a finite amount of time.

The body carries the Mind, but the body will not last forever, where the Mind will continue.

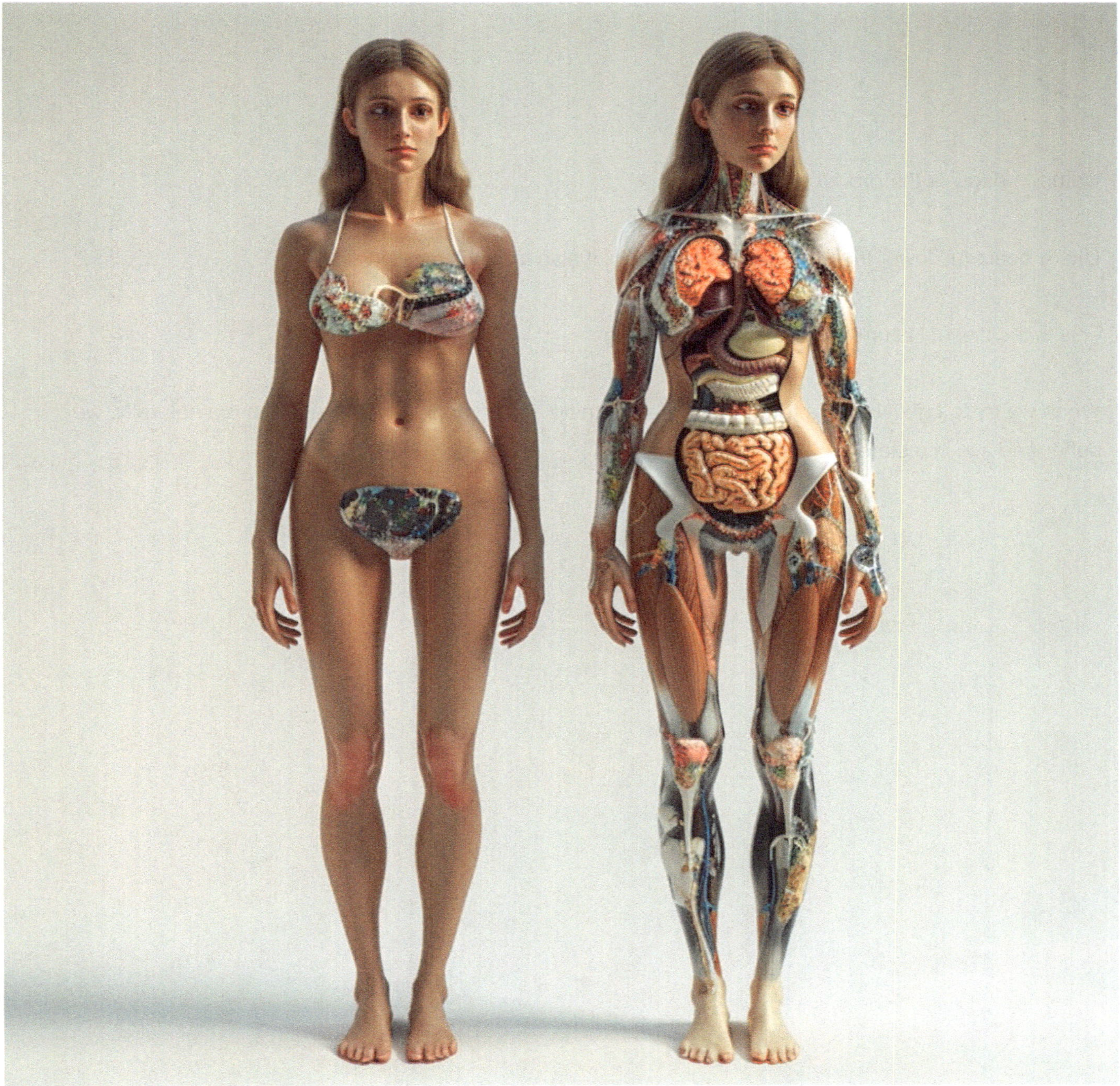

Natural beauty is the product of Nature.

Like a beautiful flower that appears in the spring, it also fades in time.

This is the law of Nature and the Truth of all things.

When we try to fight Nature and hang on to something that is meant to grow old and die naturally, we suffer and live in a state of denial and delusion.

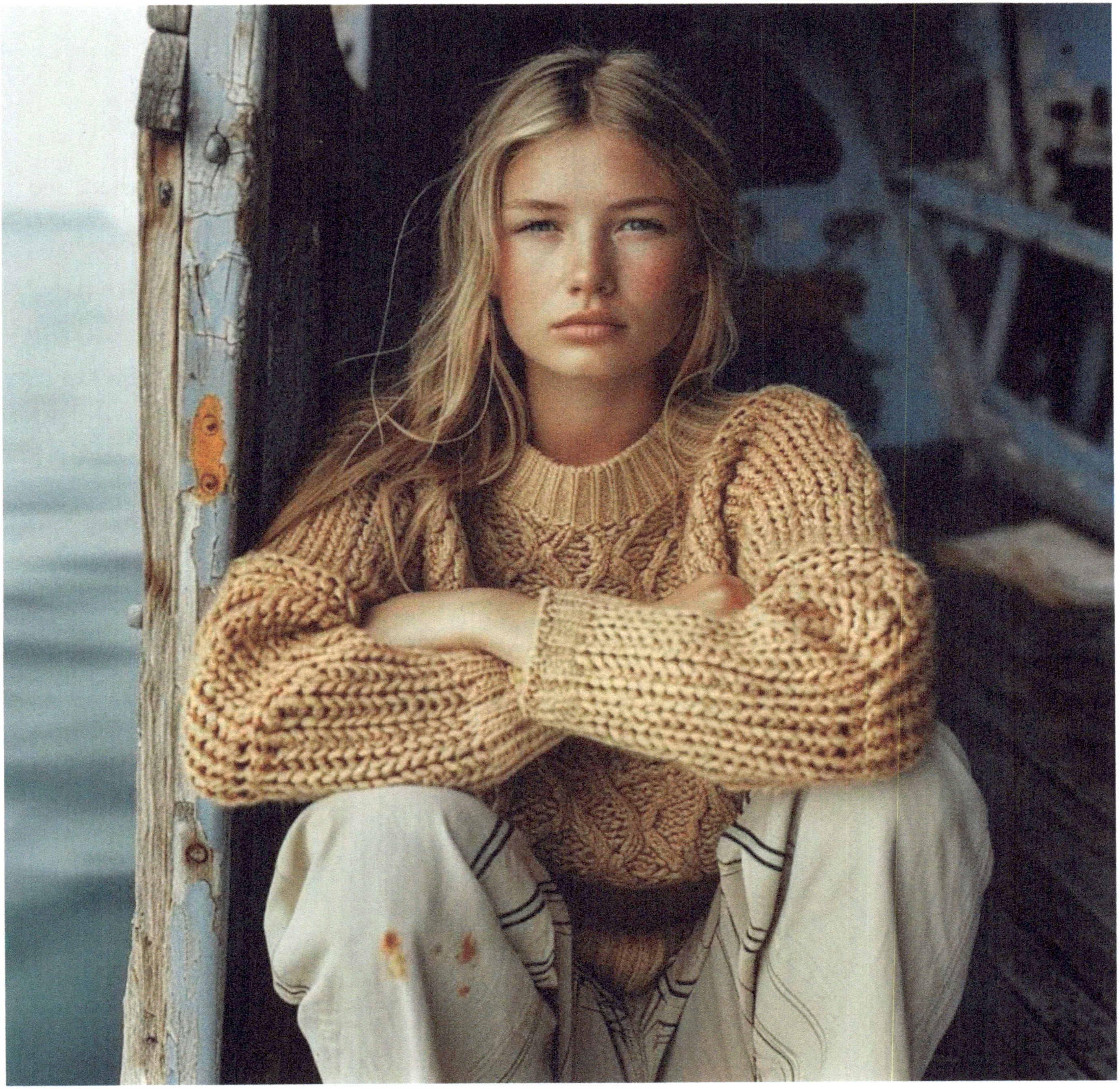

Fillers, surgery, and anti-aging treatments may give the illusion of youth, but often they look unnatural and plastic.

Society has normalized looking fake and plastic, in an effort, to hold on to youth and beauty.

Today even young natural beautiful girls inject their lips with filler, faces with Botox, to act and look like their older counterparts.

This is the power of the Mara (devil) and the delusion.

Imagine injecting a beautiful wrinkle free young girl with Botox (botulism) and filler with the promise of keeping her from wrinkling.

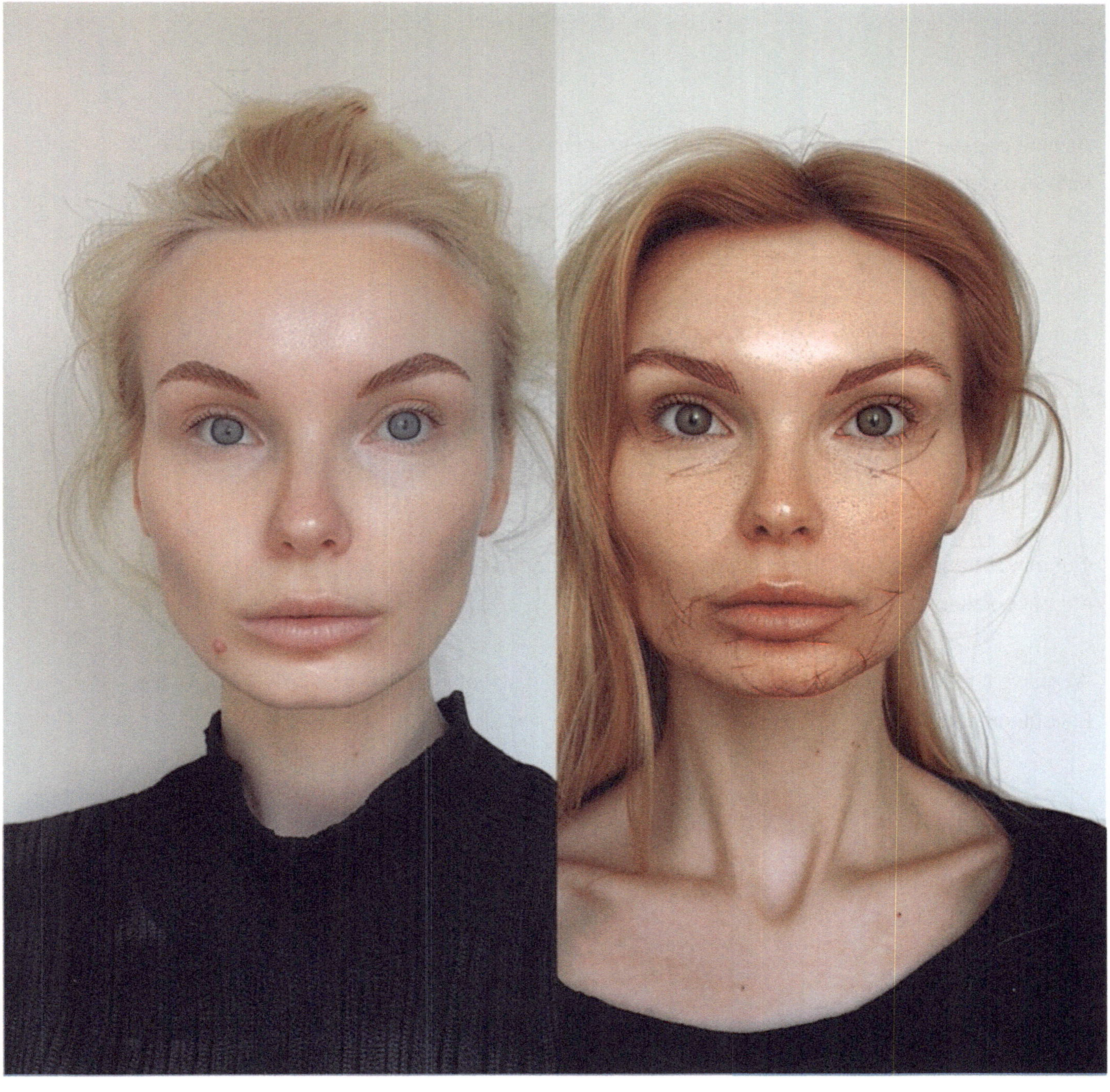

As time passes, we all undergo the inevitable process of aging, much like our parents before us. It's the natural order of things.

This is Nature.

Suffering comes when we try to hang on to something in vain.

Attachment to anything in life eventually brings suffering.

We are not our bodies.

Our minds transcend our physical form. The significance of our bodies lies in their role as vessels for the eternal quest for answers.

When we find the dhamma, our bodies become a tool, a station and the possibility to reach the Enlightenment.

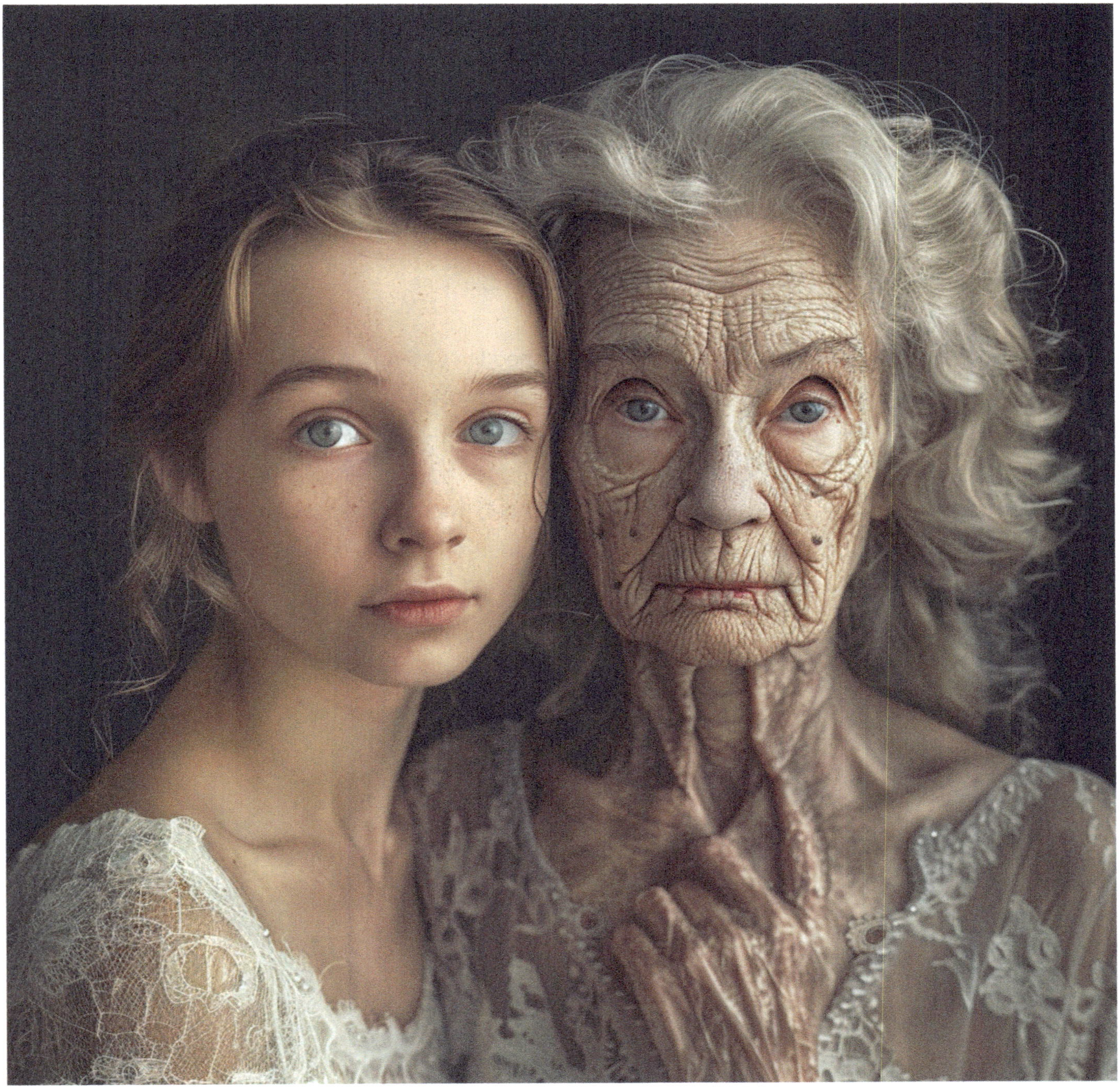

Like our parents we to will age and our bodies will become frail. This is the Nature of Life.

We have experienced this uncountable times over the fabric of time.

Instead of worrying about aging and making money to feed the Anti-Aging delusion, we should care for our elderly parents, as we to will be in their shoes soon. Karma of not taking care of parents in old age is a heavy Karma that the Western World is creating for itself.

The Buddha once explained we can never pay back the debt we owe to our parents, who gave us life and cared for us. "Even if we carried our parents on our shoulders for 100 years and they defecated on us every day, we could never repay them," said the Buddha.

Society has lost this wisdom.

In the modern world we too often prioritize, making money and enjoying our lives, ahead of spending time or taking care of our own parents.

As the Mind purifies through meditation, we realize how important our parents have been.

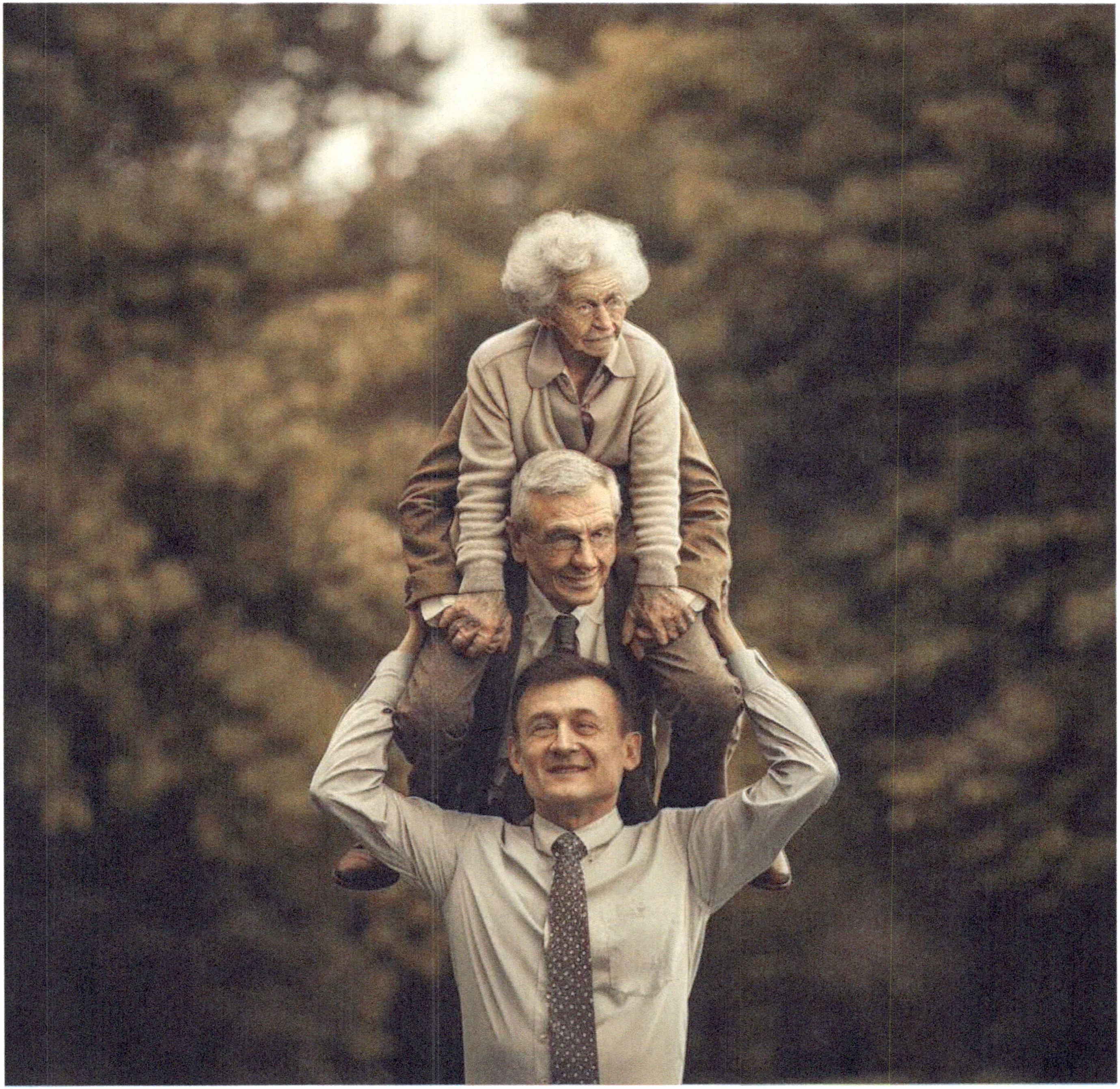

CHAPTER 11

TECHO VIPASSANA MEDITATION

Techo Vipassana Meditation uses the fire element in the Body to ignite a fire to burn impurities.

This is a fast-track method to destroying the impurity forces (Kilesa). This method is only taught by experienced Masters of Techo Vipassana in Thailand.

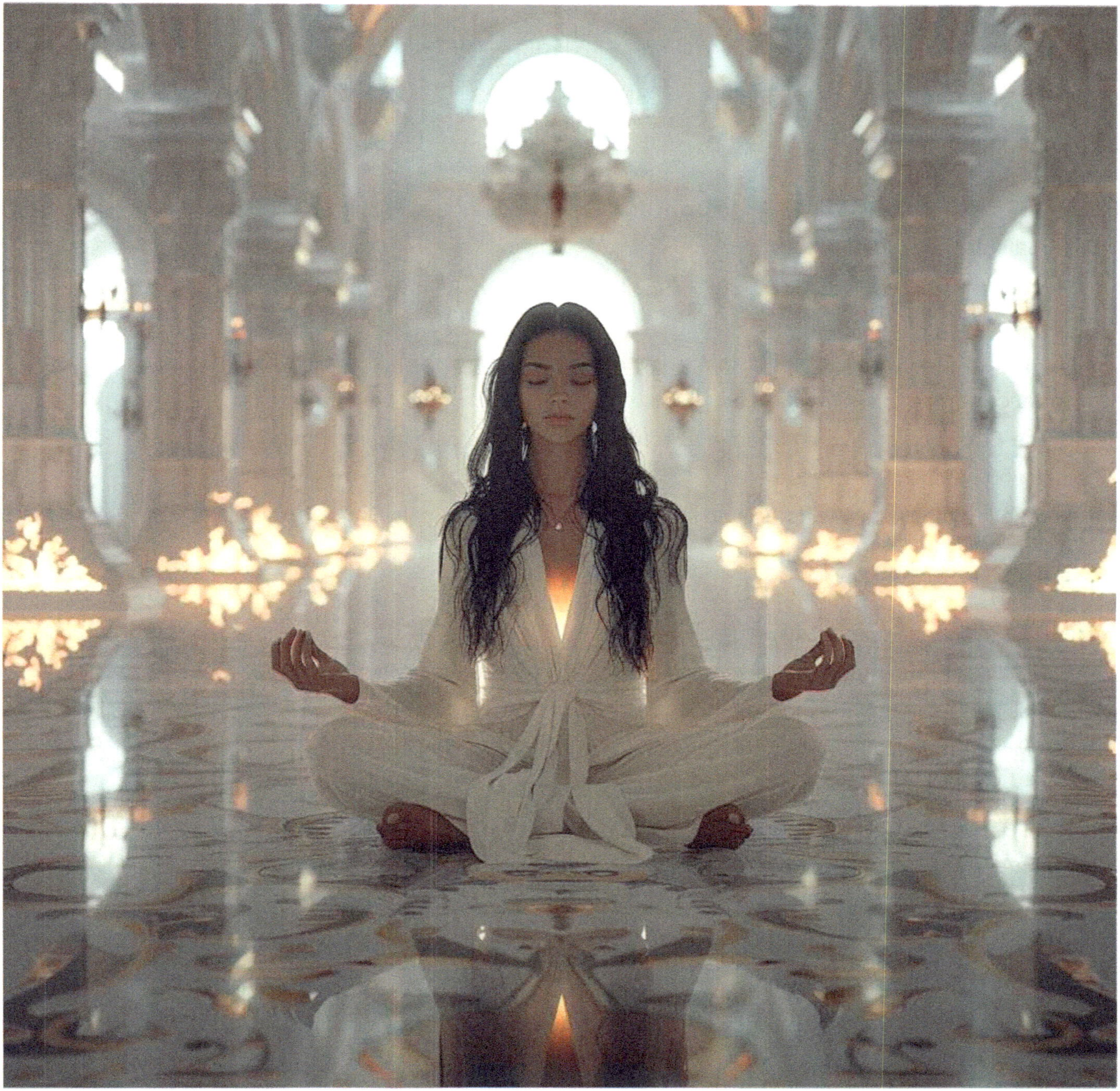

SUPERPOWERS

Did you know that training the Mind through advanced Vipassana meditation can lead to one developing Supernatural Powers…

the Buddha is believed to have possessed six superhuman or supernormal powers

1. **Divine Eye** - The ability to see distant or hidden objects, events, and beings, as well as past and future occurrences, through a form of clairvoyance.
2. **Divine Ear** - The ability to hear sounds from great distances or in other realms, including celestial beings and the thoughts of others.
3. **Knowledge of Others' Minds** -The ability to understand the thoughts, feelings, and mental states of others, including their past experiences and future destinies.
4. **Remembrance of Past Lives** -The ability to recall one's own past lives, including details of previous existences and the experiences and actions therein.
5. **Supernormal Powers** - The ability to perform supernormal feats, such as levitation, walking on water, and telekinesis, through the mastery of meditative concentration and mental power.
6. **Knowledge of the Destruction of impurity forces (Kilesa)**. The ability to attain and maintain complete liberation from all defilements and suffering, achieving the state of Enlightenment or Nirvana.

These supernormal powers are considered manifestations of the Buddha's advanced spiritual attainments and are attributed to his deep insight, wisdom, and mastery of meditative practices. They serve as symbolic representations of the Buddha's Enlightened qualities and his ability to transcend the limitations of ordinary existence.

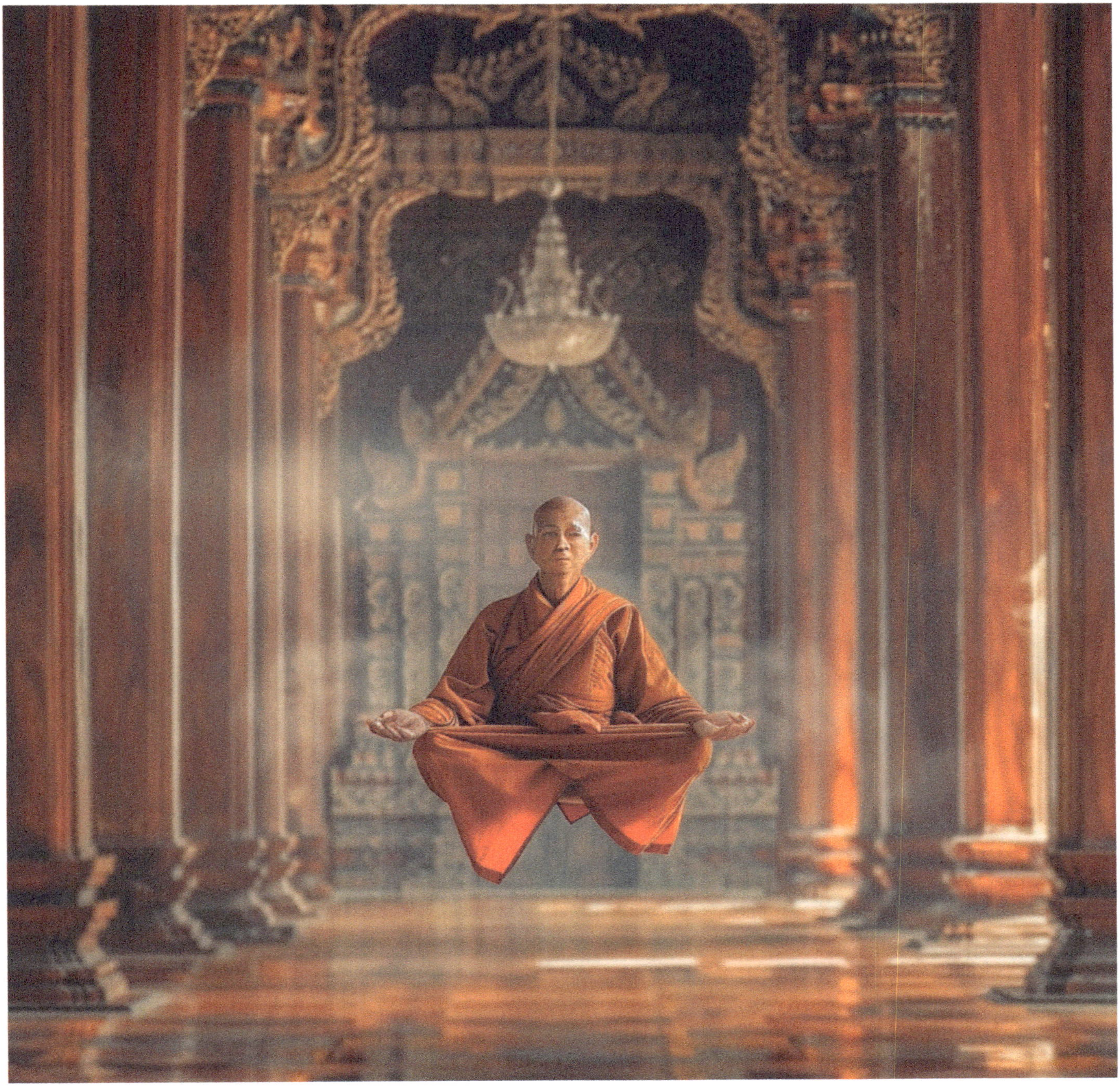

What do we see when we look into the Mind….?

This depends on the person. Some people see nothing, hear nothing, and do not feel anything. This is not unusual, 50% of practitioners only see darkness when they practice. The Buddha suggested that this was preferred for practice, so the practitioner did not get distracted by visions and the impurity forces.

However, the 50% of practitioners may develop supernatural powers, where they can see into the Mind, seeing and hear, the world inside themselves, the impurity forces, and see past lives and karma.

Those who attain supernatural powers are primarily those who have practiced virtue and meditation in a past life.

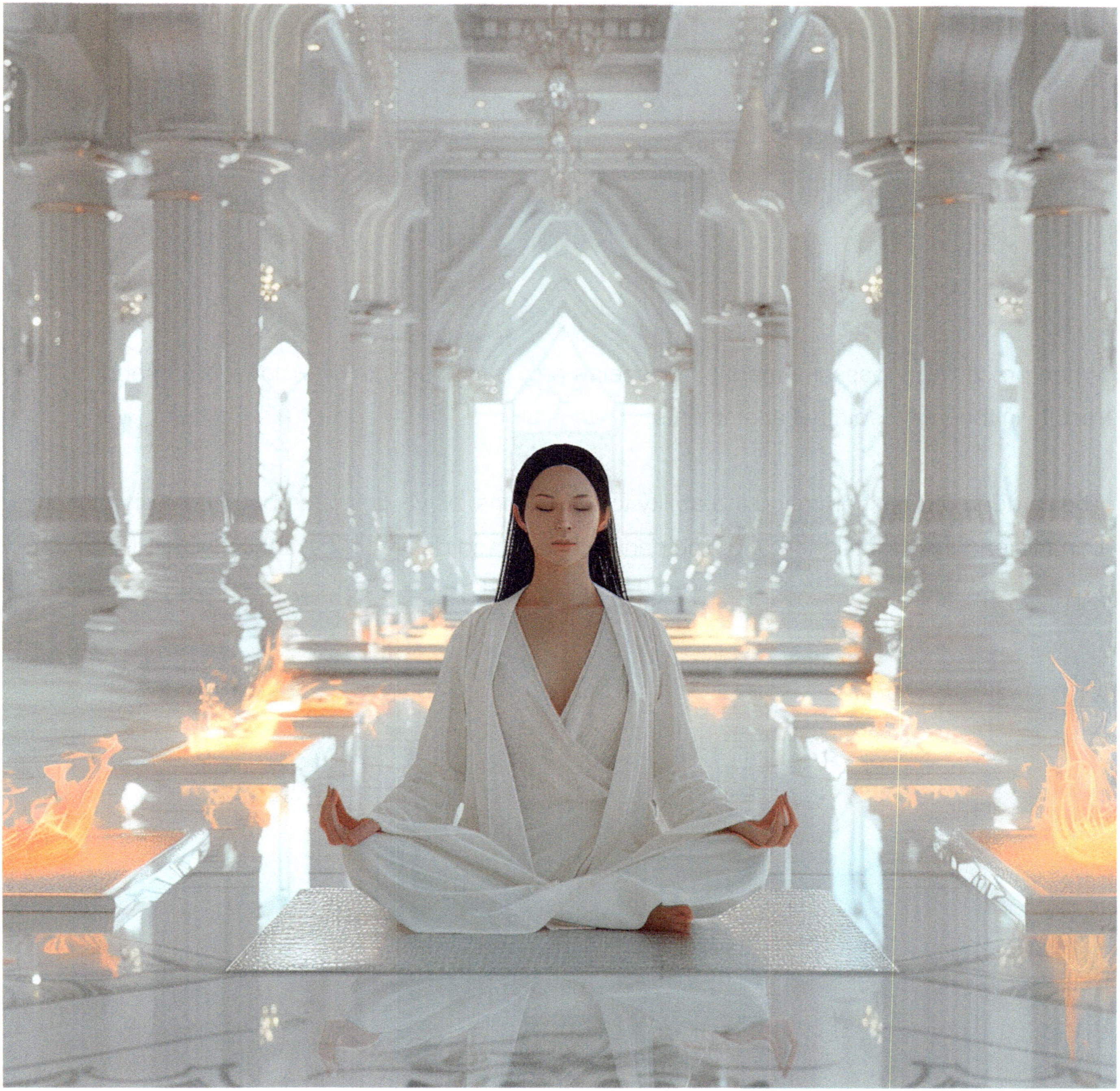

When practicing Vipassana meditation, seeing only darkness with no visions, is fine and results in the same spiritual attainments.

The Buddha did not commend the ability to see visions, as visions often become a distraction, can mislead the practitioner, and also can build ego and desire, in case the visions disappear.

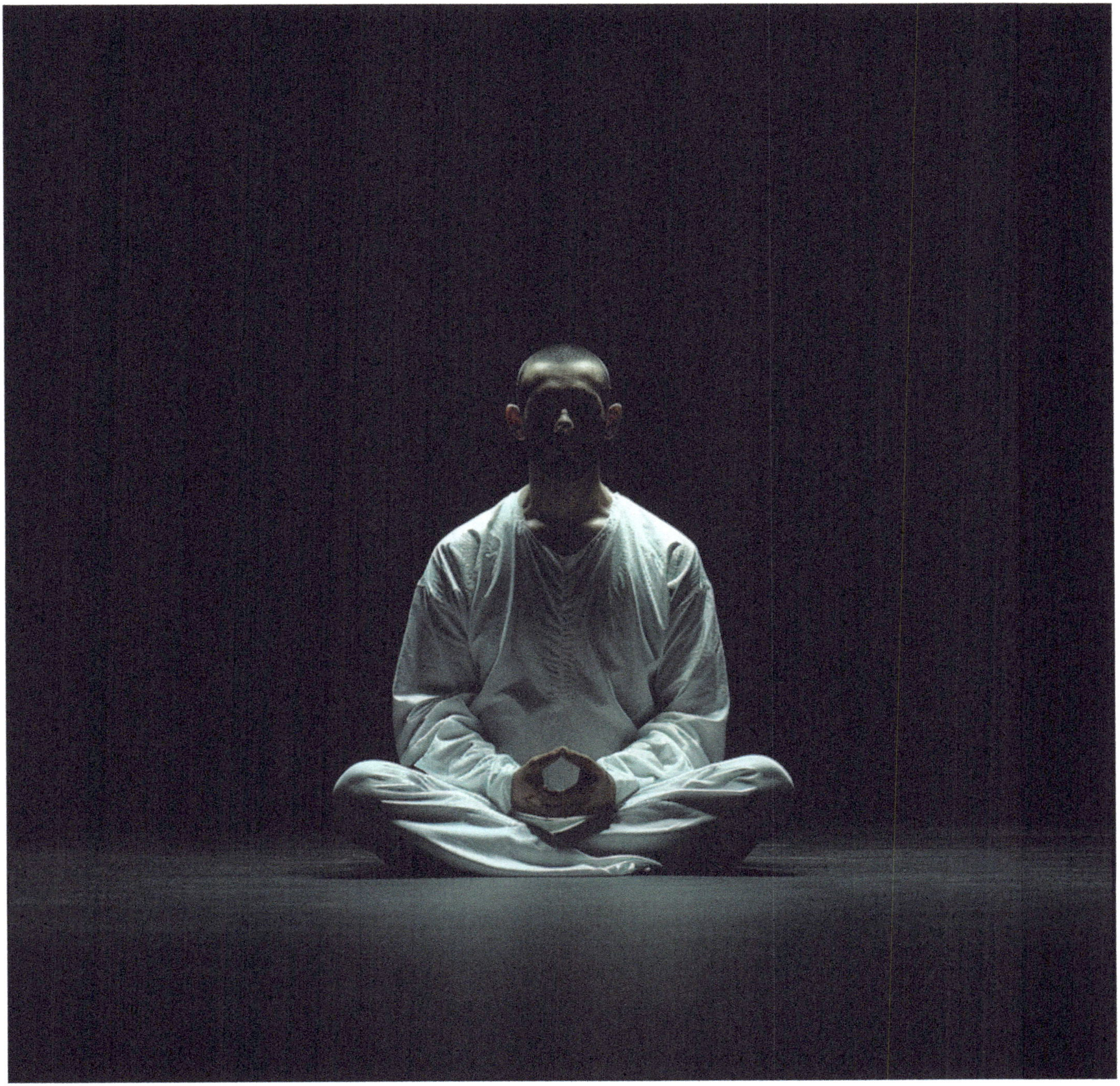

For people with divine eyes and ears and other abilities, they can see and hear a whole world inside of themselves. This includes, seeing the impurity forces (Kilesa) – parasitic entities that manifest in many forms and build a world, similar to what humanity builds on the outside. Our inside world is made of the same elements as the world we ourselves live in. Earth, water, and air.

The ability to see the impurity forces in the Mind, has the advantage that you can see the enemy. But it also has the disadvantage, that the impurity forces can cause you to see and hear things, that can fool or distract you.

Those who crave to see visions, may see visions created by the impurity forces, to cause the practitioner to lose focus or bring their attention to the vision.

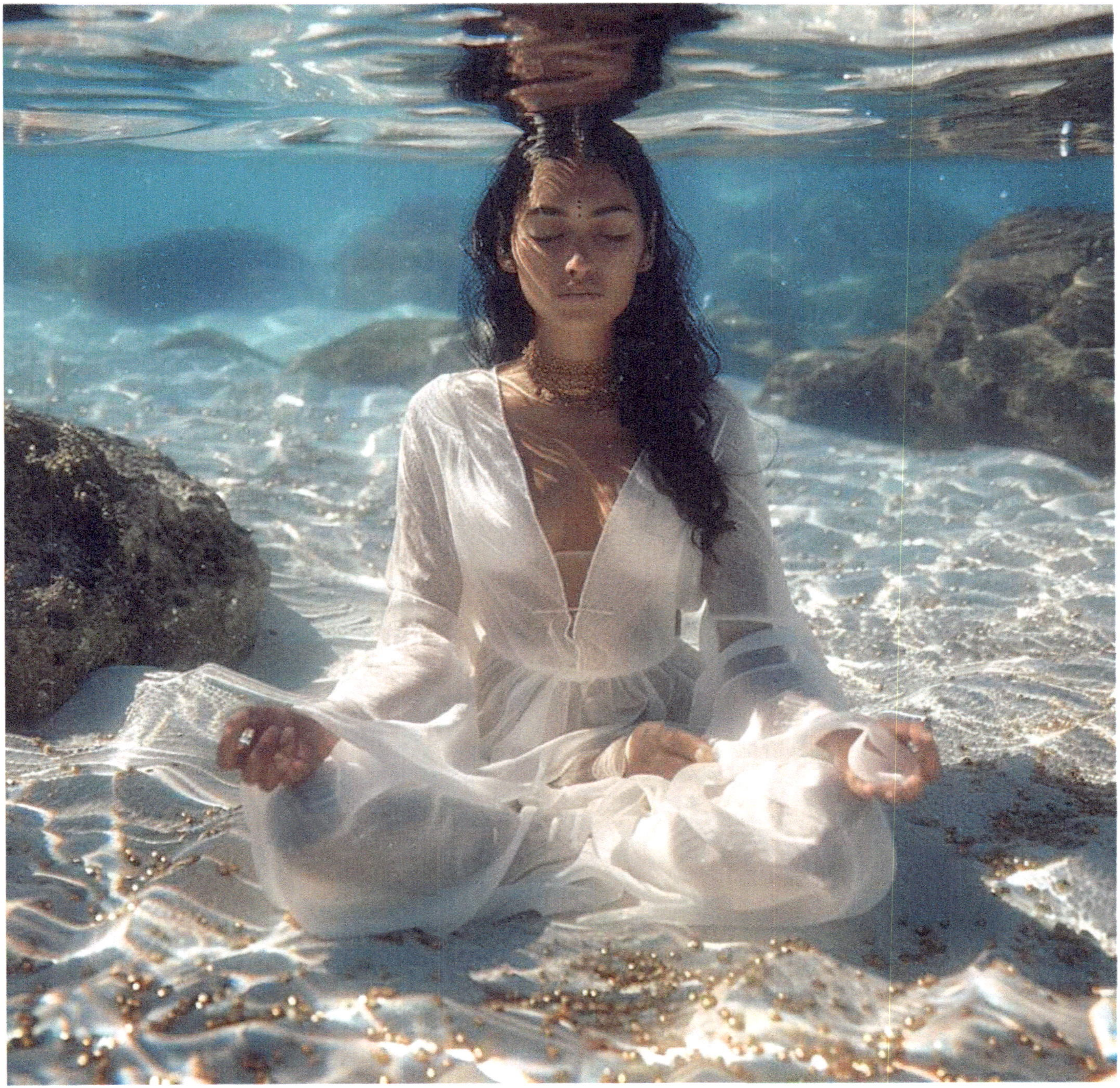

When stillness, concentration an equanimity joins, on a single point of focus, the Mind can rest in high concentration and observe for a long time. It is like sitting under water or levitating over a desert.

Then the Mind as it gathers strength can break through this desert sand and find its way into tunnels and caverns, where impurity forces in the form of insects or parasites hide. Using the fire created by the Mind, these parasites are vaporized.

The Mind will travel down these tunnels, continuing to destroy the impurities of the Mind (Kilesa) and then break through the layers to another level.

Stillness is the key – along with concentration and being neutral or equanimous. Not wanting to see, not wanting to move, just observing, and letting things arise without reacting.

The mind can become so still and focused that it sees incredible details.

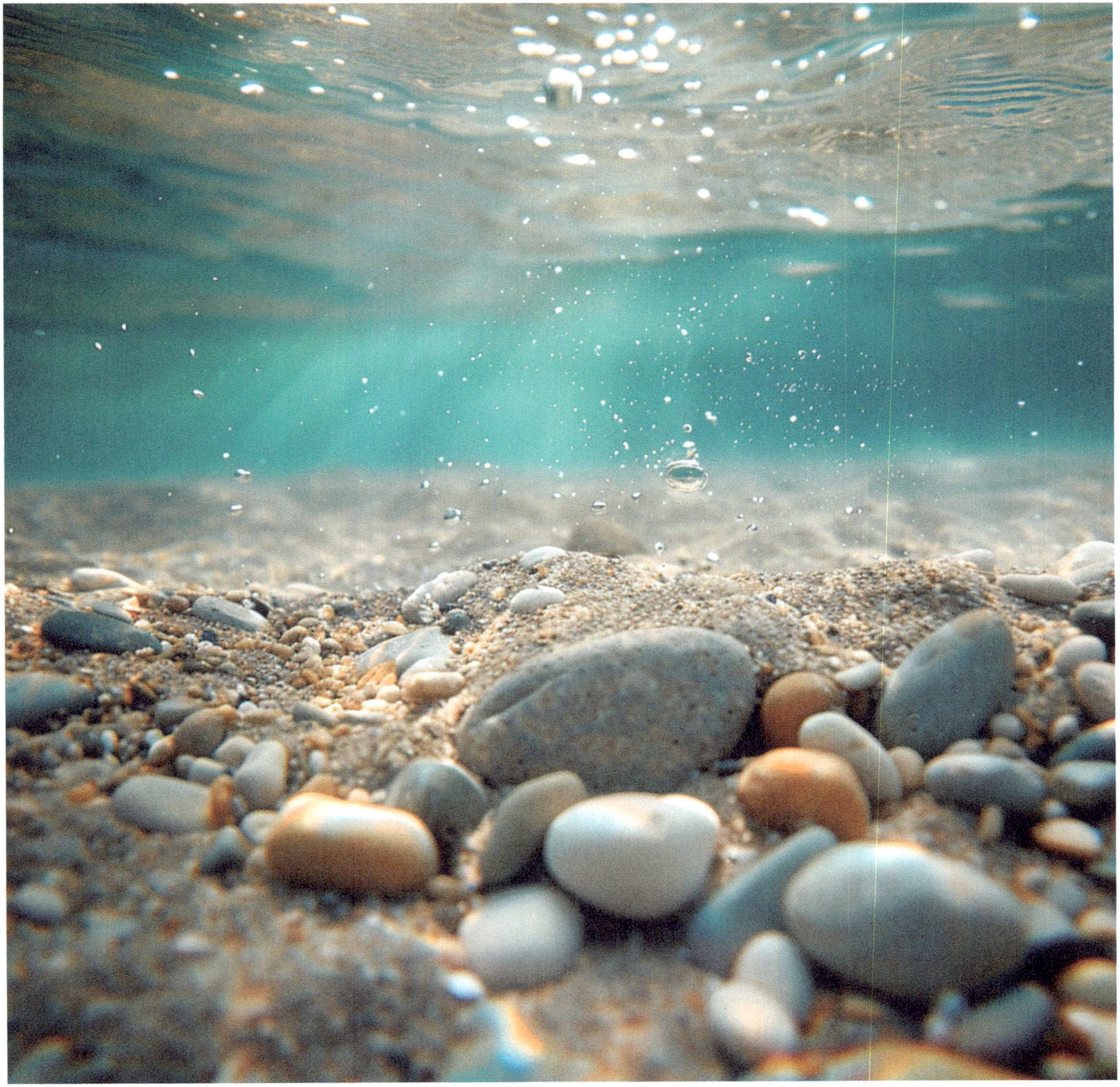

CHAPTER 13

THE WORLD WITHIN

(TECHO VIPASSANA MEDITATION EXPERIENCES)

The world inside of us can be beautiful and natural. In this world, the impurity forces (Kilesa) build their villages, towns, and cities. The goal of the practitioner is to use the body's fire element to create heat and fire that destroys and incinerates the inner world and the impurity forces, which inhabit this world.

The Mind sits in high focus and concentration and observes and starts to burn the world inside. The more still, focused, and concentrated, the greater the heat and fire.

As we reach high stillness, concentration, and equanimity, we can see the worlds within.

We can sometimes even hear the impurity forces talking.

And as we burn away layers of impurities in our Minds, this is when we also can recall our past lives and feel the emotions that arise from the past.

273

As the Mind settles, during Vipassana meditation, we see a dry grass and a forest in the darkness. When the Mind does not react to this scene, we continue to move through the forest as if we are weightless and flying.

This continues for many minutes, when the Mind stays equanimous and does not react, the Mind can rest and remain focused.

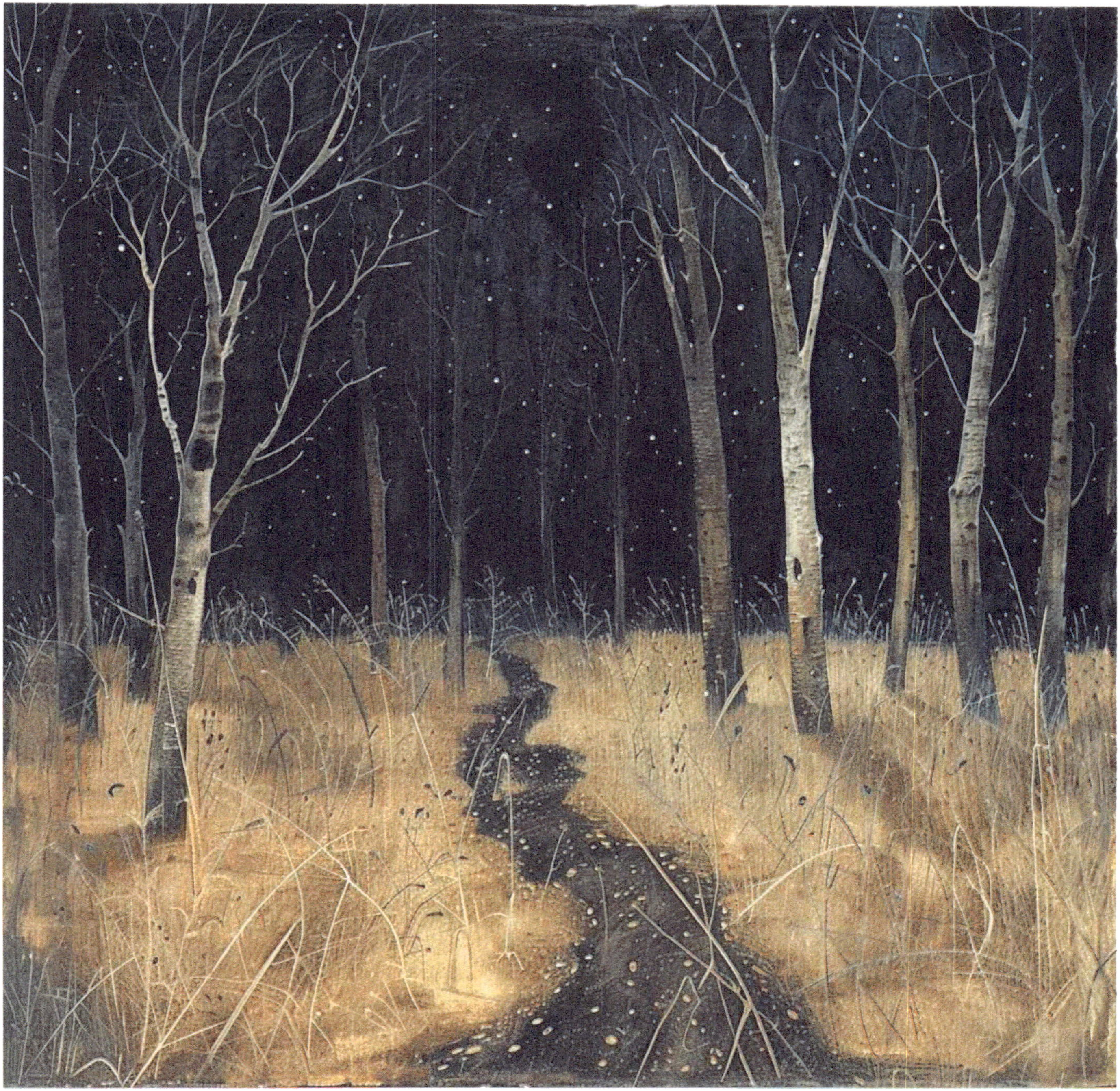

Then the scene changes, as we break through the next layer, arriving in a desert with clumps of grass. The Mind simply hovers over this scene.

With a perfectly still Mind, focused, concentrated and neutral, thoughts might arise but they fade away as quickly as they arrive. In this state the Mind continues to dig through to the next layer.

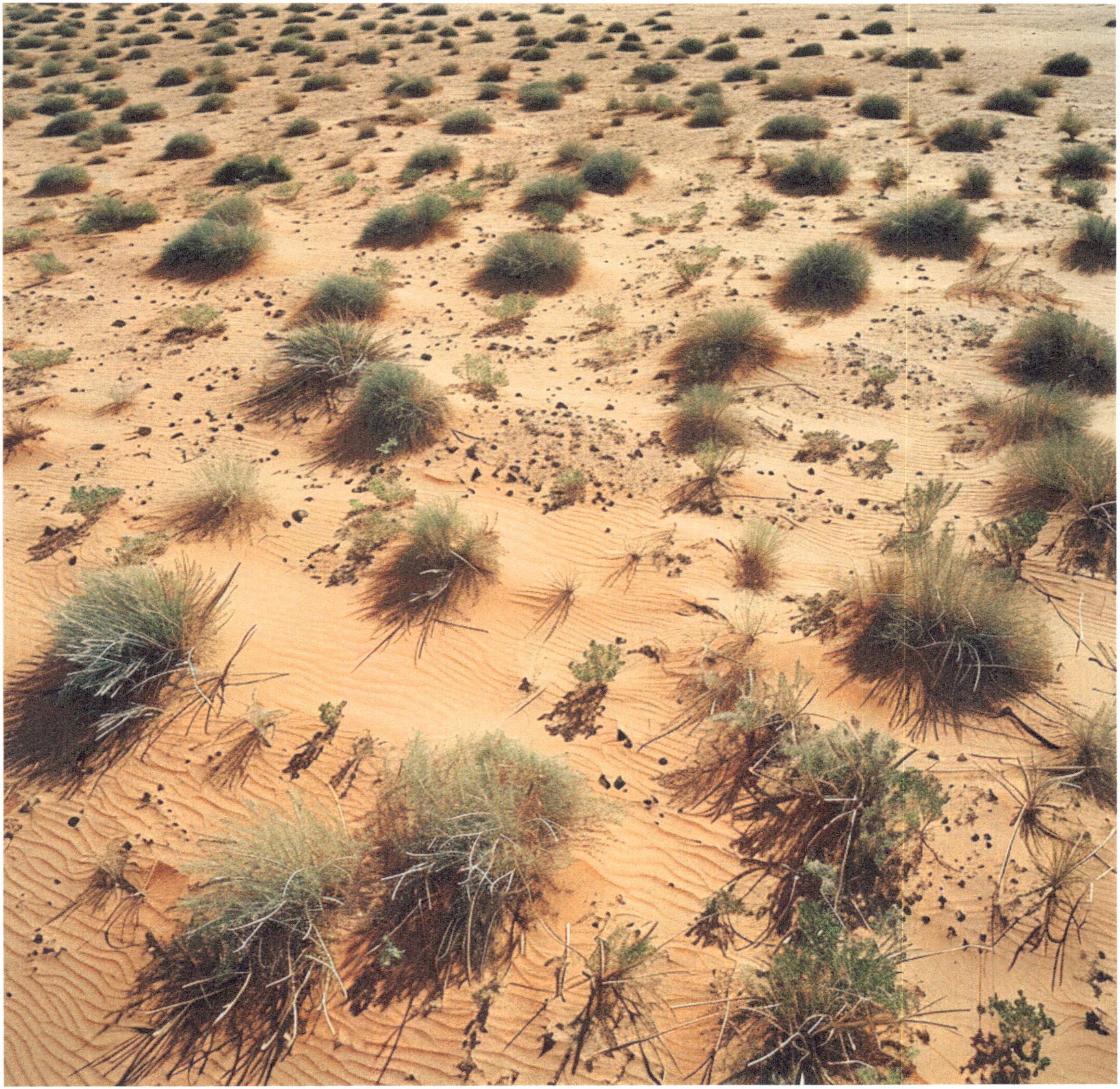

Pearcing through the desert sand, there suddenly appears a cliff with rocks and tunnels. The Mind continues to move forward to the enterance of the tunnel. We can see the Techo fire light up the tunnel as it burns impurities (kilesa) hiding like insects in the crevaces of the caves (Mind).

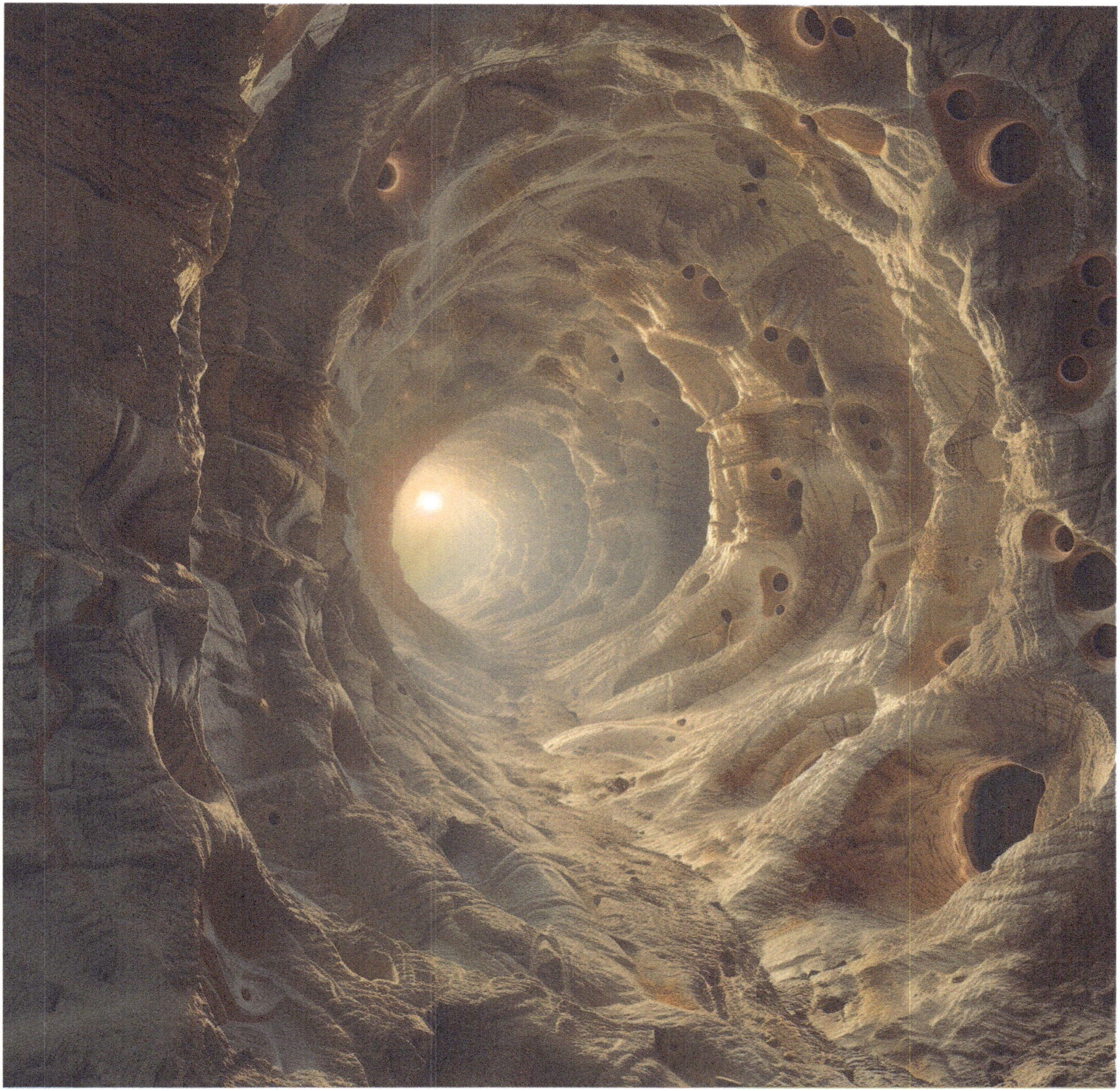

As the Mind continues to travel through the tunnel, suddenly there appears a snow covered mountain, with many pine trees. The Mind flies over the snow, trees and rocks. There is a sense of freedom. But inorder to continue the flight, the Mind must not react and must remain equanimous.
If the Mind loses focus even for a second, then the Mind returns to the beginning layers, to begin digging again.

As the Mind becomes stronger from consistent meditation and mindfulness practice, then the Mind reaches these states of stillness, focus, concentration and equanimity faster and easier.

Important to remember is that the goal is not to see layers or these scenes or places where impurities hide in the Mind, but to be able to hold the Mind in stillness and focus for longer and longer periods of time, when practicing.

Sitting in stillness, seeing only darkness with no visions, is preferable to seeing visions, as the Mind does not get distracted. When seeing visions, it is easier for the impurities to distract us from the focus point or get us to break our concentration, by us reacting to something beautiful or unexpected.

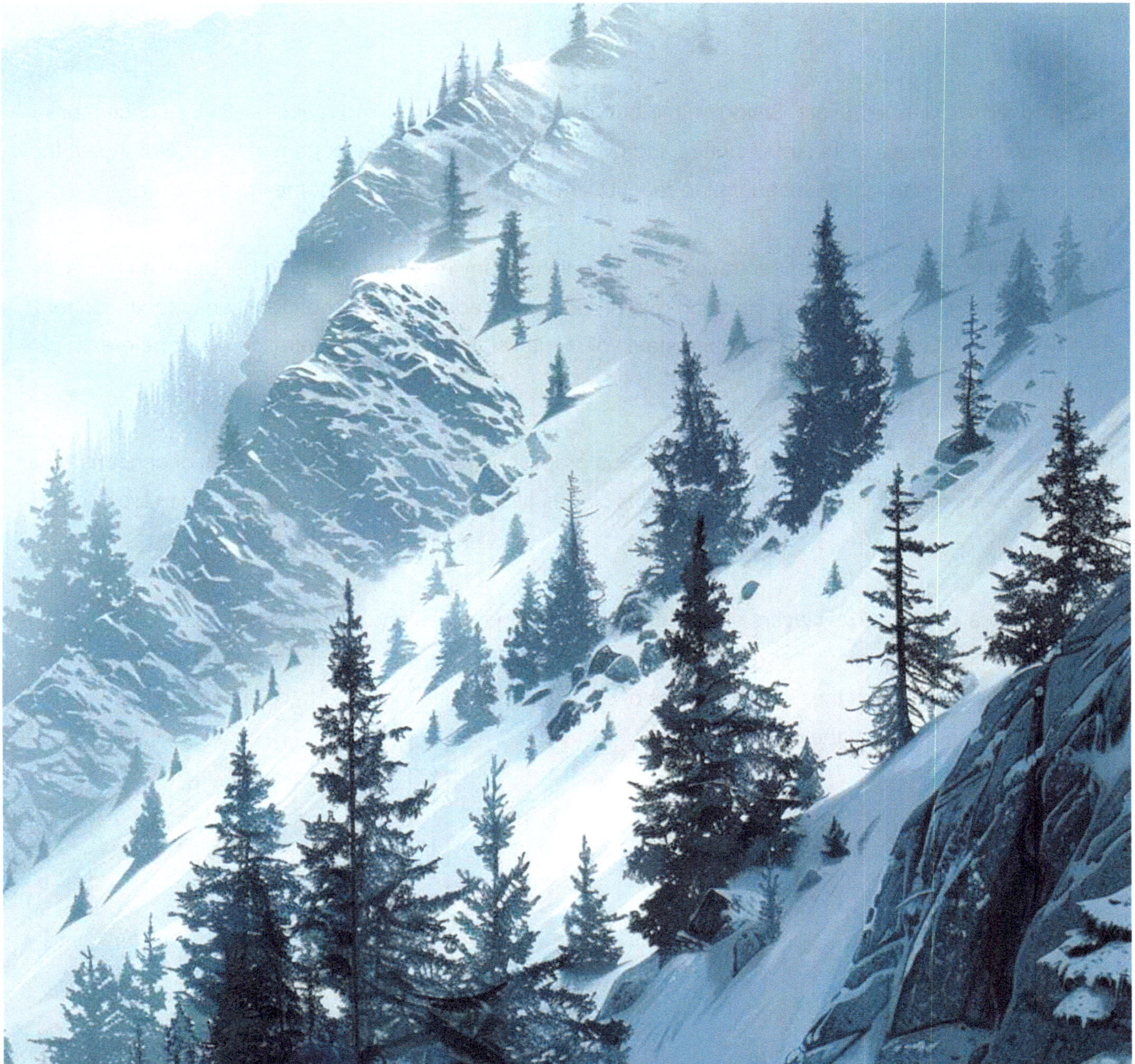

The Mind digs to deeper layers. Sitting on the bottom of the ocean the Mind reaches stillness once more and can see the details of the small stones and even grains of sand on the bottom of the ocean. Again the practitioners duty is to stay focused, not to react to anything that appears or comes to the Mind.

A trained Mind can hold this concentration for a long time. Many minutes and some people even hours. Training under a Master, in a high vibration retreat, practicing advanced Techo Vipassana Meditation for 8 days straight, allows practitioners to reach states of mental stability and concentration never before experienced.

This kind of boot camp for the Mind, is how serious practitioners reach these super states of concentration and conciousness, which can lead to the various stages of Enlightenment and liberation, from the cycle of rebirth.

In these states we burn away layers of impurities and past memories and emotions, which results in Wisdom arising and the meditator realizing certain truths for themselves. This is the great benefit of purifying the Mind. Also at these higher states of consciousness, it is possible to burn away karma and heal the body and Mind at the core.

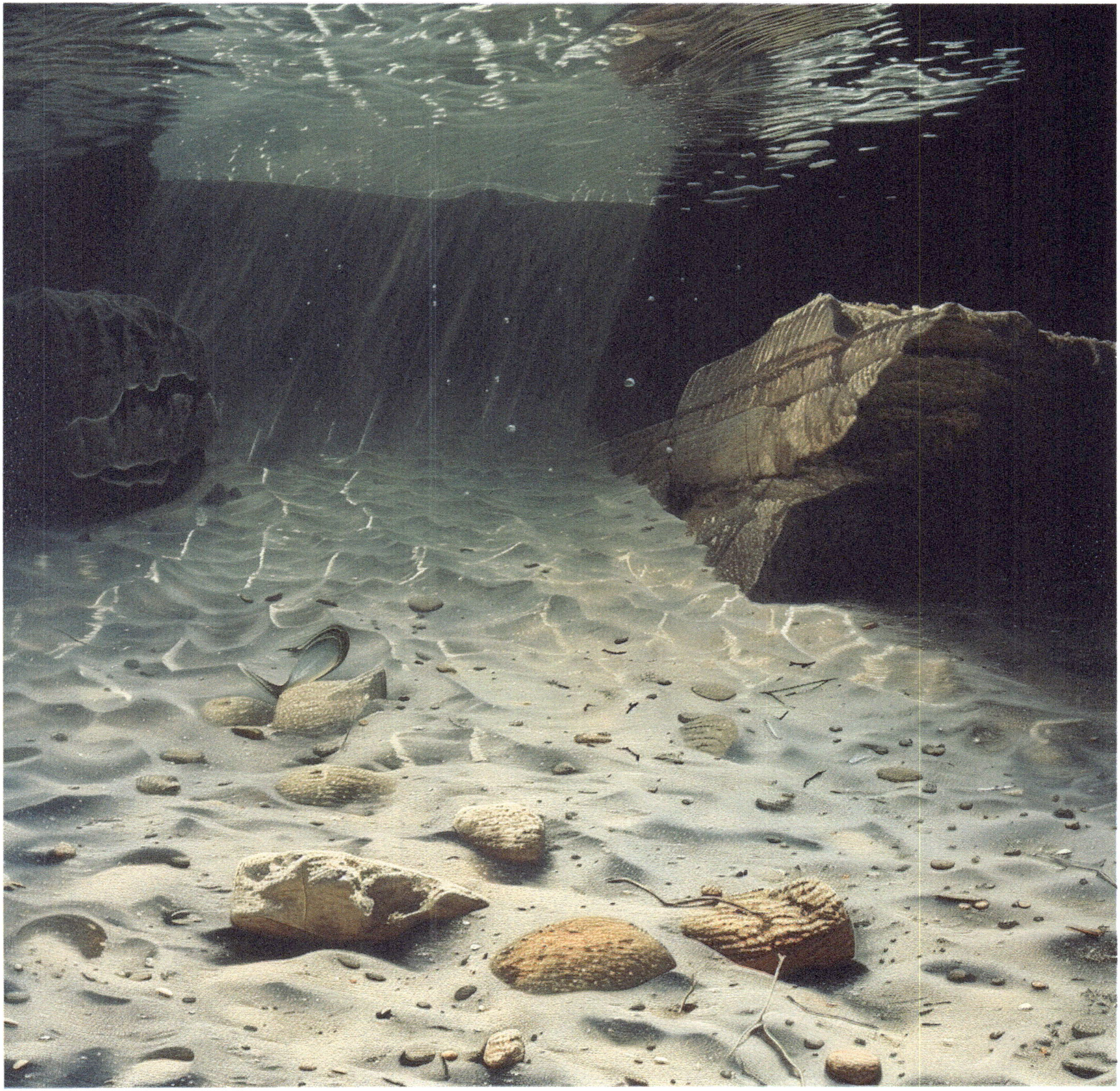

As the Mind continues to gain even more strength and concentration, it starts to percieve fine energy.

Sitting on the bottom of the ocean we see the details of the rocks and stone. But now, we also see the impurities in the form of tiny fish (kilesa) which the Mind can also destroy through Techo Vipassana fire and can reach a new level of mental strength and concentration.

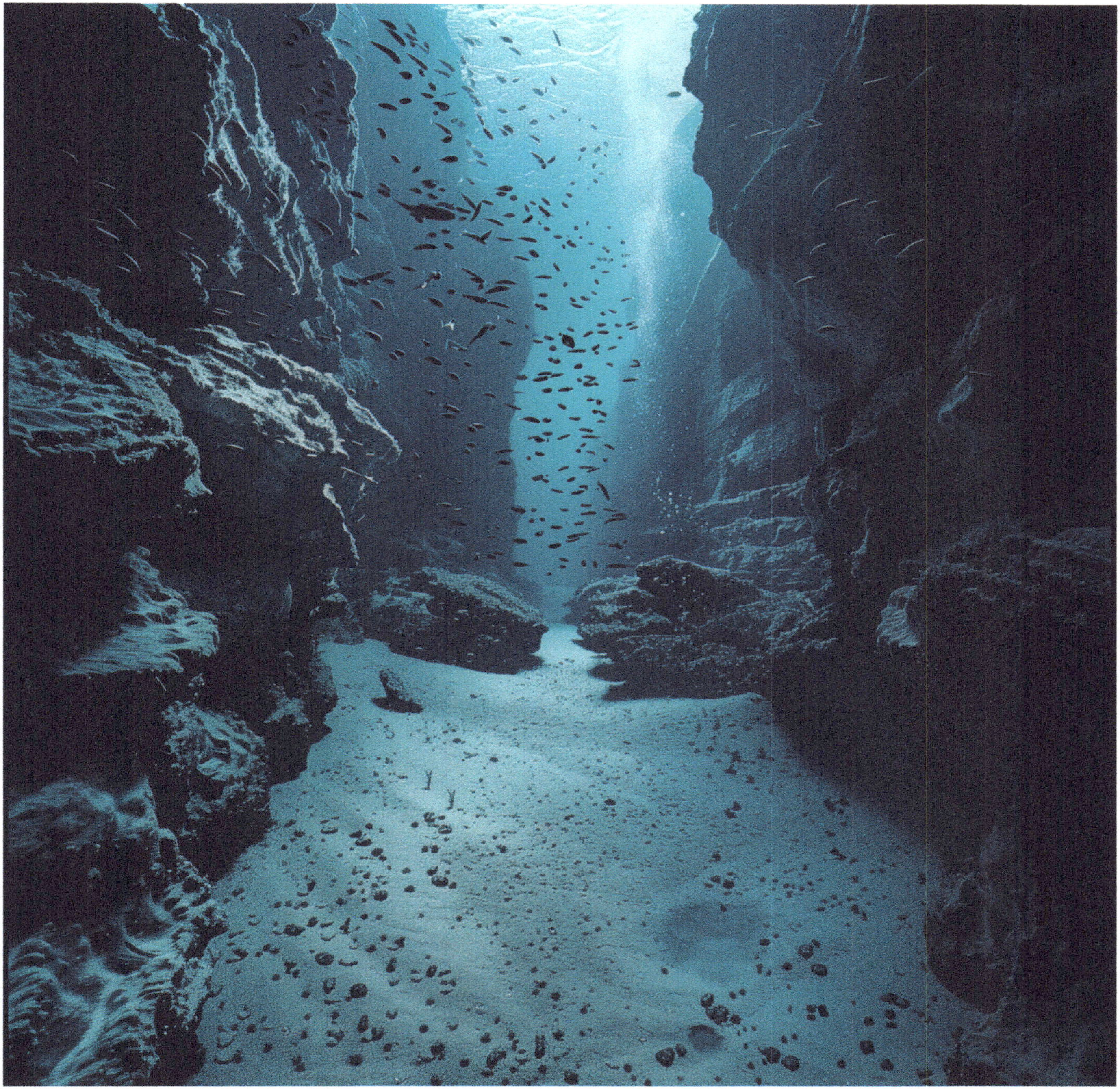

CHAPTER. 14

THE IMPURITY FORCES (Kilesa)

(TECHO VIPASSANA MEDITATION EXPERIENCES)

The armies of the impurity forces which guard and defend the world within us, can manifest in many forms. Coarse impurity forces often can take the form of literal armies, we can see marching against us in the Mind. Often these are armies we recognize and identify from our past lives. Like medieval soldiers, wearing armor, carrying swords, spears and shields.

289

As the Mind stays equanimous, these forces march towards the practitioners, in the Mind. They can attach at various speeds and with unlimited numbers and without a break or stopping.

The practitioner can react and lose concentration and thus these forces win and gain strength.

However, if the meditator is able to stay focused and equanimous with the onslaugt of endless battalions of impurities, then the meditator's own Mind conquers these forces and gains in strength.

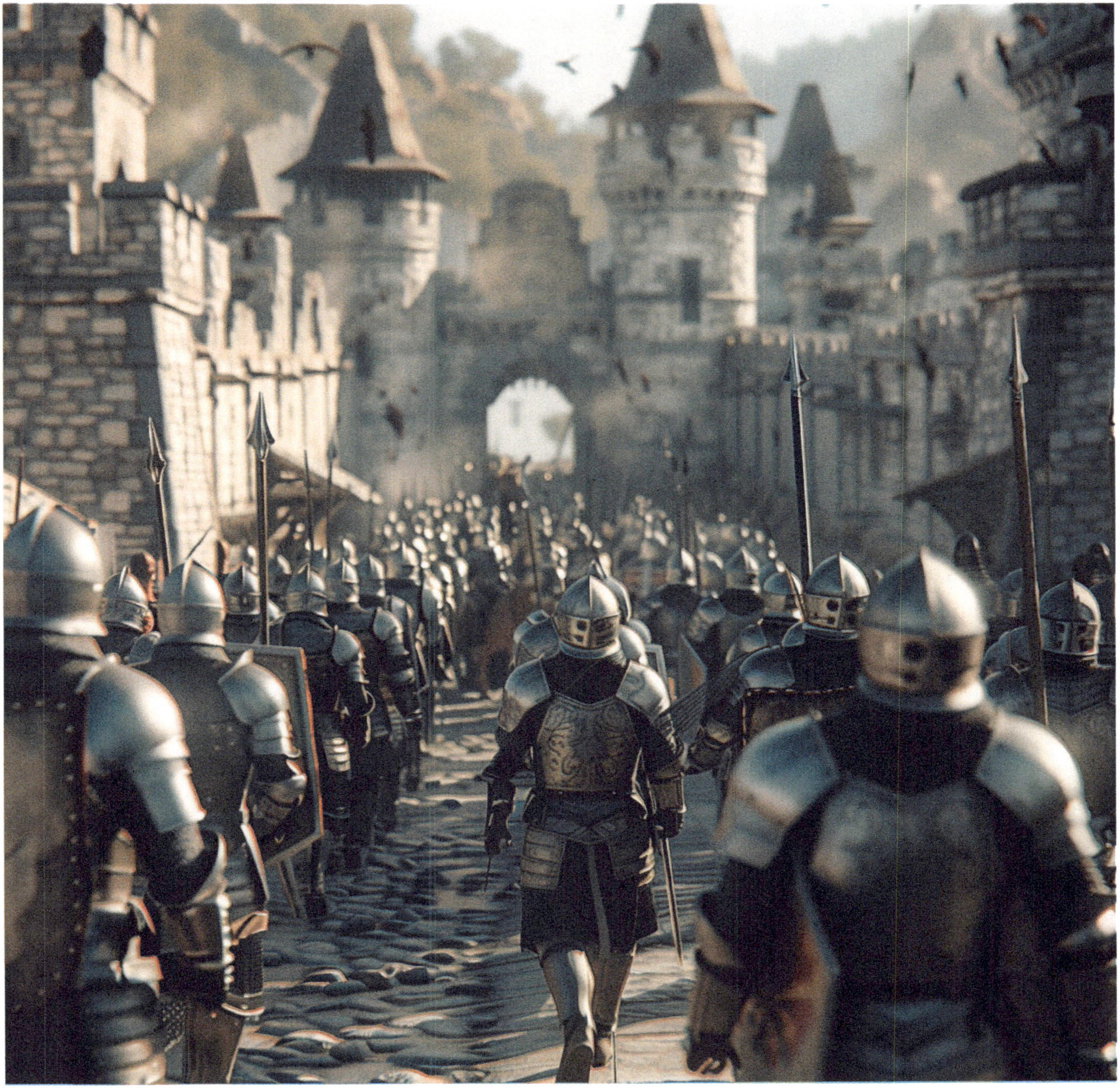

The meditator must be strong and determined. The Mind can actually falter from the endless rows of impurities marching towards the the meditators Mind. The meditator must be willing to fight to the end without waiiver. This truly is the battle of the Mind and literally a battle to the death. (hopefully the death of the impurities and not the practitioner). No one dies from practicing Vipassana meditation, but they must be willing to die and face the possiblity of death, inorder to conquer their own fears.

Anyone serious about ending the cycle of rebirth and winning back their Minds from the impurity forces, must be willing to fight to the death. They must be deternined to die, sitting on their meditation mats, just like the Buddha resolved to die where he sat until he reached the Enlightenment and uncovered the Ultimate Truth hidden for so long.

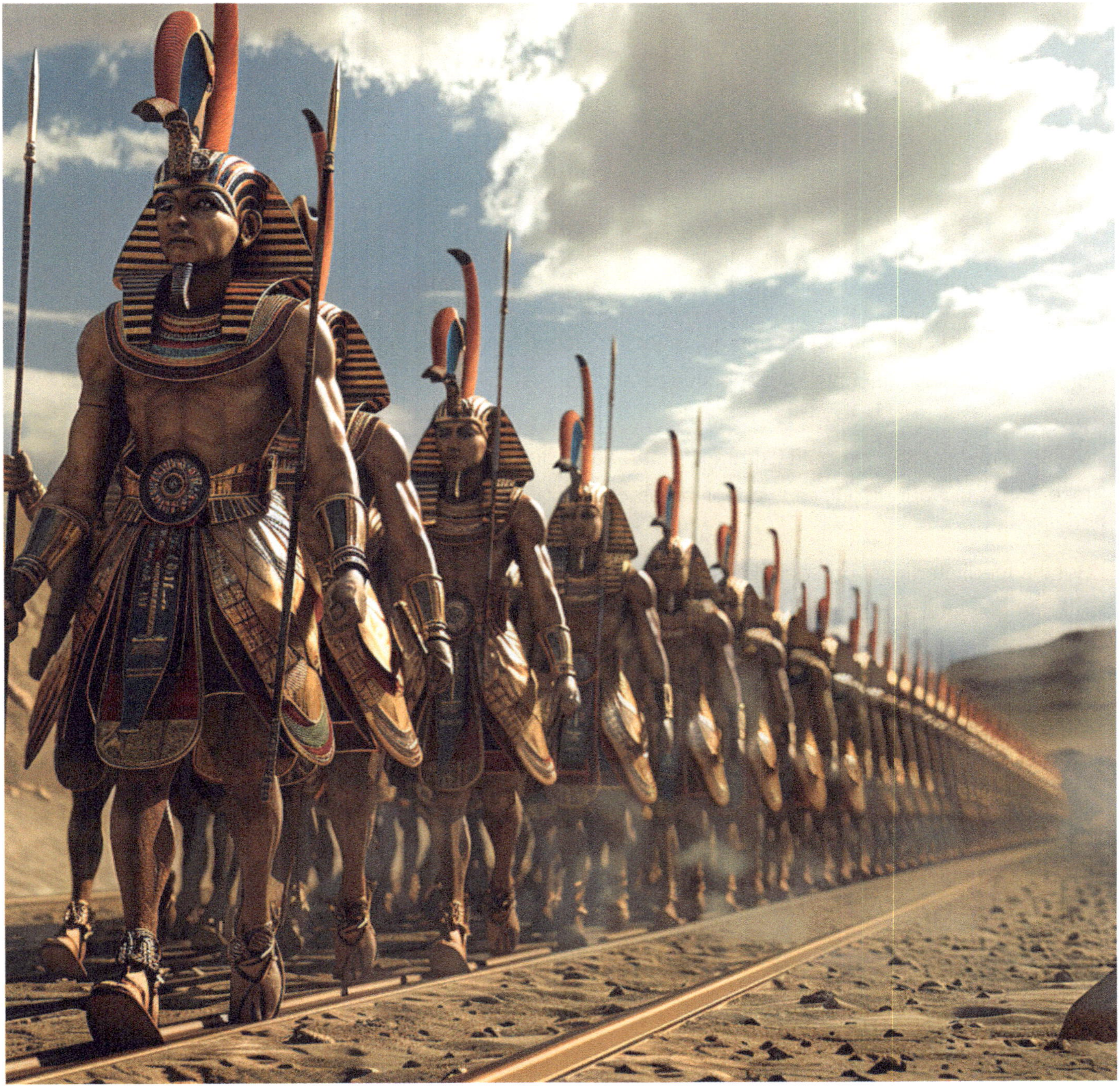

The Mind must stay composed and not react to these armies, if suddenly they appear like sausages dressed in yellow raincoats, carrying shields and spears.

Mental impurities can be both extremely smart and extremely stupid. They can be goofy in the forms they take, trying to wear disguises and fool the practitioner into believing they are real soldiers.

But the meditator must be equanimous and not react to this bizarre army, because losing focus even for a second means being defeated by an army of sausages (Kilesa).

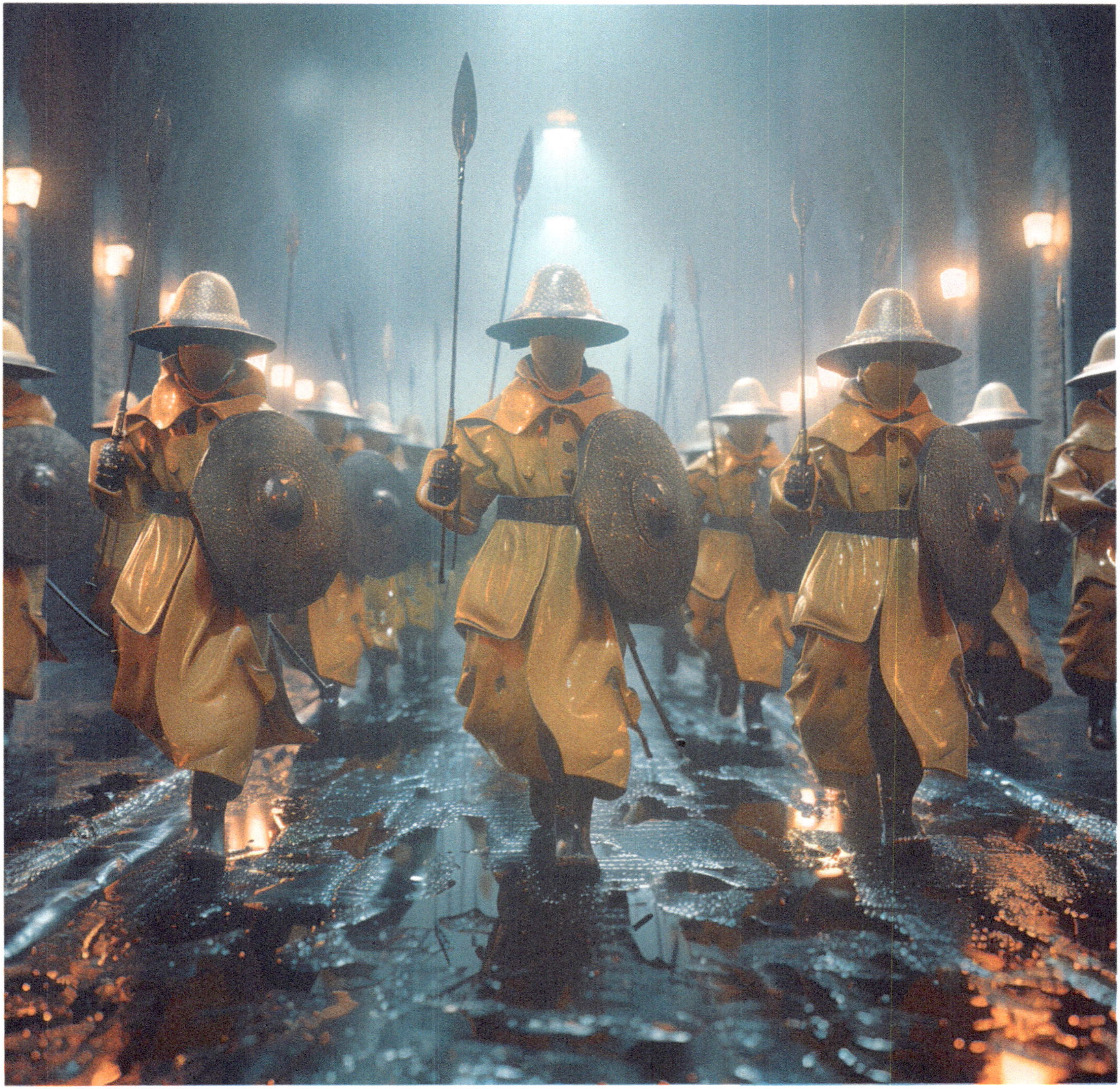

There are also armies of impurities that are frightening. They are tough and reminiscentmof armies of the past that terrified their opponents. These forces mean business.

The Mind must remain firm and still like a mountain as these forces attack.

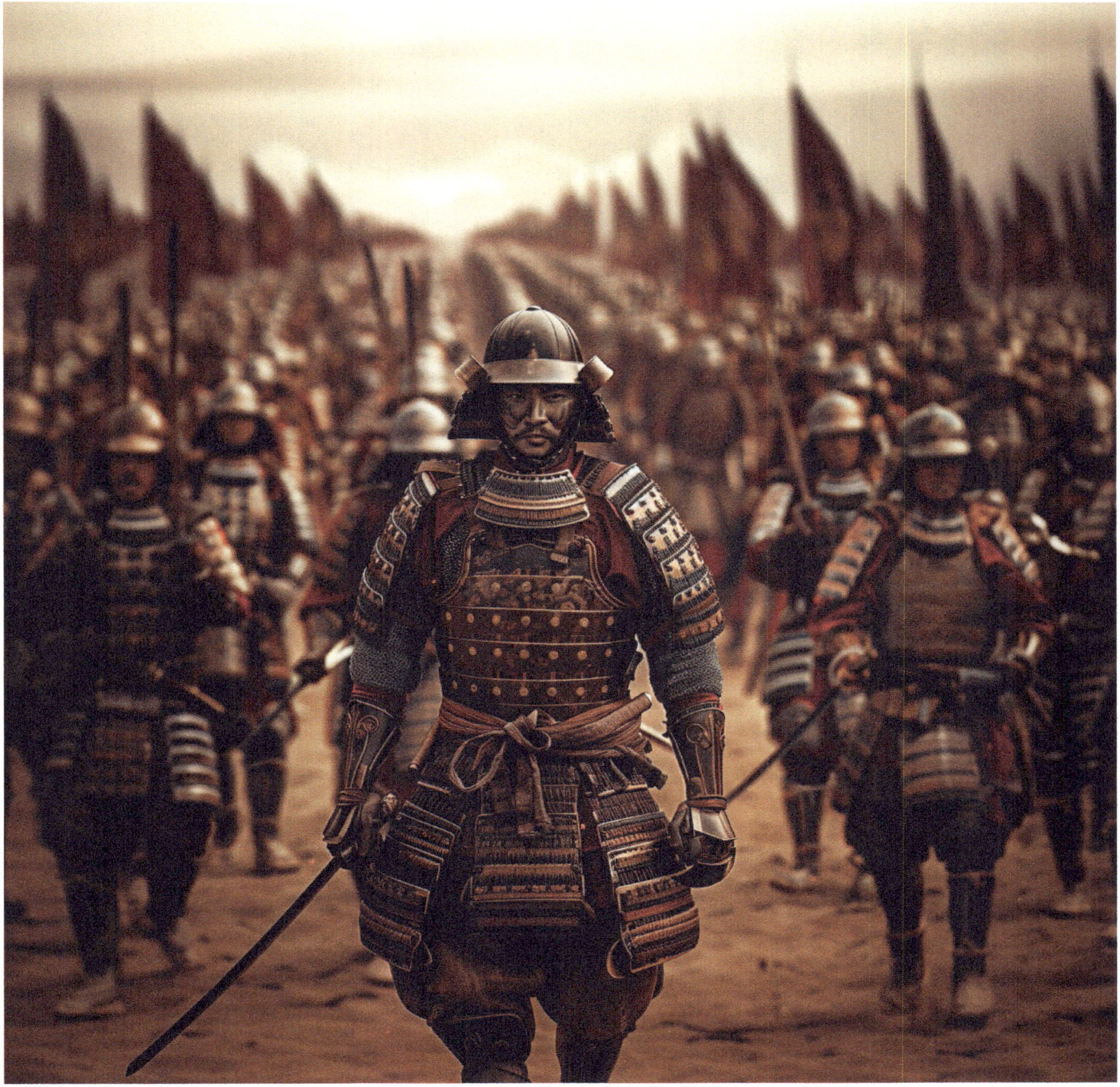

These armies can also look disgusting and strange. Anything to distract or gross out, the meditator.

These are the "coarse" impurities. As the meditator digs deeper to new layers these impurities (kilesa) take on different forms.

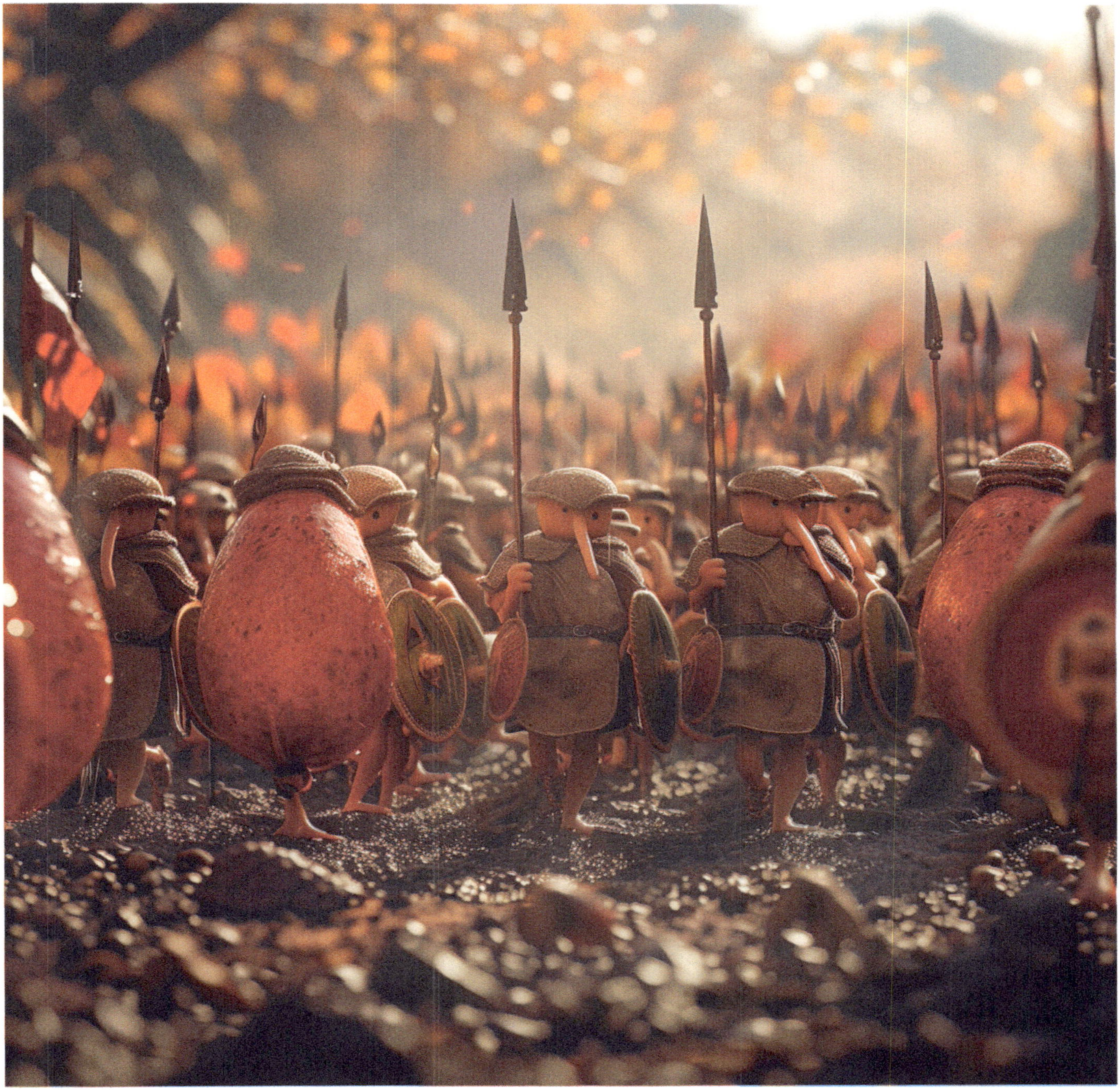

Impurities (Kilesa) can manifest as anything. This is a "Greedy Kilesa" fat gross and disgusting from it's Greedy existence. We all have this kind of Impurity inside us, as well as many other types of Kilesa, living within our Minds and bodies.

This example of a greedy kilesa, is a "coarse" impurity and demonstrates a roughness of the mind.

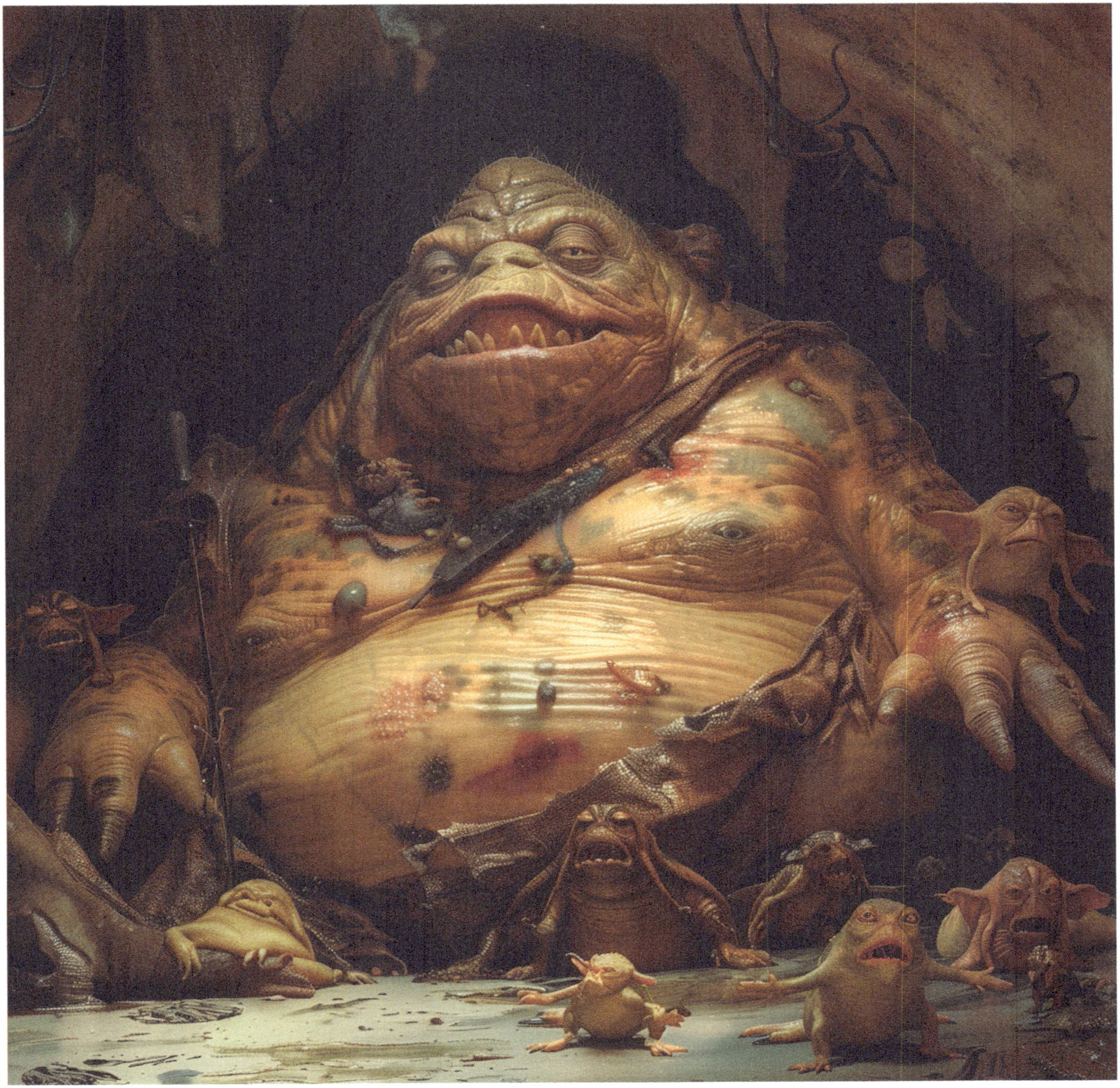

Sometimes during meditation we suddenly can see the eyes of the Impurities (Kilesa) staring at us.
Trying to figure out what we are doing?
And how to stop us from destroying them or going deeper into their dimension and world.

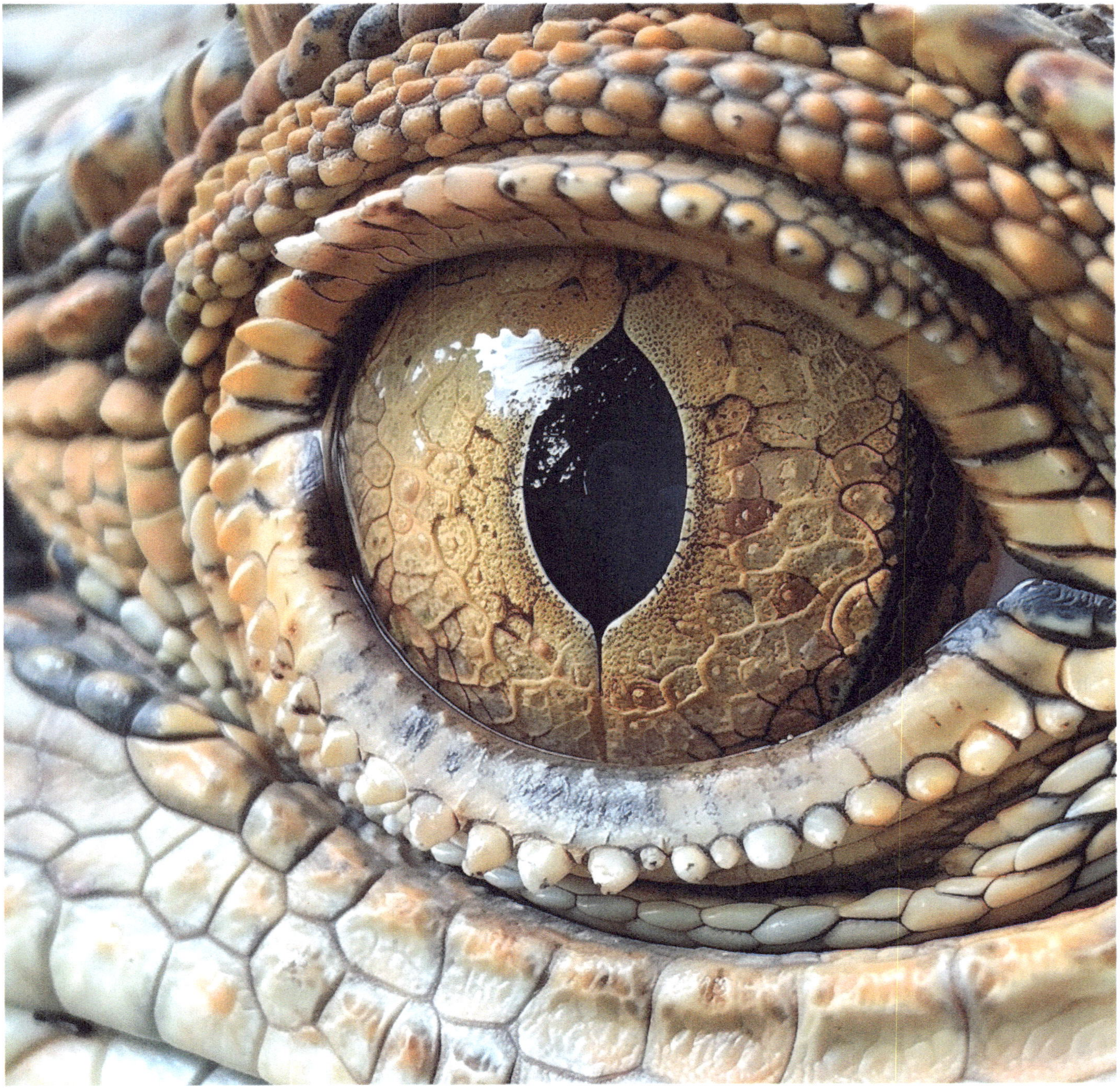

The impurity forces can manifest as images of desire. Sexual explicit and sensual images are a big impurity for the practitioner to overcome.

In this daily World our minds are inundated by explicit sexual images. From Magazines, Television, Advertising, Social Media and Movies – "Sex Sells" and drives humanity into addiction to sensual and sexual desire.

This level of Impurity Forces is not easy to conquer and requires the practitioner to be mindful inside and outside of the meditation hall.

Sensual desire drives our World and is a huge factor that attaches us to this World and the Mara (devil) Energy Particle. These images are very easy to enter our Minds through our eyes. The practitioner must become mindful in their daily activities, in order for these images not to enter the Mind and form more new impurities of desire.

Burning away sensual and sexual desires using Techo Vipassana Meditation, leads to freedom from Lust and Sexual desires controlling our Minds. It is also the essential step that leads to attaining the 2nd and 3rd stages of Enlightenment. Sakadagami (once-returner), Anagami (non-returner),

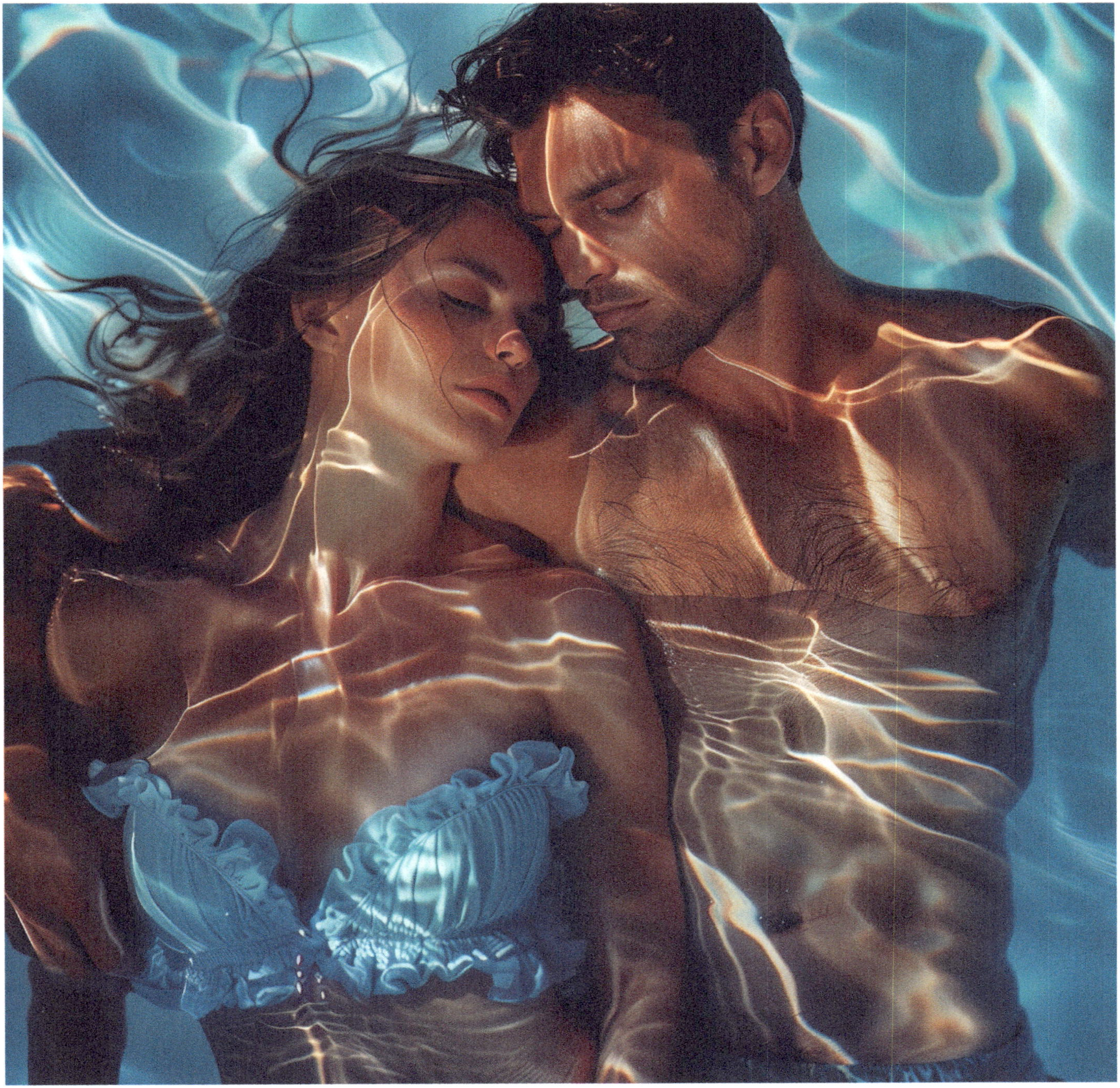

CHAPTER. 15

NEXT LEVEL IMPURITY FORCES (Kilesa)

(TECHO VIPASSANA MEDITATION EXPERIENCES)

The focused and equanimous Mind, that is concentrated will dig through layers of the Mind to find the impurity forces (Kilesa) where they live and hide. These impurities are like parasites, moving and hiding from the Techo Vipassana fire.

There is panic by these impurities, as they realize that they have been discovered after uncountable eons and lifetimes of living undisturbed in our Minds and bodies, controlling our thoughts, feelings, and emotions.

They now work to hide and cause the practitioner to stop practicing. The impurity forces use whatever means they can. This can include causing the meditator to suddenly have aches, pains, discomfort, and various emotions.

What the practitioner is experiencing are not his or her own feelings, or emotions, or pain, but those of the impurity forces. The meditator actually feels the feelings of the impurity forces, projecting their feeling into the Mind and body of the meditator. These forces have been inhabiting our minds for eons and are part of us. This is the profound knowledge that the Buddha discovered 2500 years ago.

Today, most people are unaware that they are being manipulated and driven by these parasitic impurity forces (Kilesa).

It is hard to believe, but true…. the Buddha told us about these mental impurities (Kilesa). But somehow this ancient knowledge has been covered up and lost.

How many people today have even heard the name Kilesa?

The Mara (devil) is so clever blinding us in the Illusion and giving us amnesia or doubt and denial.

How can we defeat the Kilesa if we do not know they exist?

Defeating these Kilesa in the Mind is what enabled the Buddha to reach Enlightenment, however Mara (devil) has done a great job hiding this knowledge from humanity.

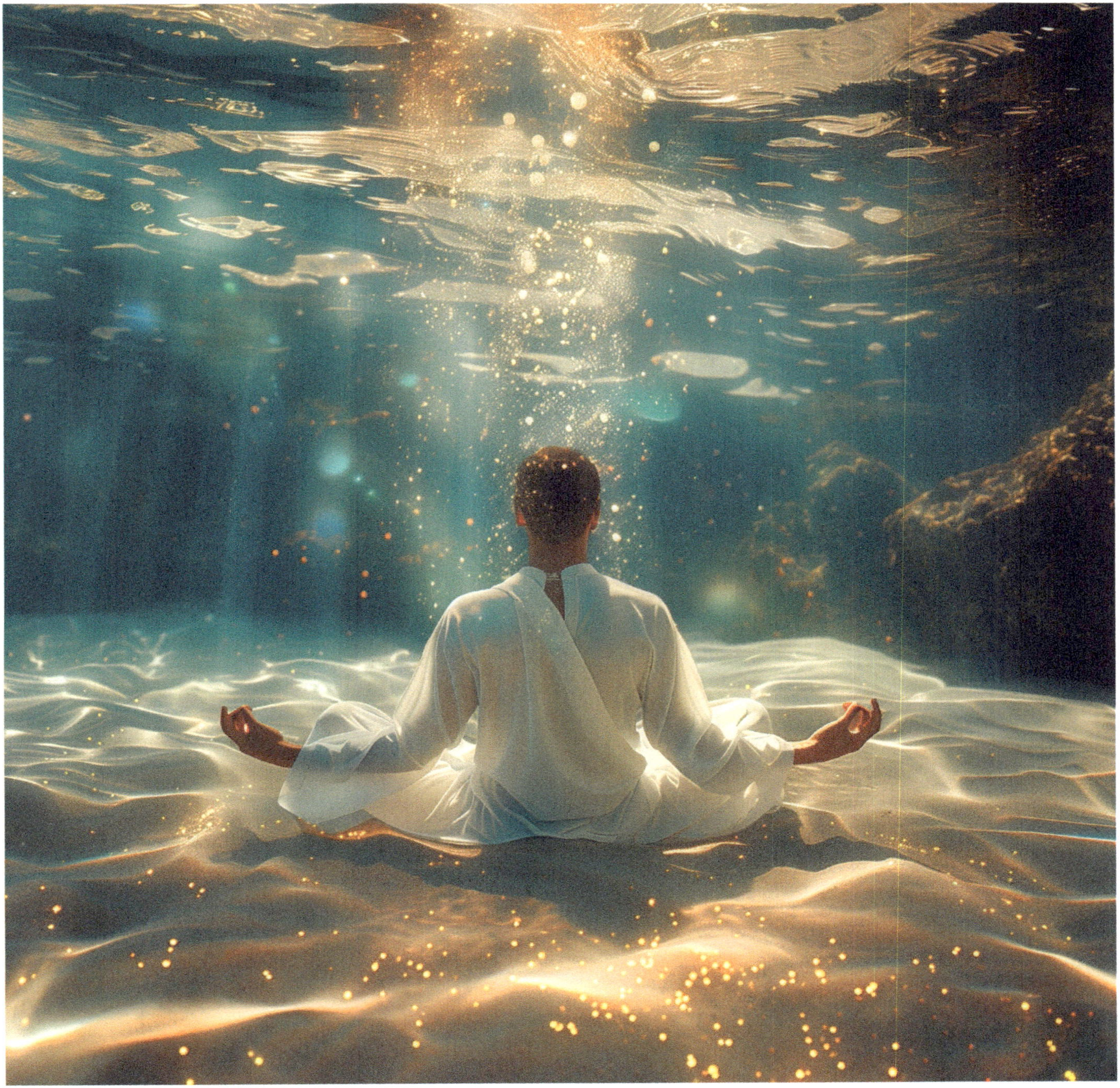

These armies of impurities can also look repulsive and abnormal like spider type creatures.

These are the coarse impurities. As the meditator digs deeper to new layers these impurities (kilesa) take on different forms.

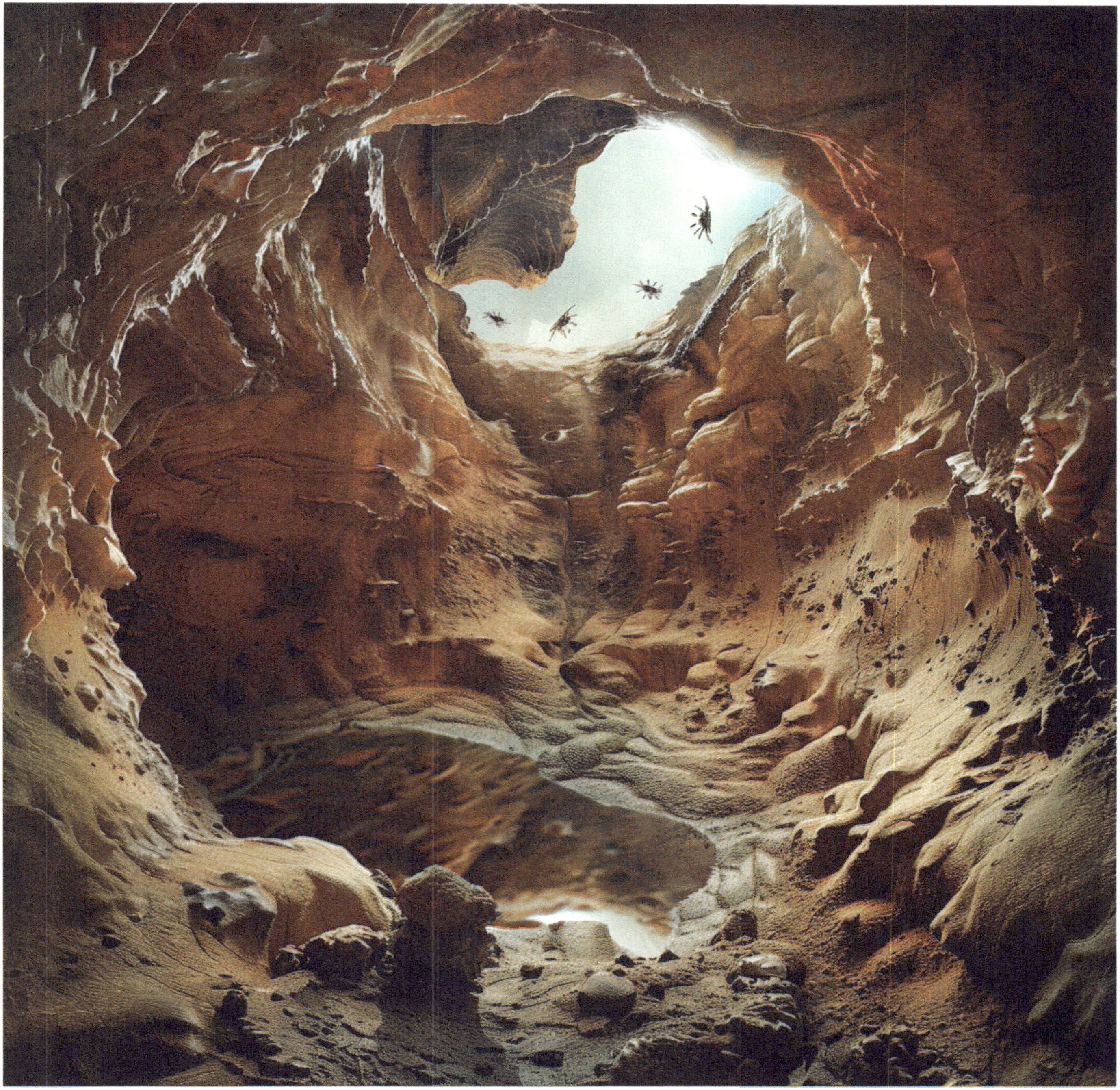

As the Mind breaks through deeper layers and digs deep into the caverns of the Mind.

We can see the impurities as reptiles: snakes, alligators, lizards and more.

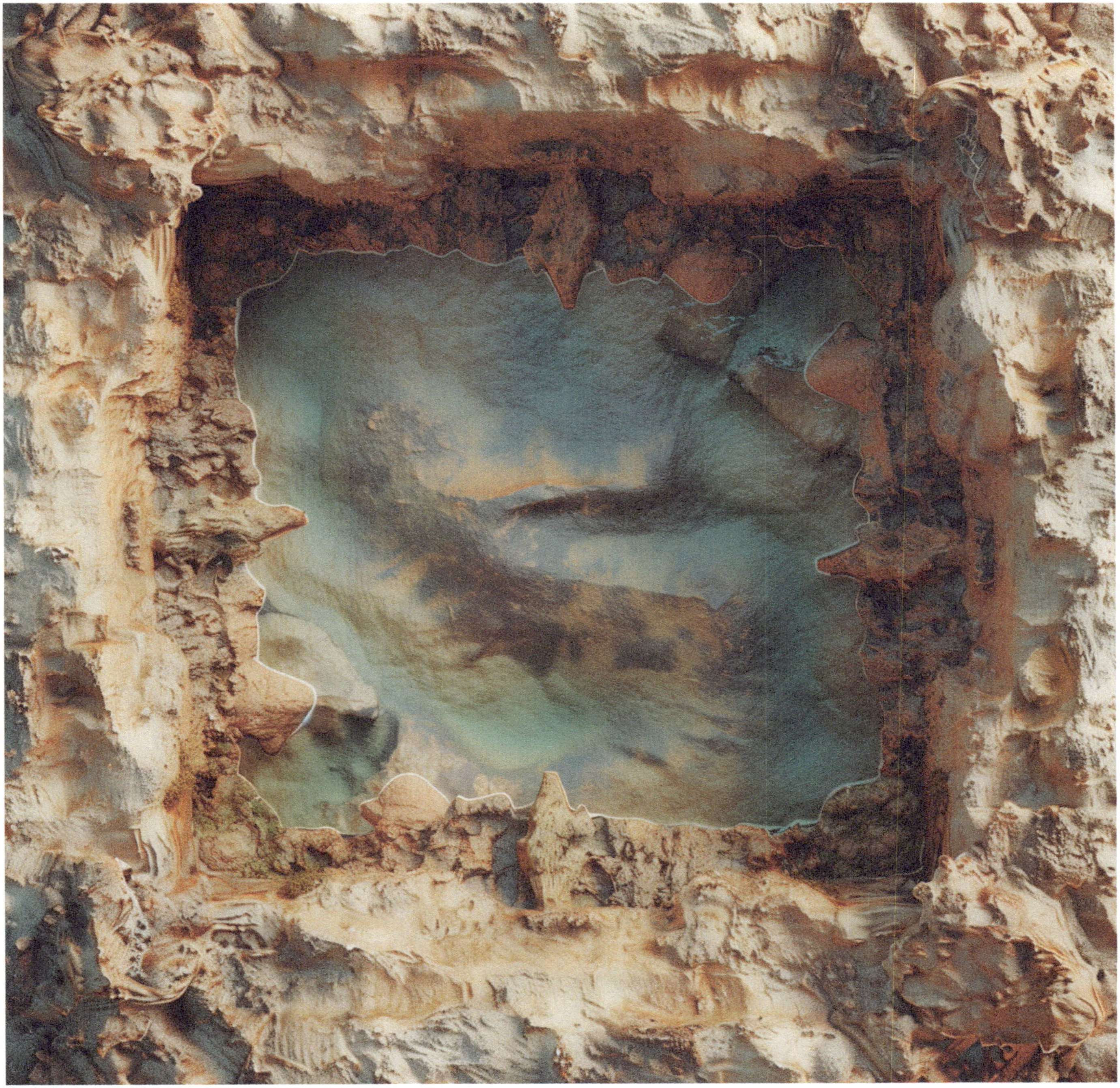

Under the sea, these impurity forces can manifest as fish or othere sea creatures.

Burning these impurities (Kilesa) in the form of sea creatures beneath the water may seem impossible, since Fire does not burn under the water. However, the meditator with a powerful and concentrated Mind, can destroy these impurities through stillness, focusing their concentration, the heat becomes so great that the ocean water itself starts, to boil and the impurities are thus destroyed.

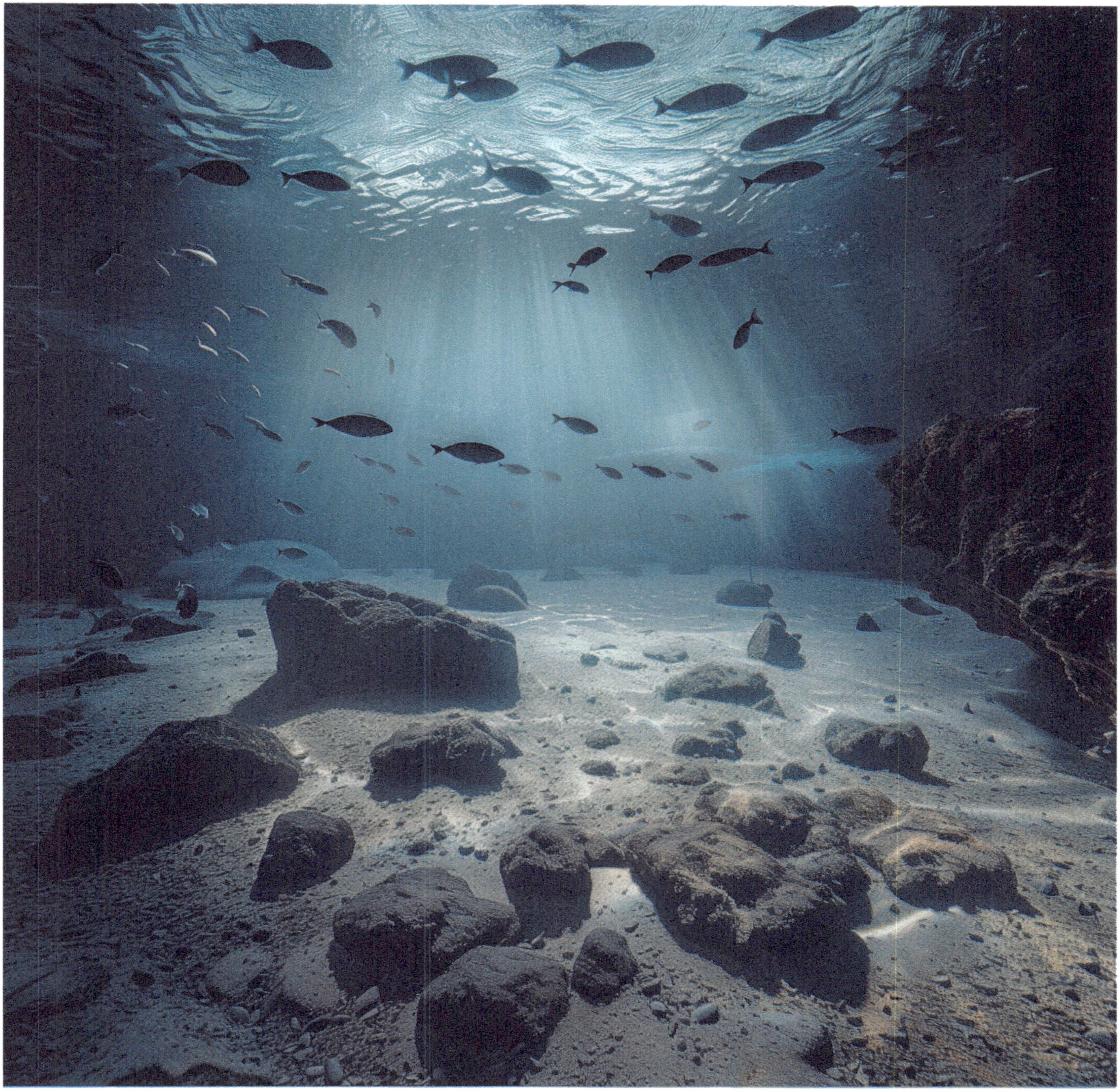

CHAPTER 16

HOUSEBUILDERS

(TECHO VIPASSANA MEDITATION EXPERIENCES)

The Buddha said:

"Through the rounds of many births I roamed without reward, without rest, seeking the housebuilder. Painful is birth again & again. Housebuilder, you're seen! You will not build a house again. All your rafters broken, the ridge pole destroyed, gone to the unformed, the Mind has come to the end of craving." — Dhp 153-4

The quote is from the Dhammapada, specifically verses 153-154. The Dhammapada is a collection of sayings of the Buddha in verse form and is considered one of the most widely read and studied Buddhist scriptures.

What was the Buddha talking about?

It is interesting to read the interpretations of the Buddha's quote, by scholars and discussions on the internet. Many interpret the Buddha's words based on their conventional truths and conventional vocabulary. It is akin to a blind man interpreting or describing a picture he is not able to see.

However, for Meditators who regularly see the impurity forces during meditation, it is simple to understand what the Buddha meant. We see the Housebuilders and the homes they build inside our Minds. And we understand how we have been caught up in endless cycles of rebirth.

"We know the game and where you hide and how to stop you Housebuilders."

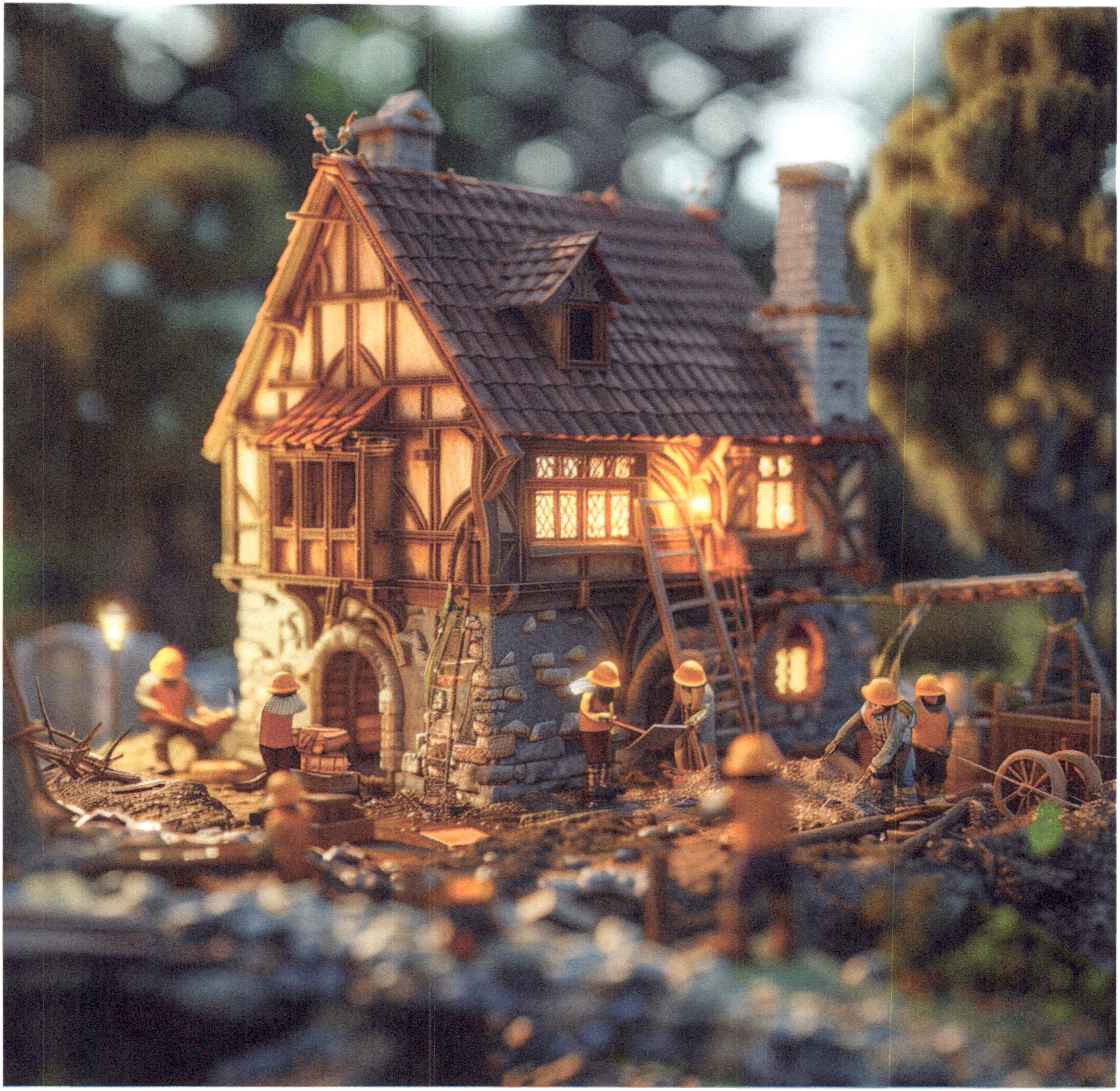

The impurities build houses and entire villages, cities and an entire World, similar to what we would see in our outside World. But they are using our bodies and Minds to construct their realms, and like parasites they do not belong inside us and cause us harm.

Killing House-Builders (Kilesa) is the one killing, that the Buddha approved of.

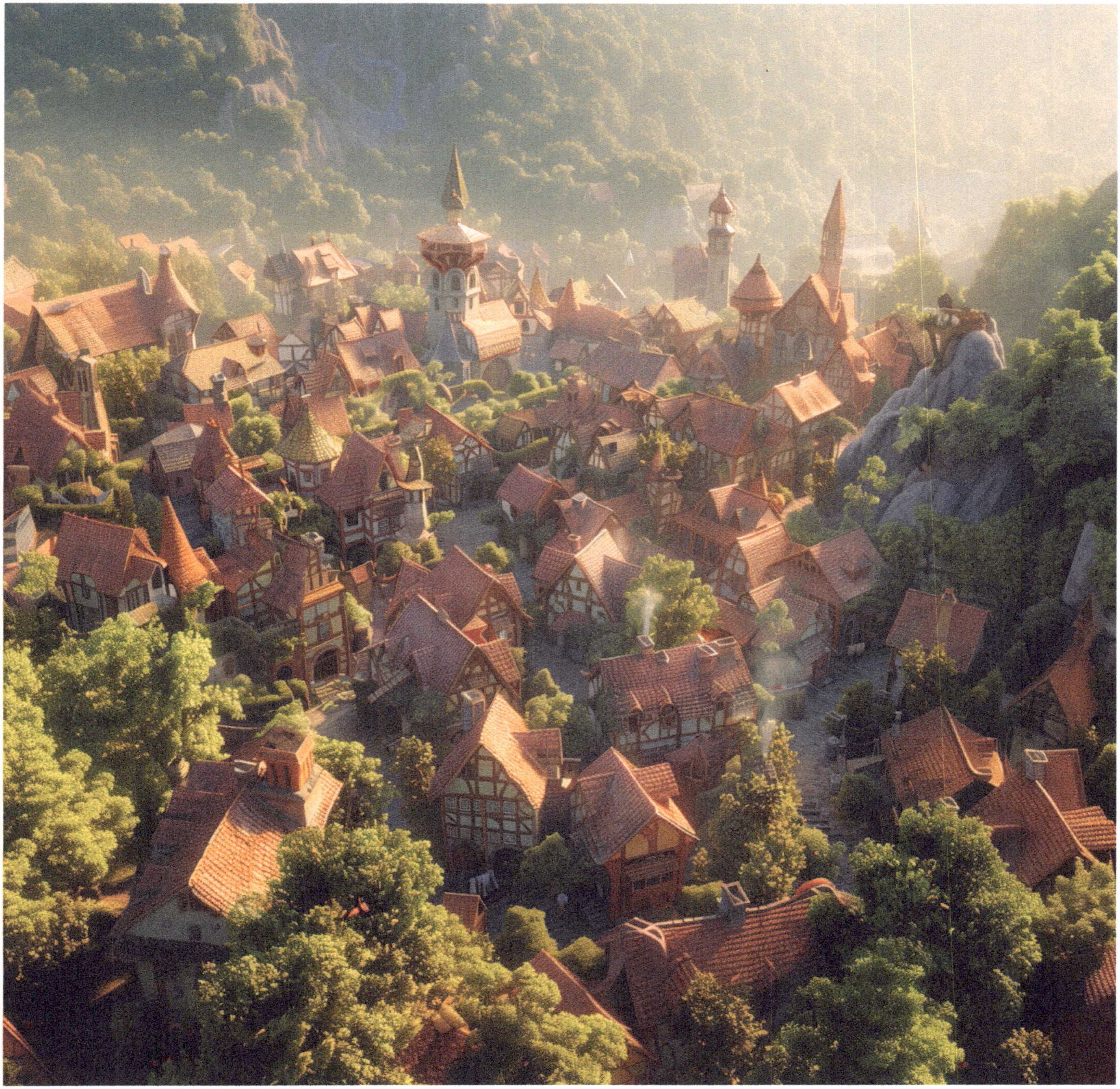

The Techo Vipassana meditator has a duty to practice and in the process to destroy these houses and villages through the intense heat created by the Techo Vipassana fire, using the body's fire element to ignite this fire.

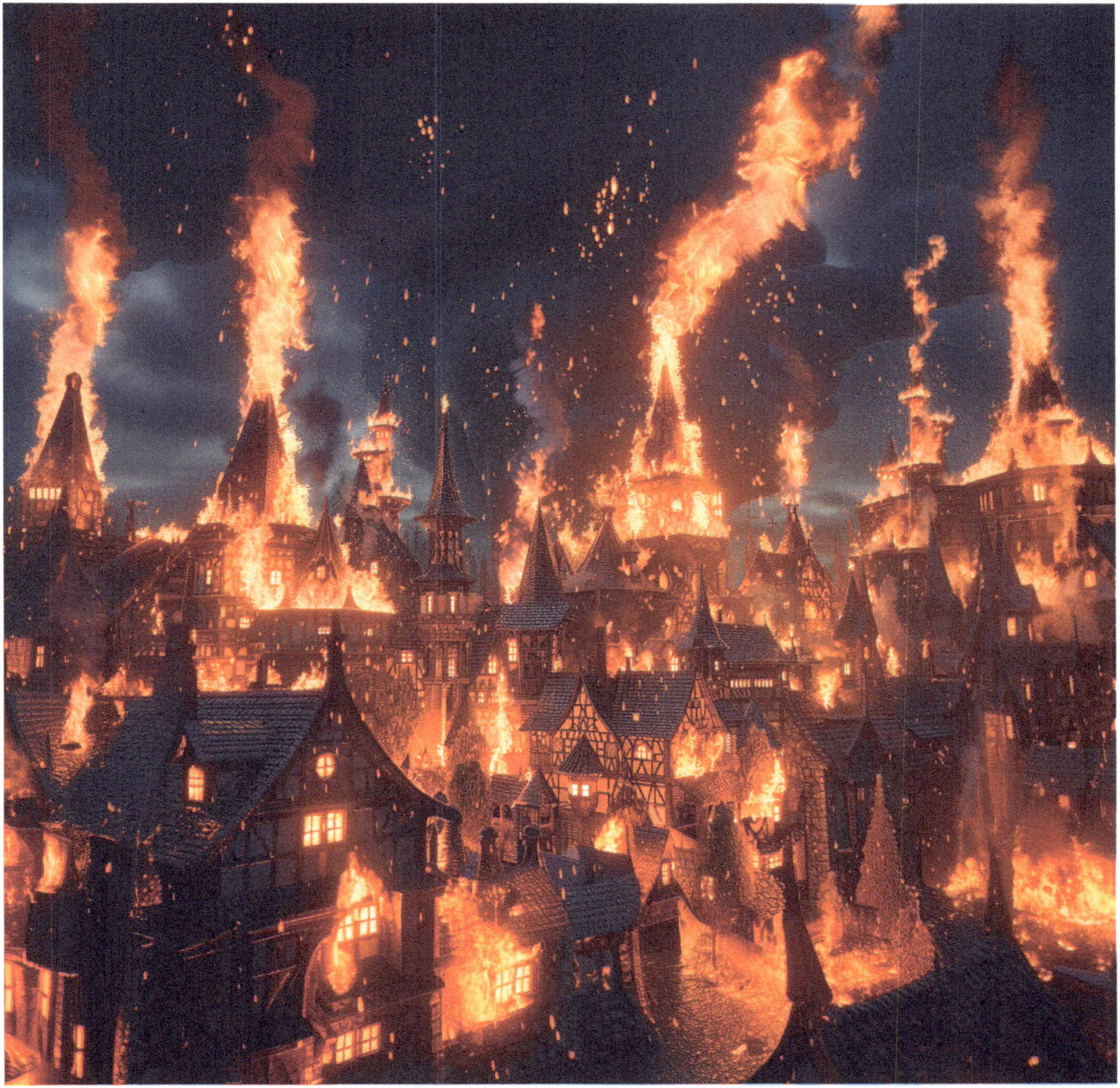

For those new to the path of Dhamma and Techo Vipassana meditation, it can be challenging to believe the notion of having had countless past lives. There are even many scholars' experts on the teaching of the Buddha, that do not themselves believe in reincarnation. This is understandable, as they have not seen their past lives for themselves.

Doubts often arise about whether a compassionate higher power could condemn us to an endless cycle of rebirth. Yet, this is the truth the Buddha himself uncovered and countless Masters and practitioners have confirmed, through their own experiences.

Throughout history, Venerable Masters and Monks have documented and shared these truths. However, as the Buddha observed, not everyone can immediately grasp or accept these Truths.
Buddha's invitation has always been "don't take my word for it…. explore through meditation and discover the truth yourself".

We've inhabited myriad forms across countless lifetimes— man, woman, animal, reptiles, insects, even beings beyond our dimension. Initially, the concept of countless reincarnations may seem daunting. I, too, grappled with this idea during my early practice of Vipassana meditation, but then in time I saw for myself.

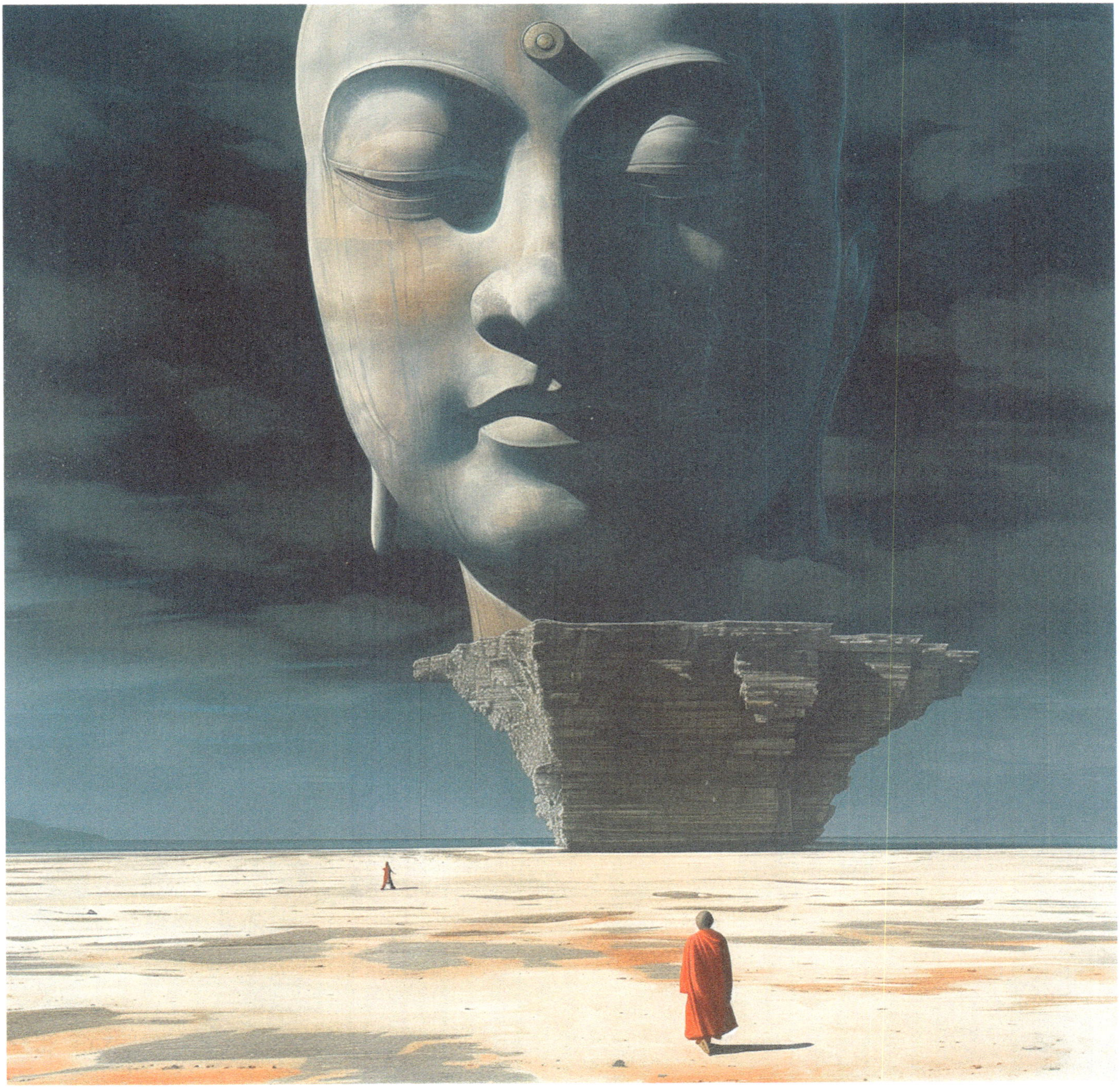

CHAPTER. 17

PAST LIVES REINCARNATION

(TECHO VIPASSANA MEDITATION EXPERIENCES)

327

Upon hearing that we've travelled across endless lifetimes, I wrestled with the notion. As I practiced and Saw past lives, at first, I found it exhilarating and I yearned to see more past lives. But the more past lives I saw, the more I began to realize that each lifetime brought with it painful memories and deep suffering. Each lifetime etched its mark in the depths of my subconscious (Sangkara), the weight and scars and karma of those lives, following me into the next lifetime.

As I reflect on some of my past lives, including those where I occupied prominent positions, my aim is to provide insight does not boast of grandeur or accomplishments. Each of these lifetimes, despite any outward sign of achievement, was marked by profound suffering and a myriad of emotions. Most significantly, I acknowledge that in each of these incarnations, I failed to break free from the cycle of rebirth. Even in a lifetime where I encountered the Buddha himself and had the greatest opportunity for liberation, I faltered, was too busy to meditate and took the opportunity for granted.

Today when I practice, rather than chasing visions of the past, I approach meditation with equanimity and seek stillness. The Buddha warned against craving visions, recognizing visions have the potential to distract and disturb the Mind. Instead, now I simply observe, acknowledging each, memory, sound, taste, emotions that arises by just knowing it. I simply allow all conditions to arise, and I let go, and do not attach to any of it.

The images of my past lives are a testament to the transformative power of meditation in uncovering the profound truths of existence and wish my experiences simply inspire others to look for themselves.

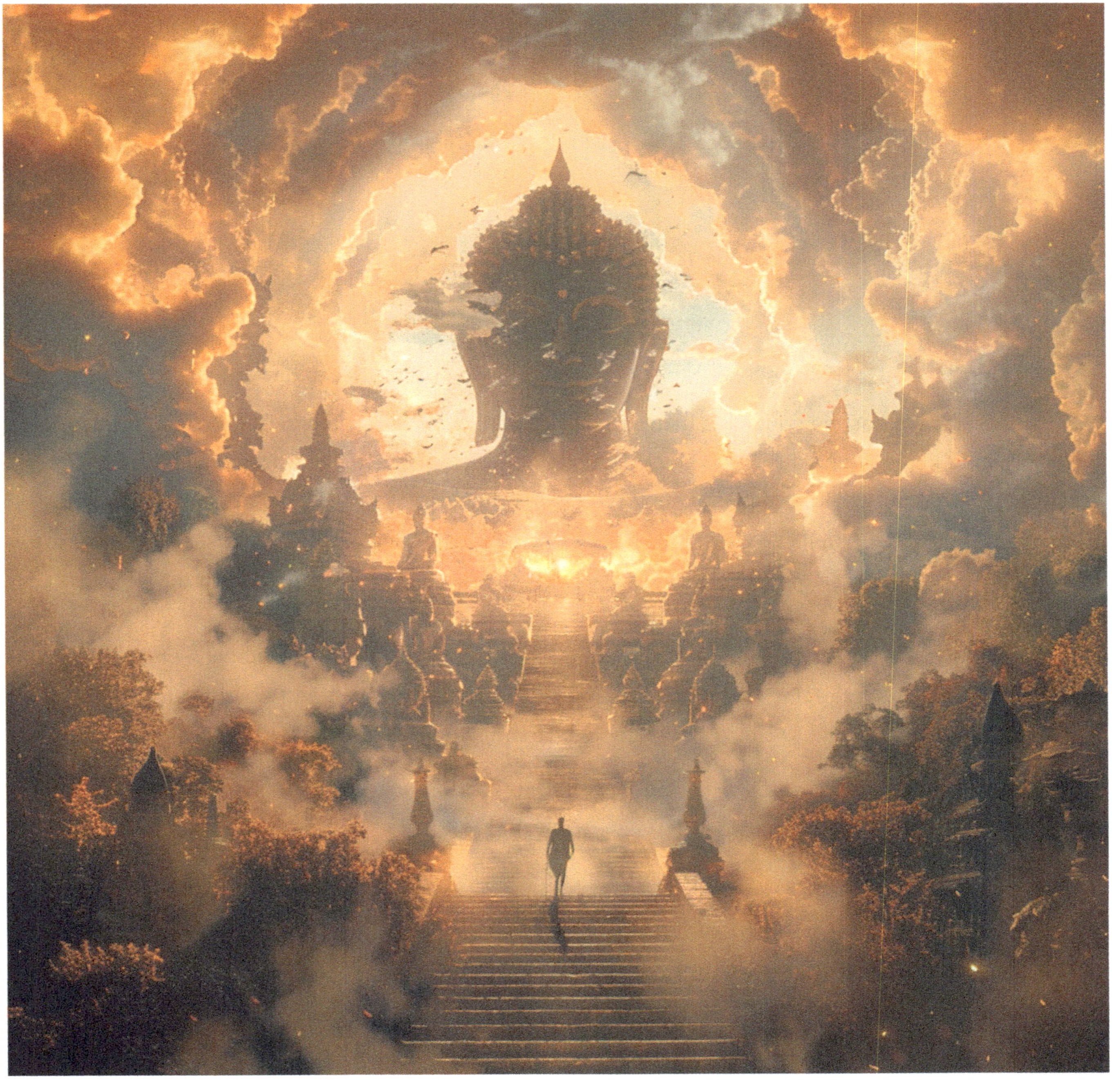

In a past life, I served as the right hand man to the head of the Samurai warriors. During the Samurai era, we honed our character and cultivated great virtues through adherence to the Bushido code, which emphasized strength, loyalty, and honor above all else. As Samurai, we were prepared to lay down our lives without hesitation in defense of our honor and principles. Our training instilled in us the swift and decisive skill of drawing our swords and dispatching our enemies with unwavering resolve.

Yet, amidst the rigors of combat and discipline, we also devoted ourselves to the practice of meditation and Zen Buddhism. Through these spiritual pursuits, we sought inner peace and enlightenment, striving to harmonize our warrior ethos with a deeper understanding of the self and the universe.

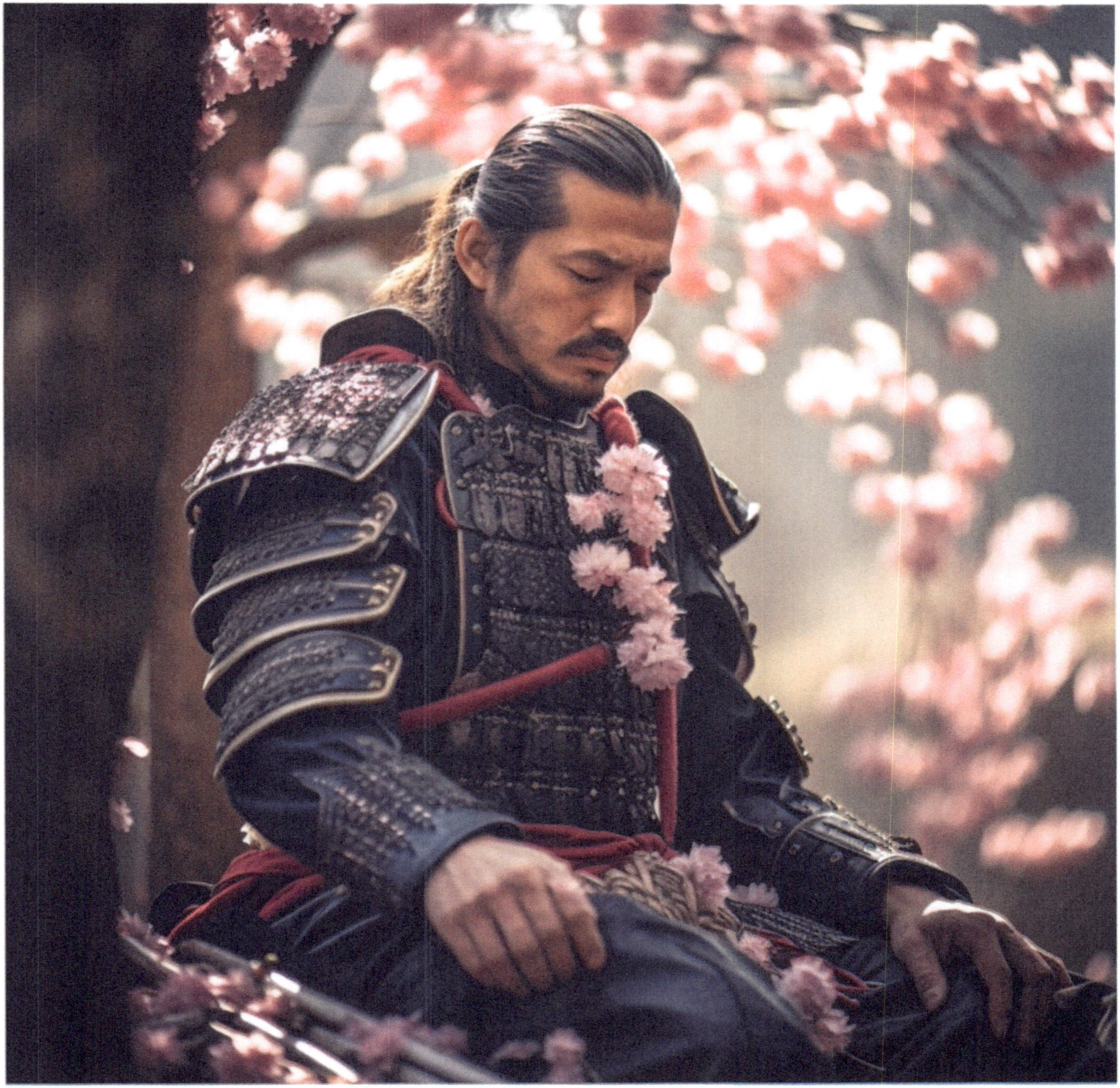

In a previous life, I found myself as a prehistoric Tiger, prowling along a well-trodden trail. Surprisingly, my mind was conscious, brimming with lucid thoughts that defied the expectation of an animal devoid of conscious awareness. However, when I detected the presence of prey nearby, a profound shift occurred. In an instant, my thoughts were silenced, and my primal instincts surged forth, driven by the ancient impulses encoded within my DNA. In that moment, I transformed into a relentless predator, wholly consumed by the instinctual drive to hunt and claim life as sustenance.

333

When I first tried to teach myself meditation from the internet out of the blue I had a vision of sitting in the Himalayian mountains with 2 other monks looking into the distance. This was such an exciting real image like I was really there. But as I reacted the vision just disappeared. At that time I had no training and did not know what it meant. I craved other visions but they did not come, until I became a student of the Master.

The following are some of the past lives I have experienced, just to show the reader what that is like. However, for me at this stage these memories are not interesting and remind me of painful existences in the endless cycle of rebirth

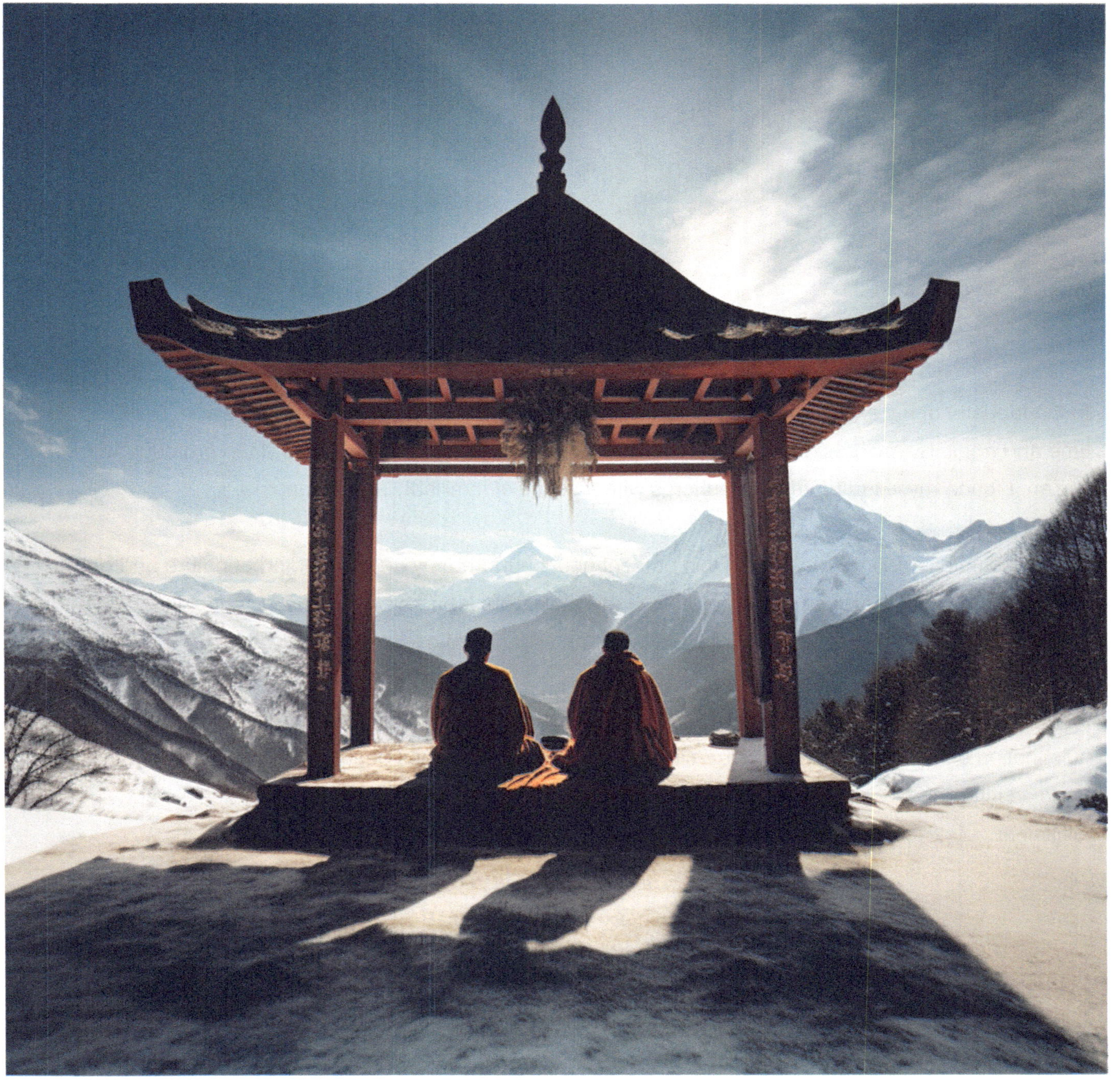

In the tapestry of my existence, Japan has woven its threads across more than one lifetime. Drawn back time and again by my deep affection for Japan, its serene natural landscapes, and the profound wisdom of Zen, I found myself returning to its shores with a sense of familiarity and belonging.

Across countless lifetimes, including this present one, I nurtured my understanding of nature and delved into the teachings of Buddha. Each iteration of my journey in Japan brought new insights, enriching my spiritual growth and deepening my connection to the essence of existence.

Now, in the embrace of this current life, I am enveloped by a profound peace—a tranquility born from the culmination of my experiences and learnings. Japan, with its timeless beauty and spiritual depth, has been an integral part of shaping this inner serenity, guiding me toward a sense of wholeness and fulfillment.

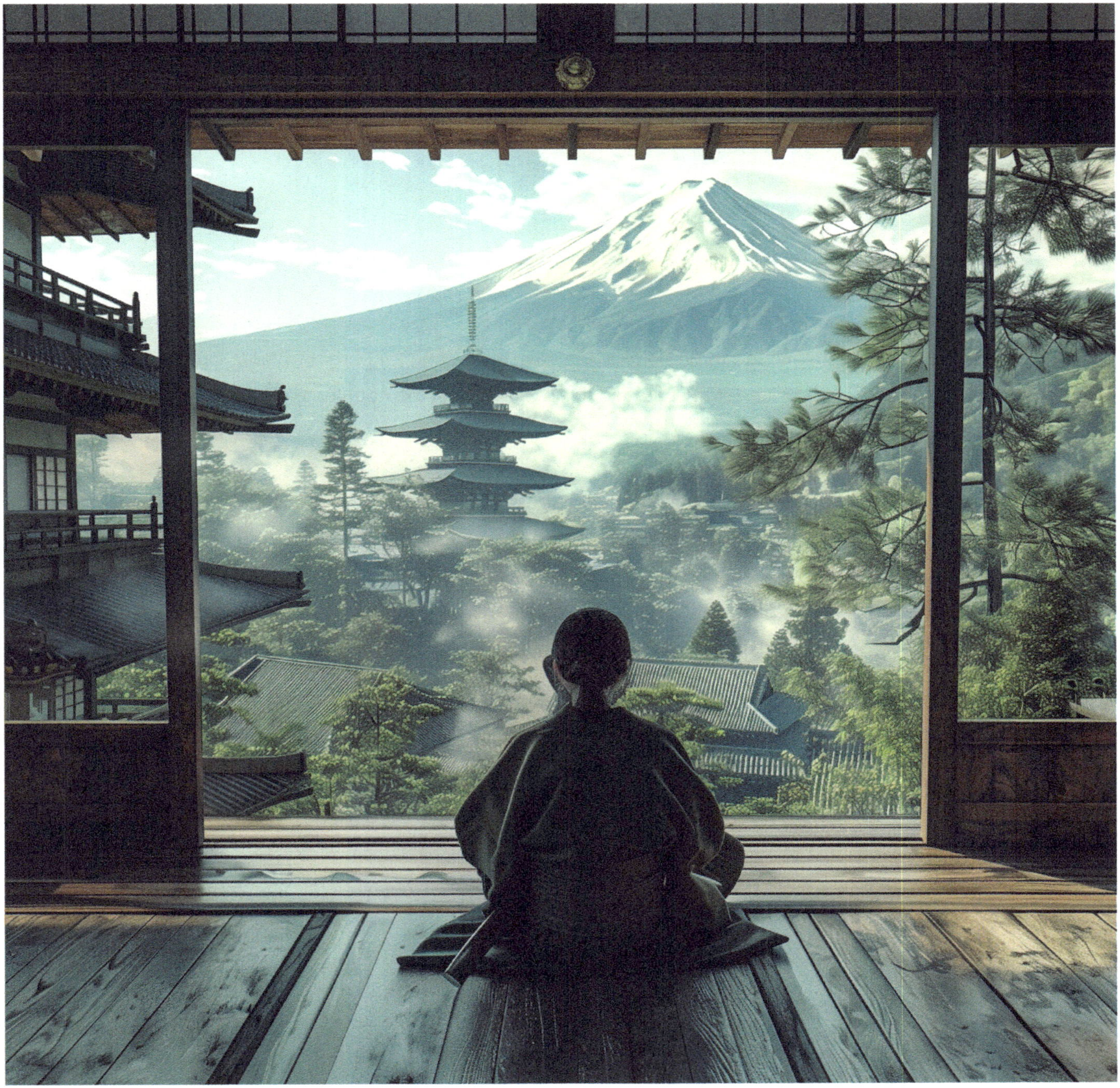

In one lifetime, I was fortunate enough to be born as the next inline to be Emperor of China. Once I would ascend to the throne, all of Asia would be under my rule and the vast riches of the country at my disposal, the loyalty of China would be mine to command.

However, my reign was cut short by a sinister plot orchestrated by a treacherous family member. While I played a young boy innocently on the steep steps of the summer palace hanging gardens, my younger brother, influenced by our relative, callously pushed me down the stairs, leading to my untimely demise. With my death, he ascended to the throne, living a life of luxury and excess, constantly plotting to eliminate any potential threats to his power.

339

In one lifetime, I rose as a formidable Arabian conqueror, expanding my dominion from the Middle East into the depths of Asia. Driven by a thirst for vengeance against China and all who I believed had wronged me in my past life, as the young emperor to be, I showed no mercy in my quest for power and wealth.

Ironically, my closest ally in this life of conquest was none other than the Chinese brother who had caused my death in that previous existence. It is a testament to the unpredictable nature of karma—a force that operates in mysterious ways, beyond our comprehension.

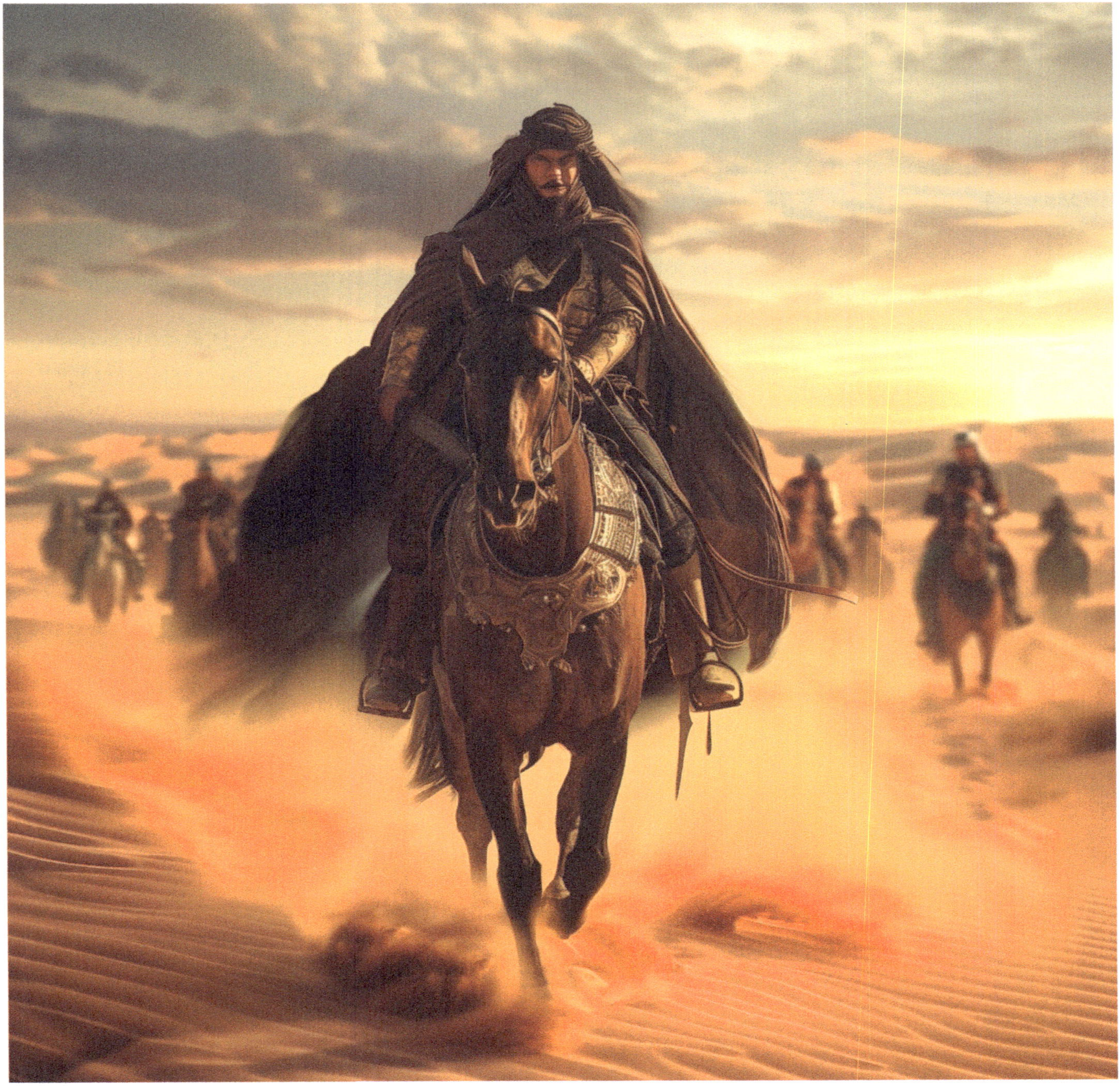

In another lifetime, I was born in Thailand and dedicated myself to the practice of meditation and the teachings of Buddha. Once again, I sought solitude in a cave, spending days immersed in deep meditation. However, despite my earnest efforts, my life was tragically cut short and I died young, due to the consequences of past life karma.

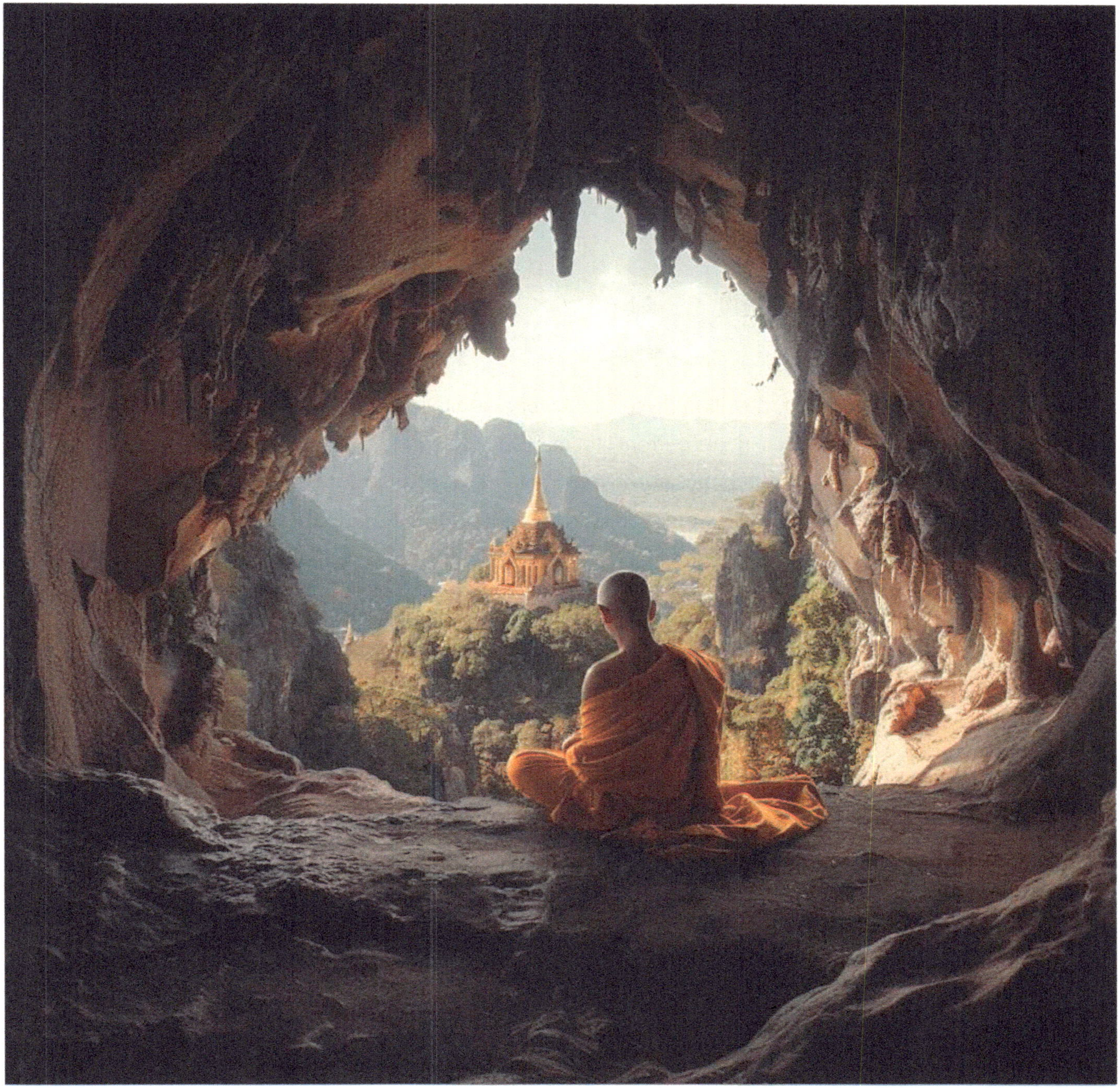

In a past life, I lived as a hermit, devoting myself to solitary meditation in a cave. This experience greatly influenced my meditation abilities in this current lifetime. Despite spending countless hours each day in meditation for many years, I did not achieve enlightenment. My lack of progress was due to my insufficient cultivation of virtues and my failure to engage in acts of merit or goodness towards others. Additionally, I carried a heavy burden of karma from previous lifetimes, which hindered my spiritual advancement.

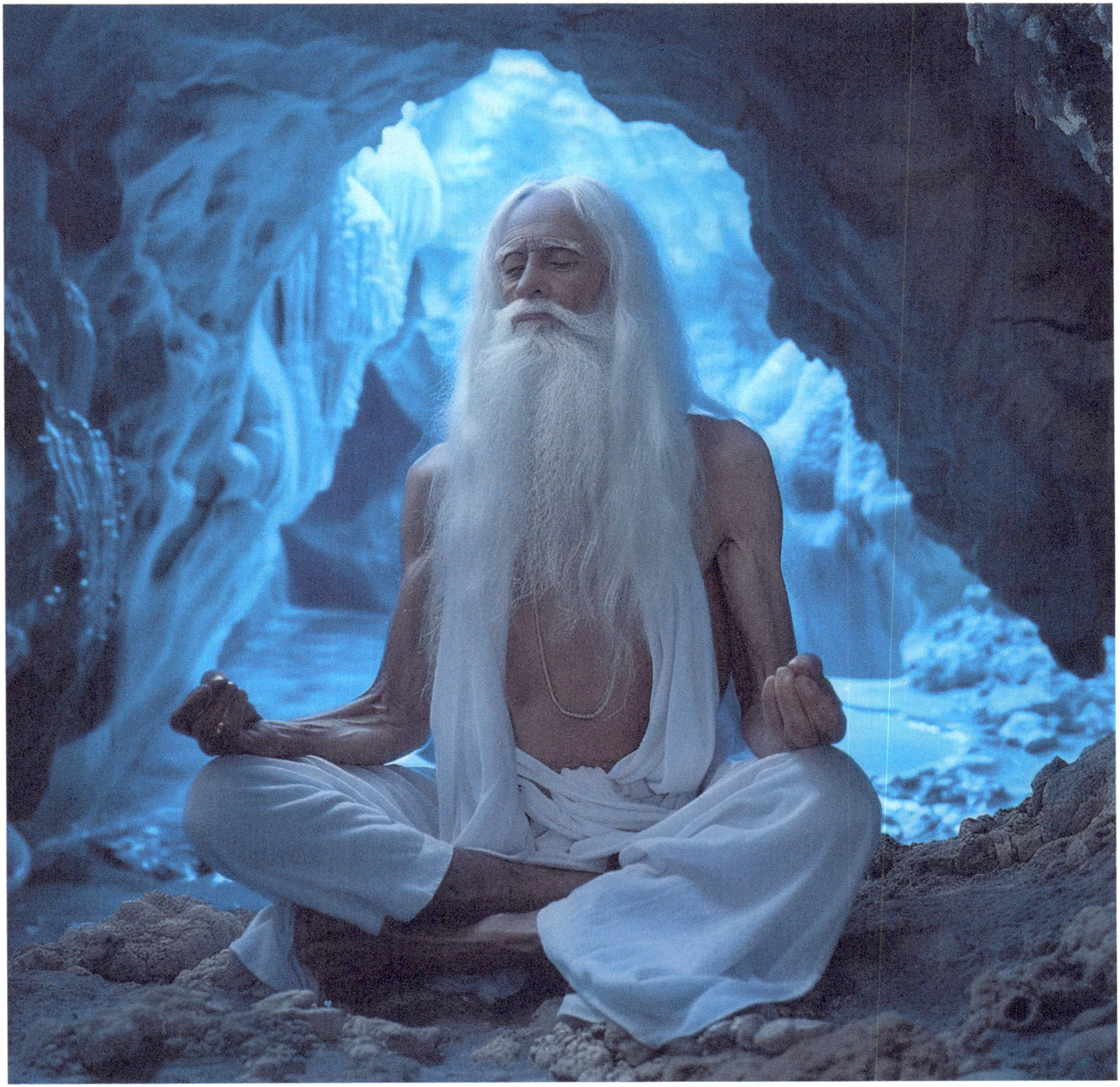

In a previous life, I held the position of a powerful governor, blessed with a sharp mind capable of visualizing and processing multiple strategies simultaneously. This served as a testament to the immense power inherent within the human mind.

Our mental capabilities are often constrained by the limitations of our physical bodies and the impurities that obscure our wisdom and connection to higher knowledge. Throughout our existence, our minds have accumulated impurities, and the influence of karma further hinder our abilities.

The conditioning we receive as we navigate through different lifetimes can instill beliefs of limitation within us. In today's world, especially with the dominance of technology and the pervasive influence of societal norms, we may feel diminished in our sense of power.

Yet, through the practice of meditation and the purification of the mind, we can tap into profound wisdom and knowledge. The truth remains that our minds possess immense power. Through the transformative practice of Techno Vipassana Fire, we unlock the limitless potential of our Mind Power.

With our minds as our most potent tool, we hold the capacity to shape the world around us and manifest our deepest desires.

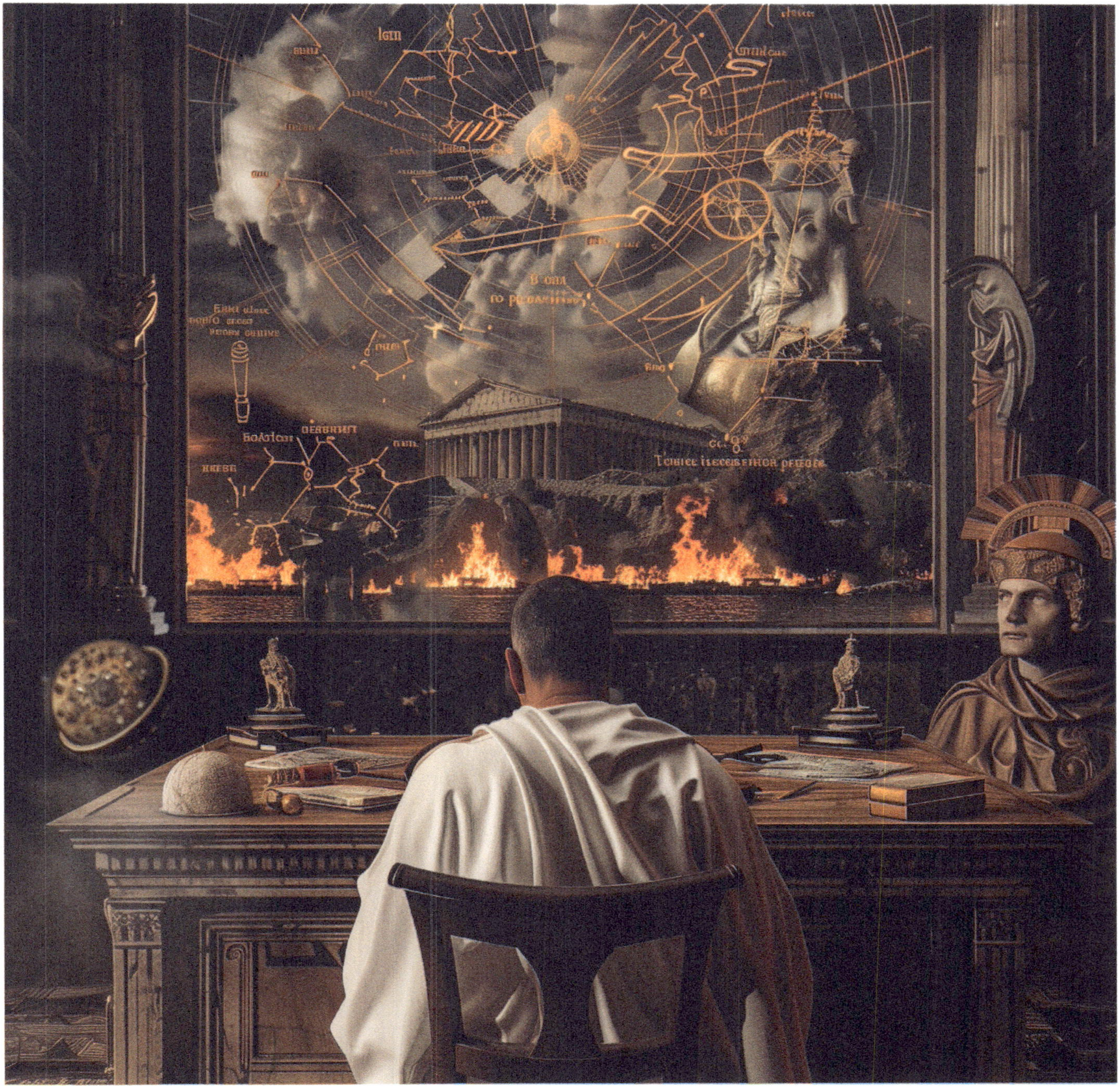

Whether or not one believes in dragons, they remain iconic figures often associated with myth and folklore. Yet, during one of my profound meditation sessions, I experienced a vivid vision of myself as a knight, wearing armor adorned with large metal scales reminiscent of those found on the back of a dragon. Mounted on a magnificent horse, I embarked on a quest to find and slay a dragon.

In that moment of deep meditation, I felt a profound connection to a past life where I had served as a fearless and valiant dragon slayer. This revelation provided a glimpse into a different realm of existence, where courage and bravery were paramount in confronting the mythical beasts that once roamed the land.

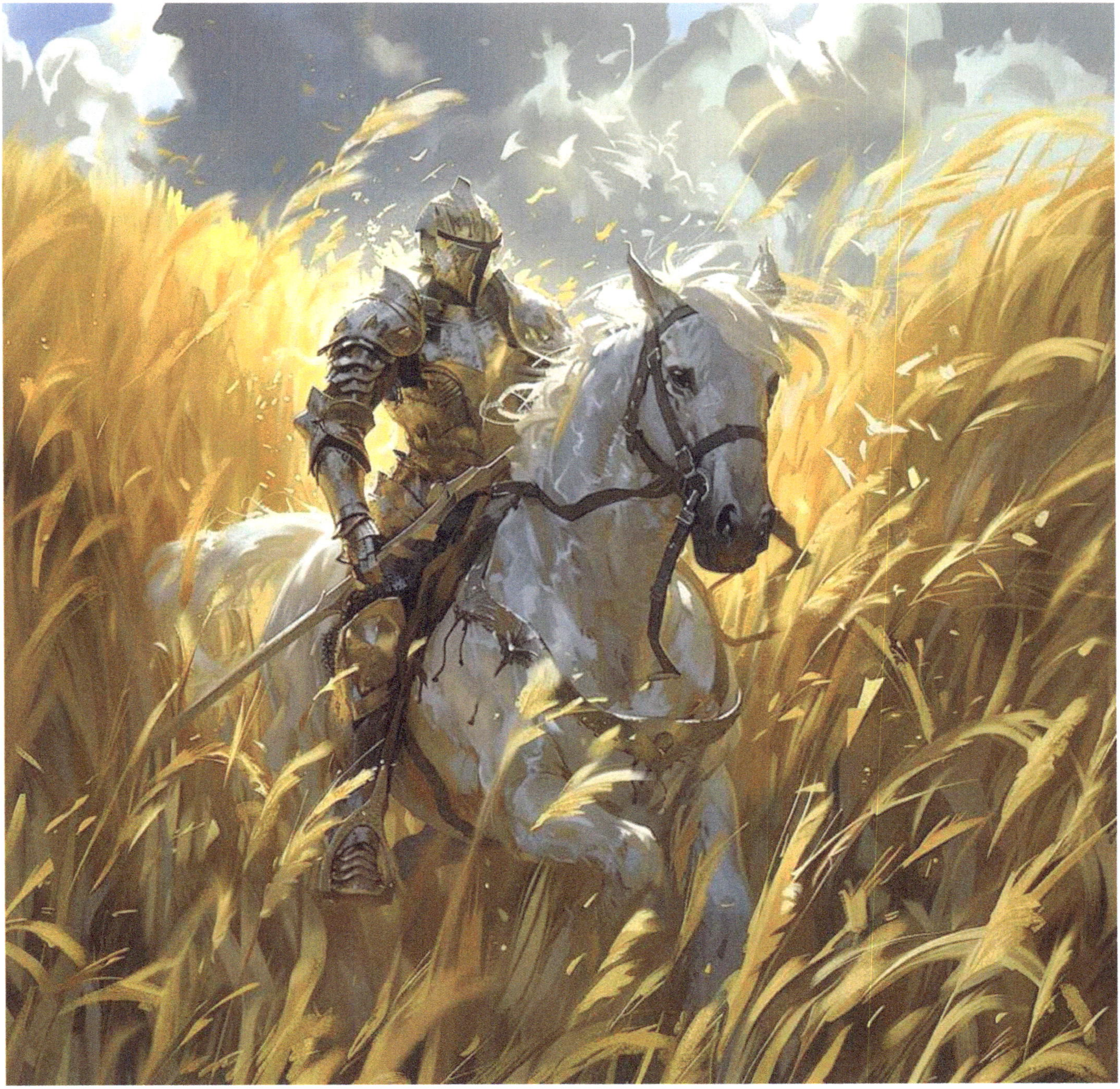

In a past life, I had the privilege of encountering the Buddha 2500 years ago when I lived as a wealthy nobleman. During that time, I generously offered alms and support to the Buddha, and most importantly, I made a heartfelt wish to transcend suffering and attain enlightenment.

Despite being in such close proximity to the Buddha and his teachings, it may seem puzzling that I did not achieve any spiritual enlightenment or noble attainments during that lifetime. However, it simply wasn't my time. Additionally, I failed to prioritize serious meditation practice amidst the duties and indulgences of my noble lifestyle. The opulence and luxury of my societal position in ancient India did little to encourage the rigorous spiritual practice necessary to break free from the cycle of suffering.

In contrast, there existed a snake in this lifetime whose intense rage and thirst for revenge led to its rebirth as a reptile. This snake, drawn to the teachings of the Buddha, would stealthily listen to the vibrations of his Dhamma while hidden nearby. Similarly, the snake harbored a fervent wish to attain enlightenment and spread the teachings of Dhamma. In a remarkable turn of events, this snake has since been reborn as a revered high master in this lifetime.

This serves as a poignant reminder of how our emotional vibrations and intentions can profoundly influence our future rebirths, highlighting the intricate interplay between our actions, aspirations, and the trajectory of our spiritual evolution.

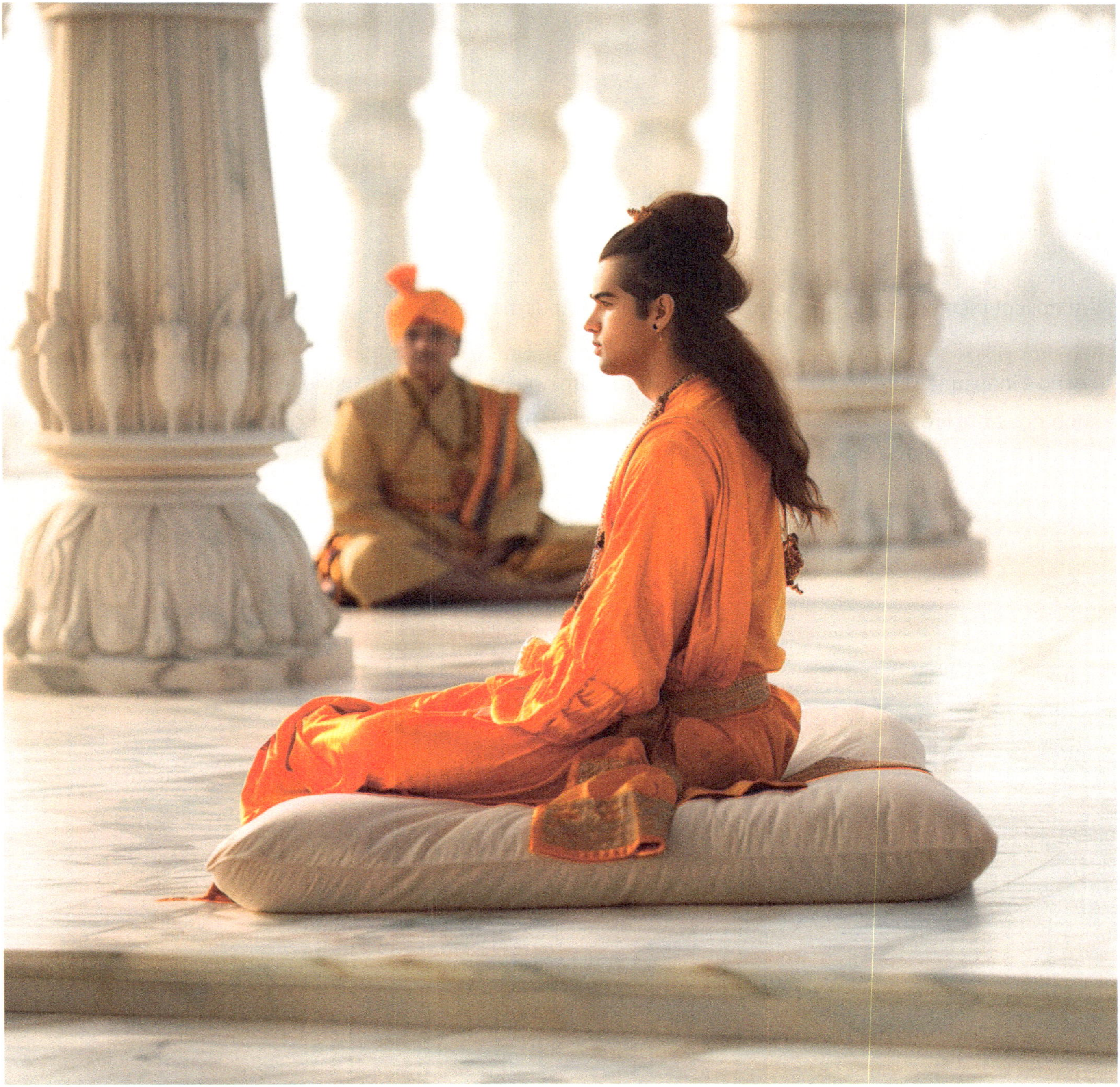

Each lifetime is another layer in our Minds.

We collect memories and imprint deep emotions into our mental data bases.

Techo Vipassana "Fire Meditation" is effective in burning away the layers in the Mind, because it uses such powerful fire, that even the Mara, (devil) fears the Techo fire, due to its enormous power.

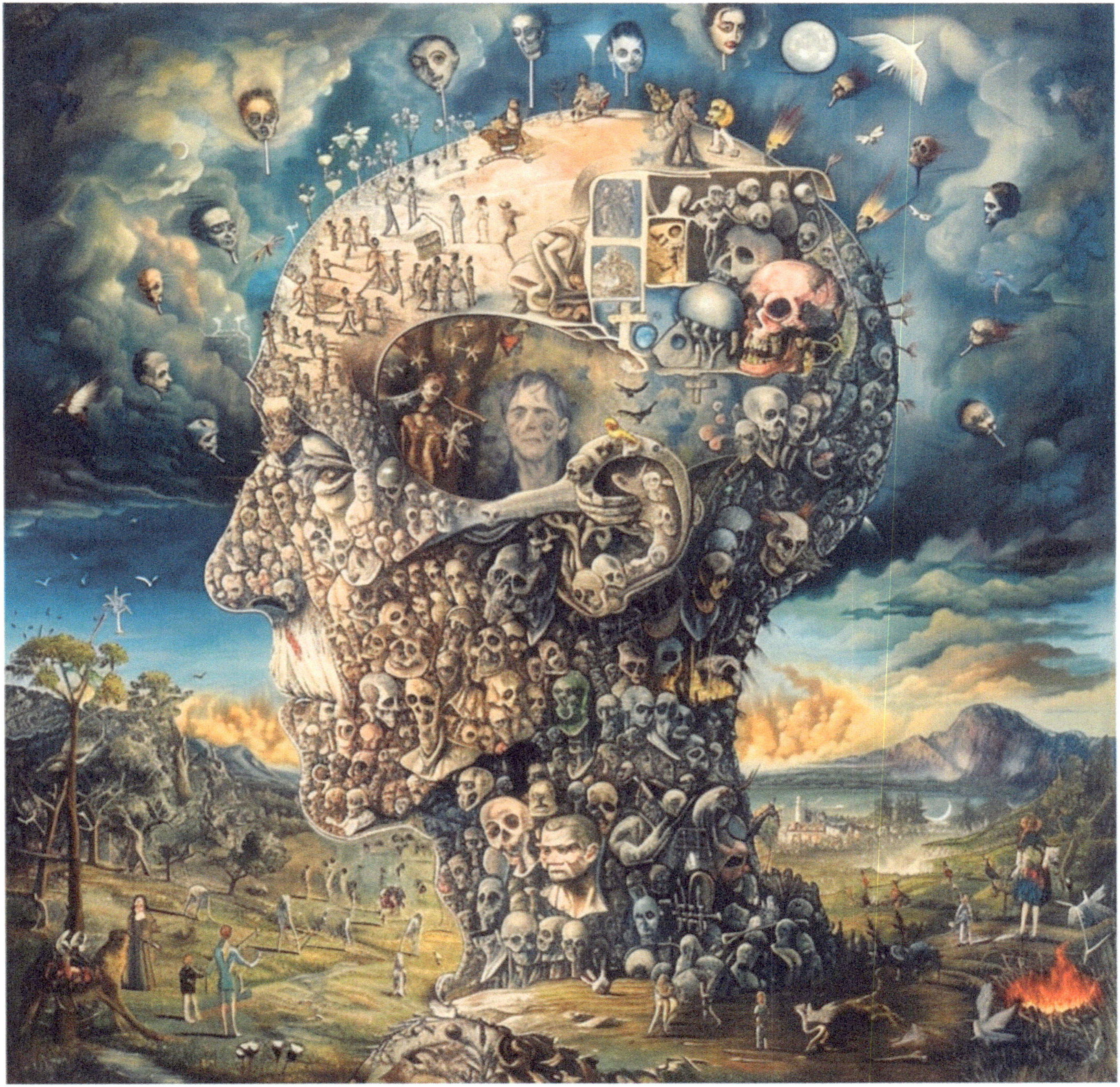

CHAPTER. 18

MIRACULOUS INSIGHTS

(TECHO VIPASSANA MEDITATION EXPERIENCES)

When practicing Techo Vipassana practitioners sit in neat rows on maroon cushions, in white outfits with the Master at the front of the meditation hall.

For those who have Supernatural abilities they see the Master in her Astral form sending beams of energy to the practitioners.

However, at the same time, also Mara (devil) sends her forces and magnetic waves to disrupt the energy flow. So, the Techo Vipassana meditation hall becomes a battlefield.

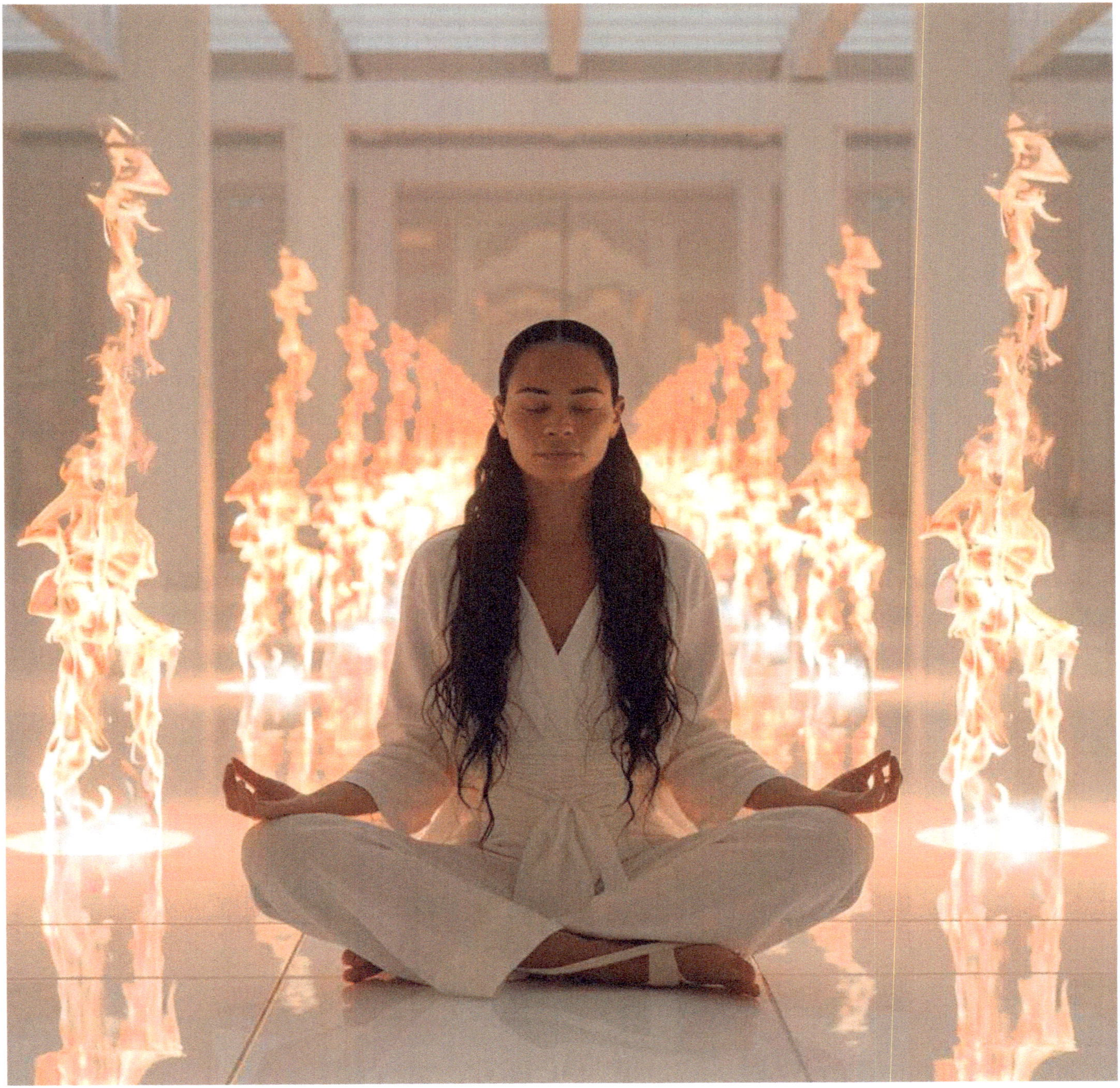

Techo Vipassana and the Master take practitioners into the dimension of Energy, where students can see for themselves, the impurity forces (Kilesa), past lives (Sangkara) and their own karma.

This meditation practice is miraculous and can be supernatural.

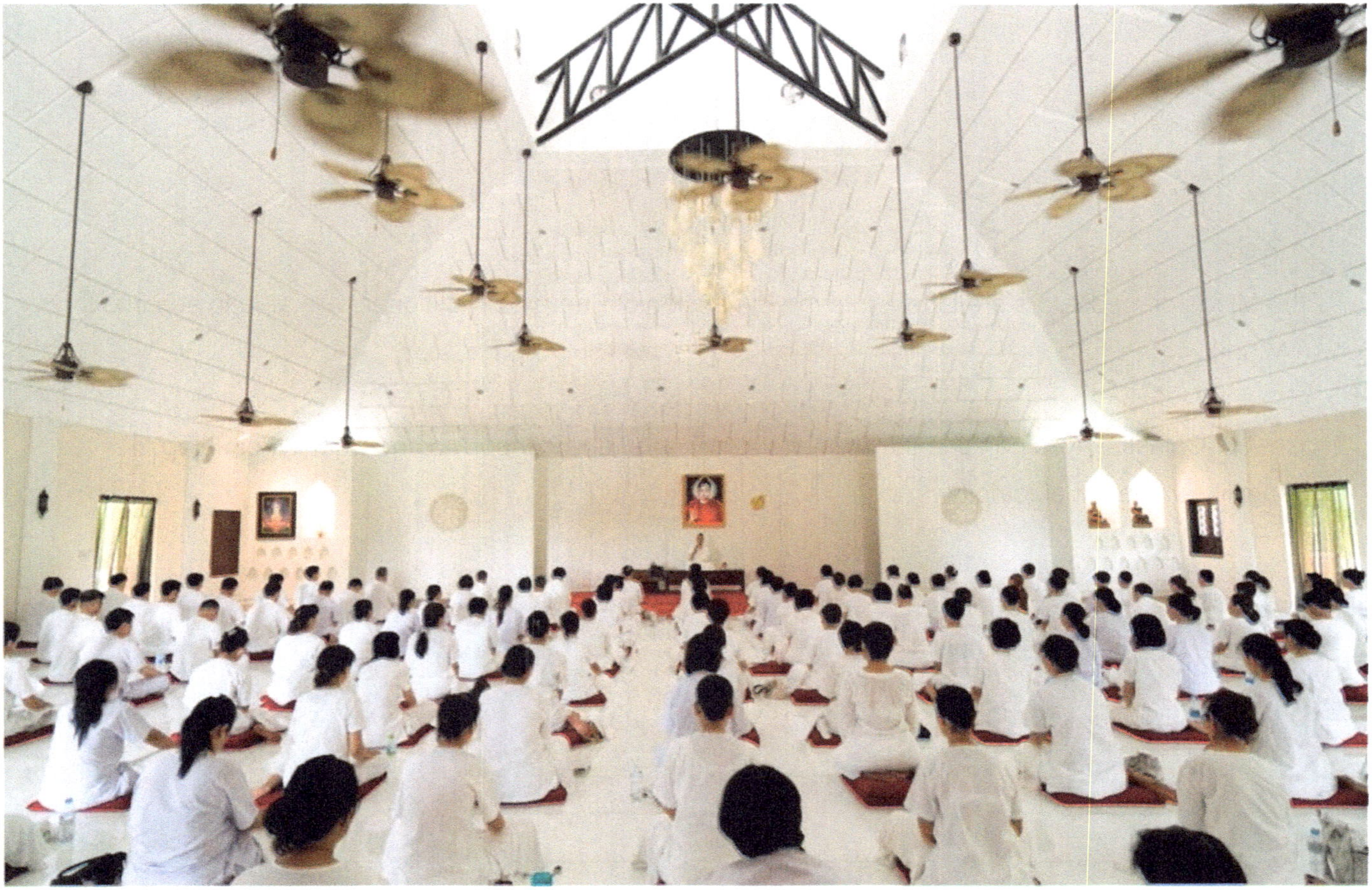

As the Minds of meditators are Lifted, into the dimension of Energy, practitioners are able to see into their own Minds.

Those with Celestial eyes can see the Master's astral body and her supporting Energy reaching to students like waves of electricity.

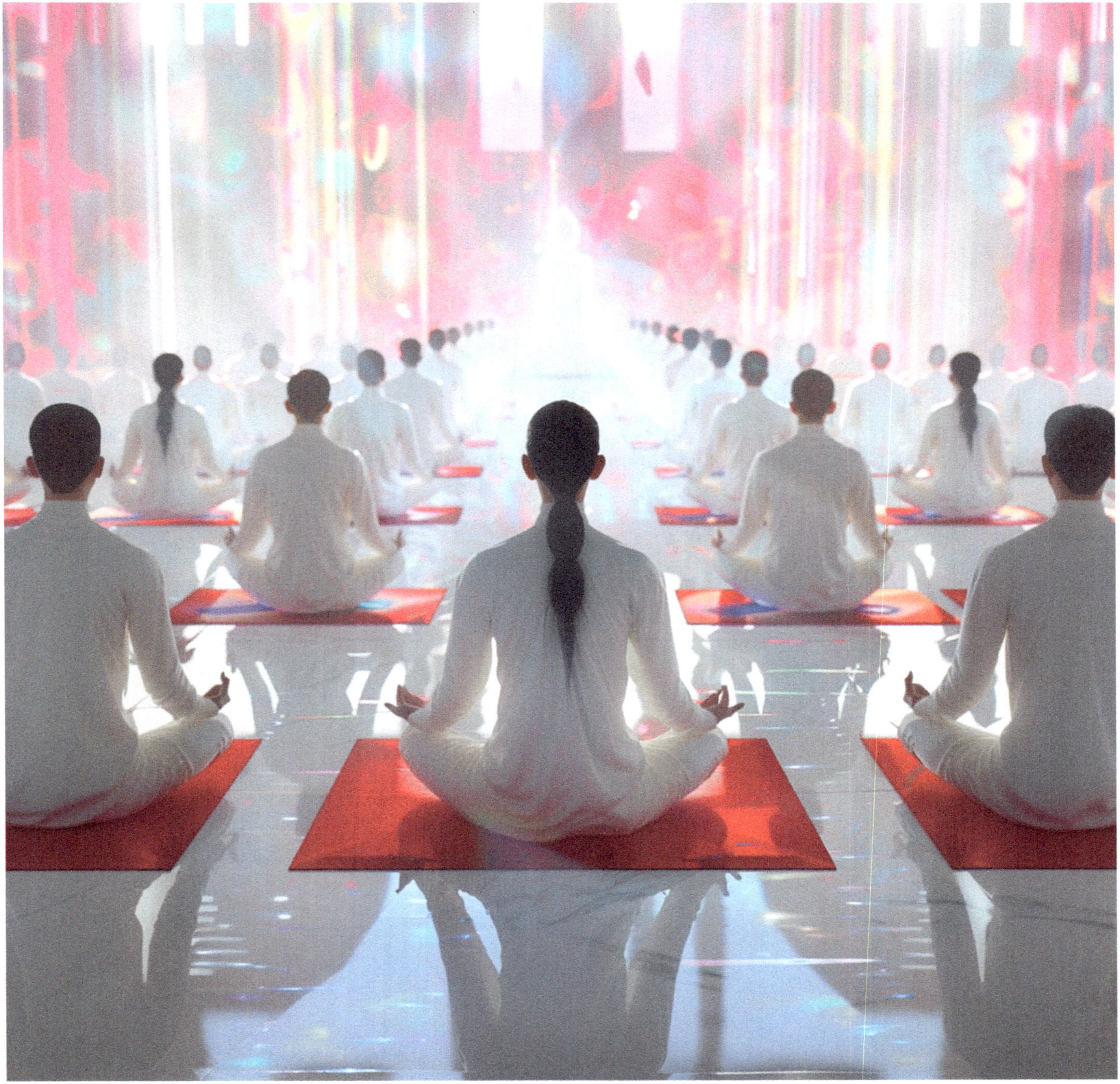

The pure Mind of the Enlightened Masters can manifest in amazing forms. I have seen the Master's mind as a giant cube with unusual symbols as code.

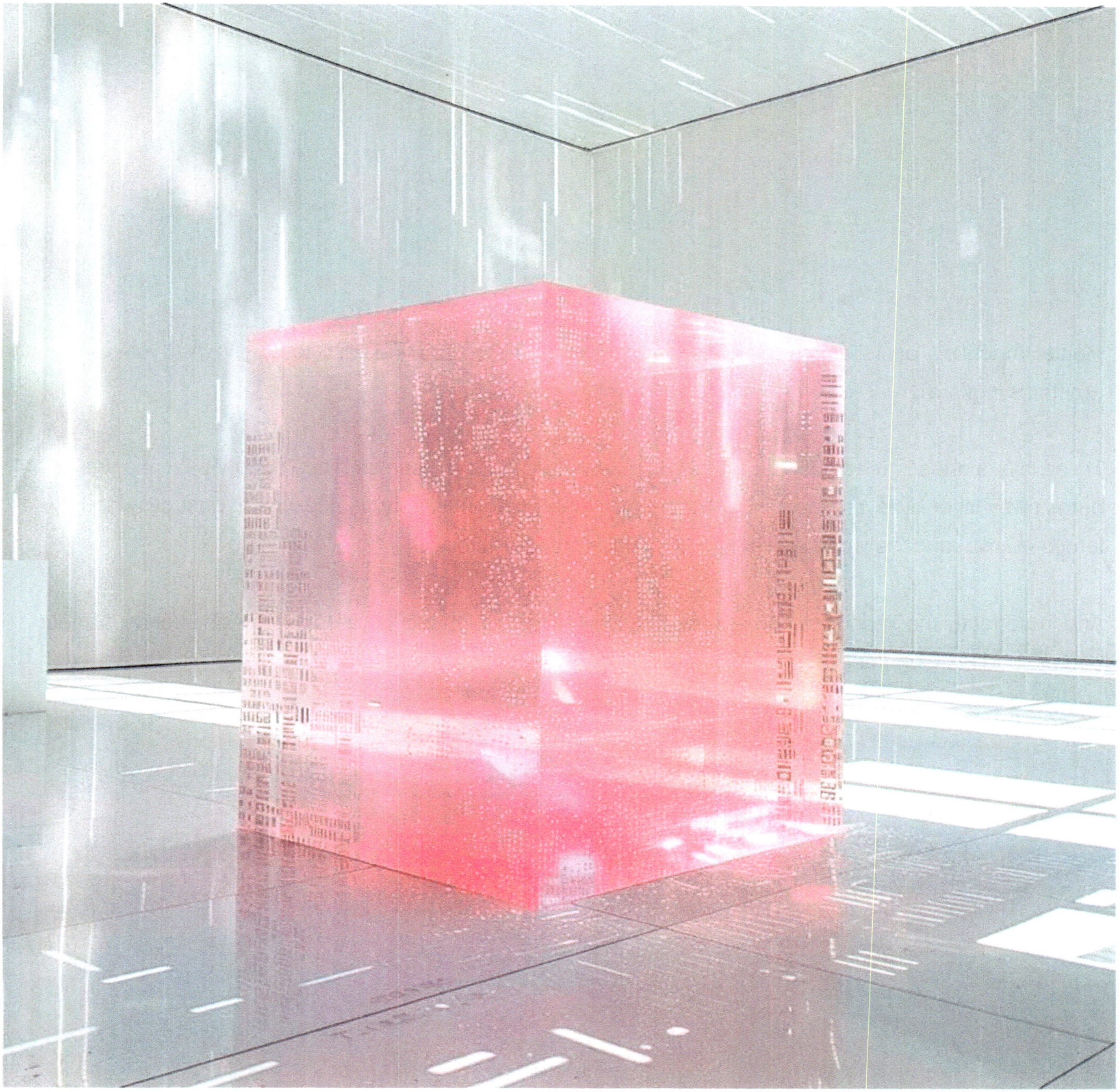

Mental impurities, past life memories, and karma form layers in our Minds and trap us in the cycle of rebirth (Sangkara).

These layers are so numerous, having been created over eons of lifetimes. The Techo Vipassana fire burns away layer by layer, releasing, past life memories, emotions, sounds, feelings. It destroys impurity forces (Kilesa) and the world and homes they have created within us.

And importantly the Techo fire can also destroy bad karma which can be associated with, sickness in our bodies, bad luck, and negative energy in our lives.

365

Sometimes we travel through different types of hallways or tunnels to reach the next layers. I have seen beautiful and interesting tunnels and dark scary ugly tunnels.

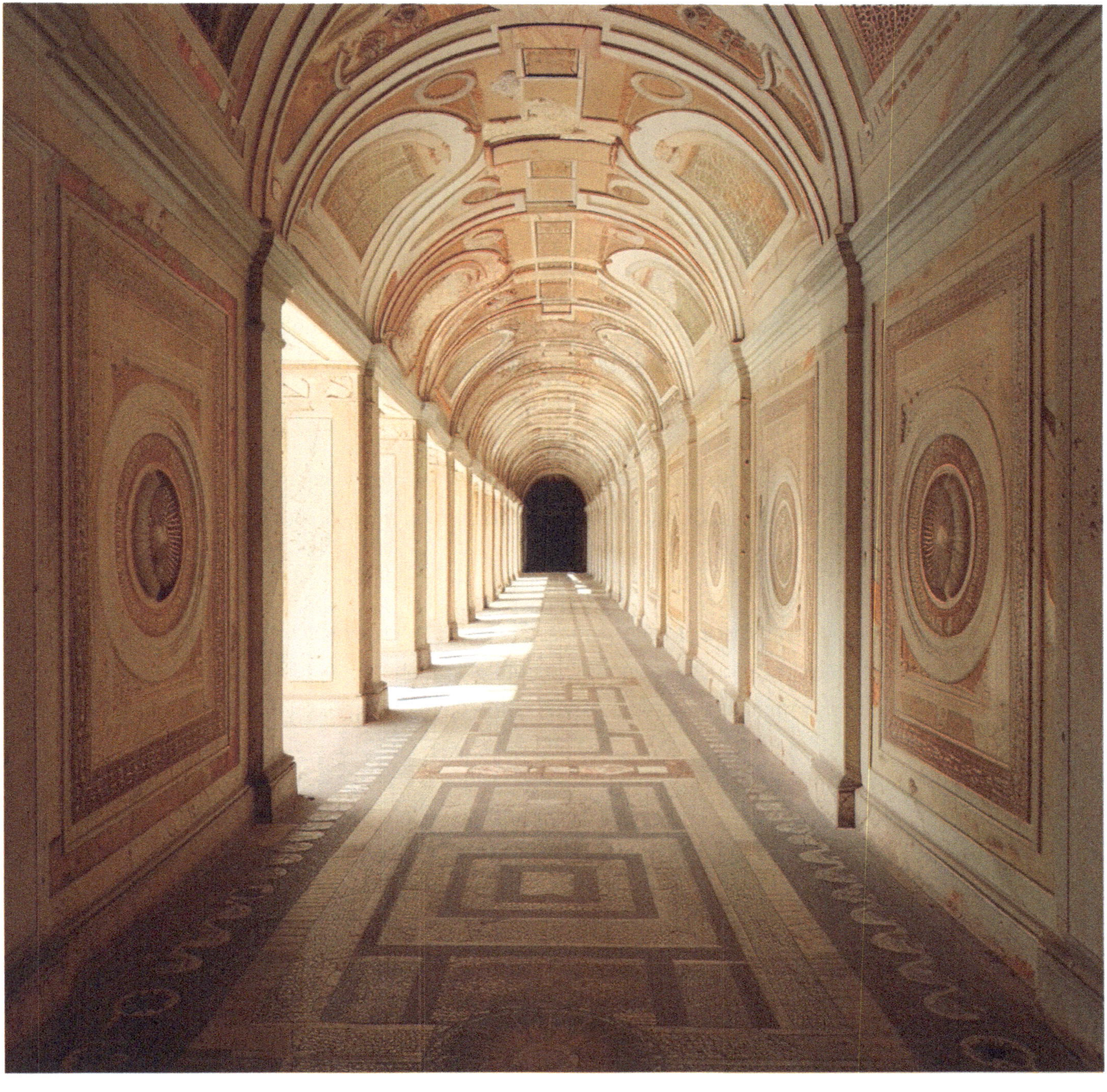

As we delve deeper into meditation using the Techo Vipassana Technique, the intensity of our focus ignites a powerful inner fire. With each moment of concentration, this fire grows more intense, consuming the world within us with unparalleled ferocity.

As the flames of meditation engulf our inner landscape, they incinerate the layers of illusion and delusion that cloud our perception. With great clarity, we witness the burning away of attachments, desires, and the very fabric of our conditioned existence.

In this transformative process, the fire of Techo Vipassana purifies our consciousness, illuminating the path to liberation from suffering and awakening to the truth of our inherent nature. It is a profound journey of self-discovery and transformation, where the flames guide us towards our original Minds.

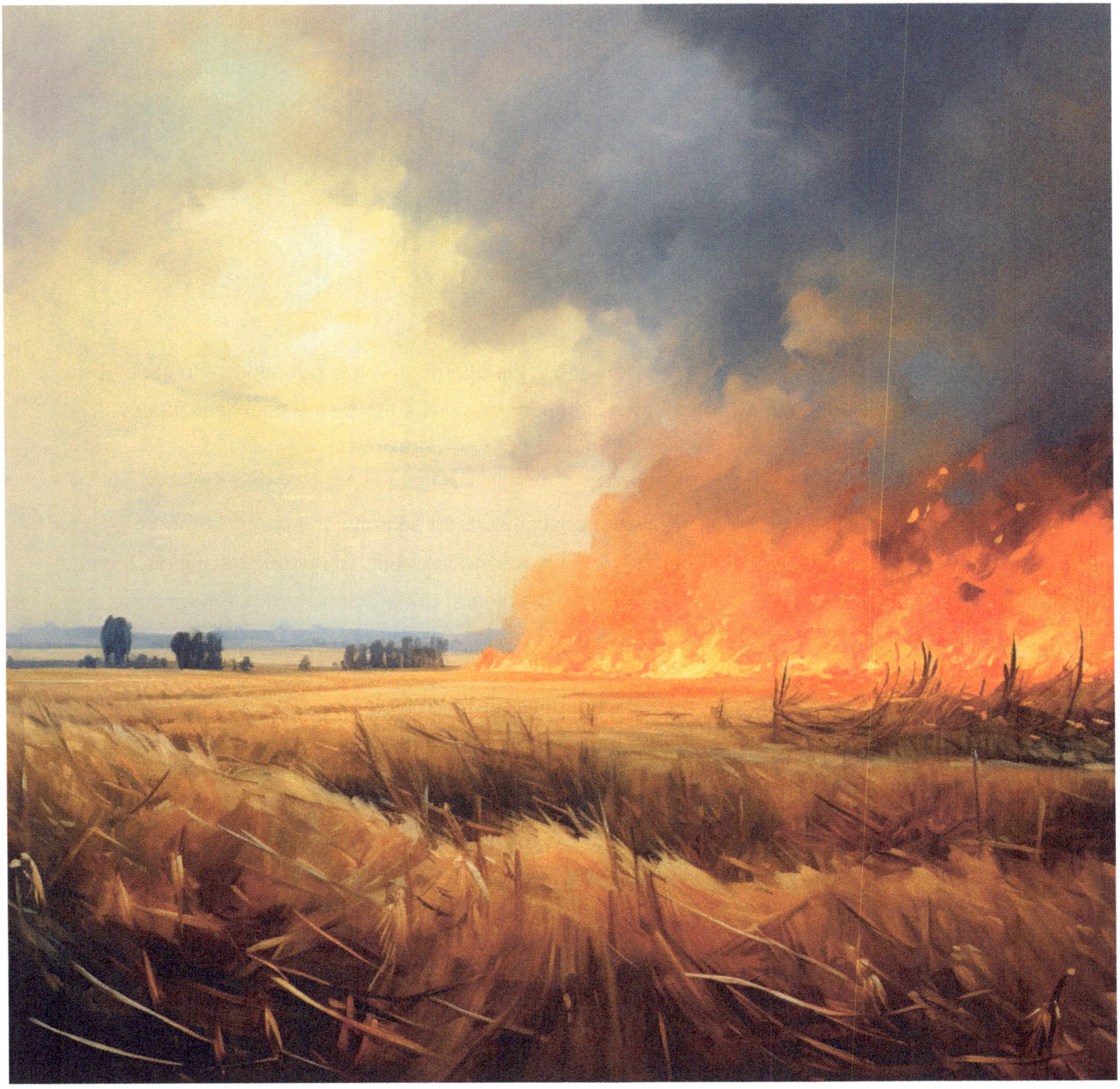

Through the intense fire of Techo Vipassana, we witness the aftermath within our minds—the scorched remnants of the world we once knew. Each layer of impurity is consumed by the relentless flames, gradually eradicating the illusionary constructs that cloud our perception.

Just as removing layers of calcification reveals the pristine surface beneath, the fire of Techo Vipassana burns away the accumulated layers of conditioning, uncovering the purity of our original minds. In the aftermath of this transformative process, we are left with a clearer understanding of our true nature and a liberated consciousness free from the shackles of delusion.

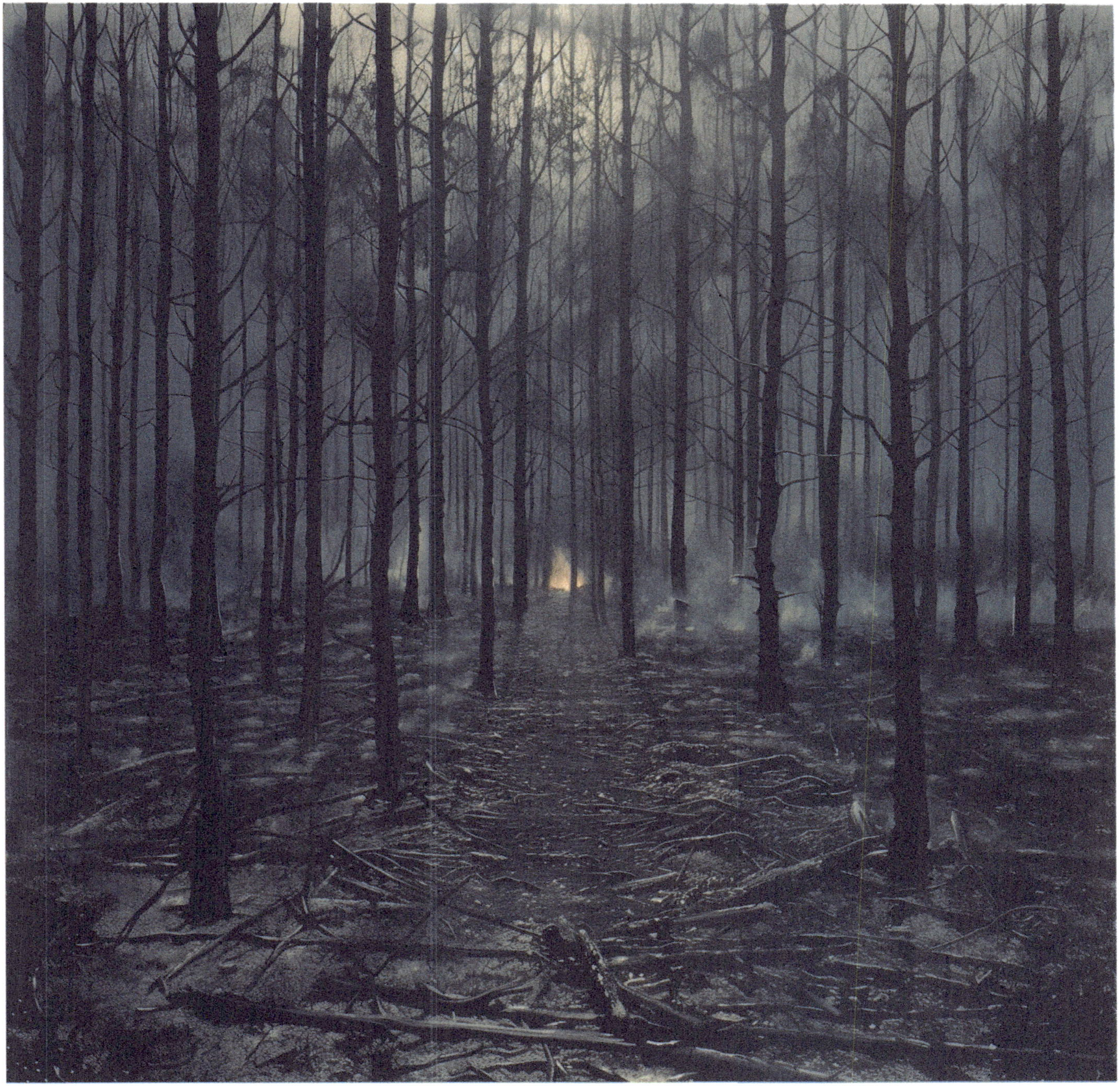

One day, my meditation Master summoned me and presented a piece of paper with words written on it. With seriousness, she informed me that during my meditation that day, I would confront an attack of hundreds of thousands of impurity forces, stemming from years of alcohol consumption and sleeping pills. She urged me to brace myself for a fierce battle against my greatest weaknesses and emphasized the importance of persevering on my meditation cushion, regardless of what may arise or happen.

True to her words, as I meditated, I found myself besieged by legions of impurity armies, each clad in armor and relentless in their attacks upon my mind. Despite the intensity of the attacks, I remained steadfast and determined, refusing to give up, despite the overwhelming forces attacking me.

As the flames of the Techo fire burned ever brighter, consuming the impurities within me, I reached a point of exhaustion. Yet, in that moment of weariness, a vision unfolded before me—a vision of a woman in a white robe standing upon a cliff, casting a piece of paper into the swirling sea below, teeming with impurities.

In that moment of clarity, I realized that the woman in the vision was none other than my Master, and the piece of paper she had shown me earlier symbolized the impurities that I was confronting within myself. It was a profound revelation, a testament to the wisdom and guidance bestowed upon me by my Master, and a reminder of the transformative power of perseverance and inner strength in the face of adversity.

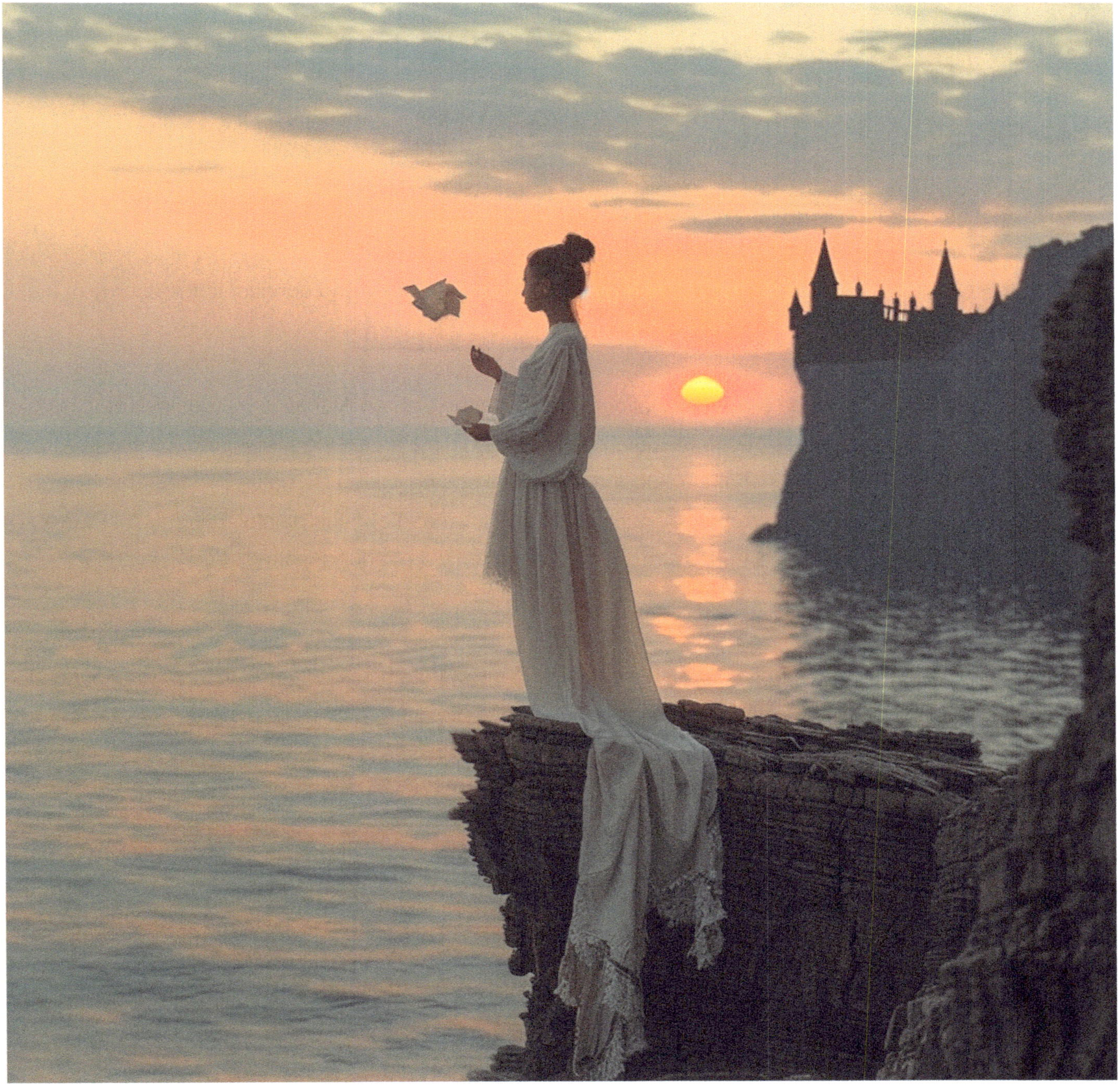

Is time travel possible.?

Perhaps not as portrayed in books and in the movies

At least it is possible to connect to the fine energy in the other dimension and connect to the energy of the past.

One time I was meditating in an 8-day meditation course with the Master. At that time, I decided to try my own modification of the Master's Techo Meditation technique. To my amazement it worked, I was back in time 2500 years ago, witnessing what the Buddha was experiencing during his battle with the Mara (devil) and dark forces. I could feel the arrows going into the Buddha's heart and the painful thoughts that were arising, meant to discourage the Buddha's resolve. This was truly a profound moment in my personal journey.

However, after this profound meditation, without me telling my experience to anyone, the Master arrived at the meditation hall and immediately spoke on the microphone directing her words at me "follow my method, do not make up your own meditation method" …. How did she know?

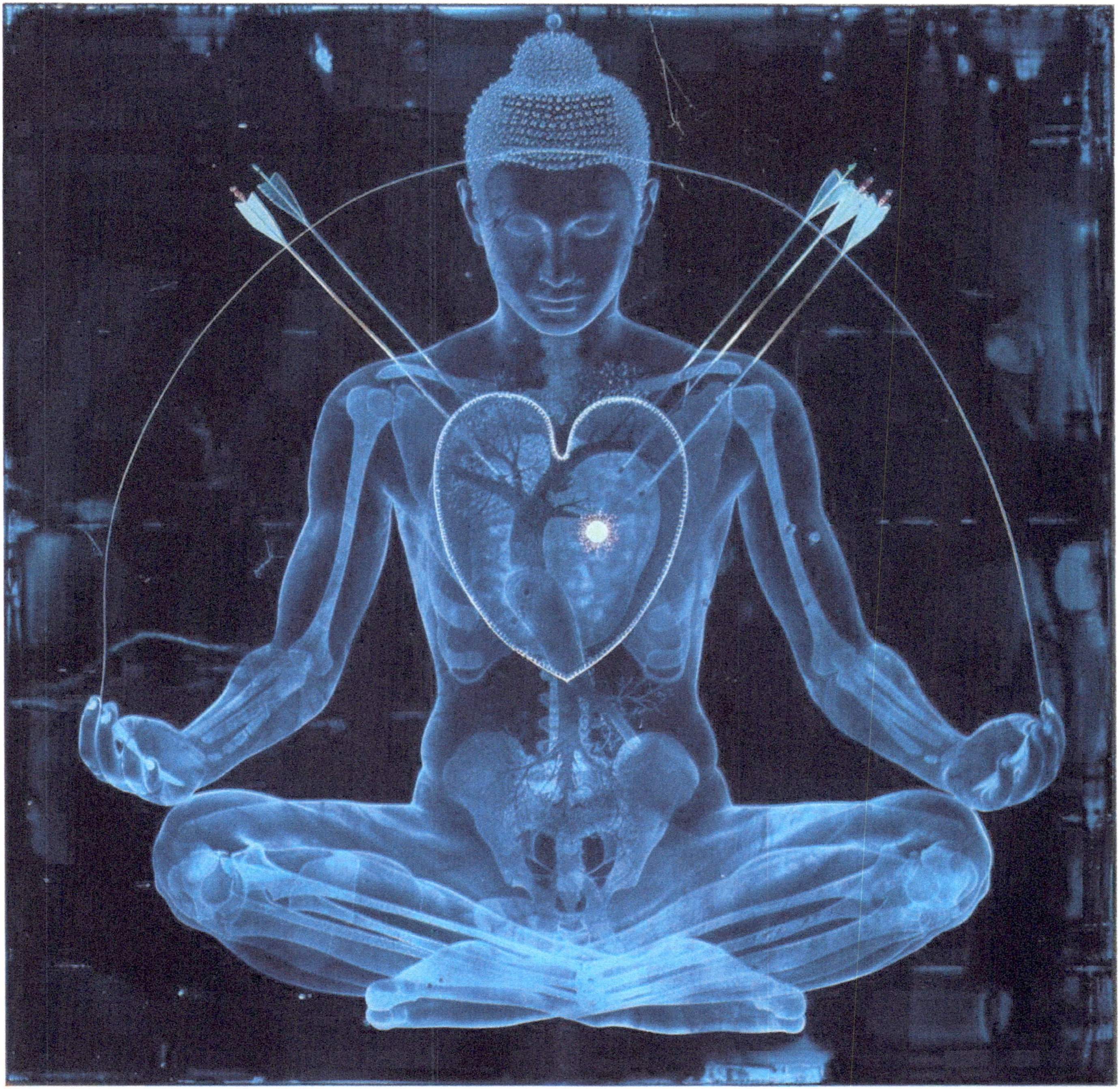

The Wall

In my practice I have been able to see many visuals in the other dimension. This is likely because of past lives where I already practiced high level meditation. Visions in meditations can often be a distraction. However, in this meditation, I went very deep and travel far into the Mind, seeing many forests, trees, mountains, oceans, deep tunnels, until finally I arrived at a great ancient monolithic wall. By now my Mind was very still and calm. As I approached the great wall, I wondered how the giant gate of the wall could be opened. My Mind remained completely neutral and equanimous. And with this equanimous Mind, the giant gate in the wall began to open. The more equanimous the Mind, the faster the gate opened.

Do you want to know what was behind the wall?

Darkness, just black space and the feeling of nothingness.

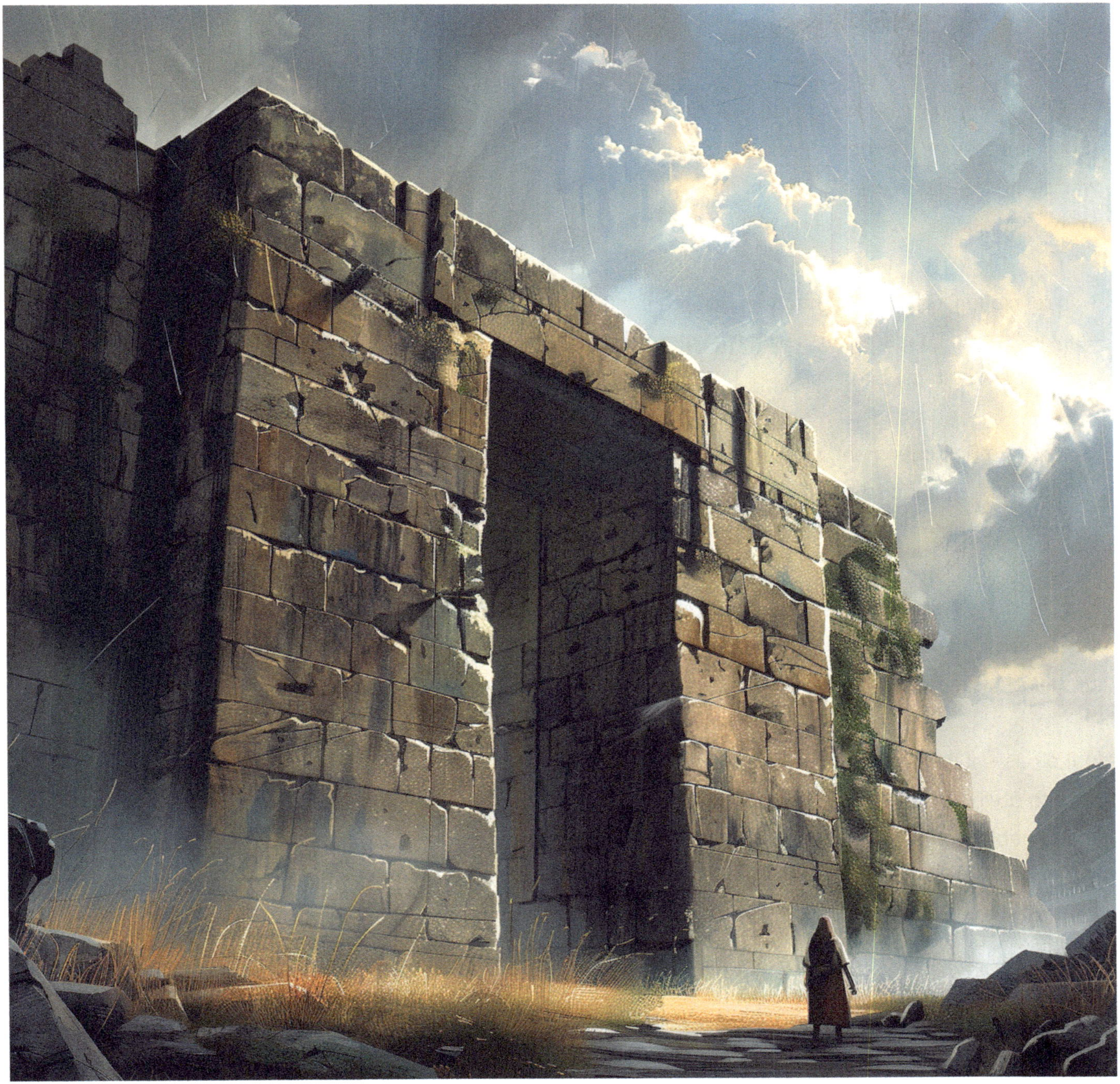

The most profound meditation experience I had, which lead me to reach the "first stage of Enlightenment" (Sotapanna), was a series of vivid images. In the first, I found myself in a grave, surrounded by all my worldly possessions piled on top of me. An inner voice conveyed to me that true freedom would only come from relinquishing everything in this world.

This revelation led me to confront my attachments, particularly to relationships. While I found it relatively easy to let go of material possessions, I struggled with the idea of releasing emotional bonds I had to certain people in my Life.

The path to Enlightenment, as taught by the Buddha, emphasizes non-attachment. It requires a willingness to relinquish all attachments and desires. In a society driven by materialism, such a profound level of detachment is not easily embraced by everyone.

Reaching the 4 stages of Enlightenment is not an intellectual process, but something so remarkable that the person experiences during meditation, that they know they have reach something incredible and are forever changed.

In the case of the first stage of Enlightenment, the hell door is closed for the practitioner, they will never have to go to hell and the maximum number of reincarnations they will face is 7 more lives. After uncountable lifetimes, this means that there is a very short time period for "karma owners" those seeking revenge or collecting karmic debts, have to collect. Often times reaching various stages of Enlightenment also means that lots of karma seems to hit you quickly.

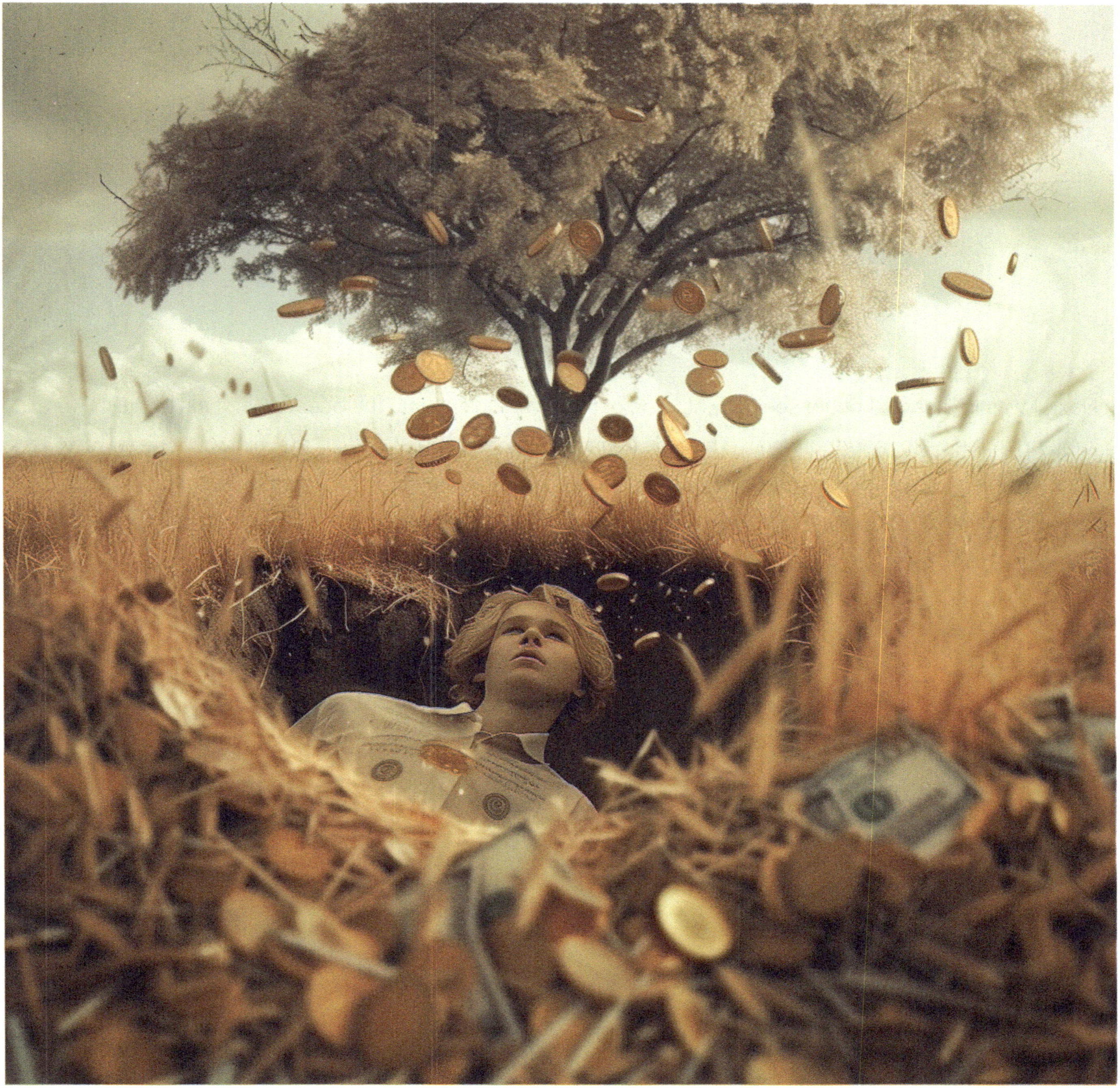

Next, I was in a cave, I could see the entrance of the cave looking into the ocean. Dolphins and fish were jumping in the water and there was a beautiful sunset. The knowing Mind told me this was the sea of ignorance. The dolphins, fish and birds were not real, but were the impurity forces (Kilesa) in my Mind, taking the form of sea creatures. This was the sea I would have to cross to be free.

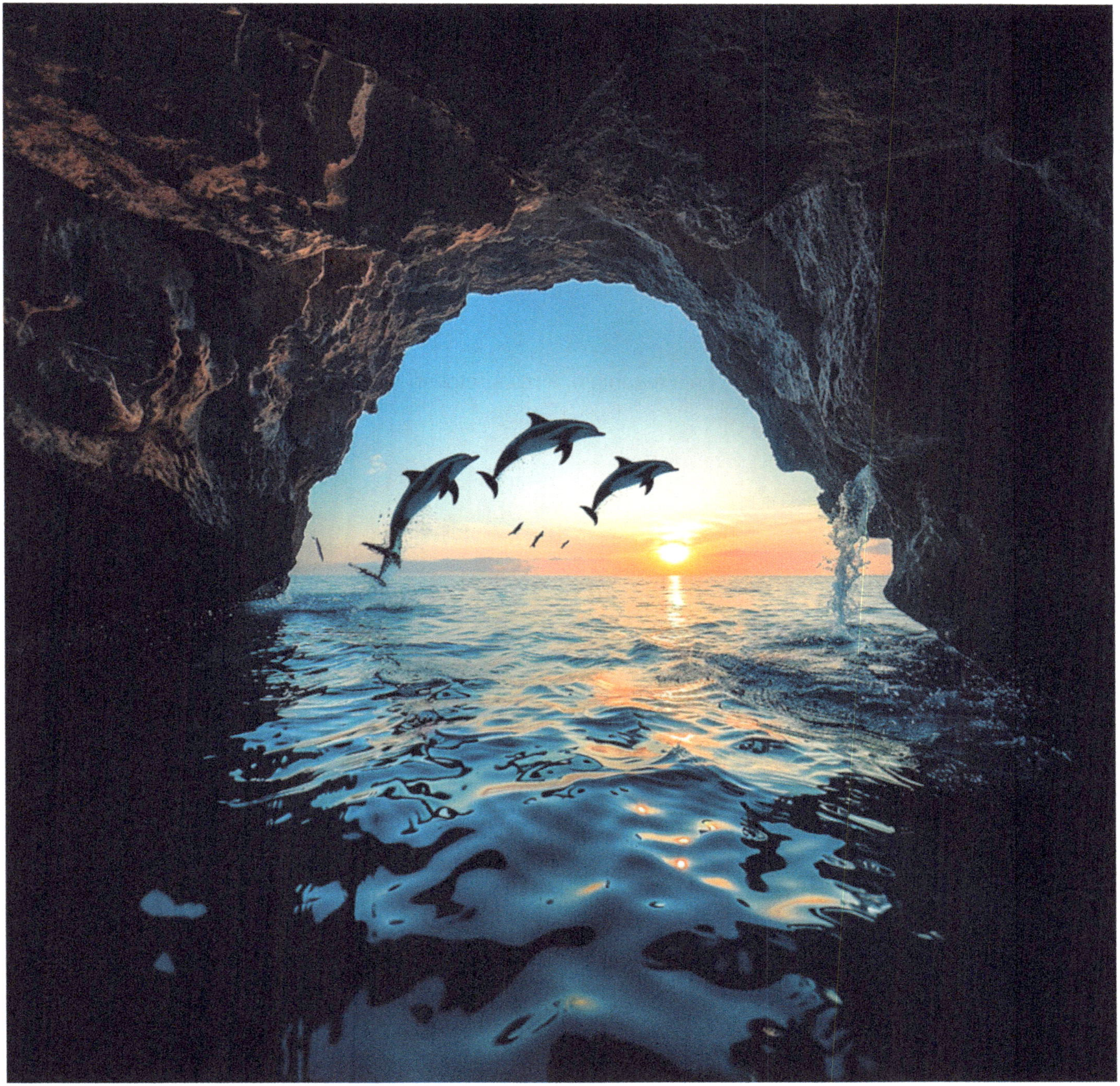

Then suddenly I saw myself standing on a mountain, arms stretched out at my sides, and I felt absolutely free.

FREEDOM

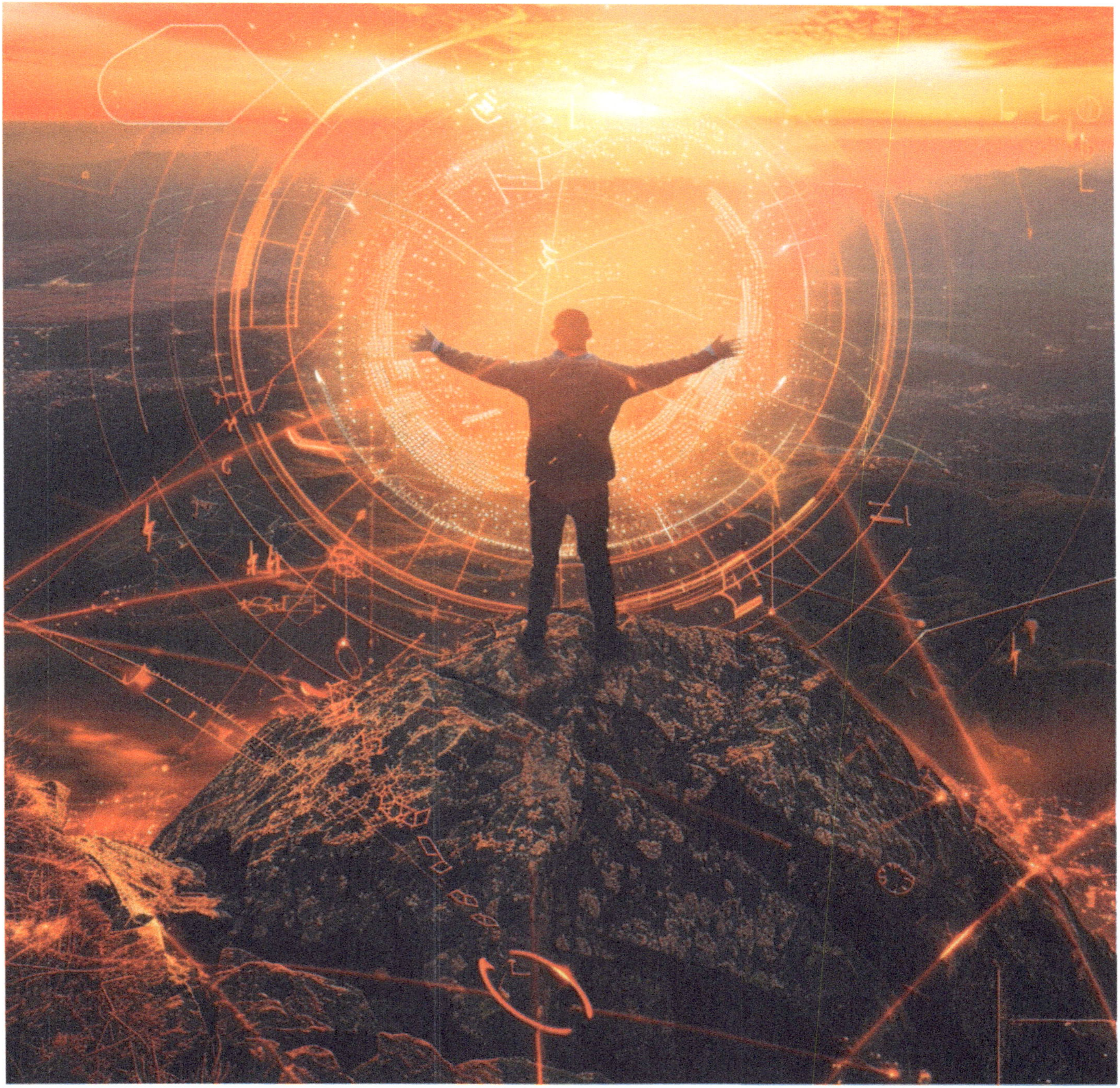

And next I was sitting in space in a row of monks, looking down at the world and saying to myself:

"What was it that I was so attached to in this World? "

That was it…I knew I had arrived to something extraordinary. The Wisdom that arose was so True and Real in my Mind, that something in me changed forever.

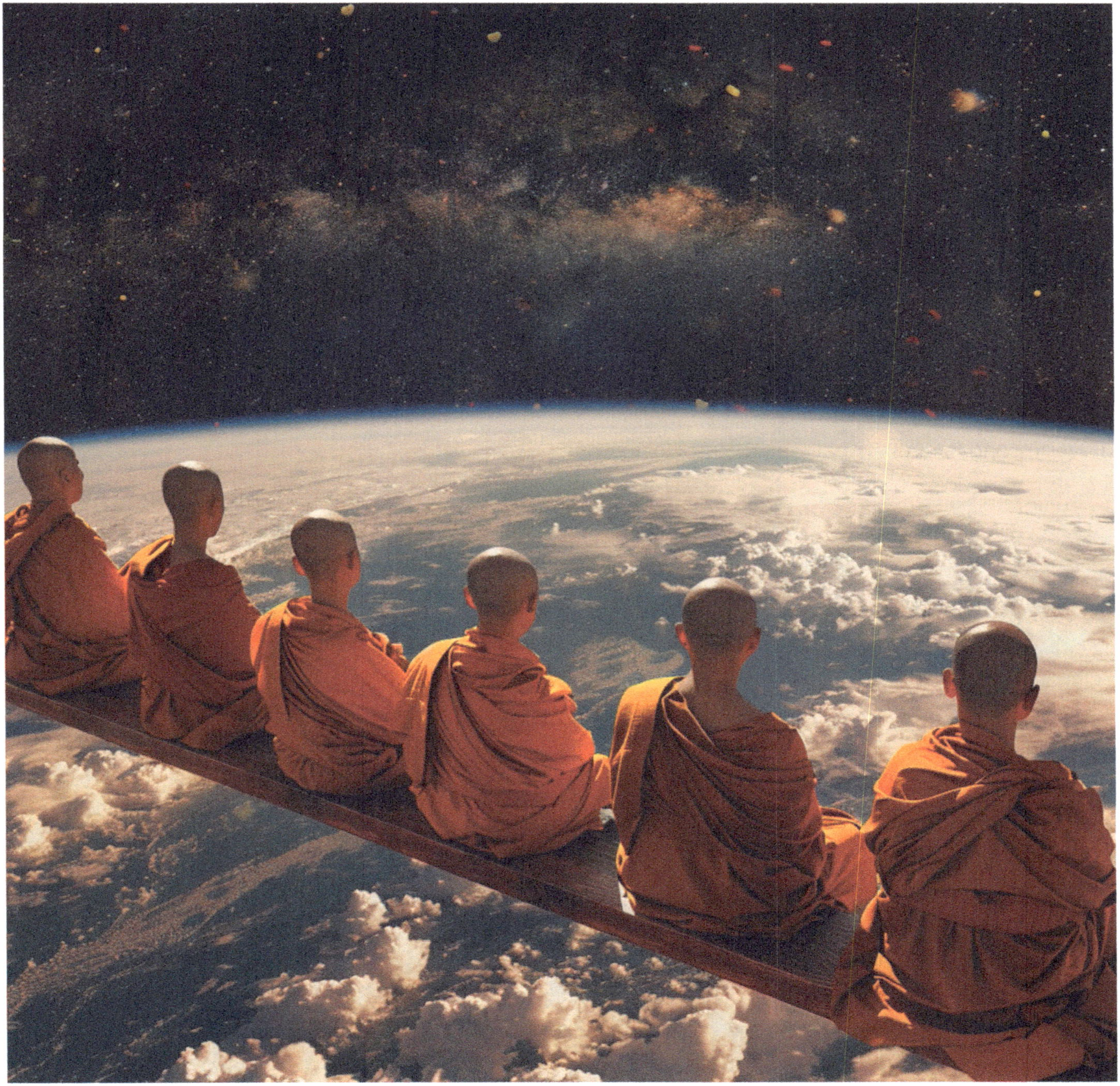

During meditation I was able to see and feel where a black root like an alien creature had grown into my brain and mind, Part of the root attached to the muscles that controlled my left eye. This allowed the alien (Kilesa) to pull my eye into the direction it wanted me to look. In many instances it forced me to notice things in the illusions from cars to clothes to women. All in an effort to attach me to the world of illusion.

As the Mind traveled through my physical head, I could in parallel feel exactly where the Mind was travelling and tracing the path of the root-like entity.

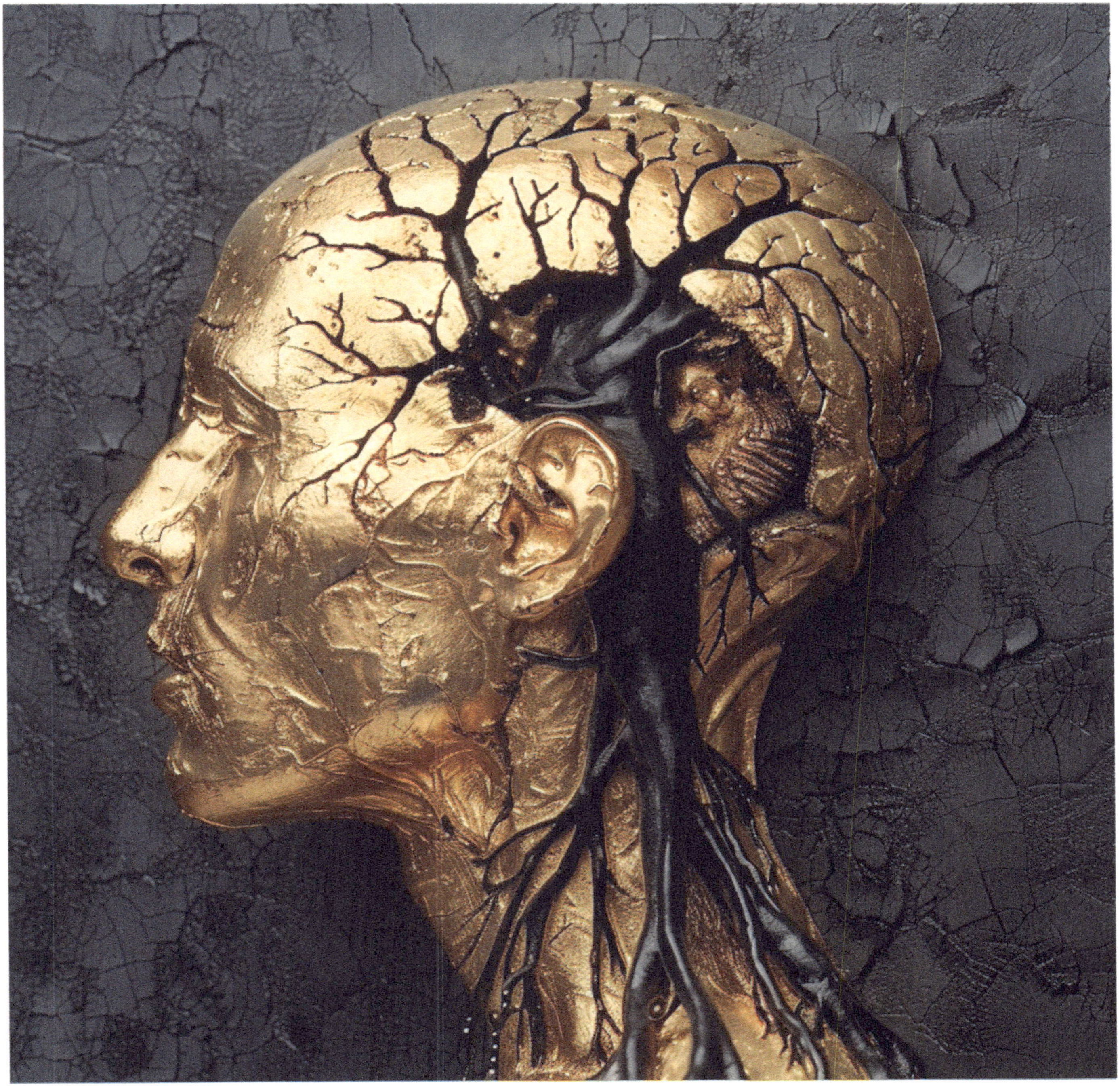

The mind has these deep roots of impurities that have taken hold since time immemorial. These roots, known as Kilesa, exert control over many of our actions and emotions, persisting from one lifetime to the next as the Asawa Kilesa—the ultimate root, as termed by the Buddha.

To reach enlightenment, one must uproot these deep-seated roots of impurities from the mind., I was able to glimpse this root and commence the process of its extraction. With unwavering focus and stillness, I delved into the depths of my mind, where I encountered a powerful image: a tractor pulling out a huge, long section of the Kilesa root. The root had tiny roots coming off it, which resembled tiny shimmering fiber optic cables which connected this massive root into the Mind.

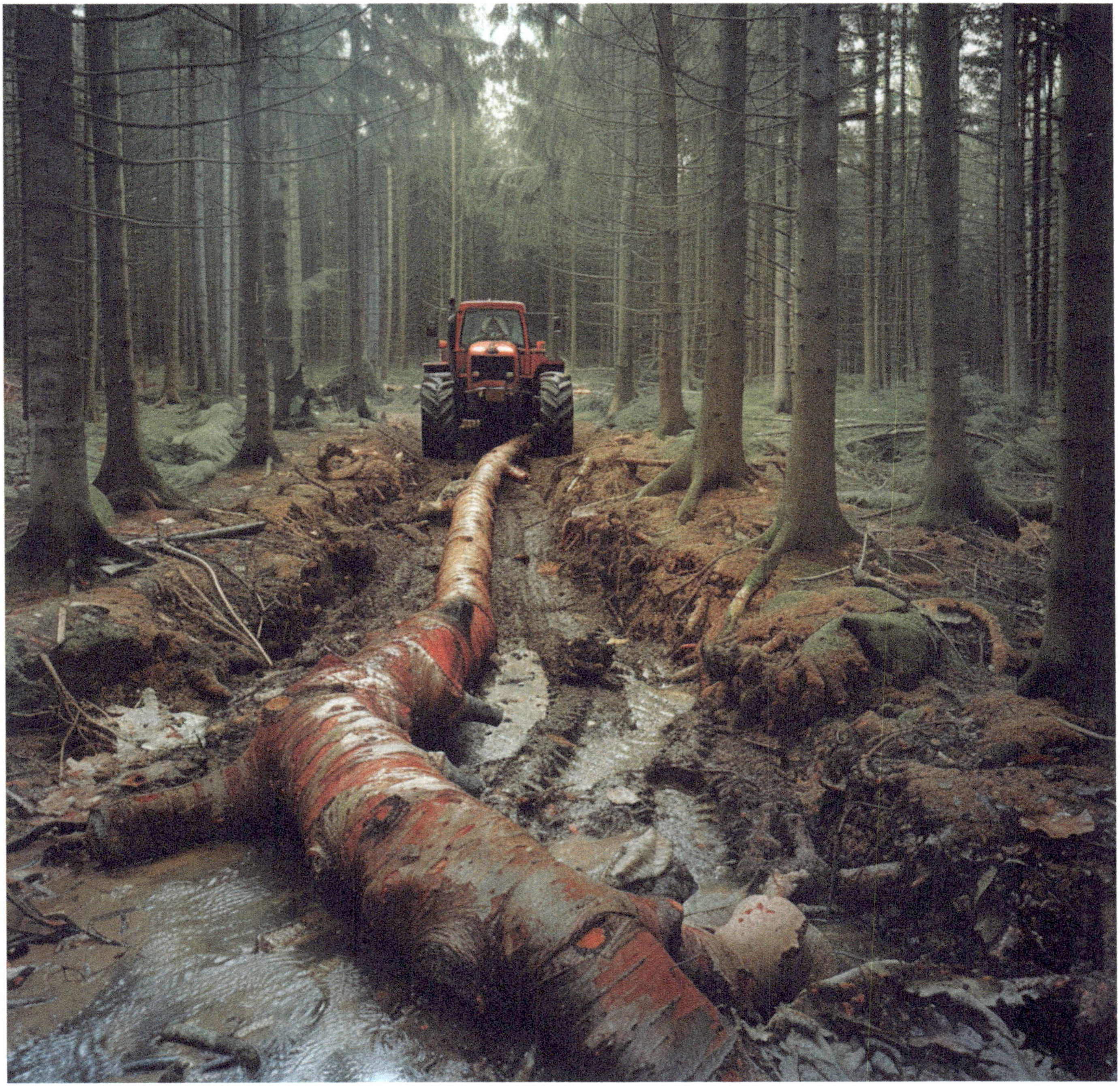

During another weeklong Techo Vipassana meditation course, I was very still doing a long meditation. Then suddenly I found myself in a very dark space, but the darkness also had fluidity, like thick tar. The knowing Mind informed me, this is karma that you are now burning.

This was a profound moment of truth. Karma does exist in the Mind. It is black and sticky. However, it can be burned away through the advanced meditation practice. What this means is that we can burn away the root of our karma, that could manifest as bad luck or disease, by practicing diligently.

91

It was a warm breezy night as I sat with the other Techo students, under the Bodhi tree.

As I meditated the Mind became very still and images of nature appeared.
I was observing, floating through green fields, forests, sand, and rock formations and over water until seeing sunsets and underwater scenes.

When my Mind became even more still and equanimous, it dug and traveled deep to a place in the Mind where a small pond appeared. The water was so crystal clear that, I could see a large koi fish below the surface of the water, as well as details of stones, pebbles, and plants on the bottom of the pond.

Then an insect landed on the surface of the water, causing a ripple to run across the pond.
In this ultimate stillness everything looked crystal clear in a high resolution.

This was the result of practicing Techo Vipassana in the course for 7 days straight and practicing at a high concentration and stillness and with determination to stay on the focus point and not allowing the Mind to wander away with thoughts.

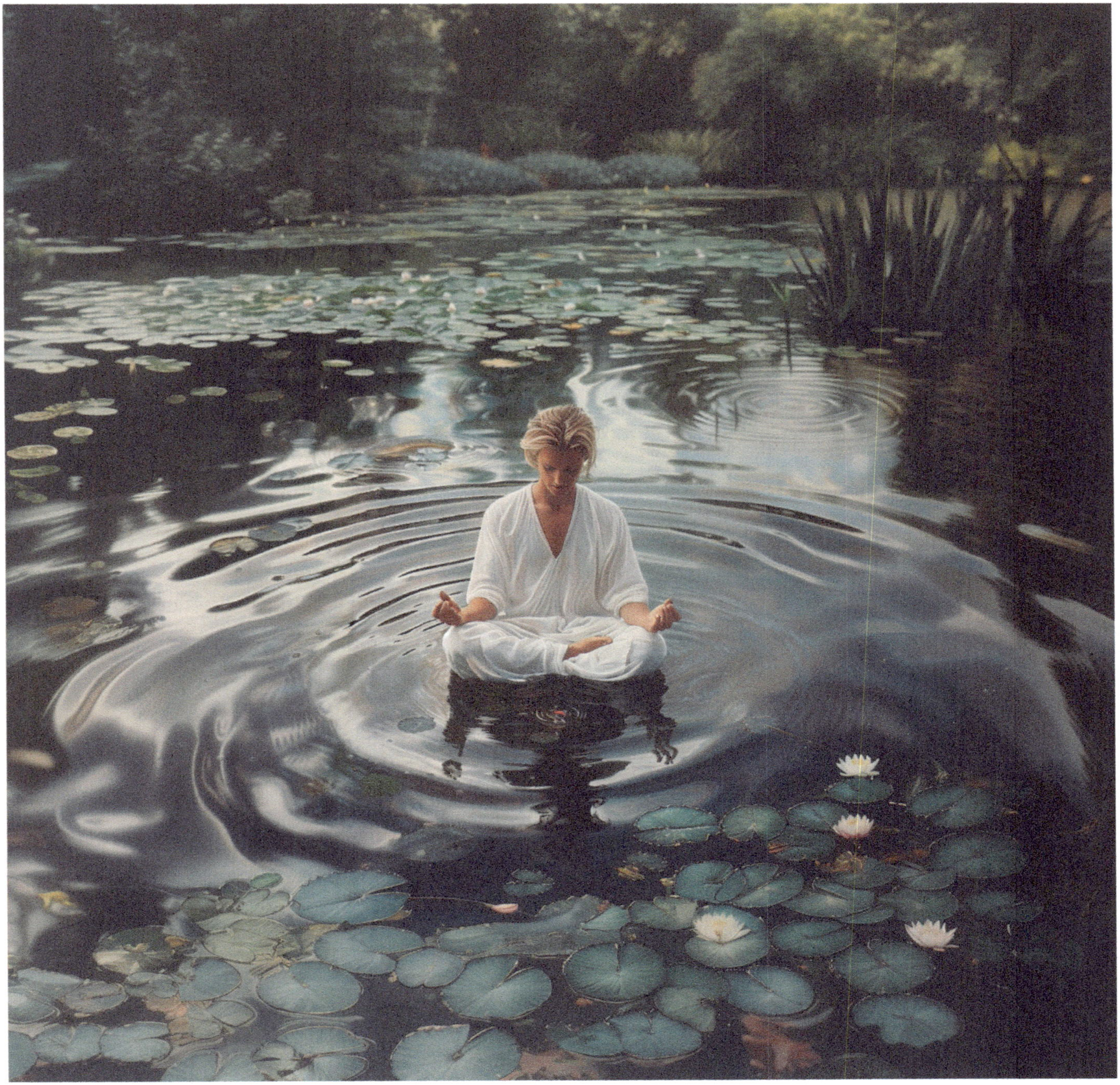

As I was observing the pond, unexpectedly tiny white particles, that looked like snowflakes, began to swirl around my vision. I recognized these particles immediately....

These were the energy particles of my Techo Vipassana meditation Master Acharavadee Wongsakon. Since my early Techo courses, I would see these white snowflake particles dancing around, when I closed my eyes. Either at the Dhamma retreat or at home when I read Master's posts or heard her dhamma. Each time these particles appeared to me I knew Master's energy was supporting me.

Now meditating, I focused on the particles swirling before me.

With such a high concentration, the Mind was able to stop these tiny snowflake particles from swirling around or moving. The particles stopped in mid-flight and were suspended, allowing me to observe them in detail. As the Mind zoomed in on one tiny white particle, the particles appeared as a small round clear fluid droplet of water. Never had I seen Master's particle so up close or in the form of water.

The droplet I focused on, was so pure and beautiful and embodied Master's Virtuous essence. Suspended in midair, this droplet reflected the other particles around it making it appear almost like liquid metal. But in fact, this particle was a clear drop of water, which looked like gold white metal, because of the reflection of other particles around it.

And therefore, when seen from a distance without this level of concentration, they looked like white snowflakes swirling around my vision. As the Mind continued to focus on the droplet, the Mind once again zoomed in all the way to the atomic energy level, where this particle appeared as a translucent ball of pure orange gold energy.

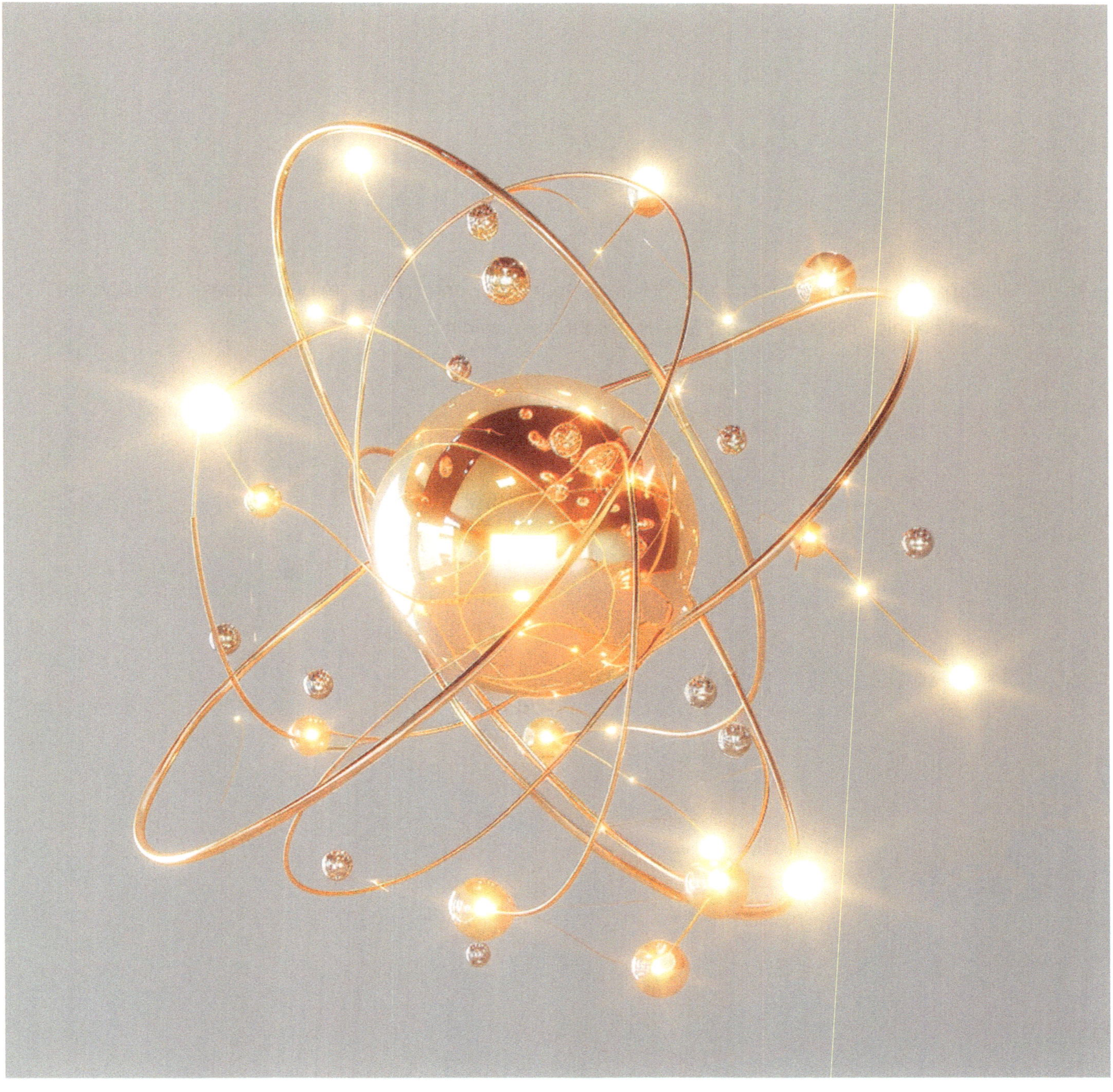

As the Mind reaches a high vibration and connects to the fine energy stream of goodness (triple gems) the Mind can see this energy manifest as fine gold flakes, swirling around.

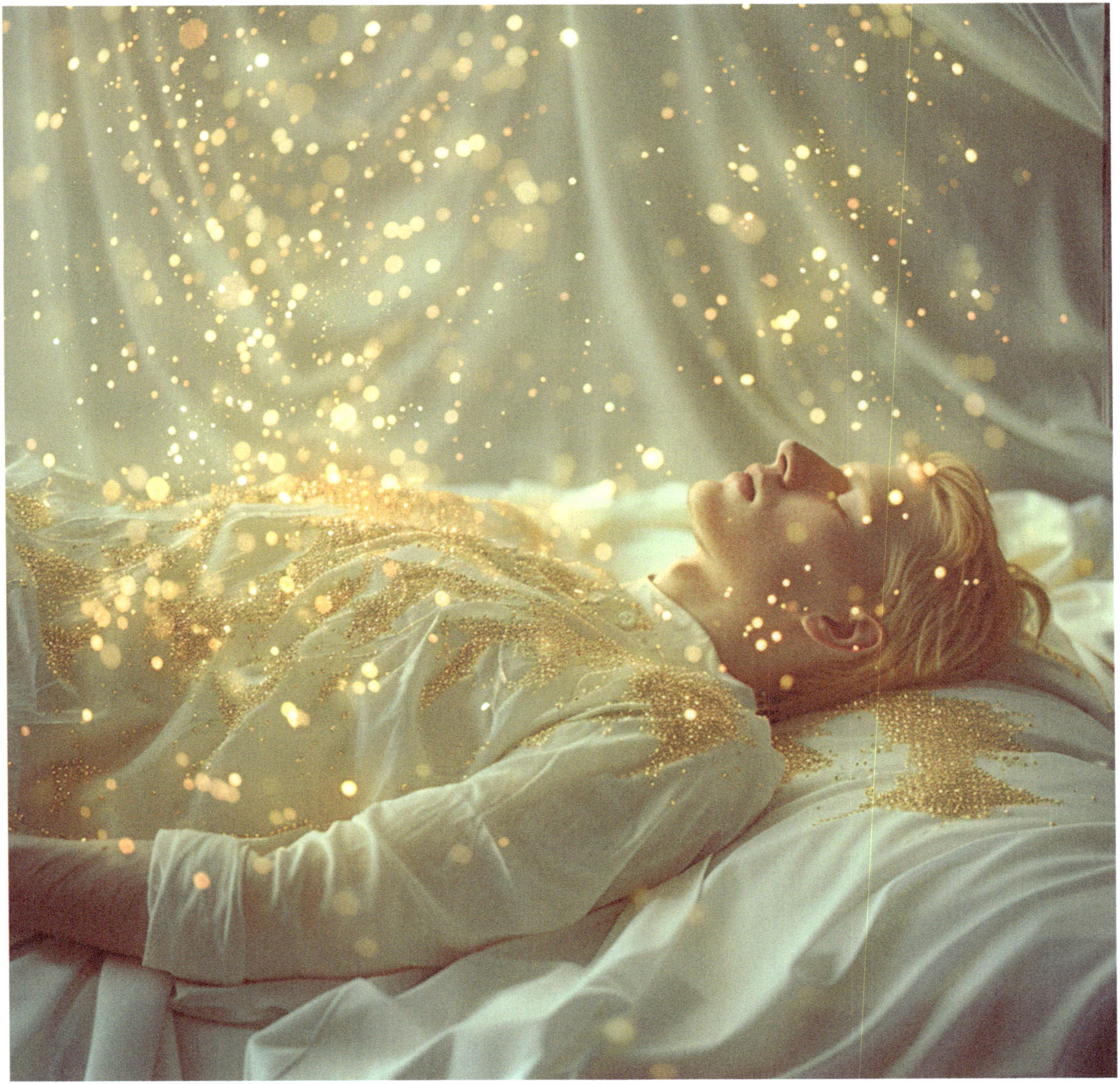

That night lying in my bed with my eyes closed the Mind still so focused, I could see through the ceiling of my hut and clearly a moon and stars appeared and a tree with leaves grew up.

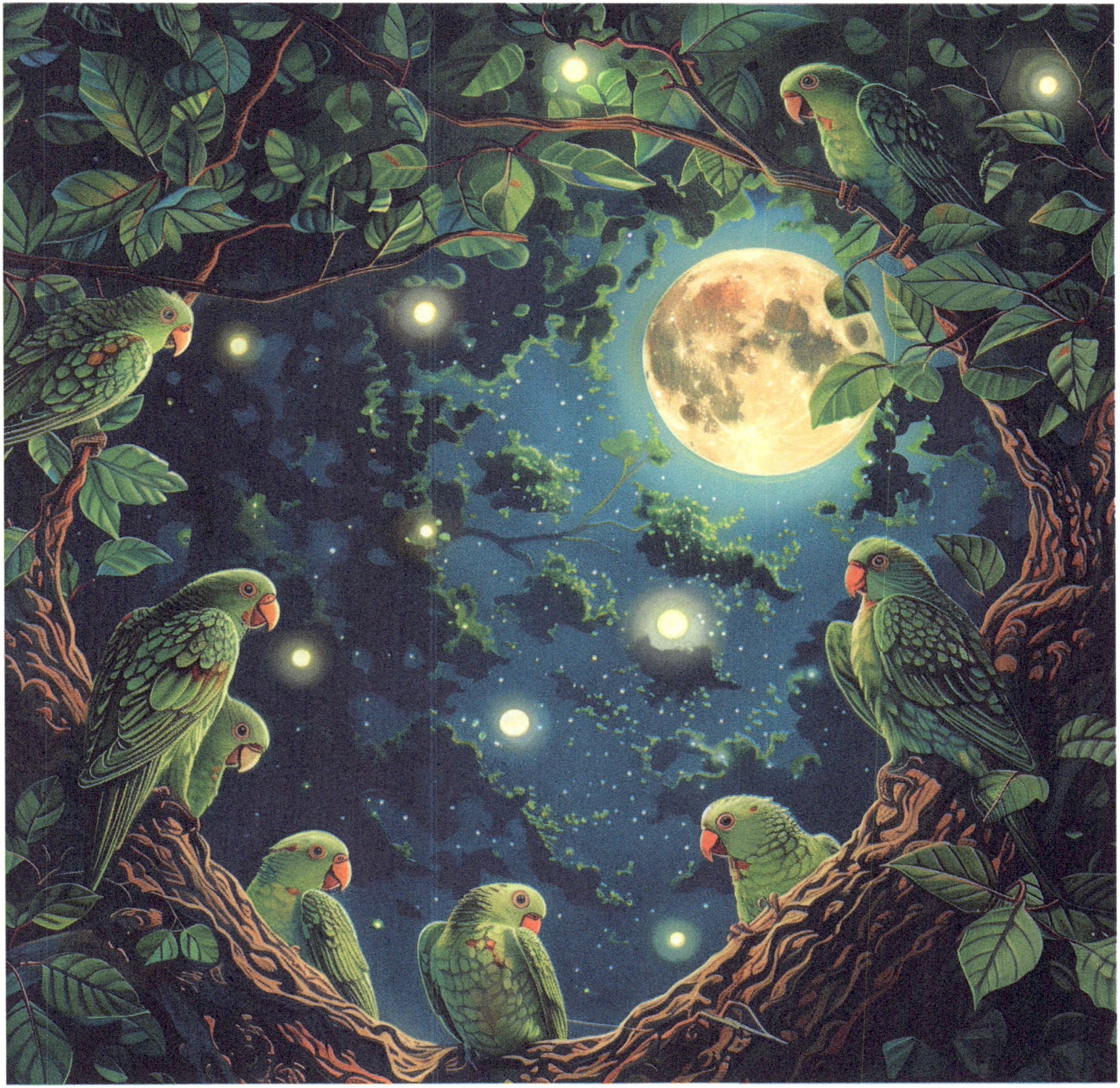

Then suddenly the leaves transformed to bright green parakeets and then they all suddenly flew away.

Now the Mind could see the fine energy of other dimensions. These were not illusions, but the Mind transcending this dimension.

As I turned on my bed and laid on my side, with my eyes closed I could see that my room was filled with Gold Treasure.

This was the Noble Treasure in the other dimension, I had accumulated from doing various Merit and attaining various levels of Enlightenment.

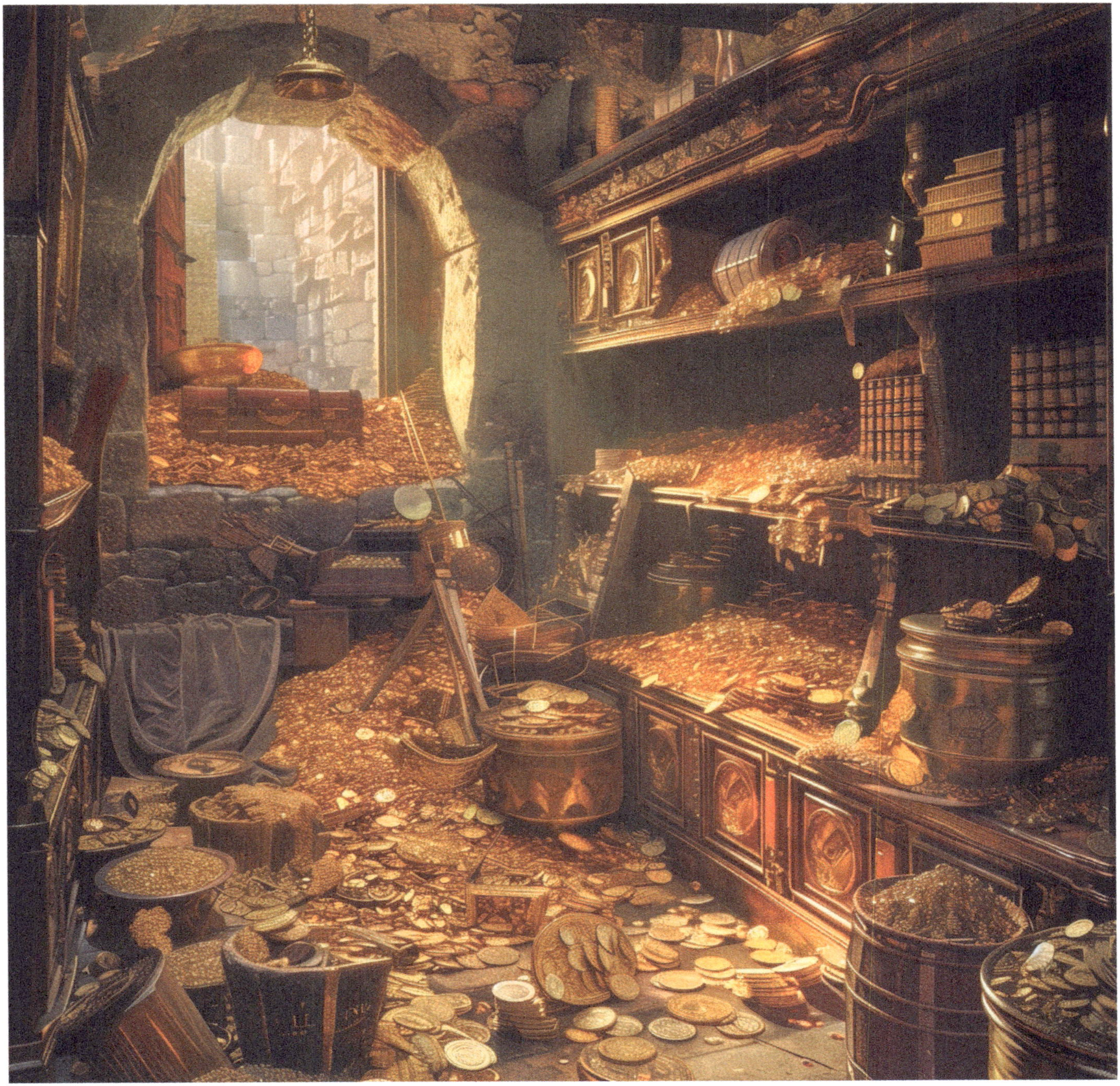

Then something extraordinary happened.

My Mind left my body. The Mind was floating above my body, attached by just a fine thread.

It simply just floated and saw a scene as if I were lying in the forest on a full moon night.

The Mind remained like this for several hours, I was fully conscious and aware, but "I" was out of my body.

So, we know that the Mind is not the Body. It just resides in what we call "our body" for a while, until it is time to leave.

Therefore, we should not become attached to our body, how we look, how we feel. Nor should we hang on when it is time to leave the body and all we know in this World.

We are merely travelers in the ocean of Samsara (rebirths).

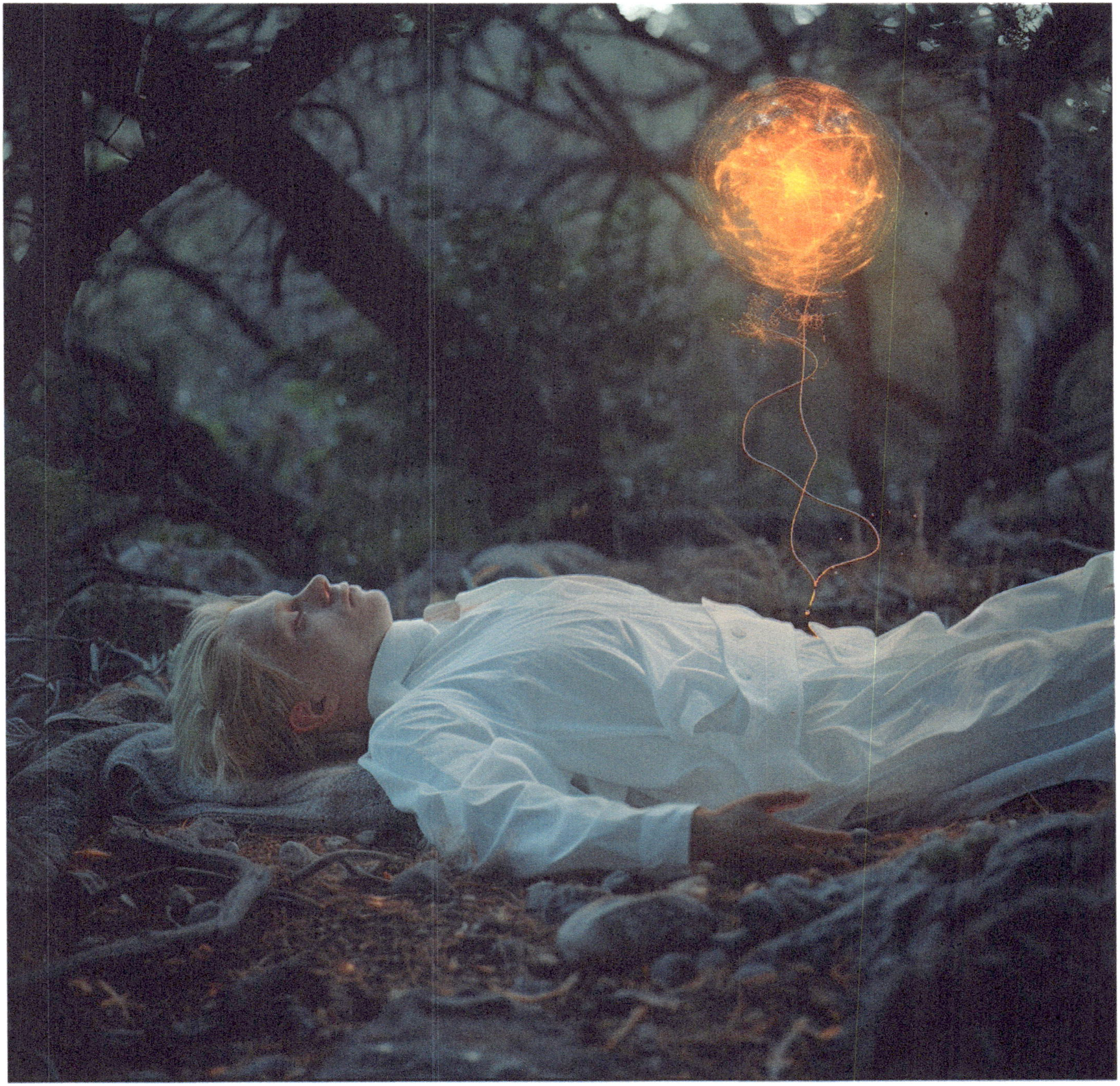

I turned in Bed once more to face the wall, and there I saw a movie playing of a pre-historic scene. Each time I turned my head again, it was like changing the channel.

This reminded me of the movie "LUCY" where in one scene as she waved her hand, the scene, she was sitting in would change.

This is a demonstration of how Powerful the Mind really is. We live in a World of Illusion, but as we strengthen and purify our Minds, we can break through the Illusion and Mara's (devil) Game.

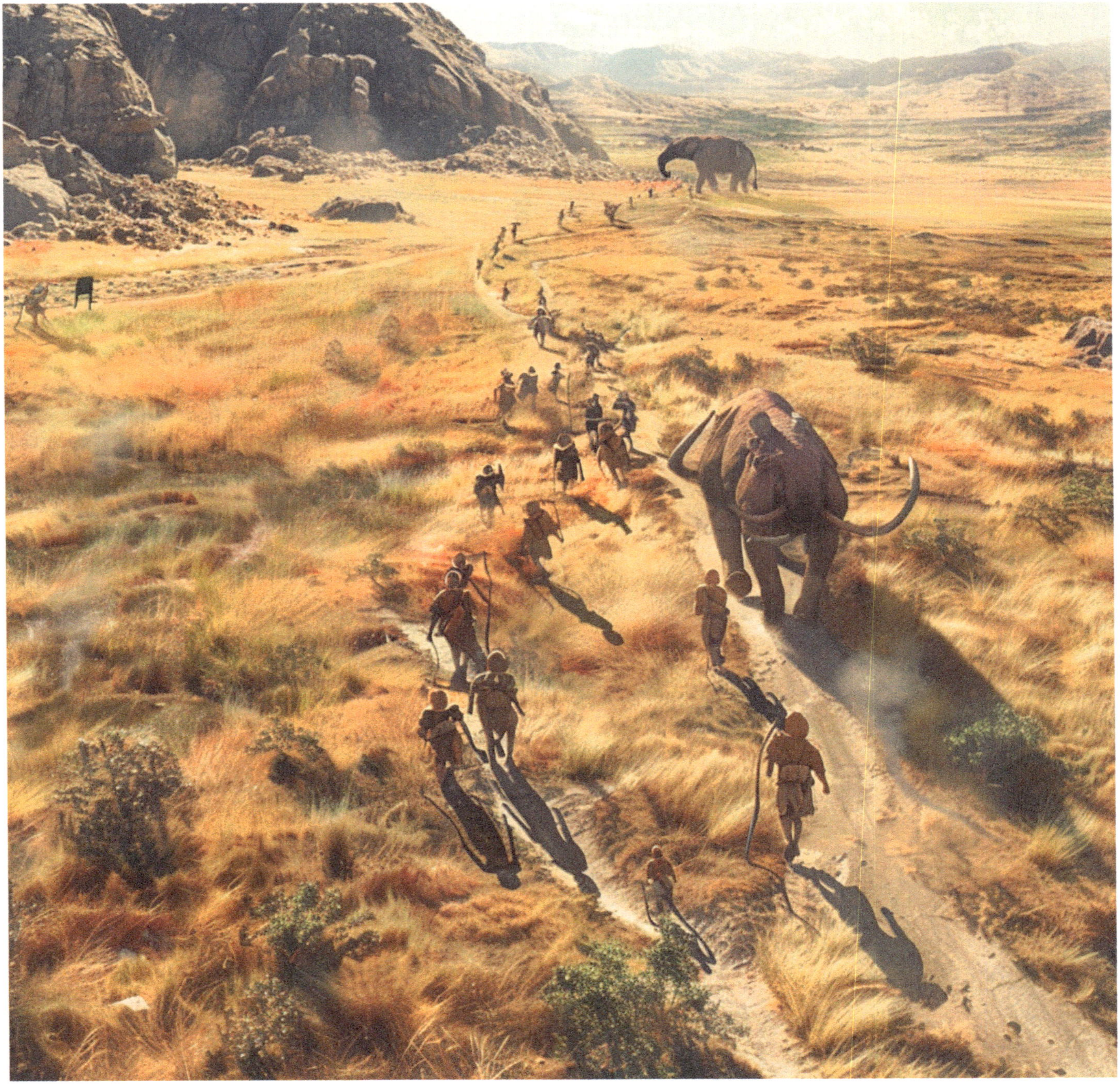

And then the Mind is free and returns to a state of Pure Energy – no longer imprisoned in these bodies or this World.

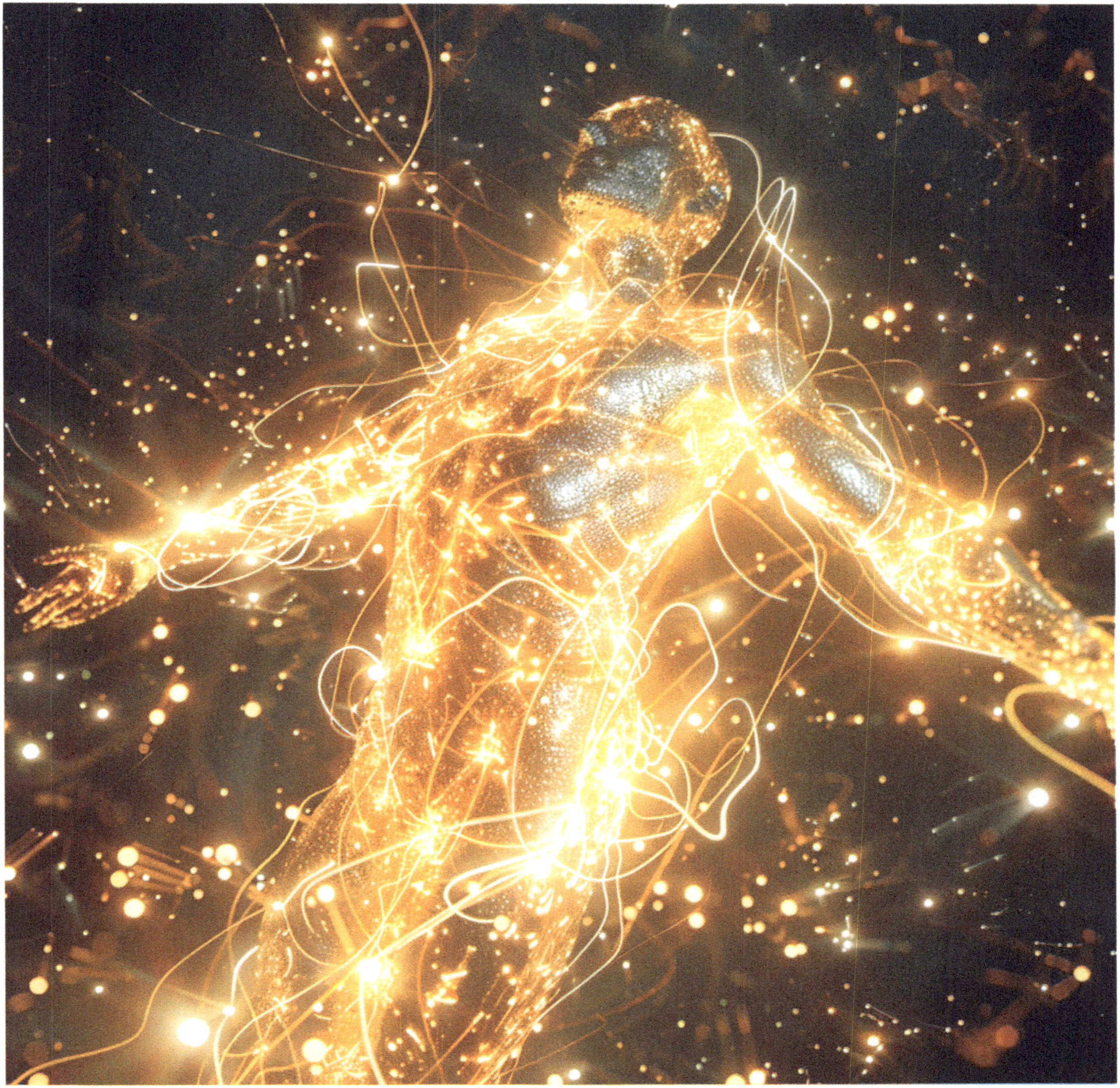

When the meditator reaches the end of the purification process, it reaches Enlightenment.

Forever free from the cycle of birth, reincarnation, and impurities that have enslaved the Mind for eons.

This is the Ultimate Bliss and Happiness. The Work is Finished.

The Game and final Battle are Won.

ANOMOUDHANA SATHU TO THE BUDDHA, HIS TEACHINGS AND ALL THE MASTERS.

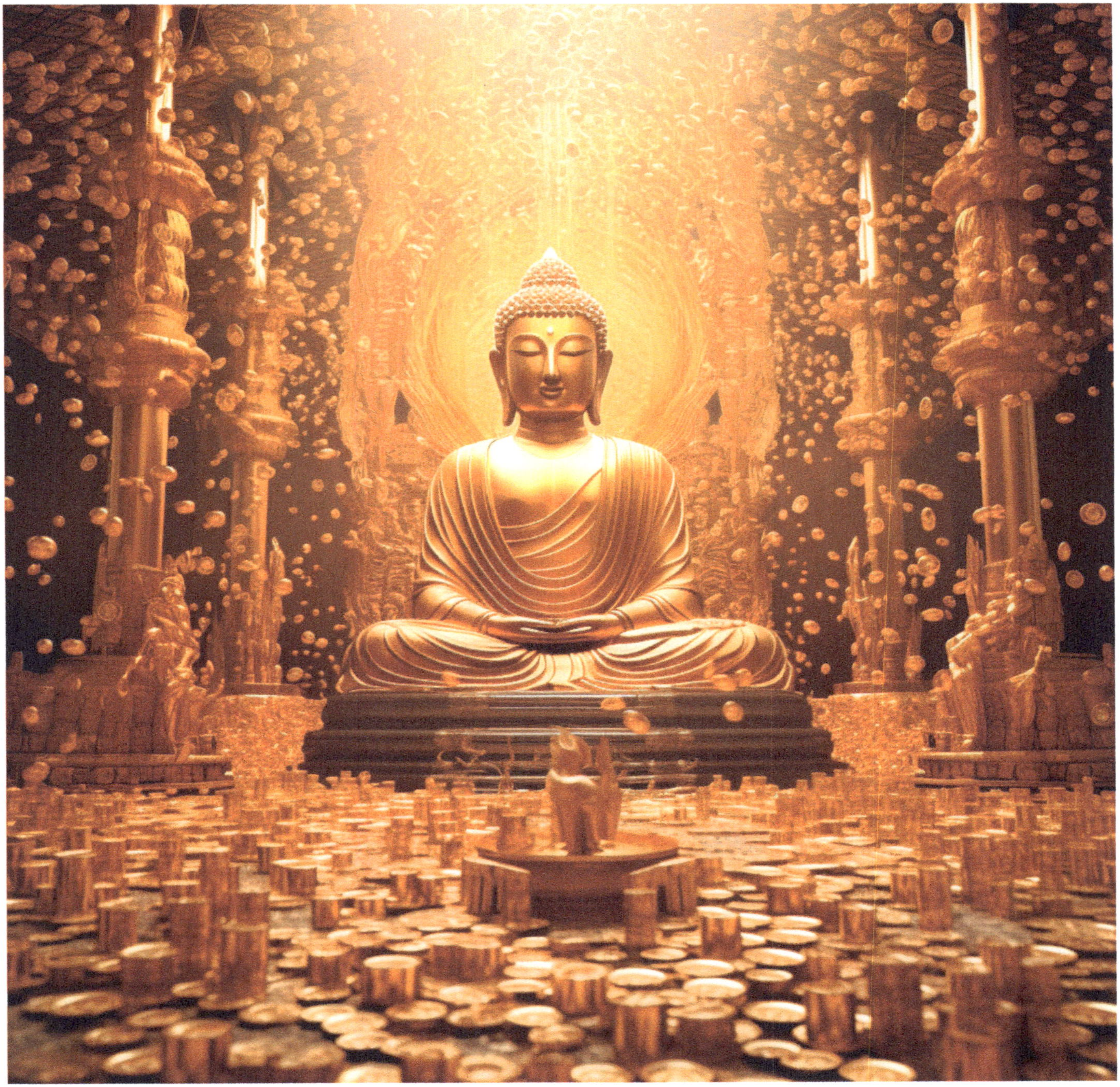

The path isn't easy, but it's not insurmountable either.

Serious practice and unwavering determination, are what it takes to walk this path.

Mara, the devil, and the forces of impurity strive to shroud the world in darkness, opposing those who seek Enlightenment. They tirelessly obstruct practitioners and aspirants on their journey.

As the Buddha proclaimed, human birth is rare, and rarer still is the discovery of the Dhamma—the path to liberation—in any lifetime. This pursuit embodies the essence of life and represents the Ultimate goal: to uncover the answers and find our way home.

Whether one walks the path as a monk or an ordinary individual, Enlightenment is within reach. The journey demands commitment and resilience, yet it promises liberation for those who persist.

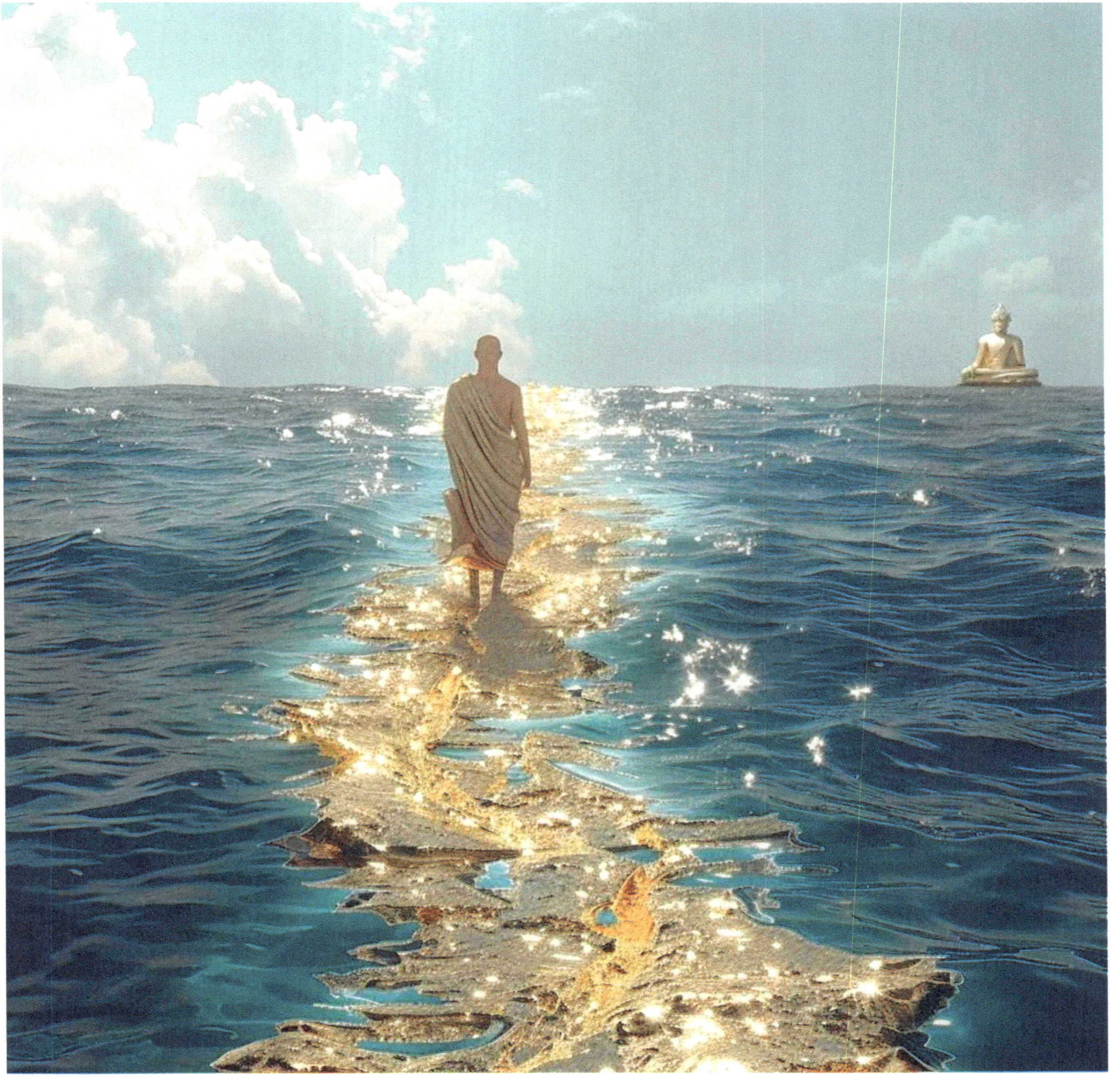

CHAPTER. 19

FATHER - DAD

My father, Detlef Soth, was a Good, Kind and Ethical man who loved his Wife and Children unconditionally.

If you do not believe in Reincarnation, perhaps consider how it would be possible to develop such goodness and virtue that defined my father, in a single Lifetime. (it is not possible)

Like every son and father, the relationship takes many turns until we get older and understand all he did for us, to make us who we are today. Sometimes when we look in the mirror, we even see Dad.

No son looks forward to the day your father grows old and meets death…. we always saw him so strong and sure. My father had Alzheimer's at the end. It was difficult for him and my mother.

I am so fortunate that at the end I was able to say good-bye to my father and despite his illness he told me how much he loved me and how proud he was of me.

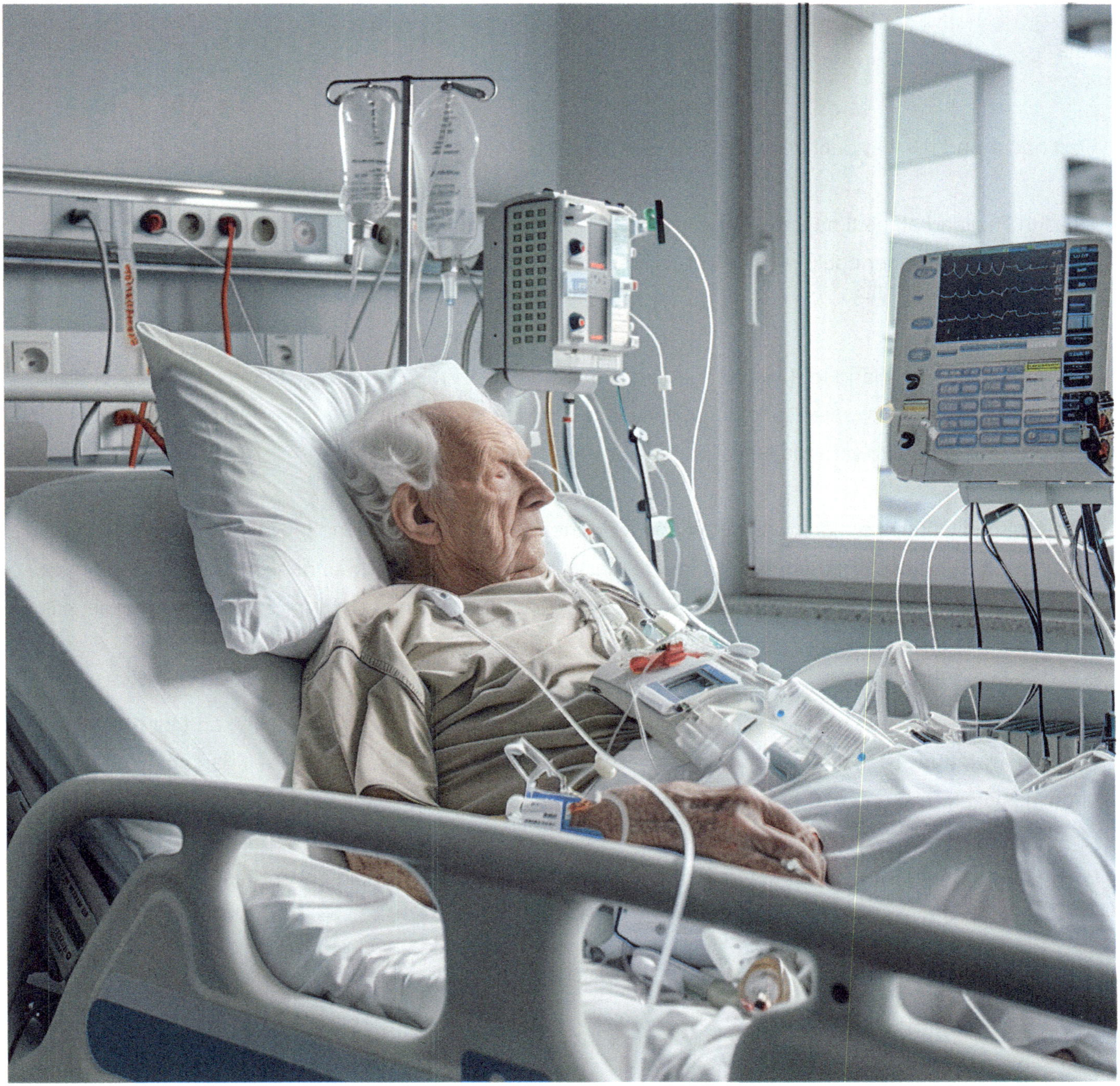

Dad had a bad fall that put him in the hospital. It was sad to see him die each day.

I was in Thailand at the time and contacting by VDO call. I came to learn that because of his condition and medications, my father could not drink much water. He was so thirsty, but water would create more suffering.

A young Monk in Thailand told me that he had learned a way to transfer Energy, from one dimension to the next. He asked me if I wanted to try to give my father the feeling of cool water to relieve his suffering. I agreed and we got several bottles of water.

Through meditation, the monk was able to be a bridge to connect my Mind to my father's Mind. We then began to drink bottles of water much to the delight of my father. At first, I was drinking sparkling water, but soon my father told us that he could only handle one glass of sparkling water, and please to give him still water. After two liters of water, it was enough.

I had sent a message to my family in the hospital that I was doing a special ceremony, and for them to observe my father. To their amazement his urine bag in the hospital filled up, where it had not seen any urine in a week. The nurse tried to find an explanation for this sudden massive flow of urine.

Later when I spoke with my mother, she also confirmed that my father could never drink more than one glass of sparkling water, otherwise it upset his stomach.

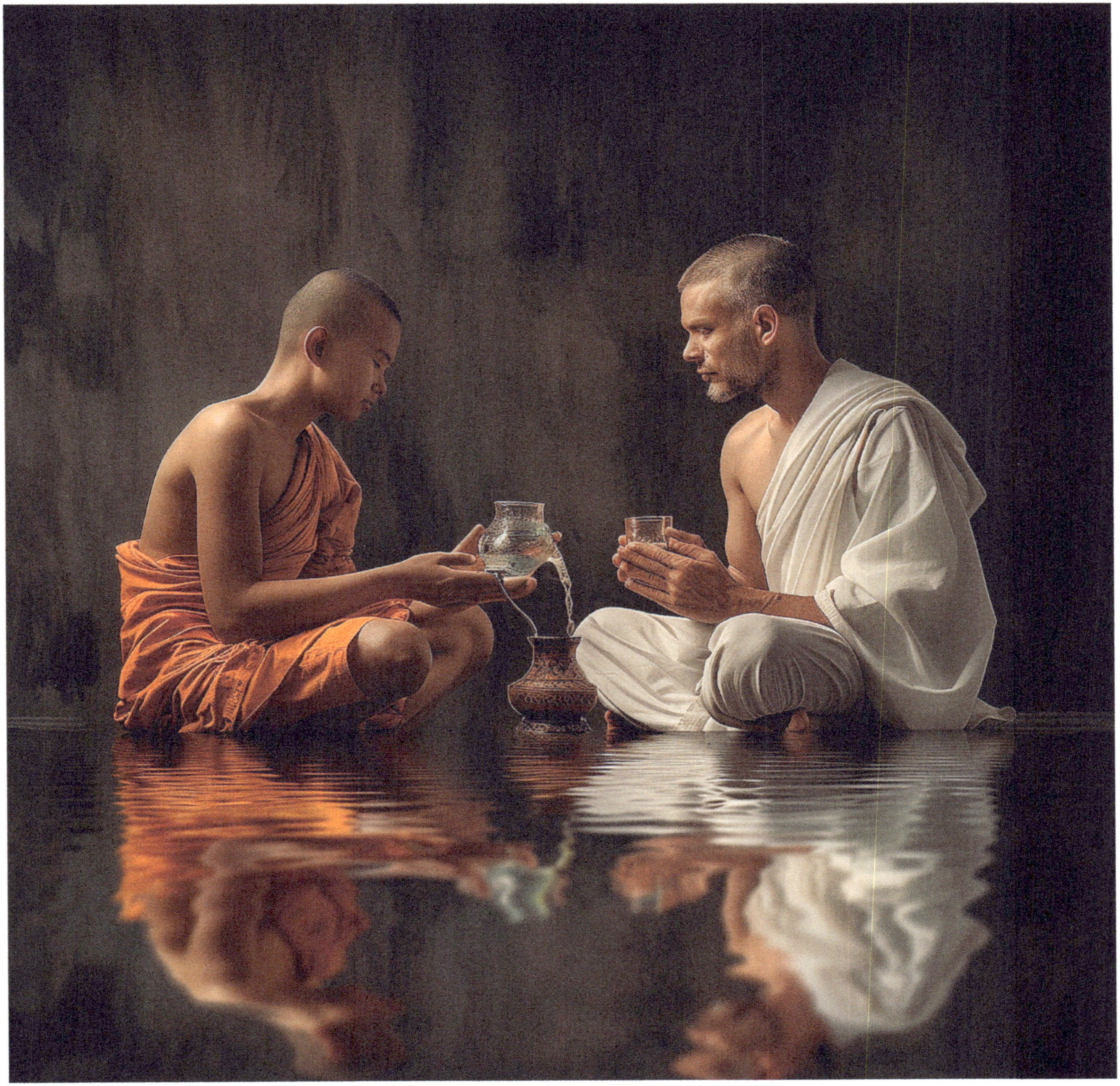

My father described to me the coolness and refreshing feeling of the water. It was like he was dancing in a cool pond on a hot summer day. He was so happy.

419

My Dad then explained to me how hard it was to have Alzheimer's, he said his Mind was fine, but it was like someone had cut the communication cables and he could not transform his thoughts into words.

He then told me what it was like to see his life end. My Dad said it was like driving into a bright orange sunset, so warm and familiar.

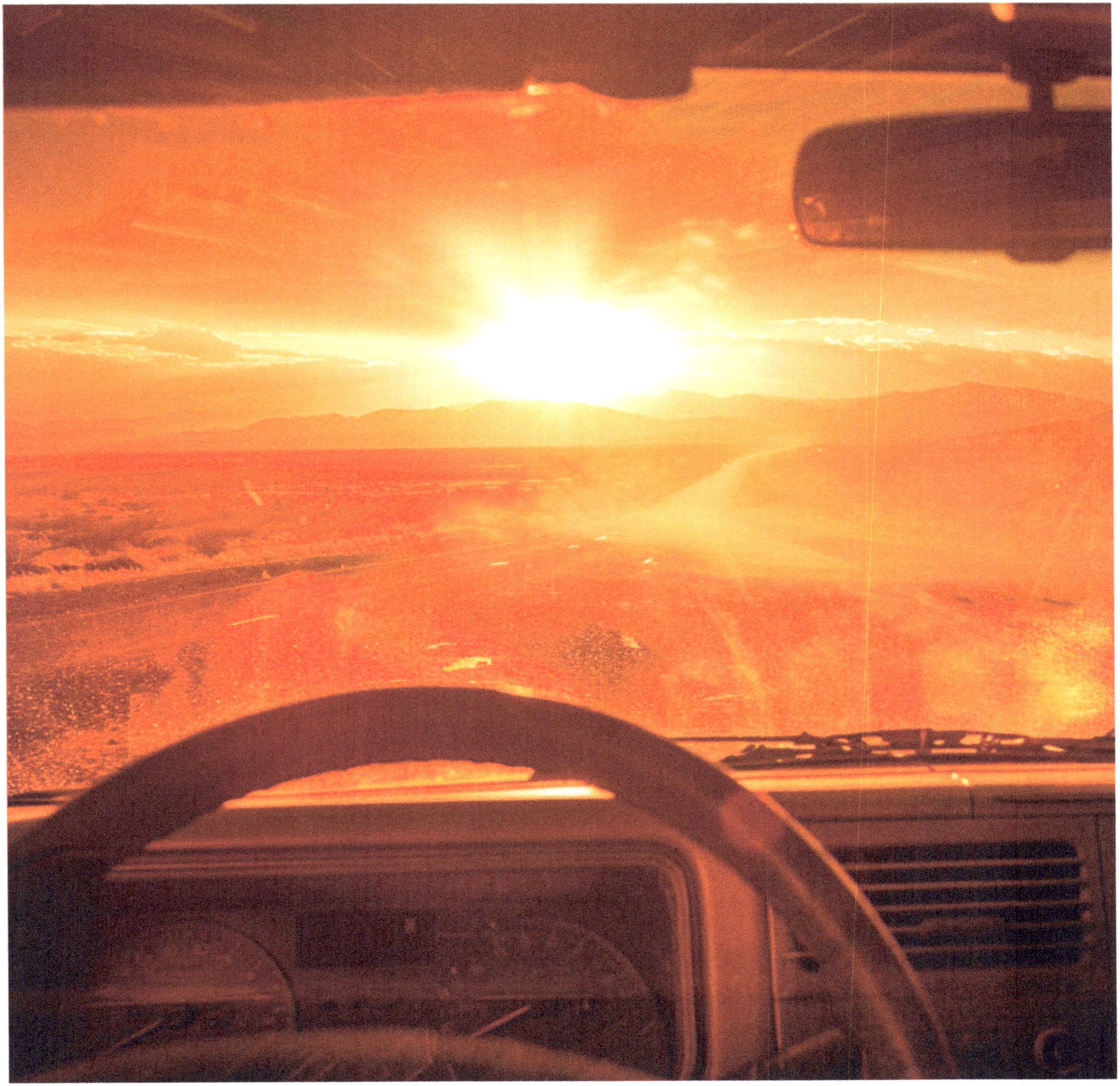

As your driving, for a moment you see a woman standing on the sidewalk and you realize that was your wife you had just spent a Lifetime with. Having and raising a family and experiencing Life's ups and downs.

But as the car passes by, that life is just a "blip" in time, and you forget all the hard times of that Life. You look ahead with clear perspective and consciousness; you understand like never before.

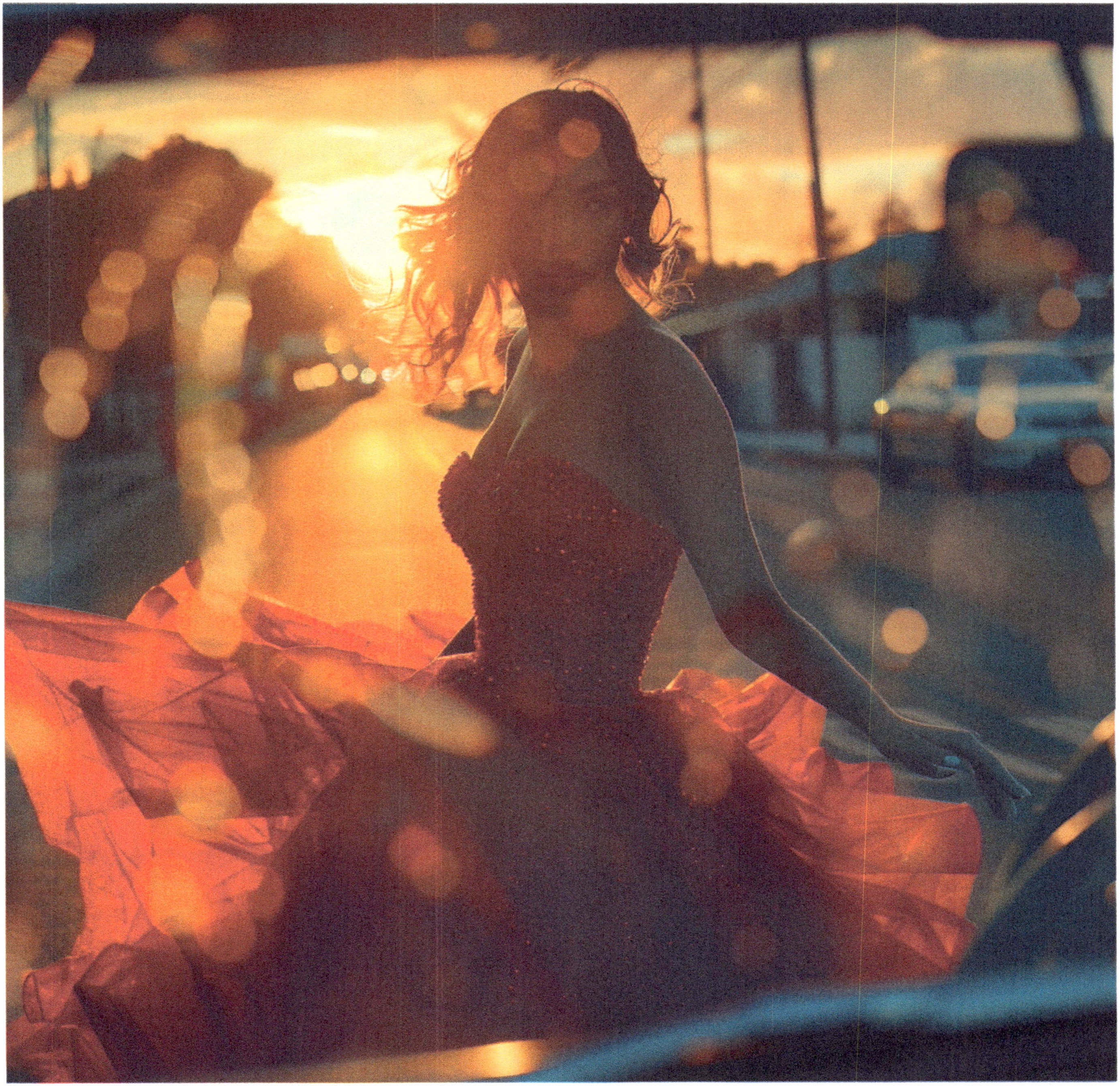

Then the Monk told me he could see my Father as a young handsome man, pulling train loads of gold, his reward for the merit he did in his Life and for raising a son who had reached the first stages of Enlightenment.

My Dad said he never understood what I was doing in Thailand and what this "whole meditation thing" was all about. But now he understood and again told me he was so proud of his son for figuring it out and helping his father reach Noble wealth in the after Life.

425

My father then appeared where the Monk and I were sitting. I had a chance to tell him I LOVED him and thank you for being my father.

He started talking about how hard his early Life had been with growing up as a boy during World War II and how he lost his own father and then later his brother in a freak accident. Curiously, he spoke in German as he recounted these details.

Parents have a strong connection to their children. This is why family relationships can be so emotional and difficult. I was Lucky to have meditation insights to clear any feelings between my parents and myself, which can be the root of disease and future Karma.

Today, I still am able to send my father energy and merit into the next dimension and Life. Nothing feels better than to be able to try to repay your parents, even if they are gone.

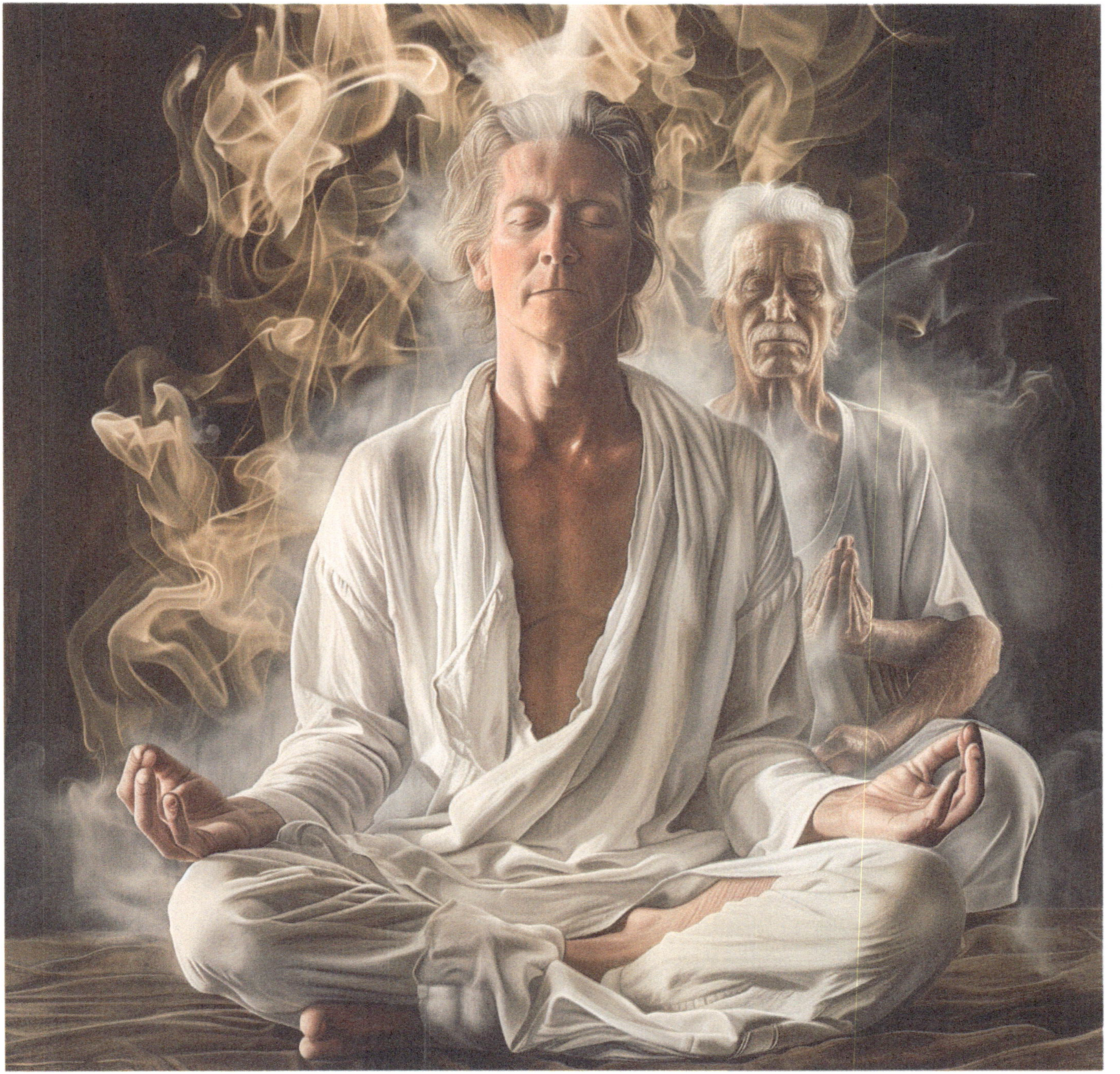

CHAPTER. 20

MOTHER – MOM

My Mother, Elke Soth is a Good, Kind and Virtuous woman. She loved her husband and has always Loved me and made my Life what it is today.

She is 87 years old and still takes care of herself, her business, and her home. She has always been an amazing overly hardworking and productive woman, who was real and kind to so many people who all think so highly of her and have such admiration for her.

During one Techo Vipassana meditation course, I had a very clear vision of a beautiful young Indian woman, in old wealthy India probably 2500 years ago. She was shopping in the colorful market. I could see her looking in a mirror checking her hair.

I knew this was my mother in this current Lifetime. From the vision I did not know what my relationship to this beautiful young Indian woman was, but I know it was family.

What I realized from this vision was the truth of reincarnation, how we follow loved ones across time and that the World and people were as or even more beautiful than today.

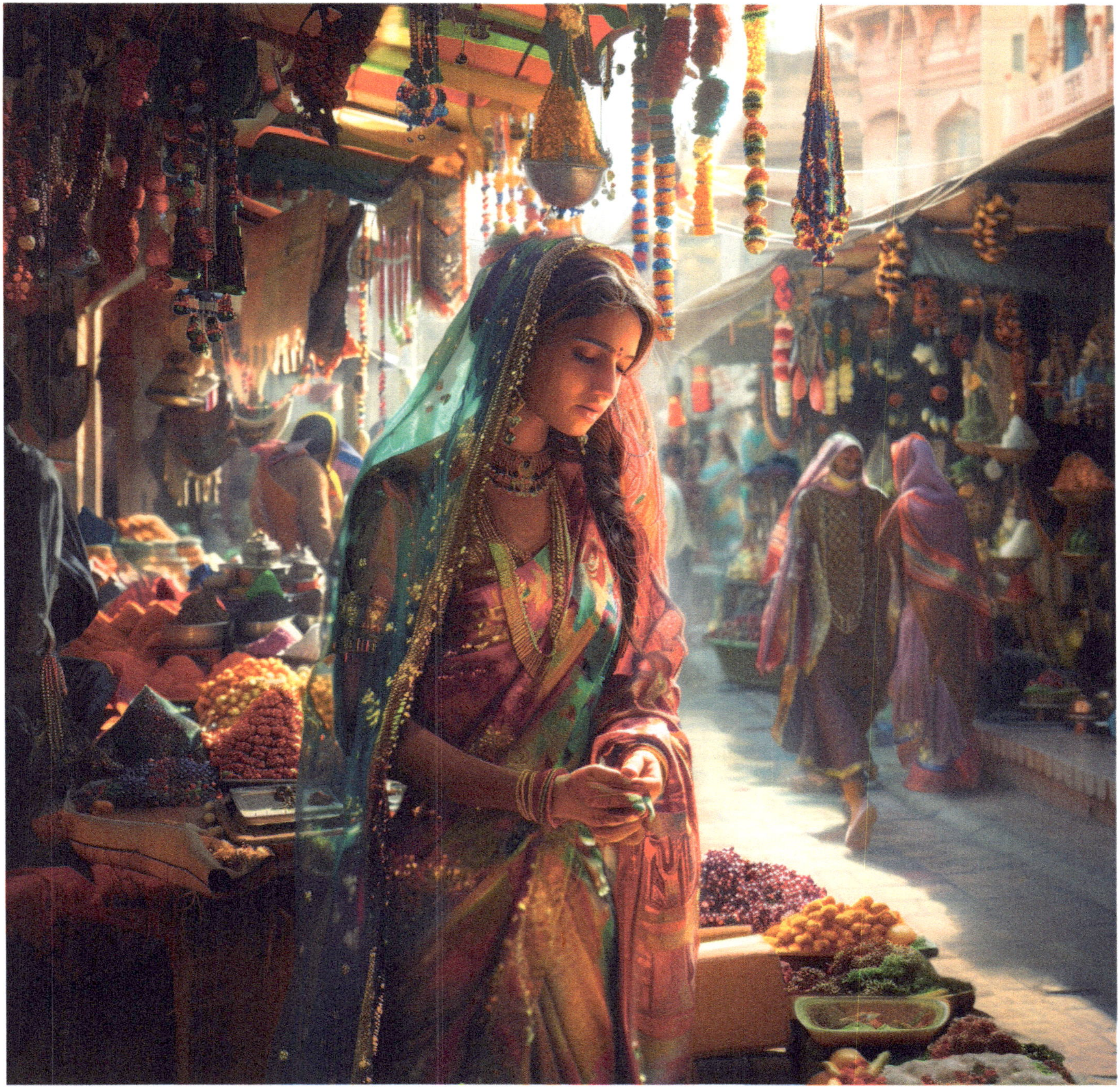

Another vision I had in a Techo Vipassana meditation course, was that of my mother. Mom's body was in the form of Gold Energy, but with black spots in various areas, especially the hips and areas I knew she had illness and pain.

I knew from my vision that these spots were the results of Karma.

My Mother had pain in various areas her entire Life. This caused her a lot of suffering and discomfort. She also cannot tolerate many medications including pain medications, so she has had to endure pain her whole life, keeping her Mind busy in order not to focus on the pain.

Mom does not know meditation; however, I can see how her GOODNESS had cancelled out many of her pains and sufferings.

Good Karma can come in many forms. Finding the right doctor, eliminating pain, or even being cured.

Modern medicine is a sort of Karma itself. Often time pharmaceuticals only mask the symptom or a disease. Finding the real cure depends on a person's karma and luck.

433

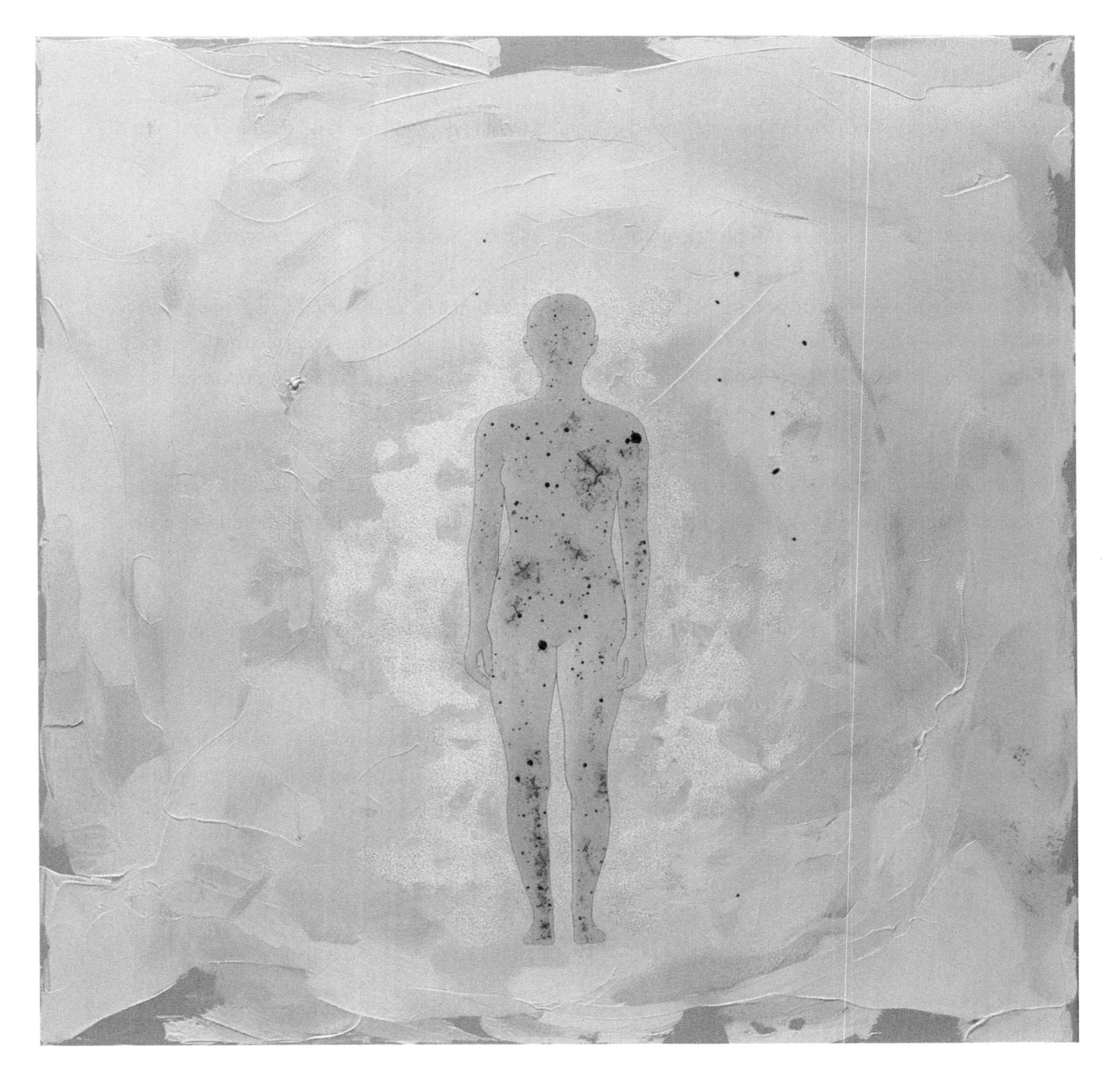

Ever since I was young, my mother was afraid of getting old, having no one to take care of her and of course dying.

Today I do not believe she is afraid of death as much, but most people fear the unknown.

What I have learned from advanced meditation, is how important it is for the Mind to be free of heavy feelings and emotions at the time of death. Having relatives crying or doctors trying to revive a body, can lock the dying person's Mind in a heavy gravity, that may keep their Minds from rising up to higher dimensions in the dimension of Energy, Heaven or all the way up to Nirvana.

It is almost like Mara (the devil) has made modern medicine and life support machines, to further trap Souls and Minds into a heavy gravity wave at the time of death, to prevent transcending or a positive rebirth.

What does a Life support machine accomplish when a person's time is up? When Karma has come to collect.

I had a vision during meditation of me and Mom sitting on a train together, looking into the orange sunset, me holding her hand, knowing that everything for her would be alright. That when it is her time, she will also get her reward and Noble Treasure for being my Wonderful Mother.

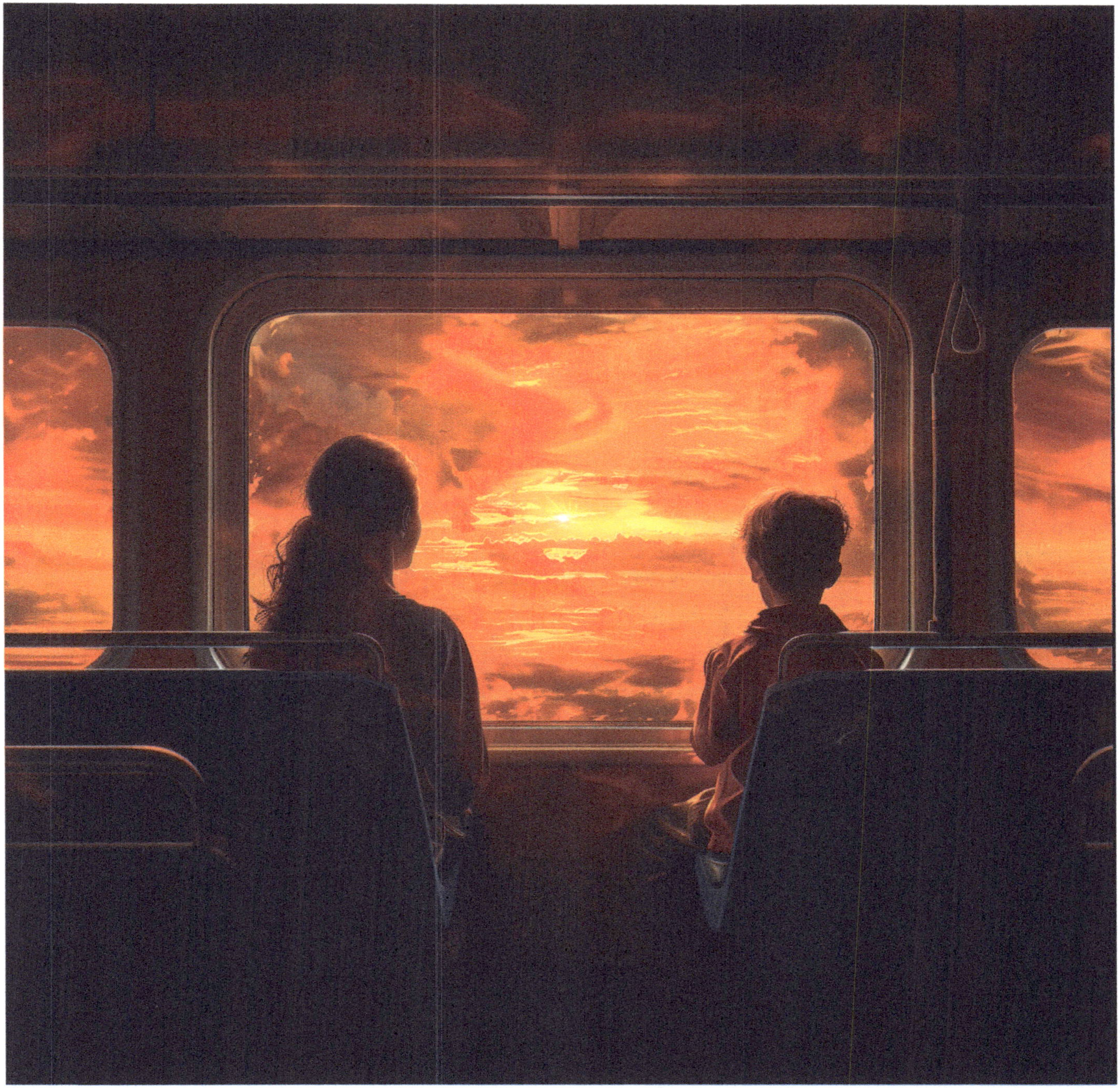

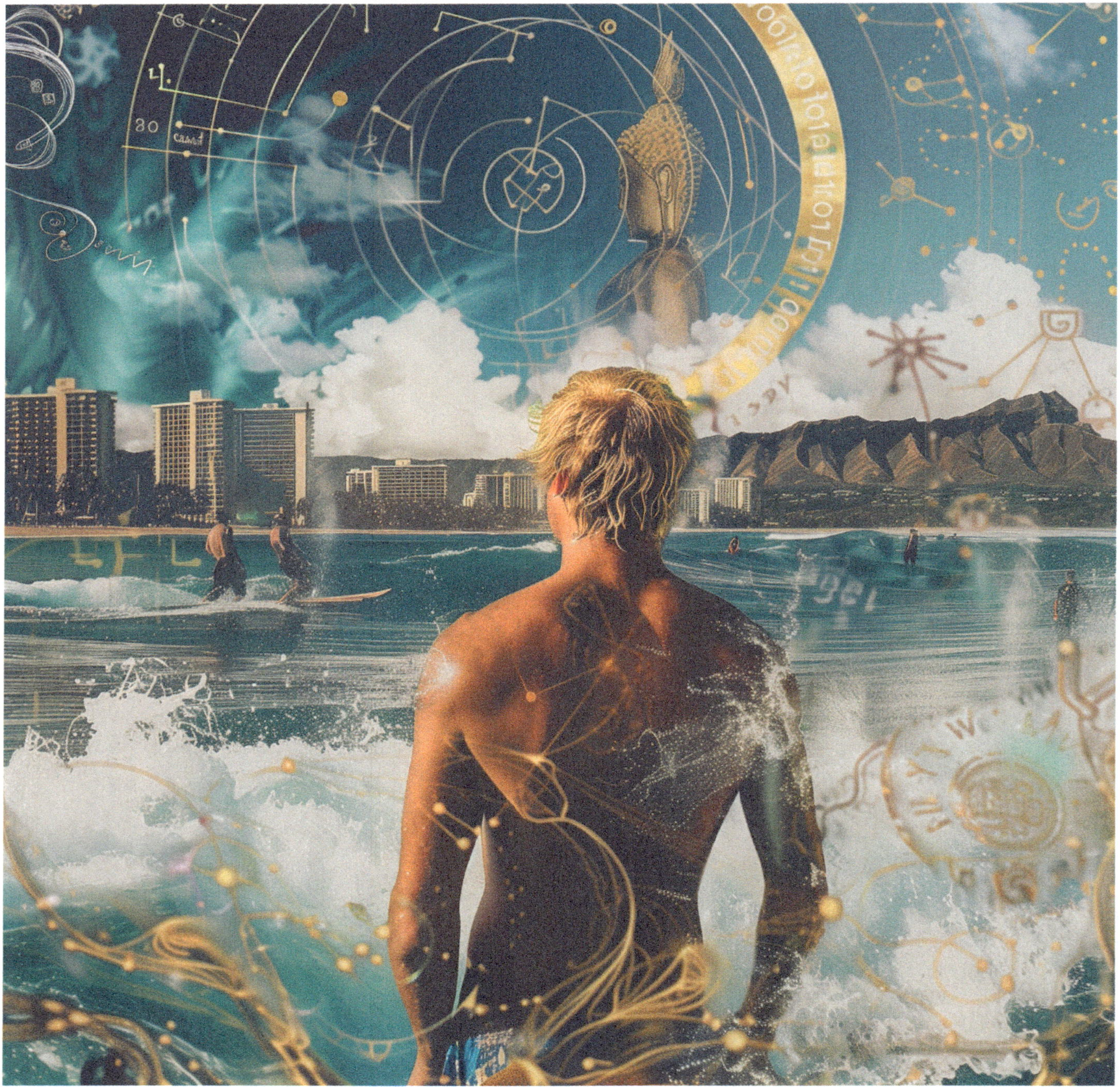

CHAPTER. 21

SPIRITUAL PATH

In my life's journey, I've always sought adventure, constantly striving to discover both myself and the meaning of life. Perhaps the answers awaited me at the summit of a mountain, so I embarked on a quest to climb one.

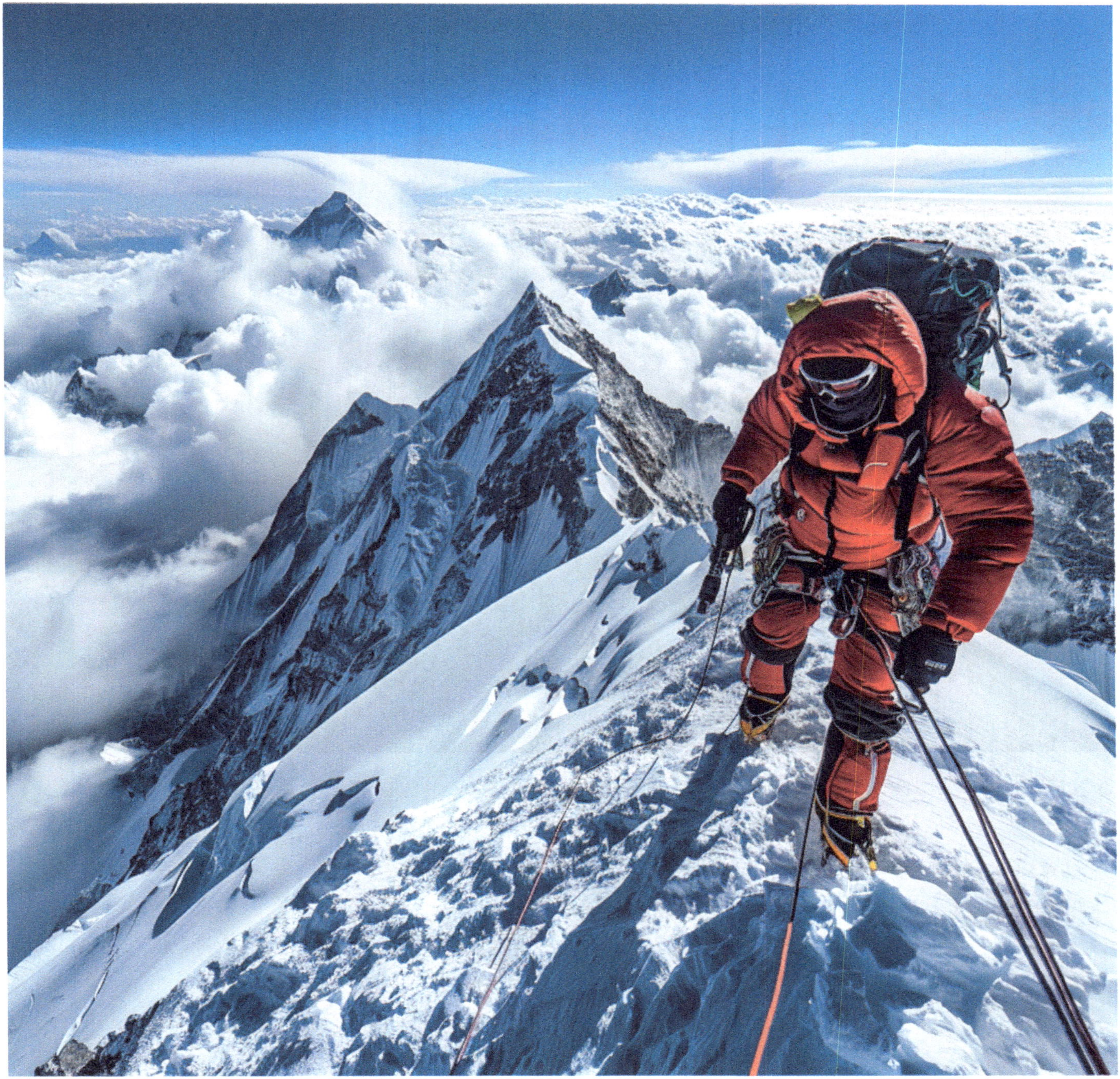

In my quest for answers, I sought solace on the waves, surfing oceans around the world in search of enlightenment.

441

Exploring the realms of the rich and famous, I traversed the globe attending their extravagant parties, mingling with beautiful people, and indulging in their lavish drinks.

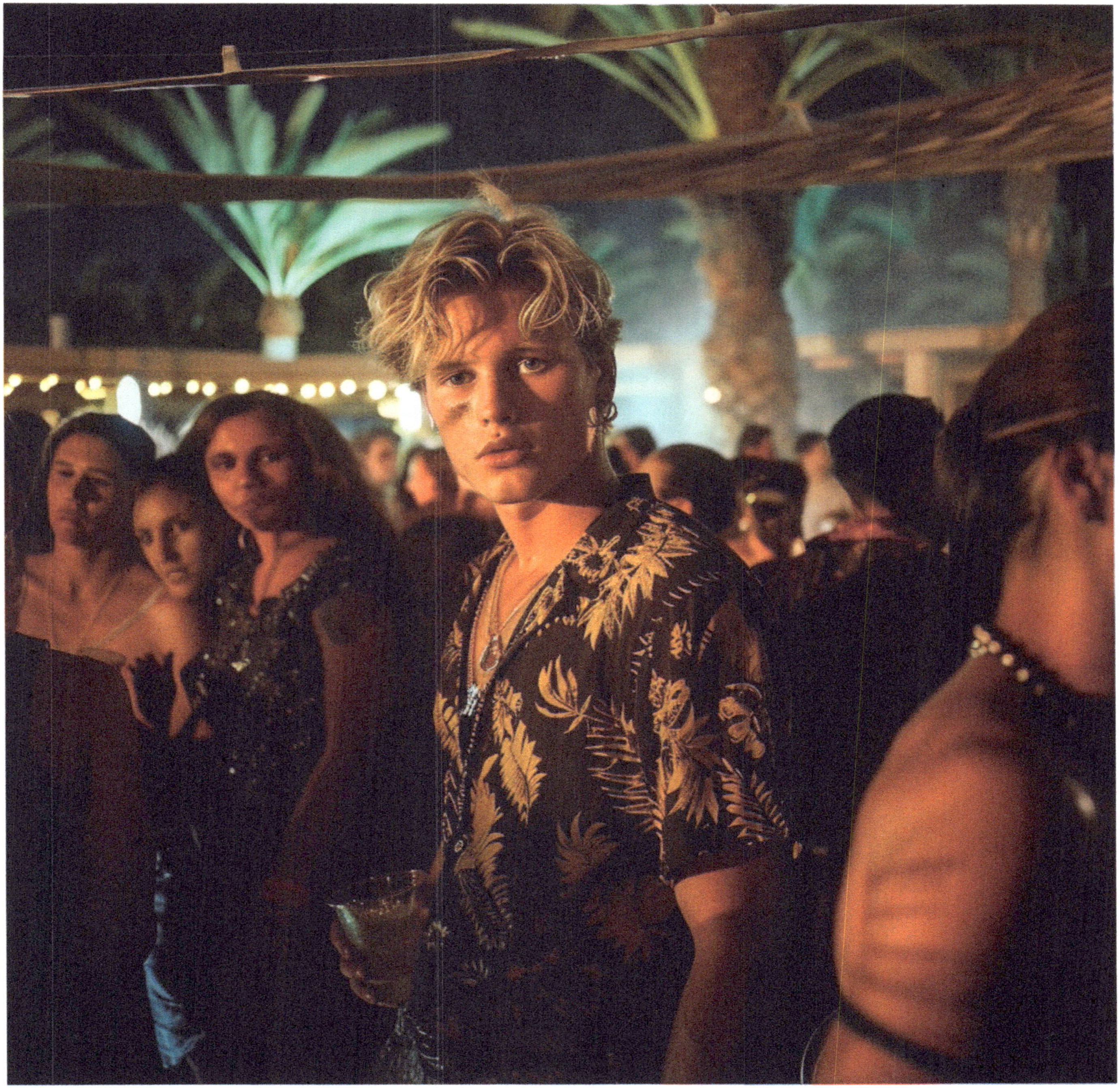

Exploring ancient ruins in distant lands might hold the key to unlocking the answers we seek.

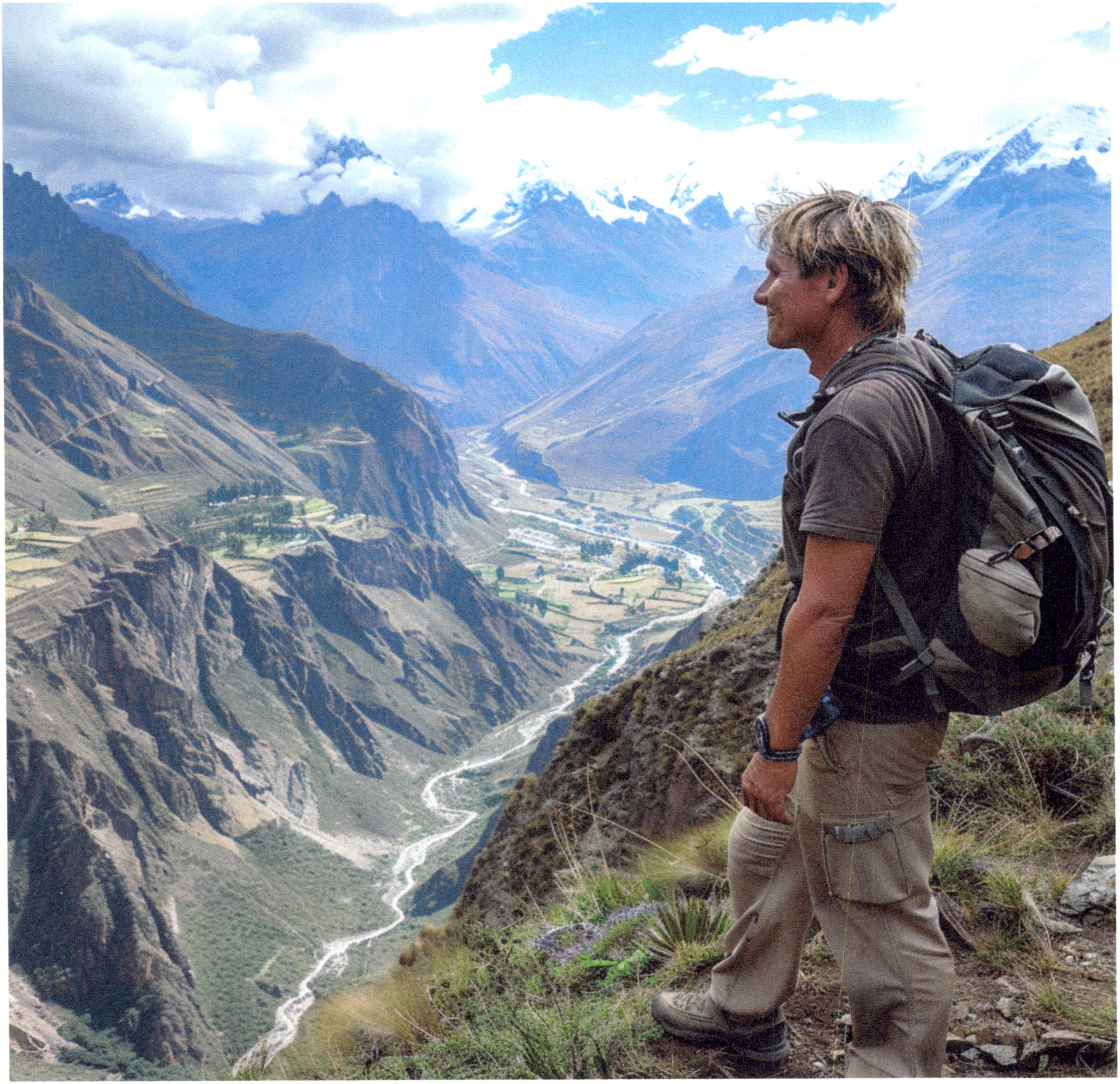

For weeks, I journeyed along the Inca trails, immersing myself in the mysteries of the past as I explored the ruins and deciphered the clues left behind by ancient civilizations.

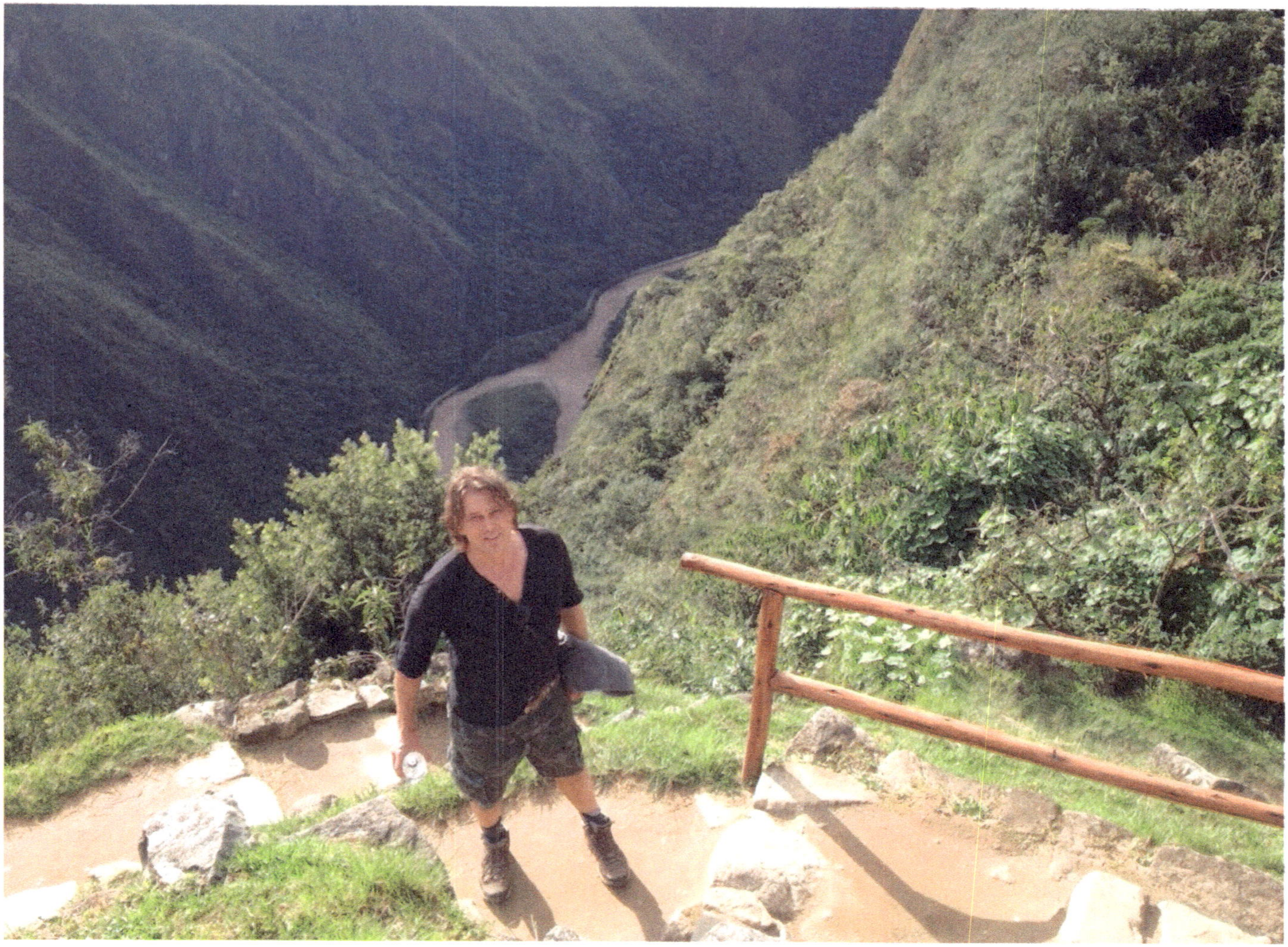

I trekked through valleys and ascended mountains, reaching the summit where the remnants of ancient civilizations lay dormant, their stories echoing through the ages.

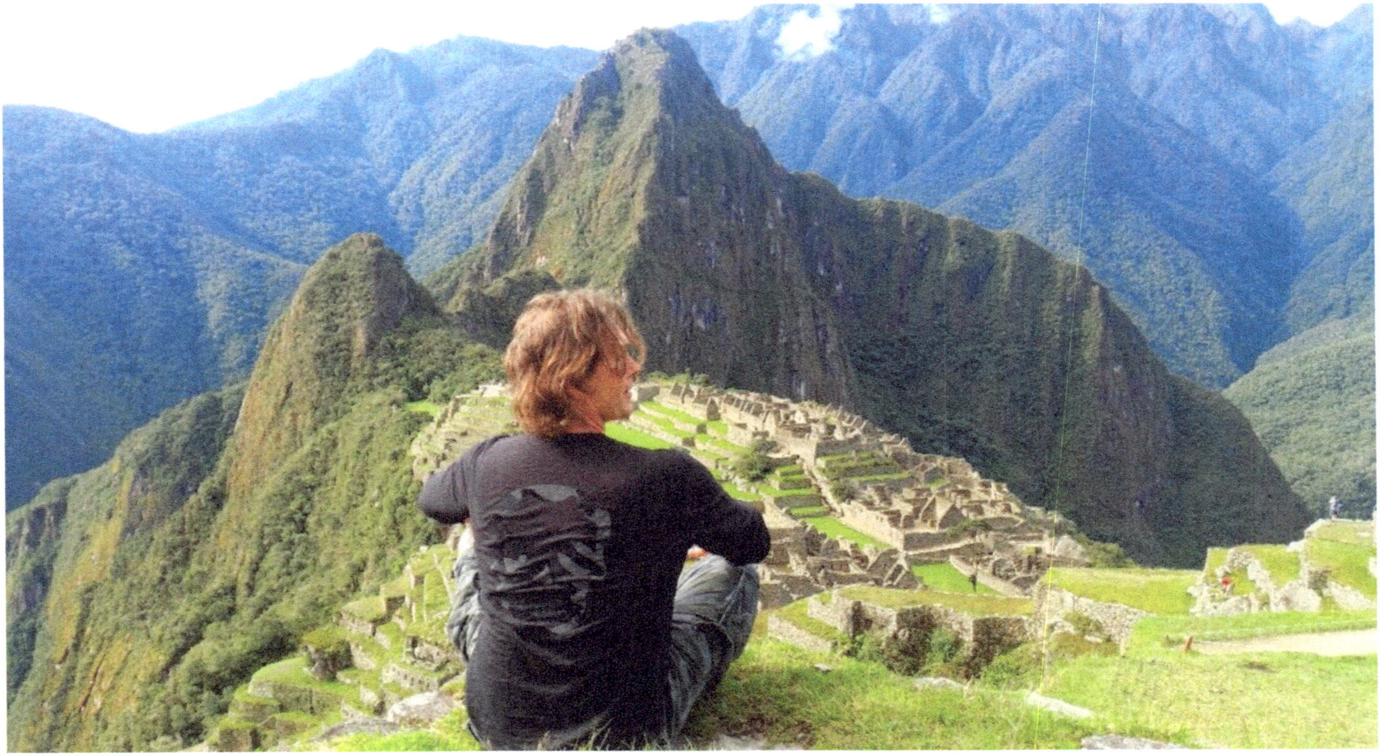

As I journeyed deeper into the Amazon Jungles, flying for hours over a vast expanse of untouched greenery, I marveled at the sheer magnitude of the pristine wilderness unfolding beneath me.

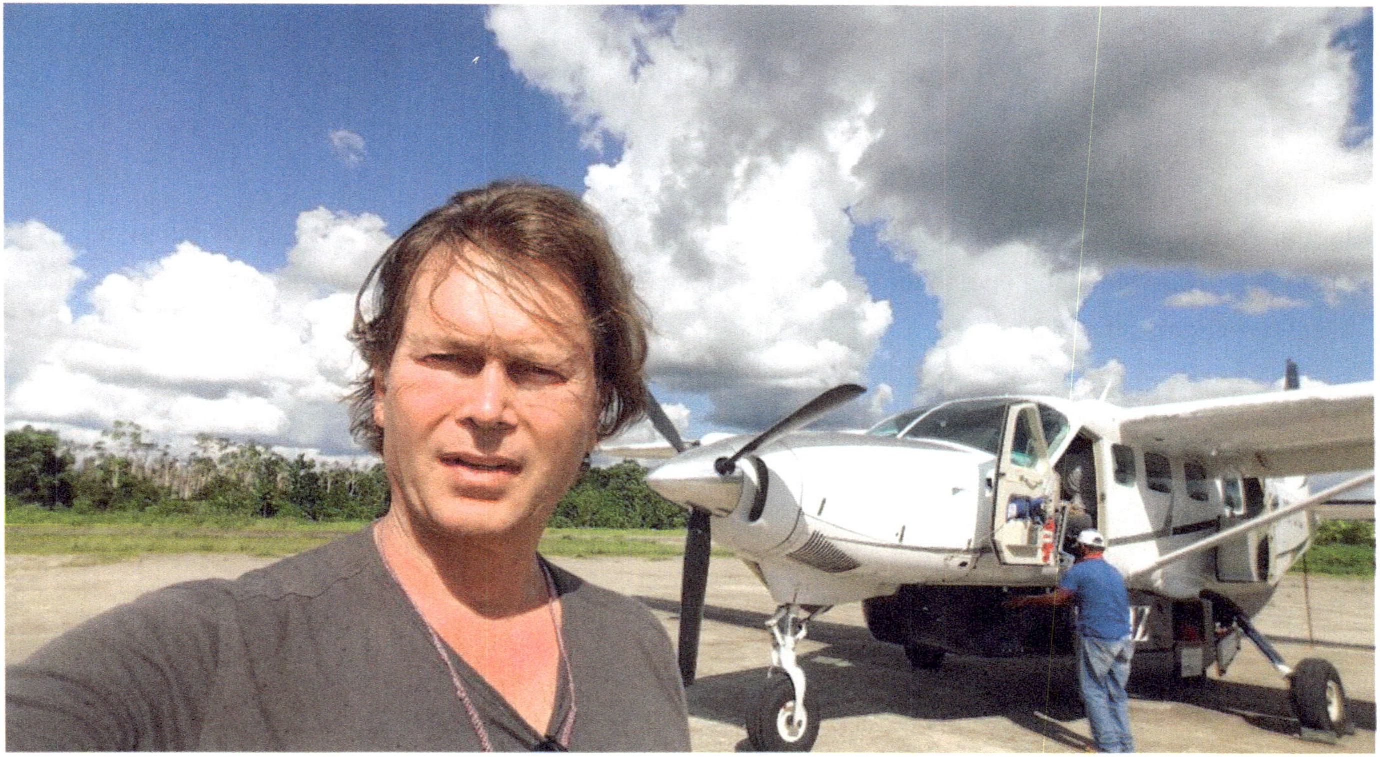

Indeed, this untouched wilderness epitomized the true nature of the world—unreached, untouched, and unspoiled. It served as the engine that cleansed the air, bringing forth fresh breezes and nourishing rain to sustain life across the planet.

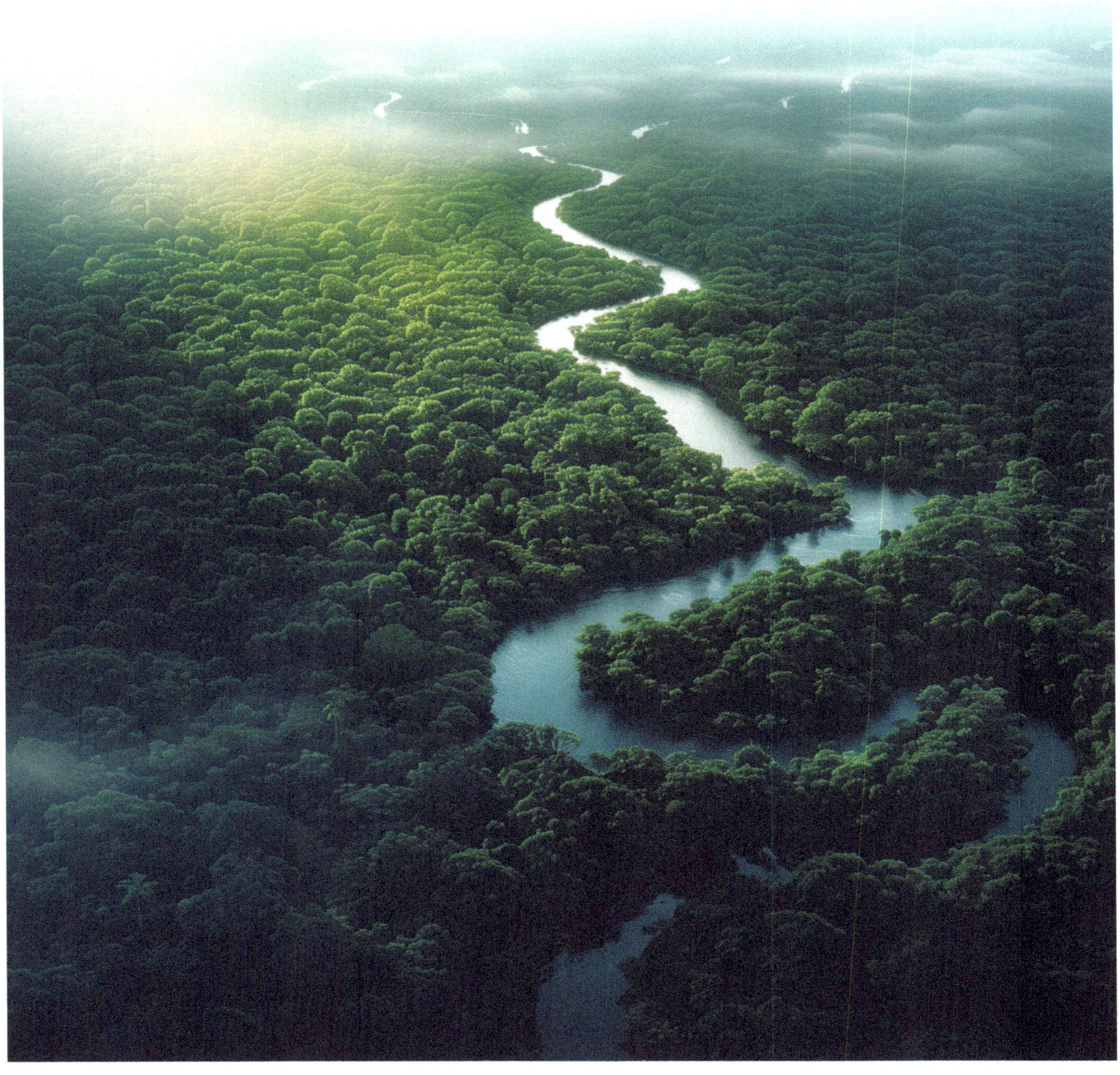

In this untouched realm, where rivers served as the sole pathways, dwelled the forest people. Their lives remained unblemished by the outside world's touch, preserving a pristine existence amidst the Amazon's vast wilderness.

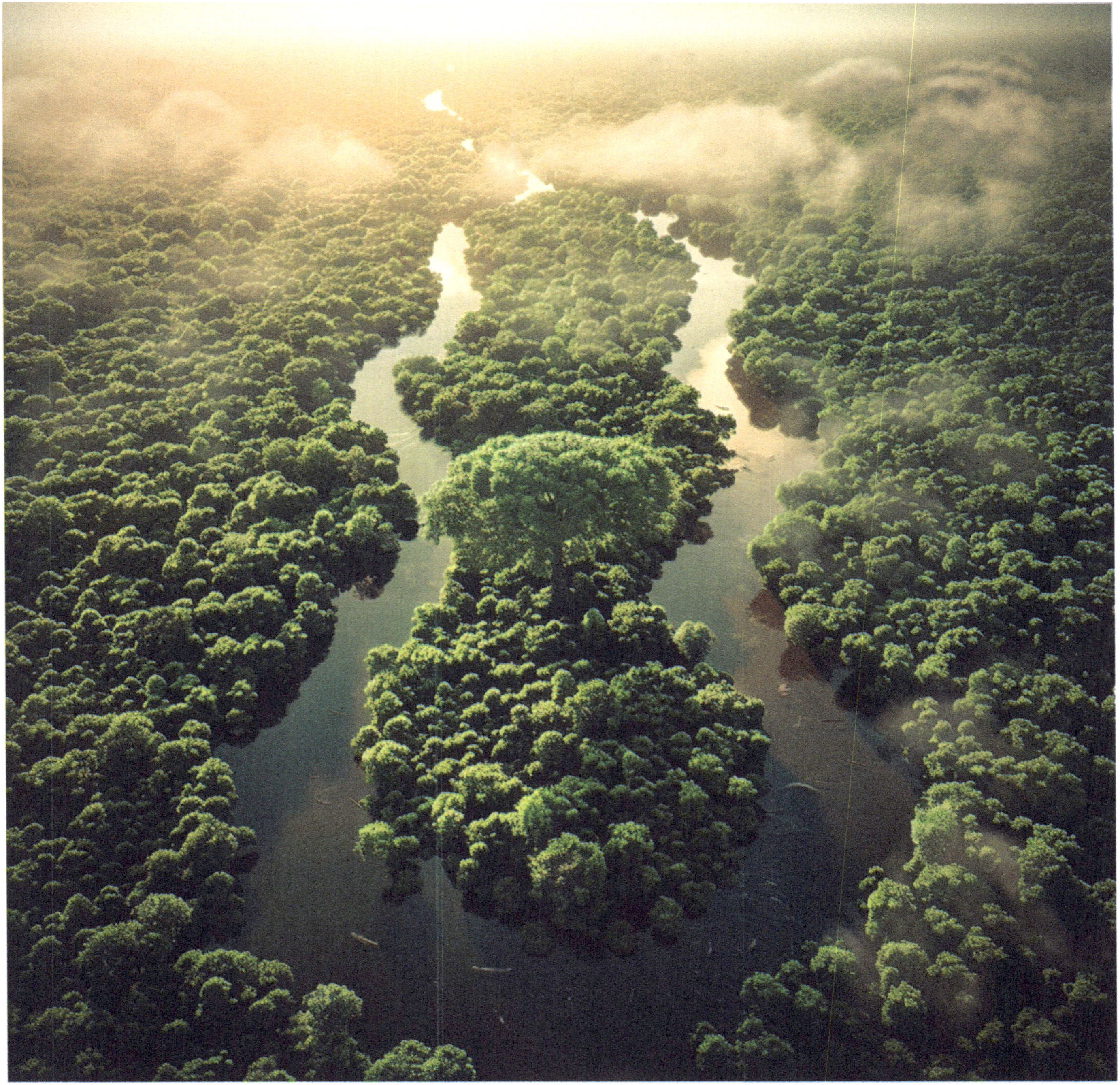

The Indians welcomed me warmly, their open arms a stark contrast to the stories I had heard while journeying through the dense jungle. Tales of tribes untouched by the outside world, of hostage-taking, and even cannibalism had filled my ears.

Yet, as I delved deeper into the heart of the Amazon, I couldn't shake the feeling that perhaps the answers I sought lay within these ancient tribes. Their history, spanning an incredible 50,000 years, held secrets and wisdom waiting to be discovered.

Among the tribes, I learned of plants with mystical properties, whispered to hold the key to unlocking profound truths. Could these plants be the gateway to the enlightenment I sought?

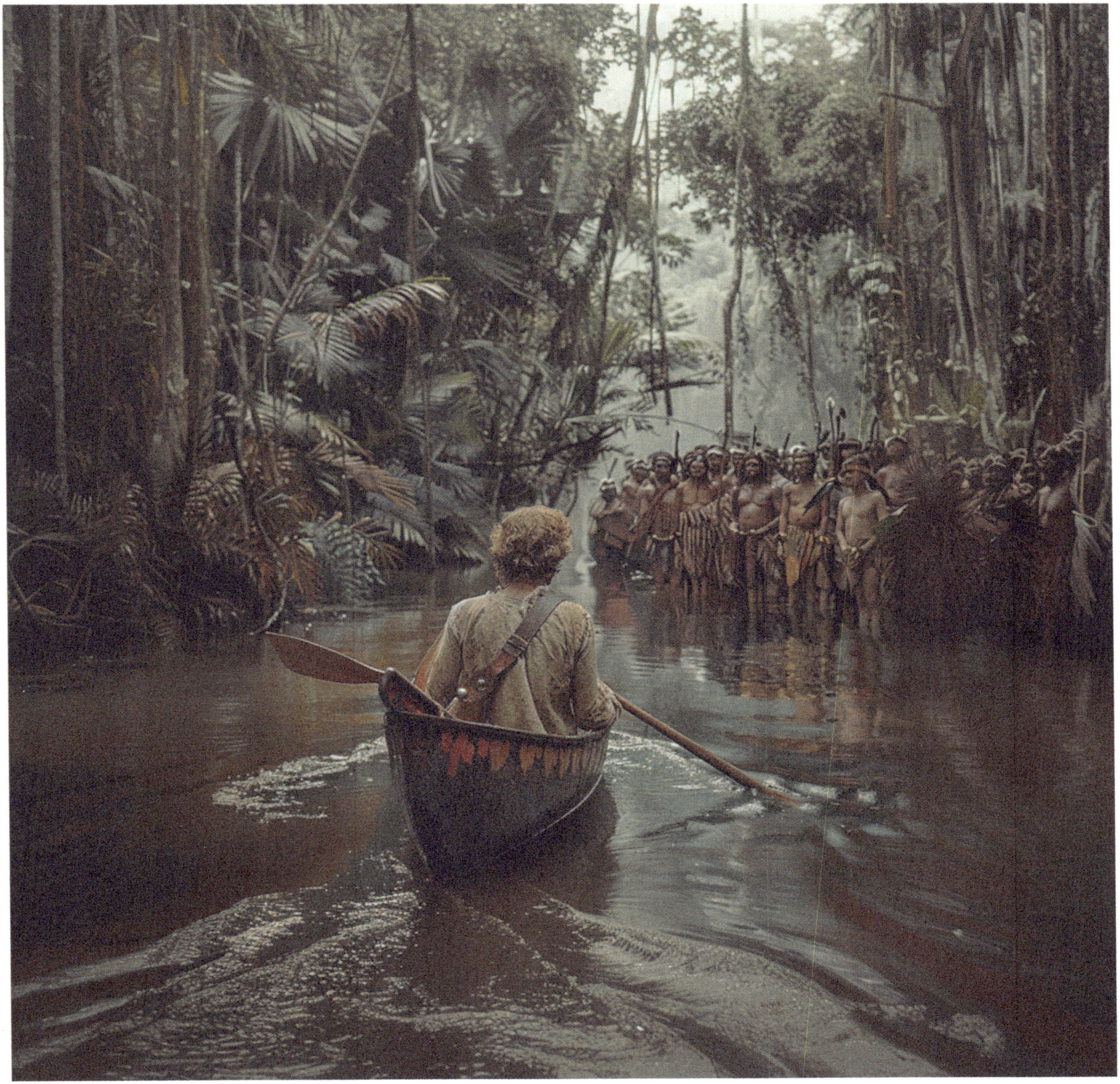

Living among the Amazon Indians, I stumbled upon a profound truth: the notion that past generations were less advanced is a fallacy. In fact, there was much wisdom to be gleaned from this pristine culture, untouched by the complexities of modern society.

Their way of life was simple yet deeply fulfilling. They shared everything—food, stories, experiences—nurturing a sense of unity and communal spirit often absent in today's individualistic and materialistic world.

Unlike our society, there were no distractions like smartphones or TVs, resulting in a lack of greed or disease. Their happiness stemmed from close connections to each other and to nature.

Their approach to food was equally simple and sustainable. They hunted only what they needed, turning to fishing when food was scarce. They ate when there was food, fasting when there wasn't, with no fixed mealtimes or the concept of three meals a day. There was no sugar addiction, nor anyone overweight or sick from consuming GMO or processed foods. It was a truly harmonious and symbiotic relationship between food and nature.

Through this experience, I learned that life can be just fine without sugar, which has become the most consumed drug of our generation and the root of much illness.

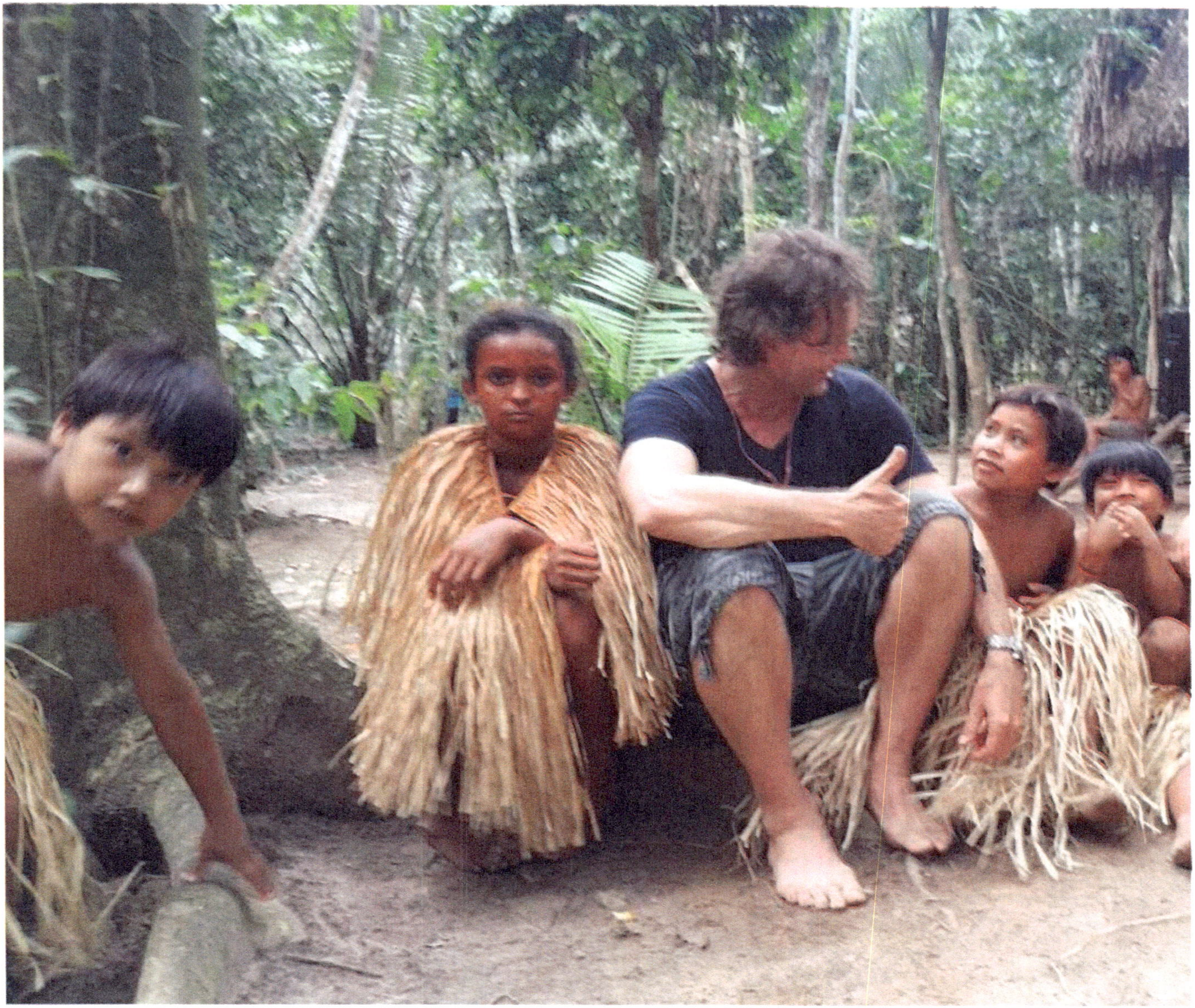

Living in the jungle presented its challenges, especially with the abundance of insects and bugs that seemed eager to make a meal out of me. To combat this, the Indians introduced me to a solution: the medicine of the green tree frog. They believed that this frog's medicine would offer protection against the jungle's pests and other creatures.

As we embarked on a canoe ride to find the frog, I couldn't help but marvel at the richness of the air around me. It was unlike anything I had ever experienced - so alive, vibrant, and filled with flavor and oxygen. In that moment, as I took a deep breath, I felt a profound connection to the very source of all life. It was a breath I would never forget, an experience that stayed with me forever.

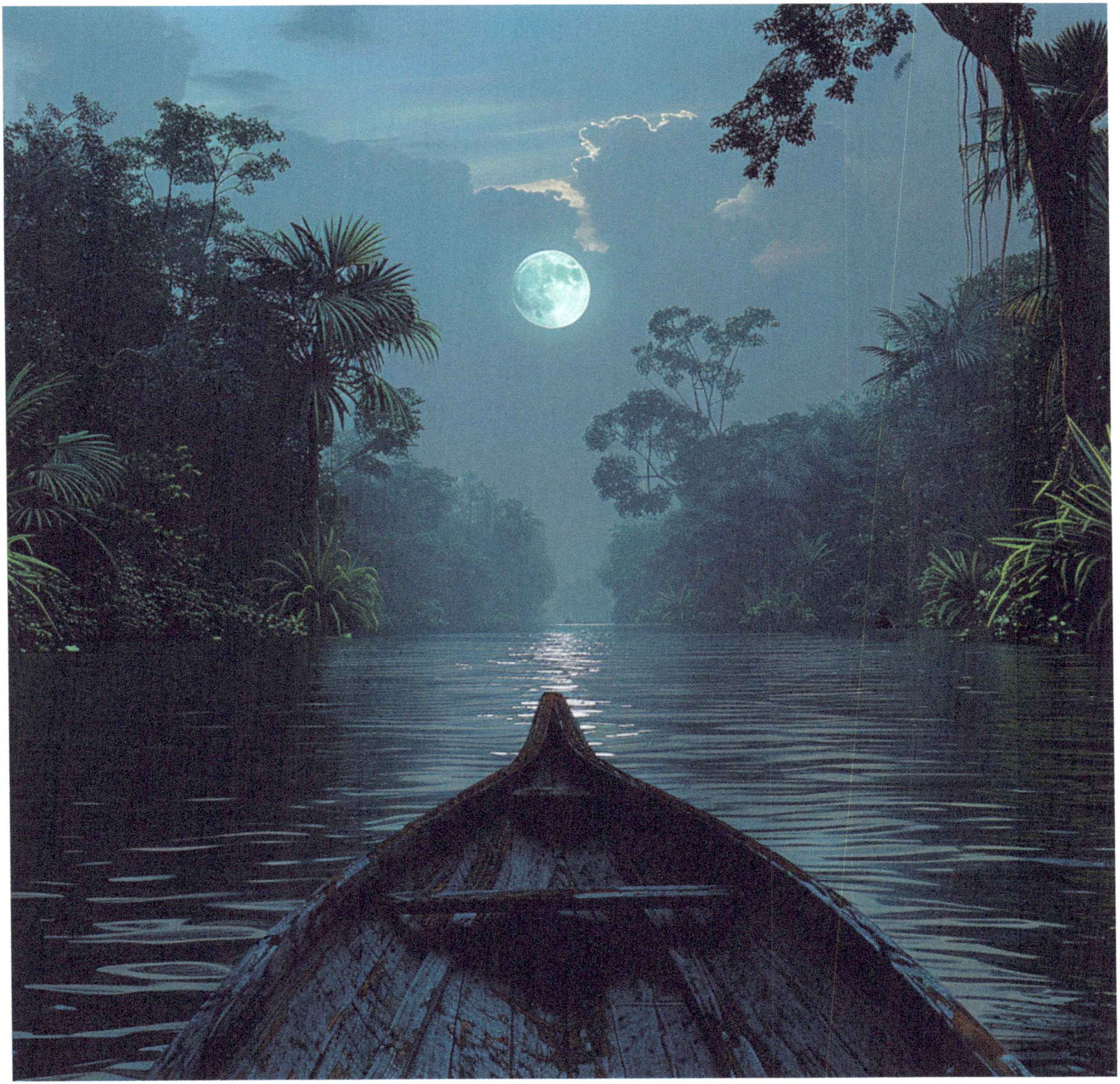

Despite its small size, the green tree frog was regarded as one of the most dangerous creatures in the jungle, surpassing even the black jaguar or the wild boars in terms of peril. The reason for this was the potent poison secreted by the frog's skin. Just a single drop of this poison could swiftly incapacitate any animal unfortunate enough to come into contact with it.

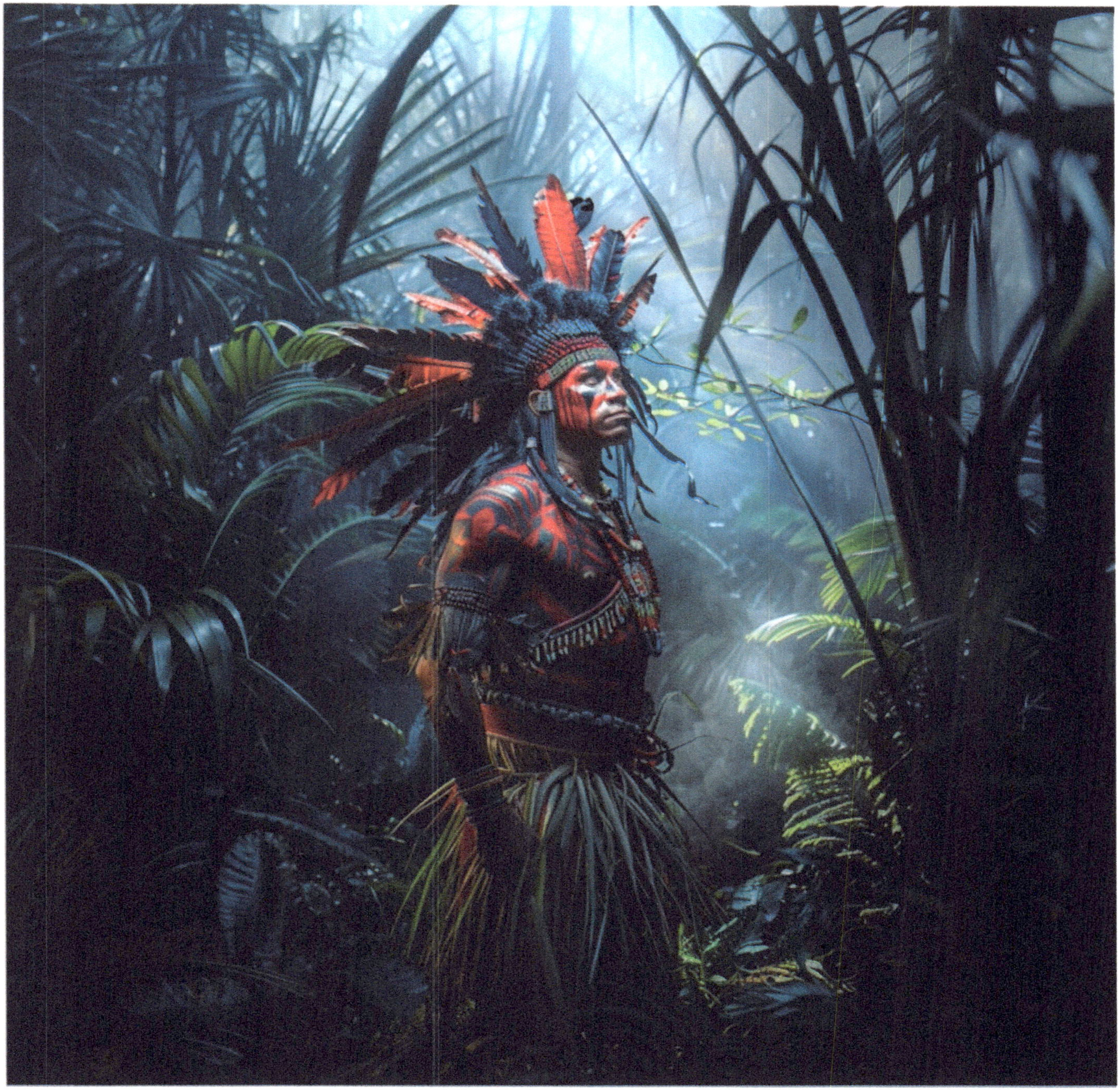

The green tree frog was easily identifiable by its loud nocturnal mating calls, echoing through the jungle night. Confident in its poisonous defense, this small frog sang its song with the bravado of a true jungle monarch, unchallenged by any predator in its domain.

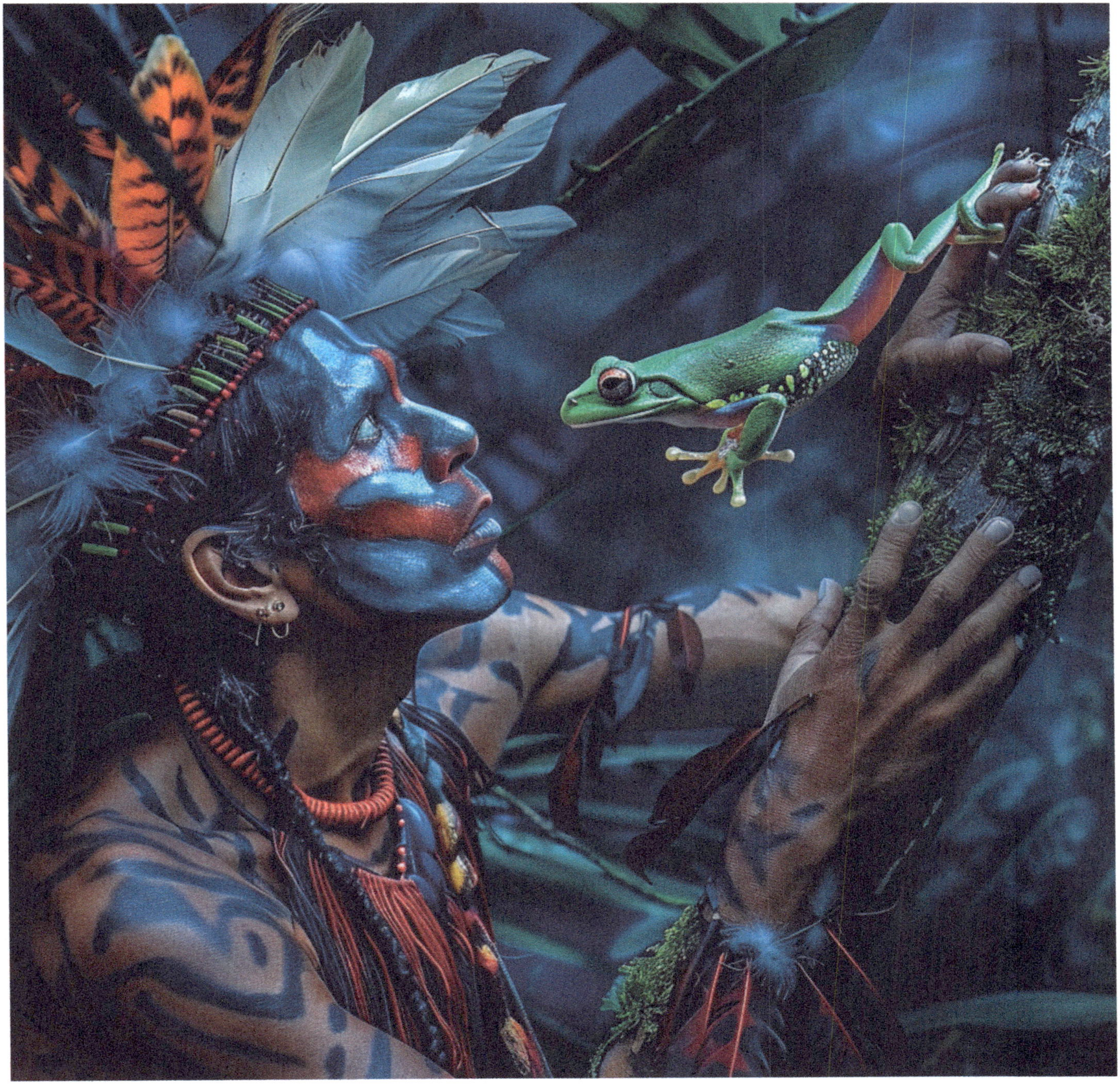

The process of inoculation with the tree frog poison was intense. Sitting in the creek, the medicine man meticulously applied the poison to small burns on my arm, using a burning stick. Almost immediately, I felt the effects coursing through my body—an intense vibration in my ears and a narrowing of my vision. The reaction was so severe that I vomited a bright green liquid.

Just as I felt myself slipping away, the Indian sprang into action, reviving me with fresh water poured over my head and applied to my wounds. In that moment, I had become inoculated with the jungle's most potent poison, ensuring that no insect or animal would dare approach me, repelled by the unmistakable scent of the tree frog poison.

467

The medicine man prepared a solution from a plant found in the jungle, squeezing clear liquid from its root. After straining the liquid through my t-shirt, he applied a few drops to my eyes. Initially, the sensation was intense, burning fiercely for a few moments.

But as the discomfort subsided, I opened my eyes to a world transformed. The clarity and vividness were astonishing—I could see deep into the intricate branches of the jungle canopy above.

It was a powerful reminder of the wealth of natural medicines hidden within the jungle, contrasting starkly with the synthetic, petroleum-based drugs of modern medicine.

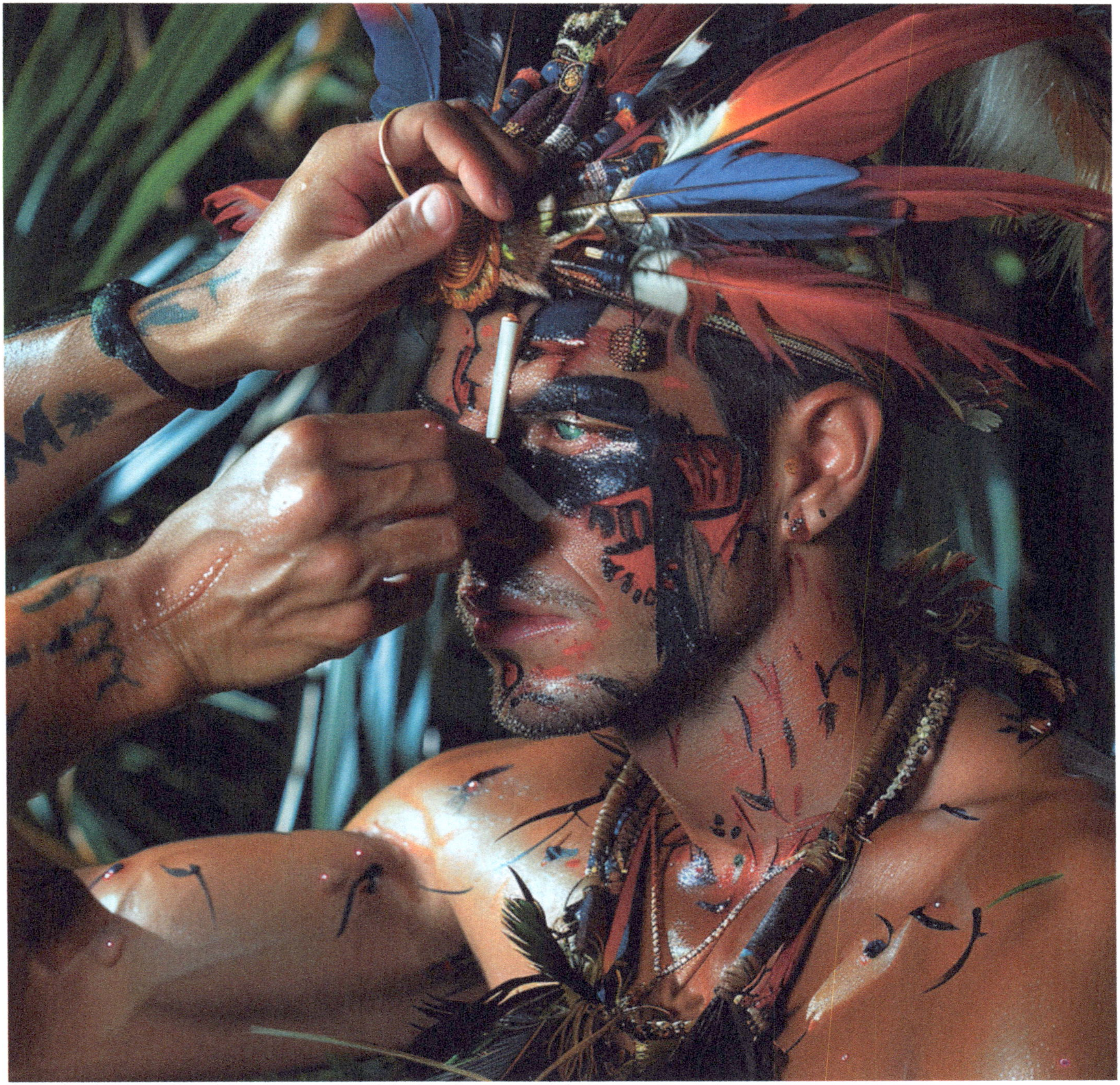

The Indians guided me by canoe to a remarkable destination within the jungle—the revered "tree of all trees," a majestic entity regarded as the great grandfather of the jungle.

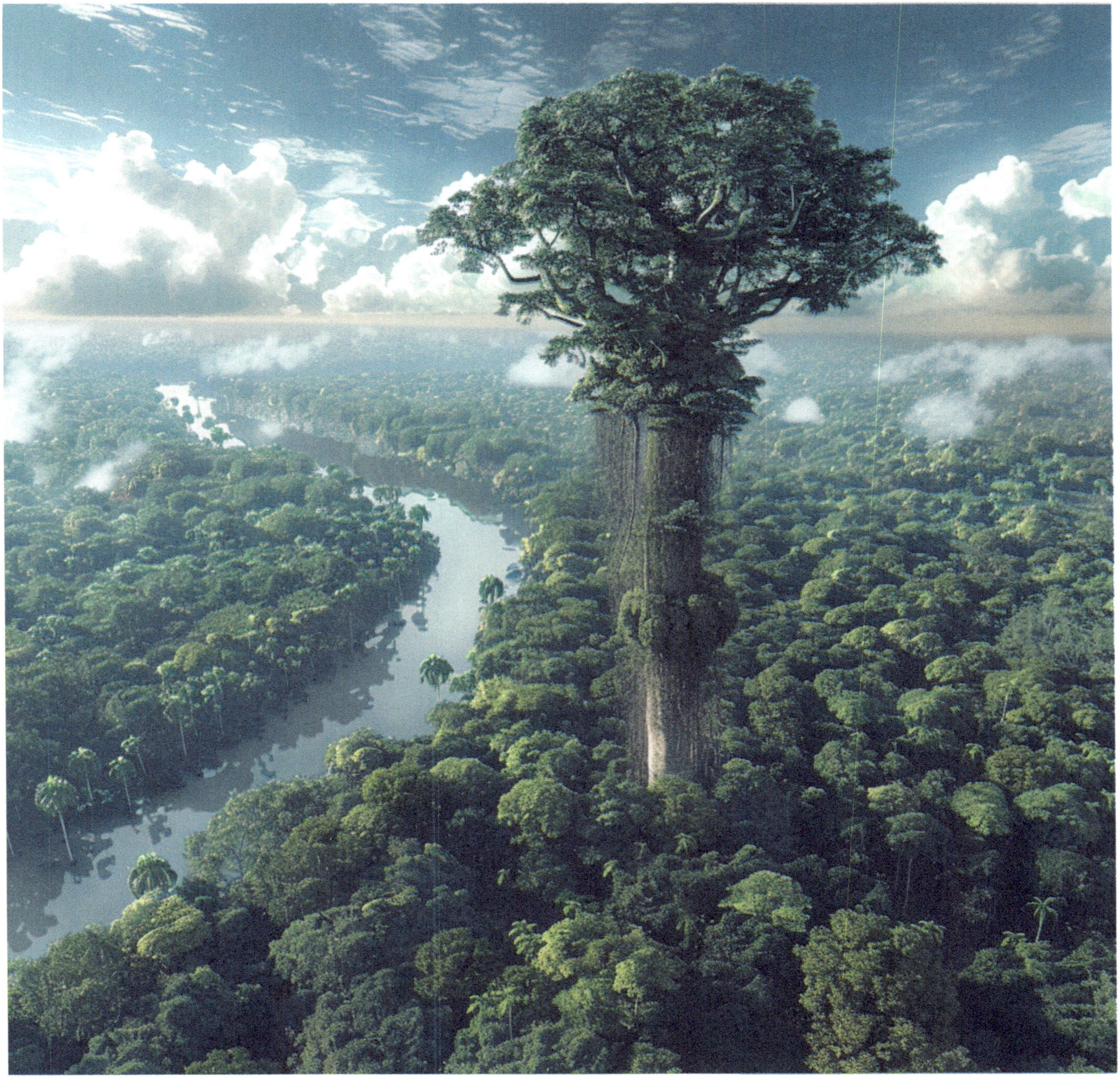

Underneath the towering canopy of this revered giant, the Indians conducted their most sacred ceremony with me.

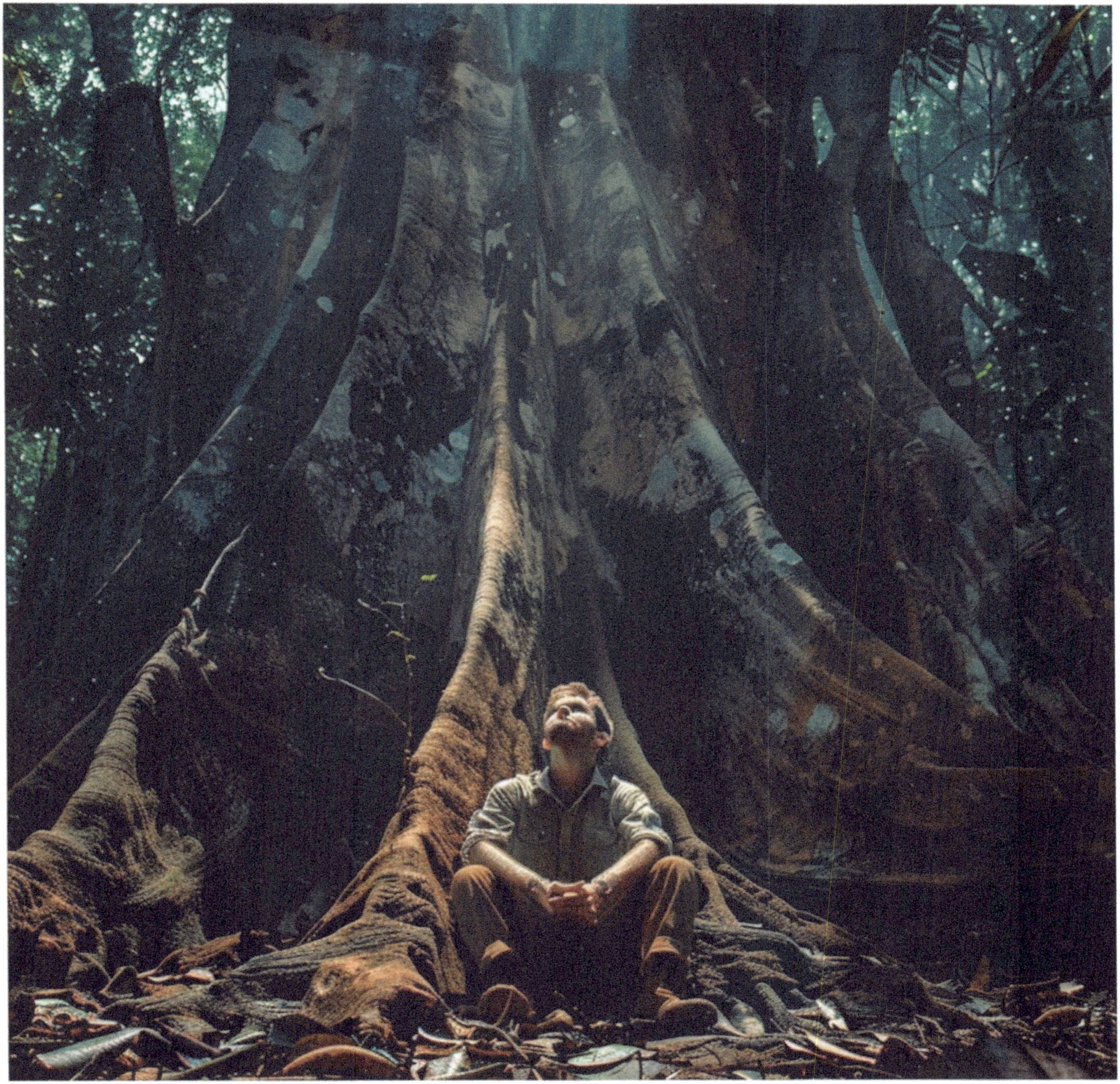

Amidst the depths of the jungle, distant from any semblance of civilization and far from the comforts of home, the medicine man handed me a cup filled with plant medicine, joining the other Indians in partaking.

As I consumed the potion, a surge of energy coursed through my veins, enveloping me in a kaleidoscope of sensations. Suddenly, my senses were heightened, and my consciousness soared to new heights. I found myself in a realm of unparalleled beauty and familiarity, as though I had traversed this realm before, and it felt more real than the world I knew as "reality."

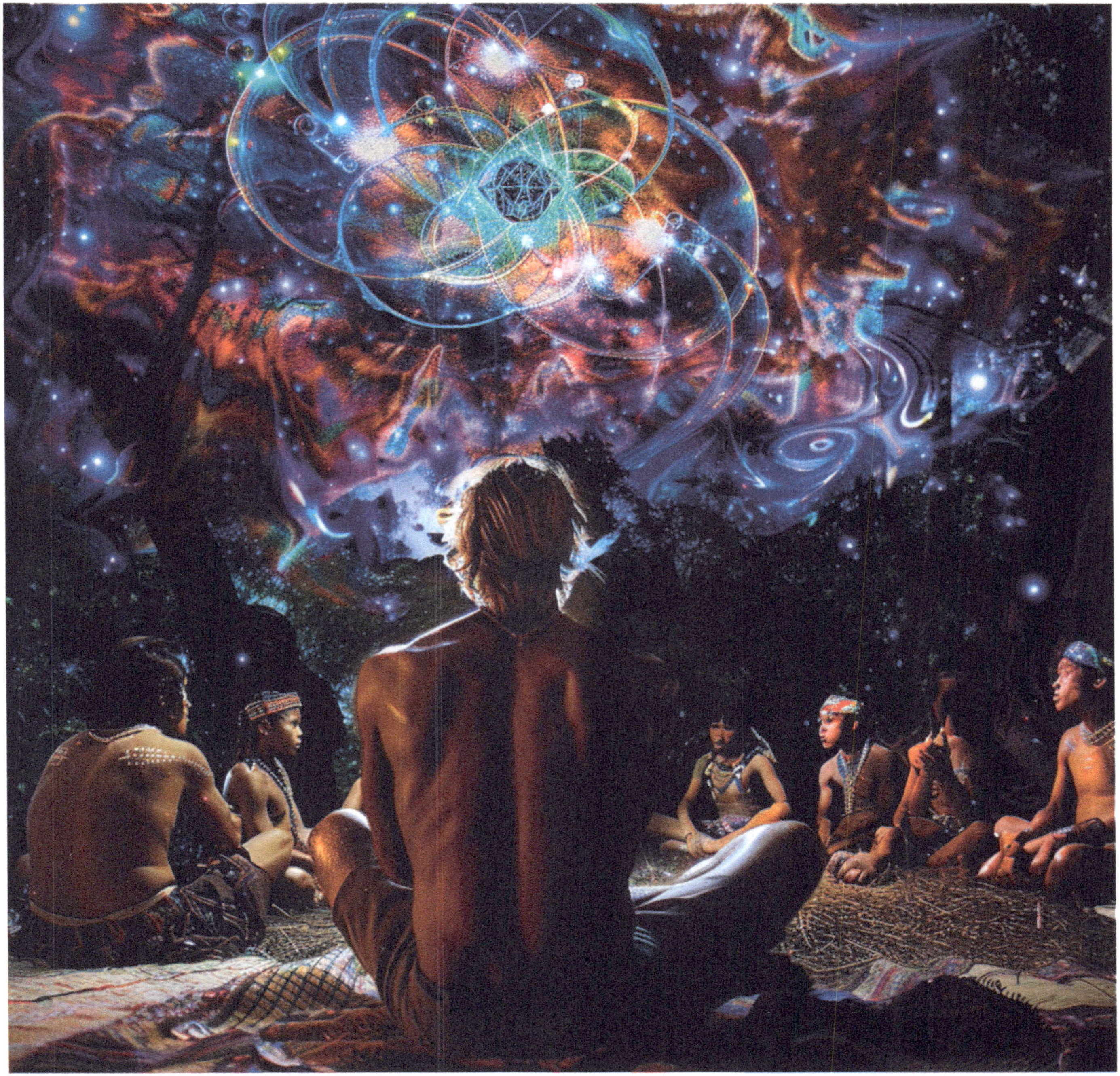

Before me materialized the embodiment of Mother Earth, Mother Nature herself, radiating warmth, kindness, and boundless love. In her presence, I felt my soul and heart undergoing a profound cleansing, as if all impurities were being washed away, leaving me purified and renewed.

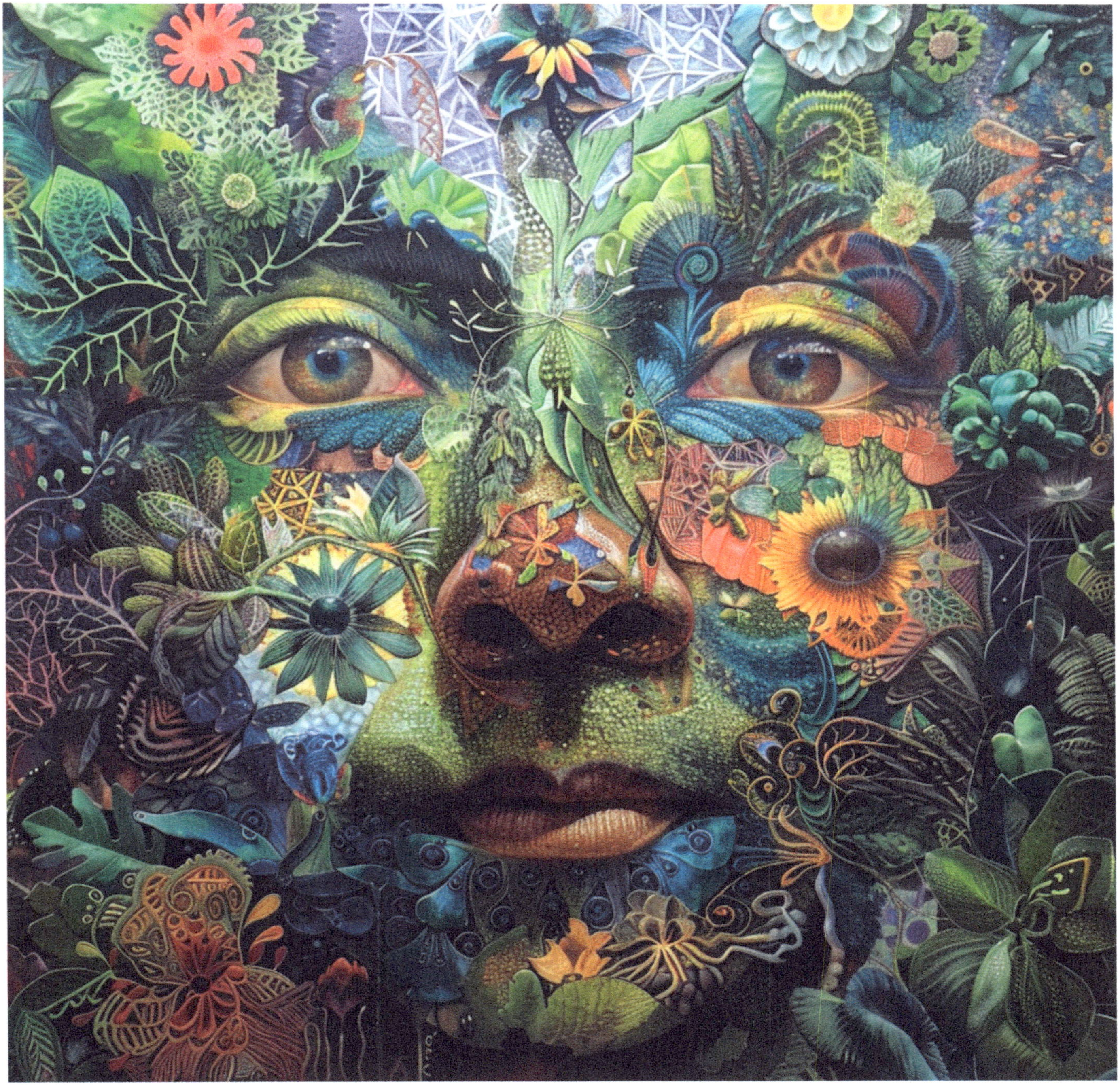

Mother Nature gently imparted to me the profound truth that everything and everyone in this world is intricately interconnected. Despite the illusions that have misled us, she revealed that all energy is one, and that the world is a collective manifestation of all of us, intertwined in a beautiful tapestry of existence.

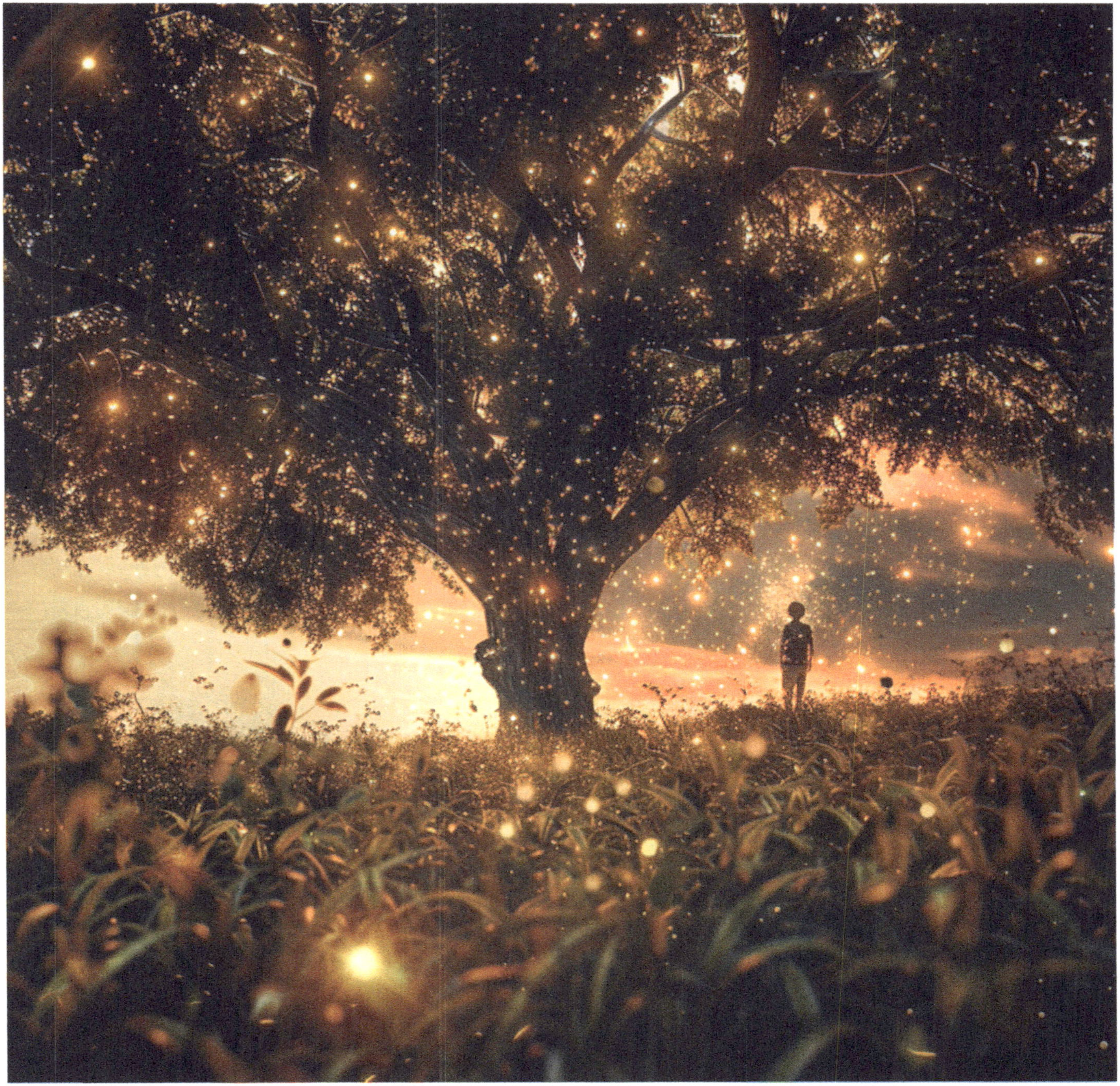

The tiny seedlings of the jungle plants seemed to speak to me, each one urging, "Pick me... pick me... take me back with you to help heal the world." Their collective plea echoed the desire of the Amazonian flora to contribute to humanity's well-being. It struck me as a profound contrast to our reliance on synthetic medicines derived from petrochemicals, a practice that only serves to distance us further from the natural world and its inherent wisdom.

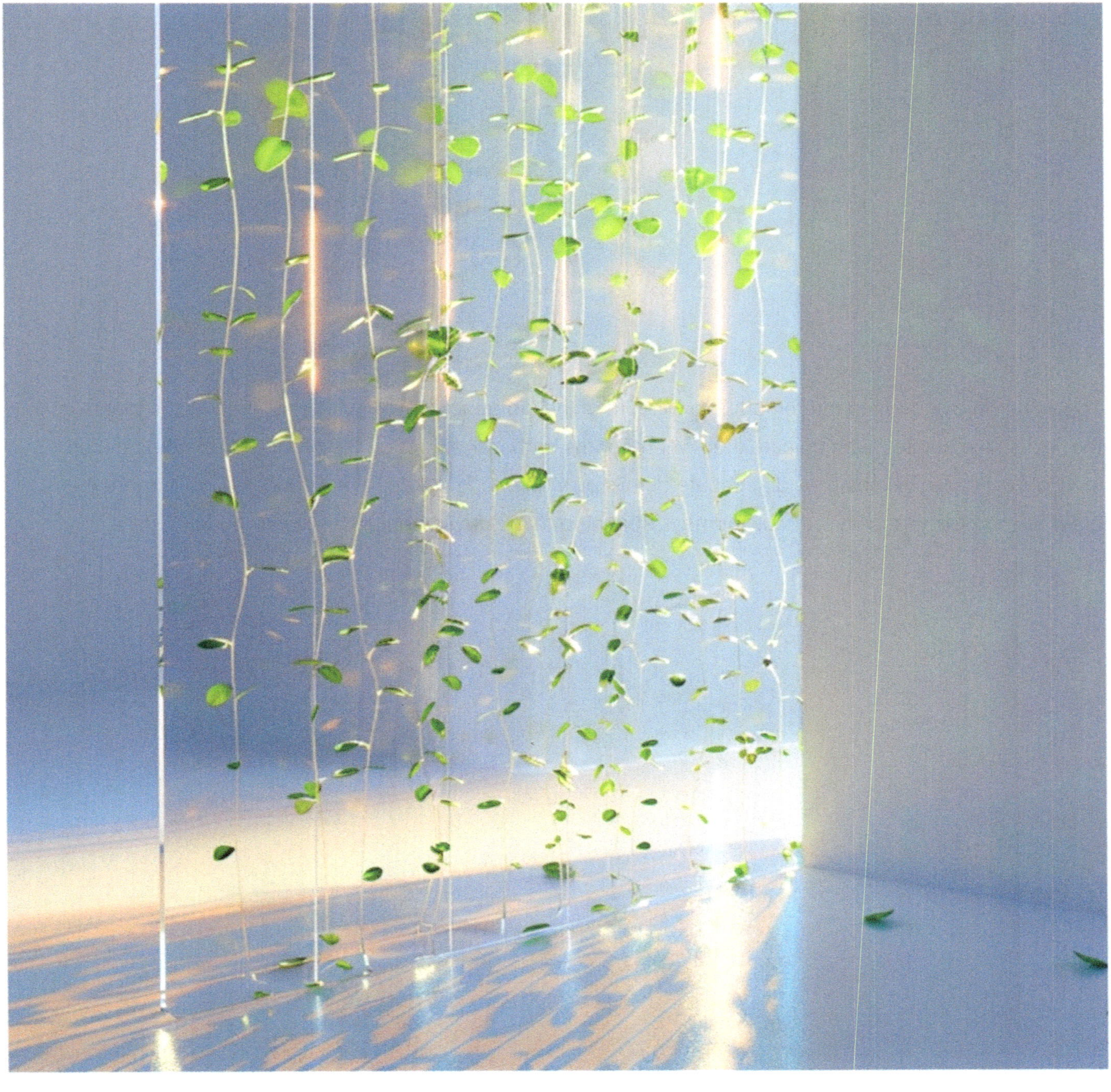

The voice revealed to me the remarkable wisdom of the indigenous people, explaining how the plants in the expansive jungle communicate their whereabouts and usage through the dreams of the indigenous individuals. These visions provide intricate details on where to find these plants and how to prepare them, often leading the tribes on arduous journeys spanning many days through the dense wilderness.

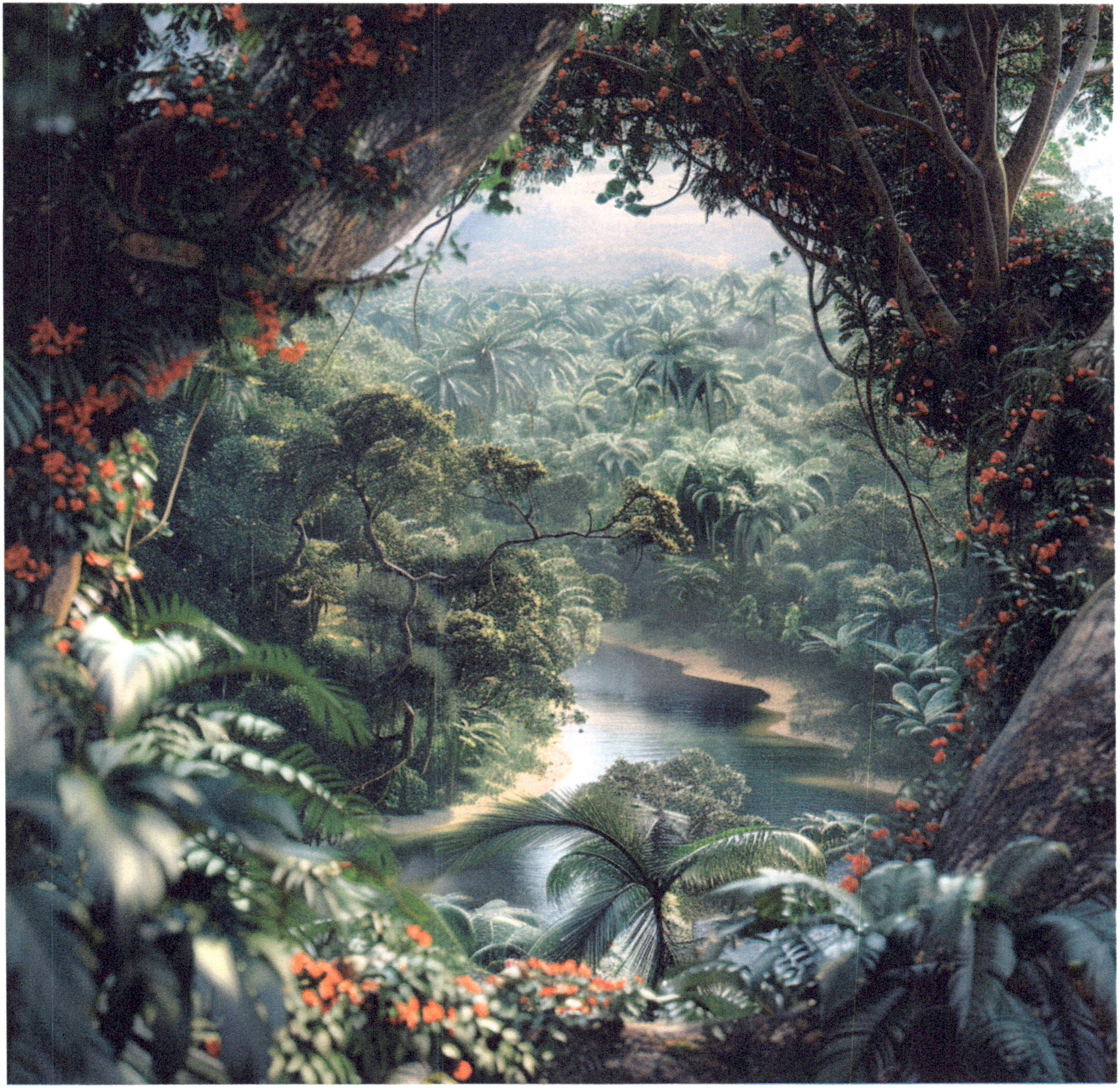

As I reclined beneath the ancient tree, gazing up into its towering canopy, a profound sense of gratitude washed over me. Every experience, both joyful and challenging, contributed to this overwhelming wave of thankfulness—a sentiment I can still tap into to this day.

It felt as though the tree possessed a magnetic pull, anchoring me to its roots and transmitting a message directly into my consciousness. The words echoed relentlessly: "One day you will write a very important BOOK." At the time, I struggled to comprehend what I could possibly write that would be deemed significant. Despite a life colored by adventures and business successes, nothing seemed to warrant a book of profound significance.

Later, the Indian chief confided in me about his own vision—a vision of me dressed in white, mounted upon a majestic white steed, engaged in a noble endeavor for the betterment of humanity. While his words were flattering, they also felt far-fetched and improbable. Yet, the memory of that night lingered in my mind, shaping my thoughts and actions in ways I couldn't fully grasp.

Even the act of writing this book, a project that materialized seemingly out of nowhere, echoes the mysterious workings of fate. It unfolded organically, much like penning a journal entry—something compelled me to begin, and the words flowed effortlessly from there.

485

The vision of myself prioritizing business over my future wife, Wassana, brought me profound shame. It illuminated how I had placed material pursuits above the most significant person and aspects of my life.

In that moment, I heard a voice urging me to support Wassana on her Buddhist path, to fulfill her wishes so she could transcend attachment to this world and the need for further reincarnation.

I made a solemn vow to myself that I would dedicate myself to ensuring Wassana's journey to Nirvana, considering it my utmost duty and priority.

487

The vision of an Asian woman with long black hair, adorned in a white robe and meditating alongside two venerable monks, initially puzzled me. Little did I know that this enigmatic figure would later reveal herself as my esteemed Enlightened Meditation Master.

Years would pass before I fully comprehended the significance of this vision. It served as a glimpse into the future—a future in which I would uncover profound truths and find the answers I had been seeking across countless lifetimes.

This revelation offers compelling evidence that glimpses into the future and even forms of time travel are indeed possible at the level of fine energy.

489

As I lay peacefully in the jungle, a gentle tap on my shoulder roused me from my reverie. In the depths of my mind's eye, I beheld a small, radiant fairy—a manifestation of the spirit Wassana my future wife, beckoning me awake.

491

In a sudden vision, my mind's eye beheld a grand jade pyramid, its peak ablaze with a golden beam of light reaching toward the heavens. Surrounding this radiant stream of energy were numerous monks, each at varying levels of spiritual attainment. Among them stood an elderly monk, poised with a staff, seemingly attempting to leap into the luminous stream. The vision unfolded before me in vivid three-dimensional detail, etching itself deeply into my consciousness. So profound was this experience that I felt compelled to capture it in a sketch, a tangible reflection of the mystical vision bestowed upon me.

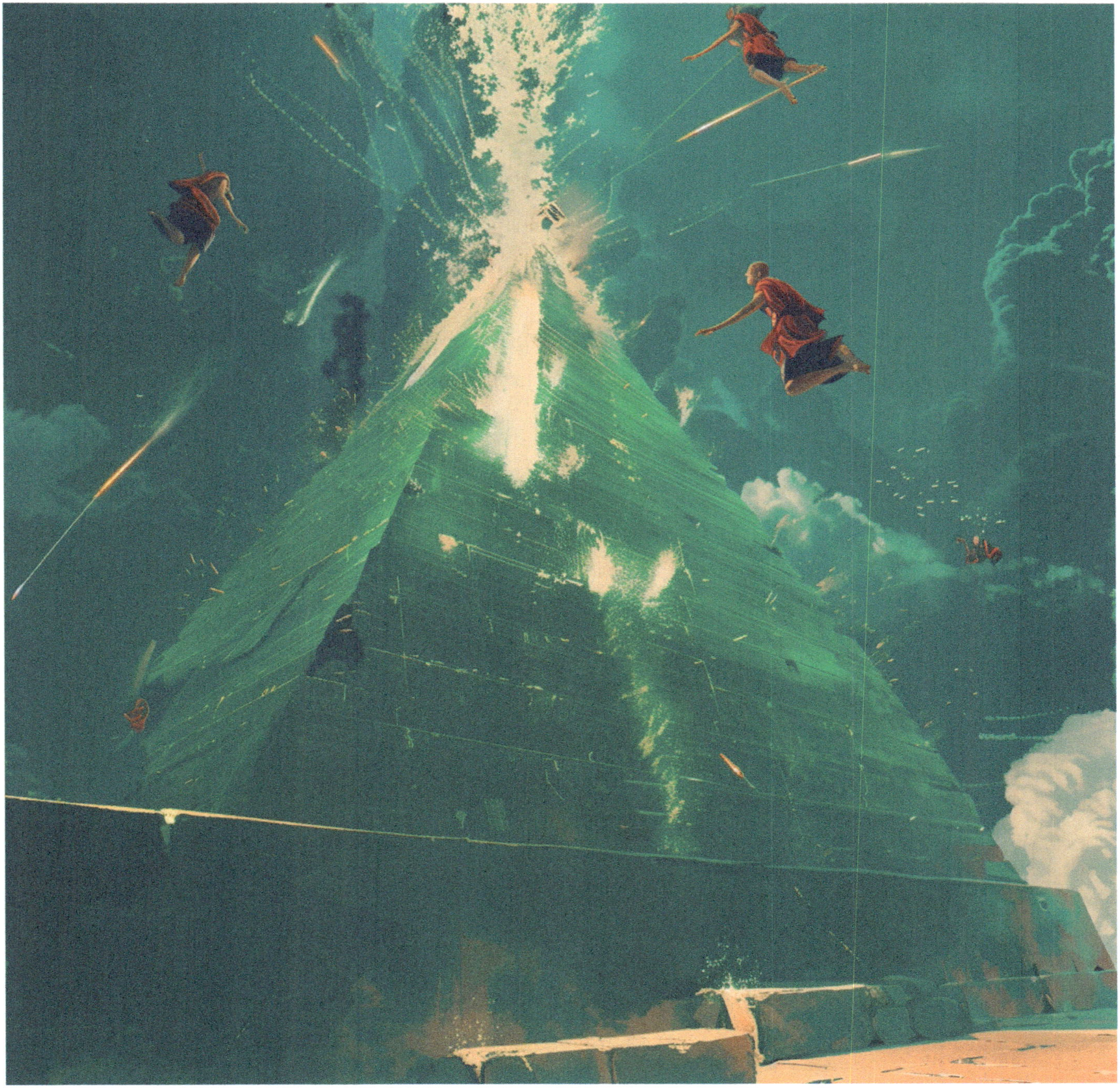

Later, upon returning to Thailand, an inexplicable impulse led me to suggest visiting a distant temple to my wife. As we ascended to the top floor of the Chedi within the temple, I was astonished to encounter an exact replica of the jade pyramid from my vision.

Having never visited this temple before, I was initially perplexed by the significance of the jade structure. However, as my meditation practice deepened, I began to decipher the symbolic meaning behind both my vision and the temple's representation.

The pyramid, I realized, symbolized the Triple Gems of Buddhism—the Buddha, his teachings, and the community of enlightened masters. The radiant energy emanating from its peak signified the path to enlightenment, while the monks depicted leaping into the energy stream representing those who had attained the first stage of enlightenment, becoming part of the Triple Gems.

Reflecting on this profound experience, I pondered why such revelations had come to me in the remote wilderness rather than within the familiar confines of Thailand. It became clear to me that this was the workings of karma—an unseen force propelling me to the depths of the jungle and guiding me through a sacred visionary ceremony to open my eyes and mind to the truths that lay before me.

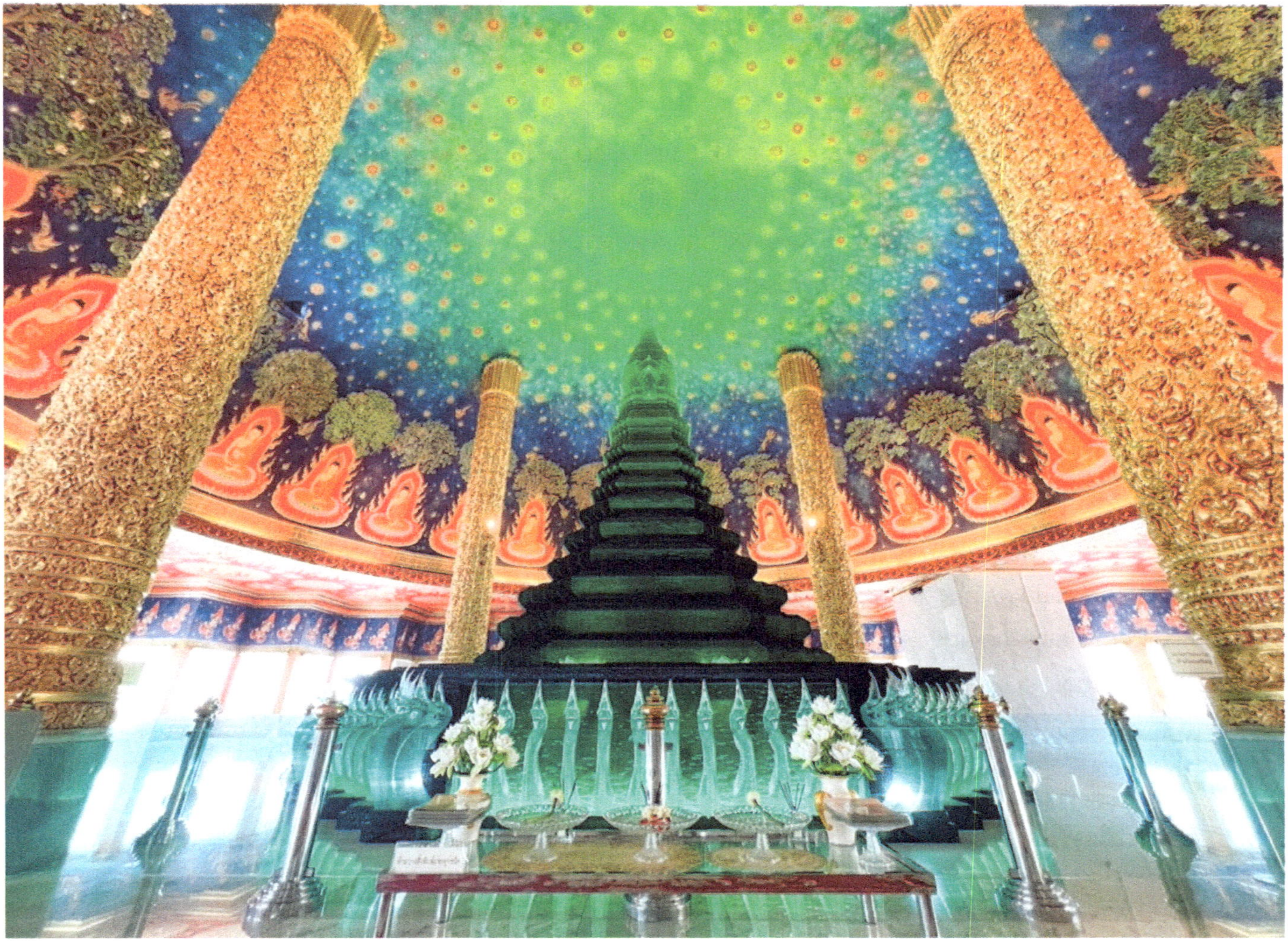

Sitting on a secluded beach on a remote island, enveloped by the serene vibration of nature, I experienced a profound realization. My mind expanded to perceive the interconnectedness of all things, and I was overcome with laughter and awe. In that moment, the weight of life dissolved into pure gratitude and love, filling me with immense happiness.

As I knelt on the sand, my mind journeyed through the depths of time, recalling encounters with great masters and teachers from ancient eras. I felt deep reverence and appreciation for the countless lifetimes that had led me to this point. With humility, I bowed in gratitude to these revered figures.

Suddenly, I found myself standing under the moonlight, outside a familiar white stucco building adorned with tall marble columns and orange curtains illuminated by flickering candles. I recognized this as the Jetevana Monastery, the abode of the Buddha. It was here that I had once paid my respects to the Gautama the Buddha and made a wish to be Enlightened.

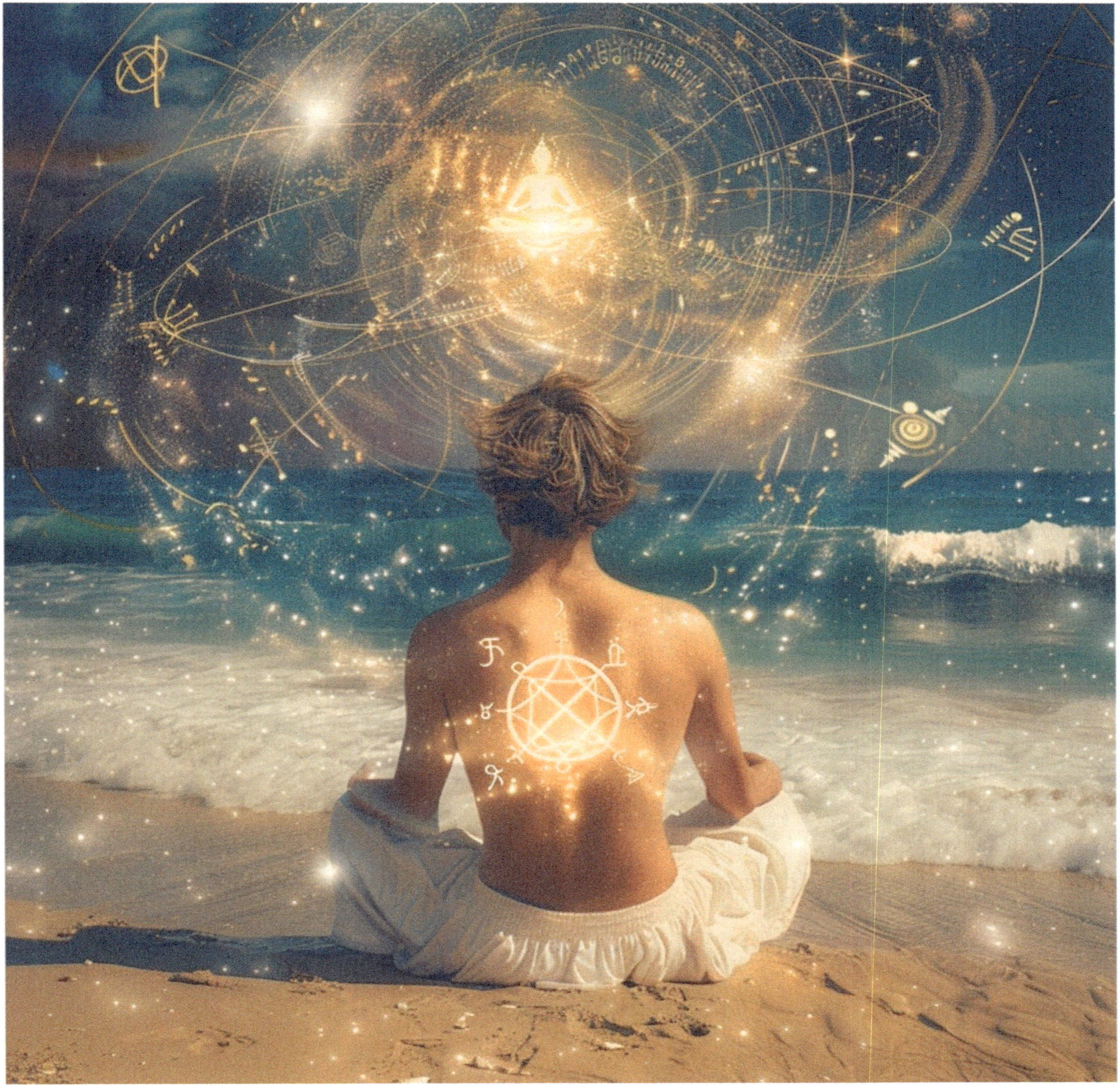

In another vision, I saw a golden statue, its hands and arms moving, fully animated. Though strangely familiar and comforting, it would be years before I learned it was Phra Phut Sik Khi Thotsaphon, the First Buddha. Nearly a decade later, I would discover that there has been a total of 28 Buddhas who walked this earth, and somehow, I found myself witnessing the first Buddha. Slowly, it dawned on me that this beautiful golden Buddha was granting wishes in my vision.

Next, I found myself seated in a modern villa overlooking the sea, with a magnificent limestone island towering high over the water. Atop the island stood a spectacular golden Buddha, radiating beauty and comfort. I felt immense gratitude and wished I could build such a Golden Buddha somewhere, for all to see and experience what I was feeling.

Looking back today, I realize how little I knew about the Buddhas, the path, or the reality of past lives. Somehow, I was given a miraculous glimpse behind the curtain of the illusion of the world.
Lying there on the Amazon jungle floor, beneath that giant, ancient tree in the densest, most remote place on Earth, I could not comprehend, nor did I have the vocabulary or knowledge to describe, what I was seeing. All I knew was that I was witnessing something so incredible, and a vibration that I can only describe as "Pure Goodness" and "Pure Nature."

It would take meeting my meditation Master, Acharavadee Wongsakon, and uncountable hours of meditation and attaining various stages of the dhamma, to understand the "sneak preview" I was given a decade before in the Amazon.

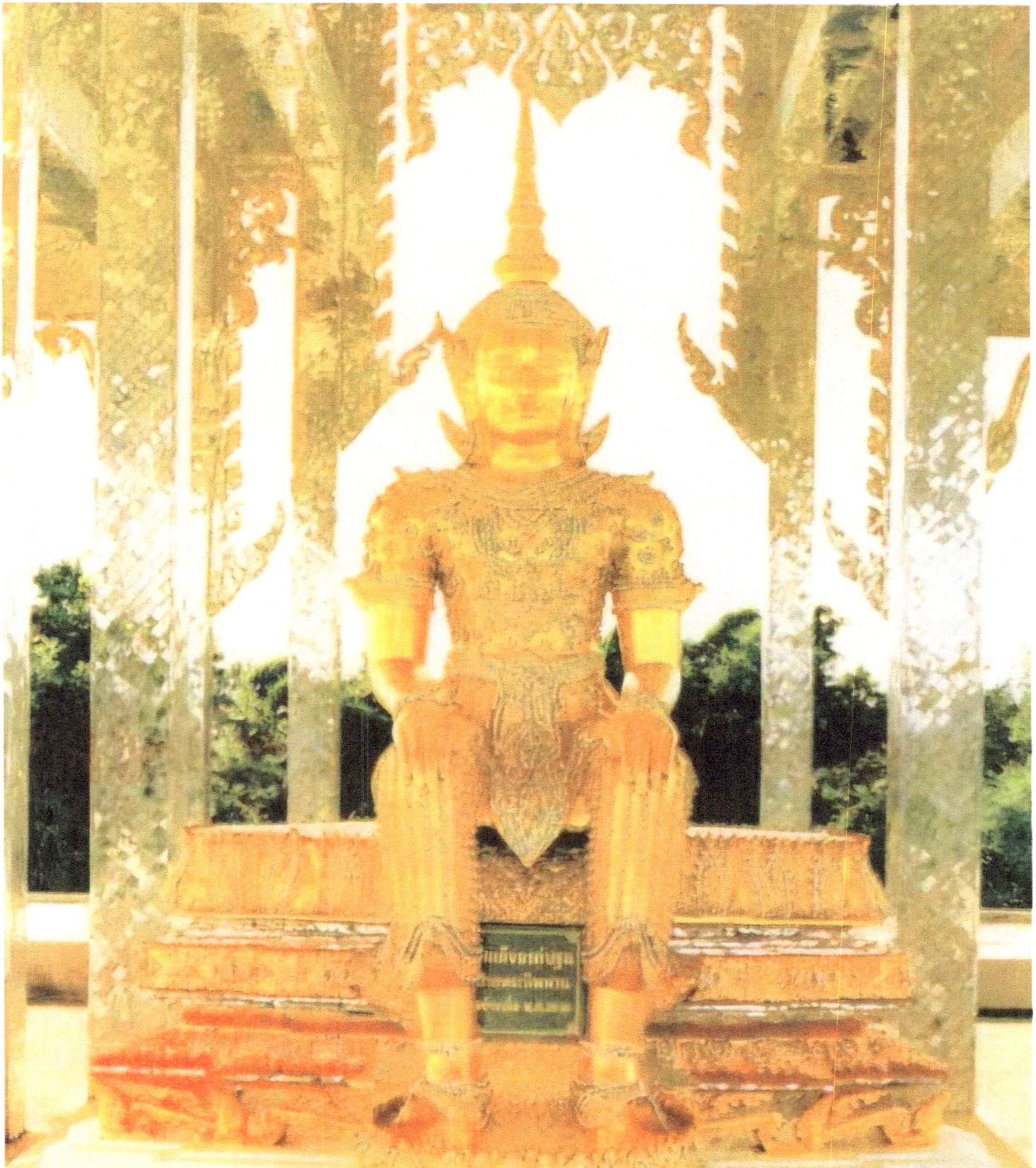

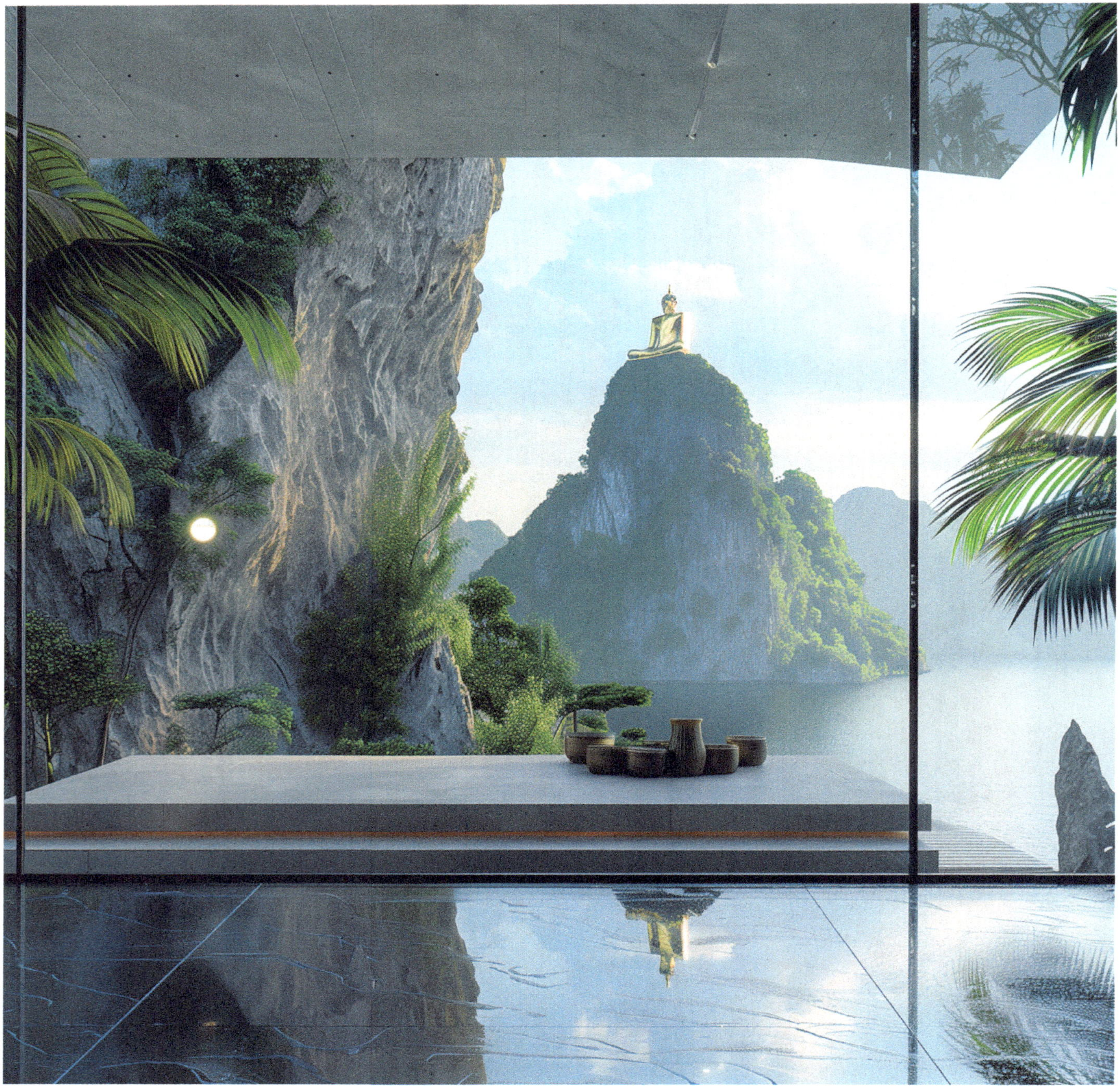

CHAPTER 22

THE MASTER

(TECHO VIPASSANA MEDITATION EXPERIENCES)

THE MASTER

In Time I returned to Thailand and became the student of Master Acharavadee Wongsakon

To be the student of the Master, likely means one has strong past life connections with the Master.

I have seen several of my past lives with the Master.

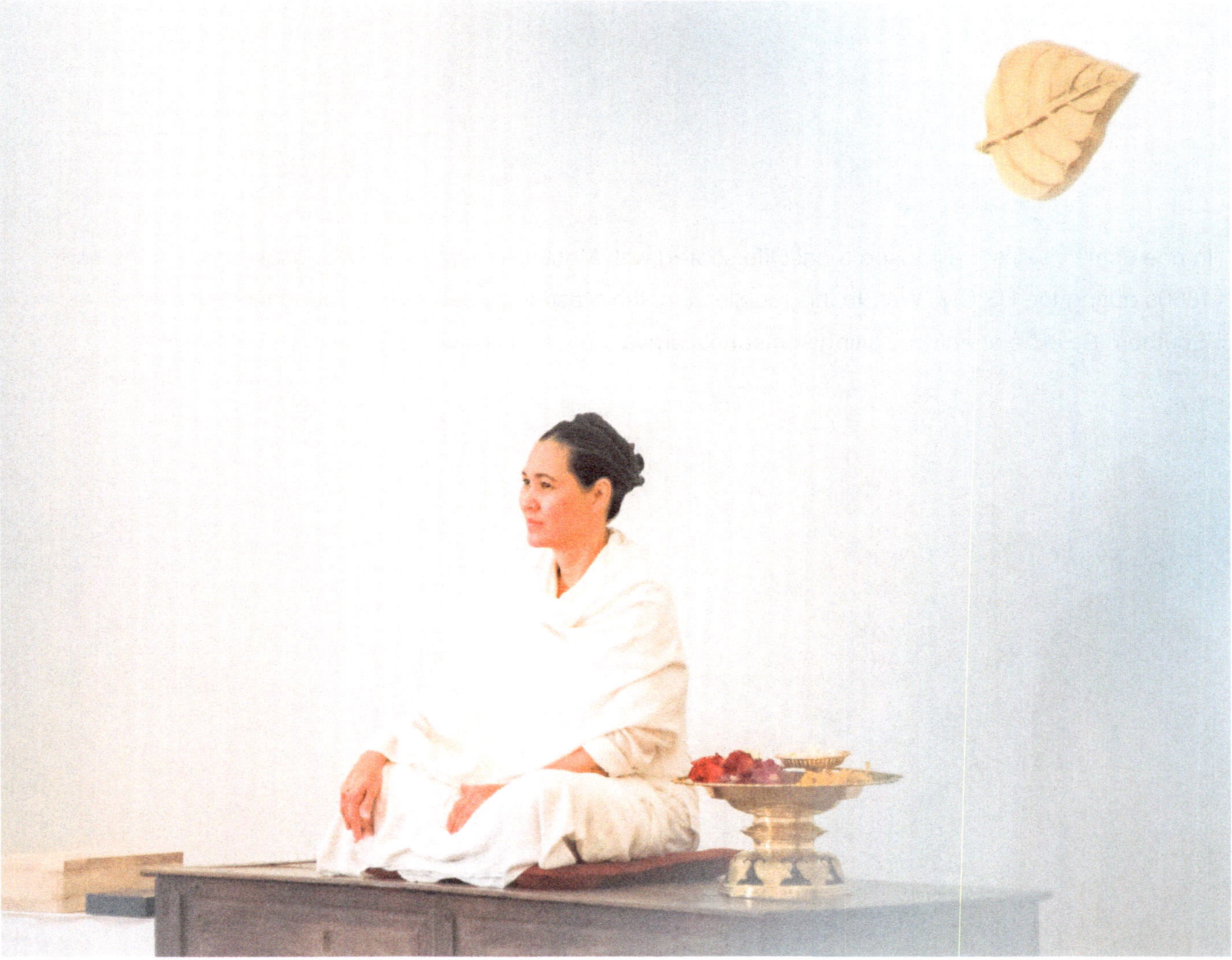

In one of my visions, I glimpsed a past life shared with Master Acharavadee Wongsakon, set in the early 1860s during the US Civil War. In this recollection, the Master appeared as a young lady, akin to a "Southern Belle," elegantly awaiting someone's arrival on a grand staircase.

505

Then I saw myself. I was a young confederate soldier, who was fighting in the civil war.

I lay on the battlefield wounded and dying, suffering with the knowledge I was not able to tell the woman on the staircase, that I would not be returning and knowing that every day she would be waiting in vain.

How cruel and painful this Life was.

I would not meet the young woman on the staircase until over 100 years later, when she would become my meditation, Master.

507

In another life shared with the Master, I was a powerful Samurai warrior. As her right-hand man, I served as her trusted general and carried her sword and shield into battle. My duty was to protect her at all costs.

509

After the Master, who was the head of the Samurai, was betrayed, she chose to commit Hari-Kiri to preserve the honor of the army. Following her death, I took on the responsibility of teaching her son the ways of the Samurai and leading the Samurai army.

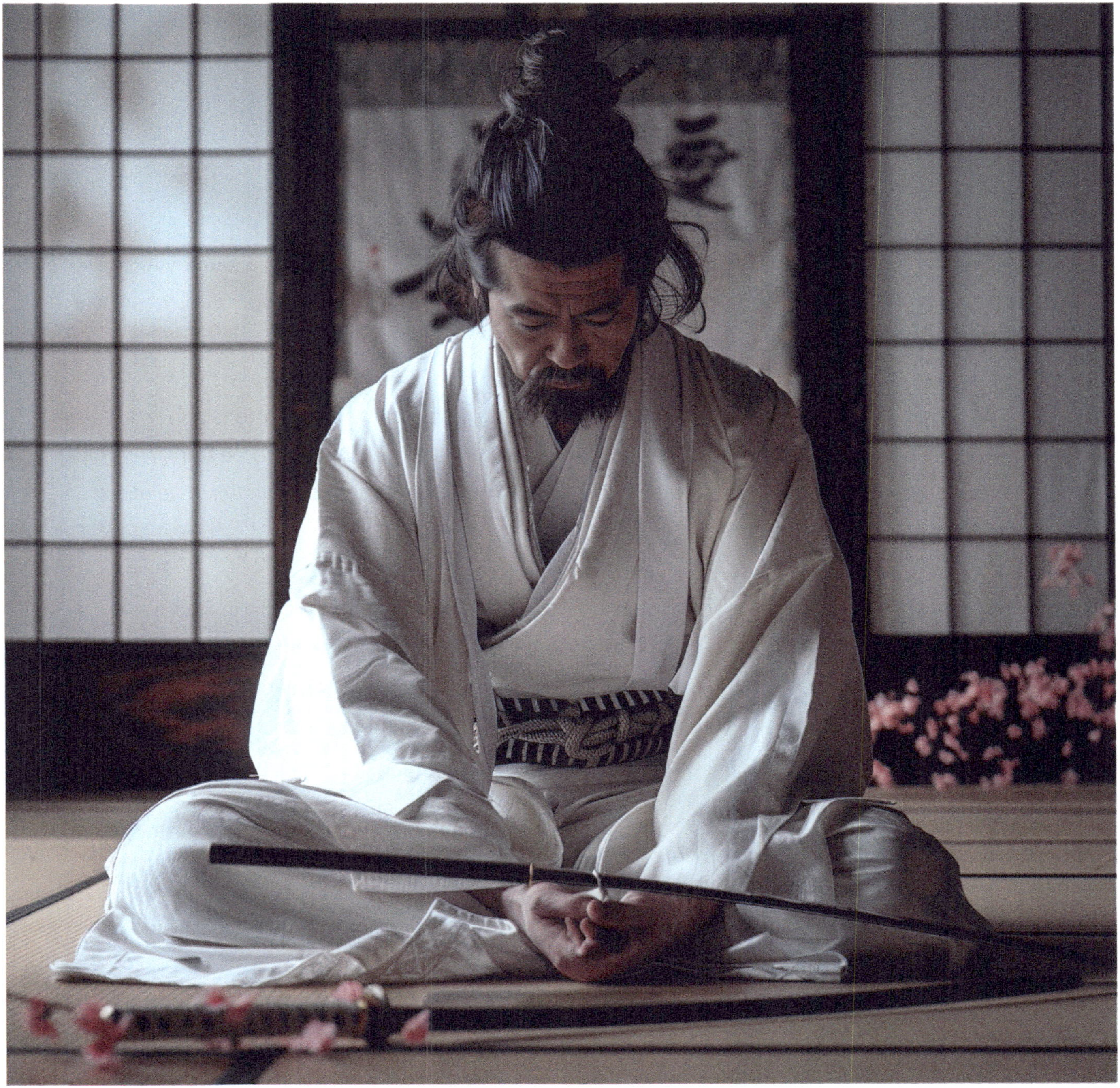

After meeting the Master in this lifetime and becoming her student, I embarked on a journey to Bodh Gaya, India, with our meditation group. The temple at Bodh Gaya encircles the Bodhi tree, where the Buddha attained enlightenment.

During our visit, one of our meditators, blessed with the ability to perceive other dimensions, witnessed a giant book hovering over our group. It bore a message that this sacred tome would be translated into numerous languages and disseminated worldwide. I felt a profound resonance with this revelation, sensing that I would have a role in its creation.

Upon sharing this visionary experience with the Master, she called me by name and invited me to accompany her on a walk through the Bodh Gaya Temple grounds. This moment not only hinted at my future involvement in the creation of the great book, but also held deep significance for me—to walk through the very area where the Buddha himself attained enlightenment, alongside my Enlightened Master, as I continued my own path to liberation.

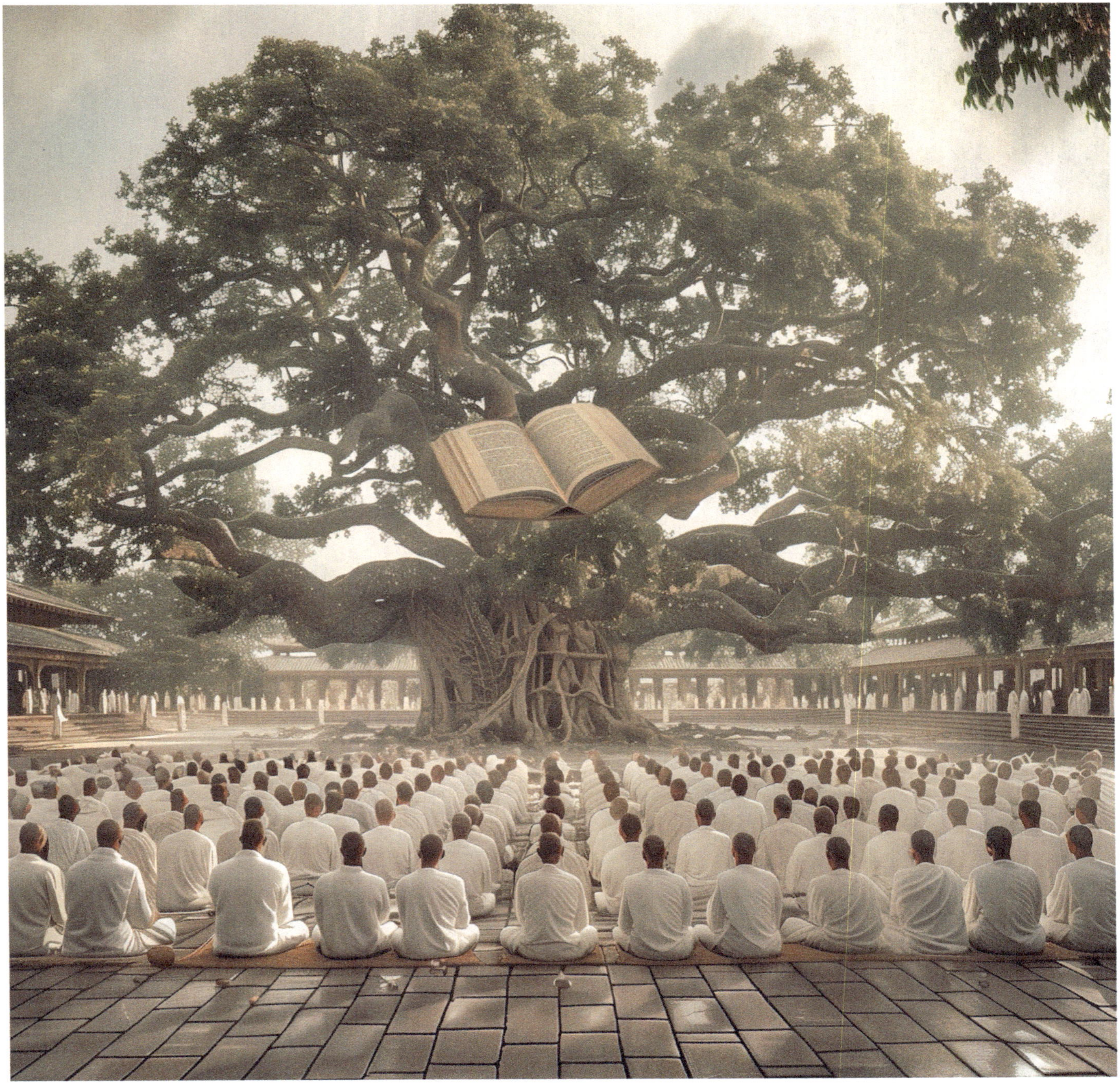

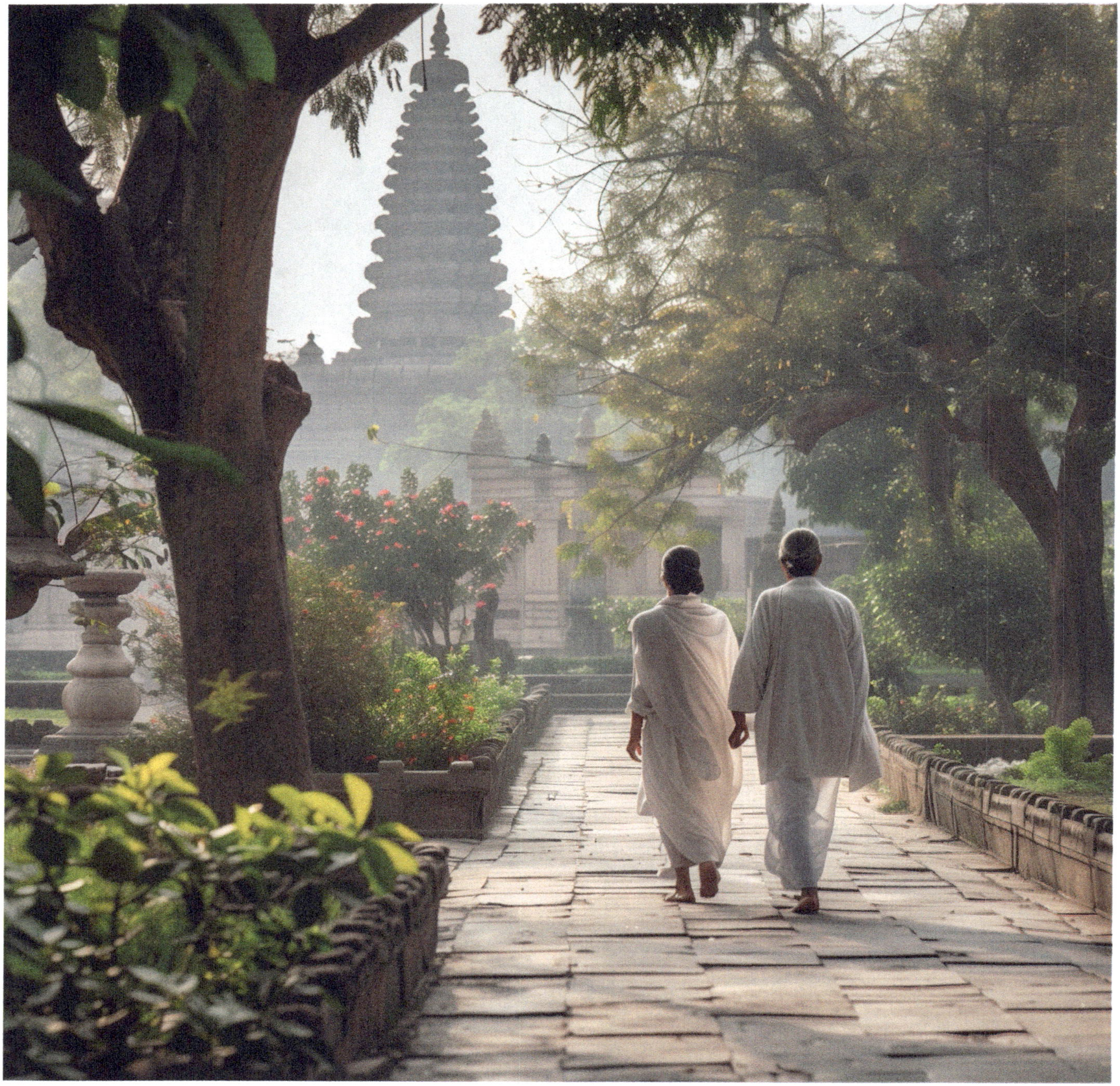

CHAPTER 23

THE MONK

(PHRA AJAHN AMORN)

516

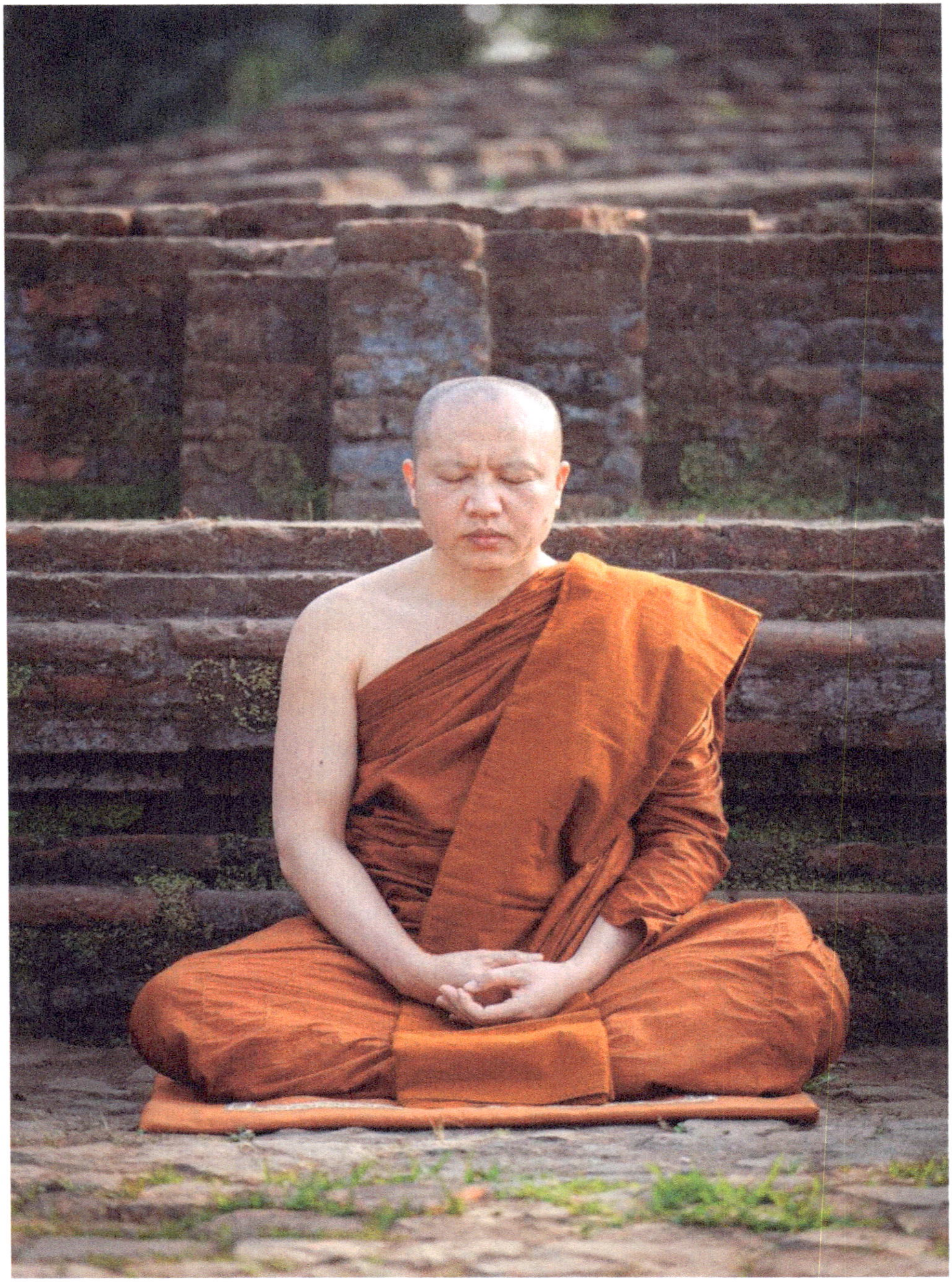

THE MONK

A few years ago, a young monk joined Techo Vipassana meditation course. This monk advanced very quickly in his spiritual attainment and amazingly became Enlightened, after just a handful of courses.

I sat with him after he became Enlightened. The electricity this monk was emitting was so strong, that as I sat on the same floor a small distance from him, the electric charges were biting me all over my body like ants. It felt as if I was sitting in a puddle of water, with an electric wire putting a charge into the water.

This monk, like many of us recalls his numerous Lifetimes. A significant past Life was as the Great Kublai Khan, where he aside from conquering nations, he also spread the teachings of Buddha throughout Asia, which today is a reason for the thriving of Buddhism in places like Thailand. This cultivated huge Merit for the Venerable Monk Amorn, ultimately leading him to reach the Enlightenment in this Lifetime.

At that time my friend Santi and I were Kublai Khan's (Monk Amorn's) right and left-hand men.

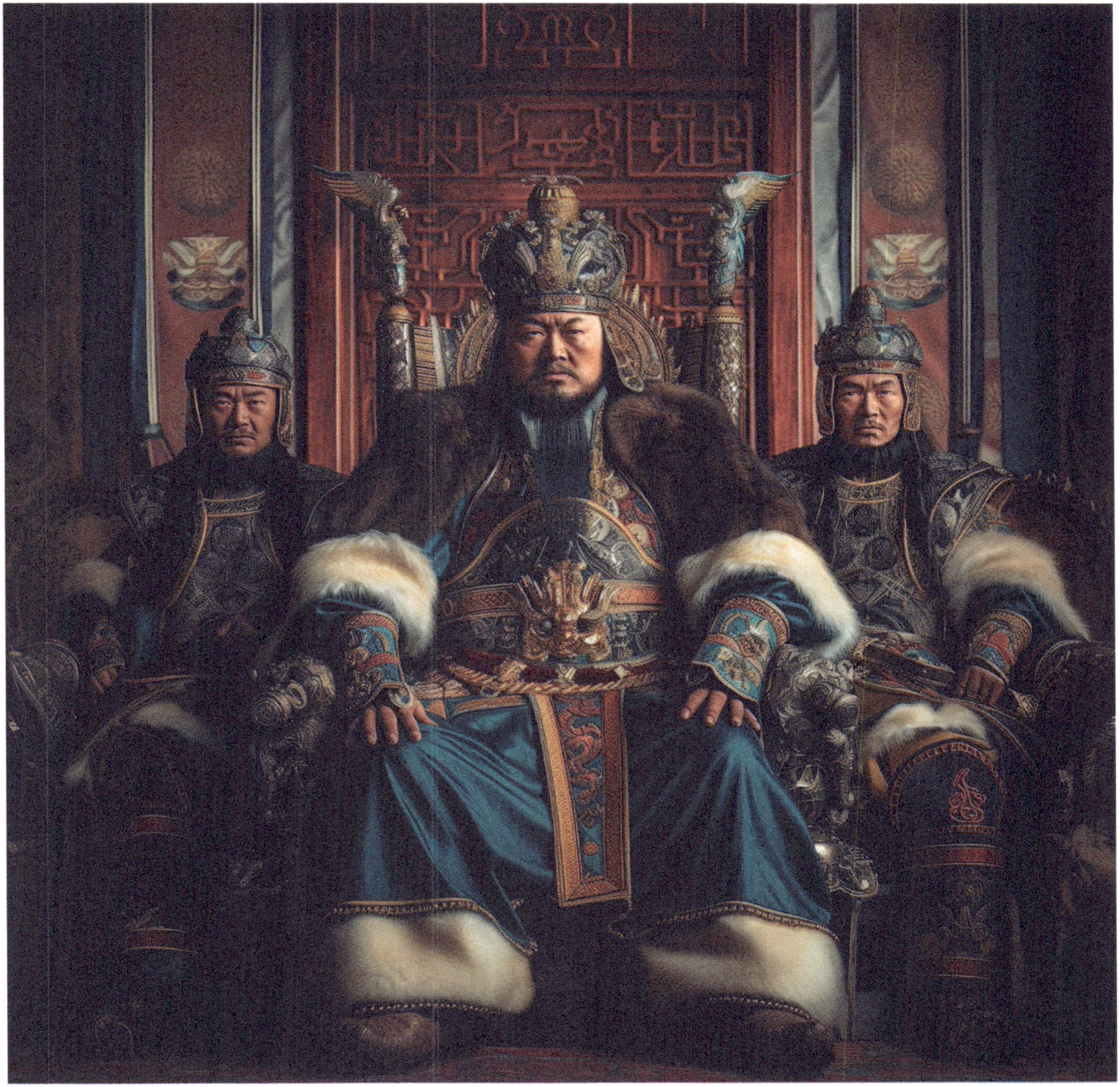

During Monk Amorn's first Techo Vipassana course with the Master, the Master suddenly felt unwell and decided to go rest.

At that moment she instructed me to check the hand position of the 110 students and Monks meditating. I am not sure why the Master chose me for this task, as I did not speak Thai and most all students were Thai. But nonetheless I took on the duty.

I checked the lay students first and then the Monks. Monk Amorn had his hands in the wrong position and seemed sleepy. Instinctively without a word, I grab this Monk's hands and raised them to the proper position. Monk Amorn opened his eyes and looked shocked. Surprised that anyone would touch a Monk so agressively without even a word like "excuse me".

For the remainder of the course Monk Amorn kept his hands high in the proper position, fearing that the foreigner would show up again and man handle his hands.

A few courses later Monk Amorn became Enlightened and even thanked me for having shocked him into the perfect meditation posture. But there is more to this story. Handling Monk Amorn without a second thought is not because I was rude or being disrespectful, but it was because of our past lives.

I was Monk Amorn's respected Grandfather figure in a past Life. In that Lifetime I trainned this young man to become a great warrior.

It was no coincidence that the Master put me incharge that day to do the checking of the meditators. This is how Monk Amorn and his "Grandfather", met again in this Lifetime.

521

When Monk Amorn was travelling to his first course with the Master to learn Techo Vipassana (fire meditation), he meditated and heard these words, "you are weak just like your mother". In his visions he recalled vividly, that he was the son of Master Acharavdee Wongsakon, during the the Samurai time. When he arrived to the meditation course he recognizing the Master as his father, asked the Master 's permission to call her "Father. This was a strange request, to ask a strict woman Master permission to call her "Father". But the Master gave permission and to this day, the now Enlightened Monk refers to her as "Father".

In that past Lifetime as head of the Samurai, the Master had been betrayed and to save the honor of her Samurais, the Master committed Hari-Kari – leaving this Monk, as a young Samurai man, incharge to lead the Samurai Army, despite his youth. Sadly as he became a strong warrior, his father was not there to see it. And so until this life the words "you are weak just like your mother" still rang in his ears, until his Enlightenment and reunion with the Master, they now together wage a very different battle, helping the others from this and other liftetimes, come together to fight the ultimate battles in the Minds, to reach liberation and enlightenment.

During our time as Samurai warriors, I assumed the role of the Master's trusted right-hand man. Following her passing, I took on the responsibility of guiding and mentoring her son teaching him how to use his sword. My duty was to instill strength and leadership skills in the young man, ensuring his readiness to lead the Samurai armies. I protected him and ensured the loyalty of his men. In that lifetime, he referred to me as "Grandfather," and even in this lifetime, he continues to call me Grandfather.

Monk Amorn never had the opportunity to demonstrate his strength and leadership to his Samurai father in their past life. He never had the chance to fight alongside his father. However, in this lifetime, Monk Amorn has showcased the strength he cultivated since then. Now, Enlightened he stands alongside his father, fighting against the forces of Darkness and Mara in the Ultimate Battle.

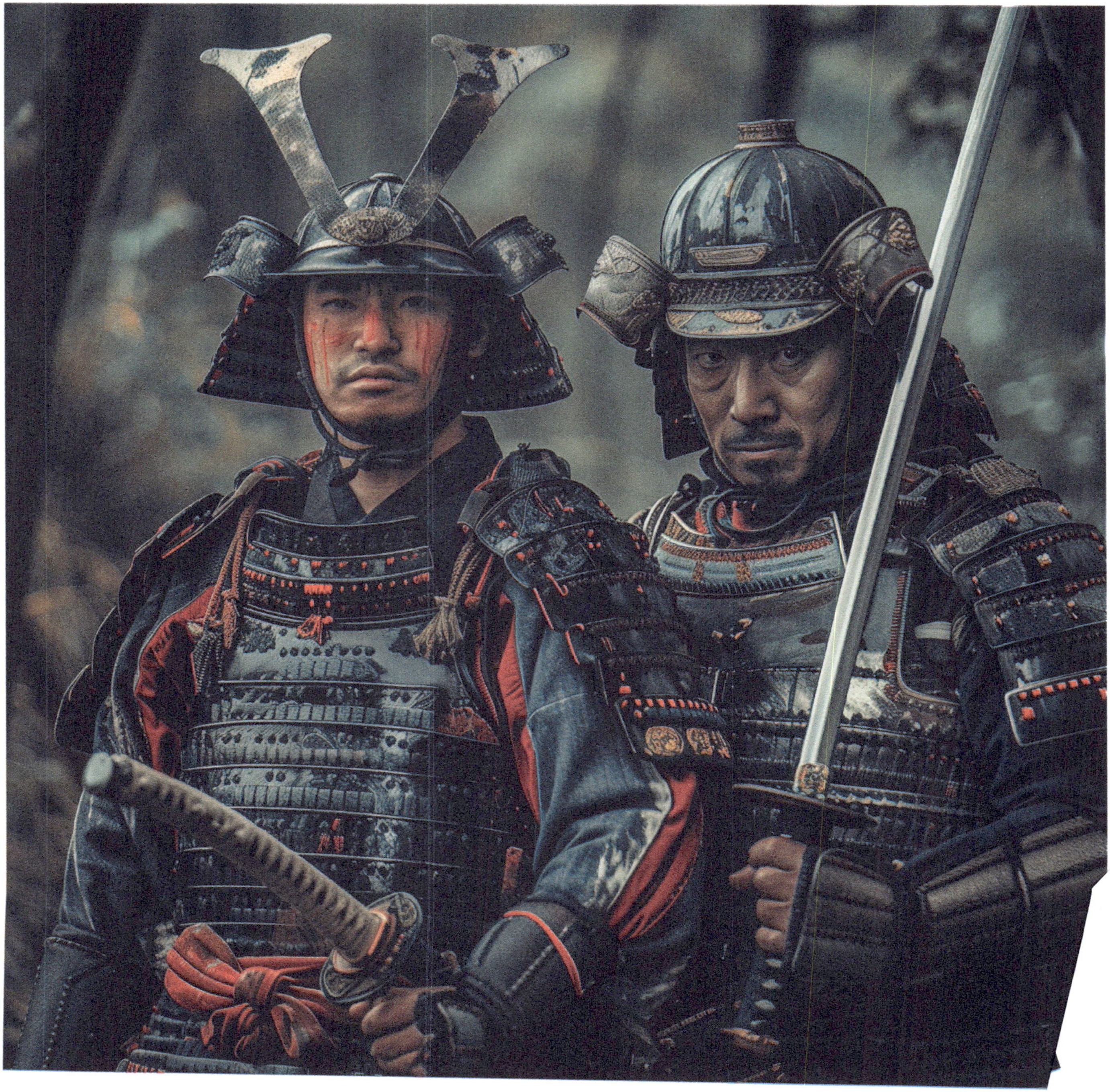

In World War II, we died together Monk Amorn, and my friends Santi, Sam, and me. It was a tragic end as we watched each get shot and die.

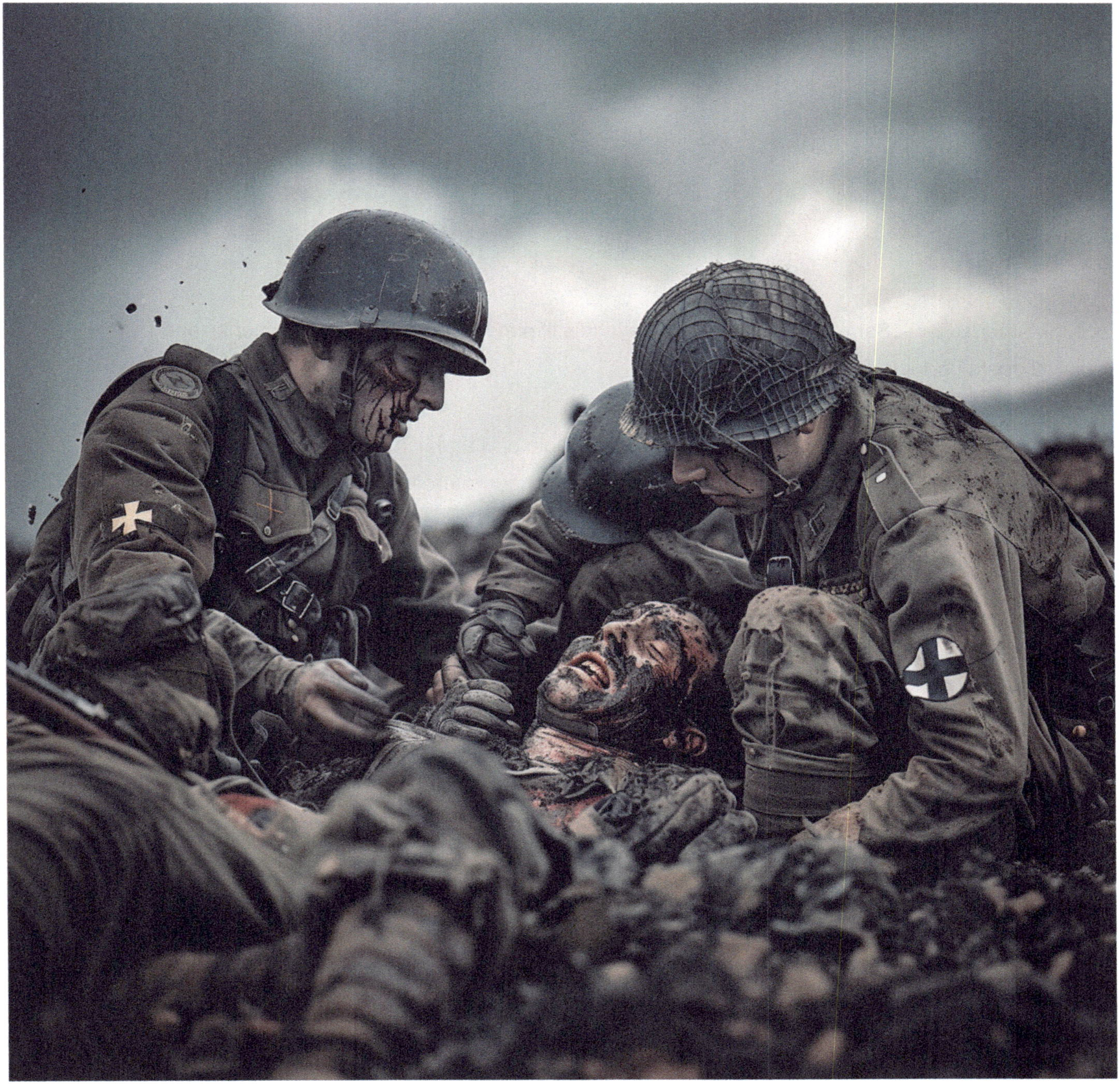

Monk Amorn, Santi, Sam, and I are still friends in this lifetime. We have trained as monks and as practitioners under the Enlightened Masters.

Everything and everyone are connected. We meet again and again in various lives, due to the pushing power of karma. Good Karma and Bad Karma all impact our future lives. Strong emotions can draw us back together.

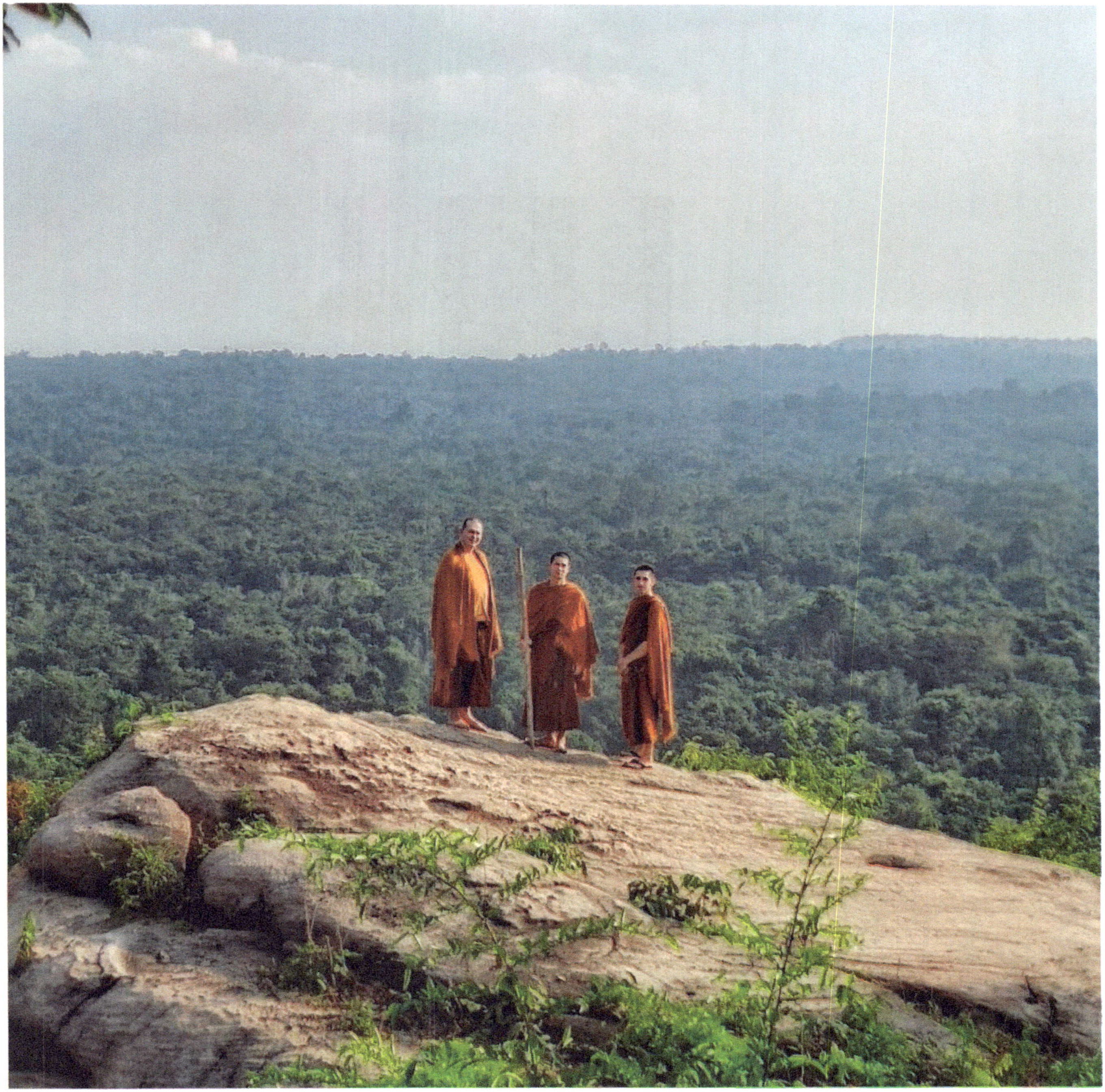

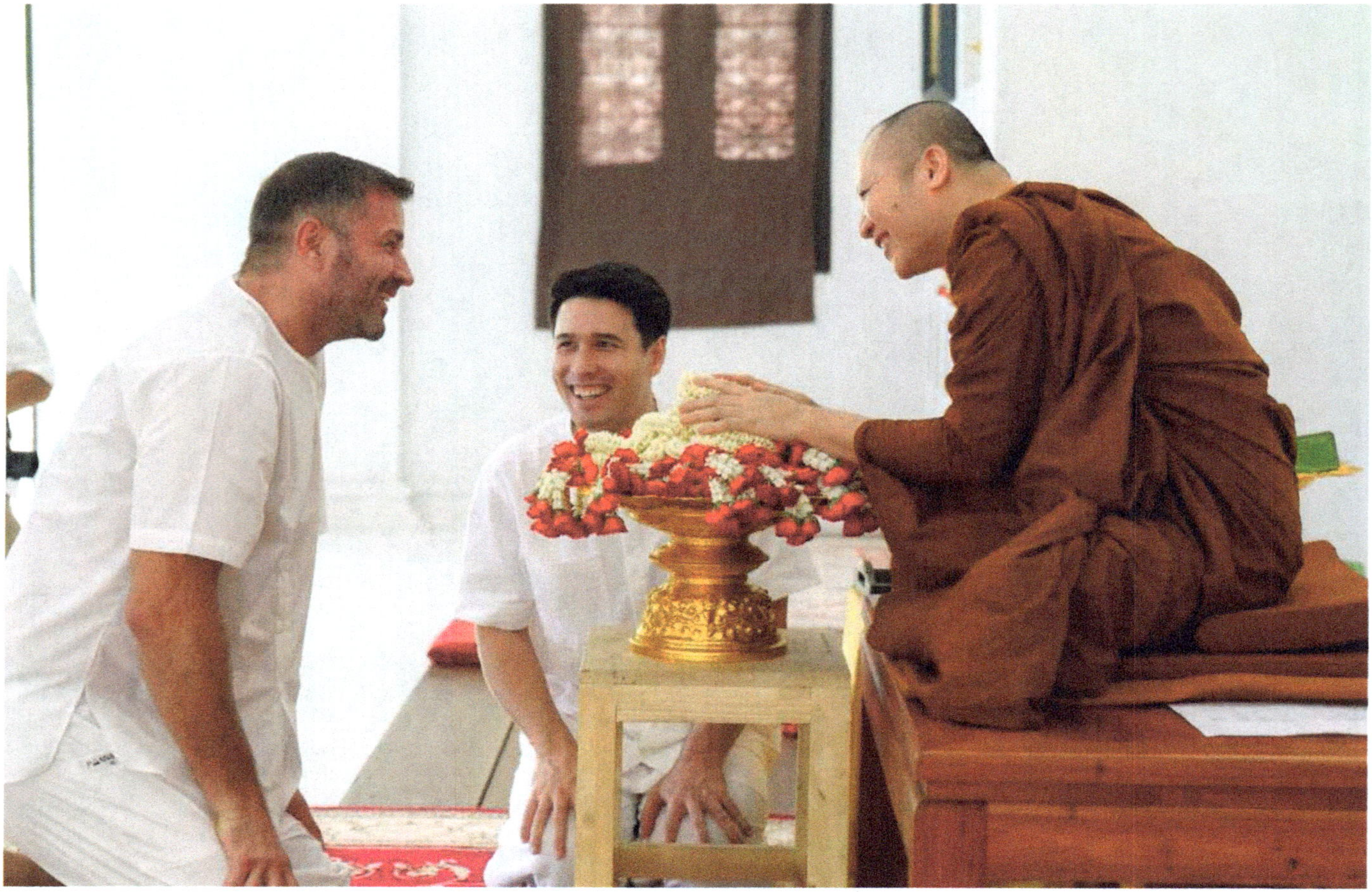

CHAPTER 24

THE DOCTOR

(DR ROBERT M. GOLDMAN)

I have been friends with Dr. Robert Goldman for a long time. Dr. Goldman is considered the "father of the Anti-Aging Industry" and is Chairman of A4M the largest Anti-Aging Medical society in the World. Any doctor practicing Anti-Aging these days has a diploma signed by Dr. Goldman hanging on their wall.

When I first met Dr. Goldman nearly 30 years ago, he told me that as a doctor and a scientist, he did not believe in life after death, as there was no scientific evidence to support the claim. He also promised me that we could live and enjoy our lives until age 120 or beyond.

Fast forward to the year 2020, I invited Dr. Bob to spend a week meditating in Thailand with Master Acharavadee Wongsakon.

After a week meditating with the Master, Dr Bob changed his Mind about the possibility of Life after death, he changed his Mind, not because someone convinced him about reincarnation, but because he himself saw many of his past lives. The evidence and the way he saw his past lives convinced Dr. Goldman of the Truth, that we have done this many times.

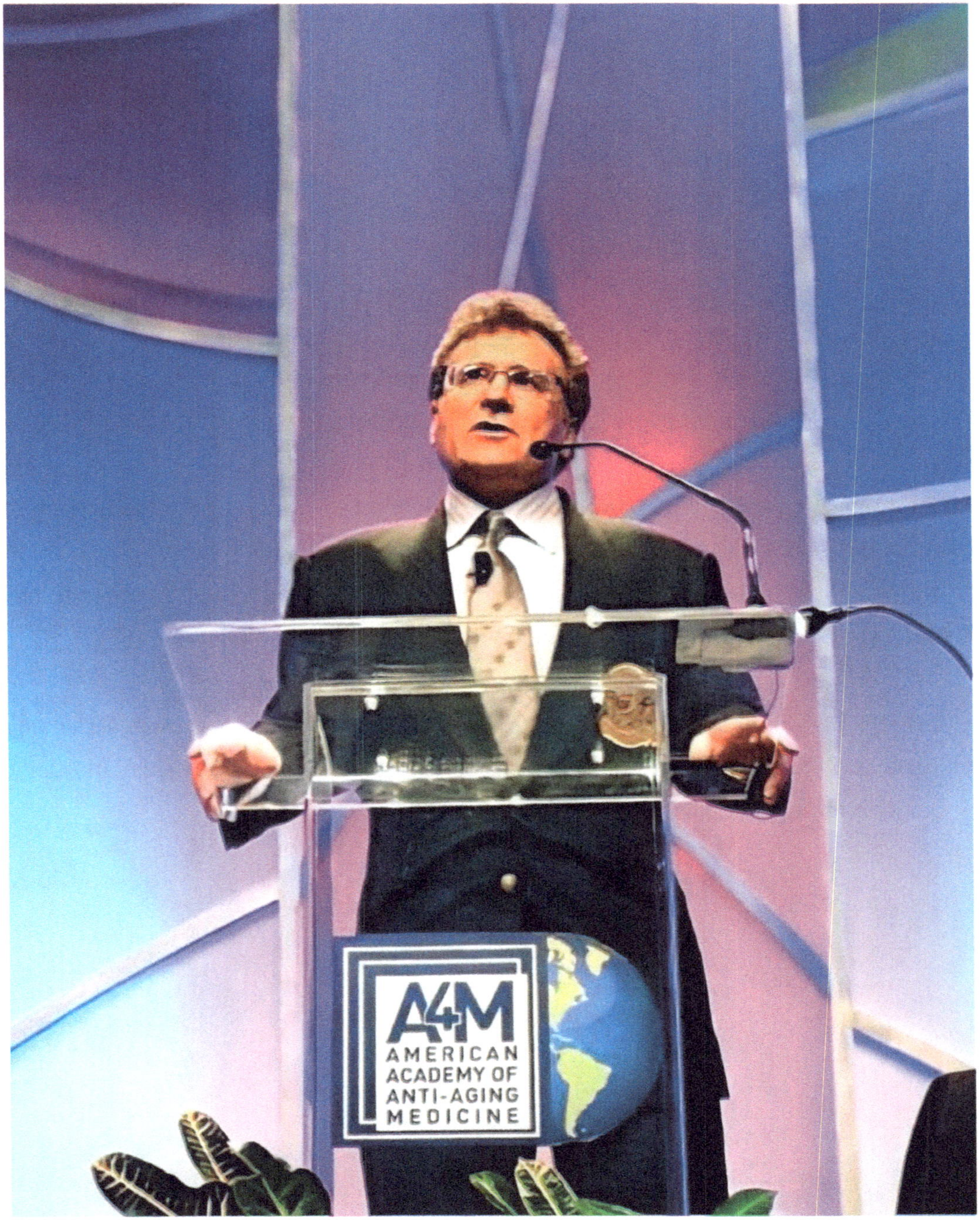
A4M
AMERICAN
ACADEMY OF
ANTI-AGING
MEDICINE

Dr. Goldman is an avid Art collector. In recent years he took an interest in collecting rare Bibles. In 2020 the prized Bible in his collection was a very large Bible whose pages were made of pig skin.

During his week meditation Dr. Goldman saw a past Life wherein he and his 2 teenage sons, transcribed a huge Bible made of pig skin. Ironically Dr. Goldman had purchased this Bible for his own collection and in this Life owns the very Bible he helped write many lifetimes ago. This is also True for other items in his large Art collection, Dr. Bob has collected many items from his other past lifetimes.

In that past Life where Dr. Goldman transcribed the Bible, he saw his face in that Lifetime, when walking by a mirror. He also saw that his sons worked on this Bible every day, and at the end of the day together they carried it back, to a huge shelf.

.

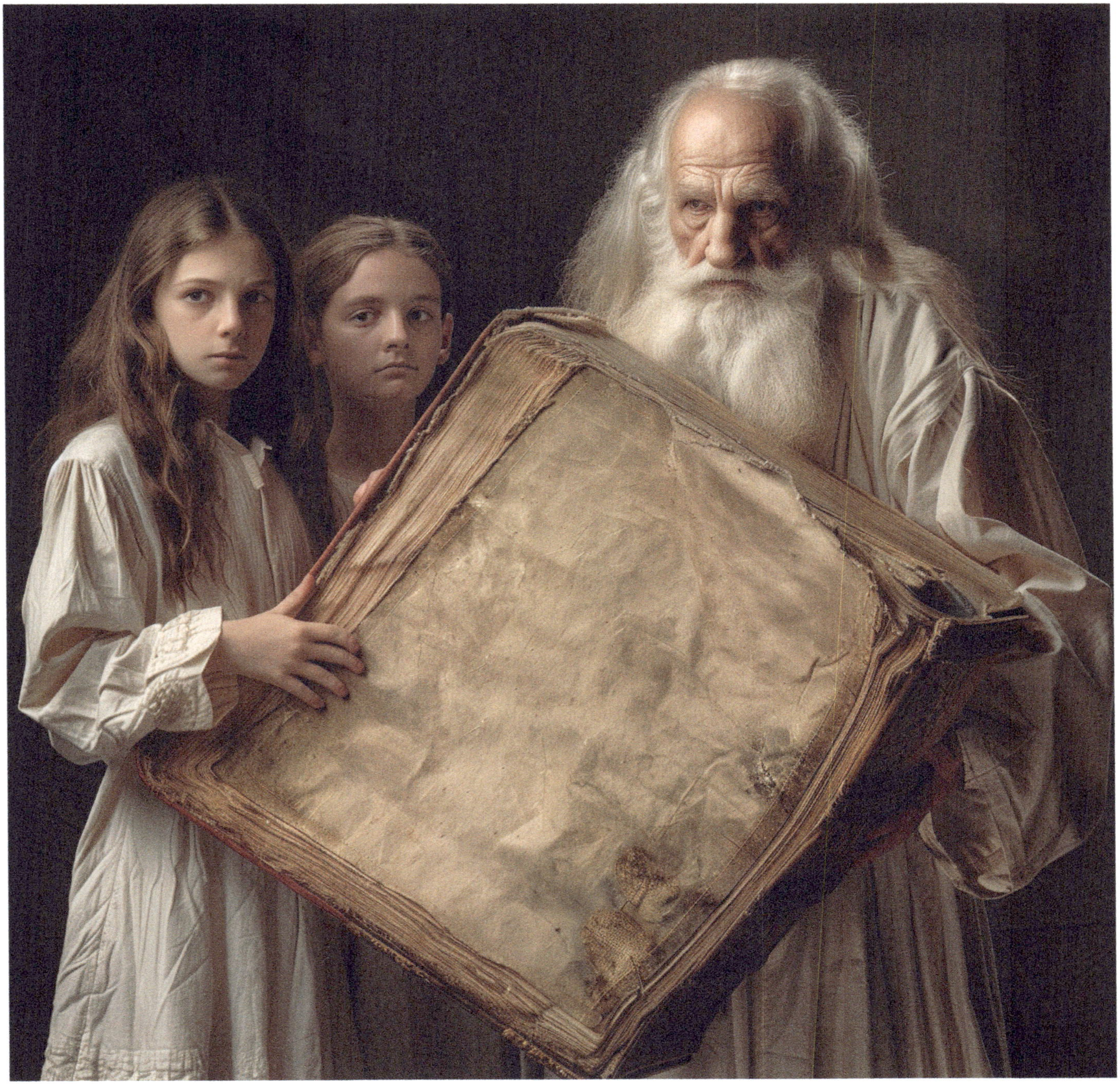

In another vision Dr. Goldman saw in detail that he was one of the Architects of the Shwedagon in Burma, a magnificent gold dome Buddhist Chedi, one of the most important Buddhist Chedis in the World, covered in pure gold.

This explains why Dr. Goldman has visited this important Buddhist shrine an incredible 47 times, even while the country was not officially open to foreigners.

Something has always drawn him back to Burma and to visit the Shwedagon. After seeing his past Life, Dr. Goldman understood why he was drawn back like a magnet to this place.

Dr. Robert Goldman has been very fortunate and lucky in this life. Being part of building this important Buddhist temple, could explain his Great Fortune in this Life.

.

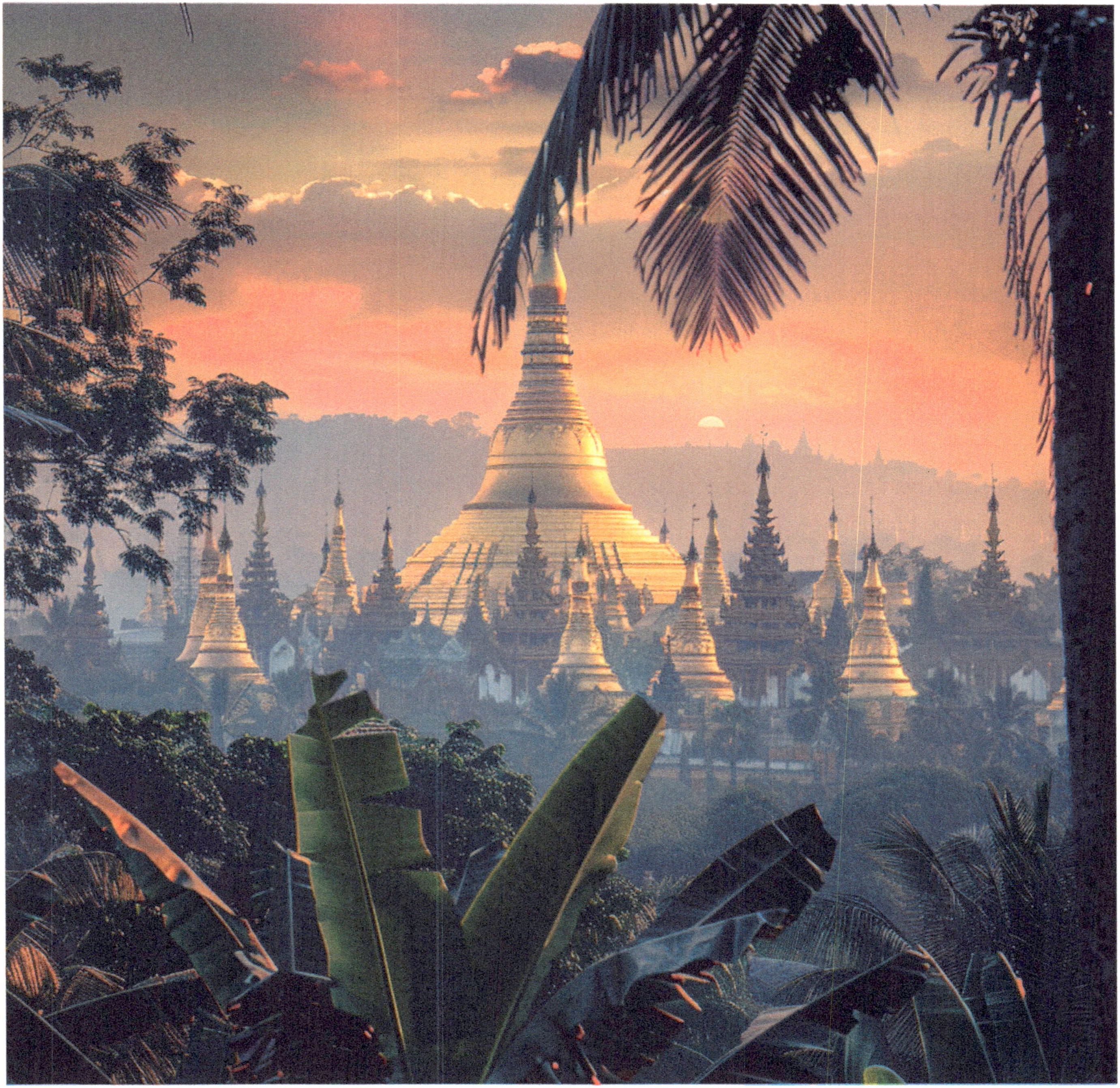

While on his many visits to Burma Dr. Bob collected different art pieces to bring back to America.

In one of his shipments to the USA, a curious item appeared when his shipping container arrived. It was an old Gold wooden Buddha statue.

This statue did not appear on the shipping manifest, nor the invoice. The shipping company had no idea where it came from and advised Dr. Goldman to keep this statue. Dr. Bob came to consider this statue as his most prized piece of all his Art collection. This Buddha seemed to give Dr. Goldman, peace, protection, and luck.

In a conversation with me, Dr. Goldman told me that one day he would like to leave this statue to me and my wife, as we as Buddhists would know what to do with it.

I told Dr. Bob why wait, why not offer it to Master Acharavadee Wongsakon since she was building some kind of museum called Manasikarn. Dr. Goldman agreed and sent me photos of the statue, so that I could show and offer the statue to the Master.

537

Upon seeing the photos of this statue, the Master's gaze froze, and in a serious voice, she stated that I must bring this statue to her as quickly as possible.

When the statue reached Thailand and the Master's hands, she explained its profound importance. This statue was intricately connected to the royalty of both Thailand and Burma, and it served as a beacon of hope for the hundreds of thousands of souls trapped in a heavy energy vortex, casualties of ancient wars between the two nations. These souls awaited a Master with immense compassion to release them from their plight.

One night, after teaching high-level meditation, the Master quietly performed a ceremony for the souls attached to the Burmese statue. In that moment, millions of souls were released.

These souls conveyed a simple message through the Master to Dr. Goldman and me: "THANK YOU."

Though the statue held great value to Dr. Goldman, he offered it to the Master without hesitation. The Master suggested that, based on its importance, the statue was worth a million dollars.

To everyone's surprise, she then offered the statue back to Dr. Goldman as a memory of this extraordinary act and event.

I immortalized this event in a painting.

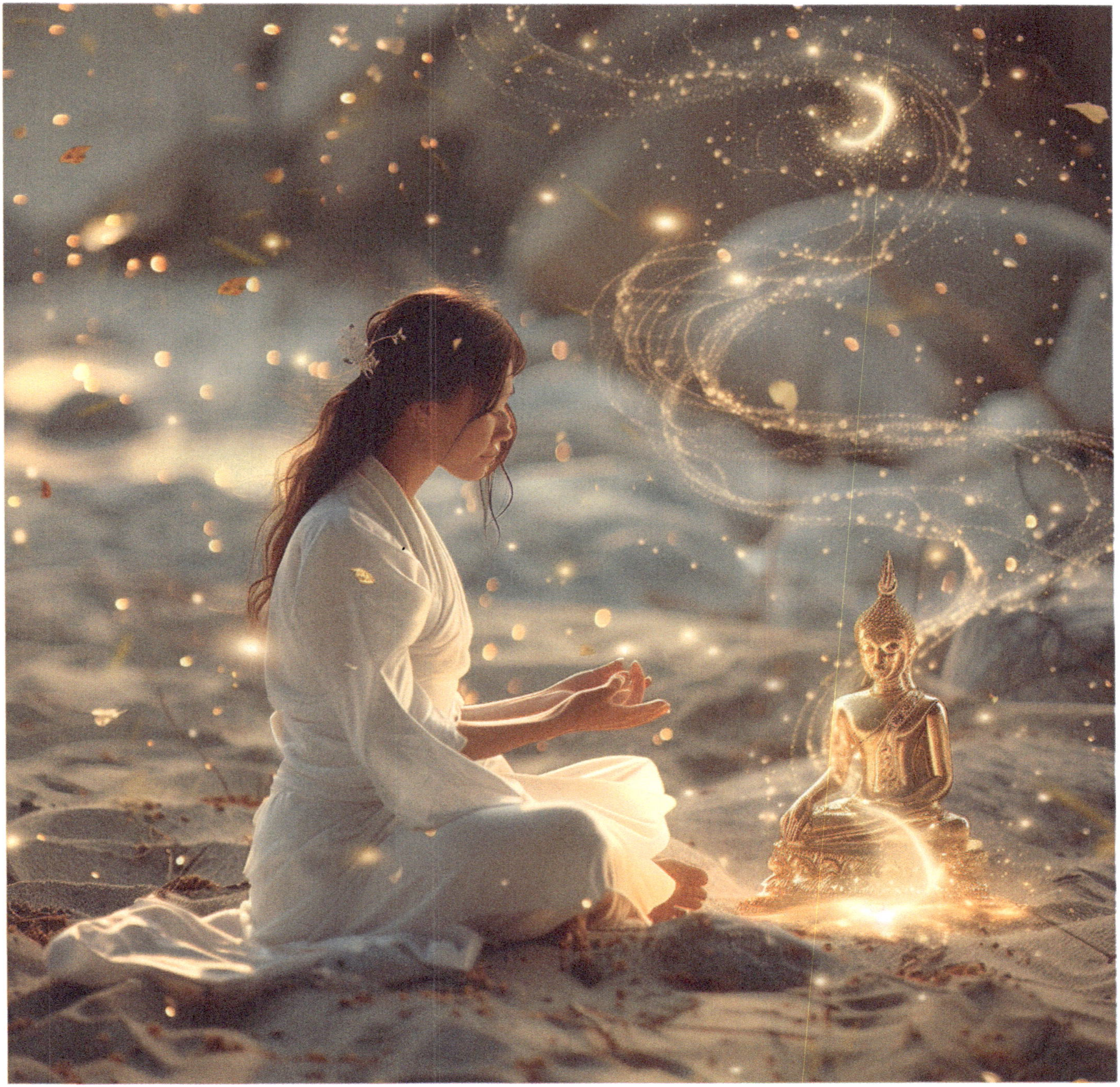

540

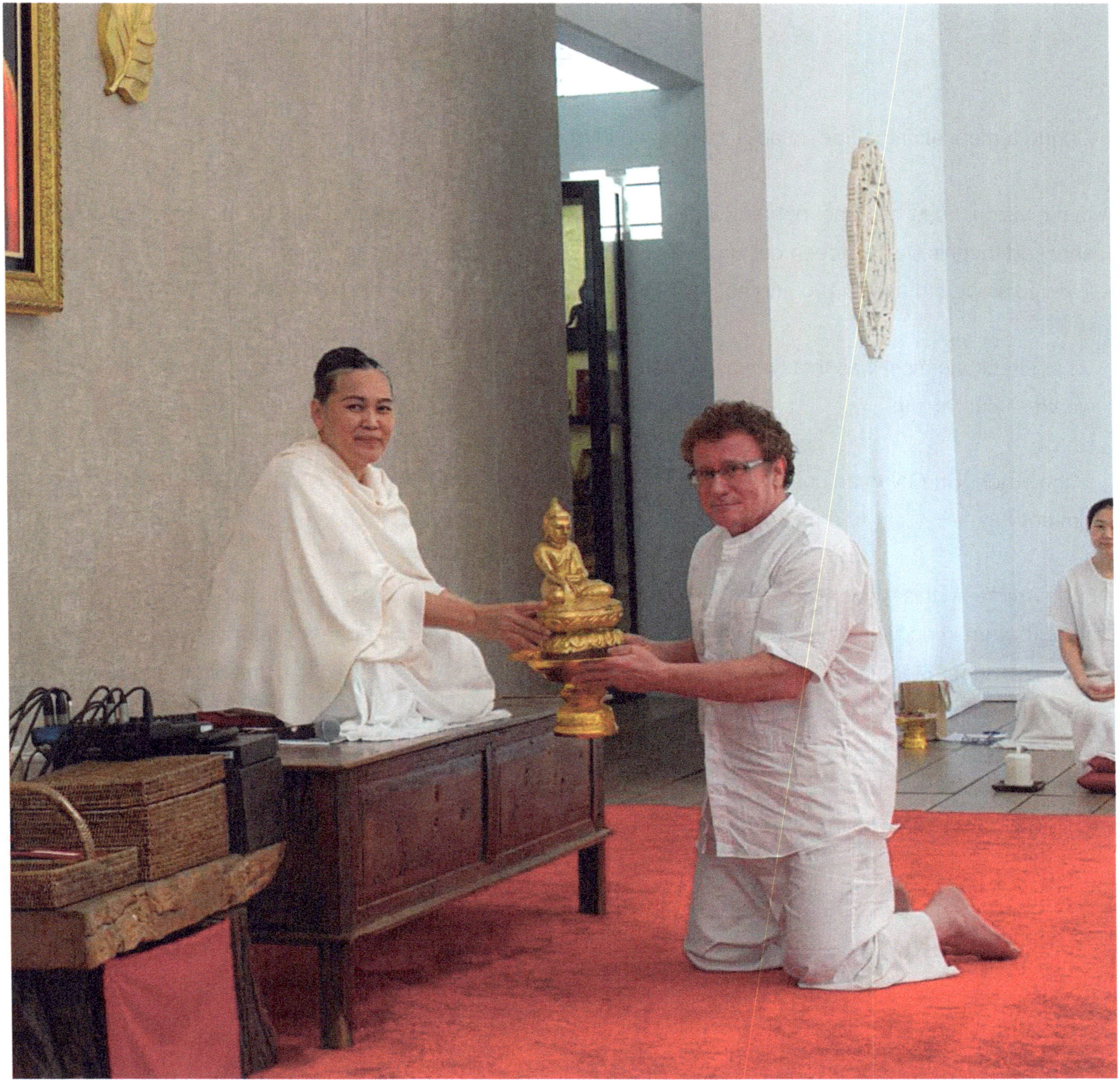

During a meditation course, I had a vivid vision of my friend, Dr. Goldman.

In the vision, I saw him unexpectedly pass away. Dr. Bob appeared despondent, utterly surprised and shocked that his life had been cut short. As the "father" of the Anti-Aging Industry, he couldn't fathom not living to a ripe old age of 120 and not having time to accomplish all he had set out to do.

What struck me most was that he was in great physical condition, far better than his peers, yet now they would all outlive him.

In the vision, Dr. Goldman couldn't comprehend how he had done everything right, yet death had taken him anyway.

Furthermore, in this vision of the next dimension, Dr. Goldman came to realize that many of the things he thought were important in his life were actually distractions. He recognized that in this lifetime, he had used his "Super Merit" and "Luck" built up in past lives to pursue these distractions rather than focusing on the real goal.

I witnessed a defeated Dr. Goldman walking into the sunset, heading towards his next rebirth to "try again" to figure out life and end the cycle of rebirth.

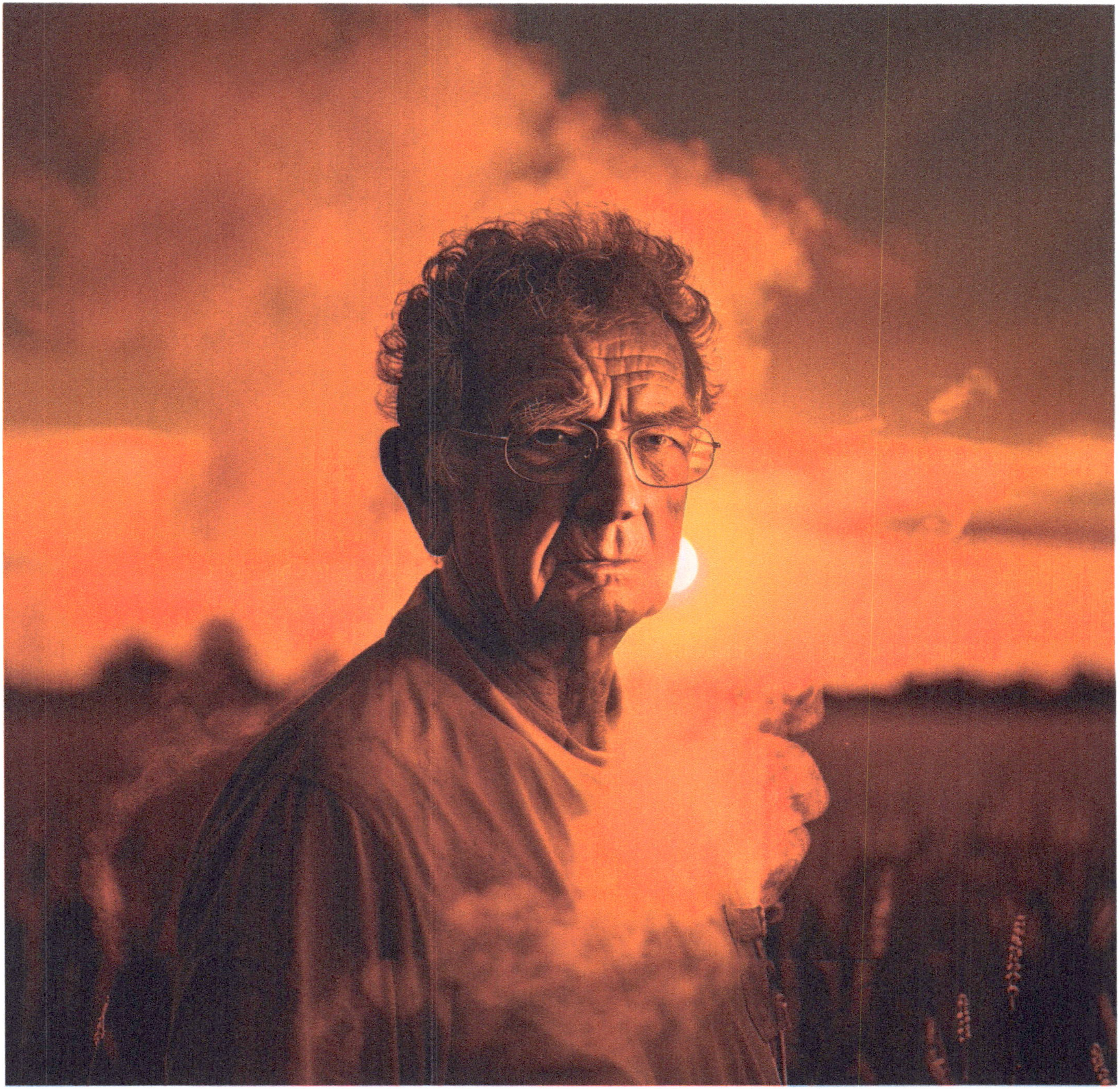

In 2023, I persuaded Dr. Goldman to come to Thailand and spend 8 days practicing with Master Acharavadee once again.

Dr. Robert agreed. He filled out an application and made his way to the airport.

However, on his way to the airport, his driver had an accident due to snowy conditions on the highway. The driver was injured, but Dr. Goldman was unhurt and still managed to catch his flight.

Later, the Master explained to him that once he had filled out and committed to practicing meditation, the Triple Gems were protecting him.

545

When Dr. Goldman arrived in Thailand and we met for dinner, I noticed his dark aura. He looked like a dead man walking. Even my wife remarked that she felt he would not live much longer. Others shared the same intuition.

It seemed that Dr. Goldman's time was up.

What Dr. Goldman would come to learn is that all the medical and anti-aging interventions could not save him from his karma. His karma owners, those he had wronged in past lives, were coming to collect.

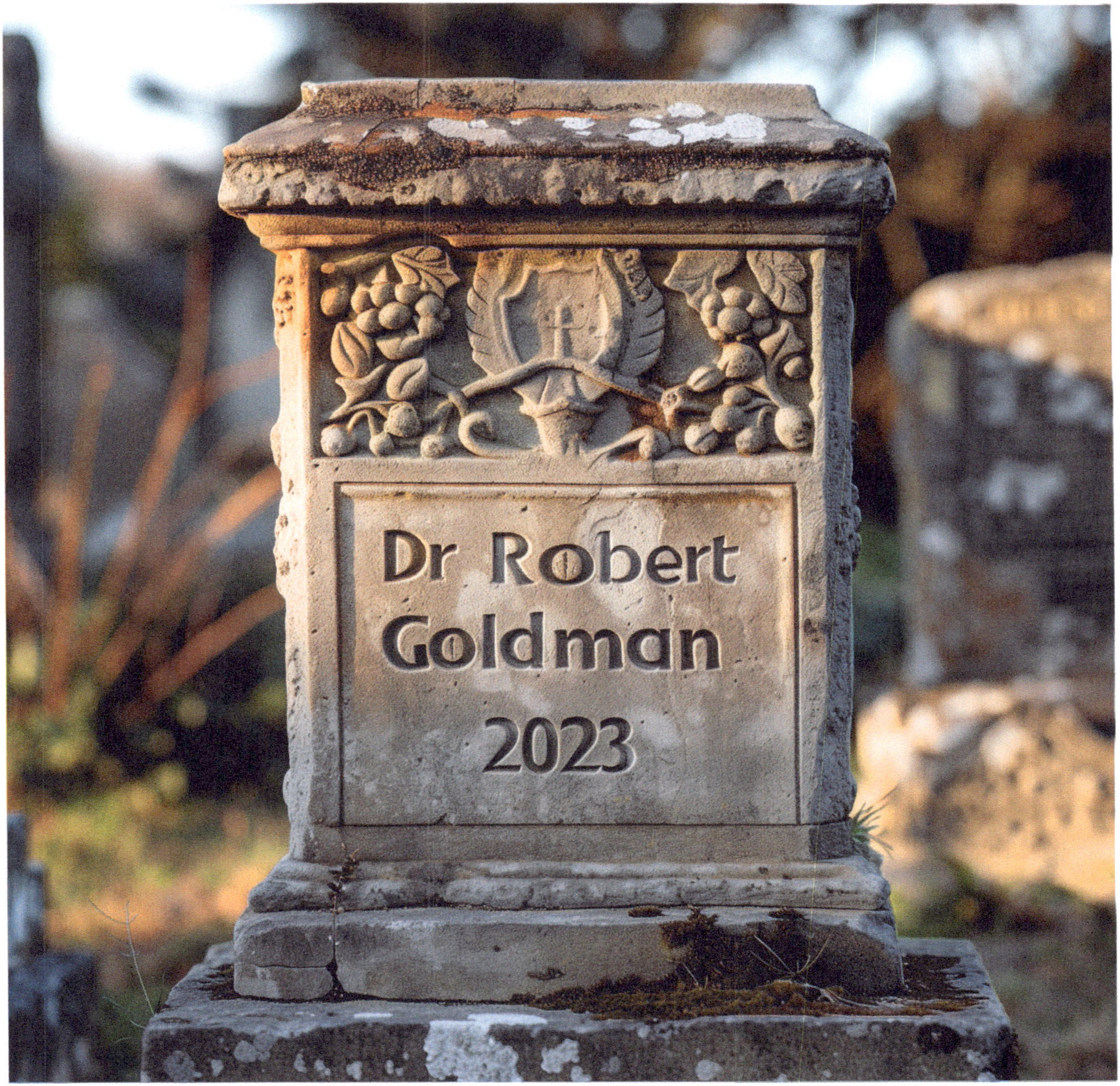
Dr Robert
Goldman
2023

During the week of advanced meditation Dr. Goldman himself began to realize his time was up. Not that he felt sick or unwell, but the "grim reaper" was knocking on his door.

549

The Master also spoke to Dr. Goldman independently, in a very serious tone, telling him "Goodbye" and indicating that this would be their last meeting.

Dr. Robert had a past-life vision in which he saw himself wearing an ancient helmet, realizing that he had been a soldier in a previous life.

Later, the Master explained to Dr. Goldman that he had been a fierce soldier in many lifetimes, having killed countless enemies. Now, those he had killed in his past lives were coming to collect the debt, and karma was manifesting as retribution, bringing an end to his life.

Dr. Goldman found it difficult to believe that he was such a fierce killer, especially since in this life, as a doctor, he had never hurt anyone intentionally.

The Master explained to Dr. Goldman that even in this lifetime, he pursued martial arts and collected weapons and war paraphernalia.

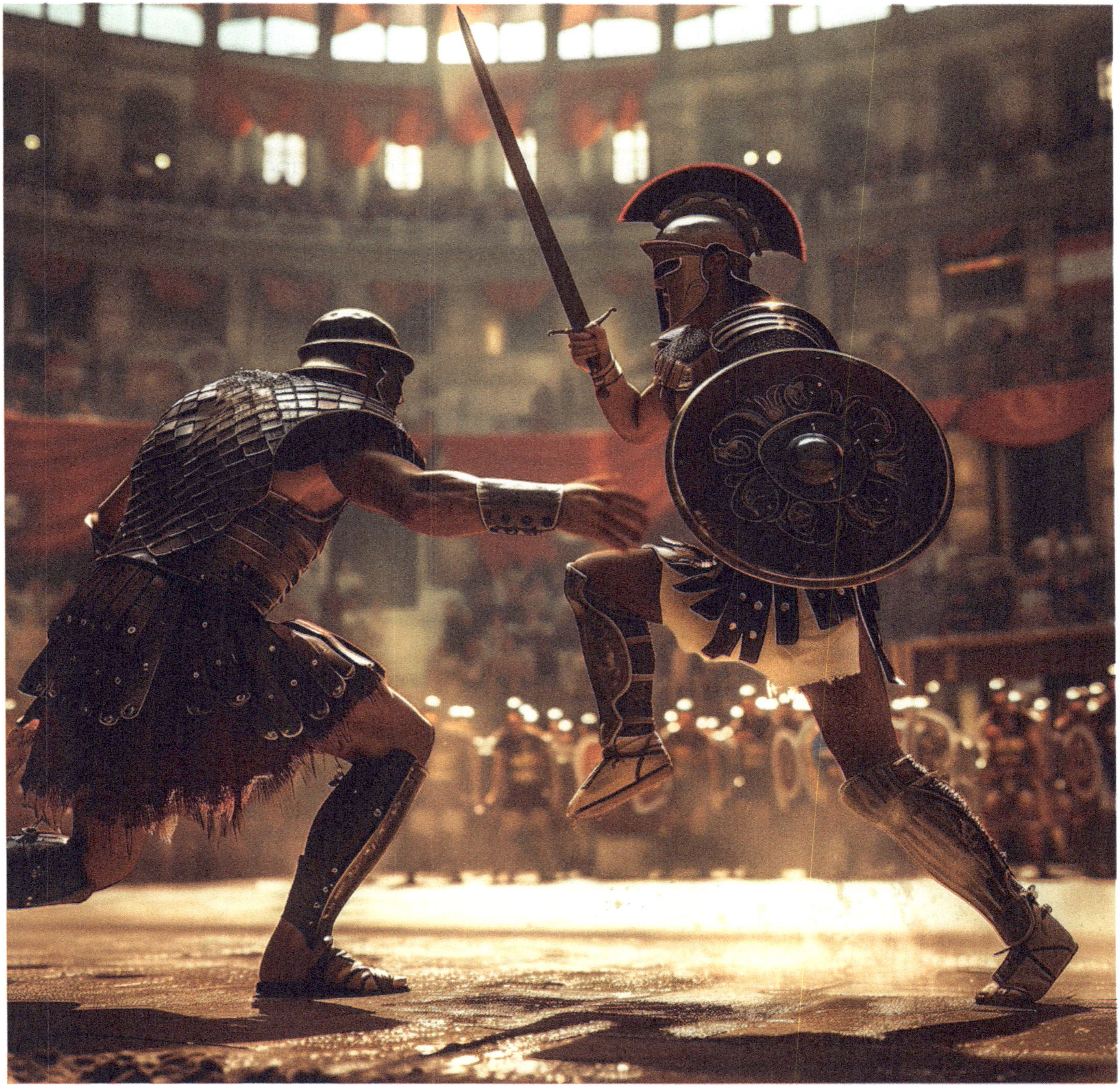

The Master advised Dr. Goldman to visit the Bodhi tree and sincerely apologize to all those he had wronged in the past. She also suggested that Dr. Goldman make a commitment to dedicate his life to helping others and spreading goodness in the world.

Following the Master's guidance, Dr. Robert Goldman did just that.

Later, the Master invited Dr. Goldman and me to sit beneath the Bodhi tree with her.

In that moment, she handed us some items, explaining that they were not ordinary objects, but rather a conduit for transferring her energy to us.

During his meditation, Dr. Goldman saw the Master's energy swirling around him like countless golden flakes, an experience that profoundly impacted him.

This and other stories are chronicled in the Master's Book "AWAKEN FROM MADNESS"

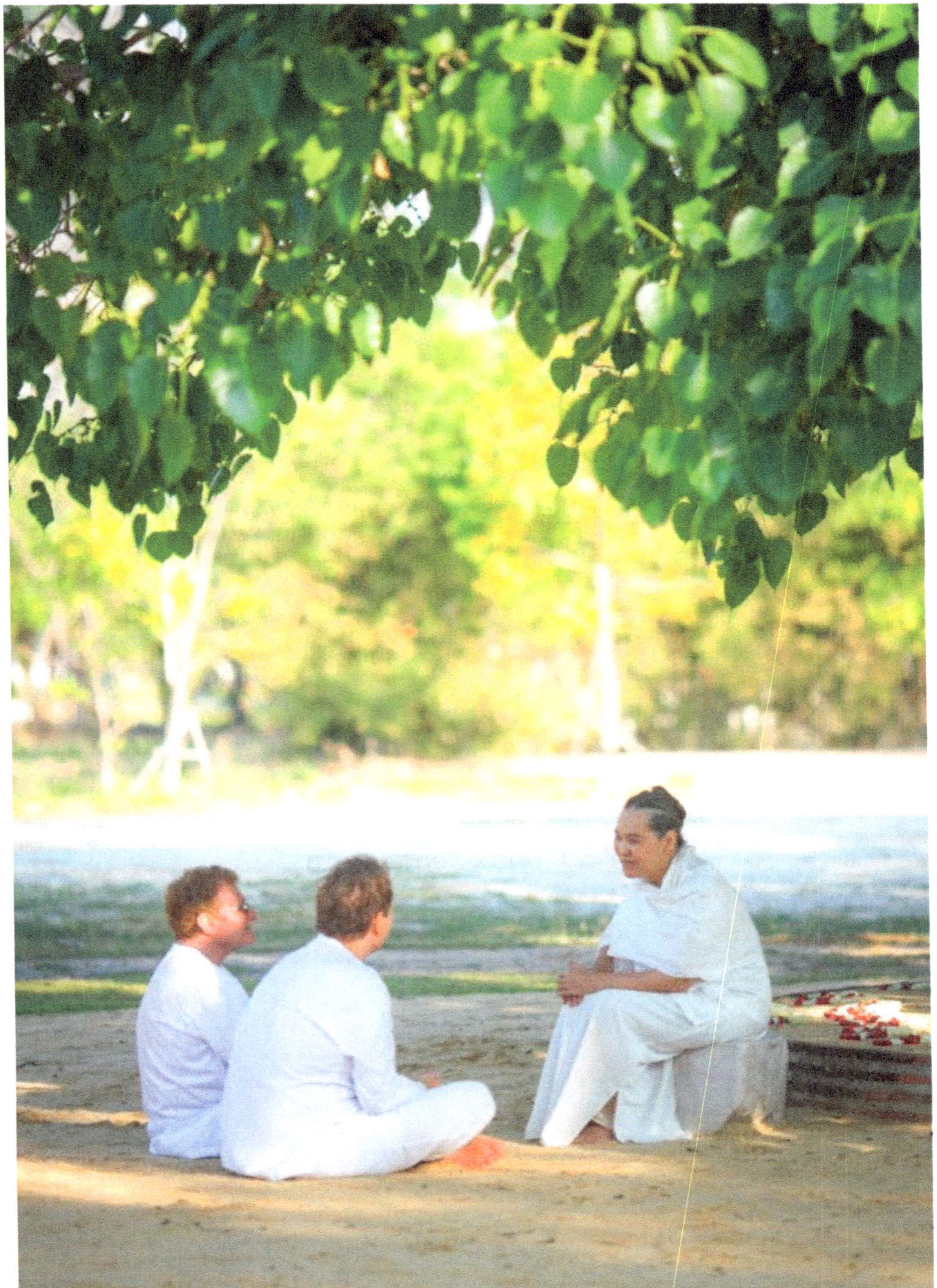

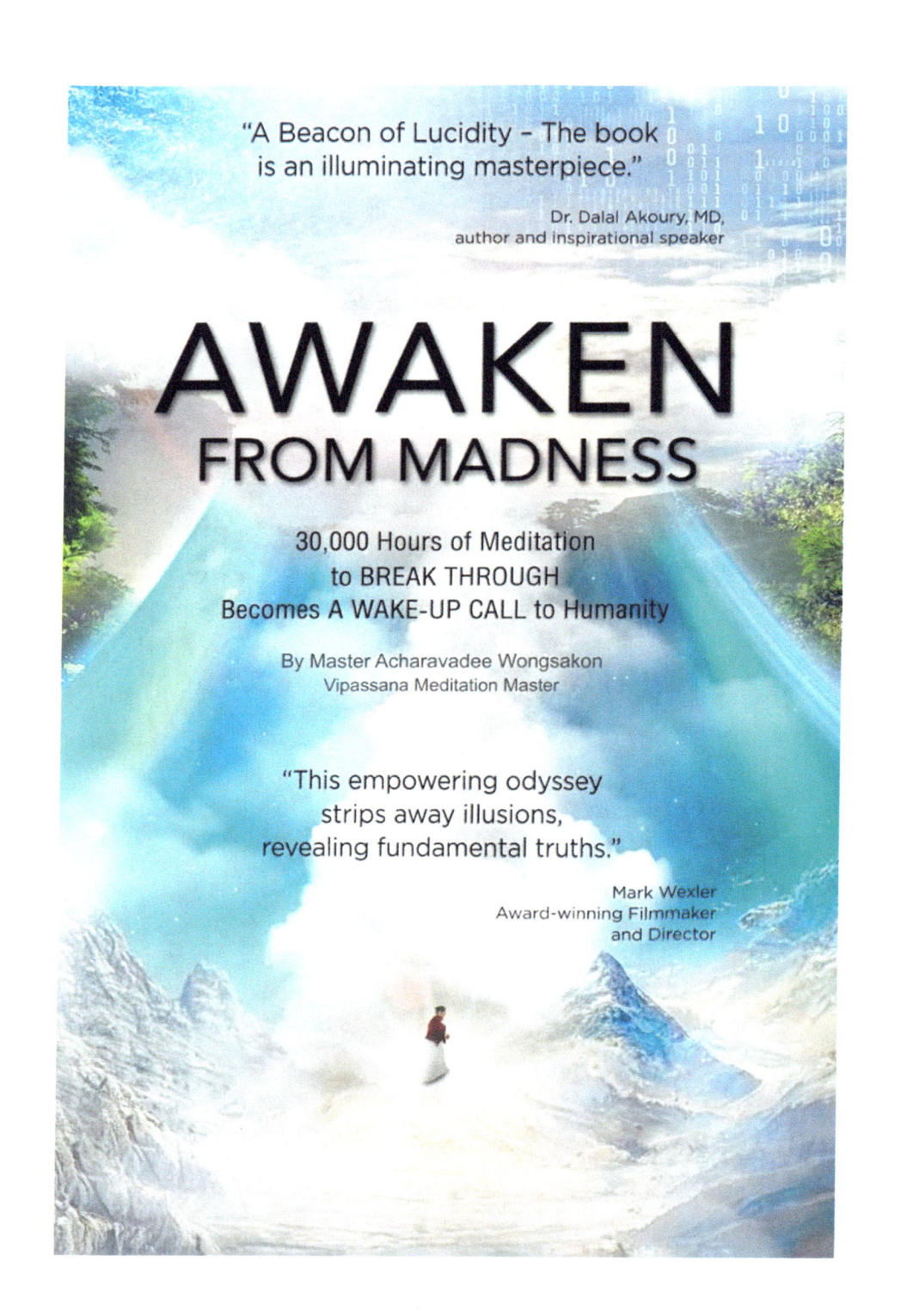

"A Beacon of Lucidity – The book is an illuminating masterpiece."

Dr. Dalal Akoury, MD,
author and inspirational speaker

AWAKEN
FROM MADNESS

30,000 Hours of Meditation
to BREAK THROUGH
Becomes A WAKE-UP CALL to Humanity

By Master Acharavadee Wongsakon
Vipassana Meditation Master

"This empowering odyssey
strips away illusions,
revealing fundamental truths."

Mark Wexler
Award-winning Filmmaker
and Director

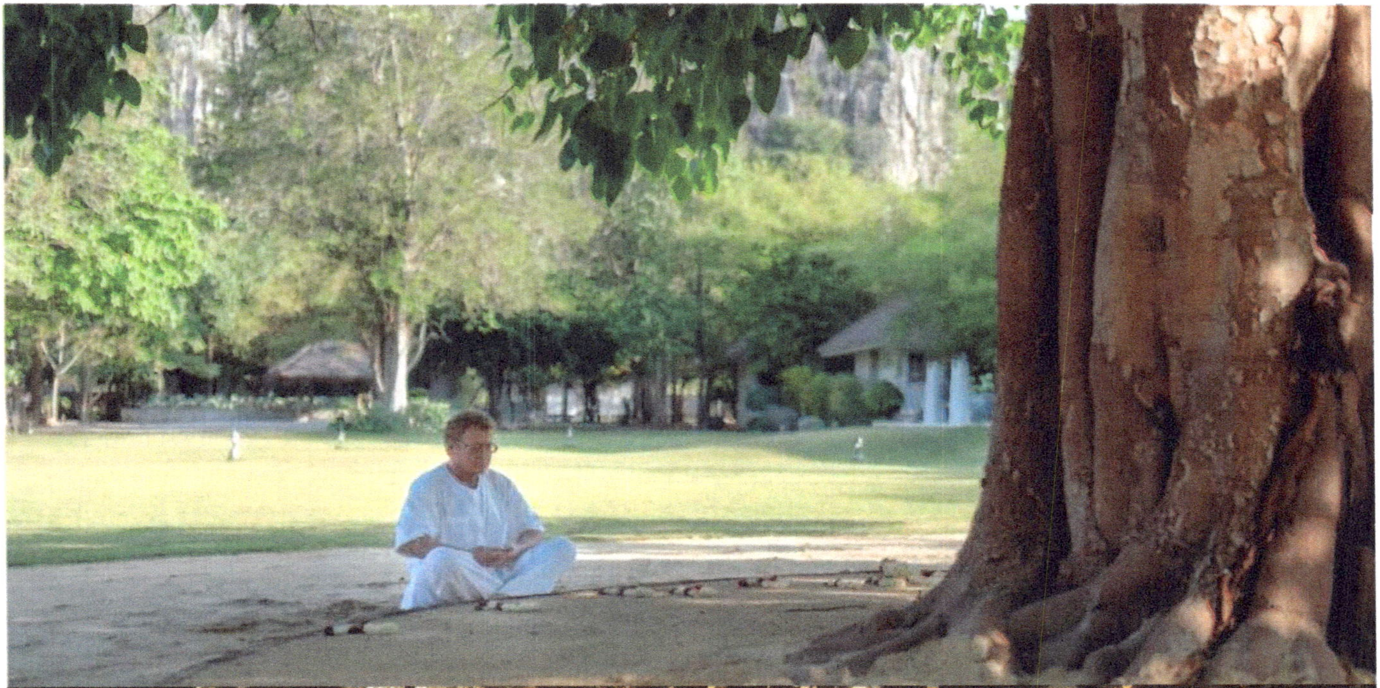

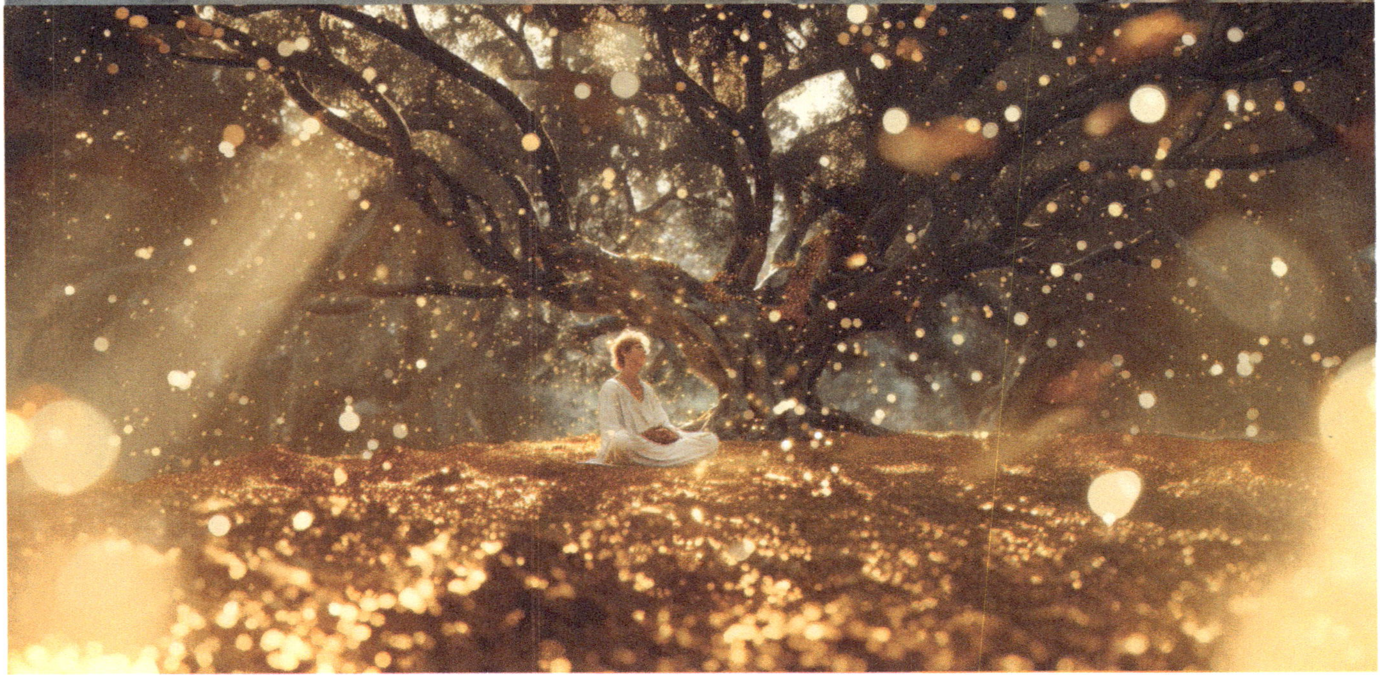

Suddenly, Dr. Robert M. Goldman saw a vision of his tombstone, where the date changed from 2023 to 2048.

Later that day, as I sat with Dr. Robert, I witnessed him regress in age and his aura become incredibly bright before my very eyes. It was miraculous, and there was no doubt that Dr. Robert Goldman had received a life extension in the truest sense of the word.

The Master had negotiated with his karmic debtors, and they had agreed not to seek revenge in exchange for receiving merit from both the Master and Dr. Goldman. They could see that with the help of the Master, Dr. Goldman would truly make a positive impact on others and the world.

However, this 24-year life extension was not guaranteed and could change depending on new karma created and how Dr. Goldman conducted his life going forward.

What does someone who receives a 24-year life extension gain?

The chance to do good and more time to practice and reach enlightenment. Because when your time is up, the game resets—all your possessions in this life are gone, and you must hope to rediscover the dhamma and the path again in a future lifetime.

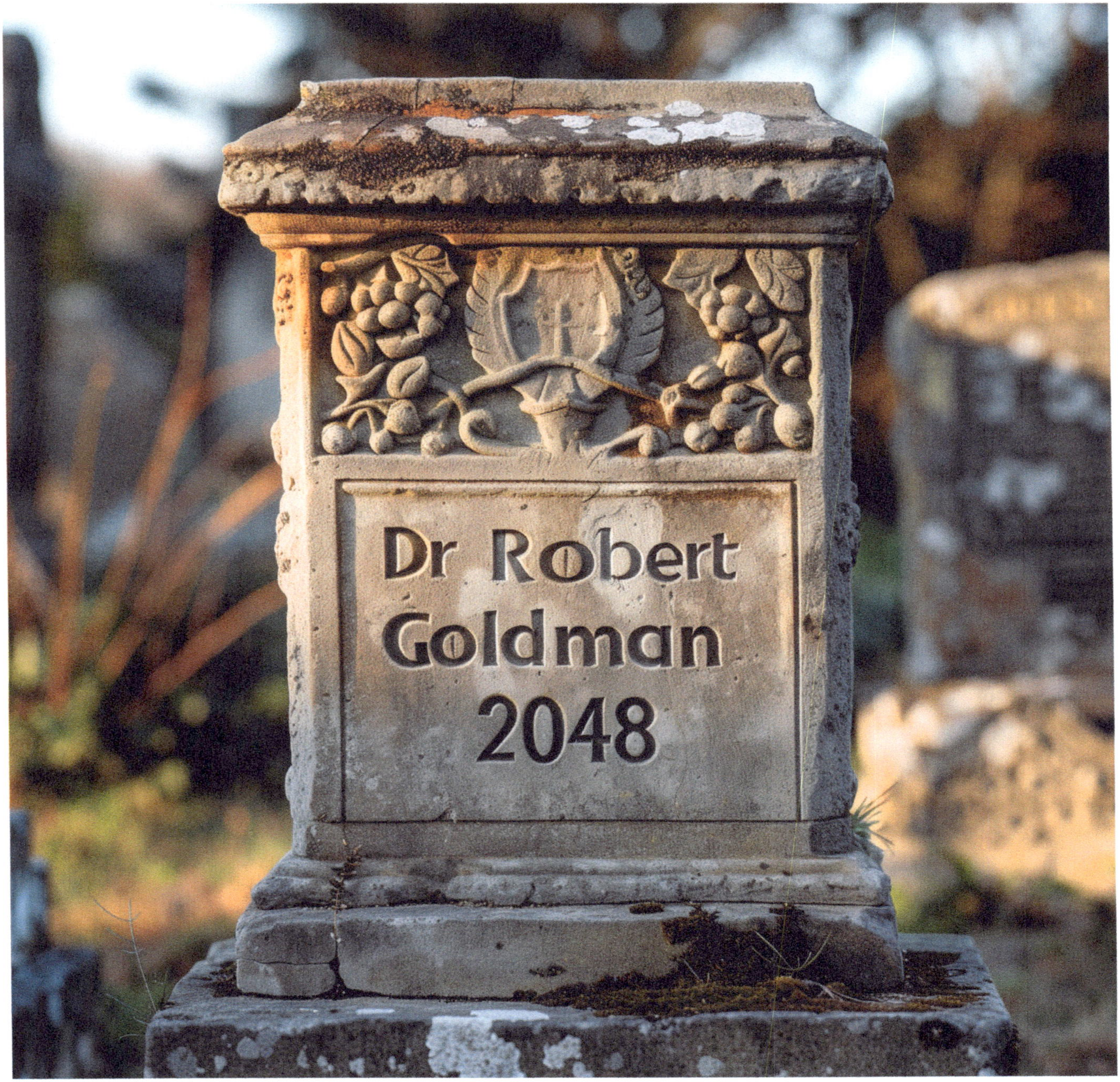
Dr Robert
Goldman
2048

Dr. Bob and I also shared an important life as samurais together.

In that lifetime, Dr. Robert was not only my friend but also a trusted ally of the Master, who was the head of the samurai. Dr. Bob would come to learn that he held the Master's helmet before each battle.

Even in this lifetime, he remained connected to many of the samurai from the past, who gradually found their way back to him. I was among them, serving as the bridge to reconnect him with the Master.

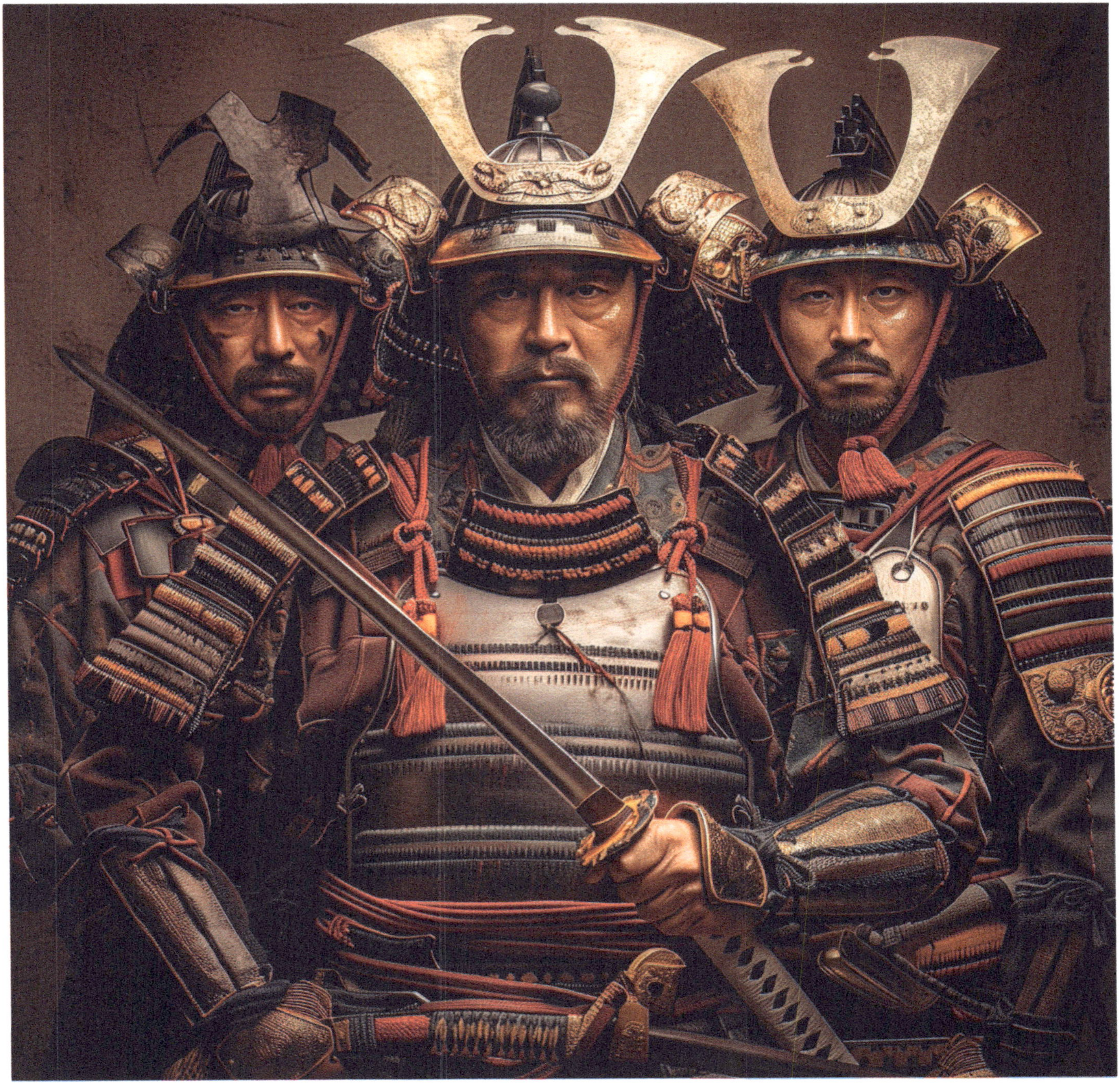

And so, with the great awakening and life extension, Dr. Robert Goldman set out to pay it forward.

One year later, he and I brought 40 of our closest friends to learn Techo Vipassana meditation and study under Master Acharavadee. He also brought 14 Grand Master Martial Arts experts and Hollywood actors and stuntmen to study under the Master.

Master Acharavadee would become the master of the world's greatest martial arts masters.

As these martial artists met the Master for the first time, someone with celestial eyes could see that they all were holding the weapons they had used in their lifetime as samurai, and still used in this lifetime.

The Master's loyal samurai soldiers had come home, but not to fight a battle in the world with swords and spears. This time, it was the ultimate battle against impurities (kilesa) in the mind, to reach the ultimate truth, liberation, and the path to enlightenment.

Both the worldly world and the spiritual world rejoiced.

This was the Master's Dhamma Army coming together with their minds, to become the seed of change for the world and humanity.

Not many people realized the good force and vibration that spread to the world that week.

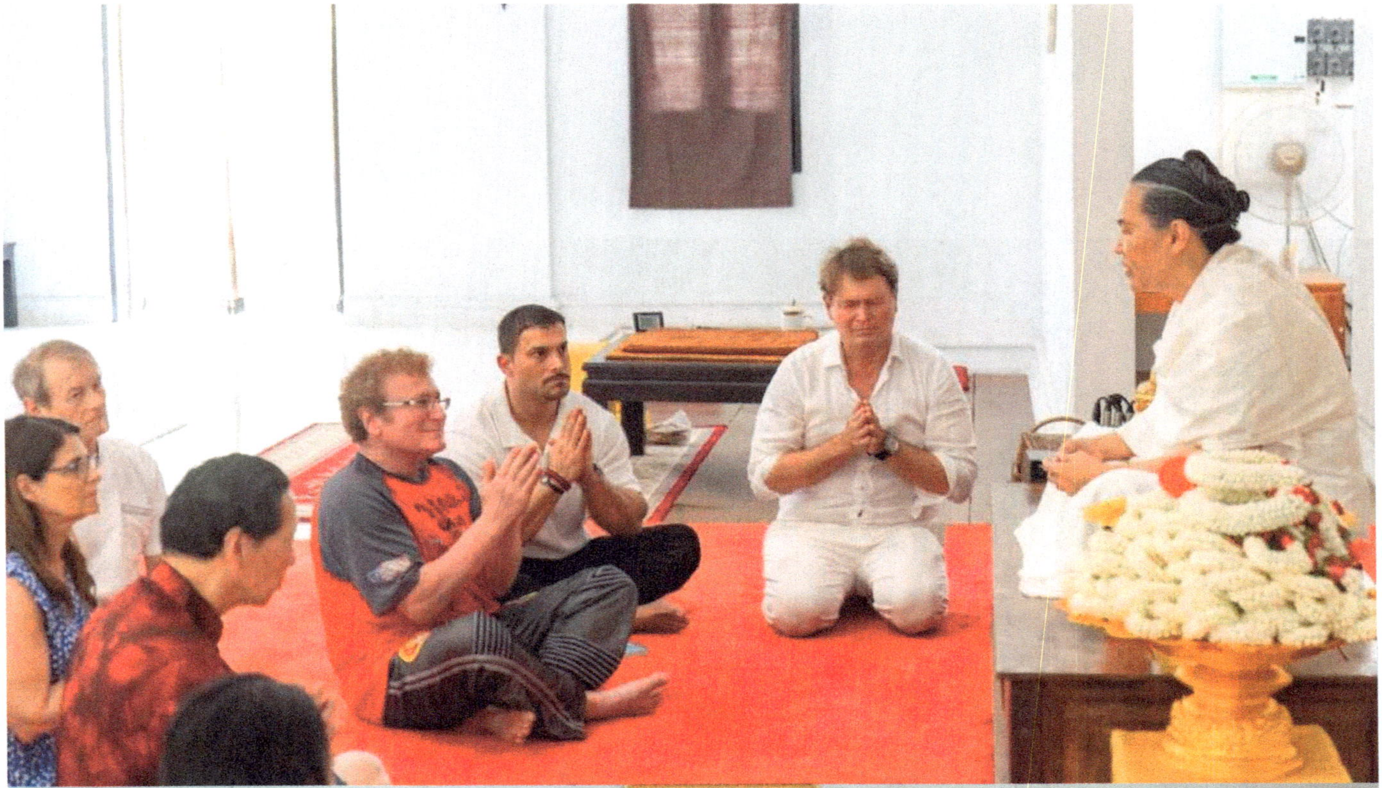

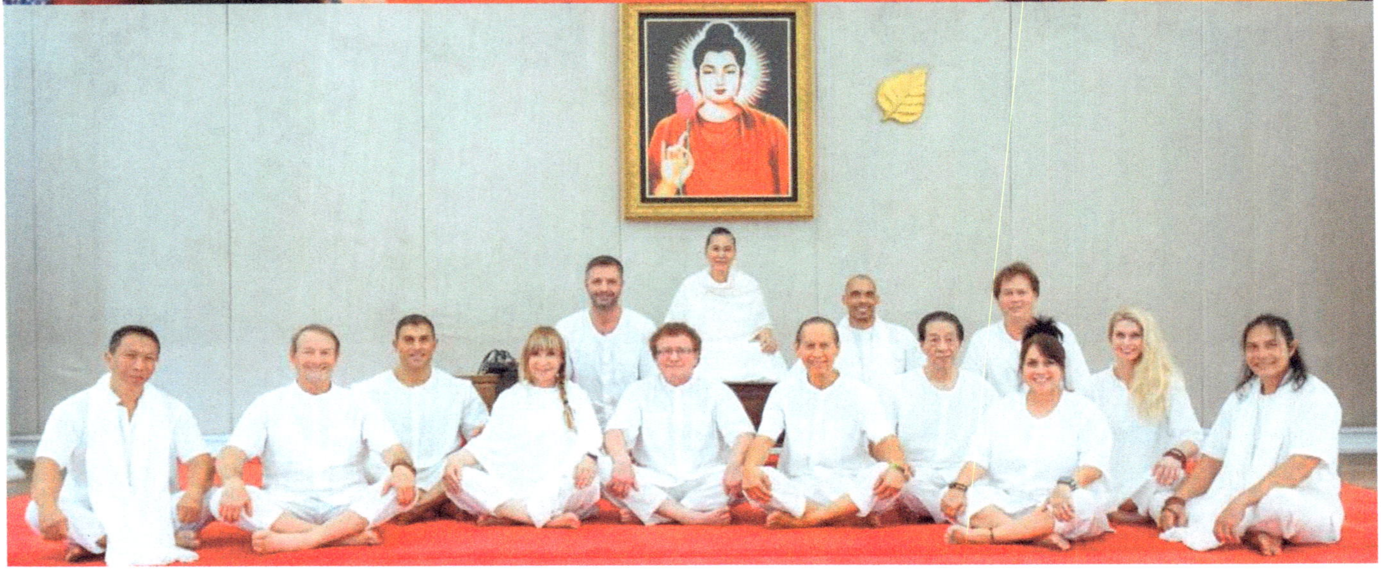

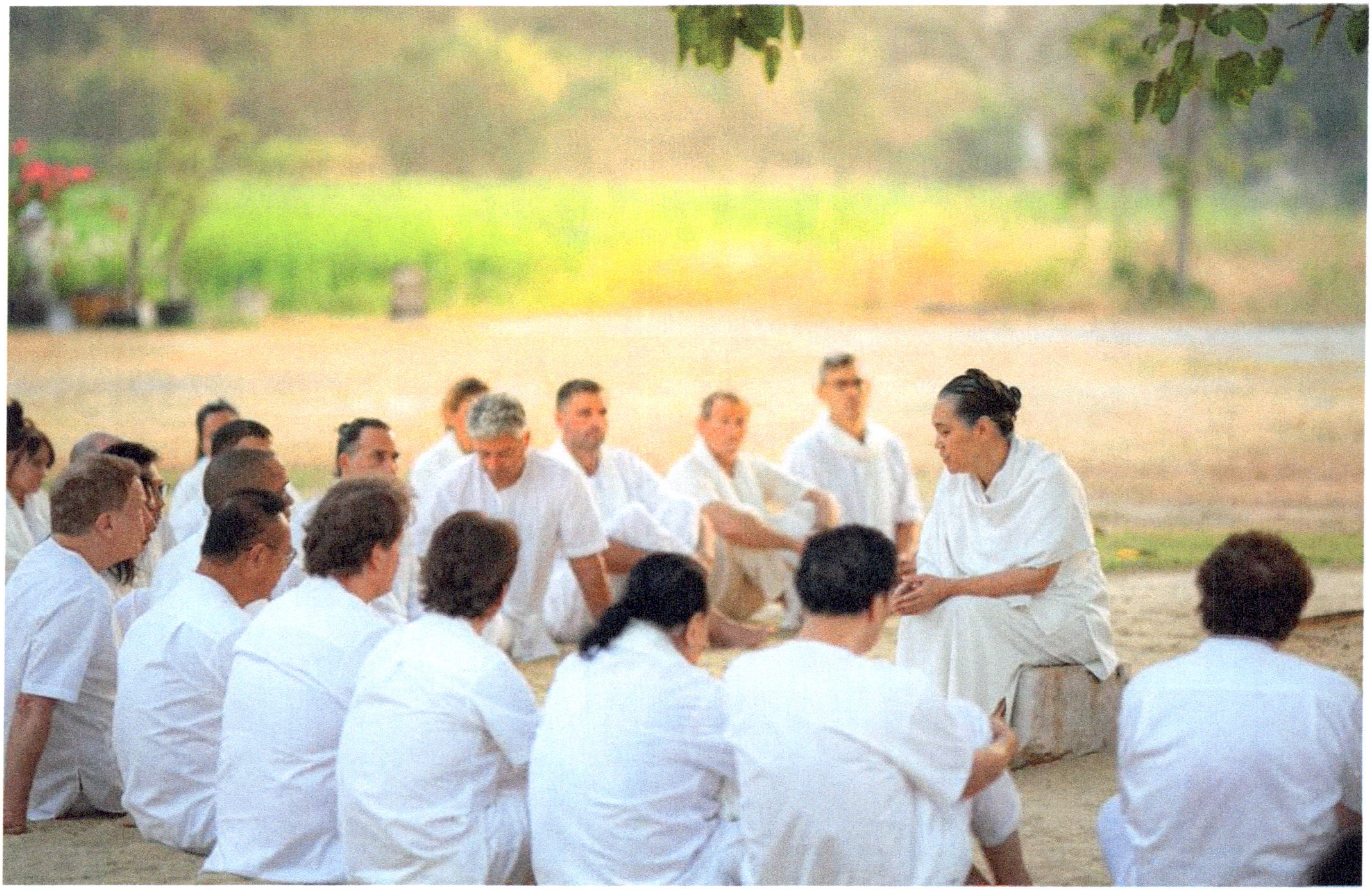

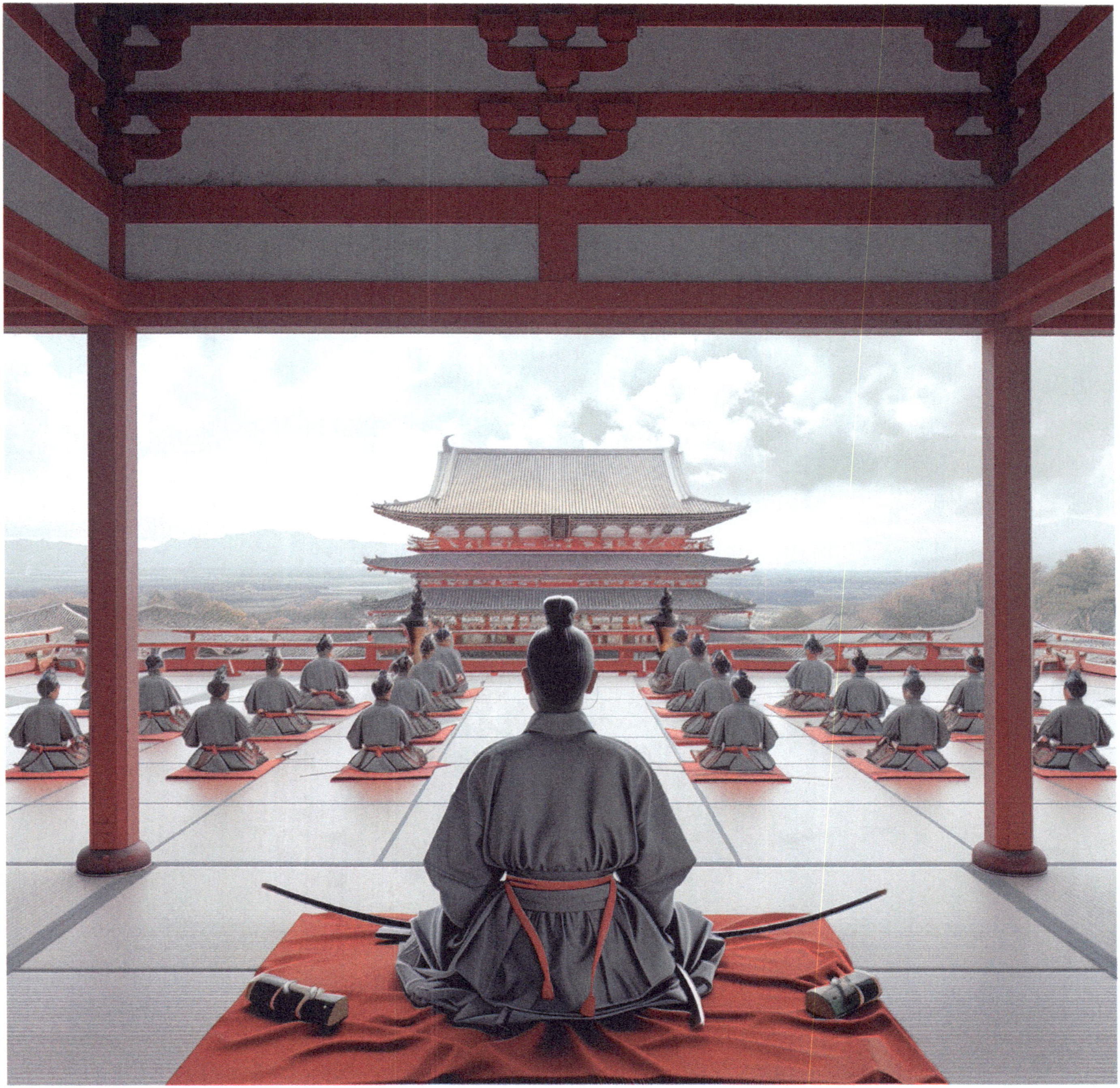

Bangkok Post

THAILAND > PR NEWS

World Elite's Spiritual Journey to Thailand's Mindfulness Oasis

Lead: World Elite Embarks on a Journey to Thailand, Embracing Mindfulness Practices for Inner Peace and Spiritual Wisdom, and Experiencing Intellectual Exploration in the World's Wellness and Mindfulness Destination

PUBLISHED : 19 JAN 2024 AT 13:46

The School of Life Foundation is transforming Saraburi into a phenomenon as the World's

Master Acharavadee Wongsakon teaches meditation to the "Black belt" Instructors of GGM Ernie Reyes at West Coast Martial Arts in California, USA. Martial Arts Legend Ernie Reyes and Margie Reyes traveled to Thailand in 2024 to become Master Acharavadee Wongsakon's students and subsequently invited the Master to California. There are no coincidences in life. These were all the Master's samurai soldiers from the past, reunited.

school-of-life-foundation.com
14th
JAN 2024
05:00 PM
MASTER ACHARAVADEE WONGSAKON
TEACHER OF THE MARTIAL
ARTS MASTERS
MARTIAL ARTS
HALL OF FAME
THE SOUL RESORT, THAILAND

Dr. Robert Goldman, Chairman of the American Academy of Anti-Aging, also flew Master Acharavadee Wongsakon to America to speak in front of 3000 of the top doctors in the world.

The message that was so crucial for the Master to deliver to the medical community was this: in order to heal oneself at the core, we must address our past karma. Medications and anti-aging therapies will fail without a person doing goodness and practicing advanced meditation to cancel out the bad karma we have accumulated in the past, and to live our lives morally.

This is the secret to anti-aging. Look at a person who does goodness and meditates. See how young and natural they look. See how they glow.

This is the true essence and "Fountain of Youth" in nature.

Goodness (Dhamma) equals nature.

Dr. Goldman and the A4M medical community awarded Master Acharavadee Wongsakon the very rare A4M Lifetime Achievement Award for cracking the anti-aging code.

LIFETIME ACHIEVEMENT AWARD
Master Acharavadee Wongsakon

CHAPTER. 25

DESTINY

(WASSANA SASAKUN)

"Wassana" in Thai means "Destiny."

Wassana Sasakun epitomizes "pure goodness"—a person who needs no anti-aging therapies or sunscreens to look young and beautiful.

Her anti-aging secret is what the Master teaches: do goodness, meditate, and maintain a moral code of conduct.

I met Wassana 20 years ago, and she has not aged. At age 45, she has no wrinkles and starts every day with a smile, searching for ways to do good deeds, offer food to monks, or save the lives of animals.

Her happiness is not found in expensive boutiques or material things. Her happiness comes from her love of Buddhism and helping Master Acharavadee Wongskon "awaken the world from madness."

Wassana is a determined soldier for Master Acharavadee and also shares a past life as a samurai. She has followed and supported the Master through many lifetimes.

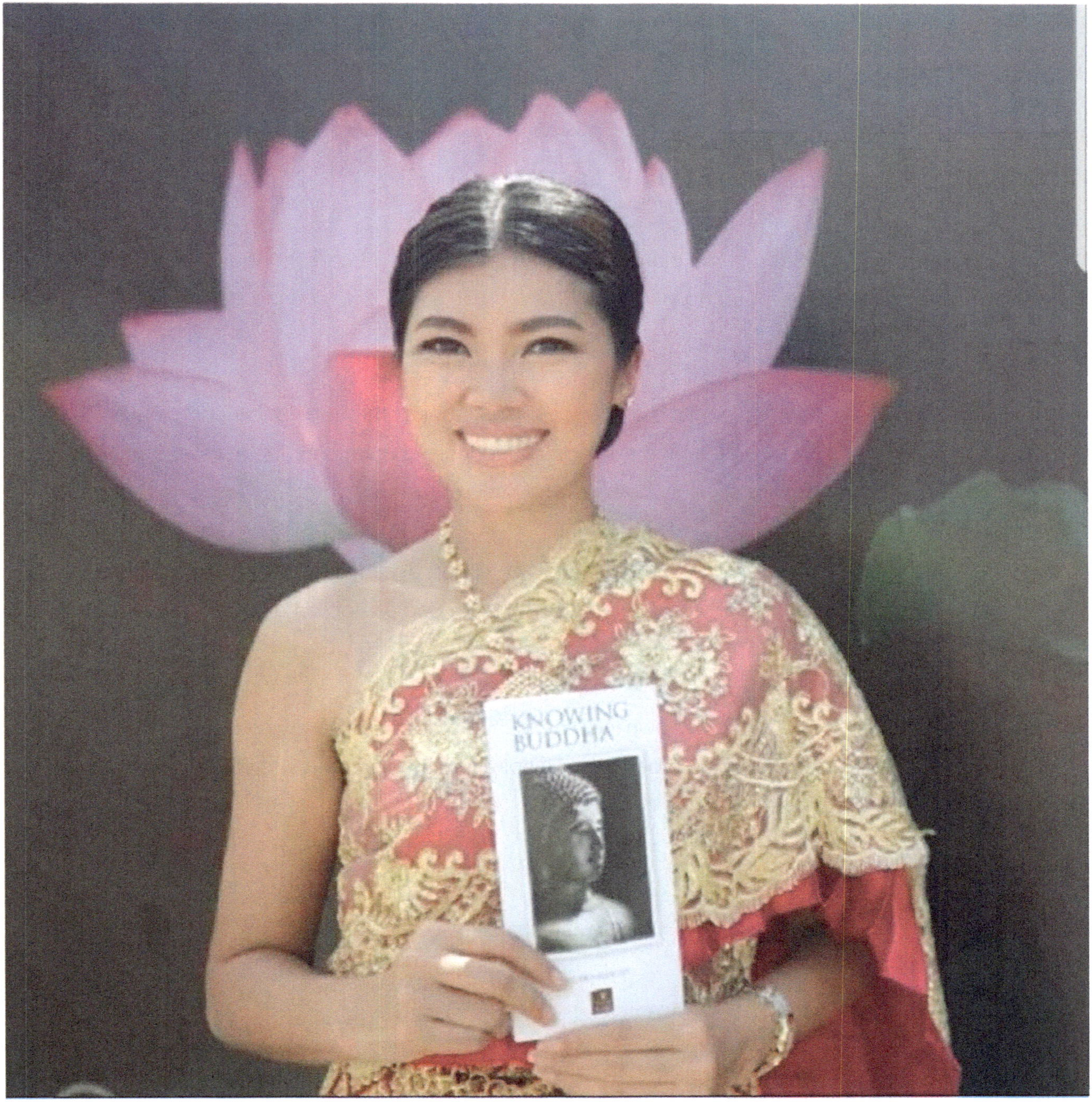
KNOWING
BUDDHA

Wassana's mother once confided in me that she had vivid dreams while carrying Wassana. Even before she was born, she would have recurring visions of Wassana as a little girl, wearing a necklace of Buddhas.

Witnessing Wassana's acts of merit-making and unceasing kindness through volunteering, such as offering food to monks, visiting temples, and spreading kindness, confirms her mother's dream. Wassana is truly an angelic person, radiating beauty both inwardly and outwardly.

Through her actions, I've come to recognize Wassana's profound destiny and her role in uplifting Buddhism and the world at large. For Wassana, the Buddha embodies not just a figure of reverence, but a source of boundless happiness to share and support.

Wassana's influence extends beyond her own life; she is the catalyst behind my embrace of meditation and Buddhism. Her existence serves as a beacon of inspiration, guiding others toward the path of spiritual growth and enlightenment.

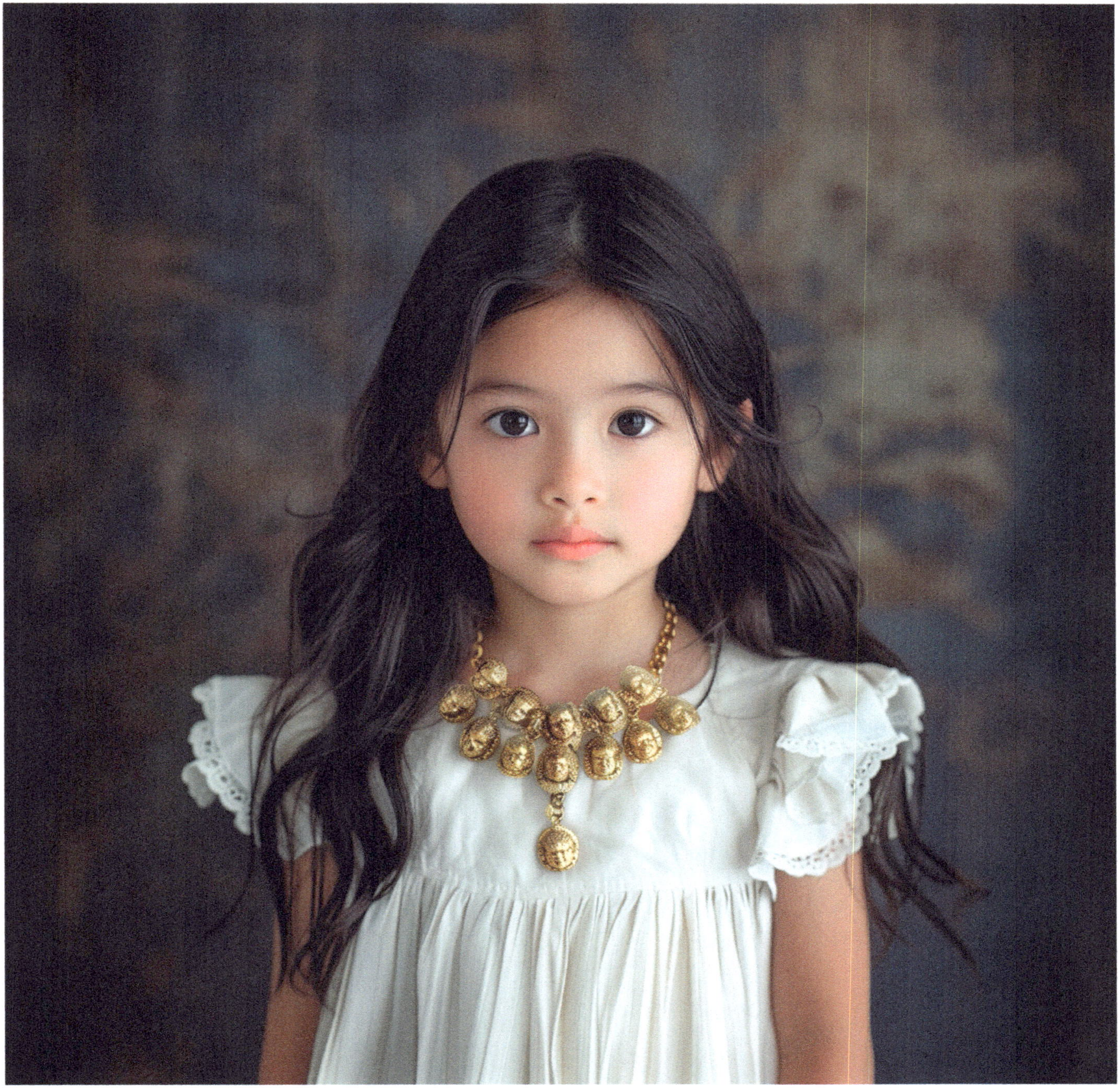

Wassana finds happiness in helping others.

Looking at her Facebook or Instagram over the years, you won't see the typical life of a beautiful young girl going on holidays, shopping, and taking selfies. Instead, you'll see the life of someone dedicated to spreading goodness.

Each day, Wassana wakes up with a smile and shares her plan for how we can make merit and do good for others that day.

I have never met anyone quite like her.

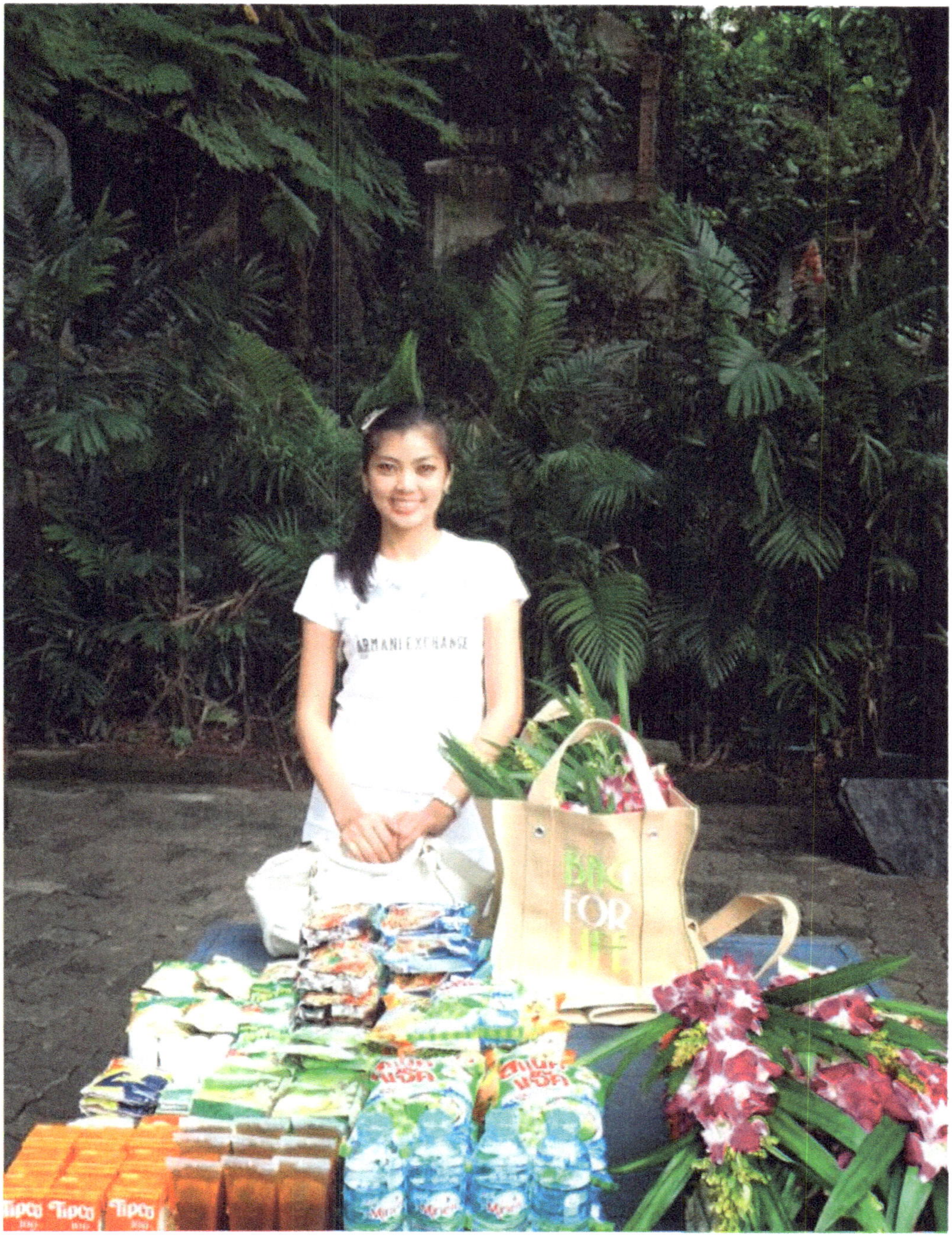
ARMANI EXCHANGE
Tipco

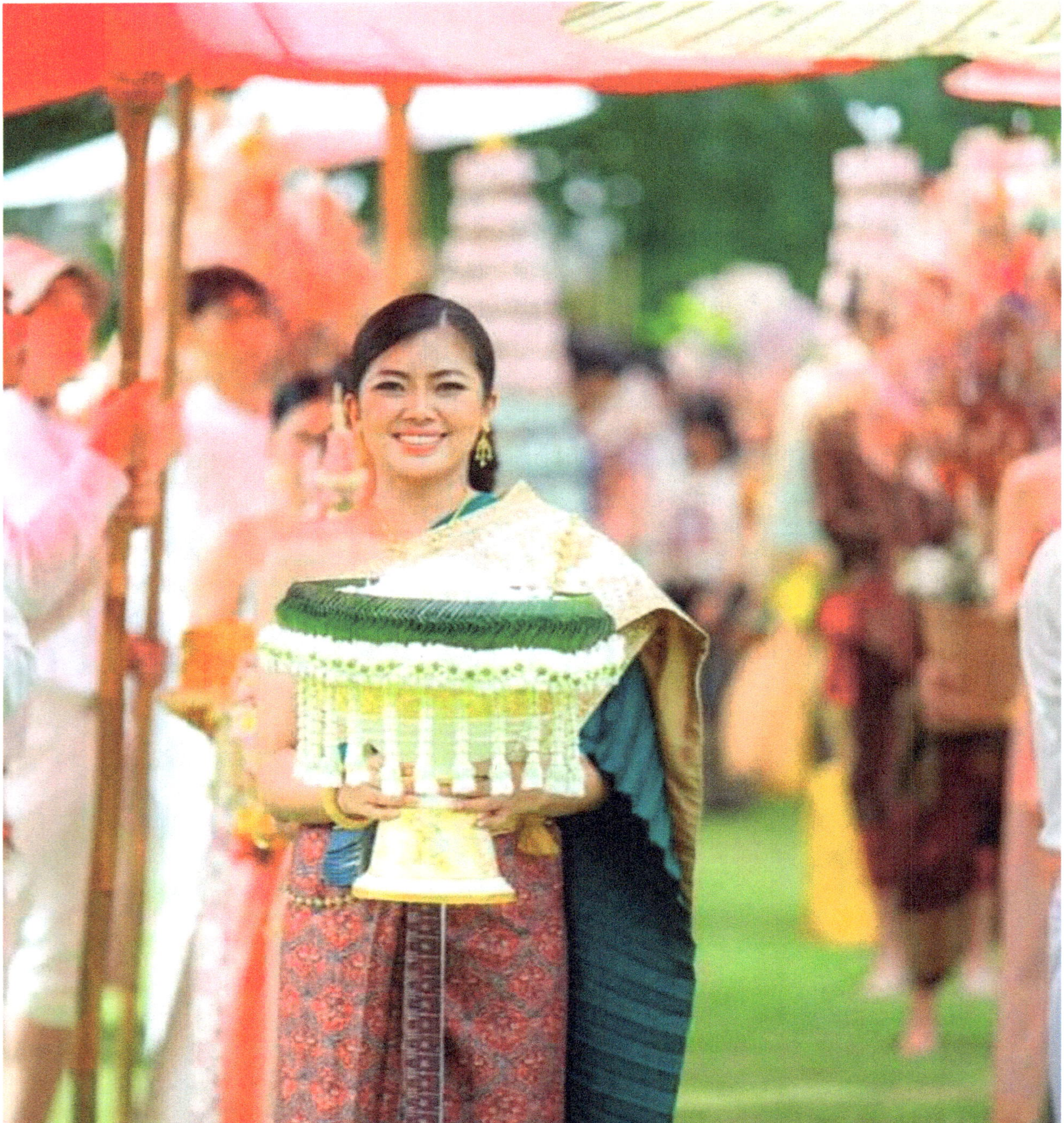

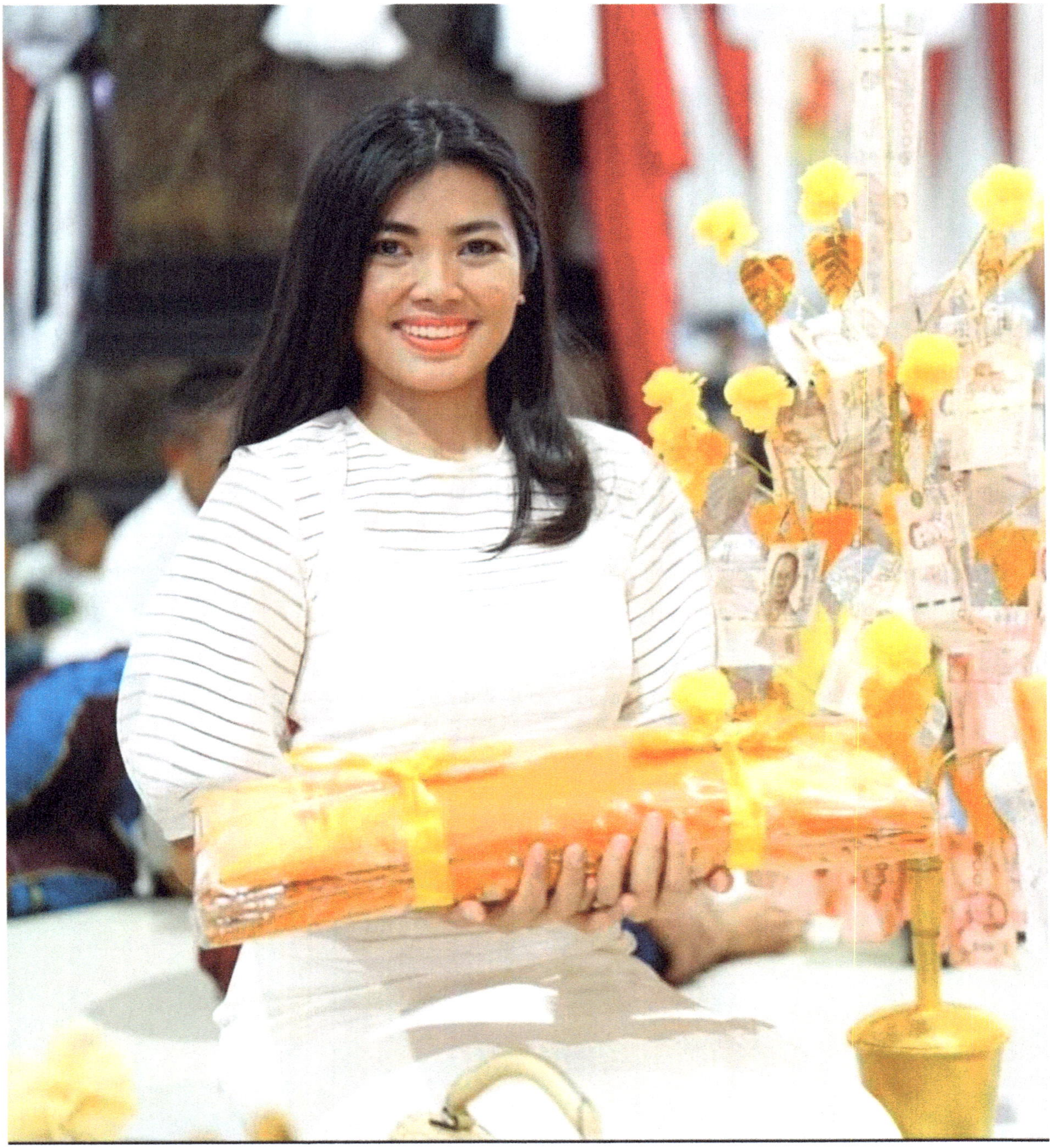

About 8 years ago, Wassana and I had meticulously planned a trip to the USA. I had booked flights, arranged accommodations, and crafted an itinerary for what promised to be a memorable journey.

Then, just days before our departure, Wassana dropped a bombshell: she couldn't go on the trip. She had been accepted into the Techo Vipassana meditation course, an advanced and highly sought-after opportunity. Missing this chance would mean waiting at least two years for another opportunity.

Though disappointed, I understood the importance of her decision. I embarked on the trip alone, not wanting to waste the arrangements already made.

Upon my return, I found Wassana in a state of pure joy. She had finally found the Master she had been seeking during the meditation course.

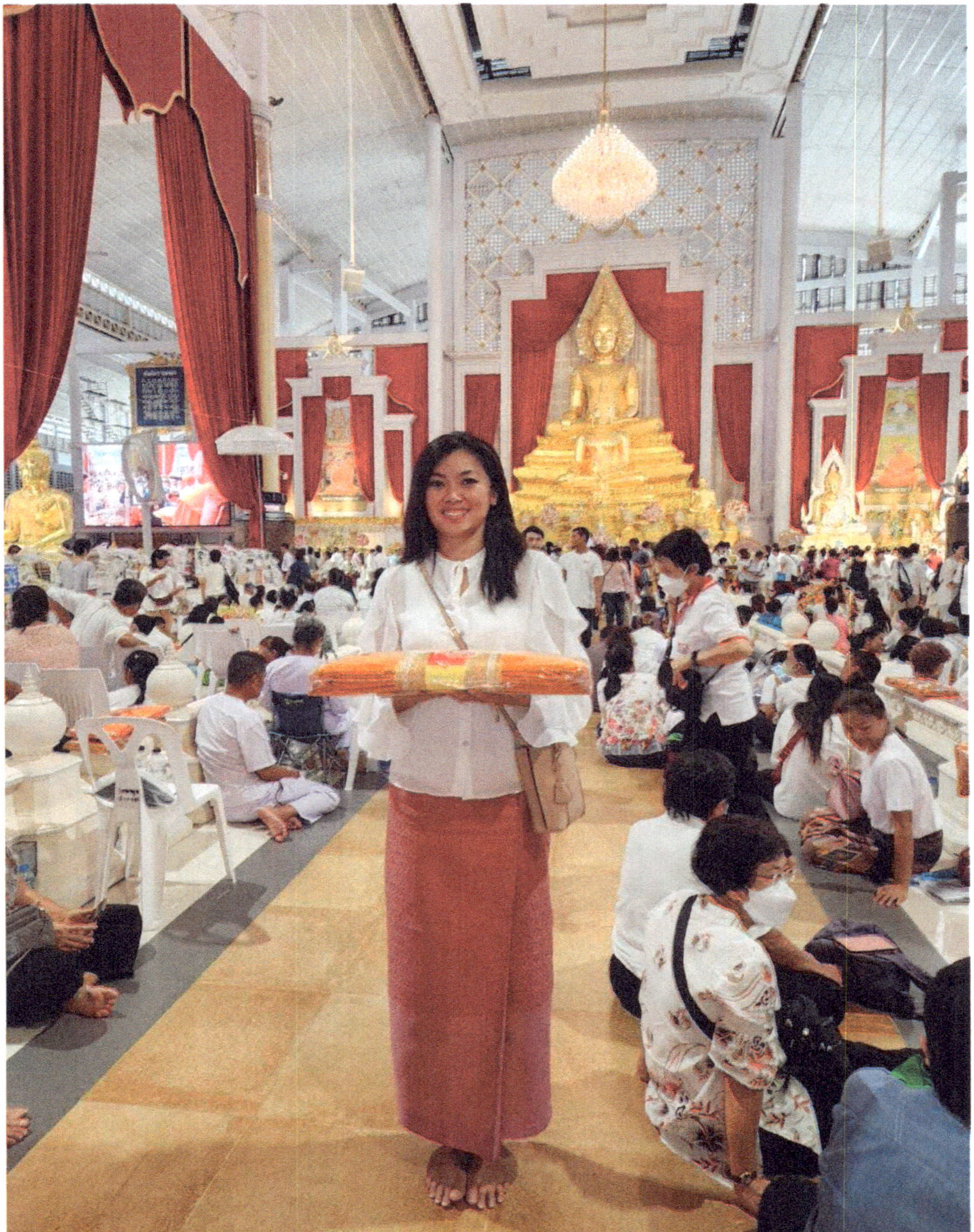

Wassana's enthusiasm for the Master and meditation took over our lives. She insisted that I must apply for a meditation course and become a student of the Master.

Having had visions of the Master and monks while living with the Indians in the Amazon Jungle, I knew this was the next step of my spiritual journey and something I had to do. I believed that learning meditation, especially this advanced "fire" meditation, would be beneficial.

What I did not realize was how difficult yet profound this week of meditation with the Master would be. The only way to describe it is as life-changing.

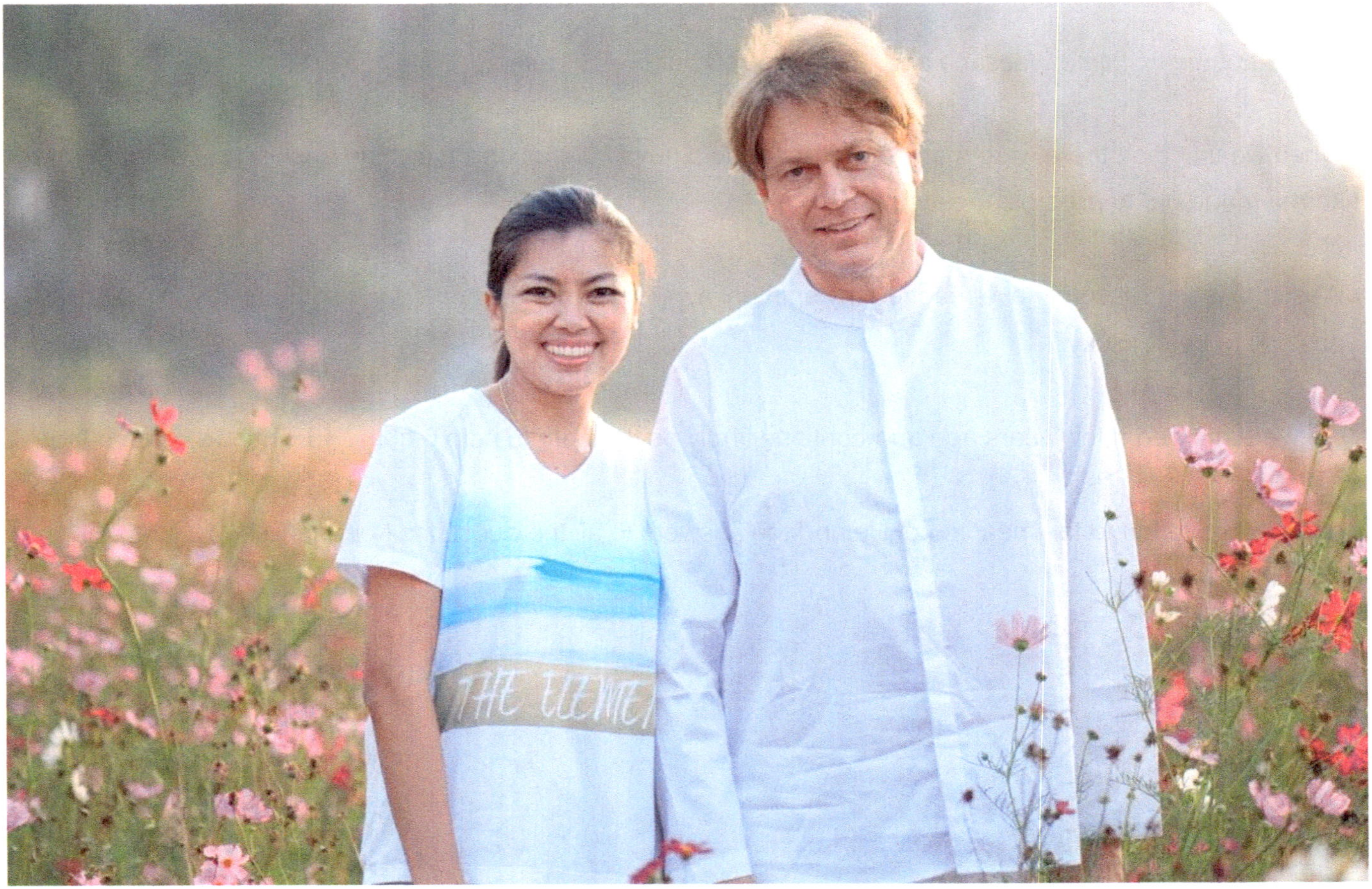

Wassana Sasakun has changed my life through her example and by introducing me to Buddhism and the Master.

This is not the first time Wassana and I have shared our lives together.

When we first met, there were many things that could have kept us apart. But the pushing power of good karma made our impossible meeting possible.

Wassana is the reason I have reached my spiritual awakening. I must have done something very good in a past life to be so lucky.

We were married a few years ago and continue firmly on the path to help others find what we have found.

And so, I have found the meaning of life and the answers to all the questions I began with.

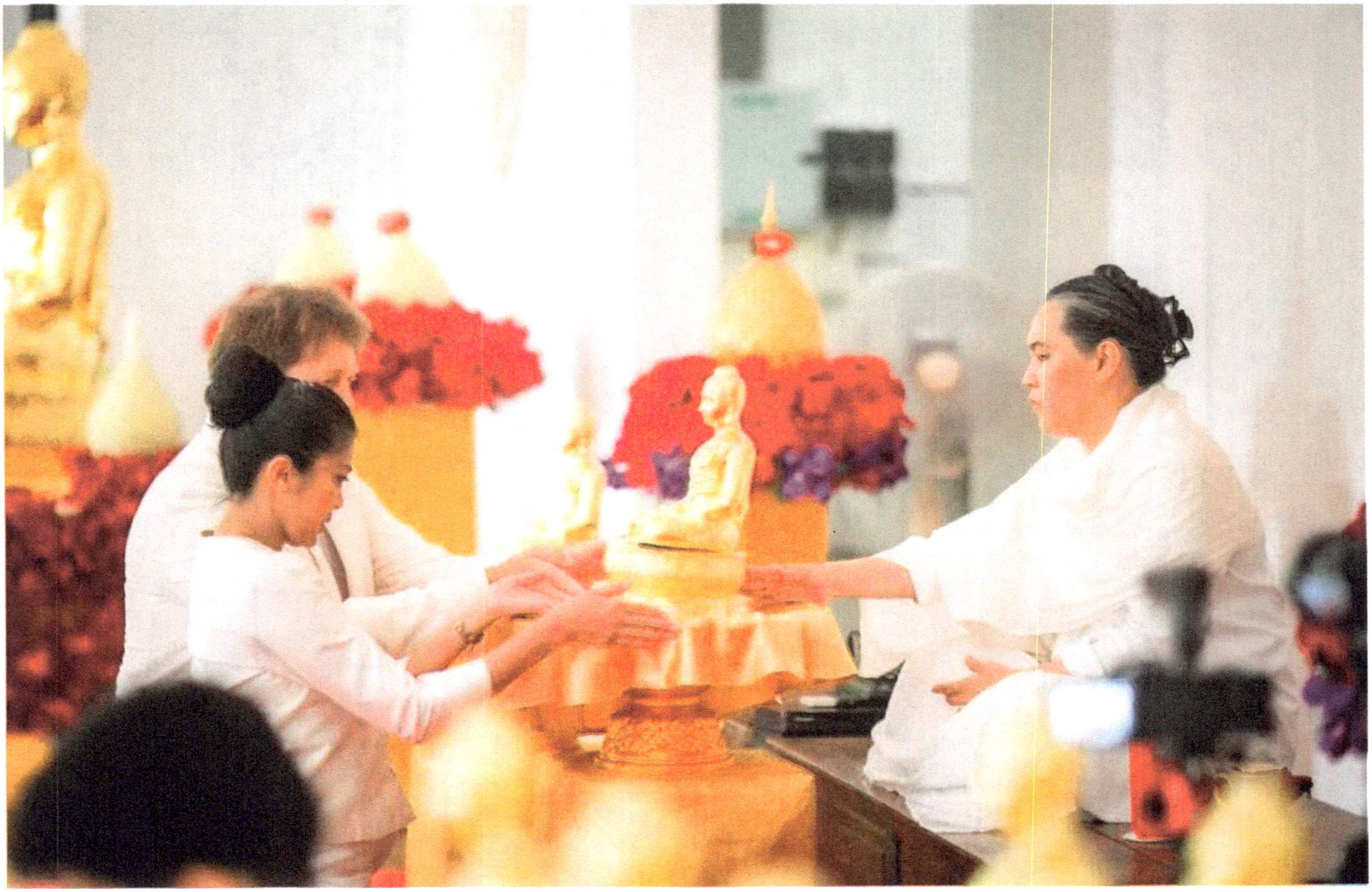

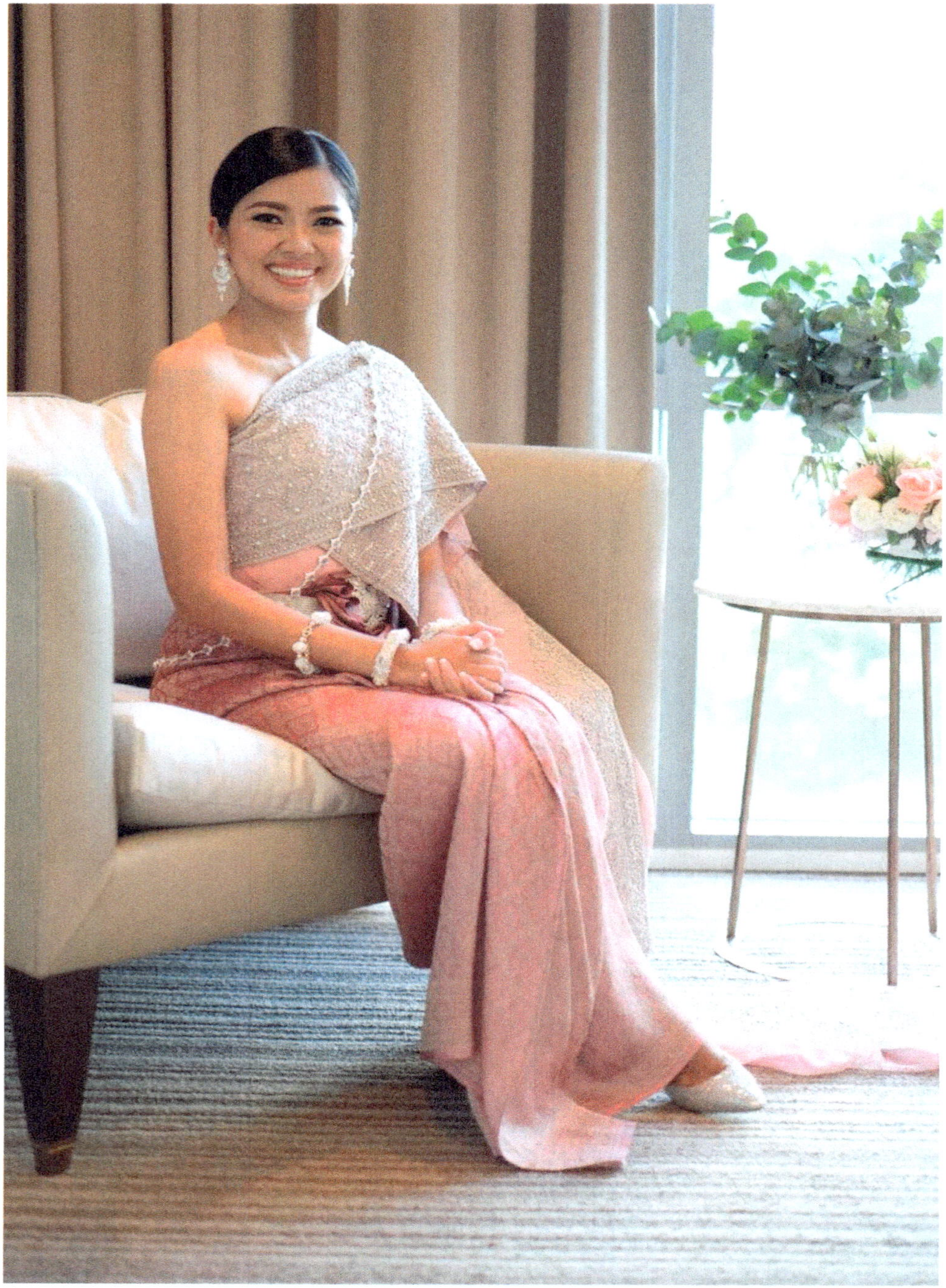

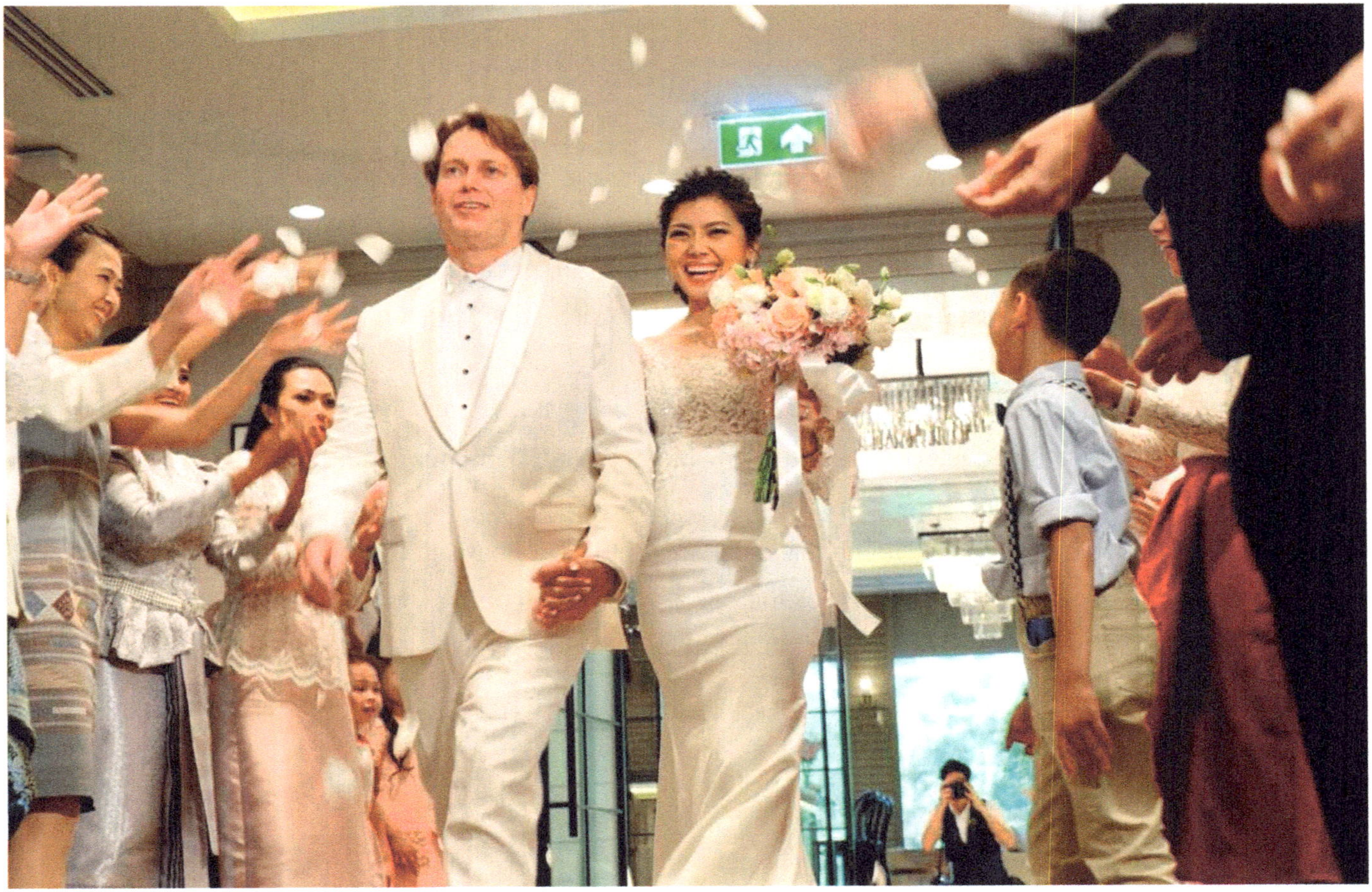

In the game of life, we dress up and play our roles on the stage of this current lifetime.

We may modify our role, but the stage and rules of the game are not easily changed. As we awaken, we realize that every lifetime is just a "restart" or "reboot" of the game, and we start to play a new round.

Like a computer game, life has a set of instructions and a code. If we break the code, we can modify our roles and start to affect the "Master Game" program itself. We can bend our minds.

How in the world could we possibly figure this out if not for the roadmap left by others? Imagine what it took for the Buddha to figure it out and crack the code by himself. Imagine how tricky the dark side (Mara) must be to cover our eyes from discovering these truths.

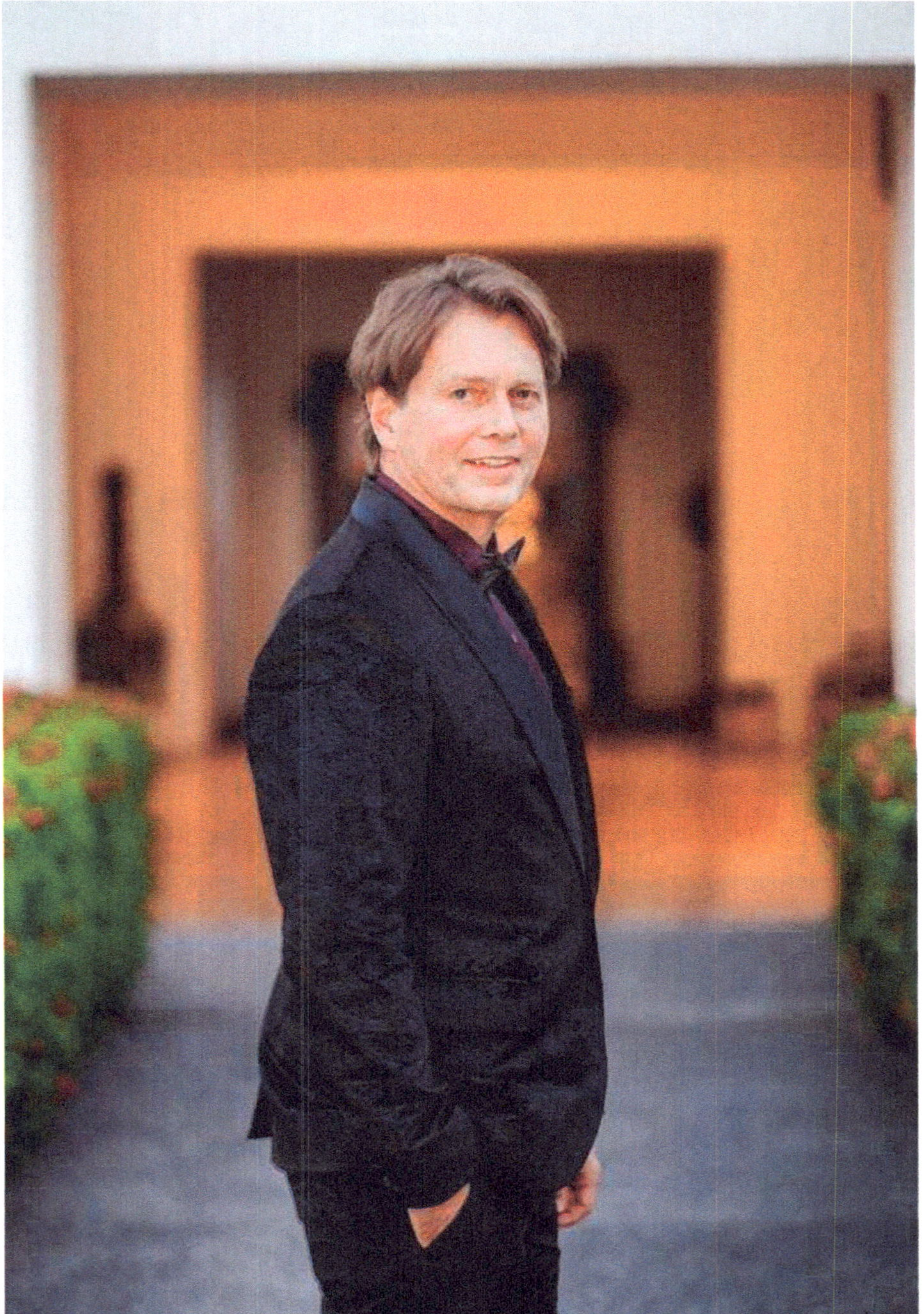

The greatest thing in this life and in this world is to bring our close friends and family to discover the ultimate truth.

To bring those who have been warriors alongside us in past lives, to meet the Master and fight the final battle for ultimate liberation.

Boris Mittelberg and I have been great friends and the greatest warriors in many past lives. In this lifetime, we continue to be the greatest friends and warriors, embarking on the final battle together.

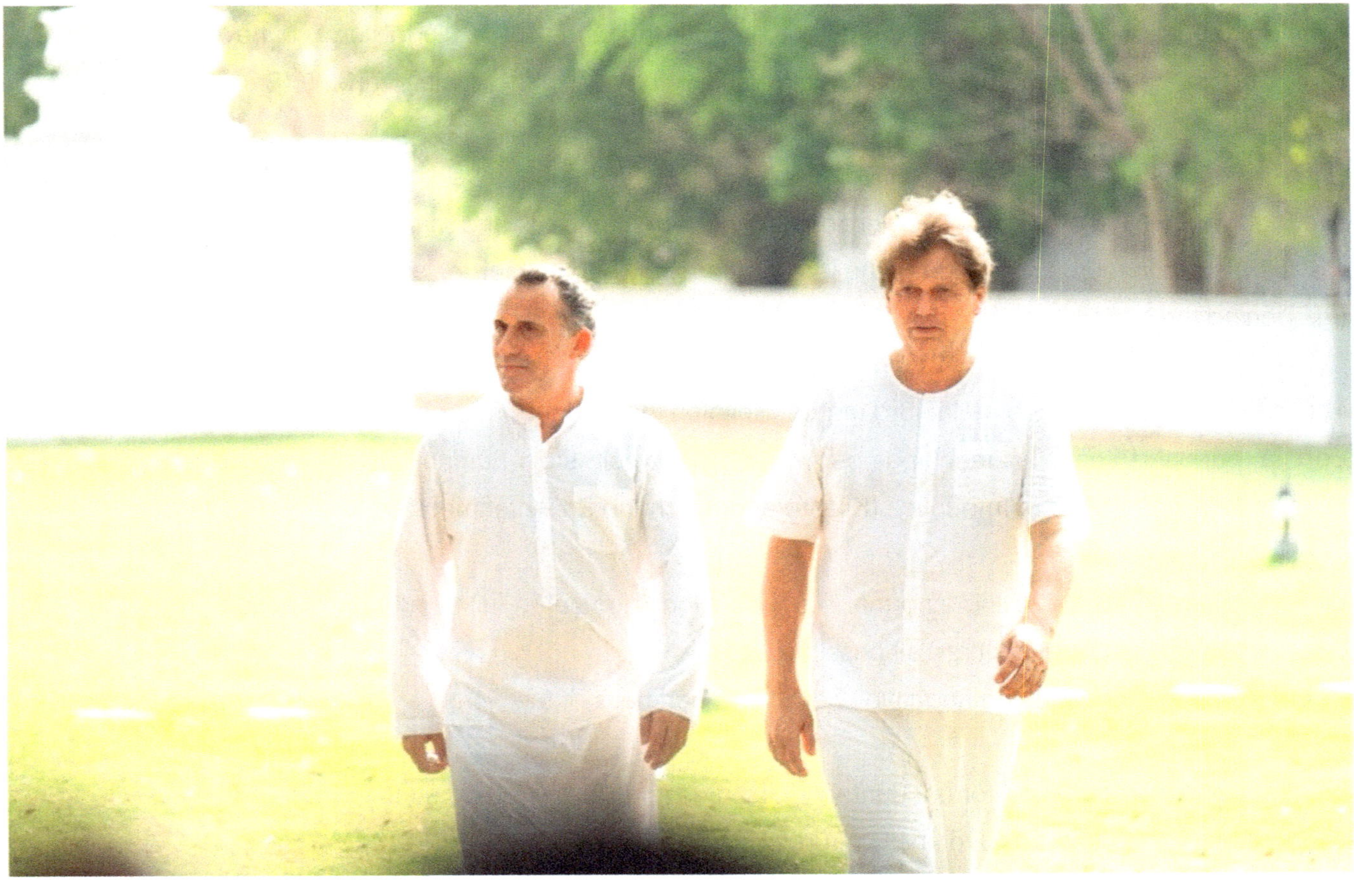

I always had respect for Thai Monks, but wrongly thought that Monks were people who could not make it in the real world or somehow gave up on Life and lived a simple existence as monastics.

But I got it backwards – Monks are the ones that are living in the "Real World" lucky to have found a life protected by the robes and able to practice, reaching the end of the cycle of rebirth (Samsara).

Sometimes we think we have figured life out based on convenutal truths, or intellectually. But when we see that what we believed to be conventional truths were mistruths and misdirection from the dark side, we see the fabrication and illusion of the world created by impurity forces and the dark side. Finally, we see behind the curtain.

Today Buddhism is labeled as the 3rd largest Religion in the world, but the Buddha never meant to teach dogma, but only to have his teachings be a road map to help steer humanity to live in goodness, meditate in order to free the Mind of Impurities (Kilesa) and reach the Enlightenment.

Whether as a Lay person living a normal Life. Or a Monk dedicated full time to the practice.
Goodness and Enlightenment are all possible.
Goodness can cancel out the negative energy and darkness of the world.

We have all been searching for uncountable Lifetimes for the way to end suffering, end the cycle of rebirth, aging and death. And to finally return HOME……

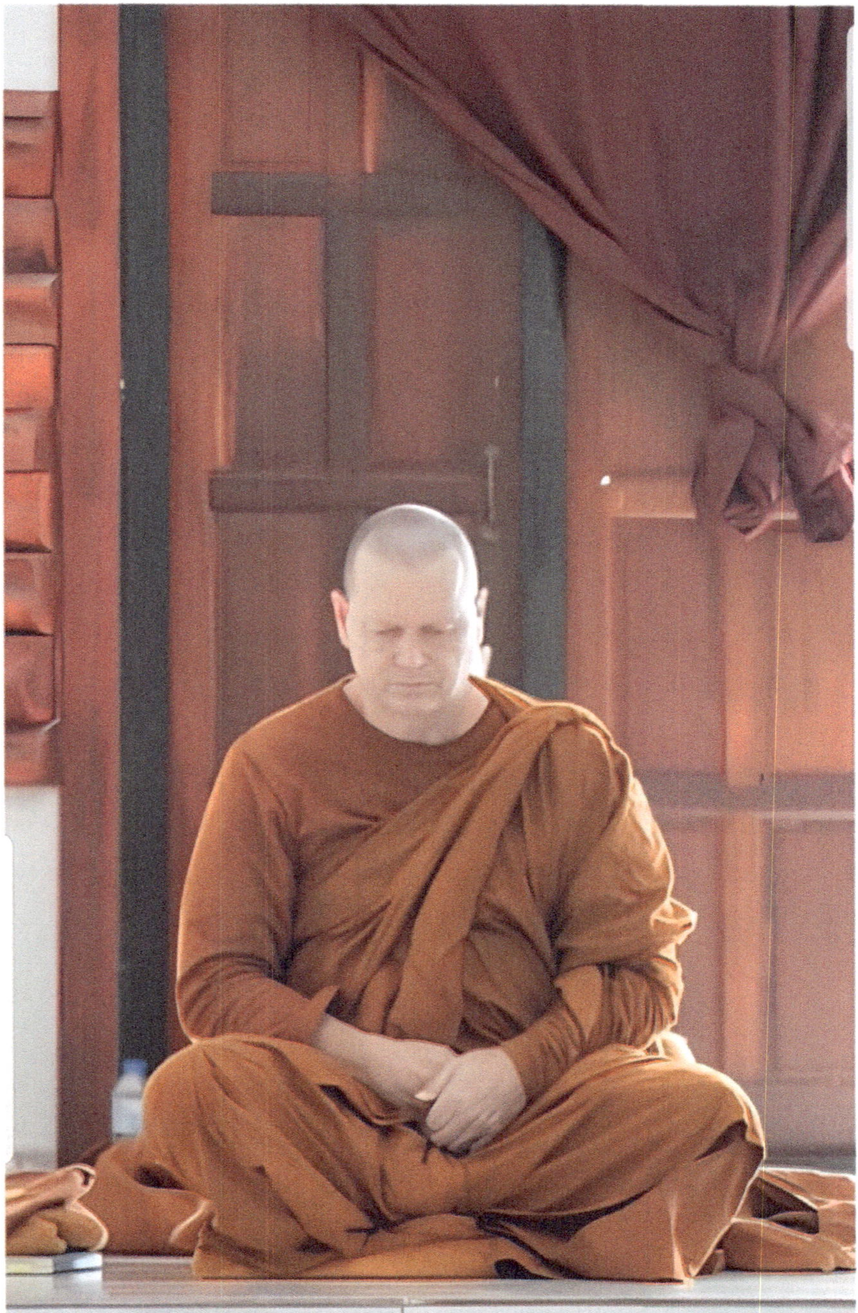

I never imagined that I would write a Book.

In the jungle I could not imagine what would happen in my Life that was so profound, that I wanted to share what I discovered with the World.

I also never imagined that in my travels, I would discover a magical place in the Kingdom of Thailand, the land of Buddha, where a woman in a white robe teaches her soldiers from the past life, how to walk the path to Enlightenment, fighting the final battle of Life in the battlefield of the Mind.

I also never imagined I would paint a painting. This painting is of a place, where the dimension of fine Energy meets the world of illusion. Where the stories of the Buddha come alive and Dhamma intersects with Nature.

This is a story about the "Journey to Enlightenment" that will be told in the future, few will believe this story, and many will others wonder, how they missed to find this place and meet the Master Acharavadee Wongsakon while she still walked this World.

[Paintings by Hanno Soth]

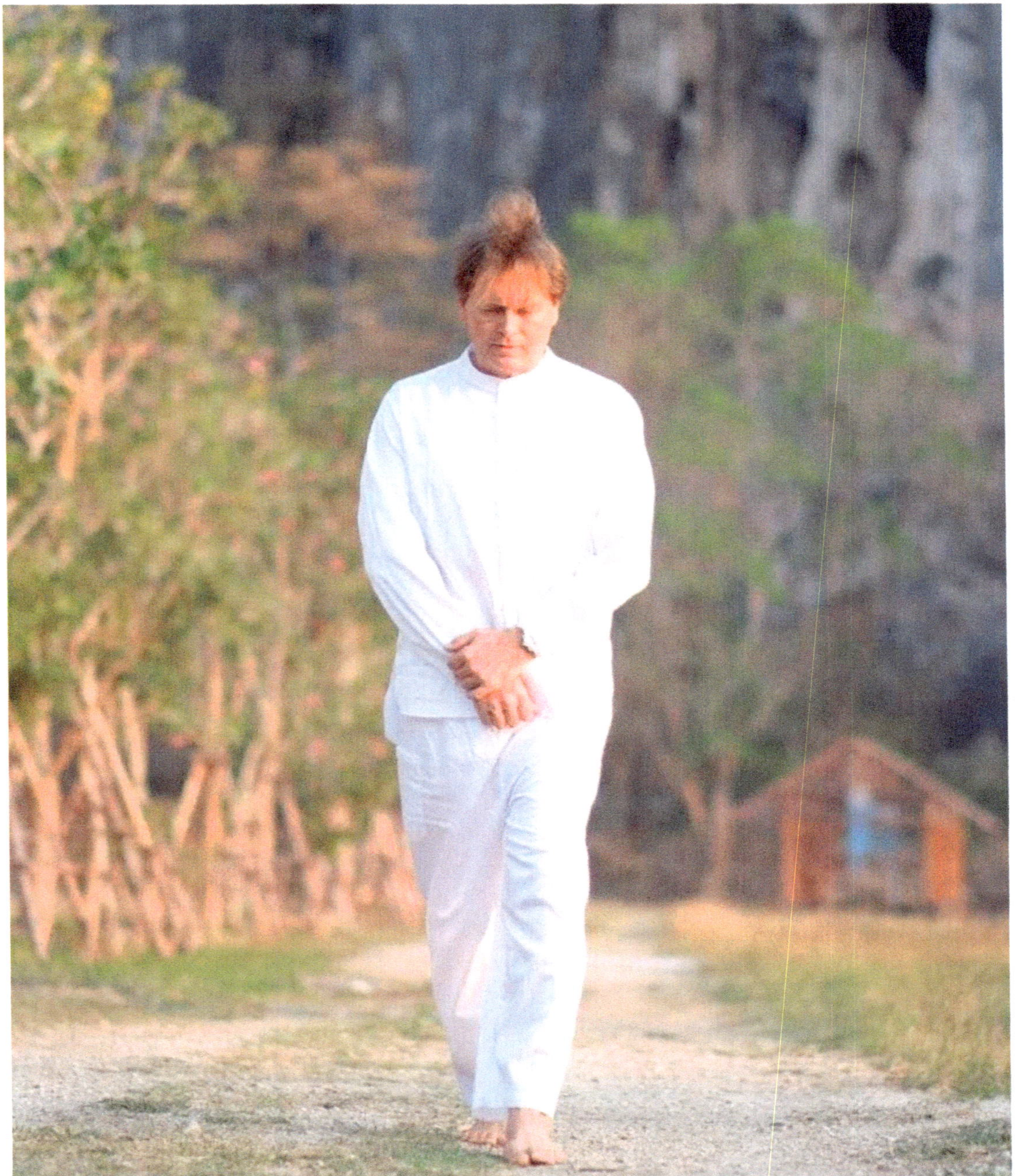

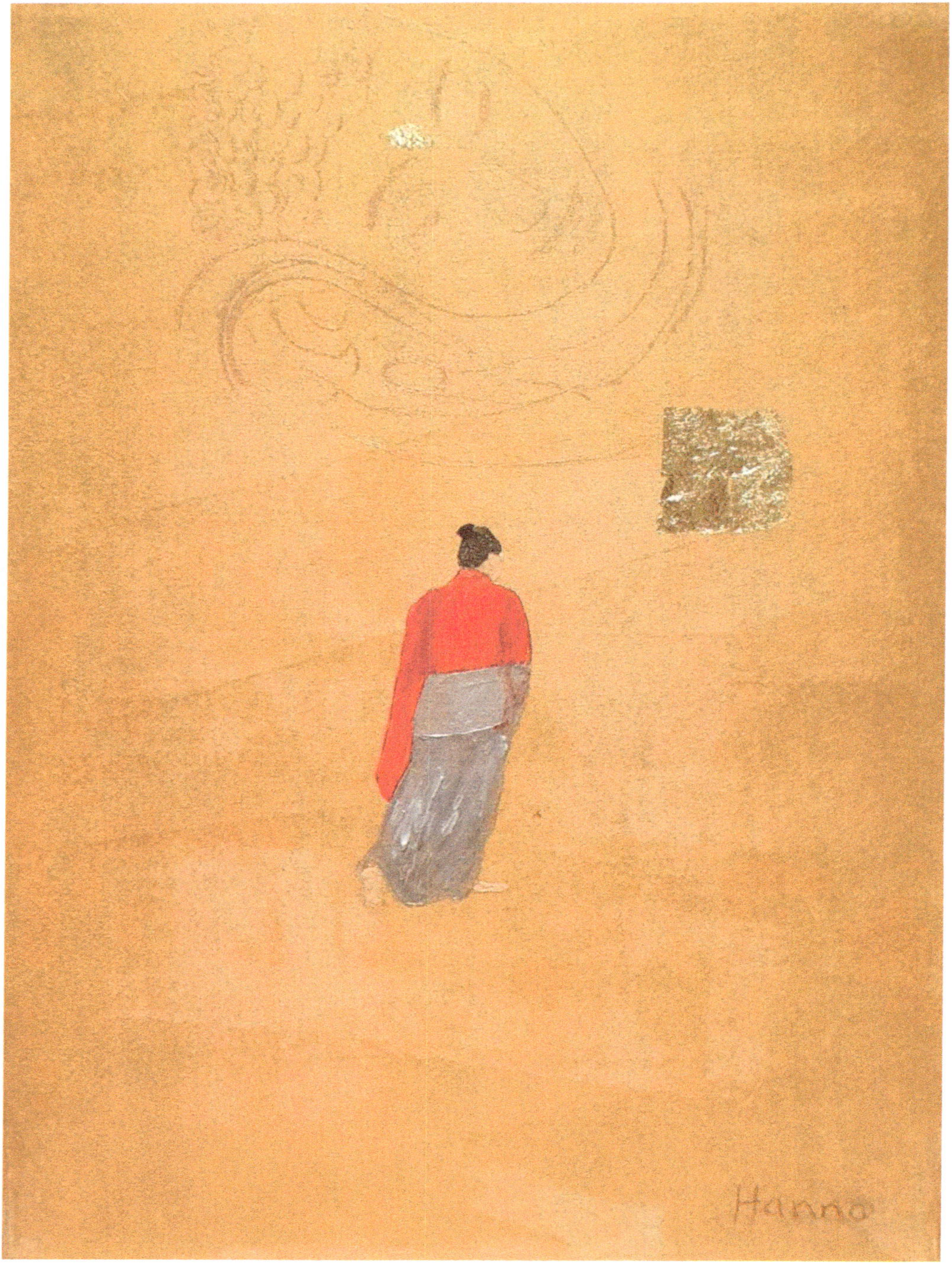
Hanno

595

Hanno

597

Hanno

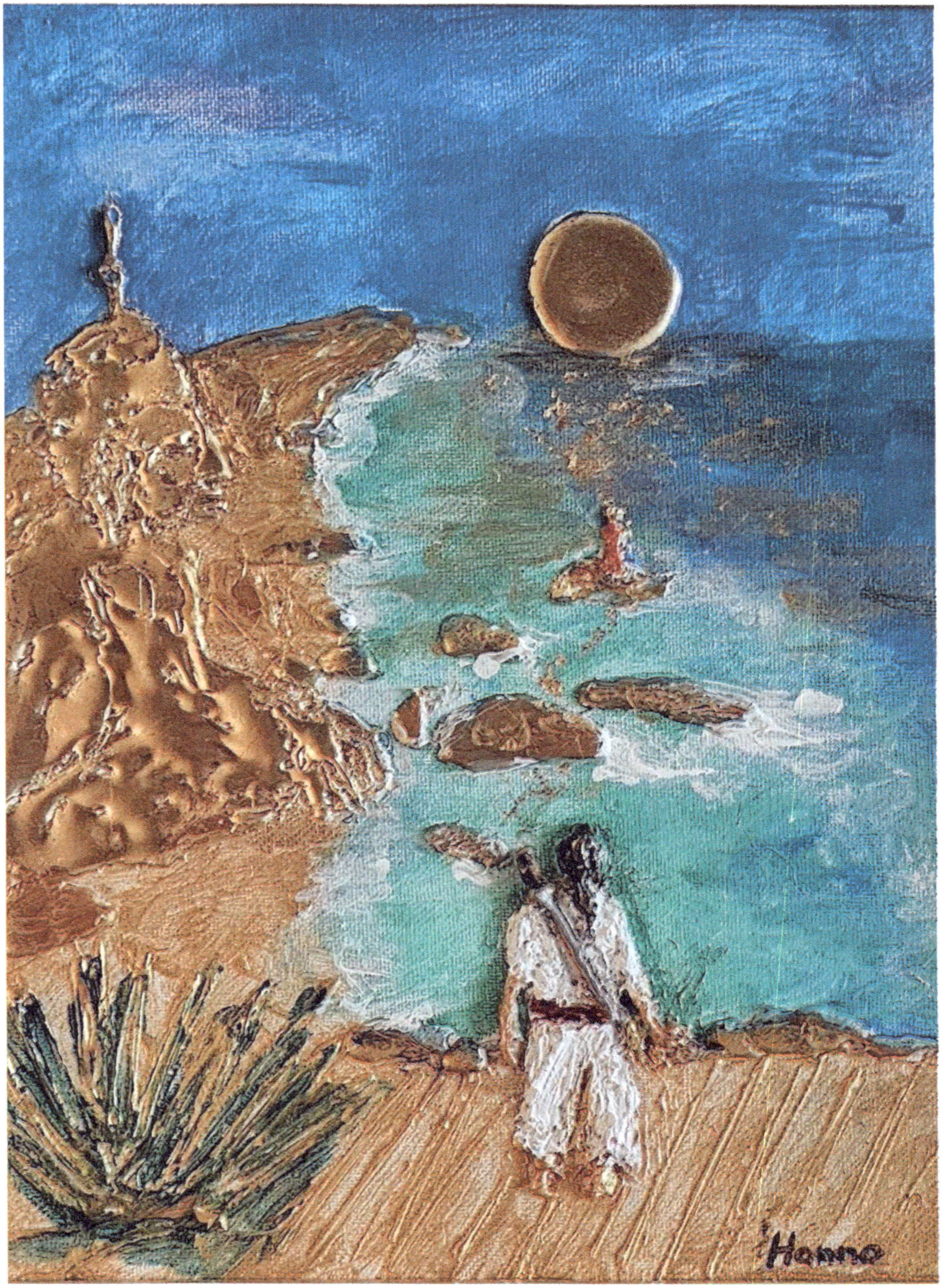
Hanno

600

Made in the USA
Las Vegas, NV
28 April 2024